America Now

Short Readings from Recent Periodicals

Modules
1. Social Networking
2. Gender Differences
3. Ethics of Consumption
4 Climate Crisis

America Now

Short Readings from Recent Periodicals
Eighth Edition

Edited by

ROBERT ATWAN
Director, The Blue Hills Writing Institute at Curry College
Series Editor, *The Best American Essays*

Exercises prepared with the assistance of

Valerie Duff-Strautmann

Jeffrey Ousborne
Suffolk University

Stefanie Wortman
University of Missouri–Columbia

Bedford/St. Martin's   Boston ♦ New York

For Bedford / St. Martin's

Developmental Editor: Christina Gerogiannis
Production Editor: Annette Pagliaro Sweeney
Production Supervisor: Samuel Jones
Marketing Manager: Molly Parke
Associate Editor: Stephanie Naudin
Copyeditor: Linda McLatchie
Text Design: Jean Hammond
Cover Design: Hannus Design
Composition: Pine Tree Composition, Inc.
Printing and Binding: Haddon Craftsmen, Inc., an RR Donnelley & Sons
   Company

President: Joan E. Feinberg
Editorial Director: Denise B. Wydra
Editor-in-Chief: Karen S. Henry
Director of Marketing: Karen R. Soeltz
Director of Editing, Design, and Production: Marcia Cohen
Assistant Director of Editing, Design, and Production: Elise S. Kaiser
Managing Editor: Elizabeth M. Schaaf

Library of Congress Control Number: 2008933110

Manufactured in the United States of America.

4 3 2 1 0 9
f e d c b a

For information, write: Bedford/St. Martin's, 75 Arlington Street,
Boston, MA 02116   (617-399-4000)

ISBN-10:   0–312–48694–4
ISBN-13:   978–0–312–48694–5

Acknowledgments

About the Editor

Robert Atwan is director of The Blue Hills Writing Institute at Curry College and the series editor of the annual *Best American Essays*, which he founded in 1985. His essays, reviews, and critical articles have appeared in the *New York Times*, the *Los Angeles Times*, the *Atlantic Monthly*, *Iowa Review*, *Denver Quarterly*, *Kenyon Review*, *River Teeth*, and many other publications. For Bedford/St. Martin's, he has also edited *Ten on Ten: Major Essayists on Recurring Themes* (1992), *Our Times*, Fifth Edition (1998), and *Convergences*, Third Edition (2009). He has coedited (with Jon Roberts) *Left, Right, and Center: Voices from Across the Political Spectrum* (1996), and is co-editor with Donald McQuade of *The Writer's Presence*, Sixth Edition (2009).

Preface for Instructors

People write for many reasons, but one of the most compelling is to express their views on matters of current public interest. Browse any newsstand, library magazine rack, or Web page and you'll find an abundance of articles and opinion pieces responding to current issues and events. Too frequently, students see the writing they do in a composition class as having little connection with real-world problems and issues. *America Now*, with its provocative professional and student writing—all very current opinion essays drawn from a range of periodicals—shows students that by writing on the important issues of today, they can influence campus and public discourse and truly make a difference.

The eighth edition of *America Now* offers a generous sampling of timely and provocative material. *America Now* is designed to immerse introductory writing students in the give-and-take of public dialogue and to stimulate thinking, discussion, and composition. Its overriding instructional principle—which guides everything from the choice of readings and topics to the design of questions—is that participation in informed discussion will help generate and enrich student writing.

America Now systematically encourages its users to view reading, thinking, discussion, and writing as closely interrelated activities. It assumes that (1) attentive reading and reflection will lead to informed discussion; (2) participation in open and informed discussion will result in a broadening of viewpoints; (3) an awareness of different viewpoints will stimulate further reflection and renewed discussion; and (4) this process in turn will lead to thoughtful papers.

The book's general introduction, "The Persuasive Writer: Expressing Opinions with Clarity, Confidence, and Civility," takes the student through these interrelated processes and offers some useful guidelines for engaging in productive discussion that will lead to effective essays. Three annotated student essays serve as models of persuasive opinion writing. Instructors may also find helpful my essay "Writing and the Art of Discussion," which can be found in the instructor's manual and at the book's companion Web site.

New to This Edition

Following is a brief overview of the eighth edition of *America Now*. For a more in-depth description of the book, see "Using *America Now*" beginning on page ix of this preface.

Fifty readings and **twenty-four visual texts**—all new and *very current*. Drawn from more than thirty-five recent periodicals, including fourteen student newspapers, each reading not only is new to this edition but has appeared within a year or two of the book's publication. With over half of its selections published in 2008, *America Now* is the most current short essay reader available. Some of the readings you will find in the eighth edition are Manuel Muñoz on assimilation, Barbara Ehrenreich on child labor, Ellen Goodman on athletic enhancements, Susan Jacoby on dumbed-down education, and Bill McKibben on global warming.

Eight new issues of current interest. Eight of the twelve thematic chapters have been updated to reflect the changing interests of students over the past two years. Sure to spark lively discussion and writing, these new topics are obesity, genetic enhancement, racial dialogue, education today, new political reforms, class struggle, immigration, and the climate crisis.

New "casebook" chapter. The book's final chapter, "The Climate Crisis: Is It Real?" contains eight selections that focus on one of today's most widely discussed issues. The expanded chapter, which also includes a student debate, can be used by instructors who want to set up classroom panels or forums for extended discussion and writing.

New "media coverage" chapter. In this edition, the topic of gender is examined from an unusual perspective: the way scientific reports on gender issues are taken up by the media and repackaged for the general public. The chapter takes a close look at how one scientific report—on the topic of whether women talk more than men—found its way into broader coverage.

Models for writing in the classroom. This edition features three new student essays commissioned to provide clear examples of personal, expository, and research-based writing on the same timely topic—the issue of stereotyping. Each essay is fully annotated and demonstrates three types of opinion writing: (1) the use of personal experience; (2) a response to reading with informal use of sources, and (3) a response to readings with full citations. The essays are supported by instruction on how and when each method is effective.

How to support opinions. The revised Introduction now offers students focused advice on the most effective ways to support their opinions.

An updated companion Web site (bedfordstmartins.com/
americanow) provides students with annotated research links for each
chapter, electronically scored ESL and Developmental Quizzes for
each chapter, and links to every online newspaper, magazine, and journal in *America Now*. The site also includes an online version of the
book's instructor's manual.

Using America Now

Professional and Student Writing from a Wide Variety of Sources

The book's selections by professional writers are drawn from recent
periodicals, ranging from specialized journals such as *Science* to influential general magazines such as *National Geographic* and *Vogue*. As
would be expected in a collection that focuses heavily on social
trends and current events, *America Now* features several newspapers
and news-oriented magazines: the *Boston Globe*, the *New York
Times*, and the *Washington Post*. With its additional emphasis on
public discourse, this collection also draws on some of America's
leading political magazines, including *Reason*, *The Nation*, *American
Prospect*, and *The Progressive*. Also represented are magazines that
appeal primarily to specialized audiences, such as the *Chronicle of
Higher Education*, *Orion*, *Wired*, and *Tikkun*. In general, the selections illustrate the variety of personal, informative, and persuasive
writing encountered daily by millions of Americans. The readings are
kept short (many under three pages, and some no longer than a page)
to hold student interest and to serve as models for the student's own
writing. To introduce a more in-depth approach to various topics, the
book includes a few longer essays, especially in the final chapters.

America Now also features fifteen published student selections —
essays and cartoons — from print and online college newspapers.
These recent works reveal student writers confronting in a public
forum the same topics and issues that challenge some of our leading
social critics and commentators, and they show how student writers
can enter into and influence public discussion. In this way, the student selections in *America Now* — complemented by Student Writer
at Work interviews — encourage students to see writing as a form of
personal and public empowerment. This edition includes eight brief,
inspiring interviews in which student authors in the book explain
how — and why — they express their opinions in writing.

To highlight models of persuasive writing, each chapter contains
an annotated section of a student paper. The comments point out
some of the most effective strategies of the student writers in the

book and offer advice for structuring sentences, stating a main point, shaping arguments, presenting examples and evidence, using quotations, recommending a course of action, and more.

Timely Topics for Discussion and Debate

Student essays not only make up a large percentage of the readings in this book, but also shape the volume's contents. As we monitored the broad spectrum of online college newspapers—and reviewed several hundred student essays—we gradually found the most commonly discussed campus issues and topics. Issues such as those mentioned on page viii of this preface have provoked so much recent student response that they could have resulted in several single-topic collections. Many college papers do not restrict themselves to news items and editorial opinion but make room for personal essays as well. Some popular student topics are climate change, gender, cultural identity, immigration, and body image, all of which are reflected in the book's table of contents.

To facilitate group discussion and in-class work, *America Now* features eleven bite-sized units and one "casebook" chapter. These focused chapters permit instructors to cover a broad range of themes and issues in a single semester. Each can be conveniently handled in one or two class periods. In general, the chapters move from accessible, personal topics (for example, obesity, networking, and identity) to more public issues (class, immigration, and climate change), thus accommodating instructors who prefer to start with personal writing and gradually progress to exposition, analysis, and argument.

Since composition courses naturally emphasize issues revolving around language and the construction of meaning, *America Now* also includes a number of selections designed to encourage students to examine the powerful influence of words and symbols.

The Visual Expression of Opinion

America Now encourages students to pay close attention to the persuasive power of language and images. Reflecting the growing presence of advertising in public discussion, among the book's images are recent opinion advertisements (or "Op-Ads"). These pieces, which focus on racial profiling, obesity, and global warming, encourage students to uncover the visual and verbal strategies of various advocacy groups trying to influence the consciousness and ideology of large audiences.

Because we live in an increasingly visual culture, the book's introduction offers a section on expressing opinions visually—with striking examples from photojournalism, cartoons, and opinion advertisements. Examples from these visual genres are also found throughout the book along with the work of such graphic artists as Nathan Huang and Peter Bagge. Another assortment of visual selections, titled "America Then," provides students with historical perspectives on "America Now." These images show that many of the issues we deal with today have roots in the past. They include a 1904 automobile ad that illustrates a trend toward conspicuous consumption, a classic Jacob Riis photograph of homeless boys from the 1890s, and a bizarre do-it-yourself weight-reduction product from the 1930s.

The Instructional Apparatus: Before, During, and After Reading

To help promote reflection and discussion, the book includes a pre-reading assignment for each main selection. The questions in "Before You Read" provide students with the opportunity to explore a few of the avenues that lead to fruitful discussion and interesting papers. A full description of the advantages gained by linking reading, writing, and classroom discussion can be found in my introduction to the instructor's manual.

The apparatus of *America Now* supports both discussion-based instruction and more individualized approaches to reading and writing. Taking into account the increasing diversity of students (especially the growing number of speakers for whom English is not their first language) in today's writing programs, the apparatus offers extensive help with college-level vocabulary and features a "Words to Learn" list preceding each selection. This vocabulary list with brief definitions will allow students to spot ahead of time some of the words they may find difficult; encountering the word later in context will help lock it in memory. It's unrealistic, however, to think students will acquire a fluent knowledge of new words by memorizing a list. Therefore, the apparatus following each selection includes additional exercises under the headings "Vocabulary/Using a Dictionary" and "Responding to Words in Context." These sets of questions introduce students to prefixes, suffixes, connotations, denotations, tone, and etymology.

Along with the discussion of vocabulary, other incrementally structured questions follow individual selections. "Discussing Main Point and Meaning" and "Examining Sentences, Paragraphs, and Organization" questions help to guide students step by step through the reading process, culminating in the set of "Thinking Critically" questions. As instructors well know, beginning students can sometimes be too trusting of what they see in print, especially in textbooks. Therefore, the "Thinking Critically" questions invite students to take a more skeptical attitude toward their reading and to form the habit of challenging a selection from both analytical and experiential points of view. The selection apparatus concludes with "In-Class Writing Activities," which emphasize freewriting exercises and collaborative projects.

In addition to the selection apparatus, *America Now* contains end-of-chapter questions designed to stimulate further discussion and writing. The chapter apparatus approaches the reading material from topical and thematic angles, with an emphasis on group discussion. The introductory comments to each chapter highlight the main discussion points and the way selections are linked together. These points and linkages are then reintroduced at the end of the chapter through three sets of interlocking study questions and tasks: (1) a suggested topic for discussion, (2) questions and ideas to help students prepare for class discussion, and (3) several writing assignments that ask students to move from discussion to composition—that is, to develop papers out of the ideas and opinions expressed in class discussion and debate. Instructors with highly diverse writing classes may find "Topics for Cross-Cultural Discussion" a convenient way to encourage an exchange of perspectives and experiences that could also generate ideas for writing. Located on the book's Web site (bedfordstmartins.com/americanow) are ESL and Developmental Quizzes that test vocabulary and comprehension skills. Electronic scoring, which can be monitored by instructors, offers immediate feedback.

The Instructor's Manual

Valerie Duff-Strautmann, Stefanie Wortman (University of Missouri–Columbia), and Jeffrey Ousborne (Suffolk University) prepared the instructor's manual, bringing to the task valuable classroom experience at all levels of composition instruction. The manual contains an essay for each chapter, offering suggestions for teaching the selections together and separately, plus suggested answers and possible discussion topics based on every question posed in the text. Anyone using *America Now* should be sure to consult the manual before designing a syllabus, framing a discussion topic, or even assigning individual selections. Liz deBeer of Rutgers University also contributed a helpful essay on designing student panels ("Forming Forums"), along with advice on using the book's apparatus in both developmental and mainstream composition classes, which is available at the book's companion Web site.

Acknowledgments

While putting together the eighth edition of *America Now,* I was fortunate to receive the assistance of many talented individuals. In addition to their work on the instructor's manual, Valerie Duff-Strautmann, Stefanie Wortman, and Jeffrey Ousborne contributed to the book's instructional apparatus. I am also enormously grateful to my son, Gregory Atwan, who also helped to fill in many elements of this edition's comprehensive instructional material.

To revise a text is to entertain numerous questions: What kind of selections work best in class? What types of questions are most helpful? How can reading, writing, and discussion be most effectively intertwined? This edition profited immensely from the following instructors who generously took the time to respond to the seventh edition: Melanie N. Burdick, University of Missouri–Kansas City; Danielle Davis, Pasadena City College; Darren DeFrain, Wichita State University; Jay L. Gordon, Youngstown State University; Thomas W. Pittman, Youngstown State University; Vicki Lynn Samson, Western Kentucky University and Bowling Green Community College; Wendy Scott, Buffalo State College; and Richard A. Williams, Youngstown State University.

I'd also like to acknowledge instructors who have reviewed previous editions, and whose ideas and suggestions continue to inform the book: Kim M. Baker, Roger Williams University; Kevin Ball, Youngstown State University; Deborah Biorn, St. Cloud State University; Joan Blankmann, Northern Virginia Community College; Diane Bosco, Suffolk County Community College; Mikel Cole, University of Houston–Downtown; Kaye Falconer, Bakersfield College; Steven Florzcyk, the State University of New York–New Paltz; Nancy Freiman, Milwaukee Area Technical College; Andrea Germanos, Saint Augustine College; Kim Halpern, Pulaski Technical College; Jessica Harvey, Alexandria Technical College; Chris Hayes, University of Georgia; Sharon Jaffee, Santa Monica College; Patricia W. Julius, Michigan State University; Jessica Heather Lourey, Alexandria Technical College; Brian Ludlow, Alfred University; Sherry Manis, Foothill College; Terry Meier, Bakersfield College; Melody Nightingale, Santa Monica College; Kimme Nuckles, Baker College; Michael Orlando, Bergen Community College; Marty Price, Mississippi State University; David Pryor, University of the Incarnate Word; Hubert C. Pulley, Georgia Southern University; Sherry Robertson, Pulaski Technical College; Lynn Sabas, Saint Augustine College; Jennifer Satterlee, Parkland College; Andrea D. Shanklin, Howard Community College;

Ann Spurlock, Mississippi State University; Linda Weiner, the University of Akron; Frances Whitney, Bakersfield College; and Martha Anne Yeager-Tobar, Cerritos College.

Other people helped in various ways. I'm indebted to Barbara Gross of Rutgers University, Newark, for her excellent work in helping to design the Instructor's Manual for the first edition. Two good friends, Charles O'Neill and Jack Roberts, both of St. Thomas Aquinas College, went over my early plans for the book and offered many useful suggestions.

As always, it was a pleasure to work with the superb staff at Bedford/St. Martin's. Jane Helms, my editor on the first edition, shaped the book in lasting ways and helped with the planning of the revision. I also am indebted to the previous edition's senior developmental editor, Ellen Thibault, who helped in so many ways to smooth the transition to my new developmental editor, Christina Gerogiannis. Christina provided excellent guidance and numerous suggestions, while doing her utmost best to keep a book that depends on so many moving parts and timely material on its remarkably tight schedule. Christina is also responsible for the student interviews that are such an important feature of this edition. Stephanie Naudin, associate editor, researched images and readings for the book, contacted the students profiled in the book, and worked energetically on the book's Web site and instructor's manual. Sophia Snyder, editorial assistant, provided top-rate support. Sandy Schechter and Martha Friedman managed text and art permissions under a tight schedule. Annette Pagliaro Sweeney guided the book through production with patience and care, staying on top of many details, and Elizabeth Schaaf managed the production process with great attentiveness. I was fortunate to receive the careful copyediting of Linda McLatchie. In the marketing, advertising, and promotion departments, Angela Dambrowski deserves warm thanks for her work, as does marketing manager Molly Parke.

I am grateful to Charles H. Christensen, the retired president of Bedford/St. Martin's, for his generous help and thoughtful suggestions throughout the life of this book. Finally, I especially want to thank Bedford's president, Joan E. Feinberg, who conceived the idea for *America Now* and who continues to follow it closely through its various editions, for her deep and abiding interest in college composition. It is a great pleasure and privilege to work with her.

Robert Atwan

Contents

1   Is There an Obesity Epidemic?   53

Are Americans wise to be concerned about their weight? Or is this worry really a misguided obsession that cruelly stigmatizes overweight people while fueling a multibillion-dollar weight-loss industry? What do we know about weight gain anyway? Is it even true that eating makes us fat? An editor of one of the nation's major alternative magazines claims that our current obsession with obesity has sadly turned fat into a moral issue. . . . Too many college students understandably eat poorly, writes a University of Kansas journalism student, and their bad habits now could have disastrous consequences later. . . . Forget most of what you've read about eating, dieting, and exercise, a *Vogue* columnist argues with a healthy combination of facts and humor; permanent weight loss is largely an unrealistic hope. . . . A popular advertisement from around 1930 offers a surefire method of losing weight.

2   Social Networking: What Are the Risks?   83

How are recent Web sites like Facebook and MySpace changing student life? Why are these sites so addictive? Will we ever be able to protect our privacy again? Is the recent surge in the popularity of "Me Media" an indication of serious community expansion or rather a distracting form of current egomania? Are we gaining instant communication but losing real human contact? Not at all, says a columnist for *Wired* magazine: The new connectivity has enhanced, not diminished, our relationships. . . . Still, whatever social values we gain, argues a *Nation* essayist, Facebook represents "one of America's largest electronic surveillance systems" and puts our privacy seriously at risk. . . . A Senior English major from the University of Arizona explores the antisocial aspects of social networking.

3   How Important Is Ethnic Identity?   108

Do you see yourself as representative of a racial or ethnic group? How important is it to your sense of identity to belong to this particular group? How do you identify yourself if, like so many Americans, you belong to more than one group? A young man, born in Ethiopia but transplanted to the United States, searches for a place where he feels he truly belongs. . . . A Mexican American closely examines one complication of assimilation: What happens to someone's name? . . .

In a short graphic memoir, a Taiwanese American considers his own loss of tradition. . . . Taking a slightly different perspective, an Ohio State University journalism student reminds us that the lines separating many ethnic groups are paper thin and that most Americans claim multiple identities.

 4   Gender Differences: Can You Trust the Scientific Reports?   135

Are there real, biologically caused differences between the ways men and women act, think, speak, and behave? Or are these differences trifling and due largely to customs and educational expectations? Can these differences and similarities be scientifically established? Are men, for example, more innately gifted in math and science? Are women innately more social? A scientific paper in behavioral psychology from a prestigious journal disproves the commonly held impression that women are more talkative than men. . . . Two representative reports, one from a leading quarterly and the other from National Public Radio, show how the media covered this scientific news. . . . An article in a feminist journal offers a thorough summary of what happens when the media report on scientific studies, especially those involving gender. . . . Why is his math department so predominantly male, wonders a University of Oregon student, who then attempts to offer an unbiased explanation.

5 / Do We Need an Ethics of Consumption?   171

Does your college store sell sweatshirts made in sweatshops? Have you ever bought fake designer goods, or something that you knew was counterfeit or produced by the labor of exploited workers? Do Americans need to act more responsibly as consumers? Do we need to develop an ethics of consumption? Can we even know when our purchases are responsible and when they're not? A popular fashion magazine argues that when we buy cheap counterfeit goods, "we are financing international crime syndicates that deal in money laundering, human trafficking, and child labor." . . . A nationally prominent author and activist takes a hard, satirical look at child labor and everyone who profits from it, including consumers. . . . A leading progressive points the finger directly at low-cost retailers like Wal-Mart whose costs are low "only because the lives of Chinese factory workers are so undervalued." . . . Why do college students who deplore unfair labor practices continue to buy from the companies accused of perpetrating them? asks a University of Maryland senior in interviews with fellow students. . . . An ad for one of the first automobiles suggests a trend toward what economist Thorstein Veblen called "conspicuous consumption" in 1899.

6   Redesigning Humanity—What Are the Limits?   204

Does someone who can speed along with artificial, high-tech carbon fiber legs possess an unfair advantage in a long-distance race? When are performance enhancements legitimate, and when should they be prohibited? Should contestants who underwent cosmetic surgery be banned from beauty contests? Is it ethical to genetically alter people so that they perform, look, or behave better? A noted newspaper columnist takes a nuanced view of what constitutes an unfair sports advantage, arguing that "technology has been used to enhance performance since the first runner put on a shoe." . . . A highly unusual fashion ad demonstrates the glamour of prosthetics. . . . Not only is it unethical to encourage teenagers to seek cosmetic surgery, writes a University of Florida journalism student, but it's also dangerous. . . . Looking at the larger issue of genetic enhancements, a major American philosopher asks whether living as we were born—whether with a hooked nose or with a crippling disease—is an act of deference to what nature intended, or rather a failure to avail ourselves of the miracles of modern science?

7 Will We Ever Transcend Race?   234

How would you describe the state of race relations in America today? Are relations improving, or are they deteriorating—or does little change? What work remains to be done, and who needs to do it? Can a dialogue between whites and blacks in this country ever amount to more than words? In a memorable passage from what is already considered one of the nation's greatest speeches on race, our 44th President acknowledges the resentments felt on both sides of America's racial divide.... An African American professor of English recounts two odd encounters on campus that demonstrate the complexities of conversation between the races and how we might succeed in getting past them.... Responding to an assignment, one of that professor's students at Bridgewater State College meditates on what it really means to be black in America.... A famous photograph captures the tension surrounding the integration of a southern school in 1957.

8   Education Today: Is Underachieving the Norm?   259

Are Americans getting dumber by the day? Is a college education now the equivalent of what a high school education was forty years ago? Who's to blame? The media? The teachers? The school system? Today's students themselves? It's one thing to become increasingly ignorant of history, geography, and science, argues a prominent social critic, but it's quite another matter to be proud of it. . . . A University of Central Arkansas student agrees and chastises underachieving fellow students who smugly proclaim that "D is for diploma." . . . Debating the pros and cons of podcasting lectures, a psychology and philosophy student at the University of South Alabama believes that this new classroom technology will definitely appeal to "the lazy, the irresponsible and the apathetic." . . . If you don't want a child's classroom to become a propaganda forum for advertisers, suggests a family psychologist, you better know what SEM stands for.

9   Signs of Change: What Can We Expect America to Be?   285

At a time when we are trying to promote democracy across the globe, it's surely worth asking ourselves: How satisfactory is our own democracy? Is it holding up as a viable political system, or is it in need of serious reform? Are too many voters still disenfranchised? How do we get young people to invest in our political future? A young writer argues that the voting age needs to be lowered to six-teen—at least. . . . The editor of a prestigious political journal be-lieves that America's entitlement programs largely ignore young people, to their detriment and to our society's. . . . If the next genera-tion is to enact major changes, claims the editor of a progressive mag-azine, it should end the old-style protests and street demonstrations and engage in "digital disobedience." . . . Change will come about only if we "set aside petty differences and join together as a unified community," writes a University of Washington student. . . . If they could not vote at the time, how did women obtain the right to vote in 1920?

10   What Does the New Class Struggle Look Like?   321

In a strong economy, upward mobility is widely expected, and class issues often appear to belong to another century. But if the economy is shrinking, how do class differences emerge? Who survives, and who doesn't? Do some people and some ethnic groups have better chances than others? In a graphic essay, a libertarian cartoonist takes an irreverent and disturbing look at the difficult and often taboo topic of homelessness. . . . Why is the American film industry so re-luctant to depict poverty and working-class issues, asks two writers in the *Nation* magazine. . . . In the United States, argues a junior at the University of Mississippi, the class struggle is inseparable from the race struggle. . . . A famous activist photographer looks at urban poverty in 1890.

11   The Border: Can We Solve the Illegal Immigration Problem?   348

Is there a solution to the problem of illegal immigration? Does changing the name of what we sometimes call "illegal aliens" to "undocumented workers" change anything? What will mass deportation accomplish, and could it even be done? What will constructing a giant wall along the border achieve? Should Americans simply accept the fact that nothing can be done at this stage and turn to other issues? A New Mexico columnist believes that offering illegal workers "a path toward citizenship" is the best and most logical solution. . . . How can we "have the audacity to label entrepreneurial immigrants 'criminals,'" asks an activist magazine publisher, "when the vast majority of undocumented workers are sincere, skilled, industrious men and women doing what they must to support their families"? . . . One of the nation's finest nonfiction authors wonders what a border wall would accomplish other than to "violate a deep sense of identity most Americans cherish." . . . A UCLA history major probes the human side of the immigration issue in a profile of an undocumented student forced to raise money to pay his college fees.

(12) The Climate Crisis: Is It Real?   381

Is the earth warming at a dangerous rate? Or is the climate crisis just a lot of hot air? Whom should we believe: Al Gore and the scientists who support his dire predictions, or the scientists who dispute those predictions? Is the science faulty? Is it biased for political reasons? Is the planetary threat imminent? And how should the public act—would anything done now be too little and too late? Or must we act immediately to avoid unspeakable catastrophe? A noted American writer and environmentalist invites us to "do something meaningful about global warming—about the biggest single threat that the entire earth has ever faced." . . . An advertisement promotes a conference featuring "the world's largest gathering of global warming 'skeptics.'" . . . One of those skeptics, a prominent African American columnist, warns that "those who have a big stake in global warming hysteria" are unlikely to appear at the conference, and "unfortunately that includes much of the media." . . . Yes, the doomsaying scientists are totally wrong, argues an author and grassroots activist—they failed to see the incredible speed at which our climate system is changing: "A fantastic spasm of altered weather patterns is crashing down upon our heads right now." . . . That's an alarmist scenario that a Johns Hopkins University student believes is complete hype, arguing that Americans have much more important issues to worry about. . . . We will lose "any chance of pulling the planet out of its current ecological tailspin," writes an African American journalist, if

climate change continues to be perceived as only a "white" issue. . . .
Two University of Alabama students spar over the validity of the scientific evidence for global warming. . . . One of the nation's most popular scientists warns against global warming in 1985.

America Now

Short Readings from Recent Periodicals

The Persuasive Writer: Expressing Opinions with Clarity, Confidence, and Civility

It is not possible to extricate yourself from the questions in which your age is involved.

—Ralph Waldo Emerson, "The Fortune of the Republic" (1878)

What Is America Now?

America Now collects very recent essays and articles that have been carefully selected to encourage reading, provoke discussion, and stimulate writing. The philosophy behind the book is that interesting, effective writing originates in public dialogue. The book's primary purpose is to help students proceed from class discussions of reading assignments to the production of complete essays that reflect an engaged participation in those discussions.

The selections in *America Now* come from two main sources—from popular, mainstream periodicals and from college newspapers available on the Internet. Written by journalists and columnists, public figures and activists, as well as by professors and students from all over the country, the selections illustrate the types of material read by millions of Americans every day. In addition to magazine and newspaper writing, the book features a number of recent opinion advertisements (what I call "op-ads" for short). These familiar forms of "social marketing" are often sponsored by corporations or nonprofit organizations and advocacy groups to promote policies, programs, and ideas such as gun control, family planning, literacy, civil rights, or conservation. Such advertising texts allow one to pinpoint and discuss specific techniques of verbal and visual persuasion that are critical in the formation of public opinion.

1

I have gathered the selections into twelve units that cover today's most widely discussed issues and topics: media bias, science and religion, racial conflict, gender differences, consumption and marketing, environmentalism, and so on. As you respond to the readings in discussion and writing, you will be actively taking part in some of the major controversies of our time. Although I have tried in this new edition of *America Now* to represent as many viewpoints as possible on a variety of controversial topics, it's not possible in a collection of this scope to include under each topic either a full spectrum of opinion or a universally satisfying balance of opposing opinions. For some featured topics, an entire book would be required to represent the full spectrum of opinion; for others, a rigid pro-con, either-or format could distort the issue and perhaps overly polarize student responses to it. Selections within a unit usually illustrate the most commonly held opinions on a topic so that readers will get a reasonably good sense of how the issue has been framed and the public discourse and debate it has generated. But if a single opinion isn't immediately or explicitly balanced by an opposite opinion, or if a view seems unusually idiosyncratic, that in no way implies that it is somehow editorially favored or endorsed. Be assured that questions following *every* selection will encourage you to analyze and critically challenge whatever opinion or perspective is expressed in that selection.

Participation is the key to this collection. I encourage you to view reading and writing as a form of participation. I hope you will read the selections attentively, think about them carefully, be willing to discuss them in class, and use what you've learned from your reading and discussion as the basis for your papers. If you do these things, you will develop three skills necessary for successful work in college and beyond: the ability to read critically, to discuss topics intelligently, and to write persuasively. These skills are also sorely needed in our daily lives as citizens. A vital democracy depends on them. The reason democracy is hard, said the Czech author and statesman Václav Havel, is that it requires the participation of everyone.

America Now invites you to see reading, discussion, and writing as closely related activities. As you read a selection, imagine that you have entered into a discussion with the author. Take notes as you read. Question the selection. Challenge its point of view or its evidence. Compare your experience with the author's. Consider how different economic classes or other groups are likely to respond. Remember, just because something appears in a newspaper or book doesn't make it true or accurate. Form the habit of challenging what you read. Don't be persuaded by an opinion simply because it appears in print or because you believe you should accept it. Trust your own observations and experiences. Though logicians never say so, personal experiences and keen observations often form the basis of our most convincing arguments.

When your class discusses a selection, be especially attentive to what others think of it. It's always surprising how two people can read the same article and reach two entirely different interpretations. Observe the range of opinion. Try to understand why and how people arrive at different conclusions. Do some seem to miss the point? Do some distort the author's ideas? Have someone's comments forced you to rethink the selection? Keep a record of the discussion in your notebook. Then, when you begin to draft your paper, consider your essay as an extension of both your imaginary conversation with the author and the actual class discussion. If you've taken detailed notes of your own and the class's opinions about the selection, you should have more than enough information to get started.

What Are Opinions?

One of the primary aims of *America Now* is to help you learn through models and instructional material how to express your opinions in a persuasive, reasonable, civil, and productive fashion. But before we look at effective ways of expressing opinion, let's first consider opinions in general: What are they? Where do they come from?

When we say we have an opinion about something, we usually mean that we have come to a conclusion that something appears true or appears to be valid. But when we express an opinion about something, we are not claiming we are 100 percent certain that something is so. Opinion does not imply certainty and, in fact, is accompanied by some degree of doubt and skepticism. As a result, opinions are most likely to be found in those areas of thought and discussion where our judgments are uncertain. Because human beings know so few things for certain, much of what we believe, or discuss and debate, falls into various realms of probability or possibility. These we call opinions.

Journalists often make a distinction between fact and opinion. Facts can be confirmed and verified and therefore do not involve opinions. We ordinarily don't have opinions about facts, but we can and often do have opinions about the interpretation of facts. For example, it makes no sense to argue whether Washington, D.C., is the capital of the United States since it's an undisputed fact that it is. It's a matter of record and can be established with certainty. Thus, we don't say we have an opinion that Washington, D.C., is the nation's capital; we know for a fact it is. But it would be legitimate to form an opinion about whether that city is the best location for the U.S. capital and whether it should permanently remain the capital. In other words:

- *Washington, D.C., is the capital of the United States of America* is a statement of fact.

- *Washington, D.C., is too poorly located to be the capital of a vast nation* is a statement of opinion.

Further, simply not knowing whether something is a fact does not necessarily make it a matter of opinion. For example, if we don't know the capital of Brazil, that doesn't mean we are then free to form an opinion about which city it is. The capital of Brazil is a verifiable fact and can be identified with absolute certainty. There is no conflicting public opinion about which city is Brazil's capital. The answer is not up for grabs. These examples, however, present relatively simple, readily agreed-upon facts. In real-life disputes, a fact is not always so readily distinguished from an opinion; people argue all the time about whether something is a fact. It's therefore a good idea at the outset of any discussion or argument to try to arrive at a mutual agreement of the facts that are known or knowable and those that could be called into question. Debates over abortion, for example, often hinge on biological facts about embryonic development that are themselves disputed by medical experts.

An opinion almost always exists in the climate of other, conflicting opinions. In discourse, we refer to this overall context of competing opinions as public controversy. Every age has its controversies. At any given time, the public is divided on a great number of topics about which it holds a variety of different opinions. Often the controversy is reduced to two opposing positions; for example, we are asked whether we are pro-life or pro-choice; for or against capital punishment; in favor of or opposed to same-sex marriage, and so on. This book includes many such controversies and covers multiple opinions. One sure way of knowing that something is a matter of opinion is that the public is divided on the topic. We often experience these divisions firsthand as we mature and increasingly come into contact with those who disagree with our opinions.

Some opinions are deeply held, so deeply, in fact, that those who hold them refuse to see them as opinions. For some people on certain issues there can be no difference of opinion; they possess the Truth, and all who differ hold erroneous opinions. This frequently happens in some controversies, where one side in a dispute is so confident of the truth of its position that it cannot see its own point of view as one of several possible points of view. For example, someone may feel so certain that marriage can exist only between a man and a woman that he or she cannot acknowledge the possibility of another position. If one side cannot recognize the existence of a different opinion, cannot entertain or tolerate it, argues not with the correctness of another's perspective but denies the possibility that there can legitimately be another perspective, then discussion and debate become all but impossible.

To be open and productive, public discussion depends on the capacity of all involved to view their own positions, no matter how cherished, as opinions that can be subjected to opposition. There is nothing wrong with possessing a strong conviction, nor with believing our position is the better one, nor with attempting to convince others of our point of view. What is argumentatively wrong and what prevents or restricts free and open discussion is twofold: (1) the failure to recognize our own belief or position as an opinion that could be mistaken; and (2) the refusal to acknowledge the possibility that another's opinion could be correct.

Is one person's opinion as good as another's? Of course not. Although we may believe that everyone has a right to an opinion, we certainly wouldn't ask our mail carrier to diagnose the cause of persistent heartburn or determine whether a swollen gland is serious. In such instances, we respect the opinion of a trained physician. And even when we consult a physician, in serious matters we often seek second and even third opinions just to be sure. An auto mechanic is in a better position to evaluate a used car than someone who's never repaired a car; a lawyer's opinion on whether a contract is valid is more reliable than that belonging to someone who doesn't understand the legal nature of contracts. If an airline manufacturer wants to test a new cockpit instrument design, it solicits opinions from experienced pilots, not passengers. This seems obvious, and yet people continually are persuaded by those who can claim little expert knowledge on a subject or issue: For example, how valuable or trustworthy is the opinion of a celebrity who is paid to endorse a product?

When expressing or evaluating an opinion, we need to consider the extent of our or another person's knowledge about a particular subject. Will anyone take our opinion seriously? On what authority do we base our position? Why do we take someone else's opinion as valuable or trustworthy? What is the source of the opinion? How reliable is it? How biased? One of the first Americans to study the effects of public opinion, Walter Lippmann, wrote in 1925, "It is often very illuminating, therefore, to ask yourself how you get at the facts on which you base your opinion. Who actually saw, heard, felt, counted, named the thing, about which you have an opinion?" Is your opinion, he went on to ask, based on something you heard from someone who heard it from someone else, who in turn heard it from someone else?

How Do We Form Opinions?

How can we possibly have reasonable opinions on all the issues of the day? One of the strains of living in a democracy that encourages a diversity of perspectives is that every responsible citizen is expected to have informed opinions on practically every public question. What do you think about the death penalty? About dependency on foreign oil? About the way the media cover the news? About the extent of racial discrimination? Do you or don't you support gun control? Are you pro-choice or pro-life? What's your position on affirmative action? Must there be a wall separating church and state? Should the United States avoid foreign entanglements or participate in humanitarian intervention where necessary around the globe? Certainly no single individual is an expert on every public issue. Certainly no one person possesses inside information or access to reliable data on every topic that becomes part of public controversy. Still, many people, by the time they are able to vote, have formed numerous opinions. Where do these opinions come from?

Although social scientists and psychologists have been studying opinion formation for decades, the subject still retains a great deal of imprecision. The sources of opinion are multiple and constantly shifting, and individuals differ so widely in experience, cultural background, and temperament that efforts to identify and classify the various ways opinion is formed are bound to be tentative and incomplete. What follows is a brief, though realistic, attempt to list some of the practical ways that Americans come by the opinions they hold.

1. *Inherited opinions.*   These are opinions we derive from earliest childhood—transmitted via family, culture, traditions, customs, regions, social institutions, or religion. For example, young people may identify themselves as either Democrats or Republicans because of their family affiliations. Although these opinions may change as we mature, they are often ingrained. Many people retain inherited opinions into their early adulthood and even throughout their entire lives. The more traditional the culture or society, the more likely the opinions that grow out of early childhood will be retained and passed on to the next generation. One reason behind the countercultural movements of the late 1960s was the enormous increase in the number of American high school graduates who went on to college, which caused a rift between the educational levels of parents and children—a generational war of values that became the subject of countless movies and books at the time.

2. *Involuntary opinions.*   These are opinions that we have not culturally and socially inherited or consciously adopted but that come to us through direct or indirect forms of indoctrination. They could be the customs of a cult or the propaganda of an ideology. Brainwashing is an extreme example of how one acquires opinions involuntarily. A more familiar example is the constant reiteration of advertising messages: We come to possess a favorable opinion of a product not because we've ever used it or know anything about it but because we have been "bombarded" by marketing to think positively about it.

3. *Adaptive opinions.*   Many opinions grow out of our willingness—or even eagerness—to adapt to the prevailing views of particular groups, subgroups, or institutions to which we belong or desire to belong. As many learn, it's easier to follow the path of least resistance than to run counter to it. Moreover, acting out of self-interest, people often adapt their opinions to conform to the views of bosses or authority figures ("follow the leader"), or they prefer to succumb to peer pressure than to oppose it. An employee finds himself accepting or agreeing with an opinion because a job or career depends on it; a student may adapt her opinions to suit those of a professor in the hope of receiving a better grade; a professor may tailor his opinions in conformity with the prevailing beliefs of colleagues; an athlete comes to agree with the dominant attitudes of her teammates. Adaptive opinions are often weakly held and readily changed, depending on circumstances. But over time they can become habitual and turn into convictions.

4. *Concealed opinions.*   In some groups in which certain opinions dominate, certain individuals may not share the prevailing attitudes, but rather than adapt or "rock the boat," they keep their opinions to themselves. They may do this merely to avoid conflict or out of much more serious concerns — such as a fear of ostracism, ridicule, retaliation, or job loss. A common example is seen in the person who by day quietly goes along with the opinions of a group of colleagues but at night freely exchanges "honest" opinions with a group of friends. Some individuals find diaries and journals to be an effective way to express concealed opinions, and many today find on-line chat rooms a space where they can anonymously "be themselves."

5. *Linked opinions.*   Many opinions are closely linked to other opinions. Unlike adaptive opinions, which are usually stimulated by convenience and an incentive to conform, these are opinions we derive from an enthusiastic and dedicated affiliation with certain groups, institutions, or parties. For example, it's not uncommon for someone to agree with every position his or her political party endorses — this phenomenon is usually called "following a party line." Linked opinions may not be well thought out on every narrow issue: Someone may decide to be a Republican or Democrat or Green or Libertarian for a few specific reasons — a position on abortion, war, taxation, cultural values, environment, civil liberties, and so forth — and then go along with, even to the point of strenuously defending, all of the other positions the party espouses because they are all part of its political platform or system of beliefs. In other words, once we accept opinions A and B, we are more likely to accept C and D, and so on down the chain. As Ralph Waldo Emerson succinctly put it, "If I know your sect, I anticipate your argument."

6. *Considered opinions.*   These are opinions we have formed as a result of firsthand experience, reading, discussion and debate, or independent thinking and reasoning. These opinions are formed from direct knowledge and often from exposure and consideration of other opinions. A person who has experienced poverty, discrimination, or disability will form attitudes about those conditions that in many respects will remain beyond dispute and will help endow her or his opinions on those and related topics with authority. Wide reading on a subject and exposure to diverse views help ensure that our opinions are based on solid information and tested against competing opinions. One simple way to judge whether your opinion is carefully

thought out is to list your reasons for holding it. Some people who express opinions on a topic are not able to offer a single reason for why they have those opinions. Of course, reasons don't necessarily make an opinion correct, but people who can support their opinions with one or more reasons are more persuasive than those who cannot provide any reasons for their beliefs (see pp. 17–18). *America Now's* twelve chapters, if the selections are read carefully and discussed and challenged in the context of the surrounding instructional material, are designed to help students learn the process of forming educated opinions that are backed up with reasons.

This list is not exhaustive, and readers are invited to think of other common sources and types of opinion. Nor are the sources and types above mutually exclusive; the opinions of any individual may derive from all six sources or represent a mixture of several. For example, someone may simply inherit an entrenched family opinion on some matter but, as time passes, come to test it so thoroughly in the context of competing opinions that it reaches the level of a considered opinion. A child growing up in a working-class home that, say, uncritically values trade unions may eventually, through a combination of experience, discussion, and a study of economics and labor history, become a highly knowledgeable advocate of trade unions. As students learn to express their opinions effectively, they will find it useful to question themselves about the origins and development of those opinions. By tracing the process that led to the formation of our present opinions, we can better understand ourselves—our convictions, our inconsistencies, our biases, our blind spots.

Participating in Class Discussion: Six Basic Rules

Discussion is a learned activity. It requires a variety of essential academic skills: speaking, listening, thinking, and preparing. The following six basic rules are vital to healthy and productive discussion.

1. *Take an active speaking role.*   Good discussion demands that everyone participates, not (as so often happens) just a vocal few. Many students remain detached from discussion because they are afraid to speak in a group. This fear is quite common—so common that psychological surveys show that speaking in front of a group is generally one of our worst fears. A leading communication consultant suggests that people choke up because they are more worried

about how others will respond than about what they themselves
have to say. It helps to remember that most people will be more interested in *what* you say than in how you say it. Once you get over the
initial fear of speaking in public, your speech skills will improve with
practice.

2. *Listen attentively.*   No one who doesn't listen attentively can
participate in group discussion. This may sound obvious, but just
think of how many senseless arguments you've had because either
you or the person with whom you were talking completely misunderstood what was said. A good listener not only hears what someone is
saying but also understands *why* he or she is saying it. One of the
most important things about listening is that it leads to one element
that lively discussion depends on: good questions. When the interesting questions begin to emerge, you know good discussion has truly
begun.

3. *Examine all sides of an issue.*   Good discussion requires that
we be patient with complexity. Difficult problems rarely have obvious and simple solutions, nor can they be easily summarized in popular slogans. Complex issues demand to be turned over in our minds
so that we can see them from a variety of angles. Group discussion
broadens our perspective and deepens our insight into difficult issues
and ideas.

4. *Suspend judgment.*   Class discussion is best conducted in an
open-minded and tolerant spirit. To fully explore ideas and issues,
you need to be receptive to the opinions of others, even when they
contradict your own. Remember, discussion is not the same as debate. Its primary purpose is communication, not competition. In discussion, you are not necessarily trying to win everyone over to your
point of view. The goal of group discussion should be to open up a
topic so that everyone in the group is exposed to a spectrum of attitudes. Suspending judgment does not mean you shouldn't hold a
strong belief or opinion about an issue; it means that you should be
willing to take into account rival beliefs or opinions. An opinion
formed without an awareness of other points of view—one that has
not been tested against contrary ideas—is not a strong opinion but
merely a stubborn one.

5. *Avoid abusive or insulting language.*   Free and open discussion occurs only when we respect the beliefs and opinions of others.
If we speak in ways that fail to show respect for differing viewpoints—
if we resort to name-calling or use demeaning and malicious expres-

sions, for example—not only do we embarrass ourselves, but we also close off the possibility for an intelligent and productive exchange of ideas. Contrary to what you might gather from some popular radio and television talk shows, shouting insults and engaging in hate speech are signs of verbal and intellectual bankruptcy. They are usually the last resort of someone who has nothing to say.

6. *Come prepared.*   Discussion is not merely random conversation. It demands a certain degree of preparation and focus. To participate in class discussion, you must consider assigned topics beforehand and read whatever is required. Develop the habit of reading with pen in hand, underlining key points and jotting down questions, impressions, and ideas in your notebook. The notes you bring to class will be an invaluable aid in group discussion.

From Discussion to Writing

As this book amply demonstrates, we live in a world of conflicting opinions. Each of us over time has inherited, adopted, and gradually formed many opinions on a variety of topics. Of course, there are also a good number of public issues or questions about which we have not formed opinions or have undecided attitudes. In many public debates, members have unequal shares at stake. Eighteen-year-olds, for example, are much more likely to become impassioned over the government reviving a military draft or a state raising the legal age for driving than they would over Medicaid cuts or Social Security issues. Some public questions personally affect us more than others.

Thus, not all the issues covered in this book will at first make an equal impact on everyone. But whether you take a particular interest in a given topic or not, this book invites you to share in the spirit of public controversy. Many students, once introduced to the opposing sides of a debate or the multiple positions taken toward a public issue, will begin to take a closer look at the merits of different opinions. Once we start evaluating these opinions, once we begin stepping into the shoes of others and learning what's at stake in certain positions, we often find ourselves becoming involved with the issue and may even come to see ourselves as participants. After all, we are all part of the public, and to a certain extent all questions affect us: Ask the eighteen-year-old if he or she will be equipped to deal with the medical and financial needs of elderly parents and an issue that appears to affect only those near retirement will seem much closer to home.

As mentioned earlier, *America Now* is designed to stimulate discussion and writing grounded in response to a variety of public issues. A key to using this book is to think about discussion and writing not as separate activities but as an interrelated process. In discussion, we hear other opinions and formulate our own; in writing, we express our opinions in the context of other opinions. Both discussion and writing require articulation and deliberation. Both require an aptitude for listening carefully to others. Discussion stimulates writing, and writing in turn stimulates more discussion.

Group discussion stimulates and enhances your writing in several important ways. First, it supplies you with ideas. Let's say that you are participating in a discussion on the importance of ethnic identity (see Chapter 3). One of your classmates mentions some of the problems a mixed ethnic background can cause. But suppose you also come from a mixed background, and when you think about it, you believe that your mixed heritage has given you more advantages than disadvantages. Hearing her viewpoint may inspire you to express your differing perspective on the issue. Your perspective could lead to an interesting personal essay.

Suppose you now start writing that essay. You don't need to start from scratch and stare at a blank piece of paper or computer screen for hours. Discussion has already given you a few good leads. First, you have your classmate's opinions and attitudes to quote or summarize. You can begin your paper by explaining that some people view a divided ethnic identity as a psychological burden. You might expand on your classmate's opinion by bringing in additional information from other student comments or from your reading to show how people often focus on only the negative side of mixed identities. You can then explain your own perspective on this topic. Of course, you will need to give several examples showing *why* a mixed background has been an advantage for you. The end result can be a first-rate essay, one that takes other opinions into account and demonstrates a clearly established point of view. It is personal, and yet it takes a position that goes beyond one individual's experiences.

Whatever the topic, your writing will benefit from reading and discussion, activities that will give your essays a clear purpose or goal. In that way, your papers will resemble the selections found in this book: They will be a *response* to the opinions, attitudes, experiences, issues, ideas, and proposals that inform current public discourse. This is why most writers write; this is what most newspapers and magazines publish; this is what most people read. *America Now* consists entirely of such writing. I hope you will read the selections with enjoyment, discuss the issues with an open mind, and write about the topics with purpose and enthusiasm.

The Practice of Writing

Suppose you wanted to learn to play the guitar. What would you do first? Would you run to the library and read a lot of books on music? Would you then read some instructional books on guitar playing? Might you try to memorize all the chord positions? Then would you get sheet music for songs you liked and memorize them? After all that, if someone handed you an electric guitar, would you immediately be able to play like Jimi Hendrix or Eric Clapton?

I don't think you would begin that way. You probably would start out by strumming the guitar, getting the feel of it, trying to pick out something familiar. You probably would want to take lessons from someone who knows how to play. And you would practice, practice, practice. Every now and then your instruction book would come in handy. It would give you basic information on frets, notes, and chord positions, for example. You might need to refer to that information constantly in the beginning. But knowing the chords is not the same as knowing how to manipulate your fingers correctly to produce the right sounds. You need to be able to *play* the chords, not just know them.

Learning to read and write well is not that much different. Even though instructional books can give you a great deal of advice and information, the only way anyone really learns to read and write is through constant practice. The only problem, of course, is that nobody likes practice. If we did, we would all be good at just about everything. Most of us, however, want to acquire a skill quickly and easily. We don't want to take lesson after lesson. We want to pick up the instrument and sound like a professional in ten minutes.

Wouldn't it be a wonderful world if that could happen? Wouldn't it be great to be born with a gigantic vocabulary so that we instantly knew the meaning of every word we saw or heard? We would never have to go through the slow process of consulting a dictionary whenever we stumbled across an unfamiliar word. But, unfortunately, life is not so easy. To succeed at anything worthwhile requires patience and dedication. Watch a young figure skater trying to perfect her skills and you will see patience and dedication at work; or watch an accident victim learning how to maneuver a wheelchair so that he can begin again an independent existence; or observe a new American struggling to learn English. None of these skills are quickly or easily acquired. Like building a vocabulary, they all take time and effort. They all require practice. And they require something even more important: the willingness to make mistakes. Can someone learn to skate without taking a spill? Or learn a new language without mispronouncing a word?

What Is "Correct English"?

One part of the writing process may seem more difficult than others—correct English. Yes, nearly all of what you read will be written in relatively correct English. Or it's probably more accurate to say "corrected" English, because most published writing is revised or "corrected" several times before it appears in print. Even skilled professional writers make mistakes that require correction.

Most native speakers don't actually *talk* in "correct" English. There are numerous regional patterns and dialects. As the Chinese American novelist Amy Tan says, there are "many Englishes." What we usually consider correct English is a set of guidelines developed over time to help standardize written expression. This standardization—like any agreed-upon standards such as weights and measures—is a matter of use and convenience. Suppose you went to a vegetable stand and asked for a pound of peppers and the storekeeper gave you a half pound but charged you for a full one. When you complained, he said, "But that's what *I* call a pound." What if you next bought a new compact disc you'd been waiting for, and when you tried to play it, you discovered it wouldn't fit your CD player. Life would be very frustrating if everyone had a different set of standards: Imagine what would happen if some states used a red light to signal "go" and a green one for "stop." Languages are not that different. In all cultures, languages—especially written languages—have gradually developed certain general rules and principles to make communication as clear and efficient as possible.

You probably already have a guidebook or handbook that systematically sets out certain rules of English grammar, punctuation, and spelling. Like our guitar instruction book, these handbooks serve a very practical purpose. Most writers—even experienced authors—need to consult them periodically. Beginning writers may need to rely on them far more regularly. But just as we don't learn how to play chords by merely memorizing finger positions, we don't learn how to write by memorizing the rules of grammar or punctuation.

Writing is an activity, a process. Learning how to do it—like learning to ride a bike or prepare a tasty stew—requires *doing* it. Correct English is not something that comes first. We don't need to know the rules perfectly before we can begin to write. As in any activity, corrections are part of the learning process. You fall off the bike and get on again, trying to "correct" your balance this time. You sample the stew and "correct" the seasoning. You draft a paper about the neighborhood you live in, and as you (or a classmate or instructor) read it over, you notice that certain words and expressions could stand some improvement. And step by step, sentence by sentence, you begin to write better.

Writing as a Public Activity

Many people have the wrong idea about writing. They view writing as a very private act. They picture the writer sitting all alone and staring into space waiting for ideas to come. They think that ideas come from "deep" within and reach expression only after they have been fully articulated inside the writer's head.

These images are part of a myth about creative writing and, like most myths, are sometimes true. A few poets, novelists, and essayists do write in total isolation and search deep inside themselves for thoughts and stories. But most writers have far more contact with public life. This is especially true of people who write regularly for magazines, newspapers, and professional journals. These writers work within a lively social atmosphere in which issues and ideas are often intensely discussed and debated. Nearly all the selections in this book illustrate this type of writing.

As you work on your own papers, remember that writing is very much a public activity. It is rarely performed alone in an "ivory tower." Writers don't always have the time, the desire, the opportunity, or the luxury to be all alone. They may be writing in a newsroom with clacking keyboards and noise all around them; they may be writing at a kitchen table, trying to feed several children at the same time; they may be writing on subways or buses. The great English novelist D. H. Lawrence grew up in a small impoverished coal miner's cottage with no place for privacy. It proved to be an enabling experience. Throughout his life, he could write wherever he happened to be; it didn't matter how many people or how much commotion surrounded him.

There are more important ways in which writing is a public activity. Writing is often a response to public events. Most of the articles you encounter every day in newspapers and magazines respond directly to timely or important issues and ideas, topics that people are currently talking about. Writers report on these topics, supply information about them, discuss and debate the differing viewpoints. The units in this book all represent topics now regularly discussed on college campuses and in the national media. In fact, all of the topics were chosen because they emerged so frequently in college newspapers.

When a columnist decides to write on a topic like same-sex marriage, she willingly enters an ongoing public discussion about the issue. She didn't just make up the topic. She knows that it is a serious issue, and she is aware that a wide variety of opinions have been expressed about it. She has not read everything on the subject but usually knows enough about the different arguments to state her own position or attitude persuasively. In fact, what helps make her writing persuasive is that she takes into account the opinions of others. Her own essay, then, becomes a part of the continuing debate and discussion, one that you in turn may want to join.

Such issues are not only matters for formal and impersonal debate. They also invite us to share our *personal* experiences. Many of the selections in this book show how writers participate in the discussion of issues by drawing on their experiences. For example, the essay by Lauren Carter, "Isn't Watermelon Delicious?," is based largely on the author's personal observations and experience, though the topic—racial identity—is one widely discussed and debated by countless Americans. You will find that nearly every unit of *America Now* contains a selection that illustrates how you can use your personal experiences to discuss and debate a public issue.

Writing is public in yet another way. Practically all published writing is reviewed, edited, and re-edited by different people before it goes to press. The author of a magazine article has most likely discussed the topic at length with colleagues and publishing professionals and may have asked friends or experts in the field to look it over. By the time you see the article in a magazine, it has gone through numerous readings and probably quite a few revisions. Although the article is credited to a particular author, it was no doubt read and worked on

How to Support Opinions

In everyday life, we express many opinions, ranging from (as the chapters in this collection indicate) weighty issues such as immigration and global warming to personal matters such as body image and our Facebook profile. In conversation, we often express our opinions as assertions. An assertion is merely an opinionated claim—usually of our likes or dislikes, agreements or disagreements—that is not supported by evidence or reasons. For example, *"Amnesty for illegal immigrants is a poor idea"* is merely an assertion about public policy—it states an opinion, but it offers no reason or reasons why anyone should accept it.

When entering public discussion and debate, we have an obligation to support our opinions. Simple assertions—*"Men are better at math than women"*—may be provocative and stimulate heated debate, but the discussion will get nowhere unless reasons are offered to support the claim. The following methods are among the most common ways you can support your opinions.

1. **Experts and authority.** You support your claim that the earth is growing warmer by citing one of the world's leading climatologists; you support your opinion that a regular diet of certain vegetables can drastically reduce the risk of colon cancer by citing medical authorities.

2. **Statistics.** You support the view that your state needs tougher drunk driving laws by citing statistics that show fatalities from drunk driving have increased 20 percent in the past two years; you support the claim that Americans now prefer smaller, more fuel-efficient cars by showing surveys that reveal a 30 percent drop in SUV and truck sales over the past six months.

3. **Examples.** You support your opinion that magazine advertising is becoming increasingly pornographic by describing several recent instances from different periodicals; you defend your claim that women can be top-ranked chess players by identifying several women who are. Note that when using examples to prove your point, you will almost always require several; one example will seldom convince anyone.

4. **Personal experience.** Although you may not be an expert or authority in any area, your personal experience can count as evidence in support of an opinion. Suppose you claim that the campus parking facilities are inadequate for commuting students, and, a commuter yourself, you document the difficulties you have every day with parking. Such personal knowledge, assuming it is not false or exaggerated, would plausibly support your position. Many newspaper reporters back up their coverage with eyewitness testimony.

5. **Possible consequences.** You defend an opinion that space exploration is necessary by arguing that it could lead to the discovery of much-needed new energy resources; you support an opinion that expanding the rights of gun ownership is a mistake by showing that it will result in more crime and gun-related deaths.

These are only a few of the ways opinions can be supported, but they are among the most significant. Note that providing support for an opinion does not automatically make it true or valid; someone will invariably counter your expert with an opposing expert, discover conflicting statistical data, produce counter-examples, or offer personal testimony that contradicts your own. Still, once you've offered legitimate reasons for what you think, you have made a big leap from "mere opinion" to "informed opinion."

by others who helped with suggestions and improvements. As a beginning writer, you need to remember that most of what you read in newspapers, magazines, and books has gone through a writing process that involves the collective efforts of several people besides the author. Students usually don't have that advantage and should not feel discouraged when their own writing doesn't measure up to the professionally edited materials they are reading for a course.

Writing for the Classroom: Three Annotated Student Essays

The following three student essays perfectly characterize the kind of writing that *America Now* features and examines. The essays will provide you with effective models of how to express an opinion on a public issue in a concise and convincing manner. Each essay demonstrates the way a writer responds to a public concern—in this case, the stereotyping of others. Each essay also embodies the principles of productive discussion outlined throughout this introduction. In fact, these three essays were especially commissioned from student writers to perform a double service: The essays show writers clearly expressing opinions on a timely topic that personally matters to them and, at the same time, demonstrate how arguments can be shaped to advance the possibility of further discussion instead of ending it.

These three essays also feature three different approaches to the topic of stereotyping. Each essay reflects a different use of source material: The first essay uses none; the second responds directly to a recent controversial magazine article; and the third relies on reading material found in this book. Thus, students can observe three distinct and common methods of learning to write for the classroom:

1. **expressing an opinion based on personal experience alone**
2. **expressing an opinion in response to an opposing opinion**
3. **expressing an opinion with reference to assigned readings**

Although there are many other approaches to classroom writing (too many to be fully represented in an introduction), these three should provide first-year students with accessible and effective models for the types of writing they will most likely be required to do in connection with the assignments in *America Now*.

Each essay is annotated to help you focus on some of the most effective means of expressing an opinion. First, read each essay through and consider the points the writer is making. Then return to the essay and analyze more closely the key parts highlighted for examination. This process is designed to help you see how writers construct arguments to support their opinions. It is an analytical process you should begin to put into practice on your own as you read and explore the many issues in this collection. A detailed explanation of the highlighted passages follows each selection.

Expressing an Opinion Based on Personal Experience Alone

The first essay, Kati Mather's "The Many Paths to Success—With or Without a College Education," expresses an opinion that is based almost entirely on personal experience and reflection. In her argument that Americans have grown so predisposed to a college education that they dismiss other forms of education as inferior, Mather shows how this common attitude can lead to unfair stereotypes. Her essay cites no formal evidence or outside sources—no research, studies, quotations, other opinions, or assigned readings. Instead, she relies on her own educational experience and the conclusions she draws from it to support her position.

Kati Mather is a senior at Wheaton College in Massachusetts, majoring in English and Italian studies. She recently spent a semester in Florence, Italy, where she spoke only Italian. In her spare time, she enjoys reading and spending time outdoors. She lives in southern Rhode Island.

Kati Mather

The Many Paths to Success—With or Without a College Education

1. Opens with personal perspective

I always knew I would go to college. When I was younger, higher education was not a particular dream of mine, but I understood that it was the expected path. Even as children, many of us are so thoroughly groomed for college that declining the opportunity is unacceptable. Although I speak as someone who could afford such an assumption, even my peers without the same economic advantages went to college. Education is important, but I

2. Establishes main point early

believe our common expectations—that everyone can and should go to college, and that a college education is necessary to succeed—and the stigmas attached to those who forgo higher education, are false and unfair.

3. Supports main point

In the past, only certain fortunate people could attain a college education. But over time, America modernized its approach to education, beginning with compulsory high school attendance in most states, and then evolving into a system with numerous options for higher learning. Choices for post-secondary education today are overwhelming, and—with full- and part-time programs

1

2

offered by community colleges, state universities, and private institutions—accessibility is not the issue it once was. In our frenzy to adhere to the American dream, which means, among other things, that everyone is entitled to an education, the schooling system has become too focused on the social expectations that come with a college education. It is normally considered to be the gateway to higher income and an upwardly mobile career. But we would all be better served if the system were instead focused on learning, and on what learning means to the individual.

It is admirable that we are committed to education in this country, but not everyone should be expected to take the college track. Vocational education, for instance, seems to be increasingly a thing of the past, which is regrettable because careers that do not require a college degree are as vital as those that do. If vocational schooling were more widely presented as an option—and one that everyone should take the time to consider—we would not be so quick to stereotype those who do not attend traditional academic institutions. Specialized labor such as construction, plumbing, and automobile repair are crucial to a healthy, functioning society. While a college education can be a wonderful thing to possess, we need people to aspire to other forms of education, which include both vocational schooling and learning skills on the job. Those careers (and there are many others) are as important as teaching, accounting, and medicine.

4. Provides examples of alternatives to college

Despite the developments in our educational system that make college more accessible, financial constraints exist for many—as do family pressures and expectations, intellectual limitations, and a host of other obstacles. Those obstacles warrant neither individual criticism nor far-reaching stereotypes. For example, a handful of students from my high school took an extra year or two to graduate, and I sadly assumed that they would not be as successful as those who graduated on time. I did not stop to consider their situations, or that they might simply be on a different path in life than I was. Looking back, it was unfair to stereotype others in this way. Many of them are hard-working and fulfilled individuals today. There is no law that says everyone has to finish high school and go to college to be successful. Many famous actors, musicians, artists, and professional athletes will freely admit that they never finished high school or college, and these are people we admire, who could very well be making more money in a year than an entire graduating class combined. Plus, we applaud their talent and the fact that they chose their own paths. But banking on a paying career in the arts or sports is not a safe bet, which is why it is so important to open all practical avenues to young people and to respect the choices they make.

We should focus on this diversity instead of perpetuating the belief that everyone should pursue a formal college education and that those who do not are somehow inadequate. There are, of course, essential skills learned in college that remain useful throughout life, even for those who do not pursue high-powered careers. As a student myself, I will readily admit that a college education plays an important role in a successful life. The skills we have the opportunity to learn in college are important to "real" life, and some of these can be used no matter what our career path. Among other things, I've learned how to interact with different people, how to live on my own, how to accept rejection, how to articulate what I want to say, and how to write. Writing is one of the most useful skills taught in college because written communication is necessary in so many different aspects of life.

5

I hope that my college education will lead to success and upward mobility in my career. But I can also allow that, once out of college, most students want to find a job that relates to their studies. In these hard times, however, that may not always be the case. I know from my own experience that other jobs—including those that do not require a college education—can be meaningful to anyone with the will to work and contribute. I'm grateful for the opportunities I've had that led to my college education, and though I do think we have grown too rigid in our thinking about the role of education, I also think we have the chance to change our attitudes and approaches for everyone's benefit.

6

The widespread belief that everyone must go to college to be a success, and that everyone *can* go to college, is not wholly true. Of course, many people will benefit greatly from a quality education, and a quality education is more accessible today than ever before. But college is not the only option. Hard-working people who do not take that path can still be enormously successful, and we should not think otherwise. We can all disprove stereotypes. There are countless accomplished people who are not formally educated. This country offers many roads to success, but we must re-

7

5. Offers balanced view of alternatives

6. Closes by summarizing position

member that embracing diversity is essential to all of us. While I will not deny that my education has helped me along my chosen path, I firmly believe that, had I taken a different one, it too would have enabled me to make a valuable contribution to our society.

Comments

The following comments correspond to the numbered annotations that appear in the margins of Kati Mather's essay.

1. Mather begins her essay with an effective opening sentence that at once identifies her background and establishes the personal tone and perspective she will take throughout. The word *always* suggests that she personally had no doubts about attending college and knew it was expected of her since childhood. Thus, she is not someone who opted to skip college, and she is writing from that perspective. As a reader, you may want to consider how this perspective affects your response to arguments against attending college; for example, would you be more persuaded if the same argument had been advanced by someone who decided against a college education?

2. Mather states the main point of her essay at the end of paragraph 1. She clearly says that the "common expectations" that everyone should attend college and that only those who do so will succeed are "false and unfair." She points out that those who don't attend college are stigmatized. These general statements allow her to introduce the issue of stereotyping in the body of her essay.

3. Although Mather does not offer statistical evidence supporting her assumption that a college education is today considered a necessity, she backs up that belief with a brief history of how the increasing accessibility of higher education in the United States evolved to the point that a college degree now appears to be a universal entitlement.

4. In paragraph 3, Mather introduces the subject of vocational education as an alternative to college. She believes that vocational training is not sufficiently presented to students as an option, even though such skills are as "vital" to society as are traditional college degrees. If more students carefully considered vocational schooling, she maintains, we would in general be less inclined to "stereotype" those who decide not to attend college. In paragraph 4, she acknowledges how she personally failed to consider the different situations and options faced by other students from her high school class.

5. In paragraph 5, Mather shows that she is attempting to take a balanced view of various educational options. She thus avoids a common tendency when forming a comparison—to make one thing either superior or inferior to the other. At this point in the argument, some writers might have decided to put down or criticize a college education, arguing that vocational training is even better than a college degree. By stating how important college can be to those who choose to attend, Mather resists that simplistic tactic and strengthens her contention that we need to assess all of our educational options fairly, without overvaluing some and undervaluing others.

6. In her concluding paragraph, Mather summarizes her position, claiming that "college is not the only option" and reminding readers that many successful careers were forged without a college degree. Her essay returns to a personal note: Had she decided not to attend college, she would still be a valuable member of society.

Expressing An Opinion in Response to an Opposing Opinion

Candace Rose Rardon's essay "Not-So-Great Expectations" tackles the difficult and sensitive question of differences in gender. Like Mather, Rardon draws from personal experience in her argument, but rather than responding to a general climate of opinion, she is writing in direct contradiction of another writer—in this case, the columnist Christopher Hitchens, whose essay "Why Women Aren't Funny" proposes a sense-of-humor gap between the sexes. This forces Rardon to structure her argument in relation to Hitchens's essay, to cite the essay verbatim, to concede points to him, and to distance herself from another writer with roughly the same position as her own. In doing so, Rardon crafts an argument—that women can be just as funny as men—that is both personal and engaged with an open dialogue.

Candace Rose Rardon recently graduated Phi Beta Kappa from the University of Virginia with a BA in English language and literature. As an English major, she welcomes any opportunity to write, whether an essay, an article, or even a short story for a fiction-writing class. When her nose isn't in a book, Rardon enjoys photography, traveling, and pursuing *her passion for music, both in late-night songwriting sessions and in performing with her friends. Although she grew up in the heart of Suffolk, Virginia, in August 2008 she began a six-month stay in London, where she hopes to master the British accent she has always wanted.*

Candace Rose Rardon

Not-So-Great Expectations

We've all no doubt heard or used the idiom, "She can't take a   1
joke," to describe that particularly sensitive soul in our circle of
friends. In his 2007 *Vanity Fair* article "Why Women Aren't
Funny," Christopher Hitchens takes this expression two steps further in his discussion of women and humor: women often don't
get the joke, and they certainly can't *make* one. As a female and
thus a part of the gender of "inferior funniness," as Hitchens so
graciously puts it, I was appalled by his argument and immediately
went on the defensive. Although I'm no comedian and would
never describe myself as "funny," I have plenty of girlfriends who
make me laugh til my sides hurt; they defy the blanket statements
abounding in Hitchens's article.

But I wasn't the only one to question his argument. Just over a   2
year later, Alessandra Stanley wrote a countering article for *Vanity
Fair* titled, "Who Says Women Aren't Funny?" Stanley asserts that,
not only are they funny, women — now more than ever — possess
established, widely embraced careers "dishing out the jokes with
a side of sexy." To me, the underlying issue stemming from this
pair of articles is a question of expectations — both of *who* and
what is funny. To near any solution in this debate of women and
humor, we must begin by raising these expectations. For starters,
what *is* actually expected of men and women? If, as Stanley writes,
"society has different expectations for women," what are these divergent requirements? For Hitchens, there is a lot of pressure rid-
ing on a man's ability to make a woman laugh. Women don't feel
this pressure, he says, because "they already appeal to men, if you
catch my drift." If I'm catching Hitchens's drift, a woman's physical attractiveness is analogous to a man's sense of humor as a necessary component in impressing the opposite sex. According to
Hitchens, it seems to be all about what one has to offer. If a
woman is attractive, there is no need for her to be funny or intelligent. Moreover, Hitchens even suggests a combination of qualities
actually becomes "threatening to men if [women] appear too
bright."

---

1. Cites opposing view concisely

2. Additional response expands discourse

3. *Extra examples broaden scope of argument*

At this point, I can't help but think of the pilot episode of *Sex and the City*, in which Miranda Hobbes brings up this exact point to her date, Skipper Johnston: "Women either fall into one of two categories: beautiful and boring, or homely and interesting? Is that what you're saying to me?" Despite Skipper's resounding "no" for an answer, it's clear Miranda has a point. Society has conditioned us into this mindset. Society has set the bar low for women — in my opinion, much lower than what women are capable of offering. This is an idea reinforced by Patricia Marx, an American humorist, former writer for *Saturday Night Live*, and one of the first two women writers on *The Harvard Lampoon*. As quoted in Stanley's article, Marx speculates, "Maybe pretty women weren't funny before because they had no reason to be funny. There was no point to it — people already liked you." Thus, if women are not expected to be funny, why should they be?

3

To take the question of expectations another step further, Hitchens cites a recent study from the Stanford University School of Medicine analyzing the different ways men and women process humor based on their responses to seventy black-and-white cartoons. Dr. Allan L. Reiss, who led the research team, explains, "Women appeared to have less expectation of a reward, which in this case was the punch line of the cartoon. So when they got to the joke's punch line, they were more pleased about it." These lower expectations translate into higher standards for what's funny. Can these women be blamed? Just because the women in the study submitted the cartoons to a higher level of analysis and scrutiny than men, that does not qualify them as unfunny and even "backward in generating" humor, as Hitchens asserts. The study essentially points out that men and women have very different expectations when it comes to what they deem funny. Dr. Reiss continues, "The differences can help account for the fact that men gravitate more to one-liners and slapstick while women tend to use humor more in narrative form and stories." Or, as Hitchens puts it, "Men will laugh at almost anything, often precisely because it is — or they are — extremely stupid. Women aren't like that."

4

4. *Challenges the meaning of statistics*

So with that in mind, I have to ask: would a woman even want to make a man laugh? A brief look at TV shows geared primarily towards a male audience answers my question. Spike TV, a network designed for young adult males, features shows with humor

5

that is often crude, immature, and just childish — not exactly the qualities any woman I know is racing to embody. Instead, women often want to make men laugh for the same reasons they'd want to make anyone, male or female, laugh — to reach common ground, establish familiarity, and build friendship. Slapstick and one-liners by their nature do not achieve those goals. Even in relationships between the two sexes, men don't usually try to make women laugh through slapstick; rather, such humor is culturally perceived as a way of fostering camaraderie between males. Essentially, Hitchens's argument is flawed here because none of this means women aren't funny. The sense of narrative in women's humor, as pointed out by the Stanford study, is simply a different idea of what is funny. It actually makes sense that women are deemed "not funny" by male counterparts such as Hitchens. If Hitchens believes women generally fall short in the humor department, and that we do so because women are slower to laugh at slapstick and one-liners, then making a man laugh is a quality I wouldn't even want.

5. Places debate in larger context

Whenever I'm faced with a problem, I always have to ask, is there a concrete solution? In other words, are there any expectations for change? Can you indeed change your sense of humor? A quick search through Amazon.com reveals scores of books that seem to think so, such as Jon Macks's *How to Be Funny* (Simon and Schuster, 2003) or Steve Allen's *How to Be Funny: Discovering the Comic You* (Prometheus Books, 1998) and *Make 'Em Laugh* (Prometheus Books, 1993). But where does our sense of humor come from in the first place? Can you develop this ability to crack a joke, or is it something we're born with? Hitchens agrees with the latter idea, writing that Mother Nature has equipped "many fellows with very little armament for the struggle" of impressing women. Stanley, though, seems to feel "the nature-versus-nurture argument also extends to humor," asserting that our sense of humor is often predetermined by our culture and society. I find some truth in both of these arguments. While the Stanford study points out the innate differences in each gender's responses to humor, our society has also conditioned these differences and continues to reinforce our expectations of each sex. Changing these expectations will be no easy task.

Finally, the question of women and humor is not about whether a woman can be attractive and funny, as Stanley's point seems to be. In fact, I find the photographs that accompany her article, portraying female comedians in seductive, alluring poses, to be just as demeaning as Hitchens's generalizations. It's about looking past stereotypes and gender lines and raising our expectations for all parties involved. I've known plenty of funny females and an equal number of not-so-funny guys. And I refuse to accept low expectations — of *who* is funny and *what* is funny.

6. Ends on an appropriate punchline

If Hitchens still wants to insist women aren't funny, well . . . *the joke's on him.*

8

Comments

The following comments correspond to the numbered annotations that appear in the margins of Candace Rose Rardon's essay.

1. Rardon is obliged to quote Hitchens's essay, but instead of a long block quotation articulating his position as a whole, she begins by citing the title and the phrase "inferior funniness," which gets at the gist of her antagonist's argument without burdening the reader with too much outside material. This concision allows Rardon to move straight into her own points. Notice how this argument is immediately personal: Rardon declares that she was "appalled" by Hitchens's position when she came across it, and that her immediate reaction was that she had "plenty of girlfriends who make me laugh til my sides hurt."

2. Toward the middle of paragraph 2, Rardon quotes Alessandra Stanley's response to Hitchens's article. Adding another voice more or less on her side helps frame the debate and contextualizes Rardon's essay within an already existing exchange of opinions. But Rardon does not buy into Stanley's argument wholesale; she announces that she'll try to probe a larger question — "*who* and *what* is funny." Rardon sets us up to expect an essay not only about genetic differences between the sexes but also about the nature of humor itself, and what we laugh at.

3. In paragraph 3, Rardon brings in two other sources to back up her view that "society has set the bar low for women—in my opinion, much lower than what women are capable of offering." The first is the HBO series *Sex and the City*, and the second (cited also by Stanley) is humorist Patricia Marx. These very divergent sources of information—a hit television show and a print humor writer—help

broaden the scope of the argument beyond the simple manufacture of one-liners. The appeal to *Sex and the City* especially offers Rardon's readers a familiar voice in doubting the dichotomy between attractive women and intelligent women.

4. In paragraph 4, Rardon attacks what would appear to be a strong plank in Hitchens's argument: a Stanford study seeming to indicate that men are more likely than women are to appreciate the punch lines of one-line jokes. Rardon employs an interesting tactic here: Instead of casting doubt on the data or the reasoning of the study as manifested in Hitchens's piece, she challenges her opponent's very conception of humor. Rardon asserts that the sort of simpleminded jokes Hitchens alludes to aren't true humor, and asks rhetorically, "Would a woman even want to make a man laugh?" The Stanford study doesn't prove, Rardon argues, that women are less funny than men, but simply that women possess "a different idea of what is funny." In paragraph 5, Rardon sketches her own delineation of the purposes of humor: "to reach common ground, establish familiarity, and build friendship." Is this an agreed-upon definition? Or is Rardon really arguing for this definition as opposed to any other definition?

5. Rardon goes on to place the Hitchens-Stanley debate in the context of the age-old argument of nature versus nurture. If it's true that men and women have different senses of humor, are their genes to blame, or is it cultural conditioning? Rardon says she sees truth in both sides but offers a strong admonition that cultural stereotypes about women are often firm and hard to crack. Even Stanley's article in defense of female funniness, Rardon points out, features female comedians in alluring poses, a reinforcement of gender roles that Rardon finds "just as demeaning as Hitchens's generalizations." By reminding us about the difficulty of overcoming preconceptions about gender, Rardon underlines the significance of an issue that might otherwise seem trivial to some readers.

6. Rardon ends with a punch line. "If Hitchens still wants to insist women aren't funny," she writes, "well . . . *the joke's on him.*" This isn't the only time the tone of Rardon's essay is humorous. What is the importance of a female writer making a few jokes in a piece defending the joke-making ability of women? More important, how should an author approaching this difficult topic balance the impulse to take a wry look at the subject — and even to crack a joke here and there — and the desire to afford it the seriousness and gravity it merits? How do you think Rardon does?

Expressing an Opinion with Reference to Assigned Readings

Our third example shows a student writer responding to an assignment that asks him not only to consider the issue of stereotyping from a personal perspective but also to refer to relevant readings from *America Now*. In "How to Approach a Different Culture," Milos Kosic uses the highly popular 2006 movie *Borat* and his physical resemblance to the central character (played by Sacha Baron Cohen) as a way to make Americans aware of how easily and unfairly they can stereotype people from other cultures. Most fans of the film are unaware of its subtitle: *Cultural Learnings of America for Make Benefit Glorious Nation of Kazakhstan.*

To lend support to some of his points, Kosic quotes from three selections found in this book (and provides the page references). At the end of the essay, he provides a "Works Cited" list to indicate the precise sources of his quotations.

Milos Kosic was born in Belgrade, Serbia, and has lived in the United States since 2007, when he relocated to study journalism at Northwest Community College in Powell, Wyoming. During his time at Northwest Community College, he wrote for the college newspaper, Northwest Trail. *Since 2008, he has attended City College of New York to study English, with a concentration in creative writing. His work at* Northwest Trail, *along with his experiences writing for the Serbian music magazine* Rock Express *and an essay for the textbook* Convergences *(Bedford/St. Martin's, 2009), encouraged him to pursue a degree in writing. In his free time, he enjoys reading and playing soccer.*

Milos Kosic

How to Approach a Different Culture?

1. Opens with a specific moment

Joss said that I look like Borat the second time we met. It was a hot summer morning, and a group of us were out eating breakfast when he let the comment slip. Joss, who hadn't yet bothered to remember my name, was visiting from out of town. We share a group of friends, and at that moment all of them laughed, shaking their heads up and down, yes, yes, and they turned to me to observe the similarities more closely. To make his joke complete, Joss raised his palm and enthusiastically added in a high-pitched impression of Borat, "High five!"

1

I didn't really care because, honestly, what Joss said was not far from the truth. With the exception of a few style differences between us—namely, moustache and haircut—my face pretty much resembles Borat's. In fact, it is so obvious that even one of my professors couldn't manage to keep it to himself, making the observation once in front of the whole class and leaving me blushing. This time, at breakfast, I didn't blush. I was a good sport about the joke and hoped only that Joss would soon move on to a new topic of conversation.

2. Increases dramatic tensions

But he didn't. He started asking me questions about Kazakhstan. He wanted to know if we sleep with our sisters there. Do we eat dogs? These questions were ridiculous for many reasons, not least of which is the fact that I am not from Kazakhstan. I'm from Serbia, which is not even geographically close to Kazakhstan, but for Joss it didn't make a difference. He gleefully asked, "Are all the women in Serbia fat?" He mentioned a famously large American actress and exclaimed, "She must have been from Serbia!" I stopped listening when he asked how much he could buy a Serbian girl for. I put my head down and prayed really, really hard that he hadn't seen the first season of *24*, in which a bunch of Serbian terrorists attempt to assassinate an African-American presidential candidate. The last thing I needed was to feel like my safety was compromised just because of my nationality.

It had happened once already, a year ago, while I was getting a haircut. One of the waiting customers was complaining loudly about Orthodox Christianity, the primary religion in Serbia, connecting it with Islamic terrorism. As the barber's scissors danced around my head, I suddenly remembered a friend of my mother's, who, after hearing that I was studying in the U.S., asked my parents, "Why did you send him right into enemy hands?"

Well, at that moment, I felt like I was in the enemy's hands. I felt an undeniable need to belong, to hide who I was and where I was from. In his article, on p. 118, "Leave Your Name at the Border," Manuel Muñoz describes this feeling, shared by many immigrants, as the

3. Supports idea with quotation

"corrosive effect of assimilation . . . needing and wanting to belong, . . . seeing from the outside and wondering how to get in and then, once inside, realizing there are always those still on the fringe" (p. 121). But then the barber chimed in, saying in his western, cowboy's accent, "I don't have anything against the Orthodox." I relaxed for a moment and responded,

2

3

4

5

"Huh, good for me that you don't." But as I turned to the customer, I realized that I may have made a mistake.

Now that I had exposed my identity to "the enemy," I expected   6
a couple of harsh words, or at least a dirty look, but it was not so dramatic. With a sudden change in demeanor, the customer was eager to hear more about Serbia, telling me about his army experiences abroad. I was the first Serb that he had met. His obvious embarrassment made me uncomfortable.

4. Approaches issue with open tone of voice

Both my interaction in the barbershop and the one with Joss   7
remind me that I am always on the outside. Dinaw Mengestu discusses his experience as an immigrant in his article "Home at Last." He is "simply . . . Ethiopian, without the necessary 'from' that serves as the final assurance of [his] identity and origin" (111). Mengestu explains his cultural dilemma as follows: it "had less to do with the idea that I was from Ethiopia and more to do with the fact that I was not from America" (111). I can identify with Mengestu's situation.

Since I've come to the U.S., I've been called a Russian, a Communist, a Texan. I have been asked all kinds of questions from   8
"Do you eat Pez in your country?" to "Do you have electricity there?" Even though my professors and American friends usually assume that those kinds of earnest questions bother me, they don't. It's quite interesting, actually, to hear people thinking about my background as something completely different from their own, a life with candles instead of electric light and with a Chihuahua on my lunch plate.

5. Establishes a broad identity

I feel almost sad when I reveal that none of that is true. As   9
Sandy Dover argues in his article "How Do You Define You?" "there are many different ways for people to distinguish themselves and identify with a myriad of cultures" (130). There have been so many racial and cultural mixtures throughout time that now it is almost impossible to define yourself as a member of one particular group. "Many 'white' people are not truly that" (130), but actually British or European. I grew up eating at McDonald's and watching *The Simpsons*. My shelves were overwhelmed with Harry Potter and Stephen King books, CDs of Creedence, Led Zeppelin, and The Rolling Stones. My favorite show as a kid was *Baywatch*. Yes, *Baywatch*. I even collected *Baywatch* sticky cards and filled a whole album. So even though I may identify myself as a

reader, fast food enthusiast, or classic rock fan, others may see me as something else entirely. Although we may claim a few identities, as Jodi Stein says in Dover's article, "a few more are often attached to [us]" (129).

I could have told Joss all of these things, but, of course, he   10
wouldn't want to know any of this; it would mean his joke was pointless. I guess it is because of people like Joss that the cousins and friends of Manuel Muñoz felt that traditional Mexican names — or "nombres del rancho" — "were names that stood as barriers to a complete embrace of an American identity, simply because their pronunciations required a slip into Spanish, the otherness that assimilation was supposed to erase" (120). Maybe changing "Milos" would make things easier for me, too, but I don't want to do that. Cultural "lines start to blur in many areas, but identities can be self-defining" (Dover, 130). I don't want to become Miles or Mike so that I can chum up with someone who judges me by my name or my nationality. My name is not only a word but part of my identity. Rather than "redefine" myself, as Mengestu puts it, I choose to believe that "there is room here for us all" (115). Aside from the obvious fact that he should avoid using Hollywood movies — and satires, no less — as reliable sources, Joss should try to learn about other cultures instead of ridiculing them. I am sure he would be surprised by the interesting things he might hear. For example, did you know that in Mongolia it is offensive to touch the back of someone's head? Or that Japanese people never make fun of another person? They simply don't see a good reason for doing it, even if you happen to look like Borat.

Works Cited

Dover, Sandy. "How Do You Define You?" *America Now*. Ed. Robert Atwan. 8th ed. Boston: Bedford/St. Martin's, 2010. 128–30. Print.

Mengestu, Dinaw. "Home at Last." *America Now*. Ed. Robert Atwan. 8th ed. Boston: Bedford/St. Martin's, 2010. 110–15. Print.

Muñoz, Manuel. "Leave Your Name at the Border." *America Now*. Ed. Robert Atwan. 8th ed. Boston: Bedford/St. Martin's, 2010. 118–23. Print.

6. Demonstrates source of quotations

Comments

The following comments correspond to the numbered annotations that appear in the margins of Milos Kosic's essay.

1. Writing often grows out of our responses to the opinions and comments of others. Note that Kosic begins his essay with a concrete reference to joking remarks made by an acquaintance. The jokes deal with the writer's resemblance to the central character of the film *Borat*, a physical resemblance that Kosic concedes in paragraph 2 isn't "far from the truth." In his opening paragraphs, Kosic deftly lays out the scene and introduces an element of dramatic tension. You should observe that he begins not with general statements about cultural differences and stereotyping, but instead with a highly specific moment.

2. In paragraphs 3 and 4, Kosic increases the dramatic tension of the scene by showing how Joss keeps joking instead of moving on to new conversational topics. Kosic lets us see the stereotypical views some Americans may have about other cultures, indicating that Joss even confuses one country (Serbia) for another (Kazakhstan). By the end of paragraph 4, we learn of the personal dangers Kosic feels as a result of stereotyping, and in paragraph 5 he expands on this feeling of danger, again using specific characters and incidents.

3. Note how Kosic reinforces his feeling of cultural conflict by introducing a quotation from one of the selections in this book, Manuel Muñoz's "Leave Your Name at the Border." You should observe how Kosic uses ellipses (. . .) to indicate that he is citing not the entire passage but only the parts relevant to his point. The ellipses point out that some text is omitted. You can check the actual passage cited on page 121, paragraph 17. Do you think he has quoted accurately and fairly?

4. Kosic ties both anecdotes together with a reference to Dinaw Mengestu's essay "Home at Last." Kosic's experiences in America — like Mengestu's in Brooklyn — have constantly reinforced his sense that he is an outsider — a nonnative individual in a culture unwilling to extend itself and learn more about the outside world. Note that Kosic responds not with anger toward those who frighten him or ask him silly, stereotypical questions but rather with an understanding that accepts the fact that they have no idea what his cultural background is like, that they consider it "something completely different from their own." Throughout the essay, he does not express anger, sarcasm, or disgust toward those who use stereotypes but instead is

approachable and open to further discussion. As a quick exercise, try rewriting paragraph 8 in an angry tone of voice.

5. In paragraph 9, Kosic illustrates a key quotation from Sandy Dover's essay with specific examples. In doing so, he makes it clear how much American popular culture he absorbed while growing up in Serbia: McDonald's, Stephen King, Led Zeppelin, and so on. These specific examples help persuade his readers that he cannot be defined by a single non-American identity.

6. To show his reliance on source material for his essay, Kosic adds a "Works Cited" list. This list, arranged in alphabetical order by the authors' last names (not in the order that the citations appeared in the essay), allows readers to find the works he cites. Note that the list provides not only the author and article title but also the full publishing information, including book title, editor, edition, place of publication, publisher, date of publication, and page references. The page reference to each specific quotation appears after the quote in the body of his essay.

The Visual Expression of Opinion

Public opinions are expressed in a variety of ways, not only in familiar verbal forms such as persuasive essays, magazine articles, or newspaper columns. In newspapers and magazines, opinions are often expressed through photography, political cartoons, and paid opinion advertisements (or op-ads). Let's briefly look at these three main sources of visual opinion.

Photography

At first glance, a photograph may not seem to express an opinion. Photography is often considered an "objective" medium: Isn't the photographer simply taking a picture of what is actually there? But on reflection and careful examination, we can see that photographs can express subjective views or editorial opinions in many different ways.

1. A photograph can be deliberately set up or "staged" so that the picture supports a position, point of view, or cause. For example, though not exactly staged, the renowned World War II photograph of U.S. combat troops triumphantly raising the American flag at Iwo Jima on the morning of February 23, 1945, was in fact a reenactment. After a first flag-raising was photographed, the military command

"Flag Raising at Iwo Jima," taken by combat photographer Joe Rosenthal on February 23, 1945.

considered the flag too small to be symbolically effective (though other reasons are also cited), so it was replaced with a much larger one and the event reshot. The 2006 Clint Eastwood film *Flags of Our Fathers* depicts the reenactment and the photo's immediate effect on reviving a war-weary public's patriotism. The picture's meaning was also more symbolic than actual, as the fighting on the island went on for many days after the flag was raised. Three of the six Americans who helped raise the famed second flag were killed before the fighting ended. The photograph, which incidentally was also cropped, is considered the most reproduced image in photographic history.

2. A photographer can deliberately echo or visually refer to a well-known image to produce a political or emotional effect. Observe how the now-famous photograph of firemen raising a tattered American flag in the wreckage of 9/11 instantly calls to mind the heroism of the Iwo Jima marines.

3. A photographer can shoot a picture at such an angle or from a particular perspective in order to dramatize a situation, make someone look less or more important, or suggest an imminent danger. A

"Three Firefighters Raising the Flag," taken by Thomas E.
Franklin, staff photographer for *The Record* (Bergen County,
NJ), on September 11, 2001.

memorable photograph of Cuban refugee Elian Gonzalez, for example,
made it appear that the boy, who was actually in no danger whatso-
ever, was about to be shot (see page 38).

    4. A photographer can catch a prominent figure in an unflatter-
ing position or embarrassing moment or can catch the same person in
a flattering and lofty fashion. Newspaper or magazine editors can

then decide based on their political or cultural attitudes whether to show a political figure in an awkward or a commanding light.

5. A photograph can be cropped, doctored, or digitally altered to show something that did not happen, For example, a photo of a young John Kerry was inserted into a 1972 Jane Fonda rally to show misleadingly Kerry's association with Fonda's anti-Vietnam activism. Dartmouth College has created a Web site that features a gallery of doctored news photos. (See cs.dartmouth.edu/farid/research/digitaltampering/.)

6. A photograph can be taken out of context or captioned in a way that is misleading.

These are only some of the ways the print media can use photographs for editorial purposes. Although most reputable news sources go to great lengths to verify the authenticity of photographs, especially those that come from outside sources, and enforce stiff penalties on photographers who manipulate their pictures, some experts in the field maintain that doctoring is far more common in the media than the public believes.

"We can no longer afford to accept news photography as factual data," claims Adrian E. Hanft III, a graphic designer, in an August 2006 photography blog. "If we are realistic," he continues, "we will come to the conclusion that much of the photography in the news is fake—or at least touched up to better tell the story. It is relatively simple to doctor a photo and everybody knows it. The fact that the term 'Photoshop it' is a part of the English vernacular shows just how accustomed to fake photography we have become. The interesting thing is that in the face of the massive amounts of doctored photos, most people still expect photos in the news to be unaltered. I think this has something to do with a human desire for photographs to be true. We know the cover photo of Teri Hatcher is touched-up but we don't question it because we *want* her to look like that. Likewise when we see news stories that confirm our beliefs we want them to be true. As photo manipulation becomes easier and easier, there is an increase in the demand for photographs that confirm what people want to believe. The market responds by flooding the world with 'fake' photography. Today people can believe almost anything they want and point to photography that 'proves' their beliefs."

Facing page: "Elian Gonzalez," taken by Associated Press photographer Alan Diaz on April 22, 2000.

Political Cartoons

The art of American political cartoons goes back to the eighteenth century; it's claimed that Benjamin Franklin was responsible for one of the nation's earliest cartoons. Almost from the start, political cartoonists developed what would become their favored techniques and conventions. Because cartoonists hoped to achieve a sudden intellectual and emotional impact, usually with imagery and a brief written message, they soon realized that exaggeration worked better than subtlety and that readily identified symbols were more quickly comprehended than nuanced or unusual imagery. The political cartoon is rarely ambiguous—it takes a decided position that frequently displays enemies negatively and friends positively. Rarely does a political cartoonist muddy the waters by introducing a mixed message or entertaining an opposing view. The cartoonist, unlike a columnist, cannot construct a full consecutive argument to support a position, so the strokes applied are often broad and obvious.

A political cartoon often combines a satirical perspective, using exaggerated humor and visual caricature, with an instantly recognized iconography. Given that they sometimes combine insulting satire and offensive imagery, cartoons can provoke more controversy than do essays and columns. The world took note of this in 2006, after a Danish newspaper printed a number of cartoons depicting the prophet Muhammad that were considered outrageously profane in the Muslim world. Caricature and stereotypes can hit harder than words and cause deep offense more rapidly than other expressions of political opinion. Let's examine a few recent cartoons and see what makes them tick. Along the way, we will look at the role of **iconography, exaggeration, irony, caricature, symbol,** and **context**.

First, a note about **context**. Chances are that if you don't know the political situation the cartoonist refers to, you won't "get" the cartoon's intended message. So it's important to remember that the cartoon's meaning depends on previously received information, usually from standard news sources. In other words, most cartoonists expect their audience to know a little something about the news story the cartoon refers to. Unlike the essayist, the cartoonist works in a tightly compressed verbal and visual medium in which it is unusually difficult to summarize the political context or the background the audience requires for full comprehension. This is one reason that cartoonists often work with material from headline stories that readers are familiar with. For many cartoons, the audience needs to supply its own information to grasp the cartoons' full meaning.

Please note, too, that the following cartoons are included for illustrative purposes only. They were not selected for their political and social opinions or for their artistic skill but primarily because they conveniently demonstrate the major elements and techniques of the political cartoon. Many other recent cartoons could just as easily have been selected.

Let's examine a cartoon that appeared in *U.S. News & World Report* on September 25, 2006. The image is unambiguous: The United Nations building is rocketing upwards as a result of a nuclear explosion, torn away from its New York City site. Note the use of iconography. **Iconography** is the use of shorthand images that immediately suggest an incident, idea, era, institution, and so on. Such images are intended to reflect immediately and clearly what they stand for. For example, a teenager with a pack of cigarettes rolled up inside the sleeve of a T-shirt is iconographic of the 1950s; a cap and gown indicates an academic; a briefcase represents a businessperson or a public official; a devil is traditionally represented with horns and a pitchfork. In this cartoon, the mushroom cloud represents a nuclear attack, and the building itself stands for the institution of the UN, which is labeled on the side in case someone doesn't recognize its familiar architecture. The cartoonist doesn't use a caption but instead includes the conventional dialogue balloon to indicate that someone is speaking. The speaker isn't pictured or identified but is clearly inside the building.

Who is speaking, and what's the point of the comment? The cartoonist expects his audience to know that a past UN secretary general, Kofi Annan, had been criticized for his soft handling of Iran's nuclear weapons program by continually issuing warnings without taking more concrete action. So the speaker is presumably the head of the UN, and the cartoon's message is that even after Iran uses its nuclear weaponry, the UN will *still* be issuing ultimatums. The cartoon thus satirizes the UN as powerless and ineffectual in the face of nuclear threat. Note how much political context the audience is asked to supply and how much information it needs to infer. Ask yourself: If you knew nothing of Iran's plans and the UN's involvement, would you be able to understand the cartoon at all? Also, imagine that you saw the cartoon without the secretary general's comment: How would you interpret the imagery?

Note, too, the cartoon's use of **exaggeration** and unrealistic depiction: Does anyone imagine that—outside of a comic strip — a nuclear blast would send an entire building skyward and totally intact,

"When It's Too Late to Warn Iran," by *U.S. News & World Report* cartoonist Doug Marlette, published on September 25, 2006.

and that we could hear a single human voice? We are, of course, not expected to understand the events literally. Nor are we even to assume that Iran *will* attack the United States. The overall effect is to call attention to the weakness of the UN by showing its leader to be someone who is all talk and no action, who futilely issues a "last warning" even after the ultimate deed is done.

Let's turn to a somewhat more complicated cartoon that demonstrates the use of four features favored by political cartoonists: **caricature, symbol, irony,** and what might be called the **pictorialization of figurative idioms.** Mike Luckovich employs all of these in a cartoon that first appeared in the *Atlanta Journal-Constitution* on June 16, 2006, and was eventually picked up by several magazines. The cartoon relies on the traditional symbols for our two major political parties—the Democrats are represented by a donkey and the Republicans by an elephant. These symbols have been used by cartoonists since the nineteenth century and allow them to instantly identify party affiliation. The use of **caricature**—the artistic rendering of

"Monkey on Your Back," by *Atlantic Journal-Constitution* cartoonist Mike Luckovich, published on June 16, 2006. By permission of Mike Luckovich and Creators Syndicate, Inc.

someone's physical features in an exaggerated manner for quick recognition—is seen in the depiction of Hillary Clinton, who is also given a badge so that readers can be absolutely certain of her identity. Depending on their political perspective, cartoonists can use caricature for purposes of quick identification or as a way to demean, stereotype, or satirize someone.

Luckovich's cartoon also demonstrates another standard cartoon feature: the tendency to literalize a common idiom. For example, the cartoonist will take an ordinary expression that suggests an image and then literally render the image. Our language is full of such expressions: "a sly fox" suggests a devious person; "don't rock the boat" suggests that we not disturb something; "know the score" suggests that we are fully aware of information; "to jump the gun" suggests doing something without thinking about it carefully. A cartoonist will often use such expressions within the cartoon for two important reasons: (1) because it is idiomatic, the expression will be quickly understood; and (2) because it contains an image, the expression will contribute to the cartoon's pictorial content. In this case, the cartoonist has Hillary Clinton refer to a "monkey on your back." The idiom was once a slang phrase for drug addicts burdened by their habits but has now shed its slang usage and become a common expression for being burdened or weighed down by something that is difficult to get rid of. Clinton means, of course, that the Republicans (the elephant) are encumbered by the war in Iraq (symbolized by the monkey). Thus, the cartoon appears to be pointing out the terrible burden the war in Iraq represents for the Republican Party.

But one reason Luckovich's cartoon received so much attention is that the cartoon seems to be saying much more. Without expressing it verbally, Luckovich's cartoon implies pictorially that Clinton may be the same uncomfortable burden or liability to the Democratic Party that Iraq is to the Republican Party. Note how the cartoonist establishes this visual analogy by suggesting through the size, position, and juxtaposition of the images that both Clinton and Iraq are equally burdensome to their respective parties. In other words, what the cartoon suggests is that a Clinton candidacy would be as hard on the Democrats as the Iraq War would be on the Republicans in the 2008 presidential election.

It's important to note that Luckovich never says this directly. To "get" the cartoon's full meaning is to understand its clever use of **visual irony**. Although it's a large literary subject, irony can be understood simply as a contrast between what appears to be expressed and what is actually being expressed. The contrast is often humorous and could be sarcastic, as when someone says after you've done something especially dumb, "Nice work!" What appears to be expressed (verbally) in the cartoon is Hillary Clinton's critical observation that the war in Iraq is a burdensome liability for the Republicans in the next election; what is actually expressed (visually) is that she represents a similar liability for her own party. The audience is also supposed to understand that Clinton herself does not recognize her liability but—given her expression and finger-pointing gesture—only her political opponent's. Thus, the audience becomes aware of something the figure in the cartoon does not perceive. This resembles the kind of dramatic irony prevalent in novels and film. We frequently know something—for instance, that a character is being lied to or tricked—that the character does not. This sort of irony—the incongruity between a character's awareness and the audience's—is an essential element of storytelling and a key ingredient of dramatic tension and suspense (as we wait for the character to finally realize what we knew all along).

We need to know a number of things to understand and appreciate Luckovich's cartoon:

1. We need to know that donkeys and elephants stand for the Democratic and Republican parties, respectively.

2. We need to know that "Hillary" means Hillary Clinton, who is a leading Democrat and was, at the time, a potential nominee for the presidency.

3. We need to know that the Republican Party (under George W. Bush) has been vigorously criticized for starting and continuing the war in Iraq.

4. We need to know what the expression "You've got a monkey on your back" means, literally and figuratively.

5. We need to understand that the pictured monkey represents the war in Iraq (hence the label).

6. We need to perceive that the cartoonist has depicted both the donkey and the elephant weighed down by equivalent physical burdens (both Clinton and the monkey are noticeably larger than the two party symbols).

7. We need to see that visually the cartoon suggests that Hillary Clinton may be as much a burden on her party as the Iraq War is on the Republicans.

Now to a third cartoon, this one from the *New Yorker* (August 7–14, 2006), which demonstrates another common feature of the cartoonist's stock-in-trade: the succinct combination of topical issues. In this case, the cartoonist's humor covers two national debates—one the use of stem-cell research and the other the oil crisis. Like the anti-UN cartoon, this one also relies heavily on iconography—the instantly recognized Capitol building in Washington, D.C. The architecture, in fact, dominates the cartoon and dwarfs the unidentified

"Of course it would be a different story entirely if we could extract crude oil from stem cells."

"Stem Cells," by *New Yorker* cartoonist Jack Ziegler, published on August 7–14, 2006. ©The New Yorker Collection 2006, Jack Ziegler from cartoonbank.com. All rights reserved.

male figures with briefcases, who might be members of Congress or lobbyists. The Capitol architecture lends the scene an aura of dignity and stateliness that is undercut by the cynical remark of the caption, which suggests that conservative pieties over the sacredness of stem cells would be easily set aside if the cells yielded crude oil. In other words, economic interests and profits would "of course" trump religious and ethical positions. The casually expressed remark suggests that the speaker would in no way protect stem cells from scientific use if they could help our oil supply.

Note that this cartoon depends almost entirely on its caption for its effect. There is nothing intrinsic to the overall drawing that necessarily links it to the caption. If there were no caption and you were invited to supply one, you might come up with any one of thousands of remarks on any number of topics or issues. The main function of the image is to set the remark in a political context. The remark can then be read as a satirical comment on how our current government works—on profits, not principles.

The relationship between the Capitol building and the caption does, however, suggest an ironic incongruity. The imposing image of the U.S. Capitol—like the UN in the cartoon on page 42, one of the world's most significant political buildings—would seem more in keeping with a principled rather than unprincipled comment. Thus, the overall image adds to the satire by making us aware of the separation between how a revered political institution should perform and how it actually does. For example, consider how the level of satire would be reduced if the cartoonist used the same caption but instead portrayed two research scientists in a medical laboratory.

Opinion Ads

Most of the ads we see and hear daily try to persuade us to buy consumer goods like cars, cosmetics, and cereal. Yet advertising does more than promote consumer products. Every day we also encounter numerous ads that promote not things but opinions. These opinion advertisements (op-ads, for short) may take a variety of forms—political commercials, direct mail from advocacy groups seeking contributions, posters and billboards, or paid newspaper and magazine announcements. Sometimes the ads are released by political parties and affiliated organizations, sometimes by large corporations hoping to influence policy, and sometimes by public advocacy groups such as Amnesty International, the National Association for the Advancement of Colored People, the National Rifle Association, or—as we see on page 48—the American Civil Liberties Union (ACLU).

THE MAN ON THE LEFT
IS 75 TIMES MORE LIKELY TO BE STOPPED BY THE POLICE WHILE DRIVING THAN
THE MAN ON THE RIGHT.

It happens every day on America's highways. Police stop drivers based on their skin color rather than for the way they are driving. For example, in Florida 80% of those stopped and searched were black and Hispanic, while they constituted only 5% of all drivers. These humiliating and illegal searches are violations of the Constitution and must be fought. Help us defend your rights. Support the ACLU. To learn more and to send your Members of Congress a free fax go to www.aclu.org/racialprofiling.

american civil liberties union
125 Broad Street, 18th Floor, NY, NY 10004 www.aclu.org

"The Man on the Left," an opinion advertisement that was part of the ACLU's 2000 campaign against racial profiling.

This selection represents only one of hundreds of such opinion ads readers come across regularly in newspapers and magazines. To examine carefully its verbal and visual techniques—whether you agree with its message or not—will help you better understand the essentials of rhetorical persuasion.

At the center of the ad (which appeared in many magazines in 2000), we see two photographs. The man on the left nearly everyone will recognize as Martin Luther King Jr. The other photo will be familiar to many Americans, especially older ones, but may not be recognized by all—it is the convicted California mass murderer, Charles Manson. The ad's headline refers only to "the man on the left" and "the man on the right." According to the headline, then, King, one of the nation's most outstanding leaders, "is 75 times more likely to be stopped by the police while driving" than one of the nation's most horrific murderers. The headline and photos are intended to attract our attention. The image of King also powerfully suggests that the issue of civil rights is still alive. (The ad's creators expect us to set aside the facts that King has been dead for decades and Manson has never been released from prison. So there is no possibility that the particular man on the left "is" more likely to be subjected to a police search than the particular man on the right. Thus, the ad's central statement cannot be taken as literally true.)

Why doesn't the headline say "Martin Luther King is 75 times more likely to be stopped by the police while driving than Charles Manson"? Why does the ad deliberately not identify each photo? One reason may be that the ACLU is counting on King's iconographic status; he's an American icon who needs no identification. But what about Manson: Did you instantly recognize him? Why doesn't the ACLU balance the photos by portraying John F. Kennedy, another American icon, as the man on the right? The main point of the ad would not be at all affected if Kennedy were on the right because the central issue is that African American drivers are more likely to be stopped than whites. Nor would the ad's message be affected if the photo on the right were simply of an anonymous, clean-shaven, white male. So, given the message, any white male could have been used instead of Manson. So why portray Manson?

Featuring Manson drives home the point that the system of stopping drivers based on their skin color is totally indiscriminate and doesn't take status, character, or virtue into account. The ACLU wants to surprise, even shock, its audience into realizing that the U.S. criminal justice system would stop and search one of America's most honored public figures while giving a free pass to one of the nation's most reviled convicts. Analyzing the ad in this way, however, raises an uncomfortable issue. If you don't recognize Manson (who was convicted in 1971 and has rarely been seen since his sentencing) and are still surprised or shocked by the headline, is it then because of the way he looks—the long hair, full beard, and glaring eyes? Does he look suspicious? If you think so, are you also engaging in a kind of "profiling," allowing yourself to think the man on the right ought to be stopped simply because he fits some kind of stereotype—a "hippie," a homeless person, a mentally ill individual? Here's a good question to ask about a visual image presented in a way that assumes you know what or who it is: What are the unintended consequences if you don't know it? In this case, what happens to the ad's message if you don't recognize either figure from the 1960s?

Besides the visual argument outlined above, the ad also expresses in smaller print a verbal argument. In print advertising, this element usually contains the ad's central argument and is known as body copy, body text, or simply text to distinguish it from the headline, illustrations, and other visuals. The argument is essentially that "humiliating and illegal searches are violations of the Constitution and must be fought." The text does not state why or how racial profiling (a term not used in the ad) violates the Constitution. In other words, it assumes our assent and offers no reasons why we must be legally concerned about the issue. There is no mention of which part of the Constitution the police violate, nor is any relevant phrase of the Constitution quoted directly.

The argument depends wholly on statistical evidence that a disproportionate percentage of certain drivers are stopped by the police. Note that the headline and the body of the text appear to cite two different sets of statistics: The headline claims that someone like King "is 75 times more likely to be stopped" than a white person, while the text reads that "in Florida 80% of those stopped and searched were black and Hispanic, while they constituted only 5% of all drivers." These two statistics are offered with no attribution of sources (Who gathered them? Is the source reliable?) nor any dates (Are they recent?). We might also wonder why only Florida is mentioned. The ad also introduces an ambiguity by mentioning the Florida statistic because we are then led to wonder what the statistic in the headline refers to. Is it only in Florida that the man on the left "is 75 times more likely to be stopped"? Or does that number represent a national figure? And is the number also meant to represent

Hispanics, or does the "75" in the headline refer only to African Americans as represented by King? To question these numbers and their manner of presentation is not to dispute their accuracy or the seriousness of the issue, but only to demonstrate the necessity of responding to statistical evidence cautiously before giving our assent to an argument.

Nearly all opinion ads (and most ads in general) are action oriented. The purpose of persuasion is to produce a change in opinion or attitude that will produce social or political action. This ad, like most opinion ads, encourages a twofold action: (1) it asks the reader to assent to an opinion (in this case, that our Constitution is being violated); and (2) it asks directly for the reader's support, which could mean both to encourage the work of the ACLU and to assist it with donations. Note the text's final words: "Help us defend your rights. Support the ACLU." Because ads must work in such a compressed verbal format, some of the words we need to pay special attention to are pronouns. A reader may wonder why the final words didn't say, "Help us defend the rights of African Americans and Hispanics" (or "people of color"), since the ad never claimed that the rights of any other group were being violated. But "your rights" is intentionally all-inclusive: It stands for you, the reader, and everyone else. In a highly abbreviated way, the ad implies that whenever anyone's constitutional rights are violated, everyone's rights are violated.

The ad contains an extra visual feature that may take a while to notice or sink in. The ad isn't just a page in a magazine; it's designed to look like the sort of wanted poster the police and FBI display to help catch criminals or the kind often seen in pictures of the old West ("Wanted—Dead or Alive"). Note the discoloration from weather and the nails attaching it to what appears to be a wooden surface. Why did the designers do this? Why take the ad's image to another dimension? And how does imagining the ad as a wanted poster affect its overall argument and our response? The ACLU's intention, it seems, is to enforce the image of criminalization. One photo is of an actual psychopathic criminal, so the wanted poster image makes sense in its depiction of Manson (though he is already in prison). But why would King, one of the greatest Americans, appear on a wanted poster? The general effect appears to be that in the eyes of the highway police who are profiling black drivers, even someone as distinguished as King would be considered a criminal. The effect and implication of the wanted poster ramp up the visual rhetoric and contribute to the shock value of the advertisement.

Writing as Empowerment

Writing is one of the most powerful means of producing social and political change. Through their four widely disseminated gospels, the first-century evangelists helped propagate Christianity throughout the world; the writings of Adam Smith and Karl Marx determined the economic systems of many nations for well over a century; Thomas Jefferson's Declaration of Independence became a model for countless colonial liberationists; the carefully crafted speeches of Martin Luther King Jr. and the books and essays of numerous feminists altered twentieth-century consciousness. In the long run, many believe, "the pen is mightier than the sword."

Empowerment does not mean instant success. It does not mean that your opinion or point of view will suddenly prevail. It does mean, however, that you have made your voice heard, that you have given your opinions wider circulation, that you have made yourself and your position a little more visible. And sometimes you get results: A newspaper prints your letter; a university committee adopts your suggestion; people visit your Web site. Throughout this collection, you will encounter writing specifically intended to inform and influence a wide community.

Such influence is not restricted to professional authors and political experts. This collection features a large number of student writers who are actively involved with the same current topics and issues that engage the attention of professionals—the environment, racial and ethnic identity, gender differences, media bias, and so on. The student selections, all of them previously published and written for a variety of reasons, are meant to be an integral part of each unit, to be read in conjunction with the professional essays, and to be criticized and analyzed on an equal footing.

America Now urges you to voice your ideas and opinions—in your notebooks, in your papers, in your classrooms, and, most important, on your campus and in your communities. Reading, discussing, and writing will force you to clarify your observations, attitudes, and values, and as you do, you will discover more about yourself and the world. These are exciting times. Don't sit on the sidelines of controversy. Don't retreat into invisibility and silence. Jump in and confront the ideas and issues currently shaping America.

1

Is There an Obesity Epidemic?

In recent years, health officials throughout the nation have grown increasingly worried about America's weight problem. In just the past ten years, the percentage of Americans thirty pounds or more overweight has risen rapidly, and experts now wonder if we are facing an "obesity epidemic." But is getting fat contagious? How serious a health issue is it? Is dieting a solution? And how much of America's concern about excess pounds is driven not by health issues but by the media's fixation on unnaturally thin bodies?

"To be fat in our culture," writes Hannah Lobel in a feature article on obesity in the *Utne Reader*, "is to be labeled not only a glutton, but also a vessel of disease." In "Shame on US," she examines America's obsession with obesity and the growing stigmatization of overweight individuals. Our weight problems cannot be solved, she suggests, until we stop overstating the issue and take a more realistic view of our bodies. Still, as University of Kansas journalism student Chelsea Durbin claims, eating unwisely can easily result in weight gain. In "Fast Food Is Fat Food," she reminds us that what might seem tasty and convenient now could be a killer in the long run.

Conventional wisdom suggests that eating fatty food will make us fat. But that commonly held notion is questioned by Jeffrey Steingarten in a controversial essay, "You Are Not What You Eat." Combining scientific fact, humor, and personal experience, Steingarten takes a skeptical view of the benefits of dieting and sees our weight as largely a result of genetic factors. "We've been giving food too much credit," he argues, "investing it with magical powers and forgetting that it's just food, source of all growth, for good and ill, and of so many of our pleasures."

HANNAH LOBEL

Shame on US

[THE UTNE READER/January–February 2008]

Before You Read

Has our country become obsessed with obesity? Is our national weight problem overstated? Do you think our society judges overweight people unfairly—or in ways that actually contribute to misperceptions about obesity?

Words to Learn

glutton (para. 1): a person who eats or drinks excessively (n.)

ubiquitous (para. 2): existing everywhere; omnipresent (adj.)

arbitrary (para. 2): subject to individual discretion, preference, or impulse; optional, uncertain (adj.)

savvy (para. 3): experienced, well informed, shrewd (adj.)

slovenly (para. 4): careless about neatness in one's dress or person (adj.)

harangue (para. 6): scolding lecture (n.)

To be fat in our culture is to be labeled not only a glutton, but 1 also a vessel of disease. Sinners incapable of keeping food from their mouths, say waistline watchers in the media, government, and health industry, are literally weighing society down. Demand for supersized coffins is on the rise! Tubby tykes are clogging schoolyard slides! A costly health crisis looms . . .

Hannah Lobel earned a bachelor's degree from Grinnell College and a master's from the Medill School of Journalism at Northwestern University. As a writer, she explores diverse subjects in her work, from the conflict in Israel to the state of America's reputation in the world. She has worked across the globe, including for the Associated Press; Berlin's Der Tagesspiegel; *the* Island Packet *of Hilton Head, South Carolina;* Cape Town, South Africa's Cape Argus; *and KPFA/Pacifica Radio in Berkeley, California. Her essay "Shame on US" first appeared in the* Utne Reader, *where Lobel currently serves as associate editor and managing editor of* Utne.com.

We are obsessed with obesity. We have become hysterical. Yes, people have gotten a bit heavier, but we're not committing mass suicide by doughnuts. The once ubiquitous mantra that "overweight" Americans have higher mortality rates than the "normals" has been debunked in the pages of the *Journal of the American Medical Association.* And the standards that peg some 66 percent of us as overweight or obese are not only arbitrary, they've shifted: Some 31 million people became overweight in 1997 when the top end of the body mass index's "overweight" category was lowered from 27 to 25.

2

If the problem of obesity is overstated, the solution—self-willed weight loss—is science fiction. As recent studies have shown, to abandon the ranks of the overweight or obese, an American must achieve some Herculean combination of the following: overcome a genetically predisposed weight; starve through the hunger that naturally stems from exercise; resist the savvy marketing cues that trick us into consuming ever larger portions; and move into a better neighborhood, one with access to fresh foods, fewer fast food joints, and safer sidewalks.

3

> *We continue to treat obesity as if it's either an original sin we're born with and must repent or a cardinal sin we choose to commit.*

We continue to treat obesity as if it's either an original sin we're born with and must repent or a cardinal sin we choose to commit. "At best, fat people are seen as victims of food, genetic codes, or metabolism; at worst, they are slovenly, stupid, or without resolve," writes Julie Guthman, an associate professor at the University of California, Santa Cruz, who tracks the politics of obesity.

4

Take the reaction to a study published in a July issue of the *New England Journal of Medicine* that found that obesity can "spread" among social networks as people (primarily males) relax their norms about what constitutes an acceptable weight. The findings set off a new wave of media panic (Are your friends making you fat? Can you catch obesity?), which made *Slate*'s national correspondent William Saletan frantic. If we start thinking of obesity as literally contagious, he warned, we're letting fat people off the hook for their bad choices.

5

The reader response to Saletan's harangue was so fervid that he banged out an apology a week later. His line of thinking: Some people, the good fatties, can't help being obese; they've just "been dealt a bad hand" by genetics. But the bad fatties, the ones who give in to their friends' insidious notions that being fat is OK, they need a good, hard shamin.' For them, "the current level of stigma isn't doing the job."

6

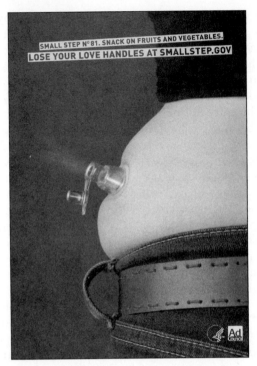

Ad Council, "Lose Your Love Handles."

Short of burning obese people in effigy, it's hard to imagine how   7
we could stigmatize fat more in this culture. Body hatred is regarded
as a feminine virtue. An estimated 8 million Americans—a million of
them men—already wrestle with eating disorders like bulimia and
anorexia nervosa, the country's deadliest mental illness.

Last fall, the Ad Council and the U.S. Department of Health and   8
Human Services skipped the shaming tack and took a more enlightened approach with their latest "Small Steps" campaign, which offered encouragement to be more active. The ads even had a sense of
humor: Two kids poked at a belly shed by someone walking on the
beach; a man coaxed his dog away from a butt lost by someone playing with his kids in the park.

The health police weren't laughing. The Associated Press par-   9
roted the backlash, noting that, while antismoking ads featured
tumor-ridden corpses and antidrug public service announcements
portrayed users wallowing in loserdom at their parents' houses, the

fat ads offered no horror or villains. "For example," the AP relayed, "none have offered a surgeon's view of fat, or dramatized a death from type 2 diabetes, or shown a person complaining about how a fat neighbor's medical bills are costing taxpayers."

Righteous myopia has a pathology of its own; it stems from our 10 unyielding faith in self-determination and our quickness to judge others' moral shortcomings. "While talk of the obesity epidemic is everywhere, honest conversation about our knee-jerk disdain for fat people is nowhere," writes Courtney Martin in *Perfect Girls, Starving Daughters: The Frightening New Normalcy of Hating Your Body*.

And that is the real shame, because our inability to see past our 11 obsession with fat is making things worse. We're sending people into prisons of self-loathing that have them seeking refuge in yo-yo diets that feed a multibillion-dollar weight-loss industry but do nothing to keep the pounds off and, in fact, often contribute to health problems later. Our narrow vision has other side effects, too. As the *Ecologist* reported in 2006, there are other culprits—endocrine disruption caused by pollution, increasing sleep deficits, the surge in prescription drugs—that may be contributing to obesity, and we desperately need to be researching them.

The plain truth is that fat people make easy targets in public pol- 12 icy and debate, just as they do on the playground. And until we are able to view our bodies as something more than never-ending renovation projects, we won't be able to make sense of our weight, no matter what the science tells us.

Vocabulary / Using a Dictionary

1. What are the roots and origins of the word *hysterical* (para. 2)?

2. Lobel characterizes an article from *Slate* as *fervid* (para. 6). What do the origins of that word suggest about the mental state of the person who wrote the article?

3. Lobel quotes a passage from an article that claims, "the current level of stigma isn't doing the job" of encouraging obese people to lose weight (para. 6). How does the word *stigma*—and its origins—support her contention that society views heavier people as "sinners" (para. 1)?

4. In paragraph 10, Lobel uses the word *myopia* to characterize common attitudes about obesity. What is the literal meaning of the word?

WILLIAM SALETAN

Fat Lies: Obesity, Laxity, and Political Correctness

[*SLATE.COM*/July 26, 2007]

Obesity is contagious like a virus. Willpower can't contain it. Stop blaming and stigmatizing fat people.   1

That's how scientists and the press are spinning a new study about weight gain, published today in the *New England Journal of Medicine*. The spin is politically correct but medically perverted. The study's findings tell exactly the opposite story: Obesity spreads culturally, individual decisions are crucial, and responsibility and stigma are part of the solution.   2

How did the story get twisted? Start with the contagion metaphor. The word *contagious* never appears in the original paper, written by Nicholas Christakis of Harvard Medical School and James Fowler of the University of California at San Diego. But it's all over their sound bites. "Obesity Is 'Socially Contagious,'" said the headline on UCSD's press release. Christakis told reporters that obesity can "spread from person to person like a fashion or a germ" and that "once it starts, it's hard to stop it. It can spread like wildfire." A government official who funded the research concluded, "It takes what was seen as a noninfectious disease (obesity) and shows it clearly has got communicable factors."   3

These metaphors spread rapidly through the media like . . . well, like bad metaphors. The *New York Times* ("Study Says Obesity Can Be Contagious") opened its report with the line, "Obesity can spread from person to person, much like a virus. . . ." The *Los Angeles Times* ("Obesity is 'contagious,' study finds") began, "Obesity can spread among a group of friends like a contagious disease," and added that the study showed a "pattern of contagion most often associated with infectious diseases." The *Washington Post* began, "Obesity appears to spread from one person to another like a virus or a fad. . . ."   4

The virus metaphor infected—actually, no, it didn't infect, it simply influenced—the authors' and the media's conclusions. "Treating people in groups may be more effective than treating them individually," Christakis argued. The *Los Angeles Times* paraphrased one expert's inference that "obesity treatment programs should move away from their emphasis on individual willpower." The *Post* said the results "lend support to treating people in groups or even whole communities." A warning against "relieving people of responsibility for watching their weight" vanished from the *Post*'s article overnight.   5

> Obviously, from a collective standpoint, it's more efficient to address   6
> obesity in a group than in one individual. But just as obviously, groups consist
> of individuals. And the gist of this study is that obesity did *not* spread through
> the sampled population like a virus or any other materially transmitted mal-
> ady. It spread culturally, individual to individual, through the relaxation of
> standards of personal discipline.

Responding to Words in Context

1. In paragraph 1, Lobel refers to a "demand for supersized coffins" as the obesity rate increases. Is this the usual context in which we see or use the word *supersized*, and what effect does it have here?

2. Lobel writes that overweight people need "some Herculean combination" of abilities "to abandon the ranks of the overweight or obese" (para. 3). What does *Herculean* mean, and why do you think the writer chose it over an adjective such as *enormous*?

3. Do you think Lobel's use of the word *fatties* in paragraph 6 is meant to be offensive or hurtful? If not, why not?

4. In paragraph 4, Lobel asserts that we "treat obesity as if it's either an original sin we're born with and must repent or a cardinal sin we choose to commit." What distinction is she making by using these religious terms?

Discussing Main Point and Meaning

1. Lobel believes that Americans have become "hysterical" about obesity, which she thinks is an "overstated" problem. How does she first bring up this point in the essay, and what kind of evidence does she use to support her view?

2. In paragraph 10, Lobel says that our society's "righteous myopia" about weight "stems from our unyielding faith in self-determination and our quickness to judge others' moral shortcomings." How do these tendencies contribute to a national "pathology" with regard to weight?

3. At the very end of her argument, Lobel writes, "until we are able to view our bodies as something more than never-ending renovation projects, we won't be able to make sense of our weight, no

matter what the science tells us" (para. 12). How is science characterized in this essay?

Examining Sentences, Paragraphs, and Organization

1. At several places in the essay (para. 2, for example), Lobel starts sentences with the word *And*. Why do you think she does this, and what effect does it have?

2. How does paragraph 3 of "Shame on US" provide a transition from the first main point of the essay to the second main point? How does this paragraph encapsulate her overall theme?

3. Lobel thinks we need to "view our bodies as something more than never-ending renovation projects" (para. 12). What do you think she means by this, and how does it tie together other threads in her argument about American attitudes toward obesity?

Thinking Critically

1. Lobel alludes to the process of public shaming and opposes it to more "enlightened" approaches (para. 8). She quotes William Saletan's essay, in which he claims, "the current level of stigma [with regard to obesity] isn't doing the job." Do you think that public shaming or the stigmatization of behavior—either overtly or in subtle ways—is ever a good idea? Historically, how have such practices been used?

2. In paragraph 11, Lobel asserts that our cultural obsession results in the prevalence of "yo-yo diets that feed a multibillion-dollar weight-loss industry but do nothing to keep the pounds off." Who benefits from America's preoccupation with fatness and thinness? Do you think it's fair of Lobel to generalize about the "weight-loss industry" as she does?

3. At the conclusion of the essay, Lobel says, "The plain truth is that fat people make easy targets in public policy and debate, just as they do on the playground." How accurate and effective is this analogy, in the context of the essay's larger point?

In-Class Writing Activities

1. In paragraph 7, Lobel writes: "Short of burning obese people in effigy, it's hard to imagine how we could stigmatize fat more in

this culture. Body hatred is regarded as a feminine virtue." Do you agree with these statements? What role does gender play in this issue? Can you think of examples from the media, popular culture, society, or your own life that support—or run counter to—Lobel's assertions?

2. By focusing on genetic predispositions, manipulative marketing techniques, class issues, the role of a culture "obsessed with fat," the connection between prescription drugs and obesity, and other factors, Lobel seems to be questioning the notion that weight loss is ultimately subject to "our unyielding faith in self-determination." In fact, one of her main points—evident in her title—asserts that we shift the "shame" of fat from the obese onto ourselves and our culture. Do you think that she goes too far with this argument and diminishes the significance of individual willpower? Write your own opinion essay on this subject, and make an argument using specific evidence.

3. Lobel takes a cynical and oppositional view of the media. She refers to journalists as "frantic" or as hysterical "waistline watchers"; she implies that they abet the scolding "health police"—as when the Associated Press "parroted the backlash" against the ad campaign mentioned in the article. Clearly, she believes that journalists are part of the problem. Considering Lobel's examples as well as your own, how do you account for distortions, biases, and misleading information in the media with regard to obesity? What "news" values and imperatives are evident in the way such a topic is covered, and do they always lead to the most useful, informative coverage?

CHELSEA DURBIN (STUDENT ESSAY)

Fast Food Is Fat Food

[THE UNIVERSITY DAILY KANSAN, University of Kansas / November 12, 2007]

Before You Read

How often do you eat fast food? Do you ever find it hard to balance the need to eat quickly and conveniently with the need to eat in a healthy way? Do you ever consider the long-term implications of your diet?

Words to Learn

ruptures (para. 1): breaks or tears apart, especially tissue (v.)
conquer (para. 4): to overcome by mental or moral power (v.)
franchises (para. 6): businesses granted the right or license to market a company's goods or services in a particular territory (n.)

It's a Thursday night and hunger is calling. Like an earthquake, your stomach ruptures with the need for food. At first you think about making something from your kitchen—Ramen noodles, PB&J, leftover spaghetti from a week ago. But none of these options sounds appealing, so you do what a majority of college students do. You go for fast food.   1

Fast food is everywhere. It's available on the main corners of a busy street and in the luxury of your own home. Fast food has be-   2

Chelsea Durbin is a junior at the University of Kansas, where she will graduate with a degree in English, and later hopes to pursue a career in writing for a magazine. As a weekly opinion columnist for the University Daily Kansan, *she explores a wide array of topics in her writing, including politics, music, religion, current issues, and campus life. When speaking to other student writers, Durbin advises them, "Follow your heart! Always write what you believe, and be proud of your writing."*

come as American as baseball, and its effects are quickly catching up with us. The nation has become a culture of fast food eating and on-the-go living, ultimately creating "fat" America. However, fast food has some advantages in the short term: people appreciate the fact that it's "fast" and "convenient."

Fast food has become as American as baseball, and its effects are quickly catching up with us.

There is no other food that you can pick up and have ready in a moment's notice. It involves no cooking, shopping, or dishwashing. All you have to do is eat and throw away the trash. In the end, you are saving an immense amount of time. Nevertheless, there seems to be a direct link in America between obesity and fast food. A typical meal from a fast food restaurant, say a serving of fries and a cheeseburger, adds up to over 1,000 calories per serving. This is about half the recommended dietary allowance for an individual per day.

In 2006, obesity levels of the average American had risen 25 percent since 2004. About one-third of all Americans over the age of 20 are considered obese. The risks involved with obesity have become a major health concern throughout our nation. Premature death from heart disease, stroke, diabetes, fatty liver disease, or cancer can result from obesity. Awareness of the effects of fast food is the first step if we want to conquer America's growing obesity problem.

Being a college student, I know how easy it is to grab something on the go that will satisfy my hunger. I have fallen victim countless times to the convenience of fast food, because life doesn't always permit enough time to cook a meal.

Recently, however, fast food franchises have begun to add new items to value meals and improved side items to encourage healthy eating habits. Salads, grilled chicken, fruit cups, yogurt, and milk have all been added to menus as options for alternative eating. Consciously choosing healthier options at fast food restaurants benefits your health in the long run, but just because these options exist does not make fast food a healthy diet. Loading on additional sides or adding lots of dressing to that salad only makes the calorie count go back up.

Understanding that the decisions we make now will ultimately affect our future is something we must be aware of. If time is on your side, go home and make yourself dinner. If it's not, choose wisely when dining out. Your body will thank you in the future.

Vocabulary/Using a Dictionary

1. When did the term *fast food* come into common use?
2. What is the basic scientific definition of a *calorie* (para. 3)? What is the origin of the word?
3. What is *diabetes* (para. 4)? Where does the word come from?

Responding to Words in Context

1. In paragraph 2, Durbin says that America "has become a culture of fast food eating." What does that mean, and what habits of mind would constitute such a "culture"?
2. Why does Durbin put quotation marks around the words *fast* and *convenient* (para. 2)? How does this punctuation change the tone or meaning of the words?
3. Durbin asserts that "about one-third of all Americans over the age of 20 are considered obese" (para. 4). What does *obese* mean in this context?

Discussing Main Point and Meaning

1. How does Durbin characterize the attitudes of college students toward food?
2. What connection is Durbin trying to make between the need for food "in a moment's notice" and the health statistics she cites in paragraph 4? What is her remedy for this?
3. What is Durbin's attitude toward the healthier menu choices now being offered by some fast food restaurants?

Examining Sentences, Paragraphs, and Organization

1. Durbin opens her essay with figurative language: "hunger is calling," and "like an earthquake, your stomach ruptures with the need for food." How effective is this opening? Does she use figurative language in the rest of the essay?
2. The essay shifts between points of view, including the second person (para. 1, for example) and the first person (para. 5). What are the benefits of this approach?

3. How does Durbin's conclusion tie up the argument and themes of the essay? Does it have implications beyond the topics of fast food and the diet of college students?

Thinking Critically

1. In paragraph 1, what food options for college students does Durbin weigh against the speed and convenience of fast food? What does this imply for the conclusion of her essay?

2. Durbin says that "there seems to be a direct link in America between obesity and fast food" (para. 3). How does she show this link, and how could she be more persuasive in establishing the connection among fast food, obesity, and negative health effects with regard to college students?

3. Do you agree with Durbin that "fast food has become as American as baseball" (para. 2)? How did this happen? Is the concept uniquely "American," and is it tied to larger aspects of American life and culture?

In-Class Writing Activities

1. As a rhetorical strategy, Durbin relies on the reader's recognition of—and identification with—a typical college student. She implies that students don't always think about long-term consequences with regard to their diets. In a brief essay, describe and analyze your own food choices over the last week; you may formulate your writing as a response to Durbin. Do your attitudes and eating habits fit her characterizations? What kind of thought and consideration—as well as external factors and pressures—went into your decisions about what and how to eat?

2. Durbin claims that fast food franchises, which are popular with college students, have added more food options "to encourage healthy eating habits" (para. 6). Do you agree with her assessment of these newer choices? Do you think such restaurants do—or should—promote better public health?

3. One of Durbin's main points is the connection between fast food and the risks associated with higher levels of obesity, which are now "a major health concern throughout our nation" (para. 4). What other factors might contribute to making Americans more overweight?

ANNOTATION Beginning with a Specific Instance

An effective way to open an essay is with an individual instance, with the concrete experiences of a single person. This writing strategy is quite common in everyday journalism: A reporter may begin coverage of a disastrous hurricane by first describing the plight of one person and then follow with an account of the overall damages. An item on increasing fuel costs might open with comments from a single consumer at the gasoline pump. In the following passage, observe how University of Kansas student Chelsea Durbin opens her essay on the dangers of fast food by putting the reader into a very particular and concrete situation. She effectively goes directly to a specific time ("a Thursday night") and a specific sensation ("your stomach ruptures with the need for food") and then drives the specificity even closer to home by putting her readers right into their own kitchens, where they could choose from several appetizing items ("Ramen noodles, PB&J, leftover spaghetti from a week ago"). Note that Durbin introduces the main topic of her essay only in the final sentence of her opening paragraph, and only in the second paragraph does she introduce generalizations on the prevalence of fast food. By opening her essay this way, Durbin invites her reader to participate directly and dramatically in the dilemma she is writing about—the immediate attractions of fast food.

Opens with specific situation and concrete details

It's <u>a Thursday night</u> and hunger is calling. Like an earthquake, <u>your stomach ruptures with the need for food</u>. At first you think about making something <u>from your kitchen—Ramen noodles, PB&J, leftover spaghetti from a week ago</u>. But none of these options sounds appealing, so you do what a majority of college students do. You go for fast food.

—From "Fast Food Is Fat Food" by Chelsea Durbin, page 62

Student Writer at Work: Chelsea Durbin
On Writing "Fast Food Is Fat Food"

Q: What was your reason for writing "Fast Food Is Fat Food"?

A: I wrote the piece to bring awareness on campus to the fact that, although fast food is easy at the moment, the negative effects of eating out for every meal are lasting. I was inspired by the films *Fast Food Nation* and *Supersize Me*.

Q: Tell us about your process for writing and revising the article.

A: It took me about a week to write "Fast Food Is Fat Food," with one rough draft and two revisions. I usually show my friends my articles before I submit them to the newspaper because I feel like having their opinions on a topic gives me insight to the views around campus. After turning it in, the article was reviewed by my editor before publication.

Q: What topics most interest you as a writer?

A: My favorite topics to cover are politics, music, religion, current issues, and campus life.

JEFFREY STEINGARTEN

You Are Not What You Eat

[VOGUE / April 2008]

Before You Read

Do you ever use the phrase "You are what you eat"? Do you believe it's true? Have you ever tried a fad diet? Why does it seem to be so easy to get fat, and so hard to get thin?

Jeffrey Steingarten began his career as an attorney, having graduated from Harvard College and Harvard Law School in 1965 and 1968, respectively. In 1989, his career took a decided turn when he began writing for Vogue *magazine, where he is currently the resident food critic. Steingarten also regularly contributes to* Slate *magazine and has written award-winning essay collections, such as* The Man Who Ate Everything *(1997) and* It Must've Been Something I Ate *(2002). As an internationally acclaimed food writer, Steingarten has traveled extensively and sampled offerings from all over the world, having tasted such rarities as deep-fried bamboo worms, roasted wasp larvae, and mashed pig's brains. On Bastille Day in 1994, he was made a Chevalier of the Order of Merit in France for his writing on French gastronomy.*

Words to Learn

pandering (para. 10): satisfying or catering to the lower desires of others in order to exploit their weaknesses (v.)

crystalline (para. 15): distinctly, sharply, and clearly defined or outlined (adj.)

euphoric (para. 15): characterized by a feeling of elation, happiness, or well-being (adj.)

aphorism (para. 17): a brief, often wittily phrased statement of truth or principle; adage (n.)

flabbergasting (para. 21): surprising and overwhelming with amazement (adj.)

bariatric (para. 27): relating to the field of medicine concerned with obesity and weight loss; relating to surgery on the stomach or intestines intended to help a patient lose weight (adj.)

And all this time, you've been walking around thinking, I totally am what I eat. It's why I look the way I do, whether I feel healthy or weak, how well I sleep, whether I'll get a cold or a stroke, how long I'll live, and how I'll die. And most important of all, how I look in a bathing suit. 1

Every one of these thoughts is more or less wrong. Because we are not what we eat. 2

Of all the warnings and urgings you've heard about food, very few of them are justified. No, eating sugar doesn't make children hyperactive. (That study was done at Yale.) Eating chocolate doesn't cause acne (National Institutes of Health). Eating salt won't raise your blood pressure unless you belong to the tiny minority of salt-sensitive hypertensives (Intersalt study). Consuming lots of salad and other raw vegetables (which used to be called "roughage") will not lessen the risk of colon cancer (Harvard Nurses' Study). Your total fat consumption will not raise your blood cholesterol. And for many people, eating saturated fat will not raise their cholesterol (Harvard's Walter C. Willett, M.D., in *Nutritional Genomics*, 2006). Most people who are actually lactose intolerant (probably two thirds of those who *think* they are) can drink an entire glass of whole milk without any discomfort—without reacting to it in any way at all (Massachusetts General Hospital study). And—get this!—exercise will not necessarily make you fit. (I'll explain that in a minute.) 3

All during the nineties, America was in the grip of an antifat obsession; everybody was bingeing on boxes of Snackwell's cookies— high-carb, high-sugar, low-fat. The percentage of fat in the American 4 diet decreased nearly every year. And yet Americans grew fatter and fatter and fatter. Some experts blame the low-fat diet itself: It seemed to encourage people to overeat carbohydrates. And get fatter. Thirty years ago, 47 percent of Americans were overweight or obese. Now it's 66 percent, or two thirds. And—as I am always way ahead of the world's food trends—you can count me in.

Let's take a break and discuss the definitions of *overweight* and *obese*. You're considered overweight if your BMI is 25.0 and above. You're obese if your BMI is at 30.0 or higher. Your BMI is your body mass index. It equals your weight (in kilograms) divided by your height (in meters) squared. Maybe that's why Americans got so fat. We're the only industrialized country that doesn't use the metric system. As a result, we can't figure out our BMI. We're fat and don't even know it.

If you're metrically challenged but have a calculator, multiply your weight in pounds by 703, divide by your height in inches, then divide by your height again. (This is my proprietary method and available only to readers of *Vogue*.) Or you can go to nhlbisupport .com/bmi/bmicalc.htm and fill in the blanks.

I hope you realize that these definitions are completely arbitrary. Don't you find it eerily convenient that the criteria are all whole numbers ending in 0 or 5? BMI doesn't work for athletes, whose high BMI is due to the weight of their additional muscles, not excess fat. And, despite what anyone may tell you, overweight people live just as long as everyone else. Only the obese are in trouble.

So, if eating fat is not what makes us fat, then what does make us fat? The truth is that our weight is strongly influenced by our genes. Jeffrey Friedman, M.D., Ph.D., of the Rockefeller University in Manhattan estimates that your body weight is just as much genetically controlled as your height. Your height! We've known this for quite some time—through studies of twins, both identical and fraternal, some raised in the same family, others who've grown up in separate families. Identical twins share all their genes and should be quite similar; fraternal twins share only half. Two unrelated adopted children share no genes, and any similarity between them comes from their environment. In the many twin studies carried out over the years, the similarity in weight between identical twins runs from 55 percent to 85 percent, and this can be understood as the influence of genes. The rest is the environment. One interesting result shows that despite the tendency to blame the obesity of a child on the family, whose members share meals and physical activity, the influence of families on the weight of their children is *very small*. Yet I've read newspaper stories about a fat little child in England whom the health authorities wanted to take away from his mother because she fed him too much.

Americans pay more than $40 billion a year to the vast dieting industry. That sum probably includes the diet articles appearing in fashion magazines, women's magazines, and men's-fitness journals. (I'm happy to point out that *Vogue* is largely blameless.) Yet you've heard the facts before: Diets don't work. Most people who lose weight gain back between one third and two thirds of it within the first year, almost all within five years. When you go on a diet and your weight falls below your usual minimum, your body thinks you are starving, and so it conserves your fat deposits by slowing you down and turning up your appetite. You'll want to eat everything in sight. 9

The flood of diet articles has several harmful effects. Pretend-ing that losing weight is easy and really fun stigmatizes the over-weight for *choosing* not to lose weight, for remaining weak and self-indulgent. It encourages people to feel that their own bodies are in pretty awful shape. Both the industry and its supporters in the press are playing on the desperation of people who hate how they look in the mirror. Pandering to their unrealistic hopes. Making weight loss into one of the central goals of life. 10

What entertained me most about the Republican primary race was monitoring the weight status of former Arkansas governor Mike Huckabee, who had lost 105 pounds over a year and apparently kept them off. Whenever Huckabee appeared on TV, I looked hopefully for signs that his stomach was spherifying into a bulge that would prove the ex-governor was backsliding. It's nothing personal—I like the fellow. He is intelligent and funny and, despite being a religious fanatic, extremely charming. But Huckabee is a freak, a sport of na-ture, perhaps a mutant. Nobody loses 105 pounds and keeps them off—or, rather, almost nobody. He sets a very bad example. 11

Obesity is largely a medical problem—a disorder or a disease. Can you imagine a popular magazine advising you to cure your dia-betes by eating a half-dozen grapefruits a day, or drive off your mi-graines by eating pizza, or quiet a heart murmur by eating dark leafy greens? The editors might end up in jail. Does it make any more sense to give the same advice to those of us who suffer from extreme chub-biness? Doesn't all this free diet advice in newspapers, magazines, and TV victimize overweight men and women who don't seem to be able to do anything about it? 12

I have a great idea. I propose that whenever a magazine publishes   13
an article that even cautiously recommends a new (or, for that matter, old) diet program, it should have to supply five pieces of information: the percentage of participants who complete the diet program;
the amount of weight these people lose; how much weight stays off
after one, three, and five years; the negative side effects of the diet;
and the percentage of dieters who experience them.

Incidentally, this is not entirely my own idea. In reality, it's not   14
my own idea in any way. In 1992, the National Institutes of Health
proposed that every diet program publish information like this; the
proposal never became mandatory, and I doubt that it is often followed. Responsible magazines should pledge to collect and publish
these statistics for any diet they mention favorably or to explain why
they can't. Though my power and control over other sectors of
Vogue's editorial staff are not absolute, I can still take the pledge myself. I will lead by example.

In the late seventies, I hit upon the ideal diet and managed to lose   15
30 pounds. For a day or two, I weighed 116; my BMI dropped to 18,
wonderfully skinny. The day my waist reached 27 inches, I spent a
fortune at Barneys on slacks and shirts, which I was able to fit into
for only the next two months and never again. Moronic? No, I have
the most crystalline memory of that euphoric moment, the first and
only time in my life that I was nearly too lean and too slender. The
diet? Two tubs of low-fat cottage cheese a day, a cup or two of
Scotch whisky to ease the pain, and a multivitamin capsule—on the
off-chance that a regimen of whisky and cottage cheese might be defi-
cient in some trace nutrient or other. I've never been prouder of how
I looked. I could wear the teeniest bathing suit that summer.

I wonder if it would work again. You're probably like those   16
people who warned me how dangerous my new diet was. But they
were mistaken. They believed that you are what you eat. Where in
the world could they have gotten that idea?

(Many of you probably believe that Jean Anthelme Brillat-   17
Savarin [1755–1826], the great French philosopher of the table, was
responsible for the aphorism "You are what you eat." Nothing could
be further from the truth. He did say, "Tell me what you eat, and I
shall tell you what you are," by which he meant he could tell where
you were born, your state of mind and health, and where you stood
on the social ladder if he knew what you eat—just what Professor
Henry Higgins could do after hearing somebody speak. It was the
German materialist philosopher Ludwig Andreas Feuerbach who in

the mid–nineteenth century first wrote the words "Der Mensch ist was er isst.")

> We've been giving food too much credit, investing it with magical powers and forgetting that it's just food, source of all growth, for good and ill, and of so many of our pleasures.

In one sense, you *are* truly what you eat. 18 If a laboratory were to remove several hundred of your fat cells and analyze them, it would be able to tell what kinds of fat you've eaten for the past several years—smoky bacon, fried chicken, vegetables stewed in olive oil, guacamole. When you eat chicken, a part of you really does become a chicken. Or, in my case, a pastrami sandwich. Otherwise, I think, we are not at all what we eat. We've been giving food too much credit, investing it with magical powers and forgetting that it's just food, source of all growth, for good and ill, and of so many of our pleasures.

Years later and 50 pounds larger, I achieved my second most dra-   19 matic loss of weight by taking the drug fen-phen for about three years. I shed 20 pounds in the first two years and kept them off for the third year. Soon after, the FDA persuaded the drug companies to remove the fen part (its full name is fenfluramine) from the market, and my weight (and that of many other temporarily happy people) reversed course and, after another year or two, climbed above the point where I had started.

Someday, I know for sure, there will be a pill that answers my   20 prayers. I've just ordered a bottle of tablets from one of those Internet pharmacies. They're called rimonabant, which according to the *New England Journal of Medicine* of November 17, 2005, is "a selective cannabinoid-I receptor blocker . . . shown to reduce body weight and improve cardiovascular risk factors in obese patients." Sounds to me like a delectable and dreamy medication. Have you ever read about the seventies? Apparently, those youngsters who smoked or ingested cannabis in the form of marijuana cigarettes or hashish would often experience a side effect that many of them referred to as "the munchies," an urge to eat everything in sight. Now, by blocking the cannabis receptor in the brain that would otherwise trigger the munchies, rimonabant successfully reduces your appetite. The mean old FDA refused to approve the drug (even though it's approved in more than 50 countries, including England and most of the European Community), using words like *depression* and *suicidality*, which the *Oxford English Dictionary* defines as "the quality or condition of being suicidal." I'll be sure to avoid open windows.

What does it mean to say that your weight is genetically determined? There are several relatively rare types of obesity caused by errors in or deletion of only one or two genes. (The most common is Prader-Willi syndrome; two others are Bardet-Biedl syndrome and Rubinstein-Taybi syndrome.) But in most cases, the genes that determine your weight are vast in number, reflecting the unbelievably complex system of sensors and signals in the body that regulate weight. Just have a look at the flabbergasting *Human Obesity Gene Map* (obesitygene .pbrc.edu/static/association_table.htm), which until 2006 was maintained by Claude Bouchard, Ph.D., and his associates at the Pennington Biomedical Research Center in Baton Rouge, Louisiana. Each of the more than 100 human genes listed in the first column has been connected, in one scientific paper or another, with some aspect of obesity listed in the fourth column, such as waist circumference, morbid obesity, body-mass index, percent of body fat in inactive people, skin-fold ratio from trunk to extremities in women and in blacks, waist-to-hip ratio, change in body weight in nondiabetics, fat-cell volume, leptin (a hormone discovered at Rockefeller University that is produced by our fat cells to help regulate appetite and energy expenditure), weight change among Chinese schizophrenics, fat mass in Thai males, obesity in sedentary individuals, weight loss on a three-month low-fat diet, percentage of body-fat loss induced by exercise training, birth weight of obese children, BMI in tall obese children, early-onset severe obesity, leptin in women, leptin in the Canadian Oji-Cree Indians. 21

There seem to be so many ways to become fat and very few to get skinny. 22

When I telephoned the Pennington center, I learned about an interesting research project: Tuomo Rankinen, Ph.D., explained to me that people have quite individuated responses to regular exercise. Some become very fit—cardiorespiratory fitness—while others do not. (All the exercisers benefited in one way or another, for example, even those who did not improve their fitness level saw their good cholesterol increase.) Rankinen and his associates are working on a map of the genes that may separate the "high-responders" from the "low-responders," and now they are narrowing their search to areas on various chromosomes that may cause the difference. 23

So, individual men and women (and their unique genes) react quite differently to fats and carbohydrates, to types of exercise, to varied environments. Someday your doctor should be able to scan all your obesity genes and prescribe a perfect combination of diet and exercise. Or maybe concoct the perfect pill or prescribe gene therapy. 24

The amazing thing is that the general public, of which I used to   25
be a member, does not understand that obesity—even just being
overweight—is without question, without need for further debate, a
genetic matter. But so far, no method has been discovered to turn the
entire system right. Does this knowledge lift our responsibility to become or stay merely overweight from our shoulders? No, our genes
only make it more difficult to lose weight. Some people would rather
blame our fattening environment. But if that were the entire problem,
then everybody in America would be fat. And if our genes were the
only problem, then America would not be getting more and more
obese. The answer is that for many of us, our genes predispose us to
gain weight when we live in "obesogenic" surroundings.

Which is why, for now, we've got to depend on the usual meth-   26
ods of losing weight.

I've read several academic evaluations of diet programs. In gen-   27
eral, a regimen of reduced calories and exercise has about the same
results as pills. The Atkins diet is more effective than a low-calorie
diet. With both, once you stop dieting, you will gain back the weight.
Bariatric surgery is considerably more successful than diet or pills;
there are three procedures, and they seem to vary in effectiveness,
with the most potent operation, called the biliopancreatic diversion,
able to help you lose up to 78 percent of your excess weight. For
some reason, it is rarely performed.

I spent part of January in Marrakech giving a little talk to an in-   28
ternational conference on obesity sponsored by Eurobese, a project of
the European Union run by the University Medical Center in Rotter-
dam, the Netherlands. This was their third meeting of four, and the
topics were (a) the success of some public anti-obesity programs and
(b) the ethical problems with such programs. Economically covering
both subjects in one fell swoop, I explained that diets don't work,
that creating false hopes is immoral, and that spending government
money on something that has no chance of success is morally wrong.
But talks by the others, who are actual experts in obesity, convinced
me that some programs do work—generally those with frequent psychological and social interventions and individualized treatment. Several public health experts have warned that the time and money spent
on programs like these would exceed the cost of obesity to society. As
with most other weight-loss regimens (except for surgery), the subjects' weight headed back up when the program was over and the
counseling stopped. Public health people typically rely on mass intervention—public education, school exercise programs, and closing
down McDonald's; they offer one prescription for all. But haven't we

just learned that there is an infinite combination of genes and the ways they regulate eating, metabolism, and energy expenditure? So, private behavior therapists might be more successful, but they are expensive and can help only a few people at a time. One of my very good friends in Paris, a great pastry chef who was morbidly obese, saw a therapist who watched him eat, then spoke with him through eight sessions. He lost more than 100 pounds.

Vocabulary / Using a Dictionary

1. What does the term *obesogenic* mean, and what are its roots (para. 25)? What other words end in *-genic*?
2. What is the definition of *regimen* (para. 27)? What connotations do its roots suggest with regard to weight loss in an "obesogenic" culture?

Responding to Words in Context

1. To help "metrically challenged" readers determine their body mass index (BMI), Steingarten offers what he calls his "proprietary method" for performing the calculation (para. 6). What does *proprietary* mean? What is the writer's tone in this parenthetical aside?
2. Steingarten says that after hitting upon his ideal diet in the 1970s, he lost 30 pounds and achieved a BMI of 18 (para. 15). On the day his waist reached 27 inches, he notes that he "spent a fortune at Barneys." What is Barneys? Why does the writer use this brand name, and what does it say about his audience?
3. In paragraph 17, the writer refers to Ludwig Andreas Feuerbach, who first said, "The man is what he eats." Steingarten describes Feuerbach as a "German materialist philosopher." What does *materialist* mean in this context?
4. Steingarten says that the "mean old FDA" refused to approve the seemingly "delectable and dreamy" weight-loss medication rimonabant; in doing so, the agency used "words like *depression* and *suicidality*, which the *Oxford English Dictionary* defines as 'the quality or condition of being suicidal'" (para. 20). Why do you think he includes this dictionary definition, and how does this paragraph connect with the tone and voice of the entire article?

Discussing Main Point and Meaning

1. In paragraph 12, Steingarten says that "obesity is largely a med-ical problem—a disorder or a disease," like diabetes. Why does this categorization matter, and how does it relate to his overall argument?

2. Genes play an enormous role in obesity, as indicated by the study showing that "the similarity in weight between identical twins runs from 55 percent to 85 percent"—regardless of whether the twins are raised in the same family (para. 8). As for other factors, "the rest is the environment," writes Steingarten. How does "en-vironment" differ from "nurture" (as in "nature" vs. "nurture"), and why is that difference important for this essay?

3. Steingarten targets the "dieting industry," generally, and the harmful effects of weight-loss articles in magazines, specifically—even as the goal of these programs and recommendations is os-tensibly to help people lose weight. How does his criticism here support his argument?

4. The article includes an apparent digression on the historical ori-gins of the phrase "You are what you eat" (para. 17). Although Steingarten puts this paragraph in parentheses as an aside, why is it important to the essay?

Examining Sentences, Paragraphs, and Organization

1. In paragraph 21, the writer provides a long, unwieldy, and even comical list of scientific subjects in obesity research. Why do you think he does this?

2. Steingarten occasionally uses one-sentence paragraphs (para. 2, for example). What purpose do they serve, and how effective are they?

3. As he concludes the essay, Steingarten recounts his attendance at an international conference on obesity. What is his tone in this paragraph, and why do you think he puts it near the end of the article, rather than at the beginning?

Thinking Critically

1. The writer considers the future possibility of an ideal diet pill that answers his prayers (para. 20), but he claims that, for now,

"we've got to depend on the usual methods of losing weight" (para. 26). What are the "usual methods," and what are they in contrast to?

2. In paragraph 11, Steingarten writes about the remarkable story of former Arkansas governor and presidential candidate Mike Huckabee, who successfully lost 105 pounds over a one-year period and kept the weight off. But Steingarten thinks that Huckabee "sets a very bad example." Why? Do you agree or disagree?

3. Does Steingarten seem credible in this essay? How would you evaluate his evidence and sources?

In-Class Writing Activities

1. Steingarten bases his essay on a well-known aphorism and cliché—one that, from his point of view, is misunderstood, misleading, and inaccurate. Choose another common saying or principle, and write a brief essay on its origins, meaning, and validity. Has its context or significance changed? Who said it? In what context? How "true" is it? How is it used?

2. In large part, Steingarten's target is the "vast dieting industry," to which Americans pay more than $40 billion a year. Have you participated in it or taken dieting or exercise tips from magazines? Have you ever tried a fad diet or exercise regimen? Is it fair to lump every product, program, and recommendation into one "industry"? What has been your experience with dieting, and have you ever made "weight loss one of the central goals of life"?

3. According to a physician and researcher in the article, "your body weight is just as much genetically controlled as your height." Steingarten repeats the last two words: "Your height!" (para. 8), as if we will not believe them. Why is this hard for us to accept? Clearly, weight and fat have different connotations and significance than height does. In a brief essay, reflect on the "meaning" of fat—culturally, historically, morally, and so on.

AMERICA THEN . . . CIRCA 1930

Reduce Easy As ABC! The Same Simple Way the Stars Use to Reduce!

Advertisements have long provided historians with insights into America's social history. A historian, for example, can follow the changing patterns of dieting and weight reduction by studying newspaper and magazine ads from the mid-nineteenth century to the present day. In the late nineteenth century and early twentieth century, one can see a clear trend toward a heavier and more curvaceous female body. But during the Jazz Age of the 1920s, a preference was quickly established for thinness. This preference was largely promoted by the rapidly expanding movie industry, which began putting a premium on slender, girlish figures. Thirty years earlier—as the advertisements testify—such female figures would have been viewed as unappealing and undernourished.

An amusing example of how weight reduction was being linked to movie-star glamour during the 1920s and 1930s is an advertisement for the Redoos-U Suit that appeared in popular movie magazines of the time. One of the earliest "lose-weight-quick" schemes in American marketing, it closely resembles many of today's products (as seen in numerous TV infomercials), with its emphasis on effortlessness and rapid results.

Discussing the Unit

Suggested Topic for Discussion

The writers included in this chapter discuss the tension between willpower, choice, and responsibility, as well as factors beyond the control of the individual—including culture, genetics, family, and the environment. How do we balance these competing pressures and forces when considering the problem of obesity? Does your view of individual autonomy versus biological determinism or social forces in this specific discussion connect with your position on other issues— personal, political, and social? How effective is self-determination and individual will, and what are their limits?

Preparing for Class Discussion

1. The three authors in this chapter are all writing about obesity, but their essays appeared in different publications, aimed at widely different audiences. What can you infer about these publications from your reading? How do you think the writers' notion of audience affected their arguments, their tone, and the aspects of the subject they chose to emphasize or minimize? Which of the essays seemed most accessible and relevant to you?

2. In the Steingarten and Lobel essays, both writers seem to say that the public is ill informed—or ill served—by the media on the subject of diet, fitness, and obesity. That seems especially true with regard to scientific information. Do you agree, and if so, why do you think that's the case? Steingarten says to his reader, "You've heard the facts before." Why do they have to be repeated? Do you think the general public is at fault for not accepting the "facts," or do you think much of the responsibility can be placed on a press that does a poor—or biased—job of making good information available? Or is the scientific information too hard to understand, or too inconclusive?

3. Whether it's been exaggerated or not, all three writers agree that there is a problem with weight in the United States—or at least a preoccupation with fat. Why do you think this issue has arisen at this particular point in American history? Has it actually gotten harder to be thin? For example, Durbin focuses on fast food, yet

fast food restaurants have been around for decades. Is the presumed "obesity epidemic" tied into any other trends in American culture at the moment? Does it seem like an inevitable by-product of a relatively prosperous, industrialized, consumer-driven society? Have there been other times in American history when a comparable public health topic was the subject of similar discussion and debate? What are the parallels?

From Discussion to Writing

1. Although all three essays directly address questions of obesity and public health, they also touch on a broad range of subjects—including fast food menus, bulimia, the role that pollution plays in weight gain, nineteenth-century German materialism, and the role of media pundits in the current debate. Write your own thesis essay on some aspect of the "obesity epidemic"—or our cultural responses to it—using the Lobel, Durbin, and Steingarten essays as your sources. You may cite these other writers and respond to them, but your thesis should be your own.

2. Both Steingarten and Lobel refer to the "multibillion-dollar weight-loss industry" with cynicism or outright disdain. Do you view it the same way? Find three examples from this "industry"—such as products, magazine advice columns, Web sites, or advertisements for diet programs—and evaluate them in light of these essays. Does the specific evidence seem to support the contention that the diet business consists mostly of "pandering" to "unrealistic hopes"? Or can you find examples that seem to run counter to Lobel's and Steingarten's arguments?

3. Lobel writes that "until we are able to view our bodies as something more than never-ending renovation projects, we won't be able to make sense of our weight, no matter what the science tells us." At the same time, Durbin frames her argument in terms of long-term planning and physical maintenance—if you are mindful of what you eat now, your "body will thank you in the future." Are these two points of view compatible? Write an essay that explores the distinction between the kind of health consciousness that Durbin advocates and the "never-ending renovation projects" that Lobel wants us to avoid. Could you make an argument in favor of regular "renovation"?

Topics for Cross-Cultural Discussion

1. Weight and obesity are national preoccupations. But do different cultures within the United States view these problems in the same way? Are obesity rates different among people with different racial, ethnic, and cultural backgrounds? Steingarten ends his essay with a reference to a Park Avenue dietary therapist, and Lobel implies that a "move into a better neighborhood" might help someone lose weight. What role do you think social class might play in this issue?

2. Superficially, it would appear that obesity is a uniquely American concern, but Steingarten refers to his participation in Eurobese, a project of the European Union. Are other countries dealing with this issue as well? How are they approaching it? Durbin notes that America has become identified with fast food, but fast food franchises are now worldwide. Is there a connection between the spread and influence of the American diet, and obesity or other dietary-related problems in an international context?

2

Social Networking:
What Are the Risks?

How often do you log on to Facebook? If you're reading this, odds are you do so frequently; 70 million people—and eight out of ten American college students—now have an active account on the social-networking Web site. Facebook, MySpace, and other social media sites offer users a chance to keep up with friends, connect with new people, share photos, and even discuss music and politics. But critics allege that the sites are just adding to an atmosphere of isolation and detachment, one already fueled by our reliance on text-messaging and e-mail in lieu of real, human contact.

Nonsense, says *Wired* columnist Regina Lynn. In "The New Communication Technology: A Challenge to Modern Relationships?" Lynn argues that our increased high-tech connectivity has improved, not damaged, the intimacy of our relationships. Text-messaging, for instance, allows us to stay close to our friends and family "across time and distance." And if it makes us less aware of the strangers we encounter in the real world, that's no great loss. "We are not going to wreck society simply because we can choose who we want to talk to at any given time, based not on proximity but on attachment and affection."

But other detractors see a danger far more sinister than personal alienation: Broadcasting yourself to your entire generation, Ari Melber tells users in "About Facebook," can put your privacy at risk. Focusing on Facebook itself, Melber agrees with Lynn that online interaction is not "merely an incubator for like-minded people to isolate themselves." Indeed, the peril for Melber is the opposite: Because Facebook legally owns its users' profiles, photos, and personal information, young people looking to connect online can become unwitting prey for advertisers, and even for snooping college administrators and employers. Calling Facebook "one of America's largest electronic surveillance systems," Melber contends that new features (such as a news feed and targeted ads) are eroding privacy rights on a site that "already facilitates all kinds of surveillance of unsuspecting users by the public."

Arizona State University student Melissa Mapes brings the issues of privacy and detachment together. In "Is Big Brother Watching Your Every Move?" Mapes concurs that Facebook presents a serious jeopardy to its users' privacy. But it isn't nosy outsiders Mapes is concerned with—it's her own friends, who use the site as an artificial way of keeping up with her that occasionally borders on spying. Probing the details of the site's architecture—public breakups, the news feed, and the ethics of unfriending a friend—Mapes sees Facebook as a mixed blessing, but she admonishes users prone to unload themselves on their profiles to tread carefully, mindful that friends are "following your life without your knowledge."

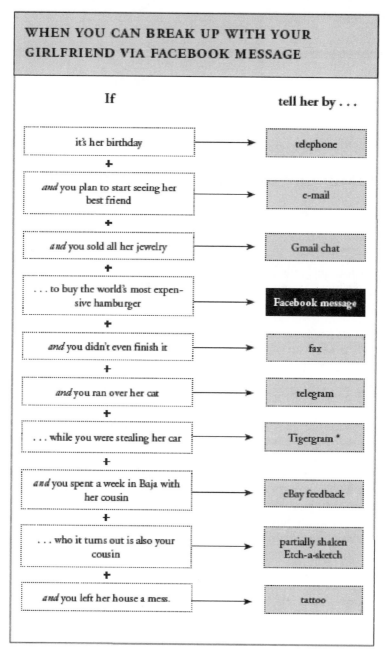

WHEN YOU CAN BREAK UP WITH YOUR GIRLFRIEND VIA FACEBOOK MESSAGE

If	tell her by . . .
it's her birthday	telephone
and you plan to start seeing her best friend	e-mail
and you sold all her jewelry	Gmail chat
. . . to buy the world's most expensive hamburger	**Facebook message**
and you didn't even finish it	fax
and you ran over her cat	telegram
. . . while you were stealing her car	Tigergram *
and you spent a week in Baja with her cousin	eBay feedback
. . . who it turns out is also your cousin	partially shaken Etch-a-sketch
and you left her house a mess.	tattoo

*(a new service from Siegfried and Roy)
From *The Facebook Book*, by Greg Atwan and Evan Lushing,
Abrams Image, 2008.

REGINA LYNN

The New Communication Technology: A Challenge to Modern Relationships?

[WIRED / September 21, 2007]

Before You Read

How does technology present problems to forming and maintaining relationships? How does Lynn complicate the definition of "relationship" in her defense of electronic communication?

Words to Learn

whimsy (para. 2): playfulness (n.)
empathy (para. 9): fellow-feeling; understanding of another person's experience (n.)

I don't remember my university offering courses on how to make   1
friends. It might have—but I didn't know about it, and neither did
any of my friends. No one ever mentioned hearing of such a thing.

Yet New York University now offers a seminar called Facebook   2
in the Flesh, reports the *New Yorker*. The idea is to help freshmen
who already know dozens of their classmates online but who worry
they don't know how to make new friends in person. That's the fear
and the whimsy behind NYU assistant dean David Schachter's deci-

---

*Regina Lynn is an author and a well-regarded sex-tech expert. Working
within a variety of formats, Lynn writes the weekly "Sex Drive" blog for
Wired.com and has also published numerous books. Her candid, humorous
style of writing has garnered much attention. In 2005, Lynn received a
Maggie award for Best Online Column from the Western Publications Association and was named one of the "top five sex experts in the U.S." by Marie
Claire magazine.*

sion to hold the workshop, even though he says he's never been on Facebook and his advice to students parallels exactly what users already do online.

The mind boggles.   3

It makes me think of the moaning and wailing surrounding mobile devices and how we supposedly don't connect "for real" anymore. How we're allegedly replacing real relationships with fake ones, true intimacy with illusion and strong social bonding with pseudo-social networking.   4

This is all because a lot of people apparently spend a lot of time conversing online rather than in the flesh. And in order to keep up with all these relationships, we're supposedly not being as attentive to the people around us as we should. Not our loved ones, mind you, but the people we encounter casually as we go about our lives: bank tellers, dog walkers, grocers.   5

Tell me again why I should spend less time with the people I love and more time with strangers?   6

Convince me that it's more important to yak with a stranger at the neighborhood coffee house than it is to text conversation with my dear friend Monique. It might look like I'm ignoring a passing acquaintance in order to "use my phone." But actually I'm checking in with a new mom who is running home, baby and business on her own while her partner's job has him commuting to Canada temporarily. (Hooray for unlimited international minutes!)   7

> *Convince me that it's more important to yak with a stranger at the neighborhood coffee house than it is to text conversation with my dear friend Monique.*

Explain to me why I am contributing to The Decline of Morals and Manners in This Society because I prefer to attend to friends and lovers through our cell phones rather than allow geography to determine who I can and can't relate with.   8

I don't dismiss out of hand the concerns about techno-communication. Daniel Goleman, a proponent of the science of empathy, intuition and emotion and a thinker I trust, writes about a mass wave of disconnection in the introduction to his book *Social Intelligence*.   9

In explaining how mood and emotion are contagious, he notes the ripple effect of rude behavior and how spreading negativity and hurt feelings damages the human web more than most people realize.   10

But rudeness is a separate issue from connectivity. Mobile devices should not make us impolite.   11

I recently caught myself flirting by text message while checking   12
into a hotel. I didn't particularly want to connect with the hotel
guy—I wanted to keep going with the sweet (and spicy) nothings.

It was an almost physical wrench to set the phone down even for   13
five minutes. Yet to do otherwise would be as churlish as carrying on
a conversation with a companion as if the clerk wasn't even there.
(Which does happen, alas, but not by me.)

We all need to accept responsibility for our manners.   14

But harnessing technology to nurture our existing relationships   15
has not damaged our ability to connect "for real." Connectivity gives
shy swains time to craft what they want to say, and it gives extroverts
layers of interaction to satisfy their craving for people contact and
shared energy.

People once took for granted the idea that meeting new people   16
was easier for some folks than others. And I think people who are not
comfortable using technology to do that, who simply can't do it, or
who have burned out or become overwhelmed by technology worry
about those who can handle it.

I think they feel left out. Like we're in a secret club they can't get   17
into, or didn't enjoy once they got through the door.

Mobile service providers know exactly what we use cell phones   18
for. Cingular's commercials about what dropped calls can do to
lovers get right to the heart of the matter. And Vodaphone has a
great one about a sleeping model, an opportunist and the trouble we
can get into with camera phones.

Just like the fears people express about Internet users "replacing"   19
love and sex with delusion and cybersex, the concerns about "everyone" interacting through devices rather than in person miss the point.
Two points.

For one thing, many of the people we're interacting with through   20
our mobiles are our intimates. They are people we feel so connected
with, we want to be with them across time and distance.

For another, we have to trust each other to disconnect when we   21
need to. I'm not going to bemoan a "dependence" on technology-
facilitated communication (as if our entire economy isn't based on
such a thing!) when we can all put down the phone or walk away
from the computer when we get overwhelmed. We are not going to
wreck society simply because we can choose who we want to talk to
at any given time, based not on proximity but on attachment and
affection.

I even believe we are strengthening human bonds through these   22
technologically supported connections.

With mobile devices especially, we're sharing the love. Our mo-   23
biles are less anonymous and more personal than online message
boards or blog comments, and we use them as extensions of ourselves
and our relationships. They define "personal tech." And the very limitation that makes flirting and lovemaking so fun also makes it too
frustrating to bother with flaming and hate speech.

I have also found that nurturing relationships through tech has   24
taught me to be more forgiving and patient. I'm a better listener, because texting forces me to slow down. I've also become better about
asking for clarification when I don't understand something, rather
than jumping to a conclusion; I don't agonize over the question,
"What did he mean by that?"

Modern relationships—whether between colleagues, friends or   25
lovers—flow between flesh and technology more easily every day.

Let's accept that we've been dazzled by the novelty of our devices   26
long enough and dust off our manners. Then let's embrace the truth
that emotions are contagious, and ensure that the emotions we inspire
in even the most casual of encounters are pleasant or at least neutral.

And then let's get back on our devices and send a text message so   27
hot, so loving, so clever that our bosom buddy cannot help but pass
that warmth on to someone else.

See you in a fortnight,   28
Regina Lynn

Vocabulary / Using a Dictionary

1. What does the prefix *pseudo-* mean? Why would critics call Facebook "pseudo-social networking" (para. 4)?

2. What does Lynn mean when she says, "The mind boggles"
   (para. 3)? Look up the origin of *boggle* in the dictionary.

3. What is a *churl*? What does it mean to be "churlish" (para. 13)?

Responding to Words in Context

1. How would opponents of the new communication technologies
   define "real relationships" (para. 4)? How would Lynn differ
   from their ideas about what makes a relationship real?

2. Lynn calls mobile phones "personal tech" (para. 23). What does she mean by this phrase? What technologies does she consider less personal?

3. What does it mean to be "dazzled" by new technology (para. 26)? How does Lynn believe we should move beyond this state?

Discussing Main Point and Meaning

1. What distinction does Lynn draw between "rudeness" and "connectivity" (para. 11)? What behaviors would she associate with each?

2. Lynn claims that those who worry about damage to human relationships from communication technologies are wrong on two points (para. 19). What are these two points? Why are they important to her?

3. Why does Lynn introduce the idea that mood is contagious? How does she imagine that this contagiousness can be both positive and negative?

Examining Sentences, Paragraphs, and Organization

1. Why does Lynn begin her essay by imagining a class about making friends? What is the purpose of foregrounding the idea of learning how to make friends?

2. How does Lynn use imperatives like the one in paragraph 6? Who is she challenging?

3. Lynn ends her essay with another imperative, this time in the first-person plural rather than the second-person singular. What does she ask people to do in paragraph 27? Does the imperative serve as an effective conclusion to her essay?

Thinking Critically

1. Lynn argues that technology has made her a better communicator. Do you find her arguments on this point convincing? List the ways she claims that technology has improved her interactions with loved ones. Which ones seem plausible? Are there any that don't seem plausible?

2. Does Lynn too quickly dismiss the casual interactions that technology can cause us to miss? Can you think of any examples that might show the value of face-to-face relationships, even when they may not be particularly intimate?

In-Class Writing Activities

1. What do you imagine a Facebook in the Flesh workshop would entail? How do you interpret David Schachter's claim that much of what he counsels students to do parallels what they already do online? Given what you know about Facebook, list some possible activities for the workshop. Then write about which ones you think would be just as effective in person. Are there any aspects of Facebook networking that would be hard to translate out of the digital realm?

2. In her essay, Lynn is concerned with maintaining basic etiquette despite the changes in communication brought about by technology. What you and your peers consider reasonably polite is likely to be very different from your parents' or especially your grandparents' notion of politeness. Working in groups, write a list of rules for etiquette in using cell phones, text-messaging, and so on. Are there any rules that you think your parents would disagree with? What is the basic goal behind any etiquette rules?

ARI MELBER

About Facebook

[THE NATION/January 7–14, 2008]

Before You Read

What are Melber's concerns about Facebook? What measures does he think users should take to protect their personal information?

Words to Learn

vulnerable (para. 3): unprotected (adj.)
rankled (para. 9): caused pain or irritation (v.)
diligently (para. 11): attentively; with steady work (adv.)

When one of America's largest electronic surveillance systems   1
was launched in Palo Alto a year ago, it sparked an immediate national uproar. The new system tracked roughly 9 million Americans,
broadcasting their photographs and personal information on the Internet; 700,000 web-savvy young people organized online protests in
just days. *Time* declared it "Gen Y's first official revolution," while a
Nation blogger lauded students for taking privacy activism to "a
mass scale." Yet today, the activism has waned, and the surveillance
continues largely unabated.

---

*Ari Melber earned a bachelor of arts in political science from the Univer-
sity of Michigan in Ann Arbor and also studied at the University of Chile in
Santiago. In addition to his work as a legislative aide in the U.S. Senate and
serving as a national staff member of the 2004 John Kerry presidential campaign, Melber is a regular correspondent for the* Nation Online *and the* Huff-
ington Post *and a contributing editor at the Personal Democracy Forum. His
writing has been featured in the* Baltimore Sun, *the* Seattle Post-Intelligencer,
the Forward, *the* Times Union, *and the* American Prospect Online. *Melber
writes that his topics often include "politics, social networking/social media,
Internet activism and anything else happening online."*

Generation Y's "revolution" failed partly because young people were getting what they signed up for. All the protesters were members of Facebook, a popular social networking site, which had designed a sweeping "news feed" program to disseminate personal information that users post on their web profiles. Suddenly everything people posted, from photos to their relationship status, was sent to hundreds of other users in a feed of time-stamped updates. People complained that the new system violated their privacy. Facebook argued that it was merely distributing information users had already revealed. The battle—and Facebook's growing market dominance in the past year—show how social networking sites are rupturing the traditional conception of privacy and priming a new generation for complacency in a surveillance society. Users can complain, but the information keeps flowing. 2

Facebook users did not recognize how vulnerable their information was within the site's architecture. The initial protests drew an impressive 8 percent of users, but they quickly subsided after Facebook provided more privacy options. Today the feed is the site's nerve center. Chris Kelly, Facebook's chief privacy officer, said that when he speaks on campuses these days, students approach him to say that while they initially "hated" the feed, now they "can't live without it." 3

Still, Facebook hit a similar privacy snag in November after it launched Beacon, a "social advertising" program that broadcast users' profile pictures and private activities as advertising bulletins. When a Facebook user bought a product on one of dozens of other Web sites, for example, the information was sent to Facebook and distributed across the user's network as a "personal" ad. ("Joe Johnson rented *Traffic* at Blockbuster," for example.) Many users had their pictures and actions morphed into advertisements without their consent, turning private commerce into public endorsements. That could be an illegal appropriation, according to Daniel Solove and William McGeveran, two law professors who specialize in digital privacy and who blogged about the issue. 4

MoveOn.org formed a Facebook group to demand that Beacon switch to "opt-in"—a default to protect uninformed users—and allow people to reject the program in one click. The group drew less than 0.2 percent of Facebook members, far less than during last year's feed protest, but this time MoveOn helped the protest group press specific reforms, generate critical media attention and even rattle some advertisers, who backtracked on using Beacon. 5

Facebook buckled, agreeing to make the ads opt-in and allowing   6
people to reject the whole program, for now. Facebook founder
Mark Zuckerberg apologized to users on the company blog, explaining the problem in the language of the new privacy. "When we first
thought of Beacon, our goal was to build a simple product to let
people share information across sites with their friends," he wrote.
"It had to be lightweight so it wouldn't get in people's way as they
browsed the web, but also clear enough so people would be able to
easily control what they shared."

Yet both Facebook and its privacy protesters largely operated   7
within the same model of privacy *control*—opt-in versus opt-out,
sharing versus concealing. The traditional concept of privacy was
largely absent from the debate: the premise that what people do on
other Web sites should never be anyone else's business. After all, why
would people want to browse the web with "lightweight" surveillance broadcasting their pictures and supposed endorsements of
products they happen to buy? And why do people continue to give
pictures and personal information to a company that reserves the
right to use their photos—and their very identities—to sell more advertising, products and market targeting in the future?

Growing up online, young people assume their inner circle   8
knows their business. The "new privacy" is about controlling how
many people know—not if anyone knows.
"Information is not private because no one
knows it; it is private because the knowing is
limited and controlled," argues Danah Boyd,
an anthropologist and social-networking expert at the University of California, Berkeley, who studied the feed controversy for a
forthcoming article in the journal *Convergence*. Facebook's Kelly also
contends that privacy is shifting from an "absolute right to be let
alone" to an emphasis on control. "We don't think [users are] losing
privacy as long as there's a control machine and access restrictions,"
he said in an interview.

The "new privacy" is about controlling how many people know — not if anyone knows.

The feed rankled because it plucked personal details that previ-   9
ously existed in a social context, limited by visitors' interest in a person, and shattered any sense of concentric circles of control by
broadcasting them across wider networks. (Students list hundreds of
acquaintances as "Facebook friends," assuming that people they
barely know don't check their profiles often.) Boyd compares it to

yelling over loud music at a bar, only to find the music has stopped and everyone is staring at you.

Neither controversy has slowed Facebook's huge growth. It quadrupled its user base over the past year and is now the most popular Web site among Americans age 17 to 25. Facebook has achieved near total penetration of the college market, with more than eight out of ten college students registered. Older Americans are also flocking to the site: it draws 250,000 new members every day. Overall, it is the fifth most popular site in the country, ranking just behind YouTube. Young and old use it to divulge loads of personal information, often oblivious to the ramifications and ignorant of the basic features of the technology they use so effortlessly to socialize.

One study at the University of North Carolina, for example, found more than 60 percent of Facebook users posted their political views, relationship status, personal picture, interests and address. People also post a whopping 14 million personal photos every single day, making Facebook the top photo Web site in the country. Then users diligently label one another in these pictures, enabling visitors to see every photo anyone has ever posted of other people, regardless of their consent or knowledge. Even if users terminate their membership, pictures of them posted by others remain online. But users can't really quit, anyway.

Like guests at the Hotel California, people who check out of Facebook have a hard time leaving. Profiles of former members are preserved in case people want to reactivate their accounts. And all users' digital selves can outlive their creators. As the company's "terms of use" explain, profiles of deceased members are kept "active under a special memorialized status for a period of time determined by us to allow other users to post and view comments."

Facebook's 58 million active members have posted more than 2.7 billion photos, with more than 2.2 billion digital labels of people in the pictures. But what many users may not realize is that the company owns every photo. In fact, everything that people post is automatically licensed to Facebook for its perpetual and transferable use, distribution or public display. The terms of use reserve the right to grant and sublicense all "user content" posted on the site to other businesses. Facebook, a privately held company, rejected a buyout offer from Yahoo! last year and recently sold a 1.6 percent stake to Microsoft, which values the company at up to $15 billion. (Rupert Murdoch's News Corporation bought MySpace, the other leading social network site, for $580 million in 2005.)

Yet the same young people posting all this personal information   14
and relinquishing their photos to corporate control still say they value
privacy. A Carnegie Mellon study found that students on Facebook
think privacy policy is a "highly important issue," ranking above terrorism, and many would be very concerned if a stranger knew their
class schedule or could find out their political views five years from
now. Of the students who expressed the highest possible concern
about protecting their class schedule, however, 40 percent still posted
it on Facebook, and 47 percent of those concerned about political
views still provided them. The study concluded there was "little or no
relation between participants' reported privacy attitudes and their
likelihood of providing certain information."

Why would young people publicize the very information they   15
want to keep private?

Critics argue that privacy does not matter to children who were   16
raised in a wired celebrity culture that promises a niche audience for
everyone. Why hide when you can perform? But even if young people
are performing, many are clueless about the size of their audience.
That's because the new generation is often proficient with technology
it doesn't fully understand. The Carnegie Mellon study found that
one-third of students don't realize that it is easy for nonstudents to
access their Facebook profiles. And 30 percent of students did not
even know they had an option to limit access to their profile.

Most people don't use the privacy settings to limit access to their   17
Facebook profile. Four out of five simply accept the default setting,
which allows their whole network to see the entire profile. In the
UCLA network, that's 50,400 people. The Boston network has
312,404 people. For comparison, the city's tabloid, the *Boston Herald*, has a circulation of 201,503. Users may think they're only sharing with the friends they can see, but they're actually publishing with
the reach of a newspaper.

Social networking sites also induce users to disclose information   18
in order to be part of the site's culture. "Allowing users into your
circle allows them to track your moves on Facebook and vice versa,"
explains technology writer Michael Hirschorn. "Even more com-
pellingly, it allows you to track, if you wish, their interactions with
other users, all from your own user page. You can play with your privacy settings to prevent this, but as you become acculturated to the
site, you realize that you have to give information to get information."

Facebook's Kelly argues that the trend is broader than a single   19
Web site. People know their actions are tracked online, he says, just

as they're tracked on streets filled with surveillance cameras, "whether privately controlled through an ATM or publicly controlled [for] legitimate anticrime or anti-terrorism purposes." In an era of massive top-down surveillance, posting information on a Web site may feel downright redundant. Just as most consumers have acquiesced to companies collecting loads of data and private information about them, many Facebook users seem resigned to the company's aggressive use of private information.

In September Facebook launched a "public search" feature to list users' profiles on search engines like Yahoo! and Google. The move could fundamentally shift the site from a (relatively) closed social network to a more exposed public directory. Students originally joined Facebook as a private campus hub, but now it touts some of their profile information to the world. (Diligent users can opt out, and visitors still need to be Facebook members to view people within networks.) The massive search function might one day make Facebook an indispensable part of Internet commerce—creating the "Google of people," as blogger Jeff Jarvis puts it. The potential loss of privacy could ultimately beat the feed controversy by several orders of magnitude, but there has been no backlash so far. 20

Ultimately, these privacy concerns do not turn on the decisions of one social networking company like Facebook, or what its future owners may do. The architecture of these sites already facilitates all kinds of surveillance of unsuspecting users by the public. Employers check Facebook to vet job applicants, for example, and some have advised users to change their profiles or photos during the application process, as the *Stanford Daily* reported last year. A 2005 survey found that one out of four employers has rejected applicants based on research via search engines. Campus police increasingly review social networking sites to investigate crimes. Arkansas's John Brown University expelled a student after administrators discovered Facebook pictures of him dressed in drag last year, a violation of the school's Christian conduct code. And a Secret Service officer paid a dorm visit to University of Oklahoma sophomore Saul Martinez based on a comment he posted on the Facebook group Bush Sucks. 21

Even if this generation of Internet users is truly developing a "new privacy" concept that prioritizes nuanced control, they largely fail on their own terms. Most users do not exercise any real authority over their information; they accept default exposure settings, post to huge networks and transfer ownership of their social media productions to 22 entertainment businesses. Thus "control" devolves to the thousands of people in their networks and the business models of ambitious companies. The entire social network ecosystem, with its detailed records, pictures and videos of formative years, can completely change on a company's whim. Most users are left relying on the kindness of strangers and the benevolence of business.

A simple way to address one of Facebook's privacy problems is   23 to ensure that users can make informed choices. Taking a page from the consumer protection movement, Congress could simply require social networking sites to display their broadcasting reach prominently when new users post information. Just as the government requires standardized nutrition labels on packaged food, a privacy label would reveal the "ingredients" of social networking. For example, the label might tell users: "The photos you are about to post will become Facebook's property and be visible to 150,000 people—click here to control your privacy settings."

This disclosure requirement would push Facebook to catch up   24 with its customers. After all, users disclose tons of information about themselves. Why shouldn't the company open up a bit, too?

Facebook's invisible audiences should also stop hiding. Responsible institutions that choose to monitor users (and minors) on the   25 site, such as schools and employers, have a special obligation to inform users and parents of the practice.

In the end, social networking sites are wildly popular precisely   26 because they disseminate information so effectively. Posting to a network is easier than e-mailing individuals, and usually more fun. One bright side is that these sites' popularity dispels the recurring complaint that the web is merely an incubator for like-minded people to isolate themselves, associating only with the people and ideas that confirm their beliefs. Young people are doing just the opposite. Their favorite Web sites are about real people in the real world—not just their like-minded best friends but hundreds of acquaintances from different facets of their lives.

The problem, of course, is that playing with reality online is   27 riskier than playing with video games and anonymous screen names. Young people are recording their lives in minute detail, enabling unprecedented experiences, exposure and evidence that will outlast their youth. Social networking is a free service, but abdicating control of personal information, photos, writing, videos and memories seems like a high price to pay.

Vocabulary / Using a Dictionary

1. How much has something grown if it has "quadrupled" (para. 10)? What does the prefix *quad-* mean?

2. Melber points out that Facebook has the right to "sublicense" content that users post to the site. What does the prefix *sub-* mean in this word, and how does it represent Facebook's legal position?

3. What language does the word *private* come from? What does it mean?

Responding to Words in Context

1. What do people mean when they say that we live in a "wired" culture (para. 16)? Why does Melber use that word?

2. Why does Melber suggest that posting personal information to sites like Facebook might seem "redundant"? What precursors does he propose to this new system of data gathering?

3. How would you describe the Beacon program, which Facebook calls "social advertising" (para. 4)? What does that phrase mean?

Discussing Main Point and Meaning

1. Melber's essay links social-networking sites with surveillance. What is the connection between self-maintained Internet profiles and information gathering? At what point did this connection become problematic?

2. How does modern advertising complicate the privacy issues Melber discusses in this essay? How has Facebook appropriated user information for advertising?

3. How does Melber think Facebook has changed the way we think about privacy? How does the "new privacy" (para. 6) differ from the old?

Examining Sentences, Paragraphs, and Organization

1. At the beginning of his essay, Melber cites a widespread protest against Facebook that arose in 2007 as a response to the company's loose privacy policies. At what points in the essay does he

return to this "revolution"? What purpose does it serve in his argument?

2. Melber begins paragraph 8 with the topic sentence, "Growing up online, young people assume their inner circle knows their business." How does the evidence he includes in the paragraph support this statement about changing notions of privacy?

3. What is the function of the sentence that begins paragraph 22? How are the two clauses related? How does the sentence further Melber's argument?

Thinking Critically

1. What did Facebook claim was the purpose of developing the advertising program Beacon? Do you think the statement made by Mark Zuckerberg on the company blog accurately represents their motivation (para. 6)?

2. Melber argues for more user responsibility and a greater awareness of privacy options, but he also suggests that Congress take some "consumer protection" actions (para. 23). What solutions does he suggest? Summarize them and then decide whether you agree that this is the proper way to handle privacy concerns.

In-Class Writing Activities

1. How would you explain the disparity between students' reported concerns about privacy and their behavior (para. 14)? Why don't their concerns translate to tighter control of personal information? Write an essay addressing why your peers are so drawn to social networking in spite of possible reservations.

2. Where do you think the responsibility for protecting privacy should fall? Write an essay in which you outline what parties should be involved in privacy control. Should individuals bear the burden? What should companies like Facebook do to help? Should the government get involved in making policies?

MELISSA MAPES (STUDENT ESSAY)

Is Big Brother Watching Your Every Move?

[THE STATE PRESS, Arizona State University/February 28, 2008]

Before You Read

Why does Mapes argue for caution in posting information to Facebook? As a college student, how does she see her peers using or misusing the site?

Words to Learn

ominously (para. 1): in a way that suggests coming misfortune (adv.)
fluctuating (para. 4): changing; unstable (adj.)

"Oh. My. God," Ashley said out loud to herself as she scanned the Facebook feed that glowed ominously in front of her, greeting her with tidbits about the digital lives of her dearest acquaintances, friends and even frenemies. "I cannot believe that Bobby is 'in a relationship' with that skank Cathy," she exclaimed. "He just messaged me the other day saying how much he missed me and wanted to see me! I am going to unfriend him right now." In the following weeks, Ashley would receive several confused, desperate messages from Bobby, wondering why she would do such a hurtful thing as unfriend him. He saw it as the lowest of low blows. She was glad because she had intended to cut him deep.

1

Melissa Mapes is a senior at Arizona State University, where she is a major in English and creative writing. As a weekly columnist for the student newspaper, the State Press, *Mapes is "always asking people what they would like to see me write about." This process led her to the idea for her essay, "Is Big Brother Watching Your Every Move?" in which she explores the effects of online social-networking sites such as Facebook and MySpace. An avid reader and writer, Mapes hopes to pursue a career that involves writing when she completes her studies.*

The story of Ashley and Bobby reflects the new relationship dysfunctions evolving along with digital communication. Facebook is now a staple of our everyday lives as college students. We have all heard how it is a phenomenon of our society, from both critical and philosophical points of view, but I wish to explore the effects online communities like Facebook are having on our personal relationships.

A phone call used to be considered a lesser form of communication, shallow perhaps. Without a face to read expressions or a body to embrace, talking can feel stilted and awkward. A Facebook message, on the other hand, can be thought out and revised until it is crafted to convey exactly what its author wishes. This was once true of the dying art of letters, but an online message is instantly delivered and catalyzes the process through convenience. Generally, messages are meant to be more personal and private, whereas a post on someone's Facebook wall is a note to all. This wide exposure motivates posters to leave witty quips on the walls of others so they can be enjoyed and admired by a vast audience.

But, the most fascinating aspect of Facebook communication, in my opinion, is the gossip and drama it brews. The fluctuating relationship status of one's friends is not only displayed on profiles, but also advertised on one's "feed." A person can stay up-to-date on the love lives of those in their network, each alteration accompanied by a whole or breaking heart—a nice little touch. If a breakup goes badly, a bitter, one-sided note may appear. This could lead to a rebuttal by the other half of the relationship, but the argument is not meant for either parts of the couple, it is meant for mutual friends on Facebook, each half of the couple trying to rally the most supporters from a specific group.

> *A person can stay up-to-date on the love lives of those in their network, each alteration accompanied by a whole or breaking heart—a nice little touch.*

Messages, notes and the like are especially enjoyed by cowards, who lack the communication skills to speak to someone in person, so instead they rant and rave via keyboard. Facebook provides the perfect forum for such folk. And to be unfriended—woohee. That person must really, really hate you. No verbal message required to get that point across.

All of us, however, feed off our Facebook feed. It provides juicy details for lunch convo or for the personal satisfaction of knowing that someone who called you a bitch in high school got dumped by her boyfriend. The pictures and photo albums allow us to follow the lives of others through concrete images. We can screen people through their profiles and judge accordingly, without seeing or speaking to them for years. We can see who's packed on the freshman thirty or got an unfortunate-looking haircut, and feel better about ourselves by comparison. It is essentially our modern world's Big Brother. So next time you log in, keep in mind that people are following your life without your knowledge.

Vocabulary/Using a Dictionary

1. What does the prefix *dys-* in *dysfunctions* mean (para. 2)? How does it modify the word *function*?

2. Look up *fascinating* in the dictionary (para. 4). What does its Latin root word mean? How is this origin related to the way we use the word now?

3. What is the root word of *rebuttal* (para. 4)? What does the word mean?

Responding to Words in Context

1. How would you describe the coined word *frenemies* (para. 1)? Is there something about Facebook that breeds frenemies?

2. What does *stilted* mean in paragraph 3? What is a stilted conversation?

3. How does Mapes use two different meanings of the word *feed* in paragraph 6? How are the two senses of the word related?

Discussing Main Point and Meaning

1. What role does Mapes think Facebook plays in the lives of college students? Would she say it is a positive pastime or a destructive one?

2. What other media does Mapes bring into her argument to compare with Facebook? In what ways are Facebook messages preferable? What are their failings?

Examining Sentences, Paragraphs, and Organization

1. What is the effect of the quotations from Ashley in paragraph 1? How does Mapes portray her speech and her attitude toward her Facebook friends? What is the purpose of using direct quotation?

2. Mapes calls the icons of whole or broken hearts that accompany updates to a user's relationship status "a nice little touch" (para. 4). What is the tone of this sentence? What does Mapes mean by it?

Thinking Critically

1. Mapes offers several ways of thinking about Facebook messages, listing both benefits and flaws. Is there any inconsistency in her views?

2. Is Mapes's comparison of the way people use Facebook to *1984*'s Big Brother accurate? Is her description of how people use the information they gather on the site true to your experience? If you've read Orwell's novel, how would you describe the way his imagined government uses surveillance?

In-Class Writing Activities

1. In her essay, Mapes focuses on a few features of Facebook that she thinks play into negative uses of the site: the ability to "unfriend" someone in your network and the status messages that declare changes in someone's relationship. Choose another feature of the site and write about how the technology affects social relationships. You may wish to criticize (as Mapes does) or to defend Facebook, but you should make sure to describe how people use this particular feature.

2. Facebook is a new phenomenon, but are the interactions that occur on it really that new? Where did the "gossip and drama" Mapes discusses (para. 4) happen before social-networking sites? Write an essay examining how earlier sites of social interaction relate to today's Web sites.

ANNOTATION Clearly Expressing the Purpose of Your Essay

In composition, your purpose is your overall goal or aim in writing. It is basically what you hope to accomplish by writing—whether it is to promote or endorse a certain point of view, rally support for a cause, criticize a film or a book, or examine the effects of a social trend. Your purpose may or may not be expressed explicitly (in creative writing, for example, it rarely is), but in essays and nonfiction it is usually important that your reader understand the purpose behind your writing. An explicitly stated purpose not only helps the reader follow your argument or perspective but also helps ensure that everything you write reflects that purpose. A carefully expressed purpose will help anchor your essay and keep it from aimlessly floating all over. Note how Arizona State University student Melissa Mapes decided to express her purpose in "Is Big Brother Watching Your Every Move?" She begins her essay with a dramatic incident involving two students. After she sets the stage with a concrete instance, her next paragraph makes it clear that the opening concrete example represents the "relationship dysfunctions" that have evolved along with new communication technologies like Facebook. She then clearly informs her reader what the main purpose in writing this essay was: "I wish to explore the effects online communities like Facebook are having on our personal relationships." Note that from the first paragraph alone—even though it effectively draws us into the subject—the reader would not know Mapes's reason for writing, the objective she wants to achieve.

Dramatic incident to introduce subject. Note that we do not know why this moment is being reported.

"Oh. My. God," Ashley said out loud to herself as she scanned the Facebook feed that glowed ominously in front of her, greeting her with tidbits about the digital lives of her dearest acquaintances, friends and even frenemies. "I cannot believe that Bobby is 'in a relationship' with that skank Cathy," she exclaimed. "He just messaged me the other day saying how much he missed me and wanted to see me! I am going to unfriend him right now." In the following weeks, Ashley would receive several confused, desperate messages from Bobby, wondering why she would do such a hurtful thing as unfriend him. He saw it as the lowest of low blows. She was glad because she had intended to cut him deep.

Clear statement of purpose

The story of Ashley and Bobby reflects the new relationship dysfunctions evolving along with digital communication. Facebook is now a staple of our everyday lives as college students. We have all heard how it is a phenomenon of our society, from both critical and philosophical points of view, but I wish to explore the effects online communities like Facebook are having on our personal relationships.

—From "Is Big Brother Watching Your Every Move?" by Melissa Mapes, pages 101–102

Student Writer at Work: Melissa Mapes
On Writing "Is Big Brother Watching Your Every Move?"

Q: What inspired you to write "Is Big Brother Watching Your Every Move?"

A: As online networking sites, especially Facebook, become more and more popular, I cannot help but marvel at how the ways we communicate are evolving. I find myself immersed in Facebook culture, where our everyday lives are tied to our profiles. I have mixed feelings about this development, so I wanted to share them with my community. I hoped to create a dialogue and find out what others think.

Q: Have you written on social networking since?

A: In my Human Relationships class, I wrote a research paper on the effects of social networking on the ways we communicate. There are a lot of well-known dangers associated with online networking sites, but the biggest danger is losing our ability to communicate in person.

Q: Do you show your writing to friends before submitting it? Do you collaborate or bounce your ideas off others?

A: Showing my writing to friends is sometimes nerve-wracking because I value their opinions. I think it is normal to be sensitive about something you put a lot of effort into, but it is essential to be open to suggestions. I have gotten used to sharing my writing, though I still get nervous at times, and it has truly helped me improve. When it comes to my column, I am always asking people what they would like to see me write about. It was a discussion with a friend that gave me the idea for "Is Big Brother Watching Your Every Move?"

Q: What advice do you have for other student writers?

A: The easiest way to be a good writer is to be a good reader. If you read a lot, it will show through in your work, and if you say you don't like to read, you just haven't found the right book yet.

Discussing the Unit

Suggested Topic for Discussion

Although Ari Melber's essay is the most overt in projecting ideas about how technologies like Facebook will progress, each of the pieces in this chapter suggests ways of thinking about how technology has changed and will continue to change the way we communicate. What would each of the authors say about the future of communications? Are they hopeful or wary? What new innovations do you expect will appear in the next decade? Will the same ethical questions apply?

Preparing for Class Discussion

1. On what evidence does each of these authors base his or her conclusions? As you read the essays in this chapter, keep track of when they call on personal experience, statistics, other writers, or news sources. How does the focus of each argument determine which authorities the author calls on?

2. The essays in this chapter raise two primary concerns about electronic communication: the fact that electronic communication makes surveillance or information gathering easier and the fear that it will result in the deterioration of personal relationships. Where do these two arguments appear in the essays? Does one of them seem more compelling or harder to dismiss than the other? How would you rank these concerns?

From Discussion to Writing

1. What technology are you concerned or excited about? Choose some advance in communication technology (the BlackBerry, for example, or video chat) and, using one of the essays in this chapter as a model, write an essay about how it will change relationships.

2. Do an Internet search for recent news articles about Facebook. What new developments to the site or new controversies have arisen since the essays in this chapter were written? Write a response to Melber's or Mapes's essay in which you discuss some news item. Do you think the story complicates the argument of the essay, or does it help support the author's claims?

Topics for Cross-Cultural Discussion

1. Facebook is a popular site not just in the United States but also in other countries around the world. How do you think Facebook works as a cross-cultural phenomenon? Why do you think it has gained popularity outside the United States?

2. Facebook has been banned in several countries, including Syria, the United Arab Emirates, and Iran. Why do you think the site would cause controversy in some cultures?

3

How Important Is
Ethnic Identity?

Jean de Crèvecoeur, a Frenchman who moved to America in the eighteenth century, wrote that an immigrant to the United States "becomes an American by being received in the broad lap of our great Alma Mater. Here individuals of all nations are melted into a new race of men." The metaphor of a melting pot, in which people of various origins are blended together to become one unified compound, has remained popular. Attempts to forge a truly homogeneous American society, however, have met with limited success — and consistent opposition.

One challenge is that ethnic identity is deeply felt and persistent, not only for immigrants but also for their children and grandchildren. In a society in which defining ourselves is increasingly important, our cultural and geographic roots, even when they are generations old, are becoming a significant source of self-understanding as well as personal pride. They can also be a source of confusion and displacement, as Dinaw Mengestu illustrates in "Home at Last." Mengestu, who left Ethiopia with his parents when he was a toddler, describes how growing up in America left him without a sense of origin. "My parents," he writes, "for all that they had given up by leaving Ethiopia, at least had the certainty that they had come from some place."

In Brooklyn, New York, itself a hodgepodge of scattered but tightly knit ethnic communities, Mengestu is finally able to discover a kind of home: On a corner where Pakistani and Bangladeshi immigrants are gathered chatting, Mengestu observes a culture and history "different from the one I had been born into, but familiar to me nonetheless." The comforting fact that these displaced men can re-create some part of their homeland in Brooklyn reminds the author that "we can rebuild and remake ourselves and our communities over and over again."

For Manuel Muñoz, a Mexican American living in a small California town, identity means an adherence to the tradition, culture, and language of one's native land. But in "Leave Your Name at the Border," Muñoz explores the complications that arise when people try to assimilate to a new culture, through the lens of a very literal form of identity: names. Growing up, Muñoz and his peers spoke English at school and Spanish at home. As a result, "Spanish was for privacy—and privacy quickly turned to shame." Muñoz links this feeling to a recent trend that disturbs him: His family has begun giving their children American names like Brandon or Kaitlyn, while old-fashioned Mexican names disappear.

For Muñoz, his unmistakably Mexican first name was always a mark of his roots, and an obstacle to the melting pot: Traditional names "stood as barriers to a complete embrace of an American identity, simply because their pronunciations required a slip into Spanish, the otherness that assimilation was supposed to erase." But does an American name really represent a loss of identity? Is a person named Ashley Sánchez more Ashley or Sánchez?

In a short graphic memoir, "A Red Envelope Day," Nathan Huang considers his own particularly bitter loss of tradition—when his Taiwanese American family decided not to give their children gifts of money for the Chinese New Year. "Since we were a large immigrant family," Huang writes, forgoing the lavish red envelopes "was a matter of financial survival." But in addition to the disappointment of missing out on cash, Huang illustrates the emptiness he feels as an important ritual dies out; the strip is a compelling contemplation of the competing pressures of preserving culture and surviving the immigrant experience.

Sandy Dover, a recent graduate of Ohio State University, takes a slightly different view of ethnic identity in "How Do You Define You?" By reminding us that the lines between many ethnic groups are paper thin, and that most Americans maintain several different but concurrent identities, Dover casts doubt on the very integrity of identity itself, particularly when it becomes entwined in politics. Dover challenges us to learn about people as people, not as members of a group, and to scrutinize seriously "what it means to be who we are."

DINAW MENGESTU

Home at Last

[OPEN CITY / Winter 2008]

Before You Read

Why does Mengestu find himself searching for a home in his adulthood? Why don't the places where he has lived before qualify as a true home for him?

Words to Learn

assimilate (para. 3): to merge into a culture; become part of the mainstream (v.)
deliberately (para. 5): purposefully (adv.)
haphazard (para. 8): random; by chance (adj.)

Dinaw Mengestu immigrated from Addis Ababa, Ethiopia, to the United States with his family at the age of two. He holds a BA in English from Georgetown University and an MFA in fiction from Columbia University. His first novel, The Beautiful Things That Heaven Bears, *was embraced by critics and has been translated into more than a dozen languages. The novel was a 2007 New York Times* Notable Book *and was named one of the ten best novels of 2007 by Amazon.com. In addition to fiction, Mengestu has written for many magazines, including* Harper's, Jane, *and* Rolling Stone, *on such global issues as the situations in Darfur and northern Uganda. When asked about how he became a writer, Mengestu responded, "I don't think most writers ever decide to write. For me, it was something that I did because I had to. It's been my way of managing and making sense of the world I live in."*

A_t twenty-one I moved to Brooklyn hoping that it would be the   1
last move I would ever make—that it would, with the gradual accumulation of time, memory, and possessions, become that place I instinctively reverted back to when asked, "So, where are you from?" I was born in Ethiopia like my parents and their parents before them, but it would be a lie to say I was from Ethiopia, having left the country when I was only two years old following a military coup and civil war, losing in the process the language and any direct memory of the family and culture I had been born into. I simply am Ethiopian, without the necessary "from" that serves as the final assurance of our identity and origin.

Since leaving Addis Ababa in 1980, I've lived in Peoria, Illinois;   2
in a suburb of Chicago; and then finally, before moving to Brooklyn, in Washington, D.C., the de facto capital of the Ethiopian immigrant. Others, I know, have moved much more often and across much greater distances. I've only known a few people, however, that have grown up with the oddly permanent feeling of having lost and abandoned a home that you never, in fact, really knew, a feeling that has nothing to do with apartments, houses, or miles, but rather the sense that no matter how far you travel, or how long you stay still, there is no place that you can always return to, no place where you fully belong. My parents, for all that they had given up by leaving Ethiopia, at least had the certainty that they had come from some place. They knew the country's language and culture, had met outside of coffee shops along Addis's main boulevard in the early days of their relationship, and as a result, regardless of how mangled by violence Ethiopia later became, it was irrevocably and ultimately theirs. Growing up, one of my father's favorite sayings was, "Remember, you are Ethiopian," even though, of course, there was nothing for me to remember apart from the bits of nostalgia and culture my parents had imparted. What remained had less to do with the idea that I was from Ethiopia and more to do with the fact that I was not from America.

I can't say when exactly I first became aware of that feeling—   3
that I was always going to and never from—but surely I must have felt it during those first years in Peoria, with my parents, sister, and me always sitting on the edge of whatever context we were now supposed to be a part of, whether it was the all-white southern Baptist church we went to every weekend, or the nearly all-white Catholic schools my sister and I attended first in Peoria and then again in Chicago at my parents' insistence. By that point my father, haunted

by the death of his brother during the revolution and the ensuing loss of the country he had always assumed he would live and die in, had taken to long evening walks that he eventually let me accompany him on. Back then he had a habit of sometimes whispering his brother's name as he walked ("Shibrew," he would mutter) or whistling the tunes of Amharic songs that I had never known. He always walked with both hands firmly clasped behind his back, as if his grief, transformed into something real and physical, could be grasped and secured in the palms of his hands. That was where I first learned what it meant to lose and be alone. The lesson would be reinforced over the years whenever I caught sight of my mother sitting by herself on a Sunday afternoon, staring silently out of our living room's picture window, recalling, perhaps, her father who had died after she left, or her mother, four sisters, and one brother in Ethiopia—or else recalling nothing at all because there was no one to visit her, no one to call or see. We had been stripped bare here in America, our lives confined to small towns and urban suburbs. We had sacrificed precisely those things that can never be compensated for or repaid—parents, siblings, culture, a memory to a place that dates back more than half a generation. It's easy to see now how even as a family we were isolated from one another—my parents tied and lost to their past; my sister and I irrevocably assimilated. For years we were strangers even among ourselves.

By the time I arrived in Brooklyn I had little interest in where I actually landed. I had just graduated college and had had enough of the fights and arguments about not being "black" enough, as well as the earlier fights in high school hallways and street corners that were fought for simply being black. Now it was enough, I wanted to believe, to simply be, to say I was in Brooklyn and Brooklyn was home. It wasn't until after I had signed the lease on my apartment that I even learned the name of the neighborhood I had moved into: Kensington, a distinctly regal name at a price that I could afford; it was perfect, in other words, for an eager and poor writer with inflated ambitions and no sense of where he belonged.   4

After less than a month of living in Kensington I had covered almost all of the neighborhood's streets, deliberately committing their layouts and routines to memory in a first attempt at assimilation. There was an obvious and deliberate echo to my walks, a self-conscious reenactment of my father's routine that I adopted to stave off some of my own emptiness. It wasn't just that I didn't have any   5 deep personal relationships here, it was that I had chosen this city as the place to redefine, to ground, to secure my place in the world. If I could bind myself to Kensington physically, if I could memorize and mentally reproduce in accurate detail the various shades of the houses on a particular block, then I could stake my own claim to it, and in doing so, no one could tell me who I was or that I didn't belong.

> *If I could bind myself to Kensington physically, if I could memorize and mentally reproduce in accurate detail the various shades of the houses on a particular block, then I could stake my own claim to it, and in doing so, no one could tell me who I was or that I didn't belong.*

On my early-morning walks to the F train I passed in succession a Latin American restaurant and grocery store, a Chinese fish market, a Halal butcher shop, followed by a series of Pakistani and Bangladeshi takeout restaurants. This cluster of restaurants on the corner of Church and McDonald, I later learned, sold five-dollar plates of lamb and chicken biryani in portions large enough to hold me over for a day, and in more finan-cially desperate times, two days. Similarly, I learned that the butcher and fish shop delivery trucks arrived on most days just as I was mak-ing my way to the train. If I had time, I found it hard not to stand and stare at the refrigerated trucks with their calf and sheep carcasses dangling from hooks, or at the tanks of newly arrived bass and cat-fish flapping around in a shallow pool of water just deep enough to keep them alive.

It didn't take long for me to develop a fierce loyalty to Kensing-ton, to think of the neighborhood and my place in it as emblematic of a grander immigrant narrative. In response to that loyalty, I promised to host a "Kensington night" for the handful of new friends that I eventually made in the city, an evening that would have been com-prised of five-dollar lamb biryani followed by two-dollar Budweisers at Denny's, the neighborhood's only full-fledged bar—a defunct Irish pub complete with terribly dim lighting and wooden booths. I never hosted a Kensington night, however, no doubt in part because I had established my own private relationship to the neighborhood, one that could never be shared with others in a single evening of cheap South Asian food and beer. I knew the hours of the call of the muezzin that rang from the mosque a block away from my apart-ment. I heard it in my bedroom every morning, afternoon, and evening, and if I was writing when it called out, I learned that it was better to simply stop and admire it. My landlord's father, an old gray-haired Chinese immigrant who spoke no English, gradually smiled at me as I came and went, just as I learned to say hello, as politely as possible, in Mandarin every time I saw him. The men behind the counters of the Bangladeshi takeout places now knew me by sight. A few, on occasion, slipped an extra dollop of vegetables or rice into my to-go container, perhaps because they worried that I wasn't eating enough. One in particular, who was roughly my age, spoke little English, and smiled wholeheartedly whenever I came in, gave me presweetened tea and free bread, a gesture that I took to be an acknowledgment that, at least for him, I had earned my own, albeit marginal, place here.

And so instead of sitting with friends in a brightly lit fluorescent restaurant with cafeteria-style service, I found myself night after night quietly walking around the neighborhood in between sporadic fits of writing. Kensington was no more beautiful by night than by day, and perhaps this very absence of grandeur allowed me to feel more at ease wandering its streets at night. The haphazard gathering of immigrants in Kensington had turned it into a place that even someone like me, haunted and conscious of race and identity at every turn, could slip and blend into. 8

Inevitably on my way home I returned to the corner of Church and McDonald with its glut of identical restaurants. On warm nights, I had found it was the perfect spot to stand and admire not only what Kensington had become with the most recent wave of migration, but what any close-knit community—whether its people came here one hundred years ago from Europe or a decade ago from Africa, Asia, or the Caribbean—has provided throughout Brooklyn's history: a second home. There, on that corner, made up of five competing South Asian restaurants of roughly equal quality, dozens of Pakistani and Bangladeshi men gathered one night after another to drink chai out of paper cups. The men stood there talking for hours, huddled in factions built in part, I imagine, around restaurant loyalties. Some nights I sat in one of the restaurants and watched from a corner table with a book in hand as an artificial prop. A few of the men always stared, curious no doubt as to what I was doing there. Even though I lived in Kensington, when it came to evening gatherings like this, I was the foreigner and tourist. On other nights I ordered my own cup of tea and stood a few feet away on the edge of the sidewalk, near the subway entrance or at the bus stop, and silently stared. I had seen communal scenes like this before, especially while living in Washington, 9

D.C., where there always seemed to be a cluster of Ethiopians, my age or older, gathered together outside coffee shops and bars all over the city, talking in Amharic with an ease and fluency that I admired and envied. They told jokes that didn't require explanation and debated arguments that were decades in the making. All of this was coupled with the familiarity and comfort of speaking in our native tongue. At any given moment, they could have told you without hesitancy where they were from. And so I had watched, hardly understanding a word, hoping somehow that the simple act of association and observation was enough to draw me into the fold.

Here, then, was a similar scene, this one played out on a Brook- 10 lyn corner with a culture and history different from the one I had been born into, but familiar to me nonetheless. The men on that corner in Kensington, just like the people I had known throughout my life, were immigrants in the most complete sense of the word—their loyalties still firmly attached to the countries they had left one, five, or twenty years earlier. If there was one thing I admired most about them, it was that they had succeeded, at least partly, in re-creating in Brooklyn some of what they had lost when they left their countries of origin. Unlike the solitary and private walks my father and I took, each of us buried deep in thoughts that had nowhere to go, this nightly gathering of Pakistani and Bangladeshi men was a makeshift reenactment of home. Farther down the road from where they stood were the few remaining remnants of the neighborhood's older Jewish community—one synagogue, a kosher deli—proof, if one was ever needed, that Brooklyn is always reinventing itself, that there is room here for us all.

While the men stood outside on the corner, their numbers gradu- 11 ally increasing until they spilled out into the street as they talked loudly among themselves, I once again played my own familiar role of quiet, jealous observer and secret admirer. I have no idea what those men talked about, if they discussed politics, sex, or petty complaints about work. It never mattered anyway. The substance of the conversations belonged to them, and I couldn't have cared less. What I had wanted and found in them, what I admired and adored about Kensington, was the assertion that we can rebuild and remake ourselves and our communities over and over again, in no small part because there have always been corners in Brooklyn to do so on. I stood on that corner night after night for the most obvious of reasons—to be reminded of a way of life that persists regardless of context; to feel, however foolishly, that I too was attached to something.

Vocabulary / Using a Dictionary

1. What does the phrase *de facto* (para. 2) mean? What language does it come from? What does it signify in a legal context?
2. What is the root of the word *assimilate* (para. 3)? How does the origin of the word relate to its current usage?
3. What is Kensington named after? Does the origin of this name support Mengestu's understanding of the neighborhood?

Responding to Words in Context

1. In pararaph 4, Mengestu describes being harassed for being black or "not being 'black' enough." What is the difference between *black* and "*black*" in quotation marks? Is there a paradox in the way people treat the author?
2. In paragraph 9, Mengestu uses the word *close-knit* to describe the immigrant community. This common usage is actually based on a metaphor. What is the literal meaning of *close-knit*, and why does it work as a figurative description of community?
3. Why does Mengestu call the gathering of men on the street corner a "makeshift reenactment" (para. 10)? What is the general sense of *reenactment*, and how does it apply to what these men are doing?

Discussing Main Point and Meaning

1. Why does Mengestu feel at home in his adopted Brooklyn neighborhood? What qualities does it have that make him feel comfortable?
2. What does Mengestu think is odd about his father's saying, "Remember, you are Ethiopian" (para. 2)?
3. What is the point of Mengestu's anecdote about going on walks with his father? Why does the father mutter his brother's name?

Examining Sentences, Paragraphs, and Organization

1. Why does Mengestu begin by stating his age? Why is age significant to this essay, and what is important about this particular age?
2. What is the purpose of the break between paragraphs 3 and 4? What does the gap signify?

3. In paragraph 9, Mengestu describes a scene from his life in Washington, D.C. What does this memory have in common with his experience of Kensington? In what ways are they different?

Thinking Critically

1. How does Mengestu actively try to make Kensington a home? What activities does he think will prove that he belongs there?

2. What would Mengestu's "Kensington night" have consisted of, and why does he decide not to hold one after all? Do you agree that it would have been an insufficient way to experience the neighborhood?

3. How does Mengestu interpret the presence of a few Jewish institutions (synagogue, kosher deli) in the neighborhood now dominated by South Asians? Why does he think it is a hopeful sign?

In-Class Writing Activities

1. What kind of relationship do you have to your neighborhood? Do you have all the street names memorized, as Mengestu does? Are you a regular at any restaurants or shops? Write a reflection on the character of your neighborhood and your place within it.

2. Mengestu takes the presence of a Jewish synagogue in Kensington as a trace of the neighborhood's history. What buildings or institutions provide clues to the past life of your community? What do they tell you about how it has changed?

MANUEL MUÑOZ

Leave Your Name at the Border

[NEW YORK TIMES / August 1, 2007]

Before You Read

Where does Muñoz live, and how does this affect the questions he raises about immigrant names? At what points in the essay does he talk about where he is from or where he has lived?

Words to Learn

camouflage (para. 2): to disguise or hide (v.)
obscure (para. 7): to darken or conceal (v.)
vilified (para. 8): treated as worthless (adj.)

At the Fresno airport, as I made my way to the gate, I heard a   1
name over the intercom. The way the name was pronounced by the gate agent made me want to see what she looked like. That is, I wanted to see whether she was Mexican. Around Fresno, identity politics rarely deepen into exacting terms, so to say "Mexican" means, essentially, "not white." The slivered self-identifications Chi-

---

Manuel Muñoz is a native of Dinuba, California, a town in the state's Central Valley that "remains the foundation of [his] fiction." After graduating from Harvard University and receiving his MFA in creative writing from Cornell University, Muñoz went on to write two award-winning collections of short stories, Zigzagger and The Faith Healer of Olive Avenue. When discussing the genre of short stories, Muñoz remarked, "I've always been attracted to stories. Like poetry, short stories can keep offering you new ways to look at lives and situations in such superb variations of style and form." His stories have been included in the New York Times, Rush Hour, Swink, Epoch, Glimmer Train, Edinburgh Review, and Boston Review. A current resident of New York City, he works in the managing editorial department of Grand Central Publishing.

cano, Hispanic, Mexican-American and Latino are not part of everyday life in the Valley. You're either Mexican or you're not. If someone wants to know if you were born in Mexico, they'll ask. Then
you're From Over There—de allá. And leave it at that.

The gate agent, it turned out, was Mexican. Well-coiffed, in her   2
30s, she wore foundation that was several shades lighter than the rest
of her skin. It was the kind of makeup job I've learned to silently
identify at the mall when I'm with my mother, who will say nothing
about it until we're back in the car. Then she'll stretch her neck like
an ostrich and point to the darkness of her own skin, wondering
aloud why women try to camouflage who they are.

I watched the Mexican gate agent busy herself at the counter,   3
professional and studied. Once again, she picked up the microphone
and, with authority, announced the name of the missing customer:
"Eugenio Reyes, please come to the front desk."

You can probably guess how she said it. Her Anglicized pronun-   4
ciation wouldn't be unusual in a place like California's Central Valley. I didn't have a Mexican name there either: I was an instruction
guide.

When people ask me where I'm from, I say Fresno because I   5
don't expect them to know little Dinuba. Fresno is a booming city of
nearly 500,000 these days, with a diversity—white, Mexican, African-
American, Armenian, Hmong and Middle Eastern people are all well
represented—that shouldn't surprise anyone. It's in the small towns
like Dinuba that surround Fresno that the awareness of cultural difference is stripped down to the interactions between the only two
groups that tend to live there: whites and Mexicans. When you hear a
Mexican name spoken in these towns, regardless of the speaker's
background, it's no wonder that there's an "English way of pronouncing it."

I was born in 1972, part of a generation that learned both En-   6
glish and Spanish. Many of my cousins and siblings are bilingual,
serving as translators for those in the family whose English is barely
functional. Others have no way of following the Spanish banter at
family gatherings. You can tell who falls into which group: Estella,
Eric, Delia, Dubina, Melanie.

It's intriguing to watch "American" names begin to dominate   7
among my nieces and nephews and second cousins, as well as with
the children of my hometown friends. I am not surprised to meet
5-year-old Brandon or Kaitlyn. Hardly anyone questions the incongruity of matching these names with last names like Trujillo or

Zepeda. The English-only way of life partly explains the quiet erasure of cultural difference that assimilation has attempted to accomplish. A name like Kaitlyn Zepeda doesn't completely obscure her ethnicity, but the half-step of her name, as a gesture, is almost understandable.

Spanish was and still is viewed with suspicion: always the language of the vilified illegal immigrant, it segregated schoolchildren into English-only and bilingual programs; it defined you, above all else, as part of a lower class. Learning English, though, brought its own complications with identity. It was simultaneously the language of the white population and a path toward the richer, expansive identity of "American." But it took getting out of the Valley for me to understand that "white" and "American" were two very different things. 8

Something as simple as saying our names "in English" was our unwittingly complicit gesture of trying to blend in. Pronouncing Mexican names correctly was never encouraged. Names like Daniel, Olivia and Marco slipped right into the mutability of the English language. 9

I remember a school ceremony at which the mathematics teacher, a white man, announced the names of Mexican students correctly and caused some confusion, if not embarrassment. Years later we recognized that he spoke in deference to our Spanish-speaking parents in the audience, caring teacher that he was. 10

These were difficult names for a non-Spanish speaker: Araceli, Nadira, Luis (a beautiful name when you glide the *u* and the *i* as you're supposed to). We had been accustomed to having our birth names altered for convenience. Concepción was Connie. Ramón was Raymond. My cousin Esperanza was Hope—but her name was pronounced "Hopie" because any Spanish speaker would automatically pronounce the *e* at the end. 11

Ours, then, were names that stood as barriers to a complete embrace of an American identity, simply because their pronunciations required a slip into Spanish, the otherness that assimilation was supposed to erase. What to do with names like Amado, Lucio or Élida? There are no English "equivalents," no answer when white teachers asked, "What does your name mean?" when what they really wanted to know was "What's the English one?" So what you heard was a name butchered beyond recognition, a pronunciation that pointed the finger at the Spanish language as the source of clunky sound and ugly rhythm. 12

My stepfather, from Ojos de Agua, Mexico, jokes when I ask him about the names of Mexicans born here. He deliberately stumbles 13 over pronunciations, imitating our elders who have difficulty with Bradley and Madelyn. "Ashley Sánchez. ¿Tú crees?" He wonders aloud what has happened to the "nombres del rancho"—traditional Mexican names that are hardly given anymore to children born in the States: Heraclio, Madaleno, Otilia, Dominga.

My stepfather's experience with the Anglicization of his name— Antonio to Tony—ties into something bigger than learning English. For him, the erasure of his name was about deference and subservience. Becoming Tony gave him a measure of access as he struggled to learn English and get more fieldwork. 14

This isn't to say that my stepfather welcomed the change, only that he could not put up much resistance. Not changing put him at risk of being passed over for work. English was a world of power and decisions, of smooth, uninterrupted negotiation. There was no time to search for the right word while a shop clerk waited for him to come up with the English name of the correct part needed out in the field. Clear communication meant you could go unsupervised, or that you were even able to read instructions directly off a piece of paper. Every gesture made toward convincing an employer that English was on its way to being mastered had the potential to make a season of fieldwork profitable. 15

It's curious that many of us growing up in Dinuba adhered to the same rules. Although as children of farm workers we worked in the fields at an early age, we'd also had the opportunity to stay in one town long enough to finish school. Most of us had learned English early and splintered off into a dual existence of English at school, Spanish at home. But instead of recognizing the need for fluency in both languages, we turned it into a peculiar kind of battle. English was for public display. Spanish was for privacy—and privacy quickly turned to shame. 16

> *English was for public display. Spanish was for privacy—and privacy quickly turned to shame.*

The corrosive effect of assimilation is the displacement of one culture over another, the inability to sustain more than one way of being. It isn't a code word for racial and ethnic acculturation only. It applies to needing and wanting to belong, of seeing from the outside and wondering how to get in and then, once inside, realizing there are always those still on the fringe. 17

When I went to college on the East Coast, I was confronted for the first time by people who said my name correctly without prompting; if they stumbled, there was a quick apology and an honest plea 18 to help with the pronunciation. But introducing myself was painful: already shy, I avoided meeting people because I didn't want to say my name, felt burdened by my own history. I knew that my small-town upbringing and its limitations on Spanish would not have been tolerated by any of the students of color who had grown up in large cities, in places where the sheer force of their native languages made them dominant in their neighborhoods.

It didn't take long for me to assert the power of code-switching   19
in public, the transferring of words from one language to another, regardless of who might be listening. I was learning that the English language composed new meanings when its constrictions were ignored, crossed over or crossed out. Language is all about manipulation, or not listening to the rules.

When I come back to Dinuba, I have a hard time hearing my   20
name said incorrectly, but I have an even harder time beginning a conversation with others about why the pronunciation of our names matters. Leaving a small town requires an embrace of a larger point of view, but a town like Dinuba remains forever embedded in an either/or way of life. My stepfather still answers to Tony and, as the United States–born children grow older, their Anglicized names begin to signify who does and who does not "belong"—who was born here and who is de allá.

My name is Manuel. To this day, most people cannot say it cor-   21
rectly, the way it was intended to be said. But I can live with that because I love the alliteration of my full name. It wasn't the name my mother, Esmeralda, was going to give me. At the last minute, my father named me after an uncle I would never meet. My name was to have been Ricardo. Growing up in Dinuba, I'm certain I would have become Ricky or even Richard, and the journey toward the discovery of the English language's extraordinary power in even the most ordinary of circumstances would probably have gone unlearned.

I count on a collective sense of cultural loss to once again swing   22
the names back to our native language. The Mexican gate agent announced Eugenio Reyes, but I never got a chance to see who appeared. I pictured an older man, cowboy hat in hand, but I made the assumption on his name alone, the clash of privileges I imagined between someone de allá and a Mexican woman with a good job in the United States. Would she speak to him in Spanish? Or would she raise her voice to him as if he were hard of hearing?

But who was I to imagine this man being from anywhere, based on   23
his name alone? At a place of arrivals and departures, it sank into me

that the currency of our names is a stroke of luck: because mine was not an easy name, it forced me to consider how language would rule me if I allowed it. Yet I discovered that only by leaving. My stepfather must live in the Valley, a place that does not allow that choice, every day. And Eugenio Reyes—I do not know if he was coming or going.

Vocabulary / Using a Dictionary

1. What does *Angl-* mean in *Anglicized*? What happens when a name is Anglicized?

2. What is the root of the word *bilingual*, and what does the root mean?

3. Why does Muñoz's stepfather call traditional names "nombres del rancho" (para. 13)? Use a Spanish dictionary if you need to determine the meaning of the words. What does the phrase signify?

Responding to Words in Context

1. What does Muñoz mean when he mentions the "slivered self-identifications" that do not exist in Fresno (para. 1)? What contrast is he setting up?

2. In paragraph 9, Muñoz argues that pronouncing their names "in English" makes his relatives and friends "complicit." To whom or what are they acting as accomplices? What are they helping to make happen?

3. Muñoz describes assimilation as a "corrosive" process in paragraph 17. What is the literal meaning of *corrosive*, and why does he use it figuratively to discuss the effects of one culture on another?

Discussing Main Point and Meaning

1. Why does Muñoz think it is a shame to pronounce Spanish names with an American accent? What is lost when the names are Anglicized?

2. Why did Muñoz's stepfather stop going by "Antonio" and start using the name "Tony"? How are his motivations different from those of the generation younger than him?

3. How did Muñoz and his bilingual peers deal with their knowledge of both Spanish and English?

Examining Sentences, Paragraphs, and Organization

1. What purpose does Muñoz's observation of the airport gate agent serve in his argument? How does he interpret her?
2. What does the list of names at the end of paragraph 6 illustrate?
3. Muñoz writes *about* names in this essay, and he also frequently writes out the names themselves. Why does he include so many names in his argument, when just a few would have illustrated his point? What do they add to the essay?

Thinking Critically

1. Why were the children in Muñoz's school embarrassed by the teacher who pronounced their names correctly? How does the adult writer explain the teacher's motivations, and how does his understanding contrast with the children's reaction?
2. How does Muñoz think his experience in Dinuba differed from that of people who grew up in big cities? When he meets other children of immigrants in college, how do they strike him as different from himself?
3. At the end of the essay, Muñoz returns to the gate agent announcing the name "Eugenio Reyes," and he imagines the man who would bear that name. What does Muñoz's picture of Eugenio Reyes assume about the name? And why, in the next paragraph, does he reproach himself for conjuring this picture?

In-Class Writing Activities

1. Many people think at some point in their lives about changing their first names. Have you ever thought about changing yours? Write about a time in your life when you wanted to change your name, and consider your reasons. How do they differ from the reasons of Muñoz and his classmates?
2. Muñoz writes that language is about "not listening to the rules" (para. 19). Does this contradict what you have learned in English or foreign-language classes? Summarize in writing what you think he means by this statement. Does knowing more than one language make it easier to challenge the rules?

NATHAN HUANG

A Red Envelope Day

[NEW YORK TIMES / February 18, 2007]

Before You Read

Why does Huang remember this "red envelope day"? What is significant about the holiday in general and about this one in particular?

Words to Learn

boast (panel 5): to brag (v.)

Nathan Huang graduated from the Art Center College of Design in 2005 with a bachelor of fine arts. A professional artist, illustrator, and comic, he currently resides in Brooklyn, New York, where he works within a variety of mediums. His work has appeared in the New York Times, Esquire, *and the* Washington Post, *in addition to many other publications and companies. Huang writes that he began making comics in junior high school, "most of them unintentionally funny," and that he "hasn't stopped since."*

Vocabulary / Using a Dictionary

1. What does the root *-gram* mean in *hologram?* What language does it come from?

2. What is the dictionary definition of *custom?* How is the word used most frequently now?

Responding to Words in Context

1. Why does Huang describe his family as "overwhelming" (panel 1)?

2. Huang describes his nemesis as "particularly annoying" (panel 4). Why does he choose this adverb to modify *annoying?*

Discussing Main Point and Meaning

1. What benefits and drawbacks does Huang see to having a large family?

2. How does the main character's desire to outdo his rival backfire on him?

Examining Sentences, Paragraphs, and Organization

1. How does Huang picture adults in his comic? How does he draw them differently from the way he draws children?

2. How does Huang use space to convey his message? Which drawings are crowded, and which contain empty space?

Thinking Critically

1. What is the purpose of Huang's Chinese counterpart in this comic? He plays a literal role in the story, but what is his thematic significance?

2. What is Huang's perspective in this comic? From what vantage point does he write it? How does he know what the adults decided to do about the red envelopes?

3. What is the tone of the narrator's last line in panel 11? What does he think about the adults' decision?

In-Class Writing Activities

1. Choose one of the Chinese New Year traditions Huang describes and write about its symbolism and the values it represents. How does it reflect the family's hopes for the New Year?

2. In the last panel of this comic, the main character remains silent rather than offering an interpretation of the story he has just told. If you were going to write a "moral" to Huang's story, what would it be? What lesson, if any, does this comic teach?

SANDY DOVER (STUDENT ESSAY)

How Do You Define You?

[THE LANTERN, Ohio State University / January 10, 2007]

Before You Read

How do people determine their ethnic identity? When they have multiple heritages, what decides which one dominates?

Words to Learn

inhabitants (para. 3): people who live in an area or a structure (n.)
myriad (para. 5): a large number of something (n.)

Sandy Dover is a recent graduate of Ohio State University with a degree in journalism and minors in religious studies and sexuality studies. As a student, he regularly contributed to the Lantern, the daily student newspaper of Ohio State University. The topics he explored range from issues of diversity to pop culture and sports. Currently seeking publication for recently penned books, Dover describes himself as "an artist of various degrees at heart, and eager to make my writing voice my livelihood."

Hollywood has been stirring up quite a controversy lately over ethnic, religious and racial issues. Last fall's blockbuster *Borat* conveyed anti-Semitism and prejudice against Arabs from Alabama to Kazakhstan; comedian Michael Richards berated African-Americans with slurs during a live comedy event. On the Ohio State University campus, these issues have a visible impact, even if it's not an immediately clear one. Eighty-five percent of OSU's students are Caucasian American (Anglo-American, white) according to last year's student breakdown. Statistics suggest the campus is only getting whiter.

But how would you define yourself? Depending on that definition, in ethnic terms, are you even defining yourself correctly? Diversity is a major theme at OSU and the ethnic ties to identification are reasons for the university to be conscious of student makeup. But some students, like 20-year-old Jodi Stein, claim multiple identities. "I would say I am Jewish," Stein said. "When someone asks my nationality, I say 'Israeli.'" An Israel-born, Akron-raised nursing major, Stein said although she claims a few identities, a few more are often attached to her. She says she also believes herself to be white.

The ethnically Hebrew population is thought to have migrated from Eastern Africa, settling in what is now the Middle East. Many of them mixed with people of Slavic heritage in Eastern Europe, and others mixed with various peoples of the Eurasian continent. The native inhabitants of the area were not (and still are not) purely Anglo,

Scene still: *Borat: Cultural Learnings of America for Make Benefit Glorious Nation of Kazakhstan*, 20th Century Fox, 2006.

if at all. Self-identification can be problematic. For instance, even Michael Richards has identified himself as being a Jewish convert. As Ali G, *Borat*'s Sacha Baron Cohen has stirred controversy by posing as an Anglo-British man assimilating into a "black" urban hip-hop culture. Despite this, Cohen is in fact not only ethnically Jewish, but is also a very strict follower of the Jewish faith.

Stein said she believes "being white or black is solely based on   4
the color of your skin." She said her beliefs about color do not equal ethnicity, which validates her concurrent white, Israeli and Jewish identities. Dan Wandrey, meanwhile, a 21-year-old industrial design student, is the product of an African-American father and an Anglo-American mother with Dutch and German roots. He said he felt as if others make judgments on his ethnicity. "White people know I'm not white, black people know I'm not black," he said.

Clearly, there are many different ways for people to distinguish   5
themselves and identify with a myriad of cultures. Generalizations about race in America are often sweeping. Many "white" people are not truly that, as the classification's root is Anglo (or Anglo-Saxon), and refers to people of England, Great Britain and western Europe.

> *Generalizations about race in America are often sweeping.*

Black people are not truly "black," but   6
the term was an overt way for Spaniards and Portuguese to classify Africans in slavery. Also, at least half of Europe's population is technically non-white. Eastern and southern Europeans are predominantly Slavic, Italian or Spanish, and many of those people are mixed with African, Jewish, western Asian and Arab ancestry. Latinos, or Hispanics, were originally products of Spanish and Native American heritage, and later, Caribbean and South African slaves of African descent.

The lines start to blur in many areas, but identities can be self-   7
defining. Maybe the elderly rodeo director who told Cohen in *Borat* to shave his mustache so that he doesn't "look like those Muslims" should meet a few of those people on the Ohio State campus. And we all should take a look at what it means to be who we are.

Vocabulary/Using a Dictionary

1. What is the meaning of *con-* in *concurrent* (para. 4)? Why does Dover use this word to describe Jodi Stein's multiple identities?

2. Look up *distinguish* (para. 5) to determine its Latin root. How does Dover use the word?

Responding to Words in Context

1. What do colleges mean when they say they want to promote "diversity" (para. 2)?
2. What does Dover mean when he says that Jodi Stein's belief about skin color "validates" her multiple identities (para. 4)?

Discussing Main Point and Meaning

1. Why do some of the students Dover talks to claim multiple identities? What does this say about the groups to which they belong?
2. What is Dover's purpose in this essay? What does he want to convince his readers about?

Examining Sentences, Paragraphs, and Organization

1. What is the purpose of the first sentence in paragraph 3? Why does Dover trace the roots of Hebrew ethnicity?
2. What would you identify as the thesis of this essay? What sentence gives the most succinct summary of Dover's point?

Thinking Critically

1. Dover begins his essay with two examples from Hollywood: the movie *Borat* and comedian Michael Richards's comments in a comedy club. How similar are these examples? Why does he put them together?
2. Why does Dover comment on Michael Richards's and Sacha Baron Cohen's identifications? What point is he making?

In-Class Writing Activities

1. One of the peers Dover interviews, a man with both African American and European ancestry, notes, "White people know I'm not white, [and] black people know I'm not black" (para. 4). What does his statement reveal about identity? Write a response in which you consider how much of our identity is defined negatively.
2. Besides *Borat*, what recent movies or TV shows employ ethnic stereotypes, either unthinkingly or in order to critique them?

ANNOTATION Establishing a Main Point

As you learn to express your opinions clearly and effectively, you need to ask yourself a relatively simple question: Will my readers understand my main point? In composition, a main point is sometimes called a *thesis* or *thesis statement*. It is often a sentence that summarizes your central idea or position. It need not include any factual proof or supporting evidence—that is supplied in the body of your essay—but it should represent a general statement that clearly shows where you stand on an issue or what exactly your essay is about. Although main points are often found in opening paragraphs, they can also appear later on in an essay, especially when the writer wants to set the stage for his or her opinion by opening with a relevant quotation, a topical reference, or an emotional appeal.

This is the way Ohio State University student Sandy Dover proceeds in "How Do You Define You?" He begins his essay with topical references (the film *Borat*, the Michael Richards incident) and quotations (from a fellow student) that prepare the reader for his main point, which he introduces in his fifth paragraph. "Clearly," he writes, "there are many different ways for people to distinguish themselves and identify with a myriad of cultures." The central point of Dover's paper is that people have multiple ways of identifying themselves.

In one sentence, Dover states the main point of his essay.

<u>Clearly, there are many different ways for people to distinguish themselves and identify with a myriad of cultures.</u> Generalizations about race in America are often sweeping. Many "white" people are not truly that, as the classification's root is Anglo (or Anglo-Saxon), and refers to people of England, Great Britain and western Europe.

—From "How Do You Define You?" by Sandy Dover,
page 128

Student Writer at Work: Sandy Dover
On Writing "How Do You Define You?"

Q: What inspired you to write "How Do You Define You?"

A: I was inspired to write the piece based on what I saw (and still see) as social untruths in American society, specifically where ethnicity and race are concerned. I felt that my article deserved to be seen by the student populace so that I could help raise some eyebrows and get people to think about who they and others really are.

Q: Are your opinions unusual or fairly mainstream, given the general climate of discourse on campus?

A: My opinions seem to be unusual, based solely on the idea that I wrote about how ethnicities are improperly categorized, instead of hitting on the typical "black and white together" cliché discourse.

Q: How long did it take for you to write this piece? Did you revise your work? Work on multiple drafts? If so, how many drafts did you create? What were your goals as you revised?

A: I wrote this piece in a day, but I made sure to collect the necessary interviews beforehand. I revised, though it was pretty much as I wanted it as I was writing it. I really wanted a concise, truthful piece that people would understand. I don't usually show my writing before submitting, because I feel confident in my writing and I don't want to have my words swayed. However, the discussion with Dan Wandrey and Jodi Stein in the piece helped give my stance more solidarity and credibility, along with more soul—my point of view became more substantiated by their words.

Q: What topics most interest you as a writer?

A: I'm most interested in topics that revolve around the college experience, God and spirituality, fitness and training, cultures and ethnicities, and the NBA.

Q: Are you pursuing a career in which writing will be a component? Do you have advice for other students who are interested in pursuing writing as a career?

A: Since graduating, I've made writing a LARGE component of my career, working as a full-time novelist and freelance writer. My advice for student writers is to begin as early as possible for your college newspaper, which will allow you to start to develop an audience; also, stand firm in what you are— if you're a good columnist, push for that and don't accept anything less, and if you're a good reporter, do that. Make sure that you keep your authority; lastly, don't write because you want to win a popularity contest. College is too short to waste time for idle things, so do what you really want to do, because that's what college is for—for you.

Discussing the Unit

Suggested Topic for Discussion

How does each of these authors represent the United States as a country built on the mixing of racial and ethnic groups? What do you think each of them would say about the melting pot or the salad bowl or other metaphors used to describe the country's diversity? Do the authors suggest any ways in which America fails to live up to its promise of diversity?

Preparing for Class Discussion

1. How would each of these authors define "home"? What goes into making a new home in the United States?

2. Think about how Mengestu and Muñoz comment on language— both the languages they encounter in the United States and the language of their native countries. How does language help define the immigrant experience?

From Discussion to Writing

1. Choose one of the essays in this chapter and write about why childhood is important to the narrative or argument. How does childhood experience enter into the writing? What perspective does a child have on immigration that an adult might not have?

2. Write an essay comparing how two of the authors in this chapter portray the blending of cultures in the United States. To what extent do they admire that blending, and when do they seem to resist assimilation?

Topic for Cross-Cultural Discussion

The authors in this chapter are African, Asian American, and Mexican or Hispanic American. Do their ethnicities affect the life they find in the United States? Think about the differences among the three writers' stories, and discuss whether any of those differences might be attributed to the authors' ethnic origins.

Gender Differences: Can You Trust the Scientific Reports?

Whether there are real, biologically caused differences between the ways men and women act, think, speak, and behave has remained an important sidebar in the debates over feminism and nature vs. nurture. If, besides trifling physical differences, men and women are more or less exactly alike psychologically, doesn't that indicate conclusively that they should be treated alike? But what if they aren't? And what does either result mean for our understanding of who we are—just the output of an immutable genetic code or the product of our experience, culture, tradition, and surroundings?

Attempts to probe these differences, however, have often encountered serious controversy. Former Harvard University president Lawrence Summers found himself in hot water, and eventually resigned his post, when he suggested that the achievement gap between men and women in academic sciences might be due to innate differences between the sexes. Some scientists, including cognitive psychologist Steven Pinker, argued that Summers's remarks were based in sound science, but others objected that the claim was nothing more than sexism.

Can science tell us whether men and women are indeed programmed differently? This chapter takes, as a case study in the question, a scientific paper in behavioral psychology published in a major scientific journal—and the reactions to it from the national press.

The paper, "Are Women Really More Talkative Than Men," published in the journal *Science* by Matthias R. Mehl and colleagues, employed a complex statistical model to answer an age-old question: Do women use language more often and more voluminously than their male counterparts?

Sociologists and chroniclers of popular wisdom had held that women utter more words a day than men do—20,000 vs. 7,000, according to one famous estimate. By monitoring the speech patterns of men and women in both the United States and Mexico, Mehl and his colleagues found that "the widespread and highly publicized stereotype about female talkativeness is unfounded." The participants in the study used about the same number of words per day on average, regardless of gender.

This result swept through the media, provoking a healthy number of words itself—from attempts to debunk the research to meditations on gender roles and stereotypes. Two representative pieces are Richard Knox's "Study: Men Talk Just as Much as Women," reported on National Public Radio, and "He Said, She Said" from the *Wilson Quarterly*, which summarizes the study without scientific or statistical jargon. Knox places the study in the context of much-debated gender roles: The finding is important, he concludes, because it undermines stereotypes that hold not only that women are more talkative but also that they are more emotional and willing to connect with their peers—while men are taciturn and detached. The fact that men use as many words as women should give pause to anyone who blindly accepts these prejudices.

But Knox, through a follow-up with the researchers, adds a complication to the conclusion—the words men and women use may be quantitatively equal, but they aren't qualitatively equal. Knox reports that the researchers of the study plan to announce that "women tend to talk more about relationships. Their everyday conversation is more studded with pronouns. Men tend to talk more about sports and gadgets, and their utterances include more numbers." Does this belie the conclusions that he and other reporters and analysts have drawn from the *Science* study?

Moreover, as you read both reports, carefully compare the language and assertions they make with the abstract of the original study. Do these reports take any conclusions out of context, or inflate them to serve the sensationalist motives of the press? How does summarizing the study damage the robustness of its findings? Beth Skwarecki, in "Mad Science: Deconstructing Bunk Reporting in 5 Easy

Steps," offers a breakdown of the errors and half truths rampant in media reporting of science, specifically the science of gender. "Nowhere do scientific findings get more mangled than when they're about the differences between men and women," Skwarecki writes. By taking into account the bias of reporters and the public, loaded words, sensational headlines, and the possibility of bad science, and by reading the actual studies, the public can get a much better sense of the often sober and measured conclusions those studies make.

The chapter concludes with a column by Joseph Vandehey, a math major at the University of Oregon, that studies the phenomenon of imbalanced math departments from the inside. Vandehey proposes a number of theories to explain his testosterone-heavy department but concludes that, in the end, both genetic differences and social conditioning are to blame. "Difference does not mean hierarchy," he writes, emphasizing that instead of lamenting or ignoring the differences between the genders, we should explore them honestly—and starting out from a premise of social equality.

MATTHIAS R. MEHL et al.

Are Women Really More Talkative Than Men?

[SCIENCE / July 6, 2007]

RICHARD KNOX

Study: Men Talk Just as Much as Women

[NATIONAL PUBLIC RADIO, *All Things Considered* / July 5, 2007]

EDITORS, WILSON QUARTERLY

He Said, She Said

[WILSON QUARTERLY / Autumn 2007]

Before You Read

Before discovering these essays, did you believe that women talked more than men? Why do you think you assumed that women talk more than men, that men talk more than women, or that no assumption can be made? Had you read or heard information that influenced your opinion on the subject?

Words to Learn

extrapolate (para. 2, Mehl): to infer (v.)

covert (para. 3, Mehl): concealed (adj.)

empirical (para. 7, Mehl): derived from experience or experiment (adj.)

unfounded (para. 7, Mehl): not based on fact (adj.)

tentatively (para. 5, Knox): hesitantly (adv.)

disparity (para. 8, Knox): difference (n.)

systematically (para. 9, Knox): methodically (adv.)

stereotype (para. 16, Knox): an oversimplified opinion or attitude held in common by members of a group (n.)

debunked (para. 17, Knox): exposed the falseness of something (v.)

constraints (para. 18, Knox): restrictions (n.)

studded (para. 20, Knox): marked (v.)

MATTHIAS R. MEHL et al.

Are Women Really More Talkative Than Men?

Sex differences in conversational behavior have long been a topic   1
of public and scientific interest (*1*, *2*). The stereotype of female talkativeness is deeply engrained in Western folklore and often considered
a scientific fact. In the first printing of her book, neuropsychiatrist
Brizendine reported. "A woman uses about 20,000 words per day
while a man uses about 7,000" (*3*). These numbers have since circulated throughout television, radio, and print media (e.g., CBS, CNN,
National Public Radio, *Newsweek*, the *New York Times*, and the
Washington Post). Indeed, the 20,000-versus-7000 word estimates appear to have achieved the status of a cultural myth in that comparable
differences have been cited in the media for the past 15 years (*4*).

In reality, no study has systematically recorded the natural con-   2
versations of large groups of people for extended periods of time.
Consequently, there have not been the necessary data for reliably estimating differences in daily word usage among women and men (*5*).
Extrapolating from a reanalysis of tape-recorded daily conversations
from 153 participants from the British National Corpus (*6*), Liberman recently estimated that women speak 8805 words and men 6073
words per day. However, he acknowledged that these estimates may

---

*Matthias R. Mehl is an assistant professor of psychology at the Univer-
sity of Arizona. He earned an MA in psychology from Friedrich-Alexander
University in Germany and a PhD in social and personality psychology from
the University of Texas at Austin. As an extensive researcher, Mehl describes
his three main areas of interest as "naturalistic person-environment interactions, . . . social interactions, coping, and health, . . . and developing alternative assessment methods that can complement psychology's long-standing
reliance on self-reports." His writing has appeared in a variety of journals
and publications. In 2007, he received the Honors College Outstanding Professor and Advisor of Psychology Award at the University of Arizona.*

be problematic because no information was available regarding when participants decided to turn off their manual tape recorders (4).

Over the past 8 years, we have developed a method for recording   3
natural language using the electronically activated recorder (EAR) (7). The EAR is a digital voice recorder that unobtrusively tracks people's real-world moment-to-moment interactions. It operates by periodically recording snippets of ambient sounds, including conversations, while participants go about their daily lives. Because of the covert digital recording, it is impossible for participants to control or even to sense when the EAR is on or off. For the purpose of this study, the EAR can be used to track naturally spoken words and to estimate how many words women and men use over the course of a day.

In the default paradigm, participants wear the EAR for several   4
days during their waking hours. The device is programmed to record for 30 s every 12.5 min. All captured words spoken by the participant are transcribed. The number of spoken words per day can then be estimated by extrapolating from a simple word count, the number of sampled sound files, and the recording time per sound file.

We addressed the question about sex differences in daily word   5
use with data from six samples based on 396 participants (210 women and 186 men) that were conducted between 1998 and 2004. Five of the samples were composed of university students in the United States, and the sixth, university students in Mexico. Table 1 provides background information on the samples along with estimates for the number of words that female and male participants spoke per day (8).

The data suggest that women spoke on average 16,215 (SD =   6
7301) words and men 15,669 (SD = 8633) words over an assumed period of, on average, 17 waking hours.

Women and men both use on average about 16,000 words per day, with very large individual differences around this mean.

Expressed in a common effect-size metric (Cohen's d = 0.07), this sex difference in daily word use (546 words) is equal to only 7% of the standardized variability among women and men. Further, the difference does not meet conventional thresholds for statistical significance (P = 0.248, one-sided test). Thus, the data fail to reveal a reliable sex difference in daily word use. Women and men both use on average about 16,000 words per day, with very large individual differences around this mean.

TABLE 1

Estimated number of words spoken per day for female and male study participants across six samples. $N = 396$. Year refers to the year when the data collection started; duration refers to the approximate number of days participants wore the EAR; the weighted average weighs the respective sample group mean by the sample size of the group.

Sample	Year	Location	Duration	Age range (years)	Sample Size (N) Women	Men	Estimated Average Number (SD) of Word Spoken Per Day Women	Men
1	2004	USA	7 days	18–29	56	56	18,443 (7460)	16,576 (7871)
2	2003	USA	4 days	17–23	42	37	14,297 (6441)	14,060 (9065)
3	2003	Mexico	4 days	17–25	31	20	14,704 (6215)	15,022 (7864)
4	2001	USA	2 days	17–22	47	49	16,177 (7520)	16,569 (9108)
5	2001	USA	10 days	18–26	7	4	15,761 (8985)	24,051 (10,211)
6	1998	USA	4 days	17–23	27	20	16,496 (7914)	12,867 (8343)
					Weighted average		16,215 (7301)	15,669 (8633)

From Matthias R. Mehl et al., *Are Women Really More Talkative Than Men?*, Science 317:82 (6 July 2007). Reprinted with permission from AAAS.

A potential limitation of our analysis is that all participants were   7
university students. The resulting homogeneity in the samples with
regard to sociodemographic characteristics may have affected our estimates of daily word usage. However, none of the samples provided
support for the idea that women have substantially larger lexical
budgets than men. Further, to the extent that sex differences in daily
word use are assumed to be biologically based, evolved adaptations
(3), they should be detectable among university students as much as
in more diverse samples. We therefore conclude, on the basis of available empirical evidence, that the widespread and highly publicized
stereotype about female talkativeness is unfounded.

References and Notes

1. R. Lakoff, *Language and Woman's Place* (Harper, New York, 1975).

2. L. Litosseliti, *Gender and Language: Theory and Practice* (Arnold, London, 2006).

3. L. Brizendine, *The Female Brain* (Morgan Road, New York, 2006).

4. M. Liberman, *Sex-Linked Lexical Budgets*, http://itre.cis.upenn .edu/~myl/languagelog/archives/003420.html (first accessed 12 December 2006).

5. D. James, J. Drakich, in *Gender and Conversational Interaction*, D. Tannen, Ed. (Oxford Univ. Press, New York, 1993), pp. 281–313.

6. P. Rayson, G. Leech, M. Hodges, *Int. J. Corpus Linguist*, **2**, 133 (1997).

7. M. R. Mehl, J. W. Pennebaker, M. Crow, J. Dabbs, J. Price, *Behav. Res. Methods Instrum, Comput*, **33**, 517 (2001).

8. Details on methods and analysis are available on *Science* Online.

9. This research was supported by a grant from the National In-stitute of Mental Health (MH 52391). We thank V. Dominguez, J. Greenberg, S. Holleran, C. Mehl, M. Peterson, and T. Schmader for their valuable feedback.

RICHARD KNOX

Study: Men Talk Just as Much as Women

An article in this week's issue of *Science* blasts the popular myth that women are more talkative than men. 1

Researchers outfitted 396 college students—345 Americans and 51 Mexicans—with devices that automatically recorded them every 12½ minutes, which amounts to 4 percent of a person's daily utterances. 2

The researchers found that women speak a little more than 16,000 words a day. Men speak a little less than 16,000 words. The difference is not statistically significant. 3

Psychologist Matthias Mehl of the University of Arizona says the three top talkers in the study—uttering up to 47,000 words a day— were all men. So was the most taciturn subject, who spoke only 700 words a day, on average. 4

Mehl says he and his colleagues were surprised at the outcome. They had tentatively bought into the popular stereotype that women are the more talkative sex. 5

But they were skeptical of the widespread claim that women use three times more words a day then men. 6

The claim got prominent attention with the publication of a 2006 book called *The Female Brain*. Its author, Louann Brizendine, has 7

Richard Knox is a correspondent for the Science Desk of National Public Radio. In addition to degrees from the University of Illinois and Columbia University, Knox has also held yearlong fellowships at Stanford and Harvard universities. While working for the Boston Globe, *he covered health and medicine and wrote a series of award-winning articles on medical errors in 1995. Since coming to National Public Radio in 2000, Knox has reported on a wide array of issues and topics, including "the impact of HIV/AIDS in Africa, North America, and the Caribbean; anthrax terrorism; smallpox and other bioterrorism preparedness issues; the rising cost of medical care; early detection of lung cancer; community caregiving; music and the brain; and the SARS epidemic."*

been widely quoted claiming that "a woman uses about 20,000 words per day while a man uses about 7,000."

Other sources have claimed an even greater disparity.   8

But until the *Science* study published this week, its authors say,   9
no one had ever systematically recorded the total daily output, in natural conversations, of a sizable number of people.

Mehl says the supposed talkativeness of women is often men-   10
tioned in pop-psychology books.

"The typical scenario is—a man comes home from work at   11
night, has used 6,850 words and with 150 left over just wants to
relax and not talk," Mehl says. "And the woman welcomes the husband with about 7,856 words left over. And that's where all the
problems start."

Mehl guesses that the talkativeness claim "evolved as an explana-   12
tion for what scientists call the demand/withdrawal pattern." That is,
the situation where a woman demands to talk through problems and
her male partner withdraws emotionally.

"We use our gender magnifying glass and over-generalize from   13
that," Mehl says. "Instead of saying that men tend to talk less and
women tend to talk more, we say 'Women always talk and men never
talk.'"

Even so, the researchers, based at the University of Texas as well   14
as at Arizona, didn't expect the verbal output between the sexes to be
virtually equal.

Mehl acknowledges that many will have trouble believing the re-   15
sults, since it contradicts their own perceptions.

"This is the way the stereotype has been maintained in the past,"   16
he says. "It is fairly easy to see what you want to see—to jump on
the very chatty woman that you certainly find and say, 'See, women
talk a lot' and to overlook the very talkative man."

Mehl says the stereotype needs to be debunked. Not only because women are harmed by the "female chatterbox and silent male" stereotype, but because men are disadvantaged by it, too.

Mehl says the stereotype needs to be   17
debunked. Not only because women are
harmed by the "female chatterbox and silent
male" stereotype, but because men are disadvantaged by it, too.

"It puts men into the gender box, that   18
in order to be a good male, we'd better not
talk—[that] silence is golden," Mehl says.
"The stereotype puts unfortunate constraints
on men and women—the idea that you can

only happily be a woman if you're talkative and you can only be happy as a man if you're reticent. The study relieves those gender constraints."

The new report doesn't mention any differences in what men and women talk about. But the researchers have analyzed the content of everyday conversation and will publish that in the future. 19

In general, they found that women tend to talk more about relationships. Their everyday conversation is more studded with pronouns. Men tend to talk more about sports and gadgets, and their utterances include more numbers. 20

No surprise there. 21

EDITORS, WILSON QUARTERLY

He Said, She Said

> **The Source:** "Are Women Really More Talkative Than Men?" by Matthias R. Mehl, Simine Vazire, Nairán Ramírez-Esparza, Richard B. Slatcher, and James W. Pennebaker, in *Science*, July 6, 2007.

Not to mince words, but women have a reputation for being much chattier than men. In 2006, neurobiologist Louann Brizendine, in *The Female Brain*, attached some numbers to the stereotype, estimating that "a woman uses about 20,000 words per day while a man uses about 7,000." Those numbers poured into the media, cited in *Newsweek*, *The New York Times*, and *The Washington Post*, and 1

The Wilson Quarterly *is published by the* Woodrow Wilson International Center for Scholars, a nonpartisan institution based in Washington D.C. Since it began in 1976, the Wilson Quarterly has sought "to overcome the specialization and information overload that prevent the public from following developments in significant realms of knowledge" and addresses such issues as politics, policy, religion, science, and "other fields that bear upon our public life." The journal features the writing of many academics and specialists and in 2006 won an Independent Press Award from the Utne Reader.

were also reported on CBS, CNN, and National Public Radio, taking on the stature of scientific fact.

But according to Matthias R. Mehl, a psychology professor at the   2
University of Arizona, Simine Vazire, at Washington University in St. Louis, and their colleagues at the University of Texas, Austin, up to now "no study has systematically recorded the natural conversations of large groups of people for extended periods of time." Mark Liberman, a University of Pennsylvania linguistics professor, attempted last year to fill the void, analyzing tape-recorded conversations of 153 participants he discovered in a British archive. He found that the women spoke 8,805 words per day versus the men's 6,073, but noted that his findings were not conclusive, since his subjects were free to turn the recorders on and off.

Mehl and his colleagues tested 396 university student volunteers   3
using an electronically activated recorder that "operates by periodically recording snippets of ambient sounds, including conversations, while participants go about their daily lives." Data from the study reveal that women spoke on average 16,215 words per day and men 15,669, a statistically insignificant difference. But the most talkative 17 percent were equally split between men and women. And the three biggest chatterboxes, gushing more than 40,000 words in the course of a day? All men.

Data from the study reveal that women spoke on average 16,215 words per day and men 15,669, a statistically insignificant difference.

While Mehl and his associates admit that their study sample—all   4
students—wasn't typical of the whole population, they believe that sex differences among the general public would be about the same. Their conclusion: "The widespread and highly publicized stereotype about female talkativeness is unfounded."

Vocabulary / Using a Dictionary

1. Do you know what an *ambient* sound is (para. 3, Mehl)? After you define the word, provide some examples of ambient sound.

2. What is the meaning of *homogeneity* (para. 7, Mehl)? What other words include the prefix *homo-*?

3. What does it mean to be *disadvantaged* (para. 17, Knox)? What are some synonyms of the word?

Responding to Words in Context

1. What do the researchers in the Mehl study mean by *lexical budgets* (para. 7, Mehl)?
2. What is the definition of *everyday conversation* (para. 19, Knox)? How does it differ from *daily utterances* (para. 2, Knox)?
3. Is a *taciturn* subject (para. 4, Knox) different from one who is *reticent* (para. 18, Knox)?

Discussing Main Point and Meaning

1. The Mehl study proves that we cannot say that women talk more than men. Do Knox's article and the *Wilson Quarterly* summary also "prove" anything about how people perceive one another?
2. If one gender turned out to be more talkative than the other, what problems would men and women run into?
3. Despite the conclusive results of Mehl and his colleagues' research, what are the limitations of their study?

Examining Sentences, Paragraphs, and Organization

1. Why does Knox include a sentence that gives the number of subjects, their nationalities, and how often they were recorded, at the start of his article (para. 2, Knox)?
2. The information for Knox's article comes from outside materials. When discussing his sources, Knox mentions in paragraph 1 that the Mehl study was published in *Science*. In paragraph 7, he also includes a claim made in *The Female Brain* by Louann Brizendine. Does it matter that he calls one source a "study" and one a "claim"? Does it make a difference that one paragraph includes a periodical name, but that the paragraph about the book does not include publication information?
3. Where do the Knox article and the *Wilson Quarterly* summary overlap with the Mehl study? Where does the Knox article go further in its examination of the study?

Thinking Critically

1. A stereotype may be true or untrue. Knox's article works to eliminate the stereotypes we hold about the talkativeness of men and

women. Are there any benefits to having stereotypes in the first place? How are they harmful?

2. How is the "demand/withdrawal pattern" noted in paragraph 12 (Knox) distinguished from the pattern of women talking more than men?

3. The Mehl study is important because before it happened, "no [other] study . . . systematically recorded the natural conversations of large groups of people for extended periods of time" (para. 2, Mehl). Do you think one study can definitively confirm that women talk the same amount as men? Why or why not?

In-Class Writing Activities

1. Much is emerging in the media about differences between men and women physically, psychologically, and now physiologically. To see just how divided we think men and women are, go to any bookstore and explore sections devoted to gender, health, psychology, or other topics. Knox's article and the *Wilson Quarterly* summary are attempts to refute the stereotype of women's and men's talkativeness (or unwillingness to talk) and to show how it is an exaggeration. The stereotype of *what* men and women talk about persists as researchers study the content of conversations (women, Knox notes, talk about relationships more often, whereas men frequently talk about sports and devices). Can you think of other stereotypical behaviors for men and women? Write an essay about one such behavior and use your personal experience as evidence for your argument. Or if you feel that you and others have been put in a "gender box" (para. 18, Knox) by some stereotype, expose the reality of the situation.

2. Knox interprets much of the data from Mehl's study in order to write his article about men talking as much as women. Examine Knox's article alone and summarize his article in several paragraphs of your own. For a summary, quote as little material as possible directly from the text. Simply condense the main points into your own words.

3. The Mehl study was performed with the use of the EAR (electronically activated recorder), which records speech, but only at random intervals. In this way, Mehl and his colleagues were able to estimate the number of words different people used over the

course of a day—but they did not actually count each word spoken. Research the EAR and discover more about how it works. Then write a brief essay on how valid you think data recovered with such a device is, taking into account the length of time devoted to Mehl's study, the amount of time during which speech was recorded, the subjects' willingness to participate, and the equipment used in former studies.

BETH SKWARECKI

Mad Science: Deconstructing Bunk Reporting in 5 Easy Steps

[BITCH / Spring 2008]

Before You Read

Do you think most scientific articles are free of bias? If the article has to do with gender-related issues, are the scientists involved in the study unaffected by stereotypes? Do you think most of what you read or see in the media is held to the same standards you hope to find in the scientific community?

Beth Skwarecki is a freelance writer and photographer who currently resides in Ithaca, New York. She graduated from Alfred University in 2002 with a BA in biology and worked for several years as a Web developer and computer programmer. This background lends authority and understanding to her scientific and technical writing, but Skwarecki has also written about such varied topics as knitting, photography, bicycling, and sustainable foods. With her personal interests ranging from juggling to travel to trapeze lessons, Skwarecki has a "tough time keeping more than one hobby or all-consuming interest at a time."

Words to Learn

evolutionary (para. 3): relating to the development of species (adj.)

robust (para. 4): strong (adj.)

mutate (para. 6): to change (v.)

salient (para. 6): notable or noticeable (adj.)

innate (para. 10): inherent (adj.)

dubious (para. 11): questionable (adj.)

fodder (para. 18): material (n.)

congruity (para. 19): harmony or agreement (n.)

reconcile (para. 20): to restore (v.)

predation (para. 25): the act of being made prey (n.)

ebb (para. 42): decline (n.)

catty (para. 46): mean (adj.)

British scientists have uncovered the truth behind one of modern culture's greatest mysteries: why little girls play with pink toys. Is it because toy companies flood whole store aisles with the color? Or because well-meaning relatives shower girl babies with pink blankets and clothing? Nope. According to the men in lab coats, it's purely biological. 1

Apparently, women are hardwired to like pink because our cavewoman foremothers spent their days gathering red leaves and berries amongst the trees while their husbands were out hunting. Later, women needed to notice red-faced babies and blushing boyfriends. And why do men like blue? Because it's the color of the sky. 2

This evolutionary just-so story takes up three pages of a 2007 issue of *Current Biology*. To back up the assertion that pink is a universal girly preference worth examining, the authors refer to a 1985 study finding that little girls use more pink and red crayons in their drawings than little boys do. 3

Dig further, however, and the story completely falls apart. British women do prefer pink, but the author's claim of a "robust, cross-cultural sex difference" turns out to be neither. The scientists compared British natives with Chinese immigrants to Britain, and glossed over the differences. For example: The girliest color in the British results, a purplish-pink, was in fact the Chinese men's favorite. 4

Nowhere do scientific findings get more mangled than when they're about the differences between men and women. According to the science pages, women aren't just biologically hardwired to prefer pink to blue. We're also predisposed to backstab one another in the workplace, cry in the boardroom, and have both lower IQs and less of a sense of humor than men. 5

Some misleading stories come from bad science, where the study authors' conclusions aren't supported by their own data. Others are well-conducted studies whose conclusions mutate upon contact with the mainstream media. Newspapers and websites are prone to playing fast and loose with their reports on studies, often neglecting to reveal salient facts about a study's sample group or methodology.

The fact is that science articles aren't designed to be read by nonscientists. College and grad students in the sciences are trained in how to do it: They review papers and discuss them in journal clubs; learn how to question methodologies (Is that sample really big enough? Was that the right test to use?); and learn how to be critical of authors' interpretations (Do the results really mean what they say they mean?). Students also know to look at context for each study, looking up previous papers on the subject, reviewing the authors' previous work, and searching out any evidence of bias that might color a study's findings.

Journalists looking for a quick story, however, do little such research. And in an age where news sites, wire services, and blogs pick up stories with lightning-fast speed, bad research gets around. When London's *Sunday Times* reported on a 2007 study claiming that men get dumber in the presence of blond women, the paper got the name of the journal wrong, citing the *Journal of Experimental Psychology* rather than the *Journal of Experimental Social Psychology*. Nearly every subsequent news article repeated the error because they were content to simply reword the *Times'* version of the story rather than finding and discussing the study itself.

The *Times* reported that blond-exposed subjects "mimic the unconscious stereotype of the dumb blonde." But that's not exactly what the study tested. Rather, subjects—most of them female—fared slightly worse on online trivia quizzes after rating hair color (is she a blond, brunet, or redhead?) on pictures of beauty queens. You could just as easily say that beauty queens make people dumb, or photos of dazzling smiles make people dumb. It seems this study made the news mostly because it could be illustrated with photos of Marilyn Monroe and filled out with dopey quotes from blond models and actresses, as well as blond jokes from the *Times* itself.

Ben Goldacre, who writes the "Bad Science" column for the UK's *Guardian*, speculates that science stories come in three varieties: the wacky story, the breakthrough story, and the scare story. Most widely reported studies on gender seem to fall into the wacky category—the supposed innate preference for pink is one of them—and

Most widely reported studies on gender seem to fall into the wacky category—the supposed innate preference for pink is one of them—and their media strength is that they tend to support existing stereotypes of women, reassuring readers that social stereotypes do, in fact, reflect reality.

their media strength is that they tend to support existing stereotypes of women, reassuring readers that social stereotypes do, in fact, reflect reality.

We can't put all the blame on mainstream media, of course. Scientists are part of the same culture as the rest of us, and they too have biases that shape their hypotheses and interpretations. The scientific community can also be as fad-driven as popular culture, creating a climate in which many researchers simultaneously geek out over one specific theory while competing ideas get lost or abandoned. So let's learn how to read between the lines of these dubious articles. Next time you see an article reporting that women are happiest when they're picking up their man's dirty socks, try asking these questions:

1. Do the Conclusions Fit a Little Too Well with Cultural Stereotypes?

Science has the capacity to surprise and amaze us, but sometimes it's more satisfying when you can jump up and say, "Yes! I knew it all along!" Which is why articles touting the awesomeness of traditional gender roles are an evergreen subject in the science pages.

A 2007 study from the American Society for Cancer Research journal *Cancer Epidemiology Biomarkers and Prevention* titled "Physical activity and breast-cancer risk" found fame in such headlines as the BBC's "Housework cuts breast-cancer risk." That's not to mention the 2006 study on housework and cancer in Canadian women, the 2005 study on housework and cancer in Chinese women, or the 2004 study . . . you get the idea. [See "Home Is Where the Cardio Is," *Bitch* no. 27]

The reality? Being physically active seems to help prevent cancer, and the researchers behind the recent studies have been counting housework as physical activity. Housework, sports, and active jobs all had significant effects in reducing cancer risk, and the authors think the key may be frequent, low-impact exercise.

An author on several of these studies, Christine Friedenreich, told the *Calgary Herald* that in past studies, researchers counted jobs like construction work as physical activity, but not housework—and it turns out that domestic tasks are, duh, hard work.

This means that many women are getting more exercise than they (or their doctors) had realized. That should be good news for them—but instead, the message imparted by the news reports is, "Get back into the kitchen! That's all the exercise you need!"

It's worth noting that one of the study's sponsors, Cancer Research UK, answered questions about the 2006 study on its website, pointing out that for many of the older women in the study group, housework was their primary form of exercise. The organization went on to address charges of sexism directly, making sure to mention a related 2006 study that found housework cuts the risk of bowel cancer for both men and women, concluding, "There's absolutely no excuse for men to dodge the dusting!"

2. Does the Study Agree with the Headline?

Behind every junk-science headline is a scientific journal article. Sometimes the university or organization that was home to the study sends out a press release to mainstream outlets, hoping for attention; other times, journalists simply scan the abstracts of academic journals for newsworthy fodder. Chances are a story will make the papers if it's got some kind of hook—weird (like the idea that housework has curative properties), controversial (like claims that men are smarter than women), can be illustrated with bikini babes (like the dumb-blond study), etc. Especially for online news outlets, these hooks are valuable because they make good linkbait: the kind of thing they hope you'll forward to friends or post on your blog.

The *London Times* probably hadn't read the full study titled "Prejudice against women in male-congenial environments: Perceptions of gender-role congruity in leadership" when they summarized it under the headline "Office Queen Bees Hold Back Women's Careers" in a 2006 article. The paper's charge—that "women bosses are significantly more likely than men to discriminate against female employees"—may indeed have surprised the study's authors.

The actual study went something like this: Participants weren't put in a boss's role, but an observer's. They read a purposely vague description of a manager who was being considered for promotion and were asked to imagine how qualified the candidate was, and whether he or she was likely to succeed. The study made a number of interesting points that the *Times* could easily have reported on—for instance, that female managers were judged to have both very masculine and very feminine traits, possibly in an attempt to reconcile their gender with the traditionally masculine-associated role of leadership.

Both the male and female participants were optimistic about the male manager's success, but not about the woman's (except when she worked in a female-dominated industry). Sounds pretty realistic, right? The researchers thought so too. They write, "Participants' predictions about the [female] candidate's future salary . . . mirrored the fact that women earn less money in the same position [than] men do in real life." So where are those "queen bees" that the *Times* so gleefully name-checked? Exactly.   21

It's not difficult to track down the science behind the story. Look for the names of the researchers, the journal their work appeared in, and (if you're lucky) the title of the article. Type whatever info you've got into Google Scholar (www.scholar.google.com), and soon you'll be looking at an abstract for the paper. Scientific journals are usually locked behind paywalls, unfortunately, so you may need to call upon a pal at a university for access to the entire study.   22

3. Can You Spot the Double Standard?

Whether it's lions fathering all the cubs in their pride, or human males getting a pass for cheating on their girlfriends, males sleeping around rarely make the news—it's the natural order, after all—unless the article is happily touting the genetic advantages a male gets from spreading his DNA around.   23

But when female cheetahs were found to do the same by a Zoological Society of London study, the study's words about "promiscuous" felines were quickly outnumbered in Google's index by the phrase, "cheetahs are sluts!"   24

Study author Dada Gottelli was quoted thus: "Mating with more than one male poses a serious threat to females, increasing the risk of exposure to parasites and diseases. Females also have to travel over large distances to find new mates, making them more vulnerable to predation." Sounds like a cheetah-specific version of certain sex-ed curricula: Don't sleep around, girls, or you'll catch lots of diseases and the male cheetahs won't respect you in the morning. Male cheetahs, however, aren't "promiscuous"—they're creating a healthier gene pool.   25

Not too surprising, then, that most of the coverage glossed over the evolutionary benefit of promiscuity for both male and female cheetahs: Multiple cubs by multiple cub daddies increases the likelihood of genetic diversity—a definite positive for a threatened species.   26

Furthermore, the study noted that the rates of infanticide in cheetahs are much lower than in other big-cat populations, likely because male competitors don't know which offspring might be theirs. But why let the facts slow down a good headline?

In a human example of a double-standard story, women were   27
found to be "worse oglers" than men, according to the *Sydney Morning Herald* summary of a study published in the journal *Hormones and Behavior*. (The *Herald* inexplicably illustrated its story with headshots of Sharon Stone and Mr. Bean.) What does that even mean, you ask? When researchers showed "sexual stimuli" (read: Internet porn) to heterosexual men and women, they expected women to look more at faces and men to look more at genitals. The newspaper reported that, in fact, "almost the reverse was true."

Actually, the study says that men looked at women's faces more   28
than women did, and men and women looked with equal frequency at the pictured genitals; women who weren't on oral contraceptives looked slightly more. So where did that headline come from?

The study authors didn't originate the "worse oglers" language;   29
they even warn in the study that they can't say why subjects' gazes lingered where they did, or whether they were turned on as they looked. So it's not fair to say that the study was about "ogling," a word that suggests that looking is lustful and perhaps inappropriate.

To say that women are "worse" at ogling, we have to believe,   30
first, that ogling is bad, and second, that men do it at some normal, baseline level that women are exceeding. The judgmental language makes it sound like women in the study were indulging a bad habit. Right there in the headline is the double standard: If men ogle, it's normal, but when women do it, they're "worse."

4. Is There Another Conclusion That Would Be Just as Valid?

Sometimes a news story is an accurate representation of the sci-   31
entists' conclusions, but the scientists' conclusions don't follow their results. Take this 2005 BBC headline: "Men Cleverer Than Women." The study, at the time of the headline yet to be published in the *British Journal of Psychology*, claims that as IQ scores rise, the gender gap widens, with 5.5 men for every woman scoring at the "genius" level of 155 or higher on IQ tests. That's all the evidence the authors (one of whom, Richard Lynn, has published similar studies on racial differences in IQ) give to support their claim.

But there is another, equally powerful explanation that's been   32
considered for years before this study came along: IQ tests—which

don't measure intelligence directly, but try to approximate it—have a wealth of gender, racial, and cultural biases.

In a 2000 survey of sex differences in intelligence called "The Smarter Sex: A Critical Review of Sex Differences in Intelligence," in the *Educational Psychology Review*, Diane Halpern and Mary LaMay write that Lynn's approach "rests on the belief that the test of intelligence is really measuring what psychologists mean by intelligence, and that it is doing so in a way that will yield a fair assessment for males and females—two assumptions that may not be justified." 33

Statistically, men do outperform women on certain types of questions, but the reverse is also true; test designers use this fact to calibrate IQ tests, balancing male-biased with female-biased questions so that men and women average the same scores on the same test. Addressing Lynn's research directly, Halpern and LaMay say, "Using data from tests that are designed to yield no sex differences to argue for a difference is psychometric nonsense." Either the tests were miscalibrated (and thus biased) or Lynn's results are a fluke: Probably the latter, since other studies (like a 1995 study on a population similar to Lynn's, done by scientists at the Flinders University of South Australia and published in the *British Journal of Clinical Psychology*) found no difference between males and females. 34

So why even report the latest study from this obviously biased researcher? Perhaps it's reassuring to believe that sexism isn't sexism, it's science; that the status quo reflects some kind of natural order; and that anyone who claims otherwise is a whiner. Or perhaps Lynn's studies make the news because he's sort of a one-man show of bunk science—after all, this is the same guy who claims that African-Americans have higher IQs than Africans because they have Caucasian genes that make them smarter. 35

Then there are the stories that point the finger at feminism for a variety of historical incidents and ills. The 2007 *Boston Globe* story titled "Stone Age Feminism? Females joining hunt may explain Neanderthals' end" is one of these. 36

The supporting study, authored by archaeologists Steven Kuhn and Mary Stiner, turned on the hypothesis that Neanderthal women participated in hunting alongside Neanderthal men. The dangers of hunting—among them, getting stomped and gored by various beasts—along with the fact that many cavegals' lives were cut short before they could produce baby Neanderthals, meant that the breeding population dwindled and the species died out. 37

But the evidence for this "stone age feminism" wasn't evidence at all. The hypothesis that the women hunted alongside the men was de- 38 veloped because the study's authors found no clues suggesting that Neanderthal women were, well, homemakers—no grinding stones and bone needles that would signal a traditional division of labor in the species. So is it possible that male and female Neanderthals hunted together successfully, and the species dwindled for some other, totally unrelated reason? And, for that matter, why not hypothesize that coed hunting parties actually contributed to the Neanderthals' longevity? More than 100,000 years of existence is nothing to sneeze at, after all. Why jump to the conclusion that feminism ruins everything? Ah, yes: because it's a story that will sell papers.

5. Is the Study Even Science?

In his "Bad Science" column, Goldacre reminds us that so-called studies may not have studied anything at all. A hair-removal cream company once asked Goldacre to come up with a formula calculating which celebrity had the sexiest walk. "We know what results we want to achieve," they told him, naming celebrities with shapely legs whose high-ranking walks could move units of their product.   39

When Goldacre refused, another scientist supplied the company with a formula, thinking it would be used as a joke. The company's press release became an article in the *Telegraph*, crediting a nonexistent "team of Cambridge mathematicians" and with no mention of the so-called study's actual source.   40

Lesson learned: If you can't find the source article, it may not actually exist.   41

In another example of non-science, BBC News studiously reported in late 2007 that humor "comes from testosterone." The article? Based on a *British Medical Journal* study recording the casual responses of passers-by to a unicyclist. The article notes that little boys had more "aggressive" responses to the unicyclist (trying to knock him over) and young men made the most jokes—typically an unimaginative variant of "Lost your wheel?"—with elderly men's jokes being less hostile ("Does it crush your bollocks, mate?"). The article also featured a graphic showing the ebb of testosterone in men over time; since young men have the most testosterone and made the greatest number of jokes, the author concludes, testosterone must be the source of humor.   42

If all you read was the BBC piece, you might think that there's a clutch of professors somewhere in England taking this theory seriously. In fact, the deliberately hilarious study was published in the *BMJ*'s Christmas issue, famous for its joke articles. (A study from the previous year was titled "Surgeons are taller and more handsome than physicians" and used a photo of George Clooney as a control.)   43

The fact that the BBC didn't pick up on the joke speaks volumes   44
about the mainstream media's unceasing appetite for gendered pot-
shots. How many of us would really be surprised to see a "legitimate" report linking testosterone and humor? Would it look
anything like the 2005 report from Stirling and St. Andrews universities in the UK that claims testosterone causes women to be "career-
driven" like men? The humbling take-home message from these
studies is that traditionally masculine traits still belong to men — even
when women share them.

Although there is an
element of humor in
how wrong the news
media can get science,
the trend isn't a harm-
less one.

Although there is an element of humor   45
in how wrong the news media can get science, the trend isn't a harmless one. While
plenty of smart people question biased headlines of all stripes, casual readers — particularly young ones — are likely to skim the
stories and tuck them away in the pocket of
their brains where stereotypes are kept. It's
bad enough when we see images of women
as passive, petty, dumb, or slutty in fiction or advertisements, but
stereotypes that come with the lofty stamp of science have the air of
being, well, factual.

After all, if women are biologically wired to be weak or catty or   46
dumb or humorless, then there's nothing wrong with writing consistently airheaded female movie and TV characters, dismissing women
in positions of power as "bitches" or "too emotional," or claiming
that institutional sexism doesn't exist, women just aren't smart
enough to be CEOs, grand masters, or surgeons. These studies reas-
sure people that media images reflect reality, that society reflects biology, and that nothing can or should be changed.

Perhaps we should just take solace in one final study, released by   47
the American Psychological Association in 2005 but picked up by
very few mainstream sources. The title? "Men and women found
more similar than portrayed in popular media."

Vocabulary / Using a Dictionary

1. What is a *bias* (para. 11)?

2. What are *curative* properties (para. 18)? If you didn't have access
   to a dictionary, how might you guess the meaning of *curative*?

3. What does it mean to *calibrate* (para. 34) or *miscalibrate* (para.
   34) something?

Responding to Words in Context

1. Skwarecki speaks of "the mainstream media" in paragraph 6 and elsewhere. What or whom do you think she's referring to when she uses the term *mainstream*?

2. What does it mean for something to be *hardwired* (para. 2)? When would you usually come across a term like this?

3. Paragraph 27 takes up the issue of oglers and "worse oglers," linking them to questions of gender. What does it mean to *ogle* something?

Discussing Main Point and Meaning

1. Explain what you think Skwarecki means when she says that "traditional gender roles are an evergreen subject in the science pages" (para. 12).

2. Even scientists can lose objectivity as they approach their subjects and research, as Skwarecki shows in her essay. What are some of the main difficulties most of us run into when we make statements about gender differences?

3. "Is the Study Even Science?" is one of the questions Skwarecki says we should ask of a scientific article. What are some of the ways to tell if a study does or does not use good science?

Examining Sentences, Paragraphs, and Organization

1. Skwarecki includes a lengthy example of media bias and cultural stereotyping in her description of a BBC story called "Housework cuts breast-cancer risk." In one sentence, she notes that "it turns out that domestic tasks are, duh, hard work" (para. 15). How does the conversational tone of this sentence influence your perception of Skwarecki's own positions as a reporter?

2. Paragraph 41 consists of one sentence: "Lesson learned: If you can't find the source article, it may not actually exist." Does this one sentence work as a complete paragraph? Why or why not?

3. Skwarecki asks her readers to challenge the viewpoints of mainstream media with five questions that test the validity of the science found in their articles. What is the effect of having Skwarecki's questions in this essay set forth as numbered points? What would the effect be without those numbered points?

Thinking Critically

1. Skwarecki opens her essay questioning a study about how men and women relate to color (if and why girls seem to prefer pink and boys blue). Do you believe that biological differences play a role in how men and women view the world? How they act in the world? How do you know?

2. In paragraph 18, Skwarecki talks about the importance of the "hook" that journalists seek when they search for studies in the academic journals. It seems that various hooks warrant attention from the mainstream outlets. How do you understand her description of these hooks? Why would the media place such importance on these hooks?

3. The essay "Mad Science" outlines many of the pitfalls and inaccuracies found in articles about gender difference. Do you think the difference between men and women is an important subject for scientific study? What kinds of differences, if any, should be studied, and why?

In-Class Writing Activities

1. In her essay about the media and "mad science," Skwarecki shows how misleading "scientific" evidence about gender difference can be, and how it is often influenced by stereotypes rather than hard facts. What gender differences do you perceive in the world? Write an essay on one particular gender difference. Explore how this difference might be the result of stereotypes. Also try to provide evidence for the "scientific validity" for this difference. Then explain how the studies you've found either practice good, sound science or, like many quoted in Skwarecki's essay, don't hold up to scrutiny.

2. This essay is concerned with how scientific studies deal with gender-related issues, but could Skwarecki's questions be applied to other kinds of studies? Come up with a list of other possible studies to which these questions might apply. Write a brief explanation of how these questions could be effectively used to question the information found in other types of articles.

3. Skwarecki's article appears in a magazine called *Bitch: Feminist Response to Pop Culture*. Is her article one that you would expect to find in such a magazine? In a short essay, explain why you do or do not think this is the sort of article you would find, and use examples from the essay to support your position.

JOSEPH VANDEHEY (STUDENT ESSAY)

Where Are All the Women Mathematicians?

[OREGON DAILY EMERALD, University of Oregon / November 8, 2007]

Before You Read

Why do relatively few women pursue mathematics as a profession? Do you think men make better students of math than women do? Are such gender differences biological, or are they the result of society and culture?

Words to Learn

quantitative (para. 4): pertaining to measurements of number or amount (adj.)

geometers (para. 4): mathematicians who study geometry, that is, the properties, measurements, and relationships of points, lines, angles, surfaces, and solids (n.)

viable (para. 6): workable; capable of being effective; capable of living (adj.)

Difference does not automatically imply hierarchy. I do not understand the instinct to rank things, to say that when two things are different, one must be better than the other. More often than not, what is considered better is a matter of personal preference (I might like vanilla ice cream over chocolate, but that does not mean vanilla   1

Joseph Vandehey is a recent graduate from the Clark Honors College at the University of Oregon with a degree in mathematics. He was the "miscellaneous" columnist for the Oregon Daily Emerald, *for which reason he "almost never [wrote] about the same issue twice," covering such topics as sociology, philosophy, nature, and literature. As an aspiring professor of mathematics, Vandehey expects to write research papers and lecture notes, but he also hopes to "write textbooks which will help students to see the beauty that I see in mathematics—textbooks which students might want to read instead of being forced to read."*

is superior). More importantly, what is "better" is often very dependent on the particular situation (I prefer vanilla ice cream directly after a meal, but prefer more exotic flavors as an in-between-meals snack). I will repeat: Difference does not mean hierarchy. So, please, dear reader, look beyond the surface implication of this sentence: Men and women are different.

At very least, the numbers of men and women who like numbers are different. In many of the mathematics courses I have taken during my time as an undergraduate, the male-to-female ratio is quite skewed, often hovering around 3.5:1 (in those classes which actually have female students). I am sure most departments have their own gender biases, but since I am a mathematician, I notice it far more in math, and it troubles me. What makes math so unattractive or unattainable for women?

Unfortunately most of the debate surrounding this subject is too politicized: People either blame everything on sexism or attempt to ignore sexism entirely. Neither ends up offering a very satisfying answer. When sexism is considered, arguments tend to focus on overt male-dominated control. These arguments both require the vast majority of males to be bigots, which they aren't, and fail to explain how any female mathematicians have succeeded.

When sexism is ignored, on the other hand, arguments tend to focus on biological differences. These arguments take into account differences between the sexes, though not all of them say that differences create hierarchies. Those which do are often quite sexist themselves (even when they claim otherwise), and those that are not are assumed to be sexist as well (even when they truly are otherwise). Some arguments even intentionally invoke the "differences are hierarchies" mindset within a scientific frame. They point out cognitive differences between men and women: Men, they say, have better spatial and quantitative abilities, and hence there are more male mathematicians. But this line of reasoning breaks down because mathematics is far more than just spatial and quantitative; it might explain a greater number of geometers and analysts but not mathematicians in general.

Some of my female colleagues have advanced one argument that rejects the "differences are hierarchies" mindset. They noticed that when a math problem is given to a group of male students, hands will rocket into the air as soon as one person thinks he might have the answer. But when the same problem is given to a group of female students, there will be much more writing and communication between the students before a hand is raised. According to this line of reasoning, the reason why there are more male mathematicians is because males are more aggressive, and are rewarded for their more active participation. However, biology alone does not hold the answer any more than male chauvinism does. It cannot just be a difference but a perception about that difference that is important (i.e., some form of sexism).

Society as well as biology must be taken into account, and society   6
has attached many negative connotations to mathematicians. We treat mathematicians as an indulgence, as people who provide nothing and make nothing of use, as eccentrics and cranks. When I was applying to college, my parents worried that I would not be able to support myself as a mathematician, that I would have a degree which would not get me a job. They encouraged me to consider an engineering degree, or any other option that would make my mathematical skills more financially viable. It took a fair amount of time to convince them that I not only wanted to be a mathematician, but I could be one. Despite many advances, certain jobs are still seen as not womanly, and I wonder how many women have been prevented from becoming mathematicians not because of a lack of ability, but because a lack of support.

> *Despite many advances, certain jobs are still seen as not womanly, and I wonder how many women have been prevented from becoming mathematicians not because of a lack of ability, but because a lack of support.*

To me, the reason for the gender gap is somewhere between the   7
extremes of non-hierarchical differences and societal expectations. Research done by the Educational Testing Service indicates that the gender gap in mathematics is slowly but steadily shrinking. Perhaps as time goes on, older, more hierarchical ideals will die off, and more and more people will realize that not only their sons but their daughters can become mathematicians.

Vocabulary / Using a Dictionary

1. Vandehey disagrees with the notion that difference always implies hierarchy (para. 1). What is the origin of the word *hierarchy*?

2. Where does the word *gender* (para. 2) come from, and what other terms share its roots?

3. What are the roots of the word *cognitive* (para. 4), and what other terms is it related to?

4. Where does the word *chauvinism* (para. 5) come from, and how has its original meaning evolved?

Responding to Words in Context

1. What functions do the words *automatically* and *instinct* have, respectively, in the first two sentences of Vandehey's essay?

2. Vandehey claims that "society has attached many negative connotations to mathematicians" (para. 6). What is a *negative connotation*?

3. What does it mean to treat something as an *indulgence*, as Vandehey says our society does to mathematicians (para. 6)?

Discussing Main Point and Meaning

1. According to Vandehey, what is the main problem with the way we view the relationship between gender and mathematical aptitude?

2. Vandehey writes that even though "scientific" arguments about gender are not always sexist in themselves, they tend to reiterate a sexist, " 'differences are hierarchies' mindset" (para. 4). How do they do this, and why do such explanations remain unsatisfactory?

3. Although Vandehey is primarily concerned with math and gender, he also thinks that broader considerations may play a role in the relatively limited number of female mathematicians. What are they?

Examining Sentences, Paragraphs, and Organization

1. In the first paragraph, Vandehey writes, "I will repeat: Difference does not mean hierarchy." Why does he use this repetition?

2. What kind of evidence does Vandehey use to support his point of view? How does it reflect his sense of his audience?

3. How would you describe the structure of Vandehey's argument, overall? Is his method effective?

Thinking Critically

1. Vandehey targets binary, hierarchical thinking—not only in terms of gender but also more generally. Do you agree with his criticism? Are there other examples where this "'differences are hierarchies' mindset" is problematic, or actually inhibits clear thinking about an issue?

2. According to Vandehey, the discussion and debate "surrounding this subject [i.e., the reason for the low number of female mathematicians] is too politicized" (para. 3). What does *politicized* mean? How are scientific accounts of this issue politicized, as well? Would it be possible for the debate *not* to be politicized?

3. In paragraph 6, Vandehey argues that society views mathematicians in a negative light, as "eccentrics and cranks" who provide little value. Do you agree with this? What would make his point stronger?

In-Class Writing Activities

1. Vandehey includes an account of gender differences based on classroom observations. From this observational evidence, some of his female colleagues propose that men are "more aggressive, and are rewarded for their more active participation," whereas women tend to approach math problems using more collaboration and communication. Does this seem like a valid theory? Have you observed other such gender distinctions in classrooms? Would you be more inclined to explain them as the result of essential biological differences, or rather as a consequence of social or cultural training and expectations?

2. In 2005, at an economics conference, Harvard University president Lawrence Summers suggested that the disproportionately small number of women in science and engineering professions might be caused, in part, by some intrinsic differences in intelligence between the two genders. His remarks were controversial, and he ultimately resigned his post. What happens if science leads us to socially unpleasant conclusions? How should we discuss such issues? If Summers is correct (and he said at the time that he'd like "nothing better than to be proven wrong"), what would the implications be? Is there any way to engage these topics without "politicizing" them?

3. According to Vandehey, he faced a lot of pressure with regard to his major and his choice of professions, both from society and from his family. He also understands the gender implications of such choices, as "certain jobs are still not seen as womanly" (para. 6). What kind of pressures have you faced, as far as choosing a field of study and looking ahead to a career? Has your gender played any role in those decisions or your sense of what opportunities are available to you? Do you think society still has entrenched ideas about "men's work" and "women's work"? Explain.

ANNOTATION The Art of Argument — Anticipating Opposition

When you take a position you think will be unpopular or controversial, an effective strategy is to anticipate the opposition you may receive. In this way, you indicate that you have thought carefully about your position, and you make it more difficult for those who resist your argument to reject your claims outright. In nearly all effective argument and debate, the writer or speaker will attempt to preempt arguments likely to be made by the other side by dealing with them first. This doesn't mean, of course, that you have answered those opposing arguments satisfactorily, but it does mean that in its response the opposing side will now need to take into account your awareness of its position.

In "Where Are All the Women Mathematicians?" University of Oregon student Joseph Vandehey opens his essay by anticipating the response that many of his readers might make to a claim that there are real differences between the sexes. His readers may assume that he considers men superior to women. Thus, Vandehey begins by making the point that differences do not necessitate rankings, that just because A is different from B is no reason to conclude that A is inferior or superior to B. In other words, even though he is advancing the claim that men and women may be different, that doesn't automatically mean he thinks one is better than the other.

Note, too, how Vandehey structures his paragraph by starting with a generalization about difference and ranking, and then reinforces his point at the end by repeating it, but this time in reference to his particular topic — sex differences.

Vandehey opens with a generalization to show that he is not supporting superiority. *By repeating his generalization, Vandehey reinforces his argument and hopes to persuade those who may disagree with his argument that he is not advocating male superiority.*	<u>Difference does not automatically imply hierarchy.</u> <u>I do not understand the instinct to rank things, to say that when two things are different, one must be better than the other.</u> More often than not, what is considered better is a matter of personal preference (I might like vanilla ice cream over chocolate, but that does not mean vanilla is superior). More importantly, what is "better" is often very dependent on the particular situation (I prefer vanilla ice cream directly after a meal, but prefer more exotic flavors as an in-between-meals snack). <u>I will repeat: Difference does not mean hierarchy.</u> So, please, dear reader, look beyond the surface implication of this sentence: Men and women are different.

— From "Where Are All the Women Mathematicians?"
by Joseph Vandehey, page 161

Student Writer at Work: Joseph Vandehey
On Writing "Where Are All the Women Mathematicians?"

Q: What inspired you to write "Where Are All the Women Mathematicans?"

A: As a mathematician, I have a lot of opinions about mathematics, and as a columnist, I have to write about my opinions; however, most people are not interested in reading about mathematics every week. This topic, I felt, was a good middle ground.

Q: What response have you received to this piece? Has the feedback you have received affected your views on the topic you wrote about?

A: All of the feedback I received was positive. I even received a detailed letter from one woman who agreed with what I wrote and told me about her own experiences in studying advanced physics after coming from a household where mathematics at least was seen as a man's domain.

Q: Tell us about your process for writing and revising your columns.

A: It usually takes me six hours total to write a column, starting from the initial idea and finishing with the submitted work. In my first draft, I attempt to get ideas I have on the subject onto the paper, even if the ideas do not relate to one another. Then in subsequent drafts, I develop continuity, clarity, tone, and a theme to hold the column together. In general, my columns represent my sole, unvarnished opinions; however, in this case I reached my conclusions thanks to talks I had in previous years with other—much older and wiser—mathematicians about their own experience with gender disparity in the classroom.

Q: What do you like to read? What do you like to write about?

A: I read a lot of science fiction and fantasy, but I also try to keep up with the local daily newspaper as well. I prefer the comics (because I like to laugh), the opinion section (because I like to understand different viewpoints), and the world news (because I like to know what goes on outside my home).

I like to write about sociology and philosophy, especially where they intersect with mathematics and logic. I also enjoy writing about nature and literature (yes, writing about writing).

Q: What advice do you have for other student writers?

A: Be honest when you write. That means more than not plagiarizing; it means writing for and from your heart. If you write just for money, or power, or even a grade, then it will read that way, and it will not be as good as it could be.

Discussing the Unit

Suggested Topic for Discussion

If the subject of gender relations is an "evergreen" topic, so is the subject of science education in the United States. The mainstream media carry regular reports that American students are "falling behind" students in other countries. All the writers in this unit are asking their readers to sort through and evaluate scientific claims — some of them (as in the case of the study Matthias Mehl coauthored) relatively technical. What kind of scientific training have you had? Do you think your science education has been adequate?

Preparing for Class Discussion

1. Writing about how popular reports warp or misapply scientific studies, Skwarecki asks sarcastically: "But why let the facts slow down a good headline?" (para. 26). Implicitly, popular journalism often brings a different set of values to its subjects than science does — and those values may clash. How does Mehl's study from the journal *Science* suggest this difference? Do you think its results would be as widely reported or quoted as Louann Brizendine's claims were? Why or why not?

2. All of the selections in this unit address directly or touch upon mistakes in science and journalism — through flawed methodology and application, cultural bias, bad reporting, and so on. How do these readings also demonstrate the mechanisms by which science and journalism can correct such mistakes?

From Discussion to Writing

1. In the Knox article, Mehl "acknowledges that many will have trouble believing the results [of his study], since it contradicts their own perceptions" (para. 15). What does the word *perceptions* suggest in this statement? How is it possible to "believe" things that contradict existing empirical evidence? Is it irrational? Is it always a "bad" thing? Write an essay attempting to explain this phenomenon. Have you ever been unable to accept such evidence? Does this tendency explain anything about human beings, generally?

2. Find a recent story in the popular press (newspaper, TV, radio, Internet, or another medium) that is based on scientific research, and then evaluate it using the questions and strategies from the Skwarecki essay. Does it fit into one of the three varieties that she lists in paragraph 18? Is its headline or lead-in misleading? Does the story reinforce a stereotype? On the other hand, is it accurate and responsible? What "values" are implicit in the article or news segment, with regard to the presentation of scientific information?

Topics for Cross-Cultural Discussion

1. How has science been used to analyze or explain differences in human beings that also have racial, ethnic, gender, or other cultural components? Is such research valid and worthwhile? Do you think such practices tend to fall into the "difference implies hierarchy" fallacy that Vandehey describes? What are the possibilities and dangers of this kind of scientific inquiry?

2. *Scientism* is often used as a pejorative term for the view that empirical, scientific inquiry of the natural world holds the primary— and perhaps only genuine—authority over reality and knowledge, meaning that science is ultimately superior to philosophy, religion, spirituality, the humanities, and other ways of apprehending and explaining the world around us. Do you think American culture tends to be "scientistic"? Why or why not?

5

Do We Need an Ethics of Consumption?

Would you buy something—a handbag, a pair of jeans, even a tube of toothpaste—if you knew someone had suffered to produce it? What if child or slave labor had been involved? Most of us recoil at the brutal and unpoliced treatment of workers overseas but won't hesitate to fund malefactors by buying their products. Where, many of us inevitably ask, is the line? Do we need an ethics of consumption, and if so, what should it be?

Take, for instance, fake designer goods—like phony Louis Vuitton bags or counterfeit Polo shirts. These often strike many of us as perfectly innocuous ways of saving a few bucks; we wouldn't spend the high prices the luxury manufacturers charge, so we're not even hurting the company by buying counterfeits. Not so, says Dana Thomas. In her investigation "The Fake Trade," Thomas attempts to debunk the myth that buying counterfeit goods is a victimless crime: Not only are we hurting the companies and designers whose ideas are being pilfered, she argues, but "we are financing international crime syndicates that deal in money laundering, human trafficking, and child labor." Thomas describes the deplorable conditions of child workers in factories that produce the cheap knockoffs, leading readers to wonder: Is buying fakes unethical? Should it be illegal?

Critic and activist Barbara Ehrenreich, meanwhile, takes a hard line on child labor, and everyone who profits from it—including consumers—in her satirical essay "Slaves for Fashion." Facetiously proposing that we consider revelations that Gap employed child sweatshop labor "not as a human rights issue but as a PR disaster," Ehrenreich is in fact arguing that declamations of child labor do not go far enough—Americans need to look to their own treatment of children before attacking the worldwide crisis. "There will always be some men, for example," she writes, "who would rather wear skirts than blue jeans impregnated with the excrement and tears of ten-year-olds."

Jim Hightower takes a more earnest approach in "The Price of Cheap Goods." Hightower points the finger directly at low-cost retailers like Wal-Mart and even Disney, which claim to be offering cheap products to American consumers. "What these moral exemplars don't mention," he writes, "is that the goods are cheap only because the lives of Chinese factory workers are so undervalued." By documenting in detail the abuses that are part of daily life in developing-world factories, Hightower appeals to his readers' sense of outrage in provoking them to think about the high cost of low-cost products.

Following is a brief examination of the groundbreaking book that made Americans aware of their powerful and irrational desire for "conspicuous consumption."

Courtney Pomeroy investigates the dilemma from a particularly college-centric perspective. In "The Ethics of What We Wear: Can We Dress Fashionably and Responsibly?" Pomeroy interviews her fellow University of Maryland students and reveals a persistent hypocrisy: Even though many say they can't countenance the unfair labor practices, they continue to shop at the same companies accused of perpetrating them. As one of Pomeroy's peers told her, "People love Gap clothes. They're going to say 'It's wrong!', but they're still going to buy those chinos."

DANA THOMAS

The Fake Trade

[HARPER'S BAZAAR/January 2008]

Before You Read

Do you own brand-name items that seem as though they should have cost more? Or have you purchased a "fake" because the name brand cost too much? Have you ever wondered where those fake brands come from?

Words to Learn

counterfeit (para. 4): an imitation meant to be passed off as genuine (n.)

slum (para. 4): a run-down, dirty part of a city where people live in crowded conditions (n.)

horrific (para. 6): having the power to shock or terrify (adj.)

antifreeze (para. 6): liquid added to automobile engines to lower their freezing point (n.)

feline (para. 6): cat (n.)

litigation (para. 6): a lawsuit (n.)

primary (para. 7): first in importance (adj.)

revenue (para. 8): income from taxes (n.)

clandestine (para. 8): done secretly (adj.)

invariably (para. 8): always (adv.)

wholesaler (para. 10): someone who sells to retailers (n.)

Before recently joining Condé Nast Portfolio *as a contributing editor, Dana Thomas served since 1986 as the Paris-based European arts and entertainment correspondent for* Newsweek. *She has written about style for the* New York Times Magazine *since 1994, and her work has been included in a variety of publications, such as the* New Yorker, Harper's Bazaar, Vogue, *the* Washington Post, *and London's* Financial Times. *Thomas is the author of the* New York Times *best-selling book* Deluxe: How Luxury Lost Its Luster, *which traces the idea of luxury across the ages. In addition to her extensive written achievements, Thomas taught journalism at the American University of Paris from 1996 to 1999 and received the Ellis Haller Award for Outstanding Achievement in Journalism in 1987.*

embroidery (para. 11): raised
  needlework (n.)
trademark (para. 13): something a
  manufacturer uses to distinguish
  its goods from those manufactured by others (n.)

guarantee (para. 17): to be secure in
  the knowledge; to be assured (v.)
verification (para. 18): a formal assertion of the truth (n.)

On a cool August evening, my family and I visited the preppy   1
town of Mill Valley, California, outside San Francisco. In the town
square was an all-American sight: a couple of kids behind a card
table selling homemade lemonade. My six-year-old wanted some, so I
gave her a quarter and sent her over to the booth. After a few minutes, I joined the kids and noticed that one, a cute eight- or nine-year-
old girl with a blonde blunt cut, had a little Murakami pouch slung
over her shoulder.

"Nice handbag," I said to her.   2
"It's Louis Vuitton," she responded proudly.   3
"No," I thought to myself as I gave it a good look-over. "It's a   4
counterfeit Louis Vuitton. And it was probably made by a Chinese
kid the same age as you in a slum halfway around the world."

Though the fashion business has muscled up its fight against   5
counterfeiting, with many brands investing millions of dollars each
year, the battle is ongoing. Since 1982, the global trade in counterfeit
and pirated goods has grown from an estimated $5.5 billion to ap-
proximately $600 billion annually. Experts believe that counterfeit-
ing costs American businesses $200 billion to $250 billion annually
and is directly responsible for the loss of more than 750,000 jobs in
the United States.

What's counterfeited? Everything. A couple of years ago, a coun-   6
terfeit investigator discovered a workshop in the Thai countryside
that produced fake versions of the classic Ferrari P4. Ferrari itself
originally made only three P4s back in 1967. The Food and Drug Administration has said that counterfeit medicine could account for upwards of 10 percent of all drugs worldwide. Unknowingly taking a
fake version of your medicine could have horrific effects on your
health. European Union officials have seen a dramatic rise in the
seizure of counterfeit personal-care items such as creams, toothpastes,
and razor blades. The television series *Law & Order: Criminal Intent*
recently highlighted this problem in an episode in which several children died after ingesting counterfeit mouthwash that had been made

with a poisonous chemical found in antifreeze. "There have been counterfeit perfumes tested by laboratories that have found that a major component was feline urine," says Heather McDonald, a partner at the law firm Baker Hostetler in New York who specializes in anticounterfeiting litigation. Counterfeit automotive brakes made with compressed grass and wood have been found in U.S. stores.

One of the primary reasons counterfeiting keeps flourishing is   7
that, as the little girl in Mill Valley proved, people keep happily buying fakes. According to a study published last year by the British law firm Davenport Lyons, almost two thirds of U.K. consumers are "proud to tell their family and friends that they bought fake luxury [fashion items]." And according to a 2003 survey carried out by Market & Opinion Research International in Great Britain, around a third of those questioned would consider buying counterfeits. Why? Because we still think of counterfeiting as a "victimless crime." Buying a counterfeit Vuitton bag surely doesn't affect the company, we reason. The parents of that Mill Valley girl probably wouldn't have invested in a real Vuitton Murakami for her, so it wasn't a loss of sales for the company.

But the reality is that we're all victims of counterfeiting, whether   8
from the loss of jobs or of tax revenue that could fund our schools and our roads, or because by buying counterfeit goods, we are financing international crime syndicates that deal in money laundering, human trafficking, and child labor. Each time I read the horrid tales about counterfeiting from my book, *Deluxe: How Luxury Lost Its Luster* — like the raid I went on in a clandestine factory in the industrial city of Guangzhou, China, where we found children making fake Dunhill and Versace handbags — audience members or radio listeners tell me they had no idea it was such a dark and dangerous world and that by purchasing these goods they were contributing personally to it. Then they invariably swear that they will never knowingly buy another fake good.

Brands as well as law enforcement have cracked down on the   9
counterfeit business severely in the past few years, here in the U.S. and abroad. I saw a difference in Hong Kong, for example: A decade ago, you could buy a fake Vuitton handbag or Burberry knapsack for a couple of bucks from a vendor in the subway; today you can't even find them on the street. There are still dealers, but now they lurk in doorways, whispering, "Rolex? Chanel?" and you hurry down dark streets to armored hideaways to close the deal. To say it's scary is an understatement. "If you can keep the stuff out of the public eye, you

are halfway to winning the battle," McDonald says. "The brands that are doing aggressive enforcement are hidden in back alleys and not on the street corners."

As long as there is a demand, however, there will be a supply. 10 Traditionally, the supply chain worked like this: An order of 10,000 handbags would be divided into 10 groups of 1,000 to be made — often by children — in hidden workshops in Guangzhou. Once completed, the items would be wrapped up and deposited in a neutral place, like the courtyard of a local school, where they were picked up by a local transporter, often simply a guy on a bike with a cart. The transporter delivered the package to the wholesaler, who would take it to another neutral place to be picked up by the international shipping agent and put in a shipping container. The goods were often packed in shipments of foodstuffs or legitimately manufactured clothing to escape detection by receiving customs officials. Each time the goods changed hands, the prices doubled. All transactions were done in cash.

But as fashion companies grew wise to the process and went after 11 the sources in China, leading to raids on workshops and busts at ports, the counterfeit-crime rings came up with new routes to supply fake goods: produce them, or at least finish them, in the destination country. Law enforcement witnessed this firsthand during a big bust this past October. The New York Police Department raided a commercial building in Queens, arrested 13, and seized around $4 million in counterfeit apparel that carried the logos of major brands including Polo, Lacoste, Rocawear, the North Face, and 7 for All Mankind. Officers also found a stash of fake labels and buttons for Tommy Hilfiger, Nike, and Adidas as well as embroidery machines. Investigators believe that the site was a finishing facility. Workers took generic items that may have been imported legally and sewed on fake logos and labels, turning the items into counterfeit branded goods.

Another trick is to import counterfeit items that are hiding under 12 a legitimate face. "Some of the counterfeiters put a whole separate coating on the bag, and you peel it off like contact paper to see the logo fabric underneath," McDonald tells me. "We seized a load of Lacoste men's dress shirts, and on the left breast pocket, where the alligator should be, there was a little generic label that read, 'Metro.' When you pulled out the threads and removed the Metro label, you found the alligator."

There's another method that is catching on rapidly: counterfeit- 13 ers who will take a legitimate logo, tinker with it slightly, apply for a trademark for the new design, then import those items under a false pretense of legality, showing the official application paperwork as their defense. For example, a company takes the Ralph Lauren polo-horse-and-rider logo and puts the polo mallet down instead of up in the air. The counterfeiter files a trademark application with the U.S. Patent and Trademark Office and gets a document that states the application is pending. "It's a legitimate document fraudulently secured, and the application will probably be rejected in six months," the intellectual-property counsel for a luxury brand explains to me. "But between now and then, the customs agents will approve the importation of the items—believing, incorrectly, that the pending application proves the importer must have a legitimate right to the trademark."

By the time the brand realizes what's going on, the lawyer says,   14
thousands of items will have been imported and the counterfeiter will have "made millions" and fled. Luxury companies discovered one operation using this technique about two years ago, and now several more have popped up. "We must be doing a good job, since counterfeiters are looking for such complicated ways to get in," the lawyer says.

People often ask me, "How do you know it's fake?"   15

Well, if it's being sold at a fold-up table on a sidewalk corner or   16
on the back of a peddler on the beach, chances are it's fake. Or if it's at a flea market. Or a church fundraiser. Or in Wal-Mart or Sam's Club or other discount mass retailers. In June 2006, Fendi filed suit in a U.S. district court against Wal-Mart Stores, Inc., asserting that the world's largest retailer was selling counterfeit Fendi handbags and wallets in its Sam's Club stores. For example, one bag was offered for $295; the legitimate Fendi handbag of the same design normally retailed for $925. In the suit, Fendi stated that Wal-Mart has never purchased Fendi products and never checked with Fendi to see if the items were real. The case was settled out of court last summer after Sam's Club agreed to pay Fendi an undisclosed sum.

> *If it's being sold at a fold-up table on a sidewalk corner or on the back of a peddler on the beach, chances are it's fake.*

If you want to guarantee that your luxury-brand purchases are   17
legitimate, don't shop in wholesale markets like those in Chinatown in Manhattan or Santee Alley in Los Angeles. "We'll go on raids on Chinatown wholesalers, and we'll find five or six suburban women standing there—customers," New York security expert

Andrew Oberfeldt has told me. "We'll say to these women, 'The dealers take you down dark corridors, through locked doors. The police say, "Open up!" The lights are turned out and everyone is told to be quiet. At what point did you realize that something was amiss here?'"

If you find an item for sale on the Internet for a price so low that   18
it seems too good to be true, it probably is too good to be true. Last fall, the U.K.-based Authentics Foundation, an international nonprofit organization devoted to raising public awareness about counterfeiting, launched myauthentics.com, a Web site that helps Internet shoppers determine if the products they are eyeing on the Web are real. It includes blogs and forums, news, myths, and tips on how to spot fakes; eBay now has links to the site. EBay also works with brands in its VeRO (Verified Rights Owner) program to find out if the items for offer on the site are genuine. If the brand deems a particular item to be counterfeit, the sale will be shut down. However, not all online sales sites have such verification processes in place. Besides, counterfeiters are known to post photos of genuine items to sell fakes. So as the old saying goes, buyer beware.

Of course, the best way to know if you are buying a genuine   19
product is to buy it from the brand, either in directly operated boutiques or in a company's shop in a department store. If you are curious about the authenticity of a used Vuitton item you purchased at a vintage shop or online, you can always contact one of the brand's boutiques.

Most important, we need to spread the word on the devastating   20
effects counterfeiting has on society today. I didn't tell the girl in Mill Valley that her bag was fake. It wasn't her fault her family had given it to her. But if I had met her parents, I would have said something. Awareness is key. Counterfeiting will never go away—it's been around since the dawn of time—but we can surely cut it down to size if we just stop buying the stuff. Without the demand, the supply will shrink. It's up to us.

Vocabulary / Using a Dictionary

1. From what word does *pirated* (para. 5) originate? What part of speech is it? What definition does the word's origin suggest?

2. In paragraph 10, there is a description of a supply chain that involves a transporter and a wholesaler. What do you think a *supply chain* is? By examining the roots of the words *transporter* and *wholesaler*, can you guess what their roles are?

3. The counterfeiter's trademark is described as "a legitimate document fraudulently secured" (para. 13). What do the words *legitimate* and *fraudulently* mean? How do you understand what is being said about the trademark?

Responding to Words in Context

1. Throughout, Thomas outlines the process of supply and demand that keeps fakes on the market. How do you understand what *supply and demand* means, given her description of how the counterfeit business works?

2. In paragraph 7, Thomas says that we buy counterfeits because we believe counterfeiting to be a "victimless crime." What do you think this phrase means?

3. Thomas has also written *Deluxe: How Luxury Lost Its Luster*, a book about the counterfeit trade (para. 8). Do the words *deluxe*, *luxury*, and *luster* have anything in common in terms of etymology? Once you know the definitions of those three words, explain what you think the title means.

Discussing Main Point and Meaning

1. In the opening paragraph, Thomas describes a little girl carrying a fake Louis Vuitton bag. Her town is named and described, as is her physical appearance. Why do you think these details are deemed necessary by Thomas?

2. Why does Thomas insist that "everything" is counterfeited (para. 6)?

3. The money that counterfeiters make and legitimate businesses lose as a result is mentioned several times in the essay. What is the effect of this profit and loss on ordinary people?

Examining Sentences, Paragraphs, and Organization

1. Thomas mentions the television series *Law & Order: Criminal Intent* as a show that has recently taken on counterfeiting as a subject. Why do you think she included it as evidence of the problem of counterfeiting?

2. Thomas includes a description of a New York Police Department raid on counterfeiters (para. 17) to illustrate which markets are

obviously illegitimate. Do you think Thomas believes that people unknowingly shop at such markets?

3. Why do you think Thomas returns, in the conclusion, to the girl with the fake bag who was mentioned in the introduction? Do you think it is an effective way to organize the argument? Explain.

Thinking Critically

1. Thomas states, "If you find an item for sale on the Internet for a price so low that it seems too good to be true, it probably is too good to be true" (para. 18). How does the Internet add a new dimension to the counterfeit market?

2. The essay mentions the duration and scope of counterfeiting: "Counterfeiting will never go away—it's been around since the dawn of time" (para. 20). How do statements like that make you more aware of counterfeiting?

3. Thomas does not tell the little girl her bag is a fake, but she says that "we need to spread the word on the devastating effects counterfeiting has on society today" (para. 20). Which effects of counterfeiting do you think are the most devastating?

In-Class Writing Activities

1. Thomas lists several very dangerous counterfeiting operations — making everything from counterfeit car brakes to fake medications — that have jeopardized the health and welfare of many unsuspecting people. Research a counterfeiting operation and write an essay that explores the venture and its outcome in more detail.

2. Do you think counterfeiting is as terrible for everyone as Thomas claims? Why or why not? Explain your position with supporting evidence. If you agree with Thomas, try to imagine scenarios not mentioned in the essay, and if you disagree with her, provide your own examples and argue with the ones provided by Thomas.

3. The statement "the best way to know if you are buying a genuine product is to buy it from the brand, either in directly operated boutiques or in a company's shop in a department store" (para. 19) indicates that Thomas sees nothing wrong with buying a name brand—it is the counterfeit that is the problem. Why do you think someone would need a name brand? Write an essay

that explores why name brands are so important that many people seek them out, even to the point of buying a counterfeit.

BARBARA EHRENREICH

Slaves for Fashion

[THE PROGRESSIVE / January 2008]

Before You Read

Have you heard reports of manufacturers using child labor in other countries? How have the companies or individuals involved responded to accusations of running sweatshops? What has been the public's response, and how do you think their response would change if child laborers were being used in this country?

Words to Learn

latrine (para. 1): an outhouse or communal toilet (n.)
condone (para. 8): to give approval of (v.)
ubiquitous (para. 9): constantly encountered (adj.)
pundit (para. 9): someone who gives opinions with authority; a commentator (n.)

facetious (para. 9): not serious (adj.)
wantonly (para. 12): carelessly or maliciously (adv.)
brace (para. 15): to get ready (v.)
excrement (para. 16): feces (n.)

Barbara Ehrenreich is an author, speaker, and activist on issues such as health care, peace, women's rights, and economic justice. She earned a PhD in cell biology from Rockefeller University and taught at the State University of New York, Old Westbury, but she eventually switched careers to full-time writing and activism. As an author, she has worked on both essays and book-length projects such as Nickel and Dimed *and* Bait and Switch. *About her decision to become a writer, Ehrenreich writes, "I cannot imagine doing anything other than what I do. Sure, I could have had more stability and financial security if I'd stuck to science or teaching. But I chose adventure and I've never for a moment regretted it."*

It was enough to make you vomit all over your new denim   1
jacket. Gap has been caught using child labor in an Indian sweatshop, and not just child labor—child slaves. As extensively reported
in the news, the children, some as young as ten, were worked sixteen-
hour days, fed bowls of mosquito-covered rice, and forced to sleep on
a roof and use overflowing latrines. Those who slowed down were
beaten with rubber pipes, and the ones who cried had oily cloths
stuffed in their mouths.

But let's try to look at this dispassionately—not as a human   2
rights issue but as a PR disaster, ranking right up there with the 1982
discovery of cyanide in Tylenol capsules.

Think of this as a case study in a corporate crisis communication   3
course: How is Gap handling the problem, and could it do better?

This is not the first time Gap has been caught using child labor,   4
but Marka Hansen, president of Gap North America, went on the air
to state that the situation was "completely unacceptable" and that
the company would "act swiftly."

Two problems here: One, it would have been nice if she had an-   5
nounced that some of the top-producing child slaves would be reas-
signed to manage Gap outlets in American malls, and that the
underperformers would be adopted by Angelina Jolie.

The other, more serious, problem is that Hansen got defensive   6
about child labor.

This is the mistake Kathie Lee Gifford made in 1996. When ac-   7
cused of using child labor in Honduras to manufacture her Kathie
Lee line of clothing, Gifford broke into tears on TV.

Maybe Hansen meant to cover herself by saying that Gap would   8
not "ever, ever condone any child laborer making our garments"
rather than saying the company does not condone child labor itself.
We already knew, from the rubber pipes and oily cloths, that Gap
does not condone much from its child laborers.

Hansen underestimated the potential support for a full-throated   9
defense of child labor. More and more American children are tried
and punished as adults today. And the ubiquitous conservative
pundit William Kristol will surely be enthusiastic, considering his recent—though possibly facetious—statement that "whenever I hear
anything described as a heartless assault on our children, I tend to
think it's a good idea."

The core of the argument, though, is that anyone who opposes   10
child labor has not witnessed its opposite, which is child unemployment and idleness.

Hansen claims to be a mother herself, so I wonder how often she   11
has returned home from a hard day in the C-suites to find her unemployed offspring Magic Marker-ing the walls and crushing the Froot Loops into the carpet.

This is what jobless children do: They rub Krazy Glue into their   12
siblings' hair; they spill apple juice onto your keyboard. Believe me, I see this kind of wantonly destructive behavior every day. Vandalism is a way of life for unemployed children, and they do not know the meaning of remorse.

In fact, corporate America should go further and make a strong   13
statement against the sickening culture of dependency that has grown up around childhood. Why are jobless children so criminally inclined? Because they know that whatever damage they inflict, the Froot Loops will just keep coming. Gap should portray its child-staffed factories as part of a far-seeing welfare-to-work program, which will eventually be extended to American children as well.

To appeal to American parents, our own child factories should   14
be run more like Montessori schools, where the children are already encouraged to regard every one of their demented activities as "work." If they're going to pile up blocks and knock them down all day, then why not sew on buttons and bring home a little cash?

Wal-Mart has already pioneered the price-cutting defense of human rights abuses, and Gap should follow suit.

But even American families will have   15
to brace themselves for the inevitable cost-cutting measures. First the cookies and milk may have to go. Then, as in India, the toilets and beds. Wal-Mart has already pioneered the price-cutting defense of human rights abuses, and Gap should follow suit.

The company can, of course, expect some   16
lingering opposition. Just as there are vegetarians and pacifists, there will always be some men, for example, who would rather wear skirts than blue jeans impregnated with the excrement and tears of ten-year-olds. Well, let them shop at American Apparel or some other "sweat-free" vendor, and if they can't find anything there, let them wear dhotis.

In a nation that cannot bring itself to extend child health insur-   17
ance to all children in need, child-made clothes make a fine fashion statement.

Vocabulary/Using a Dictionary

1. What does it mean to look at something *dispassionately* (para. 2)? What clues do you have to a definition in the prefix and root of the word?

2. Do you think Ehrenreich really believes that children's activities are *demented* (para. 14)? What sort of behavior is usually characterized that way? Why would she use that term to describe child's play?

3. Ehrenreich says that some people would rather not wear "blue jeans impregnated with the excrement and tears of ten-year-olds" (para. 16). What is the root of the word *impregnated*, and what are the usual associations with it?

Responding to Words in Context

1. What examples of children's *vandalism* (para. 12) are given in this essay? Based on your understanding of what *vandal* and *vandalism* mean, what images are conjured?

2. Ehrenreich refers to the "culture of dependency" (para. 13) that Americans accept from their children. What does it mean for a child to be *dependent* or *independent*? How are the child laborers in Indian sweatshops *dependent* or *independent*?

3. What is a *dhoti* (para. 16)? If you do not know the meaning of the word, what do you imagine it to be, based on context? What clues helped you shape your definition?

Discussing Main Point and Meaning

1. Ehrenreich's essay begins with a portrait of enslaved children working all day long, "fed bowls of mosquito-covered rice, and forced to sleep on a roof and use overflowing latrines" (para. 1). Which words in the opening paragraph carry the most weight, and why? Why would she begin an essay with such a graphic picture of child labor?

2. Ehrenreich's essay is in many ways modeled on Jonathan Swift's famous satirical essay "A Modest Proposal," which suggests that the solution to poverty in Ireland is for the poor to sell their children to the rich to eat. In actuality, Swift did *not* intend for any-

one to eat a child. In the same vein, Ehrenreich says that we should view the revelation of child labor "not as a human rights issue but as a PR disaster, ranking right up there with the 1982 discovery of cyanide in Tylenol capsules" (para. 2). What does she really mean when she calls the 1982 cyanide tragedy a "PR disaster"? How does her tone affect your reading of her essay?

3. The title "Slaves for Fashion," unlike most of Ehrenreich's essay, can be taken literally—she is referring to children enslaved in sweatshops. What does it mean in other contexts when someone uses the expression "I'm a slave for fashion"? Who is a slave for fashion in this country?

Examining Sentences, Paragraphs, and Organization

1. Paragraph 14 ends with a question: "If they're going to pile up blocks and knock them down all day, then why not sew on buttons and bring home a little cash?" How would that sentence read if Ehrenreich had instead made it a simple statement? Which version (question or statement) do you think is more effective?

2. In paragraph 8, Ehrenreich mentions that Marka Hansen, the president of Gap North America, makes the statement that "Gap would not 'ever, ever condone any child laborer making our garments.'" Later in the paragraph, Ehrenreich points out that it is apparent "Gap does not condone much from its child laborers." What is the president of Gap condoning or not condoning, according to Ehrenreich? What does she think is wrong with Hansen's statement?

3. In her examination of Gap's recently disclosed use of child labor, Ehrenreich ironically labels it a "PR disaster" rather than a "human rights issue." Where in the essay does she reveal the deeply entrenched human rights issue involved in the use of such labor?

Thinking Critically

1. Welfare-to-work is a controversial program in this country that is used to bring unemployed adults back to the workforce, and one criticism of the program is that it leads people who often need more support into the worst jobs with low pay. Ehrenreich suggests that "Gap should portray its child-staffed factories as

part of a far-seeing welfare-to-work program, which will eventually be extended to American children as well" (para. 13). How would such a suggestion be received in this country? What point is she trying to make?

2. The lives of most children in America bear very little relation to the lives of children in sweatshops in India. Do any children in this country experience situations that would be similar to what she is describing here? Was there ever a comparable situation in the United States?

3. Many large American companies have been guilty of mistreating their workers in other countries, yet people continue to buy their products. If it is true that "Wal-Mart has already pioneered the price-cutting defense of human rights abuses, and Gap should follow suit" (para. 15), what does that say about the people in charge of large chain stores? How do you think they justify the use of children in sweatshops?

In-Class Writing Activities

1. In her essay, Ehrenreich seems to be on the offensive against useless "jobless" children. Who is she really criticizing in this essay? Write an essay that argues who and what she is critical of, and explain your answer by pointing to specific selections of the text.

2. The children in the Gap sweatshop are for all intents and purposes enslaved by the company. The conditions described are intolerable for both children and adults. Have you ever held a job? Whether you have or haven't, what are your expectations of a work situation? What rights do you expect your employer to grant you? Write an essay that outlines what you believe your rights to be, and why you feel you should be granted them, keeping in mind the simple rights that were denied the children in the Gap sweatshop.

3. The Industrial Revolution saw the rise of sweatshops in this country and elsewhere, and they were condemned because those running them rarely cared about the welfare of their workers. In the late nineteenth century, sweatshops began to be exposed as unsafe and unhealthy places where the poorest people of the city often felt compelled to work. The term *sweatshop* is heard more and more once again as jobs have come to be outsourced to developing nations. What is the origin of the word *sweatshop*? Re-

search the history of sweatshops in the United States, and then write an essay explaining what a sweatshop used to be and what the term has come to mean in the twenty-first century.

<hr>

JIM HIGHTOWER

The Price of Cheap Goods

[THE PROGRESSIVE / March 2008]

Before You Read

Do you ever consider the government agencies that regulate product safety? Have you ever wondered why so many goods we buy are made in other countries? Do you think that corporations have social or moral obligations, beyond making profits? Do you take any moral considerations into account when buying the products you like?

Words to Learn

laden (para. 2): loaded or freighted (v.)

testosterone (para. 3): hormone responsible for the development and maintenance of male sex characteristics (n.)

lackadaisical (para. 6): lacking in spirit or energy; lazy (adj.)

appalled (para. 10): discouraged or dismayed (adj.)

Jim Hightower is an author, radio commentator, and speaker. He received a BA in government from the University of North Texas and has worked with and managed numerous presidential campaigns throughout the past decades. His populist political newsletter, The Hightower Lowdown, *received the Alternative Press Award and the Independent Press Association Award for best national newsletter. His daily radio commentaries are broadcast on more than 150 public and commercial stations. Hightower describes himself as "a modern-day Johnny Appleseed, spreading the message of progressive populism all across the American grassroots."*

Like a cat watching the wrong mouse hole, we're being told to   1
look to Chinese manufacturers when assessing blame for the toxic
products that are being exported from there. But wait a minute—
where, oh where, are our own country's regulatory watchdogs?

The big shock is not that Chinese-made toys are laden with lead,   2
but that America's Consumer Product Safety Commission is a toothless watchdog that employs exactly one inspector to oversee the
safety of all toys sold in the U.S. Likewise, the Food and Drug Administration has licensed 714 Chinese plants to manufacture the key
ingredients for a growing percentage of the antibiotics, painkillers,
and other drugs we buy, but provides practically no oversight of
these plants. In 2007, for example, the FDA inspected only thirteen
of them.

An even bigger shock is that our consumer protection laws are so   3
riddled with loopholes that unsafe products can legally come into our
country. Take phthalate, a chemical additive in plastics that is suspected by scientists here and in Europe of inhibiting testosterone production in infant boys. Yet, Mark Schapiro, author of *Exposed: The
Toxic Chemistry of Everyday Products and What's at Stake for
American Power*, reports that while the European Union has banned
the use of phthalates in products aimed at children under three years
of age, our government has refused to act.

Thus, China has factories that manufacture two lines of toys—   4
one without phthalates for shipment to European countries, and one
with phthalates for export to our children.

*It's common to find
child labor, sixteen-
hour days, constant
exposure to lead and
other poisons, wage rip-
offs, and other abuses
in factories that stock
the shelves of our stores
and line the pockets of
our corporate CEOs.*

The problem is not with the Chinese,   5
but with our own corporate chieftains who
have moved their manufacturing to China
specifically to get these kinds of low-cost
shortcuts in production, while simultaneously demanding that Washington cut back
on regulations that protect us consumers.
We must put our own house in order.

Such giants as Wal-Mart, Dell, and   6
Disney are profiting enormously from this
double whammy of low-cost production and
lackadaisical regulation. Not content to
profiteer, however, the top executives insist
that they should get credit for serving the
moral good. Look, they say, we are helping American families by
bringing cheap products to them.

What these moral exemplars don't mention is that the goods are 7
cheap only because the lives of Chinese factory workers are so undervalued. It's common to find child labor, sixteen-hour days, constant
exposure to lead and other poisons, wage rip-offs, and other abuses
in factories that stock the shelves of our stores and line the pockets of
our corporate CEOs.

You want cheap? What's a finger worth? A study of factories in 8
just one area near Hong Kong found that workers there lose or break
40,000 fingers on the job every year.

Or consider the cheap treatment of a sixteen-year-old boy in 9
China who works from 6 a.m. to 6 p.m., six days a week, running a
plastic molding machine to produce stuff for Wal-Mart stores. His
hands are covered with blisters, because, as he explained to a *New
York Times* reporter, the machines are "quite hot, so I've burned my
hands." The boy's reward is to be paid even less than China's
poverty-level minimum wage of 55 cents an hour.

Corporate officials here claim that they're appalled by these con- 10
ditions, but they shrug and say they simply can't keep track of what
goes on in all those factories. BS! They're the ones demanding cheap
production, even if it cheapens lives in China and endangers consumers here.

Note that Wal-Mart boasts that it's able to track every penny of 11
cost in its sprawling system of procuring and marketing products. Its
bean counters know the price of every item coming out of even the
most remote Chinese factory. The corporation simply values price
over lives.

Vocabulary / Using a Dictionary

1. What are the origins of the word *toxic* (para. 1), and what other
   words use it as a root?

2. What are the roots of the word *procuring* (para. 11), and what
   connotations does it have?

3. What does the word *antibiotics* (para. 2) mean, and what are its
   origins?

Words in Context

1. Hightower refers to government agencies responsible for consumer protection as "regulatory watchdogs" (para. 1). What
   view of business and the government does this metaphor imply?

2. What is the difference between the verbs *profit* and *profiteer* (para. 6)? Why do you think Hightower uses the latter term?

3. In paragraph 7, the writer refers to top corporate executives as "moral exemplars." What is his tone in this sentence?

4. Hightower uses the term *bean counters* to describe the people who can "track every penny of cost in [Wal-Mart's] sprawling system" (para. 11). What is a *bean counter*? Why does he use this expression, instead of a term like *account executives*?

Discussing Main Point and Meaning

1. According to Hightower, why is the recent focus—and blame— on the Chinese manufacturers and exporters of unsafe, toxic toys partially misplaced?

2. In addition to criticizing lax regulations, Hightower targets large corporations such as Wal-Mart and Disney, as well as the executives who run them. What is Hightower's criticism of these organizations and their leaders?

3. Hightower suggests that companies in the United States (and perhaps even American consumers) are complicit in the ethically questionable business practices of companies in other countries. Why would businesses in one country bear any responsibility for the businesses in another country?

Examining Sentences, Paragraphs, and Organization

1. How do the last sentences in paragraph 5 and paragraph 11 function, respectively, within the structure of the essay?

2. In paragraph 9, Hightower describes and quotes a boy who works twelve-hour days for low pay in a Chinese factory—and who has been repeatedly burned because of lax (or nonexistent) workplace standards. What is the emotional effect of this paragraph? Does Hightower use any emotionally charged language to achieve it?

3. How would you characterize Hightower's prose style? Does it sound academic? Journalistic? Serious? Comic?

Thinking Critically

1. What are Hightower's main sources for his argument? How would you evaluate them? How does he incorporate them into his essay?

2.   Hightower cites the example of phthalate, "a chemical additive in plastics that is suspected by scientists . . . of inhibiting testosterone production in infant boys" (para. 3). Is this a good piece of evidence to support his argument? Why?

3.   Near the end of the essay, Hightower uses the two-letter exclamation "BS!" as a sentence. Does he back up this assertion? Does it undercut, or does it support, the seriousness of his argument?

In-Class Writing Activities

1.   Hightower has a cynical view of corporations, whose leaders "value price over lives" and "profiteer" through questionable business practices, all the while wanting to be seen as moral exemplars. What is a corporation? What is its purpose? Do corporations have a "morality," or social obligations? What is their relationship to national goals? Do the benefits that such institutions provide outweigh the costs?

2.   "You want cheap? What's a finger worth?" Hightower asks (para. 8). Do you consider yourself morally connected to—or responsible for—the products you buy? Have you ever researched them? Do you take ethical considerations into account in your consumer spending? How have companies reacted to such issues? Choose a brand-name clothing product (or some other item) you buy regularly and research the company. Where is it made? Who makes it? What are the practices of the corporation?

3.   In paragraph 7, Hightower refers to child labor, in which young people in other countries are paid low pages for dangerous work over long hours. Should U.S. companies boycott such plants? Should our government make working with them illegal or ban their imports? What complications exist in such cases? Is child labor always bad?

The Powerful Theory of Conspicuous Consumption

If any one principle of consumption holds true for today's America, it is this: People no longer buy something merely because they need it; they buy it because it's available. How this principle of consumption became a major factor in American life and the U.S. economy is a fascinating story that begins sometime in the 1880s, with the rise of advertising, the birth of large department stores, the success of the Industrial Revolution, and the rapid expansion of mass media. It is, in effect, a story about the invention of the modern "consumer," a largely irrational creature hardly imagined in classic economics. This new phenomenon was brilliantly identified by a maverick economist named Thorstein Veblen in an 1899 book called The Theory of the Leisure Class.

Veblen (1857–1929), the American-born son of Norwegian immigrant parents, was one of the first to point out—long before radio, television, megamalls, and the Internet—the enormous power of what he memorably called "conspicuous consumption"—the desire to demonstrate one's prestige and status based on one's material acquisitions. And long before Madison Avenue discovered the power of envy (the modern consumer may be defined as someone who desperately wants whatever others possess), Veblen argued that after self-preservation, "emulation is probably the strongest of economic motives." Veblen saw emulation as wasteful and irrational; he once said that "man is not a logical animal, particularly in his economic activity."

His economic theory still retains a remarkable explanatory power and is the precursor to such best-selling books as Freakonomics *(2005), which attempt to explain the "hidden side of everything." Although Veblen would never have imagined such an item of apparel, he would nevertheless be able to explain through his theory why someone would pay hundreds of dollars for designer-ripped blue jeans. He had a keen eye for detecting "conspicuous waste." He saw that people tended to place enormous value on useless objects and skills, often because these were evidence of one's capacity for "waste-*

Thorstein Veblen (1857–1929), creator of the theory of conspicuous consumption.   The Granger Collection, New York.

ful expenditure." Too many things that we spend time and money on lavishly he considered simply "decorative" and as having no useful function; for example, he satirizes the affluent American male's preoccupation with his "lawn," which is merely a cow pasture that must be kept closely cropped but without benefit of a cow. At one point, he amusingly contrasts Americans' preference for dogs over cats. Why? Dogs are more useless and expensive to keep and therefore are afforded a higher stature as domestic pets.

Veblen received an undergraduate degree in economics from Carleton College and then took a PhD in philosophy at Yale. But his disposition and his unorthodox economic theories kept him moving from one academic position to another. In 1919, he helped develop the now famous New School for Social Research in New York City. Besides The Theory of the Leisure Class, *he published more than ten books and many articles.*

Many social leaders in New York and other large cities—people who demand and have the best of everything—are users of **Columbia** Electric Broughams, Landaus, Landaulets, Hansoms, Coupés, Victoria-Phaëtons and Opera Busses. These vehicles are built from exclusive designs, and are sold for private service only. Let us send you a handsomely printed list of prominent purchasers and our special Town Carriage Catalogue.

ELECTRIC VEHICLE CO., Hartford, Conn.

NEW YORK
134-138 West 39th St.

CHICAGO
1413 Michigan Ave.

BOSTON
74 Stanhope St.

*Member Association of Licensed
Automobile Manufacturers*

A 1904 advertisement promoting a luxury car.   The Granger Collection, New York.

COURTNEY POMEROY (STUDENT ESSAY)

The Ethics of What We Wear: Can We Dress Fashionably and Responsibly?

[THE DIAMONDBACK, University of Maryland/December 5, 2007]

Before You Read

Does shopping for clothing have an ethical component? Do you think that corporations generally value profitability over humanity? Are college students apathetic about such issues, or are they engaged with them?

Words to Learn

array (para. 1): an order or arrangement (n.)
linguistics (para. 3): the science or study of the nature of language (n.)
kinesiology (para. 4): the study of the anatomy, physiology, or mechanics of body movements, especially in humans (n.)
aforementioned (para. 5): mentioned or cited previously (adj.)

Courtney Pomeroy is a senior at the University of Maryland, College Park, where she is pursuing a degree in journalism. As a columnist and staff writer, Pomeroy contributes regularly to the Diamondback, *the school's daily student newspaper, and is interested in exploring fashion and entertainment in her writing: "As a fashion columnist I love writing about clothes and accessories but I also enjoy writing about fashion in relation to society." In her essay "The Ethics of What We Wear: Can We Dress Fashionably and Responsibly?" Pomeroy takes a closer look at the role of sweatshop labor in many of today's brand-name clothing companies. After reading a newspaper article about Gap, she wanted "to get the word out about how we take advantage of our favorite clothing stores without thinking about where our pair of jeans or sweater actually came from."*

Upon entering a Gap this season, shoppers will probably see col-   1
orful arrays of wool sweaters, pictures on the walls of stars such as
Amy Poehler and John Mayer, and smiles on the faces of the friendly
workers. But under the $60 jeans, sweater sets, and chino pants,
there lies a dirty secret. In late October, a British newspaper alleged
that Gap Inc. was using child labor in one of its factories in India. According to reports, the children found working in the factory were
confined in dirty rooms with little light and were even occasionally
beaten and stripped of pay.

Although Gap responded by saying it was glad the factory had   2
been brought to its attention, the corporation has been fighting alle-
gations and lawsuits for years about unsatisfactory factory conditions
in various cheap-labor countries around the world.

And Gap isn't the only one—trendy chain Urban Outfitters   3
openly uses non-union factories, and back in the States, the corporate
paychecks get fatter by the minute. "Profits are valued, not people's
lives," said Daniela Vann, a senior government and politics major
and member of Feminism Without Borders, the student group that
protests university gear being produced in factories with inhumane
working conditions. Amnesty International at Maryland president
and senior linguistics major Rachel Davis agrees. "I think [those com-
panies] should treat everyone else like they would treat Americans,"
she said. "It makes me really sad and it makes me upset, because of
course people love Gap clothes. They're going to say 'It's wrong!',
but they're still going to buy those chinos."

Other university students agreed with Davis, saying that because   4
these issues take place overseas, many students don't pay attention.
Junior kinesiology major Randi Baker said the issue "is definitely not
public enough." Junior hearing and speech sciences major Jill Toline
added that while she shops at some stores that use laborers working
in poor conditions, it makes her "pretty uncomfortable." "I try my
best to shop more often in stores that publicize the fact that they do
not utilize sweatshops, such as American Apparel," she said.

But some students said they aren't aware of what to look for   5
when recognizing companies that use cheap labor. And even those
more aware are correct in assuming exactly what junior elementary
education major Robyn Williams did: "I would imagine it would be
pretty difficult to find clothes that don't violate somebody's rights,"
she said. Case in point: Even the aforementioned American Apparel
has faced accusations of being anti-union and sexually abusive toward female workers.

With hope, sometime in the near future students will be able to get their trendy, brand-name gear from companies that value humanity more than cheaply made goods.

The only suggestions Vann has—for now—is to buy clothes second-hand or visit websites such as www.nosweatapparel.com, which even she admits is impractical because many people don't like to buy unfamiliar brands online. With hope, sometime in the near future students will be able to get their trendy, brand-name gear from companies that value humanity more than cheaply made goods. But the vicious cycle that takes place amongst consumers—whether it results from apathy, ignorance, misinformation or convenience—hints that we will continue to give our money to any company that offers us stylish threads while keeping its abuse of workers on the down-low.

Vocabulary / Using a Dictionary

1.   What are the origins of the word *corporation* (para. 2), and how does that origin connect to its modern meaning? What other words are related to it?

2.   What does the word *inhumane* (para. 3) mean, and how does its prefix function?

3.   What is the origin of the word *apathy* (para. 6), and what words share the same root?

Responding to Words in Context

1.   What is "cheap-labor"? What are "cheap-labor countries" (para. 2)?

2.   What is the connotation of the word *laborer* (para. 4)?

3.   In her essay, Pomeroy uses the word *trendy* twice. What associations does that word have, and how does it function in her essay?

Discussing Main Point and Meaning

1.   Pomeroy opens her essay with a vivid description of a Gap store. What contrast does she highlight? How is it sustained throughout the rest of the essay?

2. Pomeroy describes several corporations in her essay. Why do you think she chooses these companies? What image of them emerges? Do you agree with it?

3. The title of the essay asks, "Can we dress fashionably and responsibly?" What are the problems with trying to formulate an "ethics of what we wear"?

Examining Sentences, Paragraphs, and Organization

1. What are Pomeroy's style, point of view, and approach to the subject? Objective? Personal? Journalistic? Academic?

2. Several people are quoted in Pomeroy's essay. How are the quotations used? What image of college students emerges from them?

3. How would you explain or describe the overall organization of the essay? Is it effective?

Thinking Critically

1. Pomeroy cites an activist who claims, "Profits are valued, not people's lives" (para. 3). Do you see these two values as antagonistic or even mutually exclusive? Can they be reconciled? How do you weigh their relative importance, both in your thinking and in your day-to-day behavior?

2. According to one person interviewed in the story, many consumers are aware of the ethical implications of their buying habits but do not act on them: "It makes me really sad and it makes me upset, because of course people love Gap clothes. They're going to say 'It's wrong!', but they're still going to buy those chinos" (para. 3). What process is she describing? Do you ever do this?

3. Although American Apparel has tried to brand itself as an ethical corporation, Pomeroy reports that it "has faced accusations of being anti-union and sexually abusive toward female workers" (para. 5). What is a union? Do you think unions are important? How does society view them?

In-Class Writing Activities

1. This essay is called, in part, "The Ethics of What We Wear." What does the word *ethics* imply in this context? Do you think of consumption as having an ethical component, hidden or other-

wise? What about other activities? Write an essay using the formula of Pomeroy's title, but replacing the words "What We Wear" with some other activity or subject of your choice. Try to uncover and articulate its ethical aspects.

2. Essentially, all the voices and sources in Pomeroy's essay support one particular point of view about corporations and consumer habits. Can you find other credible authorities, arguments, or evidence to challenge that position? You may respond to specific aspects of her argument, or the article as a whole.

3. Near the end of the essay, Pomeroy says, "With hope, sometime in the near future students will be able to get their trendy, brand-name gear from companies that value humanity more than cheaply made goods" (para. 6). Are you hopeful about this? Do you think student consumers will behave ethically if given the information and choice to do so? Is it an issue that resonates with you? Will you reconsider your consumer habits because of this article? Why or why not?

ANNOTATION Integrating Quotations

Two types of quotations are routinely seen in nonfiction. One type, more common in essays and criticism, is the use of a famous or previously published quote. For example, a writer might begin an essay: "As Franklin D. Roosevelt once said, 'We have nothing to fear but fear itself.'" A book like Bartlett's *Familiar Quotations* is a rich source of memorable quotes and has been used by several generations of writers, artists, celebrities, and political figures. More commonly seen in journalism, however, are the quotations gathered from live interviews. In writing news or feature stories, the journalist usually needs to collect interviews from a number of people—experts, eyewitnesses, accident victims, and so on—who will have something relevant to say about a topic. But gathering the interviews is only one part of the process. The writer then needs to integrate the quotations so that they work effectively within the body of the essay.

In "The Ethics of What We Wear: Can We Dress Fashionably and Responsibly?" University of Maryland columnist Courtney Pomeroy interviewed five students with various opinions on the issue of the ethical consumption of clothing. She arranges the student quotations effectively by opening with a general statement from a campus activist and then following it up with remarks by other students who suggest the difficulties of reform: Even though consumers may be concerned and uncomfortable purchasing from certain shops, they will most likely continue to do so. Note how Pomeroy skillfully integrates the quotations from separate interviews so that they cover the major questions surrounding the issue and dramatize the impact of the issue on a particular college campus. The quotations form the body of the essay, and the fact that all are from students enhances the essay's credibility and relevance.

Two quotations establish the issue.

And Gap isn't the only one—trendy chain Urban Outfitters openly uses non-union factories, and back in the States, the corporate paychecks get fatter by the minute. "Profits are valued, not people's lives," said Daniela Vann, a senior government and politics major and member of Feminism Without Borders, the student group that protests university gear being produced in factories with inhumane working conditions. Amnesty International at Maryland president and senior linguistics major Rachel Davis agrees. "I think [those companies] should treat everyone else like they would treat Americans," she said. "It makes me really sad and it makes me upset, because of course people love Gap clothes. They're going to say 'It's wrong!', but they're still going to buy those chinos."

Two more quotations pick up on the difficulties involved despite the students' concern.

Other university students agreed with Davis, saying that because these issues take place overseas, many students don't pay attention. Junior kinesiology major Randi Baker said the issue "is definitely not public enough." Junior hearing and speech sciences major Jill Toline added that while she shops at some stores that use laborers working in poor conditions, it makes her "pretty uncomfortable." "I try my best to shop more often in stores that publicize the fact that they do not utilize sweatshops, such as American Apparel," she said.

Another student quotation summarizes an important factor.

But some students said they aren't aware of what to look for when recognizing companies that use cheap labor. And even those more aware are correct in assuming exactly what junior elementary education major Robyn Williams did: "I would imagine it would be pretty difficult to find clothes that don't violate somebody's rights," she said. Case in point: Even the aforementioned American Apparel has faced accusations of being anti-union and sexually abusive toward female workers.

—From "The Ethics of What We Wear: Can We Dress Fashionably and Responsibly?" by Courtney Pomeroy, page 195

Student Writer at Work: Courtney Pomeroy

On Writing "The Ethics of What We Wear: Can We Dress Fashionably and Responsibly?"

Q: What inspired you to write "The Ethics of What We Wear: Can We Dress Fashionably and Responsibly?"

A: I am a fashion columnist at the *Diamondback*, and this issue was something that I had wanted to write about for a long time. As a fashion columnist, I love writing about clothes and accessories, but I also enjoy writing about fashion in relation to society. A newspaper article I read inspired me to do more research, and the article was a result of my findings. I wanted to get the word out about how we take advantage of our favorite clothing stores without thinking about where our pair of jeans or sweater actually comes from.

Q: Tell us about your process for writing and revising this piece.

A: It took me about two weeks to write "The Ethics of What We Wear: Can We Dress Fashionably and Responsibly?" I revised my work several times, creating four drafts. The goals as I revised were to make my ideas flow and to create a clear opinion. I read my final draft out loud to my roommate just to make sure there were no typos or oddly worded sentences before turning it in, but I don't usually show my work to a lot of people before it is published.

Q: What advice do you have for other student writers?

A: Concentrate on writing about what you love or what interests you most. If you are passionate about the subject matter, your writing will automatically improve.

Discussing the Unit

Suggested Topic for Discussion

Near the end of her essay, Dana Thomas proposes that "awareness is key" when choosing to buy brand-name items that might be counterfeit. Courtney Pomeroy also suggests that an increased awareness of the link between cheap, appealing products and child labor will make people more ethical consumers. The implicit presumption is that, given correct and thorough information, buyers will behave more conscientiously and responsibly. Is this generally true? Do you think most consumers—or even a significant number—will make choices against their own immediate economic interests, desires, or convenience in favor of a more abstract ethical principle?

Preparing for Class Discussion

1. Ehrenreich's immediate subject is child labor, as well as the behavior of large corporations such as Gap. Yet there's clearly a much broader subtext to—and context for—her essay, especially at moments like the one in her conclusion, where she writes, "In a nation that cannot bring itself to extend child health insurance to all children in need, child-made clothes make a fine fashion statement." Do the wider implications of her argument make it more effective for you? Does she risk detracting from her primary point by doing this? How would you compare her piece to other readings in the unit? What sense of her audience do you get from her essay?

2. In "The Fake Trade," Thomas writes that "we still think of counterfeiting as a 'victimless crime'" (para. 7). Her essay, however, demonstrates that it is not. Do you ever hear this defense of behavior? Have you ever used it yourself? Can you think of examples of other supposedly "victimless crimes" that actually have victims or moral consequences? Conversely, are there activities or behaviors that you truly believe are "victimless," even if society or the legal system doesn't see them that way?

From Discussion to Writing

1. In "Slaves for Fashion," Ehrenreich quotes "conservative pundit" William Kristol: "Whenever I hear anything described as a heartless assault on our children, I tend to think it's a good idea" (para. 9). Specifically, he was referring to President George W. Bush's decision to veto expansion of federal healthcare coverage for children. As Ehrenreich does throughout "Slaves for Fashion," Kristol is using irony in the quotation—he may not literally mean what he says. Jim Hightower's essay also uses irony at certain points, which contrasts with the more sincere styles of Pomeroy and Thomas. Where else do you see such irony at work

in the essays? Do you think irony is rhetorically effective or appropriate for "serious" issues? What are the risks of being ironic? Does this approach appeal to you as a reader or writer? What other examples can you think of? Write a brief essay—ironic, if you choose—on the subject of irony.

2. Several of these writers consider the practice of corporate public relations—for example, when such companies are dealing with accusations about factory conditions. What is public relations? How do you see it functioning in our society? Does the term have any connotations for you—positive, negative, or otherwise? Ehrenreich ironically asks the reader to look at child labor "not as a human rights issue but as a PR disaster" (para. 2). Can you think of other "PR disasters"?

Topics for Cross-Cultural Discussion

1. Brands and brand identities play an important role in several of these essays. There seems to be a cultural component to brand identity, as when Pomeroy refers to the photos of "stars such as Amy Poehler and John Mayer" on the walls of the Gap store, or when Thomas describes the "all-American" girl with the "blonde blunt cut" carrying the counterfeit Louis Vuitton handbag. In fact, the world of advertising and marketing even has a term for such cultures and communities: "brand tribes." Are you a member of such a tribe? Where does the "meaning" of a specific brand come from? Do particular brands have associations with certain ethnic, racial, national, or social groups? How does this happen?

2. The articles in this unit all seem to touch upon the ethics of supply-and-demand economies—and these economies have cross-cultural implications. How do you apportion moral or ethical responsibility across those lines? What view of this do the writers of these essays take? For example, do you think the women buying counterfeit bags in Thomas's article are as morally culpable as those who rely on such underground or illicit economies to earn a living? If factories that use child labor are shut down, thereby eliminating jobs and wages for their employees, should that be an ethical consideration? Why or why not?

6

Redesigning Humanity — What Are the Limits?

In 2001, Erik Weihenmayer became the first blind person to climb Mount Everest, overcoming what would seem like an insurmountable obstacle. But, as he later wrote in *Time* magazine, critics immediately attempted to detract from his achievement. Some even cited his blindness as an unfair advantage: "I'd climb Mount Everest too if I couldn't see how far I had to fall," one said.

The line between a disability and an advantage can be fuzzier than it appears at first glance, especially when modern medicine and technology enter the equation. Consider the case of Oscar Pistorius, a South African double-leg amputee who, with the aid of two high-tech "Cheetah" prosthetics, has established himself as a formidable contender in the field of long-distance running. But are Pistorius's replacement legs, which are not subject to the fatigue that other runners experience, an unfair aid in competition? Is a sport still a sport if technology can supplement competitors' natural abilities?

In her column "Remanufacturing Athletes," Ellen Goodman argues that the race is still to the swift if he or she is running on carbon fiber legs. Analyzing the examples of a wheelchair-bound marathon runner, golf legend Tiger Woods's Lasik vision surgery, and home-run king Barry Bonds's alleged steroid use, Goodman concludes that not all efforts to improve one's abilities are unfair—after all, "technology has been used to enhance performance since the first runner put on a shoe."

Goodman does single out as unreasonable a beauty pageant in which contestants were surgically altered. "They didn't owe their beauty to their maker," she writes, "but, rather, to their remaker." But one suspects that she would not discredit the appearance of "paralympic athlete" Aimee Mullins whose prosthetic legs are fashionably (and some might say provocatively) displayed in a photograph that played a key role in the 2008 Kenneth Cole advertising campaign, "We All Walk in Different Shoes."

Cosmetic surgery, however, raises difficult questions about what we admire and how we're willing to alter ourselves to achieve that admiration. University of Florida student Rebecca Ganzak attacks the problem in her essay "Is Cosmetic Surgery Worth the Risk?" Focusing on young people who seek to add to or subtract from their bodies surgically, Ganzak contends that not only is it unethical to encourage teenagers to obsess over their physical characteristics, but also it's dangerous. Ganzak writes that even though she sought out surgery to improve the look of her nose, "I soon changed my mind after I researched the pain and cost involved—and saw a few graphic episodes of *Dr. 90210*."

The larger problem both essays address, however, is the ethics of altering people to perform, look, or behave better. Is living as we were born—whether with a hooked nose or a crippling disease—an act of deference to what nature intended, or a failure to avail ourselves of the miracles of modern science? Philosopher Michael Sandel addresses perhaps the most challenging corner of this issue: genetic engineering, or manipulating and cherry-picking genetic code in order to alter human characteristics. In "Designer Babies: The Problem with Genetic Engineering," Sandel compares the modern use of genetic screening to the ugly practice of eugenics, in which people whom an authoritarian state deems undesirable are sterilized or forbidden to breed. There's something awry, he argues, with this practice besides its being involuntary: "What's wrong with eugenics, beyond coercion, is the fact of its ambition to try to control or exercise dominion over the genetic traits of the next generation."

Sandel sees this same problem in the contemporary practice of genetic engineering. "The drive to create children of a certain character," he writes, "reflects an aspiration . . . to exercise our human will and our ability to remake human nature to serve our purposes and satisfy our desires." Meanwhile, "to appreciate children as gifts is to accept them as they come." Advocates of genetic engineering, of course, argue that parents can use it to give their children a competitive edge, or even to eradicate destructive diseases. In this argument Sandel sees the deep flaws of a society obsessed with perfection—flaws that could explode with increased control over who we are. "If genetic engineering enabled us to override the results of the genetic lottery, if it enabled us to replace chance with choice, it's likely that the gifted character of human powers and achievements would recede, and with it, perhaps, our capacity to see ourselves as sharing a common fate." Indeed, in an age of Ritalin, voluntary surgery, and medical technology that grows exponentially, are we still who we are?

ELLEN GOODMAN

Remanufacturing Athletes

[BOSTON GLOBE/May 25, 2007]

Before You Read

Should an athlete's disability be addressed or "fixed" so that the disabled athlete can compete with nondisabled athletes? What problems are then created for the world of athletics? Should such athletes compete only with others who share the disability in order to avoid these problems?

Ellen Goodman is a well-known columnist, author, and speaker. After graduating cum laude from Radcliffe College in 1963 with a degree in modern European history, Goodman went on to work for Newsweek *magazine as a researcher and later for the* Detroit Free Press *and the* Boston Globe. *She has been an associate editor with the* Boston Globe *since 1967, and her syndicated column appears in more than 450 newspapers. In 1980, Goodman was the first journalist to be awarded the Pulitzer Prize for Distinguished Commentary. She has published several collections of her columns as well as other books, including* Turning Points *(1979) and* I Know Just What You Mean: The Power of Friendship in Women's Lives *(2000).*

Words to Learn

bane (para. 7): curse (n.)

testosterone (para. 7): male hormone (n.)

duffer (para. 8): a mediocre golfer (n.)

simulate (para. 9): to give the appearance of (v.)

implanted (para. 11): inserted (v.)

ethicist (para. 12): a specialist in ethics (n.)

titanium (para. 14): a hard metallic element (n.)

bionic (para. 14): superhuman; having been enhanced through technology (n.)

Olympiad (para. 14): the Olympic Games (n.)

prostheses (para. 15): devices used as replacements for human limbs (n.)

prohibited (para. 15): forbidden (v.)

As someone who lives just a few hundred paces from the Boston Marathon course, I've cheered my share of athletes. This year, it was Masazumi Soejima at the head of the pack, propelling his wheelchair across a rainy 26 miles in 1 hour, 29 minutes and 16 seconds. It took Robert Cheruiyot an extra 44 minutes and 57 seconds to come in first on foot.   1

I take nothing away from the athleticism and grit of Soejima. But it goes without saying that he didn't "beat" Cheruiyot. Those who compete on foot and those who compete with wheels are categorically different. And succeed in different categories.   2

I make this point because of the controversy surrounding a 20-year-old South African named Oscar Pistorius. This racing phenom recently won the 100- and 200-meter races in an international competition for disabled athletes. He won on a pair of J-shaped carbon fiber blades known as Cheetahs.   3

Pistorius calls himself "the fastest man on no legs." He was born with defects in his feet and his lower legs were amputated when he was 11 months old. Nevertheless, he says, "I don't see myself as disabled." He wants to be allowed to race for the Olympic gold on his own two Cheetahs.   4

Exactly what kind of technology, training, or performance enhancements should we applaud? And what kind should we reject?

This is one of those stories tailor-made for the Olympics coverage: A great athlete overcomes enormous adversity to pursue his dream! But it's also one of the other stories now stalking sports: Exactly what kind of   5

Oscar Pistorius competing in
the men's 200-meter race at the
Paralympic World Cup.   Andrew
Yates/AFP/Getty Images.

technology, training, or performance enhancements should we applaud? And what kind should we reject?

This conversation seems to be as common as box scores and dop-   6
ing scandals. On the baseball field, Barry Bonds is creeping up on
Hank Aaron's home run record. But there is no joy in Mudville.
Bonds's achievement is tainted by the belief that he used steroids to
beef up his body and his record.

In cycling, where doping is the bane of the Tour de France, Floyd   7
Landis's inspiring win turned sour with lab reports of testosterone
shots. He is still fighting for his crown and his reputation.

Those who oppose Pistorius compare his Cheetahs to "techno-   8
doping." But it is also true that technology has been used to enhance

performance since the first runner put on a shoe and this duffer put Big Bertha in her golf bag.

Training has reached a level of technical sophistication unheard   9
of when Roger Bannister broke the four-minute mile. Athletes train in wind tunnels and travel to high altitudes. But the use of altitude tents to simulate that "high" has been decried as violating the "spirit of the sport."

And what are we to make of Lasik surgery that gave the near-   10
sighted Tiger Woods his 20/15 vision and four straight championships right afterward? Is better-than-perfect vision a kind of enhancement like doping or a correction like contact lenses?

Some years ago, I questioned a beauty pageant in which the con-   11
testants had been surgically altered and implanted. They didn't owe their beauty to their maker but, rather, to their remaker.

Similar questions about the remanufacture of athletes, says ethi-   12
cist Tom Murray, "force us to ask what is the point of sports. Whatever we think is meaningful and beautiful about sports has to do with the ways we admire natural talents and hard work and dedication."

But there are other things we don't admire. "I can climb the   13
mountains of the Tour de France faster than all the other competitors," quips Murray. "All I need is a motor."

Today, we replace hips and knees with titanium. We replace thy-   14
roids with pills. NBC is remaking the *Bionic Woman* series for a new run, and ethicists are debating the possibility of real bionic athletes. Michael Sandel, author of *The Case Against Perfection*, warns that "part of what we admire about great athletes is that we are able to see ourselves in their human achievements." Who would applaud the bionic Olympiad?

As for Pistorius and prostheses? So far, the International Associa-   15
tion of Athletics Federations has prohibited him from the Olympics. The final decision won't come till August.

But what makes his challenge so compelling is not just his ex-   16
traordinary courage and talent. His prostheses both enable a disabled man and offer an athlete high-tech equipment. They land somewhere between a sophisticated running shoe and a motor.

I don't think that Cheetahs are cheating. And I am uncomfort-   17
able with the talk of cyborgs and transhumans that surrounds this case. These stories will get harder, not easier, over the next years.

But as a fan of Masazumi Soejima, I don't think that racing on a   18
separate track is an insult. It's still the right place for the "fastest man on no legs."

Vocabulary/Using a Dictionary

1. This essay is titled "Remanufacturing Athletes." What does it mean to *manufacture* and *remanufacture* something?

2. What word is *phenom* (para. 3) short for? What is implied by calling someone a *phenom*?

3. What is a *cyborg* (para. 17) or *transhuman* (para. 17)? In what context would you expect to hear such terms?

Responding to Words in Context

1. Goodman begins her essay with a description of the Boston Marathon. What is the origin of the word *marathon*? How was the first marathon different from the one she is describing?

2. The term *performance enhancement* can be seen in either a positive or a negative light, depending on context. What is the meaning of *enhancement*? What does it mean to *enhance* one's performance in sports?

3. Why do you think the name of Pistorius's enhancement—his Cheetahs—is so important that Goodman brings it up on at least four separate occasions in the essay?

Discussing Main Point and Meaning

1. Goodman asks what we are to make of "Lasik surgery that gave the near-sighted Tiger Woods his 20/15 vision and four straight championships right afterward" (para. 10). Do you think Woods's victories should be called into question based on his surgery?

2. Allowing Pistorius to compete with "abled" athletes would add to the swirling controversy surrounding other enhancements in sports, according to Goodman. How is the use of Pistorius's Cheetahs similar to Barry Bonds's alleged use of steroids? Explain.

3. Goodman states, "I don't think that racing on a separate track is an insult" (para. 18) for Masazumi Soejima. Do you agree with her argument that separating athletes according to their physical ability can also be equal, or do you think it is an insult to tell an athlete he must compete separately?

Examining Sentences, Paragraphs, and Organization

1. Pistorius is described as wanting the chance to compete in the Olympics "on his own two Cheetahs" (para. 4). Why doesn't Goodman say "on his own two feet"?

2. Tour de France winner Floyd Landis is used as an example of the controversy surrounding sports and possible enhancements. Goodman notes, "He is still fighting for his crown and reputation" (para. 7). Why is Landis's case less clear-cut than some of his contemporaries?

3. In paragraph 11, Goodman mentions a beauty pageant whose contestants she discounts based on their use of plastic surgery. How can plastic surgery be compared with something like Soejima's wheelchair or Pistorius's Cheetahs?

Thinking Critically

1. Goodman makes the case that performance enhancements and breakthroughs in technology allow some athletes to overcome adversity and pursue their dreams of competing with others in the Olympics and other great sports events. Then she points out how such breakthroughs and enhancements can be used to lessen the achievements of athletes. Which argument do you find most compelling?

2. Athletes have trained to become faster and better than their competitors since the beginning of time — they want to win. Goodman questions the fairness of some athletes' advantages over others. What does it mean for an athlete to have an advantage over another in a sports event? Which advantages are acceptable, or fair, and which are not?

3. Goodman takes joy in watching athletes compete whether they are disabled or not. Her question explores what enhancements should be allowed in sports and who (using an enhancement or not) should compete with whom. In what areas other than sports might people suffer from a disability? What enhancements are available beyond sports to allow people to compete with one another?

In-Class Writing Activities

1. Goodman's essay includes a wealth of stories about athletes whom she respects, and some for whom she has lost esteem. Research

one of the athletes mentioned and write an essay in which you argue for or against the athlete's use of a performance enhancer in competition. Consider whether you think the enhancement provides the athlete with an advantage in a sports event.

2. Even though Masazumi Soejima (in his wheelchair) beat Robert Cheruiyot's time by 44 minutes and 57 seconds, Goodman claims that Soejima did not "win" the race, but both men competed in the same event on the same track. Why might a disabled athlete prefer to compete on the same field or track as "abled" athletes? Are there situations in which a disabled athlete would choose a different course? Write an essay explaining why a disabled athlete might or might not prefer to use the same equipment, run the same miles, or perform in the same arenas as other athletes.

3. The Olympic Games began in ancient Greece and have continued to be a popular event in modern times. Research the beginning of the Olympics and consider any differences between the games then and the games today. Write a brief essay that compares and contrasts any aspects of the Olympics that you may have watched on television with the Olympics of ancient times.

KENNETH COLE

We All Walk in Different Shoes

[VOGUE / March 2008]

Before You View

How do we see and imagine people with disabilities? Do technological advances in the treatment of the disabled change our view of humanity? Do you identify with certain brands? Do you see them as linked to your own identity?

Under the slogan "We All Walk in Different Shoes," Kenneth Cole's spring 2008 advertising campaign features a series of ten ads, which appeared in national magazines such as Vogue, Vanity Fair, Lucky, GQ, *and* Men's Health *and on billboards in New York City. Incorporating a diverse collection of people—including a Paralympic athlete, an undocumented immigrant, and a married lesbian couple and their daughter—the campaign celebrates "25 years of non-uniform thinking," as the designer himself is well known for his humanitarian and philanthropic efforts. The official Kenneth Cole Web site states, "Appearance can be a defining characteristic for us all but it's the ability to think differently that really makes a difference. Join us to celebrate those non-uniform thinkers who have the courage to truly be who they are."*

WE ALL
WALK IN
DIFFERENT
SHOES.

AIMEE MULLINS.
PARALYMPIC ATHLETE, ACTOR,
AND PRESIDENT OF THE WOMEN'S
SPORTS FOUNDATION.

KENNETHCOLE.COM
25 YEARS OF
NON-UNIFORM
THINKING.

Discussing Main Point and Meaning

1. The textual focal point of this advertisement is the slogan "We all walk in different shoes." What do these words mean or suggest in the context of the ad? How do they resonate with other familiar sayings?

2. The ad implies that clothing is an expression or representation of personal identity. Do you agree with this? Do you see your own clothing in this way? Is your sense of identity connected with the brands of clothing you choose?

3. The advertisement has no direct textual indication that Aimee Mullins wears prosthetic limbs, other than the description of her as a "Paralympic athlete." What effect does that have? How does this ad play off common perceptions of people with disabilities?

Examining Details, Imagery, and Design

1. Magazine advertisements frequently present provocative photographs of women, as this one does. How would you characterize Mullins's pose? What does it have to do with the message of the ad?

2. Describe the typeface used in the ad. What message does it convey, and what connotations does it have?

3. The ad copy uses these descriptors: "Aimee Mullins. Paralympic athlete, actor, and president of the Women's Sports Foundation." Why do you think the descriptors are in this order?

Thinking Critically

1. The ad emphasizes difference and individuality and suggests a brand identification with "25 years of non-uniform thinking." Is there anything paradoxical or contradictory about this message in the context of this advertisement, and advertising in general?

2. What was your reaction when you first viewed the ad? Did you immediately notice that the model has prosthetic legs? Did you determine this fact from the picture, or from the advertising copy? Was it immediately clear what product was being advertised?

3. Does this advertisement appeal to you? Do you find it evocative, persuasive, and effective? Do you find it exploitative or misleading in any way?

In-Class Writing Activities

1. How would you design an effective advertising campaign that used the theme of "difference" or "individuality"? What kind of language would you use? What kind of images, ideas, and cultural touchstones would you highlight? Who would your audience be? Pick a product and sketch or describe your advertisement for it. Then, explain the similarities between creating such an ad, on the one hand, and writing a persuasive essay, creating a drawing or painting, or producing a piece of fiction or poetry, on the other hand.

2. The Kenneth Cole ad does not say directly that Mullins has a disability. Instead, it refers to her being a "Paralympic athlete," which means that she participated in the Paralympics, an elite, international sporting event for the disabled. Many different terms and types of language have been used to describe people with disabilities: "crippled," "disabled," "differently abled," "handicapped," and so on. What different meanings, purposes, and connotations do these terms have? Why are some better than others? Who should decide what terms we use?

3. For these questions and exercises, you've been asked to read, think, and write about advertising. Do you think prominent ads and ad campaigns are worthy of the same intellectual scrutiny and analysis as, say, novels, poetry, philosophy, film, great art, or historical events? Or is advertising ultimately trivial? Explain your answer.

REBECCA GANZAK (STUDENT ESSAY)

Is Cosmetic Surgery Worth the Risk?

[THE ALLIGATOR, University of Florida / March 27, 2008]

Before You Read

Have you ever considered getting cosmetic surgery, or do you know anyone who has gotten it? Do you think it has become too prevalent? Are you aware of the risks associated with anesthesia?

Words to Learn

anesthesia (para. 1): a partial or total lack of sensation during medical or surgical procedures (n.)

augmentation (para. 1): the act of making larger or increasing (n.)

protrude (para. 5): to project, swell, or stick out (v.)

What would you be willing to risk for a slimmer nose? A bustier chest? Some people will dip into their life savings, spending up to $10,000 on a nose job. Others will go so far as to take a second job or apply for a loan to fund corrective surgery. You probably won't catch anyone admitting they would risk their life, however. But plastic surgery, like any procedure that uses anesthesia, can be fatal. This proved true for South Florida teenager Stephanie Kuleba, who died in March of 2008 — 24 hours after her corrective breast augmentation

1

Rebecca Ganzak is a recent graduate of the University of Florida with a degree in journalism. Interested in music and fashion, Ganzak supplements her writing by reading a variety of magazines, including Elle, Nylon, AP, *and* Vogue. *Although her essay "Is Cosmetic Surgery Worth the Risk?" first appeared in the school publication, the* Alligator, *Ganzak hopes one day to own and operate her own magazine. Her advice to other student writers is to "save everything you write, even if it isn't published . . . don't stop writing, and get published!"*

surgery—of malignant hyperthermia, an increase in the body temperature that can be brought on by anesthesia.

And yet cosmetic surgeons in Florida say they are seeing more   2
teenagers for plastic surgery than ever before. In 2005, more than 3,500 girls under the age of 18 had breast implants. I attribute this trend to celebrities and pop culture influencing the youth of America to think that corrective surgery is acceptable. If no one in Hollywood has a hooked nose, then why should a young girl find hers attractive? In 2004, more than 326,000 boys and girls under 18 had corrective surgery to fix something that made them self-conscious, according to the American Society of Plastic Surgeons.

But why do common teenage issues like body image and self-   3
esteem result in the drastic measure of going under the knife? When I am a parent, if my 18-year-old daughter tells me that she wants larger breasts or a straighter nose, I plan to kindly inform her that appearance isn't everything. And that I'm not paying for it.

> *There is plenty more that parents can offer their children than a swipe of a credit card and an introduction to their city's best plastic surgeon.*

There is plenty more that parents can   4
offer their children than a swipe of a credit card and an introduction to their city's best plastic surgeon. As expensive as it may be, parents are using this method of correction as a way to avoid actually being a parent. Moreover, despite the popularity of breast augmentation, it has a high rate of complication and often requires additional surgery within five to ten years of the original procedure. The same goes for nose jobs.

So why would parents willingly put their children through such a   5
risk? I guarantee once the teen is done obsessing over one flaw, he or she will move to another. Soon, earlobes protrude too much or calves are too little. When I was a freshman in high school, I wanted a nose job. After breaking my nose several times, the rather large bump that developed was not something I enjoyed seeing in the mirror every day. But I soon changed my mind after I researched the pain and cost involved—and saw a few graphic episodes of *Dr. 90210*.

I have been put under anesthesia before, so that thought didn't   6
scare me. However, I didn't stop to consider that the chance of death due to anesthesia is pretty common, about one in 200,000, according to studies done in 2004. And that doesn't include cases where anesthesia was a secondary or contributing factor in a patient's death. According to the *New York Times*, the agreement among surgeons is

that the risk is much higher for elderly or very sick patients, or those with certain medical conditions that are often easy to miss. Such was the case for 18-year-old Kuleba, who was, sadly, preparing to attend the University of Florida.

So if anesthesia can have this effect on anyone, why are people signing up for the unnecessary risk? If you're going to die from a surgical procedure, it had better be one that is intended to save your life in the first place.   7

Vocabulary / Using a Dictionary

1. What is the origin of the word *celebrities* (para. 2), and when did it take on the meaning it most commonly has today?

2. Where does the word *malignant* (para. 1) come from, and what other words are related to it?

3. What's the difference between *hyperthermia* (para. 1) and *hypothermia*? What is the origin of the prefixes of those words?

Responding to Words in Context

1. Ganzak uses the terms *corrective* and *cosmetic* to refer to certain medical procedures and the doctors who perform them. What is the difference between those two words?

2. According to Ganzak, one of the reasons she changed her mind about getting surgery was that she saw "graphic episodes" of a television show (para. 5). In this context, what does *graphic* mean?

3. How is the word *plastic* used in this essay? What connotations does it have?

Discussing Main Point and Meaning

1. Why, according to Ganzak, are young people and teenagers getting corrective and cosmetic surgery, regardless of its risks?

2. In paragraph 4, Ganzak writes, "There is plenty more that parents can offer their children than a swipe of a credit card and an introduction to their city's best plastic surgeon." What do you think she means? What role do parents seem to be playing in the trend toward more corrective procedures in teens?

3. Ganzak thinks that elective cosmetic surgery for teenagers is generally a bad idea. What is her main objection to it?

Examining Sentences, Paragraphs, and Organization

1. How does Ganzak use rhetorical questions to structure her essay? Are they effective?

2. Ganzak incorporates her own experience of deliberating whether to get plastic surgery. Where does she do this? Does it help her argument?

3. At various points in the essay, Ganzak cites statistics. Does she incorporate them well? How does she use them to support her case? Could they be made stronger?

Thinking Critically

1. With no qualifications, Ganzak attributes the prevalence of procedures like breast augmentation to "celebrities and pop culture influencing the youth of America to think that corrective surgery is acceptable" (para. 2). How influential are pop culture and the appearances of celebrities? Can you think of any other factors or cultural trends that might lead to wider acceptance of cosmetic surgery?

2. What view of the current generation of teens (and their parents) comes across in Ganzak's essay? Do you think it's accurate?

3. Ganzak writes, "I guarantee once the teen is done obsessing over one flaw, he or she will move to another" (para. 5). What is she referring to? Why is it important for her argument?

In-Class Writing Activities

1. Ganzak writes that her nose was broken several times and that she did not enjoy "seeing [its bump] in the mirror every day" (para. 5). Is there a specific body part or aspect of your physique that makes you self-conscious or that you especially dislike? Would you consider getting elective cosmetic surgery to change it? Why or why not? Write an essay explaining your view.

2. In paragraph 3, Ganzak claims that she would tell her hypothetical daughter that "appearance isn't everything." Overstatement

aside, do you agree? How important is physical appearance in our culture? Could you make an argument that Ganzak implicitly understates its value and significance? Does society give mixed signals about its importance? If looking more attractive correlates to finding a better job, making more money, or attracting a more appealing romantic partner, might the surgical risk be worth it?

3. Although Ganzak notes that in 2004 "more than 326,000 boys and girls under 18 had corrective surgery to fix something that made them self-conscious" (para. 2), her focus seems to be mostly on women. Can you imagine her column if it had been written by a man? Are there different expectations and standards with regard to men and women—and who's more likely to get corrective surgery? Do more women get such procedures? If so, why?

ANNOTATION Varying Sentences

When you read essays that sound choppy or monotonous or both, it is usually because the writer has constructed the same type of sentence over and over. Here's an example: "This summer I went on a trip to Spain. Our group visited three cities, Madrid, Barcelona, and Seville. Madrid was very hot and crowded. We saw a bullfight there at Las Ventas bullring. I was disgusted by the way the bulls are treated. Bullfighting is inhumane and should be outlawed." Note that the sentences essentially sound alike. The writer makes no attempt to combine thoughts or information, and the overall effect is a dull and repetitive "da-dum, da-dum, da-dum." That's why good writers make a conscious attempt to vary their sentences. Observe how University of Florida student Rebecca Ganzak uses different sentence types, structures, lengths, and openings in "Is Cosmetic Surgery Worth the Risk?"

> *Ganzak varies the length, structure, and rhythm of sentences to keep the reader's interest.*
>
> What would you be willing to risk for a slimmer nose? A bustier chest? Some people will dip into their life savings, spending up to $10,000 on a nose job. Others will go so far as to take a second job or apply for a loan to fund corrective surgery. You probably won't catch anyone admitting they would risk their life, however. But plastic surgery, like any procedure that uses anesthesia, can be fatal. This proved true for South Florida teenager Stephanie Kuleba, who died in March of 2008—24 hours after her corrective breast augmentation surgery—of malignant hyperthermia, an increase in the body temperature that can be brought on by anesthesia.
>
> —From "Is Cosmetic Surgery Worth the Risk?" by Rebecca Ganzak, page 217

MICHAEL SANDEL

Designer Babies: The Problem with Genetic Engineering

[TIKKUN/September–October 2007]

Before You Read

Do you think parents should be able to choose—and improve—the genetic characteristics of their children? What moral issues are involved? How is genetic engineering different from giving children other opportunities and advantages? Would custom-designing our offspring change our view of human beings and society?

Words to Learn

coercive (para. 3): done by force (adj.)

mandated (para. 3): required by law (v.)

conscientious (para. 10): acting according to conscience; upright, honest, dedicated; careful (adj.)

hubris (para. 11): excessive pride (n.)

contingency (para. 22): event or thing dependent on chance or uncertainty (n.)

Michael Sandel has taught political philosophy since 1980 as the Anne T. and Robert M. Bass Professor of Government at Harvard University. Sandel was a summa cum laude, Phi Beta Kappa graduate of Brandeis University in 1975 and received his doctorate in 1981 from Oxford University, where he was a Rhodes scholar. His writings have appeared in such publications as the Atlantic Monthly, *the* New Republic, *and the* New York Times. *He has authored several books, including* Liberalism and the Limits of Justice *(1998), which has been translated into eight languages. Sandel's undergraduate course at Harvard on justice has enrolled more than 12,000 students in the past two decades, making it one of the most highly attended courses in Harvard's history.*

There's a growing debate about what limits, if any, should be   1
put on genetic engineering. We are on a path in which in the not-too-
distant future scientists and technicians will be able to select genes and
may be able to shape characteristics of your children. Some people already argue that using that to select the sex of your child is fine, or
perhaps for medical reasons. But what about other features? What if
we could choose their hair color and type, their eye colors, their sexual orientation, their level of intelligence, their musical or writing
ability or sports, dance, or artistic aptitude?

There is a long tradition that defends eugenics in the name of   2
"lifting up." Now we know that the eugenics movement has a very
dark history, though it was a very respectable movement in the early
part of the twentieth century. Eugenics was discredited by the Nazis,
by genocide, the Nuremberg Laws, by the forced sterilization laws
that were enacted by the majority of American states in the 1920s
and 1930s. Yet, in its earlier days, eugenics was endorsed and embraced by social reformers, by American progressives: Theodore Roosevelt was a great supporter of eugenics; Margaret Sanger, who began
Planned Parenthood, was a defender of eugenics. Oliver Wendell
Holmes, in a famous Supreme Court case *Buck v. Bell*, upheld a
forced sterilization law, with the notorious line that "three generations of imbeciles is enough." Oliver Wendell Holmes! So eugenics
has a very respectable lineage if you look at the people who supported it, and yet it led to forced sterilization. It ultimately leads to
genocide, even though it was first done in the name of those who
have been burdened or disadvantaged.

What's the moral of the story of the dark history of eugenics?   3
Some say it's that eugenics, in its earlier version, was coercive. State
laws mandated sterilization in the so-called "feeble-minded," or in
the criminal classes, and, of course, in Hitler's genocide. There are
many today who say the only thing wrong with eugenics was its coerciveness, and if we could imagine a eugenic program that was not
mandated by the State, that was not coercive, but was chosen by the
individual parents trying to help and lift up their children, then
there's nothing wrong with eugenics.

But I think that's a mistake. I think that coercion was not the   4
only thing wrong with eugenics. What we have today with designer
children is privatized eugenics, free market eugenics, individualistic
eugenics. Without the broad social ambitions for everyone, it's really
now an instrument for privileged parents to give their kids a competitive edge. Privatized eugenics reflect a deflation of the ideal of eugen-

ics, perverse as that ideal was in its enactment, because it's no longer trying to uplift humanity, or entire societies, but just trying to get a competitive edge. I think what's wrong with eugenics, beyond coercion, is the fact of its ambition to try to control or exercise dominion over the genetic traits of the next generation. That's morally troubling, whether done on a society-wide basis or done by individual parents trying to give their kids a competitive edge.

Of course, there are objections about whether doing this can be made safe and predictable. And there is another question about making it available in a fair way, so that it would not only be an option for rich people. But what would be your objection if the designer child were an equal option for all, publicly subsidized as part of a universal health care system, and it could be done in a way that was safe and predictable?

Is there a moral objection to this genetic engineering, beyond safety, beyond fairness? After all, we tend to praise parents who give their children every advantage they can: offer them music lessons to learn an instrument, play catch with them to learn how to be coordinated in sports, help them do their homework so that they can more fully learn what they need to learn. So what's the objection to parents wanting to give their children the advantage of genes that make it easier for them to succeed in creating a pleasant life for themselves?

It seems to me that there is a reason for a set of moral considerations that go beyond safety and fairness. What makes us most uneasy about the use of genetic engineering to enhance or to create something, has to do with the fact that the drive to create children of a certain character reflects an aspiration to freedom, mastery, and control, and to exercise our human will and our ability to remake human nature to serve our purposes and satisfy our desires. It seems to me there is something flawed but deeply attractive about that.

This uneasiness, I believe, connects to a recognition that there is a way in which who we are is a gift from the universe. And this is to say that not everything we are is a product of our own doing, and not everything in the world is open to any use we might desire or devise.

An appreciation of the giftedness of life might induce in us a certain humility. What I'm trying to articulate here is, in part, a religious sensibility, but its resonance reaches beyond religion.

Let's go back to the example of designer children. It's very hard to make sense of what's precious or special about the relationship between parents and children without drawing, at least a little, on the ethic of giftedness. To appreciate children as gifts is to accept them as they come, not as products of our design or instruments of our ambition. Parental love is not contingent, or at least it shouldn't be contingent, on attributes that the child happens to have. We choose our friends and our spouses at least partly on qualities that we find attractive, but we do not choose our children—that's an important moral fact about parenting. Even the most conscientious parent cannot be held wholly responsible for the child that they had. This is why parenting teaches us what the theologian William May calls "an openness to the unbidden."

> To appreciate children as gifts is to accept them as they come, not as products of our design or instruments of our ambition.

The problem of genetic engineering lies in the hubris of the designing parents. Even if this disposition doesn't make parents tyrants to their children, still it disfigures the relation between parent and child and it deprives the parent of the humility, the human sympathies, and the openness to the unbidden.   11

Now, to appreciate children as gifts and blessings from God is not to be passive in the face of illness. It's true that medical treatment intervenes with nature, but it does so for the sake of health. It doesn't represent the same bid for mastery. Even strenuous medicine, to treat or cure diseases, doesn't constitute a Promethean assault. Medicine is at least governed by a certain norm, the norm of preserving and restoring, and that is what constitutes good health.   12

What counts as "good health" is open to argument. There is research about whether deafness or other disabilities should be cured, or if they should be part of an identity that is cherished. But even then, the disagreement comes from the assumption that the purpose of medicine is to promote health and cure disease.   13

Now there is a complexity with this idea of resisting the temptation to manage, direct, and protect our children. Because we do that as parents. Parents want to educate their children, give them every opportunity, help them learn an instrument, develop athletic skill. . . . What then is the difference, and this is not an easy question to answer, but what is the difference between providing help with health and training, and providing this help with the use of genetic enhancement? Parents spend all this money educating their children and giving them special advantages. If that's accurate, why isn't it equally as admirable for parents to use whatever genetic technology has been developed, provided it's safe, to enhance their children's chance at life, to give them a competitive edge?   14

The answer I would give to this question is that the defenders of   15
genetic engineering are right to say that there is not such a bright line
between the use of genetic technology to enhance children, and the
kind of heavily managed, high pressure child rearing practices that
are common these days. But this similarity, this parallel, does *not* vindicate genetic enhancement. To the contrary, it highlights a problem
with the high-pressure hyper-parenting tendencies that we see in our
society today. We see the frenzy of parents at soccer game sidelines or
at little league. It is a frenzy, or an anxiety even, of the parents to
manage, to hold, to direct their children's lives. I don't think there is
such a clear line between these two practices, but this suggests that
the overreaching in genetic parenting may actually shed light on the
kind of overreaching frenzied parenting that we see now.

So, let me say a word about the larger moral stance if the account   16
I have given is right. Some people would say of this drive for mastery
and life control: "That's parents exercising their freedom to give their
kids the best, and who are *we* to criticize that freedom?"

What would happen if biotechnology dissolved our sense of gift-   17
edness? There are two answers to this question. One of them is the
religious answer (which suggests that using biotechnology has us assume a role in creation that seeks to make us on par with God).
Biotechnology is, in a sense, "playing God."

The moral stakes can also be understood in secular terms. One   18
way of seeing this is to consider what would be the effect on our
moral landscape if the practice of designer parents became the common way of parenting? At least two key features of our moral culture
would be transformed. One of them is humility and the other is solidarity.

Let me say a word about humility and why it matters as a social   19
ethic. Parenthood is a school for humility. We care deeply about our
children but cannot choose the kind we want. Humility teaches us to
rein in our need for control and to live with the unexpected. One of
the blessings of seeing ourselves as creatures of nature or God is that
we are *not* always responsible for the way we are. The more we become masters of our genetics the greater burden we bear for the talents we have and the way we perform. So with the erosion of
humility comes an explosion of responsibility.

Consider the use of genetic testing. In the past, giving birth to a   20
child with Down syndrome was a matter of chance. Today, parents
of children with Down syndrome are judged or blamed. Because
people will say to them "why did you bring this child into the world?"

So the responsibility is greater because we have a choice. Parents should be able to choose what they want to do, but they shouldn't be free to choose the burden of choice that this new technology creates.

Along with the explosion of responsibility over our own fate and that of our children, comes, paradoxically, a diminished sense of solidarity with those less fortunate than ourselves. Here's why: the more open we are to chance in the control over our own success, the more reason we have to share our fate with others. Why, after all, do the successful owe anything to the least advantaged members of society? The answers to these questions lie very heavily in the notions of giftedness. They lean on the idea that our success has nothing to do with hard work, or other things within our control, but on good fortune—the result of the genetic lottery. If we regard our genetics as gifts rather than achievements for which we can claim credit, then we have no basis to claim that we are entitled to the good things in society.   21

A lively sense of the contingency of our gifts can be used in a "meritocratic" society like ours to prevent us from sliding into the idea that the rich are rich because they are more deserving than the poor. If genetic engineering enabled us to override the results of the genetic lottery, if it enabled us to replace chance with choice, it's likely that the gifted character of human powers and achievements would recede, and with it, perhaps, our capacity to see ourselves as sharing a common fate. The successful would be even more likely than they are now to see themselves as self-made and self-sufficient, and those at the bottom of society would be seen not as disadvantaged, but simply as unfit. The meritocracy would become less forgiving. So that's why humility and solidarity as features of our moral culture can help us preserve a lively sense of giftedness of our nature, of our talents, and of our achievements.   22

A related case is the use of Ritalin in classrooms. Admittedly, it is difficult to precisely draw the line between clinical Attention Deficit Hyperactivity Disorder (ADHD) and a squirmy kid in a classroom. It is a difficult line to draw and it involves judgment on the part of the parent, the teachers, the doctor, the psychologist, and the kid. I would not for a moment say that Ritalin should never be prescribed for ADHD. There are cases, clearly, of clinical ADHD where it can help a child function and overcome a real deficiency. But Ritalin is often used either to control children in the classroom who are simply squirmy and should be dealt with by closer individual attention by the teacher, and by smaller classroom size, and so on, or by college   23 students who do not have any prescription, simply to improve their performance on a test. The line can be difficult to draw between the medical use of Ritalin and the performance enhancement use.

In order to draw this line, we must have, not just some statistical understanding of the normal, because that can shift over time, but a substantive, normative conception of what human flourishing consists of. So parents are often pressured to consent to Ritalin, and I fear that they might face even greater pressures to participate in genetic engineering.   24

We can't just blame parents for responding to these pressures. How could we expect them not to? We have to take a step back and ask what is the source of those heightened, intensified pressures? There has been an enormous increase in those types of pressures having to do with the economy and society and also the educational system.   25

So, to go back to the question with which I began, beyond safety and beyond fairness, what is the source of our unease about designer children? I think it has something to do with our big questions about human nature and the limits of the Promethean project of mastery and control. It is tempting to think that bioengineering our children and selves is an exercise in freedom, but it really isn't. Because changing our nature to fit the world rather than the other way around is actually an ethical defeat. It distracts us from reflecting critically on the world. It deadens the impulse for social and political improvement. So rather than increase our genetic powers to fit ourselves into society, we should do what we can to create political and social realms that are more hospitable to the gifts and also to the limitations of imperfect human beings.   26

Vocabulary/Using a Dictionary

1. What does *aptitude* (para. 1) mean, and what is its origin?

2. What do the words *eugenics* (para. 2) and *genocide* (para. 2) mean, and what are their roots?

3. Where does the term *Promethean* (para. 12) come from, and what connotations does it have?

4. What is the origin of the word *humility* (para. 11), and how do its roots connect to Sandel's argument?

Responding to Words in Context

1. Why is the word *feeble-minded* (para. 3) in quotation marks, and why do you think Sandel includes it?

2. Sandel uses the phrases "moral stance" (para. 16), "moral landscape" (para. 18), and "moral culture" (para. 18). Why does he repeat the word *moral*?

3. According to Sandel, the "moral stakes [of this debate] can also be understood in secular terms" (para. 18). What does that mean, and why must this be true for Sandel's argument?

Discussing Main Point and Meaning

1. Sandel briefly recounts the history of eugenics in the twentieth century. He claims that some think the primary—or only—problem with genetic engineering was its coerciveness in its "earlier version" (para. 3). He thinks this view is a mistake. Why?

2. In paragraph 4, Sandel examines the distinction between the "privatized eugenics" of today and the past practices of eugenics "in the name of 'lifting up'" the public, as a whole (para. 2). How does he compare and contrast the two? What objection to his argument might paragraph 4 anticipate?

3. Considering the prospect of "designer children," Sandel writes: "It's very hard to make sense of what's precious or special about the relationship between parents and children without drawing, at least a little, on the ethic of giftedness" (para. 10). Explain what he means by an "ethic of giftedness."

4. The ability to choose "designer babies" and manipulate human beings genetically could be seen as forms of human mastery (over nature) and human freedom (from genetic limitations or defects), but Sandel disagrees. How does he counter these assertions?

Examining Sentences, Paragraphs, and Organization

1. Sandel addresses the powerful appeal of genetic engineering, and the way it reflects our desire to shape nature—human and otherwise—to fit our needs and desires: "It seems to me there is something flawed but deeply attractive about that" (para. 7). How is this sentence reflective of the essay as a whole?

2. In Sandel's brief account of genetic engineering in the twentieth century, he emphasizes that "eugenics has a very respectable lineage," including endorsements from prominent political progressives and social reformers such as Theodore Roosevelt. How does highlighting the "respectability" of eugenics near the beginning of his essay support his overall argument, which is quite critical of the practice?

3. In paragraph 22, Sandel discusses how eugenics might affect the public and society as a whole. Given that he's mostly interested in the contemporary practice of "individualistic" and "privatized" eugenics, how does this section connect to his argument?

Thinking Critically

1. Sandel claims, "What I'm trying to articulate here is, in part, a religious sensibility, but its resonance reaches beyond religion" (para. 9). What is the difference between "religion" and a "religious sensibility"? How does Sandel articulate this sensibility in the essay?

2. How does Sandel distinguish between the ways in which parents already provide opportunities, health, training, and other advantages to their children, and the practice of providing these things "with the use of genetic enhancement" (para. 14)? Do you think it strengthens his argument?

3. Sandel compares genetic engineering and the use of pharmaceuticals on children and says that "the line can be difficult to draw between the medical use of Ritalin and the performance enhancement use" (para. 23). Then he writes: "In order to draw this line, we must have, not just some statistical understanding of the normal, because that can shift over time, but a substantive, normative conception of what human flourishing consists of" (para. 24). What do you think Sandel means? Would you characterize his language here as precise or general?

In-Class Writing Activities

1. Sandel refers to bioengineering as a "Promethean" project. The tale of Prometheus is merely one of many in a long tradition of such stories. What other accounts of Promethean projects can

you think of? What lessons are we supposed to learn from them? Why do you think they are so powerful and enduring? Using at least two examples of this story—broadly understood, in versions from history, literature, or film—write an essay that explores these issues of human aspiration and human limitation.

2.   Would you consider genetically engineering your own children, either to enhance certain qualities or skills or to prevent "defects"? Why or why not? If you would, how would you address Sandel's arguments? If such eugenic practices became the norm in society, would that affect your decision making?

3.   As a response to the "growing debate about what limits, if any, should be put on genetic engineering" (para. 1), Sandel has written an argument against the prospect of "designer babies." Whether or not it's persuasive, the essay is not a piece of legislation and has no power to regulate or restrict eugenics. As a practical matter, do you think such practices should be banned or regulated? Would it be possible to do so? How do you see the American public reacting to—or participating in—this "growing debate"?

Discussing the Unit

Suggested Topic for Discussion

Writing about "enhanced" athletes and their effect on sports, Ellen Goodman claims, "These stories will get harder, not easier, over the next years." Of course, the complexities of redesigning humanity—genetically and otherwise—go well beyond sports. It appears that technological progress and medical advancements may outrun our ability to adapt cultural, ethical, and even legal frameworks to accommodate them. Do you think we will ever settle these problems and questions? Can you think of other examples of this disconnect?

Preparing for Class Discussion

1.   Both Michael Sandel and Rebecca Ganzak are arguing persuasively against the redesign of human beings, but their arguments

are fundamentally different. How would you contrast them? What is the significance of this difference?

2. Ellen Goodman notes that technologies have been used to enhance athletes "since the first runner put on a shoe." Cosmetics, piercings, and other methods of physical alteration or enhancement have existed for thousands of years. Similarly, people have practiced subtle or indirect methods of selective breeding for a long time, whether through arranged marriages or in the ways parents have determined the social and cultural circle of their children. What makes the contemporary or high-tech versions of these practices more problematic?

From Discussion to Writing

1. Michael Sandel has written a book called *The Case against Perfection*, which touches on the themes of the essay included here. Could you make the case *for* the pursuit of perfection in human beings? How would you craft such an argument?

2. Ellen Goodman's column discusses the "remanufacture of athletes" as it alters (in the words of an ethicist she cites) "whatever we think is meaningful or beautiful about sports." What do you think is "meaningful" or "beautiful" about sports? Write an essay that answers this question—and also addresses how performance enhancements affect that meaning or beauty.

Topics for Cross-Cultural Discussion

1. Aimee Mullins participated in the Paralympics, which, in a sense, is not only a sporting event but also a cultural event: It suggests a community with shared values, activities, experiences, and histories. To what degree do you think groups of people with different disabilities constitute different cultures?

2. As Sandel points out, "Eugenics was discredited by the Nazis, by genocide." What is he referring to specifically, with regard to eugenics, race, and culture? What dangers is he highlighting, if we view racially, culturally, or ethnically different groups of people as genetically different from ourselves in a fundamental way?

7

Will We Ever Transcend Race?

In 1997, President Bill Clinton initiated a national "conversation on race," promising a robust effort to tackle the divide between whites and blacks that lingered thirty years after the era of segregation had ended. Clinton's effort, even under the capable leadership of Professor John Hope Franklin, quickly collapsed, reminding Americans just how vicious and intractable the problem of race remains.

A little more than ten years later, in March 2008, the dialogue on race in America was revitalized by President Barack Obama in a dramatic speech designed to defend himself against charges that his affiliation with his pastor, the Reverend Jeremiah Wright, had compromised his candidacy. In speaking to his congregation, Wright had soundly condemned America, and his words had been broadcast repeatedly throughout the national media. Obama attempted to distance himself from Wright and at the same time to focus attention on the sensitive topic of race. Analysts were soon comparing Obama's address to some of the greatest political speeches in American history. The address is somewhat long, and much of it no longer relevant, as Obama would later denounce Wright when the pastor refused to moderate his rhetoric and continued the controversy. After Wright gave an inflammatory speech at the National Press Club on April 28, 2008, Obama announced that Wright's extreme views had caused a rift between the two men and went against the principles of the campaign. In the portion of the speech reprinted here, Obama takes an honest look at the grievances of both blacks and whites, acknowledging the difficulties of racial discourse.

234

In his essay "Teaching, and Learning, Racial Sensitivity," Jerald Walker, an English professor who is black, narrates two incidents in which race became an issue in his academic environment. In the first, a faculty member asks him to take some new puppies home to play with his sons in order to keep the dogs from developing "racist tendencies." In the second incident, another colleague admits to Walker that he hadn't invited him to the faculty basketball game because "that could be considered racist." In the first instance, Walker reacted strongly by posting an incendiary note on his door, but in the second the two men actually spoke openly about race and racism. "That's why I so appreciated the second incident," Walker says; "my colleague's honesty resulted in an open conversation about race."

Lauren Carter, one of Walker's students at Bridgewater State College, encounters a more abortive attempt at a conversation about race. In "Isn't Watermelon Delicious?" Carter relates how she felt when her friend told her that at times she could be "so white" and at other times "soooo black." The cryptic comment provokes Carter, a person of mixed race, to meditate on what it means to be black. "When am I really black?" she asks rhetorically. "When I start celebrating Kwanzaa? When I fill my wardrobe with Roc-A-Wear and Phat Farm? When I stop playing Elton John? Is that what blackness is? A holiday? A piece of clothing? A song?" Carter concludes that neither skin tone nor simple cultural artifacts make us who we are, but our heritage does. "The size of my nose is not my inheritance," she says. "The will to survive is." Carter's revelation, like Obama's speech, merely scratches the surface of what it means to be black in America today—but it's certain that without an answer to that question, transcending race in America will be no more than a dream.

The chapter concludes with the famous photograph that vividly captures the powerful resistance to segregation at a Little Rock, Arkansas, high school in 1957.

BARACK OBAMA

"Black Americans/White Americans," *from* "A More Perfect Union"

[Excerpt from transcript, March 18, 2008]

In early 2008, President Obama's campaign appeared from time to time to highlight the rift between blacks and whites more than it presented ways to heal it. In March 2008, for instance, a controversy erupted in the press over Reverend Jeremiah Wright, one of the ministers at Obama's predominantly black church in Chicago. Videos of Wright's sermons had flooded the Web, and many Americans found their content racist, radical, and unpatriotic—most famously Wright's thundering declaration of "God damn America." The media grilled Obama about his relationship to Wright and his reaction to the remarks, and thus commenced a dizzying back-and-forth. Did Wright speak for all blacks in his bitterly venomous condemnation of white America? For black Christians? For nobody but himself? Did the sermons represent an unmerited and hostile attack or a legitimate outlet for pent-up black anger?

Obama himself was quick to distance himself from his longtime paster, most notably in his now famous "A More Perfect Union" address, which can be found in its entirely on The New York Times

---

Barack Obama, as a junior senator from Illinois, made history by becoming the first African American President of the United States. Obama graduated from Columbia University in 1983 with a BA in political science and later attended Harvard Law School, graduating magna cum laude in 1991. Over the years, he has worked as a community organizer, a lawyer, and a part-time professor of constitutional law and has authored two best-selling books, Dreams from My Father *(1995) and* The Audacity of Hope *(2006). Born to a black Kenyan father and a white American mother, Obama has a unique past. As he said in his "A More Perfect Union" speech, "[Mine is] a story that hasn't made me the most conventional candidate. But it is a story that has seared into my genetic makeup the idea that this nation is more than the sum of its parts—that out of many, we are truly one."*

web site, NYT.com. *Speaking in Philadelphia, the birthplace of the American experiment, on March 18, 2008, Obama said that he strongly disagreed with Wright's sound bites but could "no more disown him than [Obama could] disown the black community." Wright and his black church, Obama claimed, represented "the kindness and cruelty, the fierce intelligence and the shocking ignorance, the struggles and successes, the love and yes, the bitterness and bias that make up the black experience in America."*

Obama went further in the speech, hinting at his own scheme for the reconciliation of blacks and whites that President Clinton had failed to achieve, one based on mutual understanding. The controversy over Wright's comments, according to Obama, underlined "the complexities of race in this country that we've never really worked through—a part of our union that we have yet to perfect." The white community would have to accept Wright's anger as a reflection of a strong black resentment and mistrust, the legacy of slavery and segregation. To "simply wish [this anger] away," Obama said, "to condemn it without understanding its roots, only serves to widen the chasm of misunderstanding that exists between the races." Meanwhile, blacks would have to acknowledge that whites harbored a similar anger. Obama admitted that one candidacy could not solve the racial divide, but was his speech a pathway to unity, or just—as critics alleged—a series of empty platitudes? Is meaningful dialogue between races even possible?

> **Obama balances his argument by conceding that whites also have grievances.**
>
> Most working- and middle-class white Americans don't feel that they have been particularly privileged by their race. Their experience is the immigrant experience—as far as they're concerned, no one's handed them anything, they've built it from scratch. They've worked hard all their lives, many times only to see their jobs shipped overseas or their pension dumped after a lifetime of labor. They are anxious about their futures, and feel their dreams slipping away; in an era of stagnant wages and global competition, opportunity comes to be seen as a zero sum game, in which your dreams come at my expense. So when they are told to bus their children to a school across town; when they hear that an African American is getting an advantage in landing a good job or a spot in a good college because of an injustice that they themselves never committed; when they're told that their fears about crime in urban neighborhoods are somehow prejudiced, resentment builds over time.

Like the anger within the black community, these resentments aren't always expressed in polite company. But they have helped shape the political landscape for at least a generation. Anger over welfare and affirmative action helped forge the Reagan Coalition. Politicians routinely exploited fears of crime for their own electoral ends. Talk show hosts and conservative commentators built entire careers unmasking bogus claims of racism while dismissing legitimate discussions of racial injustice and inequality as mere political correctness or reverse racism.

Just as black anger often proved counterproductive, so have these white resentments distracted attention from the real culprits of the middle class squeeze — a corporate culture rife with inside dealing, questionable accounting practices, and short-term greed; a Washington dominated by lobbyists and special interests; economic policies that favor the few over the many. And yet, to wish away the resentments of white Americans, to label them as misguided or even racist, without recognizing they are grounded in legitimate concerns — this too widens the racial divide, and blocks the path to understanding.

He acknowledges how the grievances of both races are exploited.

This is where we are right now. It's a racial stalemate we've been stuck in for years. Contrary to the claims of some of my critics, black and white, I have never been so naïve as to believe that we can get beyond our racial divisions in a single election cycle, or with a single candidacy — particularly a candidacy as imperfect as my own.

He demonstrates realism and understands the complexity of racial issues.

But I have asserted a firm conviction — a conviction rooted in my faith in God and my faith in the American people — that working together we can move beyond some of our old racial wounds, and that in fact we have no choice if we are to continue on the path of a more perfect union.

He reiterates main theme of speech — forming "a more perfect union."

For the African-American community, that path means embracing the burdens of our past without becoming victims of our past. It means continuing to insist on a full measure of justice in every aspect of American life. But it also means binding our particular grievances — for better health care, and better schools, and better jobs — to the larger aspirations of all Americans — the white woman struggling to break the glass ceiling, the white man who's been laid off, the immigrant trying to feed his family. And it means taking full responsibility for own lives — by de-

Grievances need to be viewed in the broader context of all Americans.

manding more from our fathers, and spending more time with our children, and reading to them, and teaching them that while they may face challenges and discrimination in their own lives, they must never succumb to despair or cynicism; they must always believe that they can write their own destiny.

JERALD WALKER

Teaching, and Learning, Racial Sensitivity

[CHRONICLE OF HIGHER EDUCATION / March 20, 2008]

Before You Read

How does Walker think people learn racial sensitivity? When do they go wrong?

Words to Learn

colleague (para. 1): coworker; someone with whom you are associated through work (n.)
vehemently (para. 4): in an aggressive or intense way (adv.)
incident (para. 7): occurrence (n.)

Jerald Walker is an assistant professor of English at Bridgewater State College in Massachusetts, currently teaching African American literature. In addition to teaching, Walker also serves as the faculty adviser of the Bridge, *a student journal of literature and fine art at Bridgewater State College. His writing has appeared in many publications, including the* Missouri Review, *the* Iowa Review, *the* North American Review, *the* Chronicle of Higher Education, Outsmart, *and the* Best American Essays 2007.

A few years back, a faculty colleague, after expressing concern   1
that his puppies would develop racist tendencies for lack of exposure
to minorities, asked if he could bring the dogs to my house to play
with my two sons, ages 1 and 3. My children—like their parents and
unlike most everyone else at the college and in our town—are of the
Negro persuasion.

I declined the request. "My boys are afraid of dogs," I explained.   2
If he knew of any racially deprived felines, I told him, he should let
me know.

When I casually mentioned the exchange to minority faculty   3
members, some of them retold it to me, putting themselves in my
shoes and performing a number of aggressive acts against my colleague.

The white faculty members I told did not put themselves in my   4
shoes. Many accused me of lying. That's because the puppies' owner,
who has since left the college, decided to deny—vehemently—that
our conversation had ever taken place. To remind him that it had, I
taped to my office door a photograph from the 1960s Civil Rights
movement: a black male leaning just beyond the reach of a German
shepherd that is being restrained by a white police officer. Beneath
the photograph I wrote: "Don't let this happen to you. Teach your
dogs racial sensitivity."

"Was *that* necessary?" an administrator asked me.   5

I assured her it was.   6

About a month after that incident, I had another interesting en-   7
counter with a different white colleague, this time while in the corri-
dor outside my office.

"Off to the pool?" I had inquired, motioning toward his large   8
duffel bag. He was a thin man, very fit-looking. I had taken him to be
a swimmer.

"Basketball," he corrected me.   9

"Oh? Where do you play?"   10

"Over in the campus gym."   11

"Open shoot-around?" I asked. "Or is there a league?"   12

"Actually, some of the faculty get together a few times a week to   13
play."

I nodded and wished him a good game. He thanked me and   14
walked away. I went into my office and sat at the computer. When I
looked up a moment later, he was standing at my door.

"I *would* have invited you to play, I just didn't, um, get around   15
to it."

Before I could respond, he left again. But he came right back. "I 16
didn't even know whether or not you played."

I smiled and said, "I'm a black male from Chicago's inner city. 17
Of course I got game!" Actually, I did not have game. From the age
of 5, I had failed to make every basketball team I had ever tried out
for, except the teen league run by my church, which had a benevolent,
no-cut policy. But I had always wanted to say, "I got game!" to
someone who might believe me.

Red in the face now, he again hurried away. I waited for him to 18
return. When he did, he looked pretty shaken up. He apologized.

"For?" I asked. 19

"Well, it's just that I wanted to ask you to play, but I didn't want 20
you to think I'd singled you out because you're black. That could be
considered racist."

"True," I said. "And it could also be considered racist not to ask 21
me because I'm black."

"You're right, you're right." He lowered and shook his head, 22
then looked up again. "I've just felt awful every time I see you. I feel
awful even talking with you about it now."

> *When blacks integrate predominantly white institutions like academe, racial incidents are bound to occur, but they are usually sparked by innocent gaffes rather than ill will.*

But he should not have. When blacks in- 23
tegrate predominantly white institutions like
academe, racial incidents are bound to
occur, but they are usually sparked by innocent gaffes rather than ill will. My former
colleague with the puppies was, in his own
unique way, simply trying to befriend me.
Things got a little tricky when, instead of
just admitting that, he accused me of fabricating our encounter.

And that's why I so appreciated the sec- 24
ond incident; my colleague's honesty resulted
in an open conversation about race. After we were done talking, I put
no photograph on my door. Instead, I went to the campus gym.

There were a dozen white men already there when I arrived, most 25
of them, I was pleased to see, feeble-looking and elderly. As I approached the court, I shot an imaginary ball toward the basket.
"Let's see who in here's got some game!" I yelled.

And then I proceeded to be trounced. While I lay on the floor try- 26
ing to breathe, I received looks from the players that seemed a mixture
of suspicion and curiosity, as if I were some kind of fraud, not the genuine article. I had seen that look in academe many times before.

The first time was from Lenny Wilkins. Lenny was my roommate   27
when I was an undergraduate at a large, predominantly white university in the Midwest. He had spent the first 18 years of his life in rural
farmland so removed from integration that he had not met a black
person before I walked into our dorm room. He confessed that several months later, but I had surmised it right off, based on the way
his eyes widened when he first saw me, the panicky quiver in his
voice when he told me his name, and how he had sat on his bed very
quietly watching me unpack.

Things were strained at first.   28

Lenny was nervous in my presence, while I, on the other hand,   29
did not want to be in a dorm room with a nervous white farmer, or
with anyone else for that matter, because, being an older, nontradi-
tional student, I did not want to be in the dorms.

Unfortunately I had transferred to the university from my junior   30
college too late to find off-campus housing, and so this was a necessary arrangement. In time, Lenny and I learned to accept our differences and each other, so much so that one night, three months into
our cohabitation and a few bottles into a six-pack of beer, he said,
"You're the first colored person I've ever known."

"I prefer 'black,'" I said, "to 'colored.'"   31

"You do?"   32

I nodded. "But that's not true for all of us. Some of us like to be   33
called 'African American.' 'Negro' was popular for a while, but not
so much these days. I'm thinking of bringing it back."

"See?" Lenny said sadly. "That's what I mean. I don't know any-   34
thing about the colored race."

Lenny was sitting on his bed and I was sitting on mine. They   35
were positioned like an L, only mine was high in the air, resting on
stilts. The beds had been stacked one directly above the other, but
neither of us had felt comfortable with that.

"I was a little afraid of you at first," he confessed. "I mean, I didn't   36
think you were a murderer or anything. I'd just been told that colored
people were, you know, different from white people."

"How so?"   37

"Well, that you love fried chicken."   38

I laughed. "And watermelon?"   39

"Yes!" He laughed, too, before adding, "And that you have little   40
tails."

"Pardon?"   41

"Little tails." He held up his hands, maybe a foot apart. Neither 42
of us spoke for a long time. And then, almost inaudibly, he asked, "Is
it true?"

I climbed down from my bed and mooned him. 43

"Was that called for?" he asked. 44

I assured him it was. 45

Or so it seemed at the time. But not long afterward, I came to un- 46
derstand that it was not my best moment, just as I have come to see
that putting the photograph on my office door was not either. Both
my college roommate and my former faculty colleague were groping
their way toward some new racial understanding, and if I could have
contained my frustration a little better, I might have been a more effective escort as they made their important journey.

I am on that important journey, too. We all are. And in those in- 47
stances when we veer from the correct path, when we momentarily
lose our way, the thing to do is to admit it and to speak truthfully
about our imperfections and failings, just as my basketball-playing
colleague did.

In other words, when dealing with the complicated subject of 48
race relations, saying "I got game!" will take you only so far.

Vocabulary / Using a Dictionary

1. What does the stem *bene-* mean in *benevolent* (para. 17). How
   does Walker use the word?

2. How does the word *predominantly* (para. 23) relate to the root
   word *domin*? What is the definition of *predominant*?

3. What is the meaning of *fabricating* (para. 23)? How does the suffix *-ate* work in the formation of this verb?

Responding to Words in Context

1. What is a *gaffe* (para. 23)? In what context is the word most frequently used?

2. Why does Walker choose the word *trounced* (para. 26) rather
   than *beaten*? What is the meaning of *trounced*?

3. What does Walker mean by *racial sensitivity* (para. 4)? He uses
   the phrase satirically at first, but which experiences in his narrative show what it means to become more sensitive?

Discussing Main Point and Meaning

1. Walker says that taping the picture to his office door and moon-ing his roommate were not his best moments. What is the basis of his self-critique? How could he have done better?

2. At the end of the essay, Walker points out the limitation of state-ments like "I got game!" Why does he point out this pronounce-ment as insufficient? What is its function in the conversation with his colleagues?

3. How do minority and white faculty members react differently to Walker's story about his dog-owning colleague? How would he explain this difference?

Examining Sentences, Paragraphs, and Organization

1. At what points in his essay does Walker use humor to convey his message? What is the function of these humorous moments?

2. What do the three anecdotes that Walker relates have in com-mon? How are they different? Why do you think he presented them in this order?

Thinking Critically

1. Walker is careful to point out the main problem with his dog-owning colleague: not that he asked a question Walker found of-fensive, but that he later denied it (para. 23). Do you agree with Walker that this is the point at which the interaction went really wrong?

2. Whose responsibility is it to teach racial sensitivity? What do you think Walker would say about the roles that minorities and whites have in this process?

In-Class Writing Activities

1. Write about a time when you either engaged in an open racial discussion or failed to do so. If you choose the former, do you think it had the positive effects that Walker attributes to commu-nication? For the latter, consider whether you passed up an op-portunity, just as Walker decides he did.

2. This essay is part of a series called "First Person," in which professors discuss and analyze their personal experiences in the academic world. What might your first-person perspective on college add to the discussion? If you were going to write a column for your student newspaper, what would be unique about your viewpoint?

LAUREN CARTER (STUDENT ESSAY)

Isn't Watermelon Delicious?

[THE BRIDGE, Bridgewater State College / Spring 2005;
revised with bibliography, 2008]

*Lauren Carter wrote "Isn't Watermelon Delicious?" as a response to an assignment
in an undergraduate African American literature course taught at Bridgewater
State College (in Massachusetts) by Jerald Walker, the author of the preceding selection, "Teaching, and Learning, Racial Sensitivity." Professor Walker generously
provided us with the actual assignment.*

Marlon Riggs' documentary *Black Is . . . Black Ain't . . .* ends with the following quotation:

> If you have received no clear cut impression of what The Negro in America is like,
> then you are in the same place with me. There is no The Negro here.
>
> —Zora Neale Hurston

Hurston's point, it seems to me, is that Negroes (or coloreds, or blacks, or Afro-
Americans, or African Americans) come in such varieties that they are impossible
to define as a homogeneous group. Much of this variety can be said to be the result
of the blues/jazz idiom, how blacks are constantly improvising new identities in an
effort to adapt to changing conditions and needs. Likewise, African American fiction
writers are constantly improvising on the theme of "blackness" in order to produce
works that attempt to offer at least partial definitions of what it means to be African
American. In your essay, work your way through the literature read in this class and
discuss how each author adds to our understanding of what it means to be black.

---

*As you read Carter's response to the assignment, observe how she successfully
blends together her personal experiences of being a young black woman with a
number of relevant literary works read for Professor Walker's course.*

Before You Read

Carter's essay is prompted by a friend's comment about behavior that corresponds to race. Where else does Carter encounter this idea? What questions does she raise about how people understand race?

Words to Learn

masquerading (para. 8): pretending or posing as something else (v.)
succumbed (para. 11): gave in (v.)
fallacy (para. 13): mistaken idea or false statement (n.)

It was just another Thursday night at Axis. White lights were flashing, music was pumping, and I was mildly buzzed. My best friend Stacey and I were making our way around the edges of the crowded dance floor, looking for a table where we could plop down and briefly escape the frenzy of the hot, crowded club. Then my favorite song came on. I don't remember what song it was; it was a long time ago and I usually had a new favorite song every other week. But at the time, the song that started playing was my favorite one, and I was ecstatic. As soon as I heard the bass line I guzzled what was left of my drink, broke out into some kind of overenthusiastic dance move, and shouted "Let's go!"   1

Stacey looked over at me and laughed.   2

"God, Lauren," she said, "sometimes you're so white, and sometimes you're soooo black."   3

It was an interesting idea. That I could be one or the other, at different times. I wondered when I was which one. So I asked her.   4

She started to answer, but the music was too loud, and I couldn't really make out what she was saying. I leaned in closer and asked her to repeat what she said, but she waved the idea away, saying we should go dance.   5

Lauren Carter graduated in 2005 from Bridgewater State College with a degree in English. While at Bridgewater State College, Carter served as editor in chief of the Bridge, *in which her essay "Isn't Watermelon Delicious?" first appeared. After graduating, she began to write for a newspaper full-time and currently works as a freelance writer for several publications. As a writer, Carter's topics of interest include music and race, and she encourages fellow student writers not to "look at writing as drudgery [but to] view it as an opportunity to express yourself."*

Yes, we should dance, I thought. My favorite song was on and   6
we were attempting to have a conversation meant for a quiet café,
not a loud, crowded club.

We never did have that conversation, and I never did get the an-   7
swer I was looking for. What, exactly, I did that was so white. And
what, exactly, I did that was so black. But the idea stuck with me.
That a behavior related to a skin tone. That my behavior related to
two different ones.

It wasn't a totally new idea. My black cousin Reagan had told   8
me for years that I acted "so white." I thought I was just acting like
me, but apparently, with my Bart Simpson t-shirt, my "proper"
speech, and my affinity for Vanilla Ice, I was masquerading as a
white girl in a black girl's body. I didn't know those characteristics
belonged exclusively to white people. I thought they belonged to
people who liked the occasional Simpsons t-shirt, spoke the way they
had learned to speak, and enjoyed listening to extremely cheesy, albeit catchy, quasi-rap music.

Or at least that's how I feel now. But then, I felt inferior—way   9
behind in the race for true blackness. I would never catch up to her.
I'd never know all the latest black sayings, never listen to all the latest
black music, never wear all the latest black clothing. I'd never be as
black as she was. Or so I thought.

But that's before I met the Ex-Colored Man. In his autobiogra-   10
phy, he switched from white to black and back again, though his skin
color never changed. When he discovered his blackness as a child, he
still looked like a white person. But internally, he realized there was
black blood running through his veins, or rather blue blood with
black ancestry in it, and he withdrew. He wasn't what he thought
he'd been. He couldn't stop thinking about his new blackness. Really,
though, nothing had changed. Externally, at least.

So it kind of surprised me when, at the end of his story, he chose to   11
become white again. This, after feeling mortified and ashamed that in a
country like America, with all its talk of democracy and freedom, the
black race could be persecuted so harshly. While I could attempt to analyze and judge his decision to forsake his blackness in order to better
his condition, decide whether he had succumbed to the race game or
merely decided to stop playing, the validity of his decision isn't as important as the fact that it could be made. That he could become white
again, simply by deciding to be. It was a miraculous transformation.
Which got me to thinking, if you can miraculously transform from
black to white, or vice versa, then how real is either category?

My sister transforms all the time, depending on who's looking at   12
her. She's black in terms of ancestry. Partially, anyway. Our mother's
Italian, her father's black. And though her hair came out extremely
nappy, her skin is light. Whiter than some "white" people's skin, in
fact. Now that she chemically straightens her hair, most people don't
know she's black unless she tells them. She can pass. Not among
black people, of course, myself included. We can all see it in her features. But to the untrained eye, amongst the world at large, she can
generally be perceived as white. So which is she? Is she what her ancestry dictates, or what other people's perception decides?

It's a ridiculous question, I know. But only as ridiculous as the   13
fallacy it's based on. When you lump a group of people together
based solely on the color of their skin, of course ridiculous questions
like these come up. It'd be the same if you lumped them together
based on eye color, height, or any other arbitrary characteristic over
which they have no control.

Funny, that we would choose to separate and define people based   14
on factors beyond their control. Well, maybe not funny. But certainly
ingenious. And an excellent way to subordinate one group in order to
elevate another. Because isn't it true that all
of these external factors, in actuality, say
nothing about a person's character, that the
only real measure of a person is in their actions, not any physical characteristic? Isn't it
true that anyone who has survived and succeeded in any facet of life did so almost
exclusively because of their intellect, their intelligence, their will to persevere, not because of the pigment in their skin or the full-
ness of their features?

> *Isn't it true that anyone who has survived and succeeded in any facet of life did so almost exclusively because of their intellect, their intelligence, their will to persevere, not because of the pigment in their skin or the fullness of their features?*

When Frederick Douglass found ways to   15
teach himself to read, it wasn't because of
his melanin content. It was because of his
desire to learn, his ingenuity, his intelligence.
After six months of torture by his brutal master Covey, Douglass
made the bold and beautiful statement: "You have seen how a man
was made a slave; now you shall see how a slave was made a man."

And when he did make that journey from slavery to manhood, it   16
wasn't because of the coil of his hair, it was because of the color of
his character. When Gabriel Prosser decided to lead a revolt in pursuit of freedom, it wasn't because of the size of his muscles, it was

because of the size of his spirit. When blacks survived slavery, it wasn't because of the width of their noses or how many calluses they did or didn't have on their hands. It was because of the survival strategies they'd developed over time, none of which had anything to do with appearance.

The folktales and spirituals that emerged out of that era weren't developed because of the shape of someone's kneecaps; they were developed because of a will to overcome seemingly insurmountable obstacles. And when Bigger Thomas, the main character in Richard Wright's famous novel, *Native Son*, became the agent of his own demise, it wasn't, contrary to his own beliefs, because of the darkness of his skin; it was because of the darkness of his mind, and all of the things he believed he would never, and so never did, achieve.   17

Maybe life would be simpler if skin color really was an indicator of character, external factors determined internal worth, and similar complexions could unite us all. Then all the dark-skinned peoples of America could heed Marcus Garvey's message and return home to Africa. We could take a giant plane to Uganda, and when it landed we could step down off it with open arms and scream, "Hello black people, I'm finally home!!" But in reality, that probably wouldn't work. Those Ugandans would only point out what I've come to realize over the past semester: that the significance of skin color is that it is the color of one's skin, and not much more. That it does not necessarily imply a common set of values, a standard behavior, a singular way of life.   18

And why should it? Aren't there a number of ways that human beings can define themselves as individuals? What about gender? Profession? Religious beliefs? Hobbies? Personality? Sexual orientation? Values? What about your attitude towards yourself, towards others, towards life? Isn't it true that race is just one ingredient in a large and complicated recipe? Why must it be the main ingredient and define all the other areas of life? I know that my life is about much more than being black, and, for that matter, being black is about much more than my skin color.   19

Which leads to the question: What is my blackness about? When am I really black? When I start celebrating Kwanzaa? When I fill my wardrobe with Roc-A-Wear and Phat Farm? When I stop playing Elton John? Is that what blackness is? A holiday? A piece of clothing? A song?   20

Funny, I never thought of being black that way. I never considered that a Dashiki would give me blackness, and I never thought that a lack of one would take it away. I always thought of black as a   21 state of mind; a way of looking at the world. Perseverance in the face of any and all obstacles. Winning when everyone says you're bound to lose. I never looked at the color of my skin as evidence of a drum, or a slice of watermelon. I never thought I had to do, have, or say anything at all to be black. I just thought I was.

I never told her so, but when Reagan said I was acting "so white," she was wrong. Whites don't have a monopoly on listening to Vanilla Ice, and even if they could have one, I doubt they'd want it. I was acting like me. I don't need to walk the streets with a sandwich board proclaiming what I am. I don't need to act out my blackness, just like I don't need to act out my eye color; it's simply an intrinsic part of who I am.

True, the color of my skin implies an ancestry that the color of my eyes does not, and I'm aware of that ancestry; I draw from it daily. But I don't need to wear Lugz and use slang to prove it. Maya Angelou wrote "I am the dream and the hope of the slave," and I haven't forgotten about those hopes and dreams. I understand the debt that I owe to my ancestors, and I pay it back every day, in my own way, that has nothing to do with what jeans I wear, and has everything to do with how I live my life. The size of my nose is not my inheritance. The will to survive is.

Stacey's statement in that nightclub was probably my first—or at least my most memorable—experience with double consciousness as civil rights activist W. E. B. Du Bois described it, of being conscious not only of how you see yourself, but how others see you; I'd never thought of myself solely in terms of white and black, but I realized the extent to which other people could. For a long time after that night I wondered where the line between black and white was, and in what moments I crossed it. I don't wonder about that line anymore. Blackness no longer boils down to a t-shirt, or a desire to dance. It's just not that simple. Blackness is the legacy left by the people that came before me, and it's the legacy I'll leave behind me when I'm gone.

References

Angelou, Maya. "Still I Rise." *The Complete Collected Poems of Maya Angelou.* New York: Random House, 1994.

Bontemps, Arna. *Black Thunder.* Boston: Beacon Press, 1992.

Douglass, Frederick. *Narrative of the Life of Frederick Douglass, an American Slave.* New York: Barnes & Noble Classics, 2003.

Du Bois, W. E. B. *The Souls of Black Folk.* Boston: Bedford/St. Martin's, 1997.

Johnson, James Weldon. *The Autobiography of an Ex-Coloured Man*. New York: Vintage Books, 1989.

Wright, Richard. *Native Son*. New York: Perennial, 2003.

Vocabulary/Using a Dictionary

1. What is the root of the word *ingenious* (para. 14)?

2. What is the meaning of the prefix *dis-*? What does it mean in the word *discovered* (para. 10)?

3. The word *subordinate* (para. 14) comes from the Latin verb *ordinare*. Look up the origin of *subordinate* to find out the meaning of the root.

Responding to Words in Context

1. What does Carter mean by "true blackness," which her cousin sees her as lacking?

2. Discussing the James Weldon Johnson novel *The Autobiography of an Ex-Coloured Man*, Carter mentions the narrator's decision to "pass" (para. 11). What does she mean by this? Why is it an important decision for the character?

3. Why does Carter call the physical features she lists in paragraph 13 "arbitrary"? What is the meaning of that word?

Discussing Main Point and Meaning

1. What does the statement Carter's friend Stacey makes assume about race? What does Carter find strange about this assumption?

2. What question does Carter take away from Johnson's *The Autobiography of an Ex-Coloured Man*? Why does she find the example of the narrator illustrative?

3. What does Carter think determines someone's race? Does she offer different possibilities? What problems does she find with them?

Examining Sentences, Paragraphs, and Organization

1. How does Carter structure the last two sentences of paragraph 23? How does the writing of these sentences reinforce her point?

2. Why does Carter begin her essay by stating, "It was just another Thursday night" (para. 1)? Why is this important to the scene she sets?

3. What is Carter's goal in paragraph 8? How does the scenario she presents there further her argument?

Thinking Critically

1. In paragraph 21, Carter claims that she "never thought [she] had to do, have, or say anything at all to be black." What does this notion assume about racial identity? Is it in line with her earlier arguments?

2. Does Carter end up underplaying the role of race in her essay? Are there any moments at which you would challenge her argument for identity based on internal qualities and not on physical features?

3. Why does Carter end by asserting that she no longer wonders when she crosses the line between black and white behaviors? What do you think has changed for her?

In-Class Writing Activities

1. Why do you think Carter and her friend never discuss the idea of being white at certain times and black at other times? What is significant about the location where she feels this conversation *should* happen? How does the personal essay work as a site for thinking through her questions? Keeping in mind the two locations Carter mentions at the beginning of her essay, write an essay about where conversations about race happen in American society and why.

2. Read the first three paragraphs of the first chapter of W. E. B. Du Bois's *The Souls of Black Folk*. Then write an essay in which you use Du Bois's ideas to analyze Carter's experience in the club.

ANNOTATION Using Parallel Structures

By using parallel structures, writers can make their sentences and paragraphs more coherent and memorable. Observe how President John F. Kennedy famously employed parallelism in his Inaugural Address (January 20, 1961): "Let every nation know, whether it wishes us well or ill, that we shall pay any price, bear any burden, meet any hardship, support any friend, oppose any foe to assure the survival and success of liberty." As you can see from this prime example, parallel structures are built by pairing ideas, balancing clauses, and repeating key words and phrases. Note, too, that Kennedy is also careful to balance sounds and rhythms at the same time.

In the following excerpt, you will see how a Bridgewater State College student, Lauren Carter, effectively draws on parallel structures for emphasis and coherence. Parallel structures inform these two paragraphs, as she uses them to balance clauses and pair ideas. Her basic structure is repeated throughout: "it wasn't because . . . it was because . . ." Note that in the first paragraph, she admires Frederick Douglass's "beautiful statement," which is also a fine example of parallel structure: "You have seen how a man was made a slave; now you shall see how a slave was made a man."

Carter points out Douglass's use of parallel structure in a famous quotation.

When Frederick Douglass found ways to teach himself to read, it wasn't because of his melanin content. It was because of his desire to learn, his ingenuity, his intelligence. After six months of torture by his brutal master Covey, Douglass made the bold and beautiful statement: "You have seen how a man was made a slave; now you shall see how a slave was made a man." 1

Carter effectively uses the phrasing "it wasn't because . . . it was because . . ." three times in this paragraph, giving her sentences a balanced rhythm and a memorable quality.

And when he did make that journey from slavery to manhood, it wasn't because of the coil of his hair, it was because of the color of his character. When Gabriel Prosser decided to lead a revolt in pursuit of freedom, it wasn't because of the size of his muscles, it was because of the size of his spirit. When blacks survived slavery, it wasn't because of the width of their noses or how many calluses they did or didn't have on their hands. It was because of the survival strategies they'd developed over time, none of which had anything to do with appearance. 2

—From "Isn't Watermelon Delicious?" by Lauren Carter, page 246

Student Writer at Work: Lauren Carter
On Writing "Isn't Watermelon Delicious?"

Q: What inspired you to write "Isn't Watermelon Delicious?"

A: It was in response to a final assignment for an African American literature course. My teacher, Dr. Jerald Walker, was also the adviser for the *Bridge* and encouraged me to submit the piece.

Q: Tell us about your writing process.

A: I always revise my work, starting with a basic framework and moving closer and closer to the end result I envision. My goals as I revised "Isn't Watermelon Delicious?" were to improve the clarity and power of the piece to communicate my point in the most effective way possible. On a rare occasion, I might bounce ideas off others, but in this case I did not. This piece was extremely personal, and I knew exactly what I wanted to say, so I did not need input from outside sources beyond what the course had given me. The books, films, and class discussions over the course of the semester had given me new ideas to think about, but ultimately when it came to sitting down and writing the piece, I knew what I wanted to say.

Q: How is writing involved in your life today?

A: After graduation I began writing for a newspaper full-time and am now working as a freelance writer for several publications.

Q: What advice do you have for other student writers?

A: Be true to your own ideas. Take what other people say about your writing into account, but know that only you truly know what you want to say and will know when you've truly said it. Don't listen to those who would discourage you as a writer or blatantly insult your work rather than offer constructive feedback, and don't be discouraged if you're not where you want to be as a writer—keep working at it and you'll get there. Don't look at writing as drudgery—view it as an opportunity to express yourself. Develop your own style, stand out, and have fun!

Racial Segregation: Little Rock's Central High School

The landmark Supreme Court decision Brown v. Board of Education *ended racial segregation legally in 1954 but did not stop it immediately in practice, as many southern states and school districts resisted the ruling and attempted to prevent black students from entering white schools. The Court had requested that the South respond with*

"all deliberate speed," but many were surprised at the extent of resistance, which involved threats, terrorism, and murder. The movement to integrate was widely covered by the newest technological development in media—television, then in its infancy. One of the major battles against integration was conducted at Central High School in Little Rock, Arkansas, where President Dwight Eisenhower had to send federal troops to enforce the new law. Photographer Will Counts documented this resistance in a number of dramatic photographs that have taken their place in civil rights history. In the photograph on the facing page, we can see an angry group taunting and threatening Elizabeth Eckford, one of nine black students seeking admission to Central High School on September 4, 1957. Years later, the young woman shown screaming at Eckford apologized for her behavior.

Discussing the Unit

Suggested Topic for Discussion

Each of the authors in this unit deliberately refers to his or her racial identity in order to make an argument. To what extent does each of these works depend on the author's personal experiences, and how much are those experiences shaped by race?

Preparing for Class Discussion

1. How has Obama's victory in the 2008 presidential election affected the country's discussion of race? In your opinion, what has Obama's victory changed about America? After reading his speech, what significance do you think he attaches to the idea of a first African American president?

2. Each of these authors offers, if not holistic remedies, at least partial solutions to the problems of race. How would you compare their different recommendations for dealing with racial issues?

From Discussion to Writing

1. What images of blackness do these authors discuss and challenge in their essays? Paying particular attention to Walker's and Carter's essays, make a list of perceptions or misperceptions

about African Americans. Where do these ideas about what it means to be black come from?

2. Although the three works in this unit address similar issues, Obama's medium, the political speech, differs significantly from the personal essay genre that both Walker and Carter write in. Write an analysis of how the medium makes a difference in how the writers deliver their messages. How does the medium affect their language or structure?

Topics for Cross-Cultural Discussion

1. America has a particularly deep history of racial division, but other countries have been in the news in recent years for their internal racial tensions. What other countries experience conflict over race?

2. In the United States, race has long been portrayed as divided between whites and blacks, but the increasing Latino population is challenging this binary. How do you think this less clear-cut dichotomy is changing or complicating discussions of race in the United States?

8

Education Today: Is Underachieving the Norm?

The first essay in this unit, Susan Jacoby's "How Dumb Can We Get?" begins with a quotation from Ralph Waldo Emerson: "The mind of this country, taught to aim at low objects, eats upon itself." Emerson made his dire assessment of the American intellect in the 1830s, and it is instructive to remember that similar sentiments have been expressed by America's intellectuals since the dawn of its history. But today, as test scores plummet, curricula are dumbed down, and *Are You Smarter Than a Fifth Grader* reveals that not a lot of people are, it may be time to ask again the old question: Are Americans getting dumber?

Jacoby herself argues that the problem is not our society's ignorance but rather its overt celebration of ignorance itself. Citing Richard Hofstadter's landmark book *Anti-Intellectualism in American Life*, Jacoby laments that if Hofstadter were alive today, "he would have found that our era of 24/7 infotainment has outstripped his most apocalyptic predictions about the future of American culture." Jacoby points to the rise of easy-to-access, lowbrow media like TV and the Internet to explain why young people can no longer find countries in the news on a map—or even care to. She goes on to argue that this pervasive attitude—"the alarming number of Americans who have smugly concluded that they do not need to know such things in the first place"—can be dangerous: The political discourse that keeps our democracy running is, Jacoby argues, increasingly un-informed.

University of Central Arkansas student Amy Widner witnesses this sort of arrogant ignorance every day in a particularly disturbing place: the hallowed halls of one of America's elite universities. In "The Pursuit of Just Getting By," Widner observes that her fellow students virtually compete to see who can study the least and perform the most poorly. Widner analyzes the incessant habit of "pretending to be dumb to look cool" at her college and concludes that it repre-sents a kind of anti-intellectualism (although she doesn't name it as such): An underachieving student proudly declaring that "D is for diploma" cheapens the learning experience that American universities are supposed to offer. "It makes college a joke," she writes, "and I'm not quite ready to believe it is yet."

Another student essay scrutinizing the intellectual mood on col-lege campuses, "Should Professors Podcast Their Lectures?" exam-ines an issue heating up at schools everywhere—the broadcasting of lectures over streaming video or iPods—and connects it to student achievement. The practice of broadcasting lectures (or coursecasting) would prove a serious detriment to student attendance and achieve-ment, Jason Shepherd of the University of South Alabama maintains: "The lazy, the irresponsible and the apathetic will start to depend on coursecasting instead of actually showing up to class." Shepherd ad-mits that coursecasting represents an impressive technological achievement with an academic use, "but only a minor one." Instead of relying on new ways to make learning more convenient, he argues, students should hit the books.

Although a virtual lecture hall may be disturbing to some tradi-tionalists, it can't compare to Structural Educational Materials (SEMs), the phenomenon Allen D. Kanner describes in "Today's Class Brought to You By . . ." SEMs are programs that large consumer-product companies create to infiltrate classrooms and advertise to kids. According to Kanner, corporations such as McDonald's and Campbell Soup use class materials like textbooks and lesson plans to advertise their products, or even their political agendas: Chevron sends out materials skeptical of global warming. The materials "are a means for corporations to promote their products and market messages to a captive audience that can't change the channel or click to a new website," Kanner says. "An additional bonus is the implicit endorsement of the school."

So if education at the grade school level has become little more than commercial entertainment, is it time to start worrying about what Americans are learning? And are our failing schools the source of our society's dumbing down? Or is it something deeper—something, even, in our culture?

SUSAN JACOBY

How Dumb Can We Get?

[THE WEEK/February 29, 2008]

Before You Read

Why are Americans becoming less literate? What factors contribute to a decrease in reading and in awareness of political and cultural issues?

Words to Learn

prescience (para. 1): forethought or knowledge of something before it happens (n.)
jeremiad (para. 7): a tirade, especially one that laments some situation (n.)
erosion (para. 12): wearing down (n.)

Susan Jacoby graduated from Michigan State University in 1965 and began her career as a reporter for the Washington Post. *Her first book,* Moscow Conversations, *was published in 1972, and since then, she has written eight books and contributed essays and articles to many publications, including the* New York Times Magazine, Washington Post Book World, Los Angeles Times Book Review, Newsday, Harper's, *the* Nation, Vogue, *the* American Prospect, Mother Jones, *and the* AARP Magazine. *Jacoby's writing explores a wide range of topics, including "law, religion, medicine, aging, women's rights, political dissent in the Soviet Union, and Russian literature." She currently serves as the program director for the New York branch of the Center for Inquiry, a rationalist think tank.*

"The mind of this country, taught to aim at low objects, eats   1
upon itself." Ralph Waldo Emerson offered that observation in 1837,
but his words echo with painful prescience in today's very different
United States. Americans are in serious intellectual trouble—in danger of losing our hard-won cultural capital to a virulent mixture of
anti-intellectualism, anti-rationalism, and low expectations.

This is the last subject that any candidate would dare raise on the   2
long and winding road to the White House. It is almost impossible to
talk about the manner in which public ignorance contributes to grave
national problems without being labeled an "elitist," one of the most
powerful pejoratives that can be applied to anyone aspiring to high
office. Instead, our politicians repeatedly assure Americans that they
are just "folks," a patronizing term that you will search for in vain in
important presidential speeches before 1980. (Just imagine: "We here
highly resolve that these dead shall not have died in vain . . . and that
government of the folks, by the folks, for the folks, shall not perish
from the earth.") Such exaltations of ordinariness are among the dis-
tinguishing traits of anti-intellectualism in any era.

The classic work on this subject by Columbia University historian   3
Richard Hofstadter, *Anti-Intellectualism in American Life*, was published in early 1963, between the anti-communist crusades of the Mc-
Carthy era and the social convulsions of the late 1960s. Hofstadter saw
American anti-intellectualism as a basically cyclical phenomenon that
often manifested itself as the dark side of the country's democratic impulses in religion and education. But today's brand of anti-intellectualism is less a cycle than a flood. If Hofstadter (who died of leukemia in
1970 at age 54) had lived long enough to write a modern-day sequel, he
would have found that our era of 24/7 infotainment has outstripped his
most apocalyptic predictions about the future of American culture.

Dumbness, to paraphrase the late Sen. Daniel Patrick Moynihan,   4
has been steadily defined downward for several decades, by a combination of heretofore irresistible forces. These include the triumph of
video culture over print culture (and by video, I mean every form of
digital media, as well as older electronic ones); a disjunction between
Americans' rising level of formal education and their shaky grasp
of basic geography, science, and history; and the fusion of anti-
rationalism with anti-intellectualism.

First and foremost among the vectors of the new anti-intellectual-   5
ism is video. The decline of book, newspaper, and magazine reading
is by now an old story. The drop-off is most pronounced among the

young, but it continues to accelerate and afflict Americans of all ages and education levels.

Reading has declined not only among the poorly educated, according to a report last year by the National Endowment for the Arts. In 1982, 82 percent of college graduates read novels or poems for pleasure; two decades later, only 67 percent did. And more than 40 percent of Americans under 44 did not read a single book—fiction or nonfiction—over the course of a year. The proportion of 17-year-olds who read nothing (unless required to do so for school) more than doubled between 1984 and 2004. This time period, of course, encompasses the rise of personal computers, Web surfing, and videogames.   6

> *The proportion of 17-year-olds who read nothing (unless required to do so for school) more than doubled between 1984 and 2004.*

Does all this matter? Technophiles pooh-pooh jeremiads about the end of print culture as the navel-gazing of (what else?) elitists. In his book *Everything Bad Is Good for You: How Today's Popular Culture Is Actually Making Us Smarter*, the science writer Steven Johnson assures us that we have nothing to worry about. Sure, parents may see their "vibrant and active children gazing silently, mouths agape, at the screen." But these zombie-like characteristics "are not signs of mental atrophy. They're signs of focus." Balderdash. The real question is what toddlers are screening out, not what they are focusing on, while they sit mesmerized by videos they have seen dozens of times.   7

Despite an aggressive marketing campaign aimed at encouraging babies as young as 6 months to watch videos, there is no evidence that focusing on a screen is anything but bad for infants and toddlers. In a study released last August, University of Washington researchers found that babies between 8 and 16 months recognized an average of six to eight fewer words for every hour spent watching videos.   8

I cannot prove that reading for hours in a treehouse (which is what I was doing when I was 13) creates more informed citizens than hammering away at a Microsoft Xbox or obsessing about Facebook profiles. But the inability to concentrate for long periods of time—as distinct from brief reading hits for information on the Web—seems to me intimately related to the inability of the public to remember even recent news events. It is not surprising, for example, that less has been heard from the presidential candidates about the Iraq war in the later stages of the primary campaign than in the earlier ones, simply   9 because there have been fewer video reports of violence in Iraq. Candidates, like voters, emphasize the latest news, not necessarily the most important news.

No wonder negative political ads work. "With text, it is even   10
easy to keep track of differing levels of authority behind different pieces of information," the cultural critic Caleb Crain noted recently in *The New Yorker*. "A comparison of two video reports, on the other hand, is cumbersome. Forced to choose between conflicting stories on television, the viewer falls back on hunches, or on what he believed before he started watching."

As video consumers become progressively more impatient with   11
the process of acquiring information through written language, all politicians find themselves under great pressure to deliver their messages as quickly as possible—and quickness today is much quicker than it used to be. Harvard University's Kiku Adatto found that between 1968 and 1988, the average sound bite on the news for a presidential candidate—featuring the candidate's own voice—dropped from 42.3 seconds to 9.8 seconds. By 2000, according to another Harvard study, the daily candidate bite was down to just 7.8 seconds.

The shrinking public attention span fostered by video is closely   12
tied to the second important anti-intellectual force in American culture: the erosion of general knowledge.

People accustomed to hearing their president explain complicated   13
policy choices by snapping "I'm the decider" may find it almost impossible to imagine the pains that Franklin D. Roosevelt took, in the grim months after Pearl Harbor, to explain why U.S. armed forces were suffering one defeat after another in the Pacific. In February 1942, Roosevelt urged Americans to spread out a map during his radio "fireside chat" so that they might better understand the geography of battle. In stores throughout the country, maps sold out; about 80 percent of American adults tuned in to hear the president. FDR had told his speechwriters that he was certain that if Americans understood the immensity of the distances over which supplies had to travel to the armed forces, "they can take any kind of bad news right on the chin."

This is a portrait not only of a different presidency and president   14
but also of a different country and citizenry, one that lacked access to satellite-enhanced Google maps but was far more receptive to learning and complexity than today's public. According to a 2006 survey by National Geographic–Roper, nearly half of Americans between

ages 18 and 24 do not think it necessary to know the location of other countries in which important news is being made. More than a third consider it "not at all important" to know a foreign language, and only 14 percent consider it "very important."

That leads us to the third and final factor behind the new American dumbness: not lack of knowledge per se but arrogance about that lack of knowledge. The problem is not just the things we do not know (consider the one in five American adults who, according to the National Science Foundation, thinks the sun revolves around the Earth); it's the alarming number of Americans who have smugly concluded that they do not need to know such things in the first place. Call this anti-rationalism—a syndrome that is particularly dangerous to our public institutions and discourse. Not knowing a foreign language or the location of an important country is a manifestation of ignorance; denying that such knowledge matters is pure anti-rationalism. The toxic brew of anti-rationalism and ignorance hurts discussions of U.S. public policy on topics from health care to taxation.   15

There is no quick cure for this epidemic of arrogant anti-rationalism and anti-intellectualism; rote efforts to raise standardized test scores by stuffing students with specific answers to specific questions on specific tests will not do the job. Moreover, the people who exemplify the problem are usually oblivious to it. ("Hardly anyone believes himself to be against thought and culture," Hofstadter noted.) It is past time for a serious national discussion about whether, as a nation, we truly value intellect and rationality. If this indeed turns out to be a "change election," the low level of discourse in a country with a mind taught to aim at low objects ought to be the first item on the change agenda.   16

Vocabulary/Using a Dictionary

1. What does the suffix *-phile* mean? What is a *technophile* (para. 7)?

2. Look up the meanings of the word *cumber*. Which one seems most relevant to Caleb Crain's description of in-depth textual analysis as "cumbersome" (para. 10)?

3. Look up meaning of the word *rational*. How does its definition help you understand Jacoby's term *anti-rationalism* (para. 1)?

Responding to Words in Context

1. Why does Jacoby think the use of the word *folks* (para. 2) is patronizing? What is the purpose of substituting *folks* for *people* in the sentence from the Gettysburg Address?

2. What two words are combined in *infotainment* (para. 3)? What does this word have to do with Jacoby's critique of anti-intellectualism?

3. Why does Jacoby call anti-intellectual and anti-rational sentiments an "epidemic" (para. 16)? What does that word imply?

Discussing Main Point and Meaning

1. What does Jacoby mean when she says that "dumbness . . . has been steadily defined downward" (para. 4)? What has changed in the past few decades?

2. How does Jacoby explain the fact that the presidential candidates talked about the Iraq War less and less as the primary campaigns went on? Why is this important to her message?

3. How does Jacoby compare recent presidents such as Bush and Clinton to presidents in the more distant past? Whom does she hold up as an example?

Examining Sentences, Paragraphs, and Organization

1. What purpose do the statistics in paragraph 6 serve? How do they support Jacoby's argument?

2. How does the first sentence in paragraph 14 set up a comparison between American citizens today and those of previous generations?

3. How does Jacoby end her essay? What is the purpose of the last paragraph?

Thinking Critically

1. Jacoby seems to agree with Hofstadter that anti-intellectualism is possibly the flip side to America's "democratic impulses in religion and education" (para. 3). What characteristics of American

ideology might lend themselves to an anti-intellectual or anti-rational bias?

2. How does Jacoby think anti-intellectualism influences the tone of political ads? How does the quote from Caleb Crain help support her argument about negative ads (para. 10)?

3. Do you agree with Jacoby that we are in an age of a "new American dumbness" (para. 15)? Do you see any cultural trends that suggest otherwise?

In-Class Writing Activities

1. Do you think Jacoby's criticisms of anti-intellectualism would apply to your college as well as to the country at large? If not, where do students get information or share ideas on public matters? If so, how would you like to see the level of discourse raised on your campus?

2. In her last paragraph, Jacoby targets standardized testing as one misguided way of educating students. Write an essay in which you discuss the role of standardized testing in schools. Would you defend the tests as a way of accounting for what students learn? Or do you think they're actually counterproductive?

AMY WIDNER (STUDENT ESSAY)

The Pursuit of Just Getting By

[THE ECHO, University of Central Arkansas / March 12, 2008]

Before You Read

How do today's college students compare to previous generations? What is the average student's attitude toward his or her courses?

Words to Learn

academic (para. 5): belonging to school, particularly college or university (adj.)

excelling (para. 6): having great success; outperforming others (v.)

Pretending to be dumb to look cool didn't make sense in high school and it certainly doesn't make sense in college. And yet I can't even begin to count how many times I've overheard fellow students play the how-low-achieving-can-you-go game before class starts.   1

"Hey man, how'd you do on the test?"   2

"Oh, man, I got a D, but I didn't study at all, so I guess it's alright."   3

"Yeah, same here. D is for diploma."   4

While I recognize the various purposes that such a conversation might serve—stress relief, nervous small talk, academic confession-   5

Amy Widner is a recent graduate of the University of Central Arkansas, where she received degrees in print journalism and international studies. While a student, she served in multiple capacities for the Echo, *the student newspaper of the University of Central Arkansas, serving at various times as reporter, head editor, opinion editor, and advertising manager. After graduating, Widner continued writing, as a reporter for the* Arkansas Democrat-Gazette. *As a reporter, she is "most interested in understanding others and being able to channel that understanding into something that the reader can also understand. I am the middleman between source and audience, the storyteller."*

als—an unfortunate, and allegedly unintentional side effect is that it gets on my nerves. These conversations, and their evil twin—the have-you-started-on-that-project-yet conversation—may be commonplace enough that they seem normal, but they indicate some very abnormal thinking.

We're in college and our education is costing someone money. In a time when it has become almost automatic to get an undergraduate degree, it seems like students are losing sight of this. But even if college is starting to feel more like extended high school, procrastinating and trying to get by doing as little as possible does not make sense. We are paying our professors to teach us as much as they can to increase our chances of excelling in the job market. Why avoid those lessons when we, our parents, and even taxpayers are spending so much for us to have access to knowledge? 6

Professors are not an enemy setting up some kind of obstacle course to be successfully navigated. The winner is not the person who completes the obstacle course with the least amount of effort. And there is no automatic prize at the end—no cheese, and certainly no job. Skills and knowledge are what help students get jobs in the real world, as well as experience working hard and getting things done on time. None of these things are achieved by avoiding work. 7

> *Skills and knowledge are what help students get jobs in the real world, as well as experience working hard and getting things done on time.*

Another aspect of this attitude that doesn't make sense is what it assumes about employers. Imagine an employer saying the following: "Hi, I'm an employer. I see you graduated from college. That must mean that you know everything you need to know to work for me, so I won't bother seeing if you have any of the skills needed for this job. I'll go ahead and pay you well while I'm at it, because you graduated from college and that's all I care about." 8

Why does all of this bother me so much? It makes students in general look bad, which decreases trust and professionalism. It shows disrespect to professors and the knowledge they're trying to share. It creates a fake atmosphere in the classroom, where the pursuit of knowledge should be the goal instead of the pursuit of just getting by. It lessens what having a college degree means. It makes college a joke, and I'm not quite ready to believe it is yet. 9

The two students having the conversation above should either be making the most of their education by completing their assignments 10 on time and to the best of their abilities, or should be too ashamed to admit out loud that they are doing otherwise. Procrastination and poor work ethic should not be what we're practicing in college, because they're not what we should be proud of and, in the end, will not be what we'll be rewarded for. So the next time we're tempted to boast at how little work we got away with on that last assignment or how close to the last minute we waited to get something done, remember: We're not fooling anybody but ourselves.

Vocabulary / Using a Dictionary

1. What is the root of the word *procrastination* (para. 10)? What is the meaning of that word?

2. Look up the word *cognize*. How is *recognize* (para. 5) related to this meaning?

3. What is the original Greek meaning of *diploma* (para. 4)? How has the meaning of the word changed?

Responding to Words in Context

1. What does Widner mean when she says that underachieving decreases "professionalism" (para. 9)? What kind of behavior does that word imply?

2. Why does Widner call the conversation between the two students "abnormal thinking" (para. 5)? What would she consider normal?

3. Widner argues that college has become "almost automatic" (para. 6) for most students. What does she mean by this?

Discussing Main Point and Meaning

1. At the beginning of her essay, Widner re-creates a conversation she frequently overhears among students. What possible explanations does she offer for why students talk this way? What underlying problem does she think the exchange reveals?

2. What is making college feel like "extended high school" (para. 6)? Why does Widner think this becomes a problem?

3. How does Widner think that underachieving hurts students in the long run?

Examining Sentences, Paragraphs, and Organization

1. In paragraph 8, Widner includes an imagined statement from a potential employer. What is the tone of this quotation? What assumptions is she trying to reveal?

2. Look at the structure of paragraph 9. How does Widner order her ideas in this paragraph? What is its purpose?

3. Why does Widner switch to the pronoun *we* at the end of her essay? Why is this important to her final warning?

Thinking Critically

1. In paragraph 1, Widner argues that if "playing dumb" in high school was misguided, it is even more so in college. Why does she think so? Can you think of some reasons why college students should be even less likely to adhere to this version of cool?

2. Why does Widner use an obstacle course as an analogy for college? What does that comparison imply?

In-Class Writing Activities

1. Have you heard similar conversations around campus? Write a response to Widner in which you compare the climate at your school with the one she describes.

2. Much of Widner's argument is based on what employers will want from students and how a college education can provide it. Try to imagine yourself in the place of someone looking to hire a new employee. Write a list of expectations you think you would have for a college graduate.

JASON SHEPHERD (STUDENT ESSAY)

Should Professors Podcast Their Lectures?

[VANGUARD, University of South Alabama/February 19, 2007]

Before You Read

What is coursecasting? How could technology be used to supplement or even replace college courses?

Words to Learn

inclined (para. 4): having a tendency toward something (adj.)
pertinent (para. 5): relevant or appropriate (adj.)

The newest fad in higher education seems to be right around the   1
corner, in the form of podcasts — video recordings made to download
onto a computer or iPod. As the popularity of podcasting grows, universities have decided to jump on the bandwagon, making class lectures available online as podcasts, or as some have more appropriately dubbed it, "coursecasting." Proponents of coursecasting are
selling it as a way for professors to connect to student culture, thus
helping to bridge the gap in student-teacher relationships while encouraging greater participation. Supporters also see coursecasting as
a way for students to catch up without forcing professors to slow

---

*Jason Shepherd is a senior at the University of South Alabama, where he is
pursuing degrees in psychology and philosophy. He has served as both the
opinions editor and editor in chief of the* Vanguard, *the student newspaper of
the University of South Alabama, in which this essay appeared. With plans to
become a researcher in the fields of philosophy and cognitive science, Shepherd
is interested in exploring topics such as philosophy of mind, consciousness,
perception, cognition, and educational policy in his writing. He frequently
reads the* Chronicle of Higher Education *and other journals in the fields of
philosophy and cognitive science, and he advises other student writers that the
best thing they can do is to "read, read, read."*

down: Coursecasting would be the end of "Can you repeat that?" Coursecasting is also seen as a way to give students who are lacking background knowledge in a certain area a chance to catch up with their more knowledgeable peers.

But the widespread use of coursecasting is potentially troublesome on several levels. First, it is likely to do the opposite of bridging the gap between students and teachers and encouraging greater participation. In an informal survey, virtually all students who welcomed the idea of coursecasting admitted that they would be more likely to skip class. A second-year student in the College of Business admitted, "Podcasting would be great. I would never have to get up and go to an 8 AM class again."

With coursecasting, attendance will be sure to drop. The lazy, the irresponsible and the apathetic will start to depend on coursecasting instead of actually showing up to class. This benefits no one. There is absolutely no way that a recorded lecture can capture the benefits of interaction or the dynamics of a classroom setting. The learning process is an active one, and its potential would be greatly diminished if the core method of transferring knowledge became dependent on such passive means.

> *The lazy, the irresponsible and the apathetic will start to depend on coursecasting instead of actually showing up to class.*

Coursecasting would encourage laziness not only among students, but potentially among some professors as well. As the focus rotates more around the coursecast, a professor may be less inclined to focus on classroom instructional methods. Professors will no longer be concerned about rushing through important information, knowing that the student can just go back and listen to the coursecast. If the original explanation was unclear, the professor could direct the student to re-listen to the same muddled explanation over and over again via coursecast until it finally sinks in. No more "Can you repeat that?" also means no more "Can you explain that again?"

As far as providing uninformed students with pertinent background knowledge, coursecasting lectures would not achieve this goal to any greater extent than better attendance. After all, we are talking about podcasts of the lectures, not podcasting supplemental materials. Besides, if some students are missing background information, they cannot ask the coursecast to fill in the blanks, but they can ask the professor in person. Better yet, those students could actually read the assigned material prior to coming to lecture. After reading, if the students don't feel confident enough in their knowledge of the subject, they can easily search the Internet for supplemental information on the subject. This would be much more effective.

Of course, there may be room to use some form of podcasting as an aid, but only a minor one. Any professor using podcasts needs to be sure that they complement classroom lectures and in no way replace any part of the classroom experience, even if this replacement is only accidental.   6

ANNOTATION The Art of Argument: Summarizing Opposing Positions

When making a case for or against a position, writers should let the reader know in advance the arguments on the other side. In this way, the reader will clearly understand the major points or positions the writer disagrees with. Note how Jason Shepherd effectively introduces in his opening paragraph the positions he will argue against in the rest of his essay. After introducing his topic in the first sentence—the growing popularity of podcasting university lectures—Shepherd then provides three reasons why proponents of podcasting (or coursecasting) support the growing trend: (1) It will help professors better connect with student culture and thus improve faculty-student relationships; (2) it will help lectures proceed more effectively by making repetition unnecessary; and (3) it will give those less knowledgeable in the subject area a chance to catch up with those who are more knowledgeable. These three reasons are effectively summarized in three sentences.

Shepherd then proceeds in the rest of his paper to question the validity of these reasons, and he offers counterevidence to show that such educational goals will not likely be reached through podcasting—in fact, the trend could make education worse. Note, too, that by setting out the opposing positions in favor of podcasting in his first paragraph, Shepherd then has the outline of his essay in place; all he has to do is to refute each position in order.

Shepherd establishes his main topic—the trend toward podcasting lectures.

The newest fad in higher education seems to be right around the corner, in the form of podcasts—video recordings made to download onto a computer or iPod. As the popularity of podcasting grows, universities have decided to jump on the bandwagon, making class lectures available online as podcasts, or as some have more appropriately dubbed it, "coursecasting." Proponents of coursecasting are selling it as a way for professors to connect to student culture, thus helping to bridge the gap in student-teacher relationships while encouraging greater participation. Supporters also see coursecasting as a way for students to catch up without forcing professors to slow down: Coursecasting would be the end of "Can you repeat that?" Coursecasting is also seen as a way to give students who are lacking background knowledge in a certain area a chance to catch up with their more knowledgeable peers.

In three sentences, Shepherd provides three reasons given to support podcasting; he then devotes the rest of his essay to rejecting these reasons.

—From "Should Professors Podcast Their Lectures?" by Jason Shepherd, page 272

Vocabulary / Using a Dictionary

1. The root of the word *apathetic* (para. 3) is *pathos*. What is the meaning of this root? How does the addition of the prefix *a-* change its meaning?

2. What does the prefix *pro-* mean in the word *proponents* (para. 1)?

Responding to Words in Context

1. What are *podcasts*? Where does that term come from?

2. Why does Shepherd describe his peers as admitting that they would skip more classes if professors used coursecasts (para. 2)? What does the word *admit* imply?

3. How does Shepherd contrast the words *active* and *passive* in the last sentence of paragraph 3? Why is this contrast important to his argument?

Discussing Main Point and Meaning

1. In paragraph 1, Shepherd lists some of the ways in which proponents of coursecasting think it will benefit students and professors. What are these benefits?

2. What problems does Shepherd think coursecasting will bring with it?

3. What role does Shepherd think coursecasting should play in college? How should professors use it?

Examining Sentences, Paragraphs, and Organization

1. What is the purpose of Shepherd's first paragraph? What information does he provide there?

2. How does Shepherd use transitions in his essay to help the reader follow his argument? Make a list of the transition words he uses.

Thinking Critically

1. How did Shepherd conduct his "informal survey" (para. 2)? What would make his findings more formal?

2. What does Shepherd mean when he says that coursecasts should "complement" work in the classroom (para. 6)? Can you think of examples of how this would work?

In-Class Writing Activities

1. Have you ever taken a course that used podcasting? If so, how did it work? If not, how do you think podcasting might have been useful to courses you have taken?

2. What educational tools do you think are most helpful in your coursework? Is there a technology you can't imagine doing without in college?

ALLEN D. KANNER

Today's Class Brought to You By . . .

[TIKKUN / January–February 2008]

Before You Read

Have you ever encountered learning materials produced by a popular beverage company, by a recognized food chain, or by some other consumer-product corporation? What do you think happens to the content of a second grader's textbook sponsored by Target, or to a reading contest for middle schoolers run by McDonald's? Is there a benefit to keeping Structural Educational Materials out of our schools?

Words to Learn

prevalent (para. 3): widespread (adj.)

plundering (para. 3): robbery (n.)

discretionary (para. 4): for any purpose one chooses (adj.)

expedient (para. 4): favorable to a particular interest (adj.)

rife (para. 5): plentiful (adj.)

privatization (para. 7): the change of something from public to private control (n.)

relevance (para. 8): appropriateness to the matter at hand (n.)

Revlon, the cosmetics company, is being taught in public schools   1
these days. The corporation provides teachers with a free curriculum that instructs students on "good and bad hair days" and asks them to list the three hair products they would absolutely need if stranded on a desert island. Meanwhile, in science class, students can conduct a

Allen D. Kanner is an associate faculty member of the Wright Institute, a clinical psychology graduate school in Berkeley, California. He also works as a child, family, and adult therapist in Berkeley and is the coeditor of Ecopsychology: Restoring the Earth, Healing the Mind *(1995) and coauthor of* Psychology and Consumer Culture *(2005). As a psychologist, he has "conducted research on the impact of daily hassles and uplifts on health and well-being in children and adults."*

Campbell Soup "Prego Thickness Experiment" comparing the thickness of Prego versus Ragu spaghetti sauces. They can also learn from the American Coal Foundation that the planet may be helped rather than harmed by increased carbon dioxide, while materials sent by Chevron challenge the existence of global warming. A first grade curriculum uses logo recognition—K-Mart, Pizza Hut, Jell-O, and Target—to teach reading while McDonald's, not to be outdone, asks first graders to design a McDonald's restaurant and instructs them on how to apply to the company for a job.

The materials, which include colorful texts, entertaining videotapes, and detailed lesson plans, are a means for corporations to promote their products and market messages to a captive audience that can't change the channel or click to a new website.

These are examples of Structural Educational Materials (SEMs), free curricula produced by major corporations and directly distributed to the nation's teachers, typically through the mail or at educational conferences. Companies spend from $25,000 to more than one million dollars per SEM. The materials, which include colorful texts, entertaining videotapes, and detailed lesson plans, are a means for corporations to promote their products and market messages to a captive audience that can't change the channel or click to a new website. An additional bonus is the implicit endorsement of the school.

The usual explanation for the success of SEMs is that desperate teachers in underfunded schools use them as a last resort. Certainly this is true, and SEMs are most prevalent in poorer school districts. But funding is not the whole story, for American schools have grappled with financial difficulties before without opening their doors to corporate plundering.

Here is why things are different today: In the 1980s, market researchers discovered that children have far more discretionary income, and influence on parental spending, than previously imagined. The result was the rapid commercialization of childhood. In 1983, American companies spent $100 million advertising to children; in 2005 the figure was $16.8 billion. In this context, schools emerged on the marketing radar screen as a golden opportunity to reach millions of children while avoiding a key obstacle: their parents. It suddenly became expedient for corporations to participate in the education of American youth.

And participate they did. There is now advertising on school buses and school bus radio programs, on gym floors and clothes, over PA systems, inside school buildings and classrooms, and on school computer screens. Math textbooks present problems using Nike, Gatorade, and Topps trading cards as examples. Pizza Hut's BookIt contest gives free pizzas to kids who read a certain number of books. Tens of millions of children have entered the contest. Exclusive contracts with Coke or Pepsi exclude the presence of other soda companies from campus. Channel 1, a twelve-minute puff news program with two minutes of advertising, is viewed by 40 percent of U.S. teens. One company, The Field Trip Factory, has organized more than 20,000 off-campus excursions to destinations such as Domino's Pizza and Toys "R" Us. In an educational environment rife with sales pitches such as these, the introduction of SEMs does not appear particularly radical or worrisome.

The use of SEMs is also bolstered by the current national shortage of teachers. The lack of qualified teachers comes mostly from baby boomer retirements and high turnover among new teachers, who are often asked to step into difficult classroom situations to teach subjects for which they are inadequately trained. This shortage is particularly acute among math and science teachers and in poor school districts, a perfect setup for SEMs. Further, many young teachers themselves were educated in schools undergoing commercialization, perhaps making them more tolerant of SEMs than their older peers.

Aiding the commercialization of schools significantly, SEMs also contribute to an ongoing attempt by the business world and conservative politicians to privatize public education. This project includes school voucher programs, charter and for-profit schools, and private testing services, all of which increase the corporate presence in K–12 education. If privatization succeeds, sponsored educational materials could become the norm.

There are several ways to stop SEMs. One approach is to ban advertising in schools, thereby eliminating SEMs. Another is to require SEMs, like textbooks, to be screened for scientific accuracy and completeness, as well as educational relevance. Fully funding schools would also work. In fact, protecting schools from commercialization is now a pressing reason to ensure that public education is well financed.

Good teaching involves passing on society's deepest knowledge and highest values. SEMs pervert knowledge and undermine values. It's time they be expelled from school.

Vocabulary / Using a Dictionary

1. What part of speech is the word *pervert* (para. 9)? What does it mean? What are other meanings and parts of speech associated with the word?

2. What is the root of the word *discretionary* (para. 4)?

3. If advertising is to be *banned* (para. 8) in schools, what does that mean?

Responding to Words in Context

1. Where have you encountered the word *commercial*? How do the definitions of the word expand your understanding of Kanner's worry about the "commercialization of childhood" (para. 4)?

2. Kanner says that every time SEMs are used, they provide an "implicit endorsement of the school" (para. 2). What is the difference between an *implicit* and an *explicit* endorsement?

3. Kanner thinks that a new teacher might be inclined to use SEMs if he or she has been "inadequately trained" (para. 6) to teach his or her subject. What does *inadequate* mean in this context? Why would an adequately trained or well-trained teacher be less likely to rely on an SEM?

Discussing Main Point and Meaning

1. Kanner notes that corporations spent much more money marketing to children in 2005 than they did in 1983 (going from millions of dollars to billions of dollars) and that the focus on schools was an attempt to "participate in the education of American youth" (para. 4). What sort of "education" does this participation create?

2. Because students and even some teachers have grown accustomed to commercialization in schools, they are less likely to see SEMs as a threat to education. Where else does this kind of commercialization take place? Are there any areas of life that still resist commercialization?

3. Sometimes one person or a group of people wants to control the majority of input into a school's curricula. Kanner says that "if privatization [of the schools] succeeds, sponsored educational materials could become the norm" (para. 7). Considering his

argument, why would privatization be dangerous and possibly lead to the wider use of SEMs?

Examining Sentences, Paragraphs, and Organization

1. In paragraph 5, Kanner mentions that "exclusive contracts with Coke or Pepsi exclude the presence of other soda companies from campus." Why do you think he stresses the words *exclusive* and *exclude* in this sentence?

2. Paragraph 1 provides an example of Revlon "teaching" students about "good and bad hair days." Students are asked to list three hair products they would need if stranded on a desert island. How does this example influence the reader's understanding of what company-provided curricula are like?

3. Kanner begins by illustrating what SEMs are and spends a great deal of time providing examples and persuading the reader about his point of view. Where does his approach shift? How does the essay change?

Thinking Critically

1. Kanner notes that schools are a particularly fruitful place to market to children because advertisers can win children over to their products with no parental screens in their way. In what ways do parents shield their children from marketers? What about teachers?

2. Advertising can take many forms, and Kanner lists many of the ways advertisers have made their way onto school grounds. Have you ever felt as if you were being sold a product in school? What form did this advertising take? Was the advertising an incentive to learn, or was it just a suggestion to buy something from a particular company?

3. Before corporations began marketing to children, places of learning were less susceptible to commercialization. Kanner tells his readers they must now fight to keep SEMs out of the schools and offers several ideas about actions readers can take. Which do you think is his most effective suggestion? Why?

In-Class Writing Activities

1. Choose one of your favorite brand names—of clothing, food, or some other item. Using Kanner's introductory examples as a

guide, write a one-page description of an SEM that features it. How can the brand be used as a learning tool? What extra materials (such as text or videotapes) will be provided to the schools? Include a paragraph that outlines both the educational and the advertising goals of the SEM.

2. Money spent on advertising to children jumped from the millions in 1983 to the billions in 2005. If corporations are willing to spend vast amounts of money to market to the nation's youth, they must think that this group is a wise financial target. Write an essay explaining what makes young people more vulnerable to marketers than an older age group (people in their twenties, thirties, forties, or older). Consider which age group in childhood is most vulnerable, and say why you think this is so.

3. Kanner states, "SEMs pervert knowledge and undermine values" (para. 9). Using one of his examples of SEMs in the schools, write an essay explaining how this is so. Before you begin, brainstorm, based on his argument, what he might mean by *knowledge* and *values*, and also consider your own definitions for those terms.

Discussing the Unit

Suggested Topic for Discussion

What will education in America look like in ten years? Or twenty? How would the writers in this chapter forecast the future of American schools and universities? What trends do you think will become important or influential?

Preparing for Class Discussion

1. How does the level of education that each of these authors addresses affect his or her take on education? What concerns are specific to primary schools? To higher education?

2. What kind of evidence do these four authors use in their arguments? What other ideas or opinions do they rely on?

From Discussion to Writing

1. Choose two of the essays from this unit and write an essay in which you compare their recommendations or solutions to

problems in education. Are these answers compatible with one another?

2. Both Widner and Shepherd identify problems or potential problems they see on their campuses. What problems do you think your college should address? Write an essay in which you identify a problem or pose a question about education at your school. How does this problem become apparent? Whom does it affect?

Topics for Cross-Cultural Discussion

1. Jacoby identifies anti-intellectualism as a particularly American problem. Do any other countries have similar cultural climates? Which countries place a much stronger value on education?

2. How does the issue of immigration affect American schools? How do children of undocumented immigrants get educated?

9

Signs of Change: What Can We Expect America to Be?

Alexis de Tocqueville, an early but prescient observer of the United States, observed that Americans "would rather be equal in slavery than unequal in freedom." At the time, America had not fought the calamitous civil war that would end the practice of human bondage and challenge future generations to consider the question of how equal we should strive to be. Are our class differences a natural product of our liberties, or are they an inexorable source of division? Can we become more equal? Should we change as a society, and if so, how do we bring changes about democratically?

This unit looks at these questions, particularly the last one, by examining the role that young people have in changing America's future. Marco Roth's essay "Lower the Voting Age!" begins the discussion by considering who should have the right to participate in electoral democracy and, at least theoretically, steer the country's future direction. Roth doesn't provide a specific proposal for dropping the age of enfranchisement, which has been set at eighteen since 1971; he argues that it "should have been lowered to 16, at least." Rather, he reasons more abstractly that expanding the franchise of voting will stir a new generation out of the political apathy that seems to pervade American life. Besides, younger teenagers may make more enthusiastic voters: "They may have just read and debated the Constitution, the Voting Rights Act, or the concept of separation of powers," Roth writes. "How many of us, as older voters, can say the same?"

Paul Starr also argues that young people have become disentitled. But in "A New Deal of Their Own," Starr focuses not on voting rights but on social programs such as Social Security and Medicaid that the government employs to help the elderly. Why, Starr asks, have young people (he focuses on the eighteen- to twenty-four-year-old demographic) gotten the short end of such entitlements? Social movements like the New Deal and the Great Society have largely ignored younger people, or have focused on those with specific needs, leaving the great majority on their own.

Starr acknowledges critics who argue that society shouldn't play nanny to anyone, especially those physically and mentally equipped to support themselves. But a more equitable society, he concludes, will mean supporting the young the way the post–World War II GI Bill did, in a way that offers opportunity for advancement to everyone but recognizes support as an investment in individuals capable of returning on it. "The challenge in creating a durable basis for social investment in the young is to reconcile these two ideals — universality and reciprocity—recognizing that as children become adolescents and then young adults, it's appropriate to premise some benefits on their efforts."

The participation of the young in America has often been caricatured in images of radical politics, such as marches and organized protests. Joseph Hart considers the future of civil disobedience in his thoughtful essay "Protest Is Dead. Long Live Protest." Hart criticizes conventional protesters who seek attention for their causes with the worn-out models of marches and celebrity speak-ins. "The problem," he tells us, "is that American peace activists have been marching down the same cul-de-sac for more than four decades, a tactic that, during one of the nation's most tumultuous periods, is proving to be a dramatic failure." Hart argues that if the next generation hopes to trigger real change, it must cultivate new and more creative forms of protest, taking advantage of new technologies and means of disseminating information—what he calls "digital disobedience."

Most surprisingly, perhaps, Hart enjoins young activists, particularly on the left side of the political spectrum, to forgo one-sided demonstrations involving shouted slogans in favor of a more interactive approach, sitting down and talking with political opponents. The "us-versus-them mentality" of the politically radical, Hart says, "alienates potential allies with the power to act and instead causes them to react defensively." University of Washington student Jeff Dickson agrees: In his essay "United We Strive, Divided We Falter," he delivers an impassioned plea for more political unity. People with a conscience can change the country, Dickson argues, but changes have come about most smoothly only after Americans have set aside petty political differences and embraced our united ideals: "It's our collective talent and diversity that make us great, and the greatest times in our nation's history have come when we banded together and worked toward a common goal."

The chapter concludes with "America Then . . . 1920." In that year, women finally gained the right to vote, although they could not legally cast a vote to give themselves that right. What they did instead was protest, demonstrate, get arrested, and argue their position whenever and wherever they could until Congress ratified the Nineteenth Amendment ensuring women the right to vote.

MARCO ROTH

Lower the Voting Age!

[n+1/Winter 2008]

Before You Read

Should the voting age be lowered, or is age eighteen the right limit for voters? What reasons exist for holding the age at eighteen? Do you think those reasons are outdated? Do voters assume certain responsibilities that a younger person wouldn't understand or handle as well as someone eighteen or older?

Words to Learn

consensus (para. 1): general agreement (n.)

righteously (para. 1): acting from an outraged sense of justice (adv.)

self-centered (para. 1): concerned with one's desires and interests (adj.)

revanchist (para. 2): relating to a political policy of revenge (usually for a previous military defeat) (adj.)

catalyst (para. 2): an agent that speeds change (n.)

stalemate (para. 2): deadlock (n.)

electorate (para. 2): people entitled to vote (n.)

imputed (para. 2): attributed or ascribed to (v.)

surge (para. 3): a sudden swell (n.)

elites (para. 3): the superior or ruling class (n.)

spectrum (para. 3): a continuous range (n.)

apathy (para. 4): lack of interest or excitement (n.)

trivialize (para. 4): to reduce to little importance (v.)

Marco Roth is one of the founding editors of n+1, *which is described as "a magazine of literature, politics, and culture . . . with an eye for the new idea, the impossible vision, the remarkable work of art." Roth graduated from Columbia University and is currently a doctoral candidate in comparative literature at Yale University. He regularly publishes essays in* n+1 *as well as other publications, such as* Nextbook *and* Critical Mass, *the blog of the National Book Critics Circle board of directors.*

exclusionary (para. 5): restrictive (adj.)

stagnant (para. 9): not advancing or developing (adj.)

indenture (para. 9): to bind oneself to a contract (v.)

The voting age was lowered from 21 to 18 only in 1971, by   1
Constitutional amendment. A response to Vietnam, the consensus of
the times was summed up in the slogan "Old enough to fight, old
enough to vote!" Simple and direct. Like most of boomer politics, the
campaign succeeded through an appeal from pride to shame: from
the righteously self-centered youth of the Age of Aquarius to an older
generation still capable of vague feelings of responsibility for their actions and the future effects of those actions. Its success, however, was
at best incomplete. As the boomers aged, spawned, developed their
own family romances, discovered market capitalism and medical
dreams of eternal life, their early promise of civic engagement was
left unfulfilled. America has never recovered from that failed promise.
The voting age should have been lowered to 16, at least—because at
18 you could still suddenly be drafted, fight, and die in a war started
by a government you had never previously voted for. It's time for our
overly cautious democratic Congress to fix that mistake and bring the
voting age down again, even if we no longer have military conscrip-
tion. Constitutional amendments, after all, are not under the oversight of either the judicial or the executive branch.

Lowering the voting age was always a good idea for American   2
democracy for reasons that have little to do with military and security questions. The old reasons are still there, along with some new
ones that have emerged since the '70s. Lowering the voting age is not
just a matter of rewarding potential soldiers with full citizenship
rights. Electoral reform that expands the franchise, historically, has
led to major social change. That change can be good or bad. On the
good side, in America and Western Europe, the abolition of property
requirements made possible the eventual enfranchisement of women
and former slaves, and laid the foundation for social democracy. On
the other hand, it opened the door to revanchist populist governments, such as those of Napoleon III and, later, Fascism. In our case,
a lowered voting age might just be the catalyst to help release our
stalled democratic, revolutionary energies. It might free us from our
two-party stalemate, and end the increasingly brutal and pointless
trench warfare for the tiny slice of the electorate known as "swing

voters" or "independents." Or—if voter psychology is as bad as cynics believe it to be—it would confirm the juvenility and irresponsibility imputed to the current "adult" electorate by the similar voting behavior of real juveniles. Why don't we find out, once and for all, what we're made of?

Why don't we find out, once and for all, what we're made of?

We should be wary of assuming that a   3
surge of voting kids will benefit any one current party. The old cliché, now backed by some researchers in evolutionary neurobiology, is that the young are naturally radical, and that as we age we become naturally conservative. (No one is a natural liberal—one of the virtues and defects of liberalism—but many become liberals all the same.) Because the young are harder to predict, harder to homogenize, despite the best efforts of marketers, the young will probably not vote as a bloc at all. There will be conservatives, teenage religious enthusiasts, parent-pleasers, shady favor-traders who will learn to barter their votes for car keys or free pizza at a rally sponsored by the nearest chapter of College Republicans. And yet the elites raised these same cautionary cries when the poor were let in. Wouldn't they simply sell their votes to the highest bidder? To the cynical all things are cynical. We must also imagine young voters who might join the army but are concerned about extended tours of duty and getting their legs blown off; others who like to play politics and debate measures seriously before taking a position and endorsing a candidate—the student-council types. There will be anarchists and globalists, environmentalists and libertarians, drug legalizers and Bible study groups, an entire spectrum. The trend ought to be toward an openness to new ideas, possibly to increased public service.

Perhaps the best reason for lowering the voting age now is that it   4
could provide a cure for American political apathy. Under the present system, Americans become politically conscious before they're allowed to vote at all. If history has been taught properly, most teenagers come into a sense of their political inheritance for the first time at 15 or even earlier. They may have just read and debated the Constitution, the Voting Rights Act, or the concept of separation of powers. How many of us, as older voters, can say the same? Flush with all this knowledge, what do the students get to do but run for student council, hand out leaflets as unpaid volunteers, and join their parents at protests? These are mere bagatelles, trivial experiences that will make it so much easier to trivialize the real thing later on. The clear-eyed teen who sees these activities as more dumb popularity

contests and silly playacting will wisely hold back, but withdrawal and guarded distance too easily become a lifelong habit. For most of us, our initial experience of democracy is of disappointment and disenfranchisement.

There are two traditional objections to lowering the voting age. When the voting age was reduced to 18, most states also lowered the age of legal majority to match. The current voting age is seen, in part, as the beginning of property-holding maturity, the age at which, in some states, one can be sole title holder of a house or stocks, or, at least, open a bank account in one's own name. The assumption governing these changes was that one ought not vote until one had a specific monetary stake in society. Or that the right to vote tacitly granted the right to acquire and manage property. Of course, we have no official property requirement for voting. Such laws, once part of the old, exclusionary mechanisms of pre-Jacksonian democracy, are now unconstitutional. You do not need to own a home, a car, or a bank account to vote; you only need to be an American citizen.   5

The other objection requires a belief that majority accords with an age of reason, which all of us now magically reach on our eighteenth birthday. Before 19th-century voting reforms, most adult men who did not own property—along with blacks and women—were thought never to reach the age of reason. Definitions of what counts as reason are too numerous to summarize here, but take one to start: Kant's.[1] Take, in fact, the journalistically friendly definition from "What is Enlightenment?" originally written for a newspaper. Enlightenment, or reason, is the ability to use one's understanding, to be able to think for oneself, free from the guidance of another: parent, doctor, priest, teacher, boss. Kant's definition is intellectual, deliberately so. He did not dream of democracy; he had no wish to shake the foundations of the monarchical Prussian state. Reason is only used for public problem solving, not private scheming. It does not and cannot serve a special interest, especially our own. This is not American reason, certainly not today. If it were, how many of us could be said to have reached the age of reason at all?   6

If adolescents can be consumers, they can certainly be voters. Americans tend now to prefer an economist's idea of reason: the ability to judge and make intelligent choices about one's interests or desires at the lowest common level, that of material survival. "Old   7

[1]*Kant*: Immanuel Kant (1724–1804), German philosopher.

enough to buy? Old enough to vote!" The same techniques used to sell clothes, video games, music, and other products to kids as young as 3 are already used to direct which buttons citizens push in the voting booth. Typical utterance of a campaign consultant: "What I think Edwards[2] has failed to understand is that he himself is one of the products placed on the market. . . . This means that—when you run for political office—you must conform your life to your political message as much as you are able." It's an easier task to conform your political message to your selfish life, and that's what we've had for eight years. What was the Bush tax cut if not the promise of free candy for all? To the consultant who spends his time off from campaigns advising corporations, there is no practical difference between a voter and a consumer. Voting is buyer's choice and buyer beware.

As buyers have special interests (shoes, guns, organic foods), so   8 there are voters' special-interest groups: people who vote for the guy who promises to fix the schools, end abortion, or provide jobs regardless of whatever else he will or will not do. If anything, enfranchising the young might create another series of interest groups to counteract some of the dominant ones. Would American youth really want to vote for people who promise to improve education by cutting funding to schools and making the students take understimulating standardized tests? (Let's assume that most children want to learn, are excited by new knowledge but are bored or humiliated or discouraged by school, the first taste of the mass society that awaits them.) Or would enfranchising the young, most importantly, create a large group with no discernible interests except in the general welfare? They are not yet lawyers, lobbyists, business people, steelworkers, or corn farmers. They might have the future good of all sorts of people at heart, before they turn into holders of any particular jobs or start down professional paths.

Perhaps it's middle-aged adults who ought to be disenfranchised.   9 Having become a government of spoiled children, with laws by spoiled children, for spoiled children, we still recognize, guiltily, that we've defrauded the real kids, out of ignorance or spite. We've licensed a growing national debt to be paid off by budget cuts in necessary social services, or ignored, only to be called in by creditors to the ruin of the US economy. We've participated in the continued defund-

[2]*Edwards*: John Edwards (b. 1953), former senator from North Carolina who ran as presidential hopeful John Kerry's running mate in 2004 and was a candidate for the Democratic presidential nomination in 2008.

ing of education and the shift to an increasingly mechanical view of the student as test taker. We've guaranteed a stagnant society in which the brightest Americans indenture themselves for the best years of their lives to pay off student loans. We've tolerated the forward-looking Pentagon planners' desire to reinstitute an arms race of small "tactical" nuclear weapons. We've allowed an indifference to, or active destruction of, the global environment. Could a bunch of 16-year-olds choose any worse?

Vocabulary / Using a Dictionary

1. What does Roth mean by the phrase *civic engagement* (para. 1)?

2. What is a *bagatelle* (para. 4)? From what foreign word does its current usage come?

3. Roth asks if enfranchising the young would "create a large group with no discernible interests except in the general welfare" (para. 8). What does it mean to *discern* something?

Responding to Words in Context

1. Words derived from *franchise* come up several times in this essay (*franchise* in para. 2, *enfranchising* in para. 8, and *disenfranchised* in para. 9). What do these words mean, and how are they related to one another?

2. Anarchists, globalists, environmentalists, and libertarians are named as a few of the groups young voters would come to represent (para. 3). Based on the roots of the words, what sense do you have of what these groups stand for?

3. Roth indicates that perhaps older voters should be stripped of the right to vote because they have "defrauded" children and participated in the "defunding" of education. What does it mean to *defraud* someone and *defund* something?

Discussing Main Point and Meaning

1. When Roth asks us to consider lowering the voting age to "find out, once and for all, what we're made of" (para. 2), what does he think we will discover? What does he think we're afraid we will discover?

2. Roth repeats "the old cliché" about the young being naturally radical while the older population is more conservative. How does Roth refute that cliché later in the essay to prove why teenagers should be allowed to vote?

3. In this essay, Roth contends that many teenagers come to understand their "political inheritance" in adolescence. What is that "political inheritance," and how does it make them good voters?

Examining Sentences, Paragraphs, and Organization

1. Roth mentions the "trench warfare for . . . 'swing voters'" (para. 2) that currently takes place in elections and says that lowering the voting age might help with the problem. What is "trench warfare"? How do you understand it in the context of this sentence?

2. What do you notice about the overall sentence construction in Roth's final paragraph? How do the sentences differ from those in previous paragraphs? Why do you think he structures his sentences that way at the end of the essay?

3. Certain people who can vote today were not always allowed to vote in U.S. elections: Women, slaves (and then nonwhites), and men without property were once barred from voting, and their enfranchisement was often slow in coming. Roth includes information on why the voting age was changed to eighteen in the 1970s. How does the inclusion of that particular piece of history affect the persuasiveness of Roth's essay? How would the essay be different if he had left it out?

Thinking Critically

1. Roth discredits the idea that voters must be of "property-holding maturity" as a reason for keeping the voting age at eighteen (a notion that, earlier in the history of the nation, was discredited as a reason for keeping women, propertyless men, and former slaves from voting). How does the world of "things" already influence teenagers in terms of their voting potential, even if they don't yet hold "property"?

2. After giving several definitions for the phrase "age of reason," Roth wonders what it means in terms of American voters today. What do you think a voter "age of reason" might mean?

ROTH Lower the Voting Age!   295

3. Roth refers to "the young," "voting kids," and "teenagers" in his argument for lowering the voting age. In paragraph 1, he says that in the 1970s "the voting age should have been lowered to 16, at least—because at 18 you could still suddenly be drafted, fight, and die in a war started by a government you had never previously voted for." What do you think is the lowest acceptable voting age and why?

In-Class Writing Activities

1. In the 1970s, the Vietnam War was seen as the catalyst for change that led to lowering the voting age to eighteen. It seemed unfair that a young man could be forced to fight in a war declared by officials he had had no part in electing. The economy, the environment, foreign affairs, and health care are only some of the issues that a teenager might feel he or she has a stake in as a voter, or that an older voter might consider a reason for excluding teenagers from the election process. Consider what issues are important or divisive today and write an essay explaining why that issue should influence the current voting age.

2. Lowering the voting age is only one question that can be raised around U.S. elections. Many voters today wonder whether elections should be decided by popular vote or by the electoral college, particularly following the victory of George W. Bush over Al Gore in the 2000 presidential election. Research the process by which our president is elected and write an essay that argues whether you think the popular vote should be more influential.

3. Roth frequently refers to the "cynics" who don't believe the voting age should be lowered. They come up with a variety of reasons why lowering the voting age would be a terrible idea. Roth, on the other hand, is very hopeful about the role younger voters would play in elections. Do you feel cynical or hopeful about our election process and current elections? Write an essay that explains what you feel cynical or hopeful about and why.

PAUL STARR

A New Deal of Their Own

[AMERICAN PROSPECT / March 2008]

Before You Read

Do you think the government should do more to help younger people enter the middle class? Have you ever had difficulty paying for health care or your education? Would it be a good idea to have younger people do voluntary service for the country in exchange for education and other benefits?

Words to Learn

pension (para. 5): a fixed amount of money, other than wages, paid to a person or a person's dependents in consideration of past services, age, merit, poverty, or loss sustained; allowance (n.)

cohort (para. 6): a group or companion (n.)

discretionary (para. 8): for any use one chooses; not designated for any particular purpose (adj.)

retrenchment (para. 8): a cutting down or off, as by the reduction of expenses (n.)

obscure (para. 12): unclear or uncertain (adj.)

Paul Starr is a professor of sociology and public affairs at Princeton University and holds the Stuart Chair in Communications and Public Affairs at the Woodrow Wilson School. After graduating in 1970 with a BA from Columbia University, he went on to receive his PhD in sociology from Harvard University in 1978. As the cofounder and coeditor of the American Prospect, *he writes extensively on issues such as "American society, politics, and both domestic and foreign policy." Starr is highly regarded as an "expert on health care," and in 1984 he received both the Pulitzer Prize for Nonfiction and the Bancroft Prize in American History for his book* The Social Transformation of American Medicine.

Americadoes not do well by its young. For years government   1
data and social-science research have demonstrated persistently high
levels of poverty and related problems among children. In a UNICEF
study last year measuring the well-being of children and adolescents
in 21 rich countries, the United States ranked next to last. According
to U.S. Census Bureau data, 17 percent of children in 2006 were
growing up in families with incomes below the poverty line—just
about the same proportion as in the 1970s.

What's less widely appreciated is that the problems afflicting   2
children now extend into young adulthood. For roughly 30 years
after World War II, young workers shared in economic growth, but
since the 1970s they've lost ground. In 1967, according to research
by Andrew Sum and his colleagues at Northeastern University, young
men ages 18 to 24 who were employed full-time earned 74 percent as
much as men 25 years of age and older, but by 2004, they were making only 52 percent as much. Young workers, especially if they
haven't gone to college, are now also less likely to find long-term,
stable jobs with health insurance and other fringe benefits; partly for
that reason, many are taking longer to start families, as Sheldon
Danziger and Cecilia Rouse point out in the introduction to *The
Price of Independence*, a new book on the economics of early adulthood. Between 1973 and 2004, median real weekly earnings dropped
27 percent for young men and 9 percent for young women.

The persistent problems affecting children and the deteriorating   3
economic position of young adults stand in contrast to the historic
improvement in the well-being of the elderly during the same period.
As late as 1965, 30 percent of the elderly lived in poverty. But in
good part due to public policy—particularly the growth of Social Security benefits and the introduction of Medicare and its continued expansion, most recently in prescription-drug benefits—the proportion
of seniors in poverty has been cut by two-thirds, dropping to 9.4 percent in 2006.

As this contrast suggests, the difficulties facing the young gen-   4
erally—both children and young adults—are the result of long-
standing limitations in social policy whose effects have been aggra-
vated by recent changes in the economy and the family. The three
great waves of social reform since the 1930s—the New Deal, the
post–World War II GI Bill, and the Great Society—failed to establish
durable policies in support of the young.

The New Deal did provide some assistance targeted to young   5
adults, such as jobs in the Civilian Conservation Corps and the

National Youth Administration and the provisions of Social Security that were originally conceived as aiding widows and their children. The youth employment programs were shut down between 1940 and 1945, however, and Aid to Families with Dependent Children evolved into welfare for single mothers and was cut back sharply in the 1990s. The survivors' benefits in Social Security do represent an important source of support for children at risk of a collapse in their family's living standards. But, particularly in fiscal terms, the greatest legacy of the New Deal is old-age pensions.

The GI Bill, in contrast, was targeted primarily to young adults.   6
Educational assistance, home loans, and health care for veterans after World War II provided a great boost to the generation that came home from the war. And because spending for primary and secondary schools also jumped during the baby boom, social expenditures overall had a strong tilt in favor of the young. By its nature, however, the GI Bill was temporary; even though the United States has since been at war, young veterans have represented a much smaller proportion of their age cohort, and veterans' programs today cannot serve the broad purposes they did in the late 1940s.

Despite its initial focus on economic opportunity, the Great Soci-   7
ety also did not create a durable source of social investment in the young. In fiscal terms, Medicare became the single greatest legacy of the 1960s, while such programs as Head Start remained tiny by comparison and the youth-oriented training programs were eliminated as ineffective. If there was one long-lasting educational innovation benefiting young adults during the 1960s, it was the rise of community colleges. To be sure, Medicaid has paid for health care for many children of the poor, but two-thirds of Medicaid expenditures have actually gone for nursing homes for the elderly.

Young workers have also acutely felt the impact of the declining real value of the minimum wage and unemployment benefits.

The result of these developments has   8
been a change in the generational impact of social spending. Instead of the focus on the young in the period after World War II, social spending has shifted increasingly toward seniors. Young workers have also acutely felt the impact of the declining real value of the minimum wage and unemployment benefits. And whereas Social Security and Medicare are entitlements, spending programs targeted to the young have been discretionary and consequently more liable to retrenchment in economic downturns.

Through their payroll taxes young workers help support Social   9
Security and Medicare, and they have every right to expect those programs will be there for them when they retire. But, in the meantime,
they need a New Deal of their own that addresses their needs for
both opportunity and security.

The historic shift in the distribution of expenditures isn't just a   10
matter of the interests of different age groups. Much public spending
on the young, particularly in education and health care, represents investment in human capital and provides a return in economic growth
with broad benefits for the entire society. But in recent decades, education spending has been virtually flat as a percentage of national income, and though health-care expenditures have grown dramatically,
the young have not been the principal beneficiaries. In economic
terms, social spending has shifted from investment to consumption.

One notable exception to this pattern has been increased health   11
coverage of children through Medicaid and the State Children's
Health Insurance Program adopted in 1997. But young adults are another matter; they are the age group in the United States most likely
to go without health insurance. According to the most recent Census
Bureau estimates, while 15.8 percent of the overall population is
uninsured, 29.3 percent of 18- to 24-year-olds have no coverage, and
the rate is almost as high (26.9 percent) among 25- to 34-year-olds.
Altogether, adults ages 18 to 34 represent 40.4 percent of the 47 million uninsured.

The reasons for this problem are not obscure. As children, Amer-   12
icans typically receive coverage via their parents, and as adults from
their own or their spouse's employer. The peak probability of being
uninsured comes around age 23 when many have lost their parents'
coverage without gaining their own. And the number of uninsured
young adults is going up because the proportion of entry-level jobs
providing health insurance is going down.

There is a parallel trend in higher education. Like health-care   13
costs, college tuition has been rising far more rapidly than overall in-
flation, and a failure to bring public policy into line has left young
adults to bear the burden. For example, the maximum Pell grant,
which covered nearly three-quarters of tuition costs at a four-year
college in the early 1970s, now covers only one-third (and only about
one in five recipients receives the maximum). At the state level, tuition at public institutions has risen sharply partly because other services, notably health care and prisons, have claimed a growing share

of state budgets. (Prison construction is also a form of spending targeted primarily to young adults—but with dramatically different implications for economic growth and social mobility from the schools and college campuses that states were building in the 1950s and 1960s.)

What is especially disturbing about these trends in public spending is that no built-in dynamic is going to restore social investment in the young. On the contrary, the aging of the population and rising health costs threaten to tilt expenditures against the young even more in the future.   14

So how can we reverse the damage to the interests of young adults from the legacies and trends of public policy? Health-care reform is essential for returning social expenditure to its function as social investment. It is crucial on two counts—first, as a method of paying for health care for the young, who are relatively cheap to insure; and second, as a general means of cost containment so as to prevent health care from draining away revenue from other social needs.   15

Beyond health care, however, the GI Bill may provide the most relevant model. It was the one concerted effort in recent history to focus public resources on expanding opportunity for young adults, and it had a big pay-off in postwar prosperity. The country was willing to support generous benefits for veterans and their families because they had made sacrifices and plainly weren't getting something for nothing. The program was premised on a norm of reciprocity—benefits in exchange for service—though for that very reason, it wasn't universal.   16

The challenge in creating a durable basis for social investment in the young is to reconcile these two ideals—universality and reciprocity—recognizing that as children become adolescents and then young adults, it's appropriate to premise some benefits on their efforts. An expanded program of college tuition grants in return for volunteer service, whether in the military, AmeriCorps, or other institutions, is a good example of that kind of approach, but far more could be done to develop a system for the young to earn support through national or local service than the relatively modest proposals currently under discussion.   17

America's young adults are not just passive victims; they can be a force in their own right, and if they have the opportunity to use their energies and talents for the public good, they can contribute to an American revival. After all, it's not just about what the country owes them; nearly half a century after John F. Kennedy, the right question is still what all of us can do for our country.   18

Vocabulary/Using a Dictionary

1. What are the origins of the term *median* (para. 2), and what other words is it related to?

2. What are the roots of *universality* (para. 17), and what other words is it related to?

3. What is the meaning of *reciprocity* (para. 16), and what are its roots?

Responding to Words in Context

1. The title of the essay is "A New Deal of Their Own." What was the New Deal? What connotations does it have for Starr's essay?

2. Starr writes that "much public spending on the young, particularly in education and health care, represents an investment in human capital" (para. 10). What is "human capital," and why does he use this term?

3. In the last paragraph of the essay, Starr refers to words from President John Kennedy's inaugural address: "Ask not what your country can do for you; ask what you can do for your country." How is this reference related to the essay as a whole?

Discussing Main Point and Meaning

1. Starr gives a brief history of several large-scale social reforms in the twentieth century. What are they, why does he do this, and how are they connected to his overall argument?

2. What has happened to the economic prospects of the young? What are some of the consequences, according to Starr?

3. What has happened to social spending for young people? According to Starr, what is the major challenge in creating social programs to help the young now?

Examining Sentences, Paragraphs, and Organization

1. Starr begins his essay with the sentence "America does not do well by its young." How does this sentence function here, and what do the first sentences of his paragraphs accomplish, generally?

2. What is the relationship between paragraph 4, and the three paragraphs that follow it? Do you find this structure effective?

3. How would you characterize Starr's writing voice, overall? Is it highly rhetorical? Does he use figurative language or call any attention to the writing itself? Does the prose style suit his subject and argument?

Thinking Critically

1. The essay includes a significant amount of economic data and statistical information. Do you find that Starr uses this evidence effectively and persuasively? Do you find any of it hard to follow or to connect with his overall argument? What can you infer about his audience from the article?

2. Starr writes, "Aid to Families with Dependent Children evolved into welfare for single mothers and was cut back sharply in the 1990s" (para. 5). What is welfare? Do you think it's a good thing? What connotations does it have, socially and politically? Why was it "cut back sharply" in the 1990s?

3. At the end of the essay, Starr claims that "America's young adults are not just passive victims; they can be a force in their own right, and if they have the opportunity to use their energies and talents for the public good, they can contribute to an American revival" (para. 18). How would you describe Starr's view of young Americans, here and throughout the essay? Do you agree with him?

In-Class Writing Activities

1. Starr refers to the "great waves of social reform" in the twentieth century, by which he means various programs of public assistance. How do you view such programs, generally? Have you ever benefited from them? Do you think they're necessary? Do you think they're well administered? How does your perception of them shape your larger political views? Write an essay describing and justifying your point of view, using evidence to back your assertions.

2. According to Starr, several past and current institutions provide good examples of positive volunteer programs, "but far more could be done to develop a system for the young to earn support through national or local service" (para. 17). Write a three-page proposal describing a program along the lines that Starr describes. How would it unite the ideals of "universality and reci-

procity"? If you disagree with the need for such initiatives, write an essay explaining your position.

3.   Starr implies that social policies such as the GI Bill helped young people join the middle class. What is the middle class? Do you identify as a member? Do you aspire to join it? What qualifies people as middle class? What levels of income, education, wealth, and status does it suggest? What values and qualities are associated with the middle class? Why is access to it important? What role should government play in maintaining it?

JOSEPH HART

Protest Is Dead. Long Live Protest.

[THE UTNE READER / May–June 2007]

Before You Read

Do you think the antiwar movement, or any movement that involves political protest, needs to reconsider its approach if it is to make an impact on policy? What are the current ways protesters make their messages heard? Can you think of fresher, more creative tactics they might use instead?

Joseph Hart is a full-time freelance editor and writer whose work has appeared in a variety of publications, including the Utne Reader, Adbusters, City Pages, *and several regional newspapers. He attended the University of Minnesota, Twin Cities, where he received a BA in English and an MFA in creative and professional writing. Hart also works as the production editor for the* Kickapoo Free Press, *an independent community newsmagazine founded by his wife, in Viroqua, Wisconsin. With the philosophy that "nothing is irrelevant to a writer," Hart has explored an array of subjects in his writing, having recently written about such topics as "the history of soil erosion control, how to simplify Christmas, the science of human collaboration, and UV coatings for furniture."*

Words to Learn

iconic (para. 1): having the qualities of an important and enduring symbol (adj.)

quell (para. 2): to suppress or subdue (v.)

mobilized (para. 3): assembled (v.)

virtually (para. 3): for the most part (adv.)

impotence (para. 4): weakness (n.)

sentiment (para. 4): attitude or opinion (n.)

tactic (para. 5): plan or procedure (n.)

tumultuous (para. 5): marked by confusion and upheaval (adj.)

boycotts (para. 7): instances of abstaining from using, buying from, or dealing with an individual or organization as a means of protest (n.)

integrate (para. 7): to bring groups together; to desegregate (v.)

partisanship (para. 8): firm attachment to a party, faction, cause, or person (n.)

singularly (para. 10): oddly or curiously (adv.)

subversive (para. 13): intended to overthrow or undermine an authority (adj.)

exploit (para. 14): to make use of to one's advantage (v.)

commemorative (para. 15): intended for remembrance or memorial purposes (adj.)

rhetoric (para. 16): exaggeration or display in writing and speech (n.)

allies (para. 20): people who cooperate with each other and act as support (n.)

collaborated (para. 20): worked with (v.)

Forty-three years ago, 250,000 people descended on Washington, D.C., to register their support for the civil rights movement. They carried signs and listened to Joan Baez sing "We Shall Overcome" and to Martin Luther King Jr.'s now-iconic "I Have a Dream" speech.   1

They were taken seriously. The U.S. Justice Department readied emergency troops to quell rioters (although no one rioted). CBS television canceled its afternoon soaps to report the protest live from beginning to end.   2

Earlier this year, when United for Peace and Justice mobilized its latest march on Washington, the event barely registered. A few TV cameras clustered around Jane Fonda, who was at her first protest in years. The networks virtually ignored the demonstration. Another day, another protest.   3

On its face, the antiwar movement's impotence is puzzling. As this issue went to press, a *Washington Post*–ABC News poll showed a staggering 67 percent disapproval of President Bush's handling of the war—a level that matches public sentiment at the tail end of the   4

Vietnam War, when street protests, rallies, and student strikes were daily occurrences.

The problem is that American peace activists have been marching   5
down the same cul-de-sac for more than four decades, a tactic that, during one of the nation's most tumultuous periods, is proving to be a dramatic failure. A generation of rabble-rousers, schooled in 1960s-style dissent, have adopted nonviolent civil disobedience not only as a default tactic, but in later years as a profession, a lifestyle, and, most disappointingly, an end in itself.

"A street demonstration is only one form of protest," says Jack   6
DuVall, president of the International Center on Nonviolent Conflict, "and protest is only one tactic that can be used in a campaign. If it's not a part of a dedicated strategy to change policy, or to change power, protest is only a form of political exhibitionism."

The 1963 march in Washington was one of many devices used   7
by the civil rights movement. Others included bus boycotts, lunch counter sit-ins, and the Freedom Rides to integrate buses—not to mention calls for armed resistance from the black power movement's militant wing. Most importantly, these tactics were in service of a long-term strategy: to rally Americans around the mainstream values of inclusion, equality, and freedom.

By contrast, today's mainstream protesters are operating in a   8
vacuum. "Many of us are disillusioned with the tactics, strategy, and partisanship within the antiwar movement," a student organizer told the *Indypendent* in early February. "There doesn't seem to be much interest in talking strategy. Action has become ritualized. And frankly, without a major shake-up of the status quo in the movement, I can't imagine how the movement could ever become a relevant force in shaping U.S. foreign policy."

Civil disobedience of the sort associated with Mahatma Gandhi   9
was used to particular advantage in the civil rights movement. Media images of black protesters facing police batons, water cannons, and savage dogs were effective because they illustrated—dramatically— the immorality of Southern-style segregation.

This unity of medium and message is singularly lacking in the   10
case of the antiwar movement. It would be one thing if Iraqi civilians were resisting U.S. tanks nonviolently (like African Americans in the 1950s, the average Iraqi citizen bears the greatest burden of U.S. policy). When a middle-aged war opponent signs a form or pays a modest fine after blocking the steps of the courthouse, however, or when an aging hippie with a multimillion-dollar film career speaks from a podium, it lacks a certain power.

The first step toward building a movement is getting people's at-   11
tention, which is not easy. There's no doubt that during the "Battle in
Seattle," the 1999 protests against the World Trade Organization,
street demonstrators found some visceral satisfaction in smashing
windows at a McDonald's or a Nike store, but the acts themselves
were unimaginative and overshadowed the cause.

One example of a successful anticorporate campaign is the Bubble   12
Project (www.thebubbleproject.com), launched in 2002 when Ji Lee, a
thirtysomething New York ad man fed up with his trade, printed
thousands of stickers shaped like blank cartoon bubbles and then
slapped them on posters and billboards around the city—an open
invitation for passers-by to fill in the blank.

The results, documented in Lee's book *Talk Back* (Mark Batty,   13
2006), were hilarious, subversive, and encouraged participation.
Now there are bubble commentaries around the world, ranging from
the political (a grinning model on an insurance company billboard
asks, "Why doesn't the government insure our health?") to the absurd (the Starbucks mermaid asks, "Have you seen my nipples?").
Although he has been fined a few times for vandalism, Lee isn't a revolutionary—he's simply trying to "transform the corporate monologue into a public dialogue," he says.

"The idea is to look for cracks in the system and exploit them,"   14
says Steven Kurtz, a founder of the group Critical Art Ensemble (CAE),
best known for its 1994 book *The Electronic Disturbance* (Autonome-
dia), an early critique of the Internet that called for digital disobedience.

One CAE project in Halifax, Nova Scotia, featured a fake cul-   15
tural tour—complete with glossy brochures, commemorative icons,
and LCD displays—that highlighted injustices in that city, including
a sewage-infested Halifax harbor. One display was mistaken for a
bomb and the police's terrorism squad took charge. By the end of the
day, the harbor was at a standstill. The larger public pegged police
paranoia and antiterrorist overkill as the real culprits.

The Yes Men, undercover impersonators who pose as corporate   16
spin doctors and show up to speak at big business retreats, turn the
rhetoric of globalism on its head. A group called Improv Everywhere
deploys hundreds of slow-motion shoppers to jam up the pace of
commerce in retail outlets like Home Depot. The Center for Tactical
Magic has dozens of tricks in its bag, including a "tactical ice cream
unit" that hands out propaganda—and ice cream—from a cart that
doubles as a high-tech communications unit during protests. These
groups aren't always linking their actions to a broader strategy for
change, but their creativity is inspiring.

When it comes to that broader strategy, another movement is   17
emerging that could lead the way for activists: collaboration and cooperation with the enemy.

There are times when it's right to fight—and fight creatively. The   18
left's us-versus-them mentality, however, represents strategic shortsightedness. It alienates potential allies with
the power to act and instead causes them to
react defensively.

> *There are times when*
> *it's right to fight—and*
> *fight creatively.*

Of course, it's far easier to shout slogans   19
than it is to sit down at the table and hash
out, say, energy policy. But that's exactly
what groups that want change are starting to do. Consider the movement to prevent the clear-cutting of Canada's rainforests on the Clayoquot Sound. Fourteen years ago, environmentalists, backed by over-
whelmingly favorable public opinion, organized what was then the
largest civil disobedience campaign in that nation's history, resulting
in 1,000 arrests. The clear-cutting continued. So instead of facing off
against the logging companies again, the activists targeted their customers—the largely U.S.-based corporations that were buying the
paper. They launched a creative education campaign with clever advertisements and other tactics to alert the public about where their
phone books were coming from.

Then activists made allies within these same corporations with   20
whom they collaborated to find alternatives to Clayoquot lumber.
"It's not about moving on from confrontation," explains Tzeporah
Berman, strategic director of Forest Ethics, an organization that grew
out of the Clayoquot campaigns. "It's about understanding which
tool you use from your tool belt. Confrontational tactics like blockades kick the door open. But if all we do is protest, without actually
helping to define the solutions, we're as thin as a placard."

Success stories like Forest Ethics serve as a model—and a reason   21
for relegating nonviolent civil disobedience to its rightful place as
only one of many approaches. Public opinion is with progressives on
a whole range of issues, from reforming health care to ending the Iraq
war. It's time we come down off our high horses, get creative, and
take back change.

Vocabulary / Using a Dictionary

1. From what language has the word *cul-de-sac* (para. 5) been
   adopted? How is it defined?

2. What does *visceral* (para. 11) mean?

3. What is a *progressive* (para. 21)? How is the word related to *progress*?

Responding to Words in Context

1. Hart quotes the president of a nonviolence center as saying, "Protest is only a form of political exhibitionism" (para. 6). What does the term *political exhibitionism* mean?

2. How is it possible to "operat[e] in a vacuum" (para. 8)? What does this expression mean?

3. What is the difference between a *monologue* and a *dialogue* (para. 13)?

Discussing Main Point and Meaning

1. Hart notices parallels between the protests of the 1960s and the antiwar protests today. What did the civil rights movement and the Vietnam antiwar movement have going for them that the current movement lacks?

2. Why do "middle-aged war opponents" and "aging hippies" (para. 10) lack the power to propel the antiwar movement forward? Who needs to speak out in order for the movement to gain force?

3. Does Hart appear in favor of any type of protest? What form of protest might he not advocate?

Examining Sentences, Paragraphs, and Organization

1. A Web site address is added to Hart's description of the Bubble Project (para. 12). Do you think the inclusion of this information is important? Why or why not?

2. Hart alludes to the civil rights movement and Vietnam war protests in various places throughout the essay. How does his inclusion of these examples show the weakness of the current antiwar movement, which is modeled on those historic events?

3. Does Hart provide evidence throughout the essay to support his final claim that "it's time we come down off our high horses, get creative, and take back change" (para. 21)?

Thinking Critically

1. Several examples are given of "thinking outside the box" for protest movements, including the takeover of public property, impersonations, and collaborations with the very organizations the protesters are trying to defeat. Do you think the creative tactics used by the Bubble Project, the Yes Men, and Forest Ethics could be successfully put into effect by today's antiwar movement? Why or why not?

2. In this essay, an environmental protester is quoted as saying, "Confrontational tactics like blockades kick the door open. But if all we do is protest, without actually helping to define the solutions, we're as thin as a placard" (para. 20). Do you agree with that statement?

3. Hart notes that Ji Lee (of the Bubble Project) has been fined a few times for vandalism. Do you think the Bubble Project qualifies as vandalism? If so, why? And if not, what makes it acceptable?

In-Class Writing Activities

1. The Bubble Project, mentioned in Hart's essay, has its own manifesto on its Web site: "Our communal spaces are being overrun with ads. . . . The Bubble Project is the counterattack" (www .thebubbleproject.com). The bubbles cover a range of topics that people have tackled in the space of a small white bubble, from political and social issues to personal and humorous ones. Come up with a list of five to ten common advertisements that you have encountered lately either in the media or on the street. Despite their familiarity to most people, describe them in detail. Then imagine bubble commentaries for those ads. Then write one political bubble and one nonpolitical bubble (it can be funny or absurd) for each one. Write a sentence that explains how the bubbles for each ad are a form of protest.

2. In paragraph 3, Hart mentions United for Peace and Justice, an active antiwar protest group, and a recent march that garnered little attention in the nation's capital. Research this organization and notice its protest tactics and any stated goals. Write a critique of the group's contribution to the antiwar effort and argue about the effectiveness of this protest, based on what you've learned from this essay.

3. The March on Washington in 1963, which offered Martin Luther King Jr. the stage for his "I Have a Dream" speech, provides the lead-in for Hart's essay. Research another famous antiwar rally or protest from the 1960s and explain where its energy and effectiveness came from. Who attended the event? Why do you think it generated the attention it did?

JEFF DICKSON (STUDENT ESSAY)

United We Strive, Divided We Falter

[THE DAILY, University of Washington / April 2, 2008]

Before You Read

Do you think America is especially polarized right now? Is it less unified than it was in the past? What does it mean to define yourself as an "American"?

Words to Learn

recession (para. 1): a state of economic decline; a widespread decline in gross domestic product, employment, and trade lasting from six to twelve months (n.)

disparity (para. 2): inequality; difference (n.)

incentive (para. 3): something that encourages or motivates effort or action (n.)

Jeff Dickson is a weekly opinion columnist for the Daily, *the student newspaper at the University of Washington, where he will graduate in 2010 with a degree in accounting and business administration. As a writer for the* Daily, *Dickson enjoys the "most obvious thrill" of opinion writing, the "chance to share your views with such a large audience." Even though writing as a career is not his ultimate goal, Dickson still finds that there is "no tool more useful in the arsenal of an aspiring business professional than the ability to communicate effectively, especially in written form."*

polarization (para. 5): a sharp division of a population or group into opposing factions (n.)

permeated (para. 5): passed through every part; saturated (v.)

festered (para. 5): undergone decay or rot; generated pus (v.)

Every day, the American media covers stories about how the country continues to deteriorate. From rising war costs to economic recessions to eco-meltdowns, it seems as if the glory days of the United States have long passed. But there is one issue plaguing our country that receives little or no press coverage, an issue that negatively distinguishes us from the golden years: There is a lack of unity between Americans.

We have become so anxious to overly define ourselves by our race, religion or political affiliation that we lose sight of the aspects that unite us. We categorize ourselves as fill-in-the-blank–Americans, according to political affiliation, or by faith—rather than simply as "Americans." People like Al Sharpton, Rush Limbaugh and James Carville have promoted such disparities between us, so much so that we have virtually segregated ourselves. Divisive media stories further invoke unnecessary and unwanted controversy upon a public that has already lost the ability to set aside petty differences and join together as a unified community.

> But as a nation of immigrants, it's our collective talent and diversity that make us great, and the greatest times in our nation's history have come when we banded together and worked toward a common goal.

Admittedly, the "melting-pot" nature of the United States has created a hodgepodge demographic, so the natural collaboration of people does not come as easily to us as it does to homogenous nations such as Japan or Germany. But as a nation of immigrants, it's our collective talent and diversity that make us great, and the greatest times in our nation's history have come when we banded together and worked toward a common goal. Just look at what we were able to accomplish during World War II. While brave soldiers were fighting overseas, women and children of all ages and backgrounds joined together in a collective effort to raise scrap metal for the war efforts. Minor demographic differences didn't matter. The fact that they were

all Americans gave everyone the incentive to do their part. And ultimately, we were able to rid the world of a great evil.

Imagine the good that could be done today if such harmonious   4
efforts were made. If we ignored the subtle differences that separate
us, recycling would increase tenfold, development of alternative fuel
would rid ourselves of our stranglehold dependence on foreign oil,
and crime rates would plummet. Certainly some sense of difference is
a positive. Rivalries and basic competition are what drive our capitalistic economy. But there are some tasks that are simply too large and
too important and require a cooperative effort.

Increasing polarization has divided the highest levels of our gov-   5
ernment, and has trickled down and permeated even the smallest of
communities. Unfortunately, this has festered into a distinct bitterness that continues to drive us apart, despite the obvious challenges
that face our nation, such as health care, climate change and a rapidly
draining Social Security fund.

It's time that we become the great generation we know we can   6
be, and implement the change that we speak of so fondly. But the
first step in leading the age of the future is to take a page out of the
golden past by setting aside our petty differences and banding together as one, united nation.

Vocabulary / Using a Dictionary

1. Dickson says that people increasingly categorize themselves according to "political affiliation" (para. 2). What does *affiliation*
   mean, and what are its origins?

2. Where does the word *demographic* (para. 3) come from? What
   are its roots, and what other words is it related to?

3. What does *petty* (para. 2) mean, and what are its origins?

Responding to Words in Context

1. Dickson claims that, given the current level of polarization and
   division in the United States, "we have virtually segregated ourselves" (para. 2). What connotations does the word *segregate*
   have?

2. Dickson suggests that the melting pot of America "has created a
   hodgepodge demographic" (para. 3). What associations does the
   term *hodgepodge* have, as opposed to other words he could have
   used to characterize America's immigrant composition?

3. According to Dickson, "harmonious efforts" (para. 4) would lead to great improvements in the country. What is a "harmonious effort," and what does the metaphorical description suggest?

Discussing Main Point and Meaning

1. What is Dickson's thesis? How does it serve to shape and organize the meaning of his essay?

2. Dickson is concerned that Americans are not unified, as they have been at times in the past. What reasons does he give to explain this lack of unity?

3. Dickson compares what he sees as our current state of disunity with the harmony of the "golden years" of the United States. What kind of problems does he believe unity will help us solve?

Examining Sentences, Paragraphs, and Organization

1. According to Dickson, "the 'melting-pot' nature of the United States has created a hodgepodge demographic, so the natural collaboration of people does not come as easily to us as it does to homogenous nations such as Japan or Germany" (para. 3). What does the metaphor of the "melting pot" suggest about the nature of American identity? Do you agree with his statement about other countries being more "homogenous"?

2. How does paragraph 3 function within the context of the whole essay?

3. In his last paragraph, Dickson writes: "It's time that we become the great generation we know we can be, and implement the change that we speak of so fondly." This sentence carries an echo of "the Greatest Generation," a label often attached to Americans who fought in World War II. Do you think that specific generations have particular characteristics, attributes, or even obligations that distinguish them? Do you consider yourself as being part of a "generation"?

Thinking Critically

1. Dickson claims that "every day, the American media covers stories about how the country continues to deteriorate," even as divisiveness "receives little or no press coverage" (para. 1). Do you think the media spend too much time discussing other problems

in America? What reasons would explain this coverage? Do you agree that the problem of our dividedness goes ignored?

2. Dickson writes that during World War II, "minor demographic differences didn't matter" (para. 3). He also says we need to ignore "the subtle differences that separate us" (para. 4) and set aside our "petty differences" (para. 6). What kind of differences is he referring to? How were they handled in the past? What do you think constitutes a "minor" or "petty" difference, as opposed to a significant or profound difference?

3. According to Dickson, "it seems as if the glory days of the United States have long passed" and that our country is no longer living in its "golden years" (para. 1). How do you evaluate assertions such as these? Do you believe that there were once "golden years," from which our country has degenerated or deteriorated? What evidence would you use to support such a claim—or oppose it?

In-Class Writing Activities

1. In paragraph 2, Dickson implies that Americans need to stop viewing themselves in terms of divisive categories or hyphenated labels, and instead see their identities "simply as 'Americans.'" Do you think this is possible, in practice? What values, attitudes, characteristics, and ideas do—or should—all Americans share in order to be "Americans"? Why would articulating them be a more complex issue in the United States than in some other countries? Explain.

2. Dickson worries that Americans tend to separate—and perhaps privilege—aspects of their identities that are distinct from being an "American" first. Do you do this? How does your sense of nationality connect to other aspects of your identity? Are there "non-American" aspects of yourself—say, cultural inheritances or religious and ethnic traditions—that you retain against a general process of "assimilation"? Do they take precedence over your American identity, or are they subsumed by it? Write a personal essay explaining your positions.

3. Dickson writes explicitly about the media's role in focusing on or exaggerating divisiveness, even as they don't (as he sees it) consider their own role in contributing to the problem. As a result, such stories "invoke unnecessary and unwanted controversy upon a public that has already lost the ability to set aside petty differences and join together as a unified community"

(para. 2). Find a recent item in the media (broadly understood) and evaluate it in light of Dickson's assertions. What aspects contribute to a story's or editorial comment's "divisiveness"? Is the conflict being covered legitimate, or is it "unwanted"? You may also choose to highlight a report that serves as evidence in a counterargument to Dickson.

ANNOTATION Effective Persuasion: Recommending a Course of Action

The primary purpose of a persuasive essay is to change someone's thinking or course of action. On election day, a newspaper editorial will encourage its readers to vote for a particular candidate; in the same paper, a film review may discourage moviegoers from attending a certain film the reviewer finds "pointless, trivial, and embarrassingly dumb"; and an opinion column in that paper may try to persuade parents to avoid buying fast food for their children. All of these pieces will offer reasons for their views, but they will also urge their readers to take some form of action. In "United We Strive, Divided We Falter," a University of Washington student, Jeff Dickson, provides an excellent illustration of how a writer can persuasively conclude an essay by recommending a course of action. In this case, Dickson suggests that Americans put aside their many minor unimportant differences and join together for larger purposes. What's effective about his essay — whether one agrees with it or not — is the way he has prepared readers for his final call to action by offering specific examples that show the effects of our current disunity and polarization along with positive examples of what can happen when Americans pull together. In doing that, he systematically moves his argument from a set of reasons supporting his position to a direct call for action.

> *Dickson suggests that our disunity will not help us solve our current challenges.*

Increasing polarization has divided the highest levels of our government, and has trickled down and permeated even the smallest of communities. Unfortunately, this has festered into a distinct bitterness that continues to drive us apart, despite the obvious challenges that face our nation, such as health care, climate change and a rapidly draining Social Security fund.

> *He then calls for national unity as the way to bring about change and recapture our greatness.*

It's time that we become the great generation we know we can be, and implement the change that we speak of so fondly. But the first step in leading the age of the future is to take a page out of the golden past by setting aside our petty differences and banding together as one, united nation.

— From "United We Strive, Divided We Falter"
by Jeff Dickson, page 310

Student Writer at Work: Jeff Dickson
On Writing "United We Strive, Divided We Falter"

Q: What inspired you to write "United We Strive, Divided We Falter"?

A: The lack of social unity in this country has been an important, yet largely ignored, issue in my mind. I always wanted to address it in my column, but never knew quite how. After talking to a friend about it, I had a better sense of what I wanted to do to approach the topic.

Q: What was your main purpose in writing this piece?

A: Unlike some of my columns, which tend to be satirical takes on current events, this article was a heartfelt sentiment about an issue that I care deeply about. As much as I appreciate and respect our diversity and our nature to debate over our differences, at times it seems as if we have engrossed ourselves in a paltry competition and lost sight of the many stronger ties that bind us together. I simply wanted to use the small soapbox I had been given to try to make people stop and think about the importance of unity—and remind them that the difference between us all is not the colossal chasm that it is sometimes made out to be.

Q: Has the feedback you have received affected your views on the topic you wrote about?

A: Not at all. There will always be people who disagree with you on any one of a number of subjects. Although it is important to consider the opinions of others, they should never dictate what you believe in.

Q: Tell us some of your favorite publications.

A: I read the *Wall Street Journal* and of course the *Daily*. As far as magazines go, I love *Sports Illustrated*, *Road & Track*, *Car & Driver*, *Fortune*, and the *Economist*. I also enjoy just perusing the headlines on my MSN home page as well as sites like Fox News and ESPN.

Q: What topics most interest you as a writer?

A: I have always really enjoyed opinion writing. Perhaps the most obvious thrill that it presents is the chance to share your views with such a large audience. But the less apparent joy is in the challenge of writing something that is both smart and entertaining.

Q: What advice do you have for other student writers?

A: Don't ever be afraid to share your thoughts and beliefs, even to an audience that may not agree with you. You might even find that you enjoy the debate.

AMERICA THEN . . . 1920

The Nineteenth Amendment:
Women Get to Vote

Between 1916 and 1918, American women staged mass picketing demonstrations throughout the nation in hopes of gaining the right to vote. The first organized attempts for suffrage began as far back as 1848, when women met at the Seneca Falls Convention to argue their case, and their campaigns continued annually, although gains were small. In 1873, Susan B. Anthony was tried in a highly publicized case for the crime of unlawful voting. Then, in June 1917, a determined core of women led by Alice Paul, the head of the National Woman's Party, launched more aggressive protests in Washington, D.C. Charged at first with petty violations of obstruction, many of the women (a number of whom were socially prominent) were sentenced to jail time. The protests and imprisonments continued into November as several of the women went on hunger strikes and others were held in solitary confinement. The protests and incarcerations captured the attention not only of the press but also of many officials who joined in support of the women's cause. Women finally achieved the right to vote when the Nineteenth Amendment to the Constitution (which passed Congress on June 4, 1919) was ratified by the thirty-sixth state on August 26, 1920, in time for women to vote in the presidential election that November. The amendment reads: "The right of citizens of the United States to vote shall not be denied or abridged by the United States or by any State on account of sex." The photograph on page 318 shows a 1916 suffrage parade that appears to be in New York City.

Discussing the Unit

Suggested Topic for Discussion

All of the essays in this unit deal with political and civic engagement—particularly in the context of young people. Indeed, these writers suggest that the current generation of teens and young adults hold the possibility of "an American revival" (to use Starr's words). Roth claims that lowering the voting age "could provide a cure for American political apathy" (para. 4), and Dickson proposes that "it's time that we become the great generation we know we can be" (para. 6). Do you share this idealism and sense of purpose? Are you politically or civically engaged? Why or why not?

Preparing for Class Discussion

1. In various ways, Roth, Starr, Hart, and Dickson all want more vigorous civil and political commitment from young people. But Hart, who focuses on protest and advocates forms of public disobedience and disruption, seems to call for much different methods than do Roth and Starr, who essentially want to work for change within government institutions. Where do you stand on these contrasting methods of political engagement? How do you view the practice of "protesting"? Are there any current issues that you think demand vigorous protest or even civil disobedience? Is it ever right to disobey laws for political reasons, or to do things such as "jam up" stores, an activity described by Hart?

2. Roth thinks that lowering the voting age might lead to an increase in public service. Starr refers approvingly to "volunteer service, whether in the military, AmeriCorps, or other institutions" (para. 17). How do you view the prospect of such programs, whether voluntary or mandatory? Do you see your political rights and your level of political engagement as a citizen tied to any national obligations or public commitments? What connection do you think there is, or should be, between the two? Do the readings provide any insight into these questions?

From Discussion to Writing

1. According to Roth, "If adolescents can be consumers, they can certainly be voters" (para. 7). He also points out, seriously or not,

that "there is no practical difference between a voter and a consumer" (para. 7). Do you agree with this assessment? Are there any significant differences between voting and shopping? Should there be? Write a compare-and-contrast essay that analyzes Roth's assertions.

2.   Hart criticizes many current activists, not so much for their convictions and ideals, but for their lack of originality and creativity. He also provides examples of campaigns that he finds imaginative and inspiring. Choose a political, social, or cultural issue that interests you. Then, come up with your own campaign to raise awareness of it and spur social or political action.

Topics for Cross-Cultural Discussion

1.   Roth describes the successful campaign to lower the voting age in 1971 as "boomer politics." He claims that this movement "succeeded through an appeal from pride to shame: from the righteously self-centered youth of the Age of Aquarius to an older generation still capable of vague feelings of responsibility for their actions and the future effects of those actions" (para. 1). In a sense, the campaign reflected the cultures—and cultural styles— of two different generations, especially the baby boomers. Does your generation have a distinctive politics, as well? How would you define it, politically and culturally? How is it different than— or similar to—what has come before? What are its values and issues? Can such things be defined in "generational" terms?

2.   According to Dickson, Americans have a tendency to define themselves as "fill-in-the-blank–Americans" and to think of their identities in terms of faith, ethnicity, race, and other factors, rather than see themselves as simply Americans. What effect does this have on our sense of ourselves as citizens and as voters? For example, does your race or religion affect your voting choices and your sense of the general welfare of the country? How does your cultural and ethnic background shape your political identity?

10

What Does the New Class Struggle Look Like?

Jacob Riis, a photographer and reformer whose work appears in this unit, became famous for a book promising to reveal *How the Other Half Lives* (1890). What Riis hit on is one of the chief difficulties of any discussion of class in our society: that each half has very little idea of how the other half lives. It can be as difficult for the rich to empathize with the poor as it is for the sighted to understand blindness. Photographs documenting the plight of destitute workers proved more powerful than newspaper descriptions or statistics on poverty because they drew a real image of the everyday lives of the urban poor.

In his graphic essay "Bums," Peter Bagge takes an irreverent and deeply realistic look at the difficult (occasionally taboo) subject of homelessness, deflating the theory that homeless people are good-for-nothing incorrigibles and, at the same time, the notion that they are hapless victims of social stratification and misfortune. The picture Bagge draws of San Francisco vagrants is a complex one: They are often addicts helpless to change their situations, although many have "an exaggerated sense of entitlement, putting on loud air guitar concerts while practically demanding change from passers-by."

After spending a day with a group of street people at a food kitchen, Bagge begins to develop a detailed image of the homeless. They are, for instance, full of advice on how to survive on the streets and are "able to find humor in their own situations, no matter how abysmal they get." Indeed, Bagge's visual depictions of his homeless characters, drawing on Depression-era archetypes of drunken hobos, inject a good deal of humor into a rather grave subject area.

This kind of sincere look at the lives of the underclass is something our popular culture has failed to provide, according to Robert Nathan and Jo-Ann Mort. In "Hollywood Flicks Stiff the Working Class," the writers bemoan the movie industry's apparent apathy for poor and working-class people, contrasting the current cinema with a nostalgic look at the classic Sally Field film *Norma Rae*, which documented the plight of workers attempting to unionize. "Making *Norma Rae* in 1979 was hard enough," Nathan and Mort write; "now it would probably be impossible. The country has changed. It's more difficult to build a mass movement for social and economic change, to find large numbers of Americans who care about social solidarity."

Nathan and Mort conclude, sadly, that "moviemakers are in the movie business, not the social change business." But like Riis, they take for granted that class in America is a phenomenon best understood anecdotally through depictions, rather than analytically through sociological arguments. Student essayist Robert Reece takes a different tack, arguing, as the title of his piece declares, that "Class Struggle Is Race Struggle in the U.S."

Reece's means of comprehending class differences is to align them with more familiar racial fissures, since "the racial and socioeconomic lines run almost parallel." Because of the disproportionate economic poverty of the black community, Reece, an African American student at the University of Mississippi, was known as "one of the 'rich kids' at my all-black high school when my parents' annual combined salary barely exceeded $45,000." Reece concludes from this enormous disparity that "a meritocratic society in the United States is an ongoing lie."

Reece finds it impossible to reconcile a situation in which one ethnic group fares so poorly with the model of a country in which economic opportunity is universal and class discrepancies are simply a product of some people's hard work and intelligence. But despite their divergent methods, both Jacob Riis and Robert Reece would most likely agree that creating a more equitable society is an imperative we all share. This chapter concludes with "America Then . . . 1890," which shows that urban homelessness is not a modern problem.

PETER BAGGE

Bums

[REASON/April 2007]

Before You Read

Can cartoons be more than entertainment? Read the following work and notice how this particular medium is being used to convey factual information. How is this cartoon different from the essays you've read, and how is it similar? Do you think you have a better understanding of people who are homeless once you have finished this piece?

Words to Learn

exaggerated (panel 1): overblown (adj.)

entitlement (panel 1): a feeling that one has a right to something (n.)

predators (panel 6): people who prey on or victimize others (n.)

debilitating (panel 7): damaging (adj.)

trauma (panel 9): physical or psychological injury (n.)

emphysema (panel 10): a severe lung disease (n.)

mercenary (panel 14): a hired soldier (n.)

grandeur (panel 17): impressiveness or greatness (n.)

paranoid schizophrenia (panel 17): a psychiatric disorder characterized by delusions and/or hallucinations (n.)

remote (panel 19): unlikely (adj.)

Peter Bagge is a visual artist who describes his style as "exaggerated and distinctively in-your-face." Bagge was briefly enrolled in the School of Visual Arts in New York City in 1977 and was the managing editor of Weirdo magazine from 1983 to 1986. His most well-known comic series, Hate, has been "hailed by critics for its brilliant characterization in its complete chronicle of the 1990s." Bagge's comics and illustrations have appeared in a range of publications, including Hustler, Mad, Oxford American, Reason, and the Weekly World News.

WHO ARE THESE PEOPLE? WHERE DID THEY ALL COME FROM? AND WHY ARE THERE SUDDENLY FEWER OF THEM NOW? WELL, FIRST OF ALL, WHEN TALKING ABOUT "BUMS," I AM IN NO WAY REFERRING TO ANY OF THE FOLLOWING:

SYMPATHETIC, THERE-BUT-FOR-THE-GRACE-OF-GOD TYPES LIKE THESE MAKE UP AROUND 90 PERCENT OF THE OFFICIAL "HOMELESS" POPULATION AT ANY GIVEN TIME. THEY ALSO ARE RARELY HOMELESS FOR LONGER THAN SIX MONTHS.

ALSO, THERE ARE SO MANY CHARITIES AND AGENCIES THAT ARE READY AND EAGER TO HELP PEOPLE IN NEED WHO ASK FOR HELP THAT IT'S ALMOST IMPOSSIBLE FOR ANYONE TO GO HUNGRY IN THE U.S. THESE DAYS...

ALL THOSE PEOPLE HOLDING SIGNS AND GLARING AT YOU AT BUSY INTERSECTIONS ARE NOT ONLY WELL-FED, THEY ALSO AREN'T HOMELESS. THEY'RE JUST LAZY JERKS!

MOST OF THE MORE OBNOXIOUS STREET PEOPLE YOU RUN INTO AREN'T HOMELESS EITHER. THEY'RE JUST PIMPS, CON ARTISTS, AND SMALL-TIME CROOKS WHO "HIDE" AMONG THE HOMELESS POPULATION TO AVOID DETECTION AND TO EXPLOIT THE SERVICES SET UP TO HELP THE NEEDY...

THESE PREDATORS ALSO USE AND ABUSE THE REAL HOMELESS, OFTEN TO A TRULY HORRIFIC DEGREE.

THIS POOR FELLOW IS ONE OF THE CHRONIC "10 PERCENTERS" — THOSE TRAGIC SOULS WHO LIVE MOST OF THEIR ADULT LIVES WITHOUT ANY PERMANENT SHELTER...

MOST OF THEM ARE MALE, AND THEY TEND TO ABUSE DRUGS AND ALCOHOL, THOUGH WHAT THEY ALL HAVE IN COMMON IS THAT THEY SUFFER FROM ONE OR MORE TYPES OF DEBILITATING MENTAL ILLNESS.

THEY ALSO MOSTLY COME FROM POOR, DYSFUNCTIONAL, AND/OR ABUSIVE FAMILIES WHERE NO ONE IS WILLING OR ABLE TO DEAL WITH THEIR MENTAL PROBLEMS, WHICH IS HOW THEY WIND UP ON THE STREET IN THE FIRST PLACE...

THE MYTH OF THE CAREFREE HOBO WHO CHOOSES TO LIVE UNDER THE STARS IS JUST THAT: A MYTH! ANYONE WHO'D OPT FOR SUCH A WRETCHED LIFE IS CRAZY BY DEFINITION!

MORE SAD BUM FACTS:

THE LIFE EXPECTANCY OF A CHRONICALLY HOMELESS PERSON IN THE U.S. IS 47...

THEY ALSO ARE 10 TIMES MORE LIKELY TO BE MURDERED, BE SEXUALLY ASSAULTED, AND COMMIT SUICIDE THAN THE GENERAL POPULATION...

ONE-THIRD OF THEM DIE FROM ALCOHOL POISONING, WHILE ANOTHER 25 PERCENT DIE FROM TRAUMA (MURDER, SUICIDE, ACCIDENTS, ETC.)

AND ALMOST ALL OF THEM HAVE BEEN IN AND OUT OF JAIL, DETOX, AND REHAB COUNTLESS TIMES, ONLY TO FALL OFF THE WAGON AS SOON AS THEY'RE RELEASED!

THEY ALSO COST THE REST OF US A FORTUNE IN EMERGENCY HEALTH CARE -- IN SOME CASES UP TO $100,000 A YEAR!

...OH, NO! NOT **HER** AGAIN!

GASP!   -WHEEZE-

FOR EXAMPLE, A RESIDENT OF A SEATTLE HOMELESS SHELTER WHO SUFFERED FROM EMPHYSEMA WOUND UP IN THE E.R. EVERY TIME SHE SMOKED A CIGARETTE -- ONLY SHE INSISTED ON SMOKING EVERY DAY!

HOSPITALS ARE SO OVERWHELMED BY THESE REPEAT VISITORS AND THEIR SELF-INFLICTED WOUNDS THAT MANY OF THEM NO LONGER OFFER EMERGENCY SERVICES AT ALL...

AREN'T YOU SICK OF CARRY-ING ME TO THE BATHROOM?

YOU'RE **NOT** GETTING A WHEELCHAIR! THOSE ARE FOR **PAYING** CUSTOMERS!

MAN! HOW **SPITEFUL** CAN YOU GET?

I ONCE SHARED A HOSPITAL ROOM WITH A WINO WHO BROKE HIS LEGS (AFTER DRUNKENLY FALLING IN FRONT OF AN AMBULANCE!), YET THE NURSES REFUSED TO LET HIM USE A WHEELCHAIR, CLAIMING HE DIDN'T DESERVE ONE!

MANY CITIES, INCLUDING SAN FRANCISCO AND SEATTLE, RECENTLY HAVE ADOPTED A POLICY CALLED "HOUSING FIRST," WHICH PROVIDES A FREE ROOM FOR CHRONICALLY HOMELESS ALCOHOLICS WITHOUT ANY SOBRIETY REQUIREMENTS...

UGH... I'M TOO DRUNK TO GET UP...

BUT AT LEAST I'M NOT IN THE MIDDLE OF THE **HIGHWAY** LIKE I WAS LAST NIGHT...

THESE BARE-BONES "BUNKS FOR DRUNKS" ALREADY HAVE DRASTICALLY REDUCED THE NUMBER OF EMERGENCY ROOM VISITS FOR THEIR RESIDENTS SIMPLY BY ALLOWING THEM TO GET HAMMERED INDOORS FOR A CHANGE.

CRITICS DERIDE THIS APPROACH AS "REWARDING" DRUNKS BEFORE THEY MANAGE TO GET SOBER, WHICH IGNORES THE FACT THAT THESE GUYS WILL NEVER BE SOBER...

I'M **ALSO** AN ALCOHOLIC, BUT I JOINED A.A. AND **CLEANED UP MY ACT**...

UNLESS THESE BUMS DO THE SAME I HAVE **NO** SYMPATHY FOR THEM!

THE SAD TRUTH IS THAT THERE IS NO "CURE" FOR CHRONIC HOMELESSNESS. ALL WE CAN DO IS APPLY BAND-AIDS, TO REDUCE THE COSTS AND RISKS.

THE LIGHTER SIDE OF BUMS DEPT.: AFTER SPENDING A DAY WITH A GROUP OF CHRONIC "10 PERCENTERS" AT A LOCAL FOOD KITCHEN, I CAME AWAY WITH A FEW SWEEPING GENERALIZATIONS, SUCH AS...

THEY TEND TO ACT "TOUGH" AROUND STRANGERS...

...MAN, IF ANYONE MESSES WITH ME I'LL CUT them.

I USED TO BE A MERCENARY, MAN.

I USED TO BE A STUNTMAN. IN HOLLY-WOOD!

GONNA GET ME SOME PUSSY, MAN...

LUTHERAN CALVARY CHURCH

I FEEL LIKE I'M BACK IN JUNIOR HIGH!

YET ONCE THEY DECIDE YOU'RE "OK" (WHICH HAPPENS IN TEN SECONDS) THEY START TO OVERLY CONFIDE IN YOU...

THE METHADONE CLINIC I USE DOESN'T TEST YOU FOR ALCOHOL BEFORE THEY DOSE YOU...

IT'S RIGHT NEXT TO A VACANT APARTMENT I'VE BEEN CRASHING IN LATELY TOO...

IT'S HEATED AND EVERYTHING! I JUST HOPE THE OTHER TENANTS DON'T FIND OUT...

YEESH...

THIS GUY'S GIVING AWAY ALL HIS VALUABLE BUM SECRETS!

I ALSO RECEIVED A LOT OF FREE ADVICE ON HOW TO BE A "SUCCESSFUL" HOMELESS PERSON...

I PREFER TO LIVE OUT IN THE NEIGHBOR-HOODS. IT'S SAFER!

...NO ONE KNOWS WHERE I SPEND THE NIGHT, SINCE I DON'T PEE AND POO ALL OVER THE PLACE LIKE SOME GUYS...

THE BEST PLACE TO WASH YOUR-SELF IS A JANITOR'S CLOSET...

THE MOP SINK IS LIKE A MINI-BATH TUB!

AND ALL THE CLASSIC SIGNS OF THE USUAL MENTAL DISORDERS WHERE ON FULL DISPLAY...

I INVENTED SUSHI!

I NEVER INVENTED ANYTHING...

THAT SQUIRREL IS AFTER MY LUNCH...

AND MY SOUL!

DELUSIONS OF GRANDEUR

CLINICAL DEPRESSION

PARANOID SCHIZOPHREMIA

THEY ARE ABLE TO FIND HUMOR IN THEIR OWN SITUATIONS, NO MATTER HOW ABYSMAL THEY GET...

I FRACTURED MY SKULL OPEN LAST WEEK...

HOW'D THAT HAPPEN?

HOW TH' HELL WOULD I KNOW?!

OH, YEAH, HEH...

MY CAR BATTERY DIED LAST NIGHT...

I NEARLY FROZE TO DEATH...

THAT'S WHAT YOU GET FOR BEING A FORD MAN...

BUT THE MOST DISTURBING THING ABOUT HANGING OUT WITH HOMELESS PEOPLE IS THE POSSIBILITY, NO MATTER HOW REMOTE, THAT YOU COULD BECOME ONE YOURSELF...

I LIKE THE WAY YOU THINK, PETE!

WE'RE SIMPATICO, YA KNOW? TWO PEAS IN A POD!

UH, SURE, HEH HEH...

NO! DON'T SAY THAT!

I'M NOTHING LIKE YOU! NOTHING!

SO THE LAST THING I WANTED WAS THIS ONE BUM'S ATTEMPTS TO BOND WITH ME!

Vocabulary / Using a Dictionary

1. What is the root of the word *obnoxious* (panel 2)?

2. *Hammered* (panel 12) in this context is slang. What does it mean here, and what else can it mean?

3. Does the word *abysmal* (panel 18) have any relationship to the word *abyss*? What do these words mean?

Responding to Words in Context

1. What does the homeless man mean when he says, "I am the new *Messiah*" (panel 1)?

2. Bagge uses the word *chronic* throughout the piece (for example, panels 7 and 13). What does it mean for someone to have a *chronic* condition?

3. What is a *life expectancy* (panel 9)?

Discussing Main Point and Meaning

1. What does Bagge want people to know about the plight of the homeless?

2. Do Bagge's drawings of the homeless people he encounters convey any sympathy for them? If he doesn't have sympathy for them, what emotion does he feel about them, and how can you tell?

3. Are you convinced by Bagge's argument that there are no "happy hobos"? Which sections are particularly convincing?

Examining Sentences, Paragraphs, and Organization

1. Bagge relies heavily on ellipses to get from one idea or thought to the next. What would the effect be if he didn't use the ellipses?

2. Bagge's commentary runs throughout this piece and holds it together, but how does his medium allow him to go beyond this commentary?

3. Cartoons can often make people laugh, but Bagge is also trying to present serious information through his medium, much like an essay. How does Bagge convey humor yet inform his audience about this tragic subject?

Thinking Critically

1. Do you agree that "all those people holding signs and glaring at you at busy intersections are not only well-fed, they also aren't homeless. They're just lazy jerks!" as Bagge claims? Why do you think he believes he can make that statement as if it were a fact?

2. Does Bagge come across as likable? Why or why not? Does anyone come across as likable in this cartoon?

3. Why does the piece seem to end so abruptly? Did you expect more?

In-Class Writing Activities

1. What kind of magazine is *Reason*? Explore the images, information about the journal, and articles of a recent issue online, and write a brief essay that describes who you think would be interested in subscribing to *Reason*. Explain who you think the audience is, and refer to specific articles as supporting evidence. You may also refer to the graphic art piece you just examined.

2. The word *hobo* began to be used in America in the late 1800s; it came to be associated with vagrants or bums, although it may first have specifically referred to migrant workers. The hobo, as Bagge mentions, has been portrayed in many different ways. Bagge hopes to dispel the myth of the "happy hobo," although he does include a picture of a scruffy man with a bag tied to the end of a stick, which is the typical portrayal of a hobo. What images of hobos have you come in contact with? Write a list of things the word calls to mind and try to connect those characteristics with your experience of them—did they come from a movie, a story, a cartoon? How does your perception of a "hobo" differ from your idea of a "homeless person"?

3. Imagine that you are an editor, and write a letter to Peter Bagge responding to his graphic art piece "Bums." Based on your experience of his cartoon, explain whether or not you would like to read others he has done. Give some idea of what other topics you'd be interested in seeing in this form and why.

ROBERT NATHAN and JO-ANN MORT

Hollywood Flicks Stiff the Working Class

[THE NATION/March 12, 2007]

Before You Read

Are workers and class issues visible in our films and television shows? Do you think movies should have messages or should advocate for political and social change? Are you aware of the role of class in your own life?

Words to Learn

evocative (para. 3): serving to bring to mind (adj.)

aberration (para. 4): object or condition notably different from the norm (n.)

redemption (para. 6): the act of delivering from sin; the repurchase of something sold; rescue (n.)

paean (para. 7): song of praise or triumph (n.)

fractionated (para. 12): separated or divided into different parts (adj.)

corrosive (para. 12): caustic, sarcastic; destructive (adj.)

Robert Nathan is the co–executive producer of the television series Law & Order *and is a member of the* Writers Guild of America. *He has written several novels and contributed articles to magazines, including* Harper's, New Republic, *and* Politics Today. *Jo-Ann Mort is director of communications at the Jewish Funders Network and is an officer of Americans for Peace Now. As a writer, Mort "specializes in Israel, the Jewish world, and economic justice issues" and is coauthor of* Our Hearts Invented a Place: Can Kibbutzim Survive in Today's Israel? *(2003). Her writing has appeared in the* Chicago Tribune, *the* Jerusalem Report, *the* Los Angeles Times, *the* American Prospect, *and the* Forward, *among others.*

Here are some words you are unlikely to hear in any of the movie clips shown during the Academy Awards this year:

Ladies and gentlemen, the textile industry, in which you are spending your lives and your substance . . . is the only industry in the whole length and breadth of these United States of America that is not unionized. Therefore, they are free to exploit you, to lie to you, to cheat you and to take away from you what is rightfully yours—your health, a decent wage, a fit place to work.

"Unionized" isn't a word you hear in many American movies. "A decent wage," now there's a phrase that doesn't crop up too often. As for the evocative "your lives and your substance," poetic descriptions of the human condition aren't generally found in contemporary entertainment.

This speech is from Martin Ritt's classic 1979 film *Norma Rae*, delivered in an impassioned sermon by Ron Leibman in the role of an organizer for the Textile Workers Union of America, a real union at the time and a predecessor to the current trade union UNITE HERE. *Norma Rae* is an aberration in recent Hollywood history. The movie portrays a realistic union-organizing campaign and the fierce corporate response at the fictional O.P. Henley textile mill in the fictional town of Henleyville. As everyone knew at the time, the mill and the town were unambiguous stand-ins for J.P. Stevens and its sixteen-year war against union organizers in Roanoke Rapids, North Carolina, and the movie accurately depicted the state of American labor in 1979.

The situation has not improved much since. The only remaining Stevens factory in the United States (owned by its successor company, Westpoint Home) is a unionized blanket mill in Maine. In other industries, union organizers are battling adversaries as unyielding as any in the days of *Norma Rae*. According to the labor advocacy group American Rights at Work, last year more than 23,000 Americans were fired or penalized for legal union activity.

On a human level, *Norma Rae* is the story of one woman, played by Sally Field, who finds redemption risking her life for economic justice, and of factory workers demanding to be treated as more than slaves. In the realm of the political, it is virtually the only American movie of the modern era to deal substantially with any of these subjects. Even today it remains iconic—a major studio movie about the lives of working people with a profound and, for its time, disturbing political message: The little guy may have a prayer of getting social justice, but he'll have to fight desperately to get it. Try to think of a contemporary American film with a similar message or a political statement anywhere near that blunt. The closest thing to a message in this year's crop of Oscar nominees for Best Picture can be found in *Babel*, which poses the rather mild question, Why can't we all just get along?

European filmmakers, like England's Ken Loach and Mike Leigh,   7
don't shy from the subject of class. Loach's *Bread and Roses* dramatized the 1990 Service Employees International Union's Justice for Janitors campaign in Los Angeles, and Leigh's entire career is virtually a paean to the working class. This is not to say that American studios don't make topical mainstream films. A kind of renaissance seemed to be blossoming in 2005, with material as varied as *Good Night, and Good Luck* and *The Constant Gardener*. But *Blood Diamond*—about the 1990s civil war in Sierra Leone partly sparked by international diamond speculators—was perhaps this season's only major studio picture that could be called politically daring, and it was a box-office disappointment. In the end, of course, financially successful or not, such movies don't fundamentally threaten the established order. They're well-crafted stories delivering conventional wisdom with considerable artistic skill.

Norma Rae was different. Its subject matter, never mind its poli-   8
tics, was enough to make a studio executive cringe: a movie about a union. On top of that, it was a story of platonic love between a Jewish intellectual and a factory worker; in Hollywood love stories, the audience wants the heroes to end up in bed. Even with a trio of creative giants—Ritt and his writers, Irving Ravetch and Harriet Frank Jr.—this was no easy sell. Casting could have helped; stars get movies made. But several leading actresses, among them Jane Fonda and Jill Clayburgh, turned down the title role. Creative issues aside, there was the problem of location. Where would you shoot the movie? Because of J.P. Stevens's influence, taking the production to most Southern towns would be impossible, and building your own textile mill, prohibitively costly. (With help from the union, Ritt found a unionized mill in Opelika, Alabama, where management agreed to let him shoot, with mill workers as extras playing themselves.) Finally, after overcoming all the odds, when released the movie was anything but an instant hit, and only after Sally Field won Best Actress at Cannes did it gradually go from dud to box-office success.

Since then, the entertainment community has kept its distance   9
from the film. One indication of Hollywood's indifference came six

years later, at the 1985 Academy Awards, when Field accepted her Oscar as Best Actress for *Places in the Heart.* "You like me," she said effusively, "right now, you like me." The audience response was nervous laughter, as if Sally Field were so needy as to consider an Academy Award a sign that she was "liked." This was, of course, not the case. Field had assumed, incorrectly, that most of her colleagues had seen her astonishing performance in *Norma Rae.* But in fact, many in the audience had no idea that she was referencing one of the picture's most memorable pieces of dialogue—her character's realization that her union organizer not merely respected her but liked her as a human being.

In the ensuing twenty years, the movie essentially disappeared. 10 Otherwise movie-literate folks only vaguely remember Norma's quest. Alas, they don't know what they're missing. With Leibman and Field, the movie has two of the toughest and most generous performances in the history of American film. The film's language is simultaneously elegant and gritty. Of powerful moments, there is no end. When Norma commits herself to the organizing campaign, she asks the local minister to lend his church for a union meeting. "That's blacks and whites sitting together," Norma says. The minister, horrified, tells her, "We're going to miss your voice in the choir, Norma." She replies, "You're going to hear it raised up somewhere else."

In an unusual twist, the movie's story played itself out in reality 11 the year following its release. Sixteen years after a successful union election at the Roanoke Rapids mill, union members finally forced J.P. Stevens to the bargaining table. The film was a key factor in a nationwide boycott against Stevens—a campaign that became a model for coalitions of union supporters and union members. The Rev. David Dyson, who helped spearhead the Stevens boycott when he was on the union's staff, recalls: "The movie came along at the two-year point in the boycott, which hadn't picked up any steam. We found Crystal Lee Jordan [now Crystal Lee Sutton, the worker who inspired the *Norma Rae* character]. . . . We put on a tour, including a great event in Los Angeles with Sally Field and Crystal Lee. The lights would come up and there would be the real *Norma Rae* and people would leap to their feet."

It's nearly impossible to imagine a similar movie that would bring 12 them to their feet today. Television, a broader medium, is different, with an audience more fractionated and therefore, theoretically, more open to content that some might label controversial. Not so long ago there was *Roseanne*, which addressed head-on the darkness of power and social class and the tribulations of working life. Last year's Emmy winner *The Office* included a story line mocking a nasty anti-union campaign; the hugely popular *Grey's Anatomy* followed a nurses' strike with obvious sympathy for the nurses—even management, in the person of doctor George O'Malley, joined the picket line as the story revealed his upbringing in a pro-union home. One could argue that the brilliantly corrosive *Rescue Me*, about Denis Leary as a New York City firefighter and the personal lives of his colleagues, is a bold step into the interior world of the working class; but firefighters are unmistakably post-9/11 heroes. What's ultimately most telling about these examples is how unusual they are, far from television's norm, at a time when most Americans are losing economic ground. One new show this season, the polished and artful *Brothers & Sisters*, is about a wealthy family in Pasadena who own a business in which workers are nearly invisible; the primary stories involve the characters' tortured love lives. Ironically, the family matriarch—albeit a liberal ACLU-ish matriarch—is played by none other than Sally Field.

It would be easy to blame the entertainment industry for the invisibility of working people fighting to better their lives. Ask writers in show business and they'll say, "Nobody cares about seeing those people on a screen" and "If audiences wanted to see that, the studios would make it" and, finally, the answer to nearly every question about the current condition of American filmmaking, "The studios have a mega-hit mentality; they don't want to make small pictures." But maybe there's another reason. Making *Norma Rae* in 1979 was hard enough; now it would probably be impossible. The country has changed. It's more difficult to build a mass movement for social and economic change, to find large numbers of Americans who care about social solidarity. If popular entertainment is, by definition, mass entertainment, what happens when no mass exists, when an insufficient number of people occupy cultural common ground? In that case, for whom would you make *Norma Rae*?   13

> *If popular entertainment is, by definition, mass entertainment, what happens when no mass exists, when an insufficient number of people occupy cultural common ground?*

"You live there, and you become one of them," Sally Field said in a documentary issued with the DVD of *Norma Rae*, "and you try to stand at their machine and thread it and run it, and . . . you learn to   14 appreciate how difficult their lives are, and chances are you're never getting out." Which, for the most part, is how things remain. The American labor movement is arguably in more trouble now than it was then. Where is the next movie that might hope to change the course of history?

Of movies about ideas and social justice, Sam Goldwyn famously said, "If you want to send a message, call Western Union." In other words, moviemakers are in the movie business, not the social change business. And so tomorrow we won't go to the tenplex and find movies about Wal-Mart workers fighting for health and pension benefits, or turn on the television and find a working-class hero struggling to pay the electric bill. (Isn't it odd that people on TV hardly ever seem to worry about gas prices?) If we are to find a *Roseanne* or a *Norma Rae* again in popular entertainment, if we are to make movies that can affect the course of history, we need to find something else first, something difficult to see on the horizon. We need to find a belief in an ideal disappearing not only from our movies but also from our lives—the notion that we do, in fact, share common ground, and that if we ignore the lives of the least fortunate in our society we may well be ignoring the future of our society itself.

15

Vocabulary / Using a Dictionary

1. What does *advocacy* (para. 5) mean, what are its origins, and what other words share its roots?

2. The writers refer to *Norma Rae* as "iconic" (para. 6). What does *iconic* mean, and where does the word originate?

3. What is a *renaissance* (para. 7)? What other words share roots with *renaissance*?

Responding to Words in Context

1. In paragraph 3, Nathan and Mort refer to a line in *Norma Rae* as being a "poetic description of the human condition." What does the adjective *poetic* suggest in this context?

2. Nathan and Mort refer to "economic justice" in paragraph 6. What do you think that phrase means here?

3. What is *platonic love* (para. 8)? Why is it significant that the film portrays only this kind of love, according to Nathan and Mort?

Discussing Main Point and Meaning

1. According to Nathan and Mort, *Norma Rae* is still an iconic movie, even if remains unusual among Hollywood films, then and now. Why was the film difficult to make back in the 1970s? Why are these problems significant to the larger point of the essay?

2. According to Nathan and Mort, what are the problems with current films and television—even the ones that attempt to include political and social messages?

3. Nathan and Mort believe that a film like *Norma Rae* would be even more difficult to make now than it was originally. Why is that the case, and why do they find this situation odd, in some ways?

Examining Sentences, Paragraphs, and Organization

1. In paragraph 12, Nathan and Mort discuss the images of working people in contemporary television shows. They refer to *Rescue Me*, a show depicting some of the struggles of firefighters, which they acknowledge as "a bold step into the interior world of the working class." But they then qualify that judgment in the same sentence by claiming, "firefighters are unmistakably post-9/11 heroes." What does this qualification mean? Do you agree with it?

2. Although Nathan and Mort are writing about the film *Norma Rae* in particular and the entertainment industry generally, their arguments are clearly meant to transcend a discussion of movies and TV. How does their conclusion serve to direct their assertions and conclusions about movies and television outward, to broader issues? Why is this important?

3. "Hollywood Flicks Stiff the Working Class" contains elements of a compare-and-contrast essay, especially in its discussion of past and present, as well as its references to non-American filmmakers. Locate some of the places in the article that show this structure at work. How are the contrasts highlighted?

Thinking Critically

1. "European filmmakers, like England's Ken Loach and Mike Leigh, don't shy from the subject of class" (para. 7), claim Nathan and Mort. What is "the subject of class," as you can

infer it from the essay? Why is class more difficult to discuss or portray in America than in other countries?

2. According to Nathan and Mort, most aspiring, contemporary "message" films are simply "well-crafted stories delivering conventional wisdom with considerable artistic skill" (para. 7). What connotations does the phrase *conventional wisdom* have? What is wrong with it in this context, from the writers' point of view?

3. Nathan and Mort suggest that the entertainment industry has a "mega-hit mentality"; in their account, Hollywood's general attitude toward the scarcity of smaller or more demanding films is: "If audiences wanted to see that, the studios would make it" (para. 13). Do you agree with that logic? What kind of movies does this system produce? What are its advantages and disadvantages?

In-Class Writing Activities

1. In this essay, Nathan and Mort are clearly calling for movies and television shows that are more politically and socially conscious. They lament the lack of "message" and "political statement" in movies; they want more films that "can affect the course of history" (para. 15). This view goes against the opinion of the famous producer Sam Goldwyn, who claimed: "If you want to send a message, call Western Union" (para. 15). What do you think of "message" movies? Do you think films should aspire to change the world? Or are they just supposed to be entertainment? Write an essay in which you take a clear position on this issue.

2. Nathan and Mort look closely at scenes and dialogue from *Norma Rae*. They also provide brief interpretations of several television shows from a class perspective and show how seemingly small details and omissions can be significant: "Isn't it odd that people on TV hardly ever seem to worry about gas prices?" (para. 15). In the same manner, choose a film or television program, and then analyze and interpret it using the lens of class. Does it portray working people at all? In what way? Does it discuss, address, or represent the subject of class? Are there stereotypes about class? Would this show or film support Nathan and Mort's contentions, or would it be evidence for a counterargument?

3. Are you aware of class—in your personal history, in your day-to-day life, in the way you view your future? What effect, if any, do you see it having on your identity? Has class, or an awareness of it, shaped you in any way? Write a personal essay that explores these questions.

ROBERT REECE (STUDENT ESSAY)

Class Struggle Is Race Struggle in U.S.

[DAILY MISSISSIPPIAN, University of Mississippi / February 28, 2008]

Before You Read

Do you see your race and your skin color as a disadvantage or a benefit? How pervasive do you think racism is in the United States? Do you ever use stereotypes? What's the relationship between race and social class in this country?

Words to Learn

scrawny (para. 1): excessively thin (adj.)

eavesdropping (para. 1): listening secretly to a private conversation (v.)

conferred (para. 2): given, as a gift or favor (v.)

ingrained (para. 4): firmly fixed, deeply rooted (adj.)

diminish (para. 5): lessen or reduce (v.)

Robert Reece is a junior at the University of Mississippi, where he will graduate in 2010 with degrees in journalism and sociology. As a weekly columnist for the Daily Mississippian, he is interested in "anything dealing with race relations in the United States" and plans on pursuing a career that involves writing. Reece encourages other student writers to "always write what you're passionate about, and that passion will show in your writing."

When I was a scrawny high school freshman, I overheard my technology teacher discussing a job opportunity with one of her colleagues. I don't recall what position she was applying for, but she was skeptical of her abilities and qualifications. She was reassured by her colleague who said, "Don't worry about it, you'll get the job because you have great qualifications, and, let's be honest, because you're white." They caught me eavesdropping, saw the look on my face and tried to laugh it off.

As a 14-year-old black kid, hearing someone who was supposed to be teaching me how to be a productive adult say something like that hurt, and the conversation was forever carved into my memory. I knew what she said wasn't right, but I didn't know why it hurt so much or why it was so true until I was much older. Peggy McIntosh, associate director of the Wellesley College Center for Research on Women, writes in her essay, *White Privilege: Unpacking the Invisible Knapsack*, "I was taught to think that racism could end if white individuals changed their attitude. But a 'white' skin in the United States opens many doors for whites whether or not we approve of the way dominance has been conferred upon us."

I don't believe that the majority of whites are consciously racist. We all make those little prejudiced remarks and stuff people into stereotypes. I don't think whites spend their time developing new ways to limit the success of minorities. But as McIntosh said, being white simply opens doors, just as "male privilege" and "heterosexual privilege" do. In some cases, being a minority makes it much more difficult to get through those same doors.

Successful people don't want to believe that they've had an unearned advantage.

I expect opposition to this column. I don't expect white people to look objectively at their lives and see the white privilege that has become so deeply ingrained in our society. Successful people don't want to believe that they've had an unearned advantage. I completely understand because I, too, have only recently begun to acknowledge the advantages I've been given in life. I grew up in a two-parent home with an income much higher than other blacks in my area. In fact, I was known as one of the "rich kids" at my all-black high school when my parents' annual combined salary barely exceeded $45,000.

As a minority, I don't mean to diminish the accomplishments of white people or give other minorities an excuse. But it can't be a coincidence that 22.3 percent of blacks and 17.7 percent of other minorities live in poverty while only 6.1 percent of whites have those same economic struggles. It can't be coincidence that 64 percent of United States inmates are minorities. In a capitalist economy, there will always be a class struggle, but in the U.S., class struggle has come to mean a race struggle as the racial and socioeconomic lines run almost parallel.

Some will argue that poor whites are at the same disadvantage as   6
poor minorities. And yet ask yourself how many poor whites have been racially profiled by a police officer. Ask yourself if anyone attributes a poor white person's lack of economic success to the lack of motivation of an entire race. And when a poor white finally pulls himself or herself from the depths of poverty and sits on the board of directors of a massive international corporation, will his hiring be chalked up to affirmative action, resulting in a lack of respect from his colleagues? Or as he stands outside the boardroom soaking in the moment, will he have to wonder whether anyone inside will have the same skin color? Rich or poor, any minority will have to deal with those problems.

As difficult as it may be for the privileged, who so desperately   7
want to cling to the notions that hard work and dedication are the only contributing factors to their success, we must acknowledge that a meritocratic society in the United States is an ongoing lie. The first step to achieving any form of equality and banishing the white privilege that plagues our nation will be admitting to the inequality that is so prevalent in nearly every institution in our country. Only then can we move forward as a society.

Vocabulary / Using a Dictionary

1. What is the origin of the word *prejudiced* (para. 3)?

2. What are the roots of the word *meritocratic* (para. 7), and what does it mean? What other words can be formed using its suffix?

3. Where does the term *stereotype* (para. 3) come from?

Responding to Words in Context

1. In a passage quoted by Reece, the writer Peggy McIntosh claims that "a 'white' skin in the United States opens many doors" (para. 2). Why is the word *white* in quotation marks?

2. How are "heterosexual privilege," "male privilege," and "white privilege" related to one another (para. 3)?

3. What does it mean to be "racially profiled"? Are such practices limited to blacks and other minorities?

Discussing Main Point and Idea

1. According to Reece and the source he cites in his essay, what is the problem with the way some white people view the nature and consequences of racism? Why is this important for his argument?

2. Why does Reece think that race, as a social determinant, is in some ways more significant than class?

3. In the conclusion of his essay, what does Reece want to see happen in American society?

Examining Sentences, Paragraphs, and Organization

1. Reece begins his column with a personal anecdote. How is it related to the theme and argument of his essay, as a whole? What are the benefits and drawbacks of introducing a piece of persuasive writing in this way?

2. In paragraph 4, Reece asserts: "I expect opposition to this column. I don't expect white people to look objectively at their lives and see the white privilege that has become so deeply ingrained in our society." How does Reece imagine his audience? How does he anticipate their objections? How does his sense of his readers shape his essay?

3. How does Reece incorporate statistical evidence into his argument? Is it relevant and related to his point? Why is it important for him to include such data?

Thinking Critically

1. Reece writes, "I don't believe that the majority of whites are consciously racist" (para. 3). Do you agree? Do you think that conscious racism is worse, or less excusable, than unconscious racism? Why do you think the writer focuses on this distinction?

2. According to Reece, he doesn't "expect white people to look objectively at their lives and see the white privilege that has become

so deeply ingrained in our society" (para. 4). What does that mean? Do you think that Reece is "objective"?

3. In paragraph 5, Reece claims that "in a capitalist economy, there will always be a class struggle, but in the U.S., class struggle has come to mean a race struggle as the racial and socioeconomic lines run almost parallel." What does the phrase *class struggle* imply about our economic system? What does it have to do with his argument about race? Do you agree?

In-Class Writing Activities

1. Reece begins his essay by recounting a conversation he overheard as a fourteen-year-old that was "forever carved into [his] memory" (para. 2). But he says he only understood the full significance of the encounter later in life, after he read an essay by Peggy McIntosh. Have you ever had an experience that seemed significant, or lingered in your mind, even if you could not describe its full meaning at the time? Have you ever made sense of a personal experience like this through reading, as Reece did?

2. Discussions of race often raise the issue of stereotyping: "We all make those little prejudiced remarks and stuff people into stereotypes," writes Reece in paragraph 3. Have you ever been stereotyped? Have you ever used stereotypes? What are some common stereotypes? Why are they so persistent and appealing? What's wrong with stereotyping? Explain.

3. According to Reece, "it can't be a coincidence that 22.3 percent of blacks and 17.7 percent of other minorities live in poverty while only 6.1 percent of whites have those same economic struggles" (para. 5). Although the writer does not demonstrate cause and effect, he implies that these figures are due to the white privilege that he describes throughout the essay. Do you think high poverty rates among African Americans are caused primarily by racism, institutional and otherwise? What other factors or explanations might be in play? Write an essay that addresses this issue. You may use Reece's column as a starting point for your response, but you must come up with your own evidence and your own argument.

ANNOTATION Developing Ideas through Comparison and Contrast

One of the most common ways to develop the central idea of a paragraph or even an entire essay is by setting up two contrasting positions. A historian, for example, examines the Battle of Gettysburg by contrasting the different military strategies of Union versus Confederate generals. Or a sportswriter contrasts the tennis tactics of Venus Williams with those of her sister Serena. Depending on the writer's goal, such contrasts can be briefly stated or comprise practically the entire body of the essay. Observe how University of Mississippi student Robert Reece effectively develops a paragraph around two opposing views—the differences between "poor whites" and "poor minorities."

Reece opens the paragraph by saying some would argue that both economic groups are similar in terms of disadvantages. He then sets out in the remainder of the paragraph a number of contrasts between the two groups that show why poor minorities are at a greater disadvantage than poor whites.

Reece contrasts two groups to support his argument on economic disadvantages.

Some will argue that poor whites are at the same disadvantage as poor minorities. And yet ask yourself how many poor whites have been racially profiled by a police officer. Ask yourself if anyone attributes a poor white person's lack of economic success to the lack of motivation of an entire race. And when a poor white finally pulls himself or herself from the depths of poverty and sits on the board of directors of a massive international corporation, will his hiring be chalked up to affirmative action, resulting in a lack of respect from his colleagues? Or as he stands outside the boardroom soaking in the moment, will he have to wonder whether anyone inside will have the same skin color? Rich or poor, any minority will have to deal with those problems.

—From "Class Struggle Is Race Struggle in U.S."
by Robert Reece, page 338

AMERICA THEN . . . 1890

JACOB RIIS

Homeless Boys

    Toward the end of the nineteenth century, a noted reformer and photographer, Jacob Riis, undertook a dramatic investigation of urban poverty. His now-famous book, How the Other Half Lives *(1890), portrayed the world of the New York City slums with an unprecedented realism that shocked and disturbed readers throughout the nation. Many of the photographs, such as "Homeless Boys,"*

Jacob Riis, "Homeless Boys," New York City.

New York City, show raggedly dressed boys living on the edge, with little family or social support. Of these boys, Riis wrote:

"Whence this army of homeless boys? is a question often asked. The answer is supplied by the procession of mothers that go out and in at Police Headquarters the year round, inquiring for missing boys, often not until they have been gone for weeks and months, and then sometimes rather as a matter of decent form than from any real interest in the lad's fate. The stereotyped promise of the clerks who fail to find his name on the books among the arrests, that he 'will come back when he gets hungry,' does not always come true. More likely he went away because he was hungry. Some are orphans, actually or in effect, thrown upon the world when their parents were 'sent up' to the island or to Sing Sing, and somehow overlooked by the 'Society,' which thenceforth became the enemy to be shunned until growth and dirt and the hardships of the street, that make old early, offer some hope of successfully floating the lie that they are 'sixteen.' A drunken father explains the matter in other cases, as in that of John and Willie, aged ten and eight, picked up by the police. They 'didn't live nowhere,' never went to school, could neither read nor write. Their twelve-year-old sister kept house for the father, who turned the boys out to beg, or steal, or starve. Grinding poverty and hard work beyond the years of the lad; blows and curses for breakfast, dinner, and supper; all these are recruiting agents for the homeless army. Sickness in the house, too many mouths to feed."

Discussing the Unit

Suggested Topic for Discussion

Historically, the United States has been distinguished socially by having no aristocracy and no hereditary class structure—that is, no monarch and no system of inheritable titles and honors. Yet it seems that important and profound class distinctions still exist in the United States. Do you think that such disparities result from America being, ultimately, a meritocratic society, in which the best and the brightest usually rise to the top, and in which the only restrictions on achievement are those we place upon ourselves? Or do you think that external factors—such as relative affluence at birth, race, and geography— have more of an influence in determining economic and social status?

Preparing for Class Discussion

1. Robert Nathan and Jo-Ann Mort claim that "European filmmakers . . . don't shy from the subject of class" (para. 7). Indeed, there's a common assumption that most Americans, in contrast, have a difficult time acknowledging and discussing class issues. At the same time, large-scale American political, cultural, and social discussions have focused more often on race in this country. Why do you think that we've generally been more inclined to deal with divisions of race than of class? As Robert Reece's essay seems to imply, can talking about race become a way of talking about class?

2. Compare Jacob Riis's photograph and brief excerpt "Homeless Boys" with Peter Bagge's "Bums" comic as representations of homelessness. How are they similar, and how are they different? Which form do you think would be more effective in influencing readers and spurring social change?

From Discussion to Writing

1. In his comic "Bums," Bagge describes the "Housing First" policy, which cities have pursued with regard to the problem of homelessness. The programs provide free rooms for people, with no requirements for sobriety. As Bagge implies in his strip, the "Housing First" policy may significantly alleviate some of the problems associated with chronically homeless "10 percenters"—cutting down on expensive emergency room visits, for example, which end up being funded by taxpayers. Still, as he acknowledges in his strip, critics of such policies say that they essentially reward bad behavior. And one may also argue that the "there-but-for-the-grace-of-God types" of homeless people (panel 4) are more deserving of free board. Investigate the "Housing First" policy and write a persuasive essay either in favor of it or against it.

2. Both Robert Reece and Peter Bagge take disturbing, confusing, or curious personal experiences and then use them to explore wider social issues. Recall an experience or source of puzzlement in

your own life — and then write an essay analyzing it and connecting it to a broader social, political, or cultural question of more general interest.

Questions for Cross-Cultural Discussion

1. Nathan and Mort refer to "the invisibility of working people fighting to better their lives" (para. 13) in the products of the popular entertainment industry. How important are such media representations in fictional movies or television shows? What is the significance of these representations? Can this question of "visibility" be applied to other racial, cultural, and ethnic groups as well? Is it just a matter of being seen, or is the type or quality of representation also significant?

2. On the last page of "Bums," Bagge writes that after spending time with some chronically homeless people at a local food kitchen, he "came away with a few sweeping generalizations" about them. Do you think that these people constitute a "culture," in themselves? What are the connections between understanding other cultures and making generalizations, as Bagge does?

11

The Border: Can We Solve the Illegal Immigration Problem?

According to recent estimates, there are nearly 10 million immigrants, most of them from Mexico and Latin America, living illegally in the United States. The problem of how to deal with them is so intractable that there's even a debate over what to call them: some tend to use the more traditional term *illegal immigrants*, while others have adopted the gentler *undocumented workers*.

Both sides of the political spectrum, meanwhile, have been in open ferment over the status of these 10 million people for decades. Some conservatives argue that they should be deported or that their entitlements — such as free emergency medical care or even, in some places, driver's licenses—should be rolled back in order to discourage more migration. Some liberals, as well as some Republicans, argue either against deportation and for the status quo (that is, tolerating the violation of the law) or for a more nuanced position: amnesty for illegal immigrants, or a "guest worker" program allowing them to stay legally for a finite period.

Marjorie Lilly falls into the second category—she says she votes Democrat but agrees with President George W. Bush—articulating the case of a legalization process for immigrants who are already in the country. In "The A-Word" (for "amnesty"), Lilly summarizes both the economic and the humanitarian argument for legalization: The enormous cost and burden of deporting the mass of illegal immigrants in the country would not be worth the value of following the letter of the law. "And besides all these reasons," Lilly adds, "there is the fact that these immigrants are working hard for low wages in conditions that are often sub-standard. There ought to be more respect for them, and concern for the way their labor rights are neglected."

In fact, a major talking point for those who aim to legalize, or at least believe in tolerating, illegal immigration is that their opponents are out of touch with the realities on the ground. It sounds logical to follow the law as it's written, and it's certainly disturbing to hear stories of people illegally poaching benefits from citizens, but the facts are, according to Lilly and others, that the lives of migrant workers are brutal and dismal, and their sacrifices are necessary to keep our economy running.

Bryan Welch goes even further, equating the current status of illegal immigrants with that of antebellum American slaves. According to Welch, in "Putting a Stop to Slave Labor," illegal immigration isn't just an unpleasant reality, but a system put in place by farmers and other employers looking to exploit the cheap labor of undocumented workers. Welch ruminates that "my fourth-grade classmates' parents were keeping local farms and businesses afloat by doing work no 'legal' laborer would do." The situation most migrant workers face, Welch says, is bitter: hard work for subsistence pay. "We know why they're here, and most of us are smart enough to figure out why we won't do anything meaningful to change the situation. We don't want to lose the cheap, efficient labor."

One controversial solution to the problem has been a security fence, or wall, erected on the 1,952-mile border between the United States and Mexico. Proponents claim that, no matter what the status of immigrants already in the country, a wall would stave off further waves of migration. But for many opponents, a wall not only is potentially ineffective but also carries sinister connotations tied to the Berlin Wall, the Great Wall of China, and other attempts to isolate populations. Charles Bowden reports from the town of Naco, which straddles the border, that the wall built there stirs mixed feelings in almost everyone but reminds him of the barrier constructed between Israel and the Palestinian territories. "It is designed to control the movement of people, but it faces the problem of all walls—rockets can go over it, tunnels can go under it. It offends people, it comforts people, it fails to deliver security. And it keeps expanding."

The poet Robert Frost wrote that before he built a wall, he'd "ask to know / What I was walling in or walling out," and Bowden's essay attempts to do just that—humanizing the issue of the wall, and of immigration, by taking a close, personal look at the people affected. "I don't understand why they put up a wall to turn us away," one Mexican tells him poignantly. "It's not like we're robbing anybody over there, and they don't pay us very much."

In "Undocumented: One Student's Story" UCLA student Jessica Chou employs the same tactic, forgoing the complex legal and economic arguments over immigration in order to probe its human side. Chou profiles one of her fellow students who braved the perilous passage from Mexico to the United States but had to raise money from his friends to pay to go to school as an undocumented student. "I don't have enough money to pay for it," the student tells Chou. "But you know, you just try to make it work." His story is only one of 10 million around which the immigration debate revolves.

MARJORIE LILLY

The A-Word

[DESERT EXPOSURE / January 2008]

Before You Read

What is amnesty for immigrants without legal status? What are the arguments for and against it?

Words to Learn

replete (para. 1): filled (adj.)
exploited (para. 2): used to the fullest extent, often for another's gain (adj.)
probationary (para. 5): on a trial basis (adj.)

Anybody who isn't confused about border issues once in a while   1
isn't being honest. The whole subject is a can of worms. It's a thicket
of issues replete with ironies. These issues often bend back on themselves, or turn in spirals.

For example, people who sympathize with Mexican farmworkers   2
and the way they're exploited tend to sympathize with undocumented
border crossers. But the Border Agricultural Workers' Union (UTAF
in its Spanish acronym) in El Paso has for a long time urged stronger
policing of the border because illegal immigrants crowd the chile
fields and push down wages. These people were proved right last year

*A graduate of Skidmore College, Marjorie Lilly writes the "Borderlines"
column and other articles for* Desert Exposure, *an alternative newspaper in
Silver City, New Mexico. From her unique location in the southwestern corner of the state—only half an hour from the Mexican border—she is able to
witness and write about important issues facing the country, including border
crossers, farmworkers, biculturalism, and the drug war. Lilly writes, "Being
known locally as a writer is fulfilling and is a tribute to sheer doggedness if
nothing else. I write to witness the pathos of the border, to marvel over this
interesting world, to reform, and to heal."*

when the relative absence of illegal workers did, in fact, drive up the price per bucket. (It made one elderly gentleman in Hatch laugh last fall when I asked him how long the price per bucket of chile had remained the same—it's been something like 25 years.)

When I hear about the number of border crossers being reduced   3
because of increased vigilance by the *migra*,[1] I admit I feel as if a wound is being staunched—the "wound" that is the border, as many people describe it. It's a relief that at least locally the number of deaths of border crossers has gone way down. Some of the bleeding of the wound has been staunched.

Obeying the law brings a feeling of intactness, and breaking it   4
brings a loss of control. This is true even though the closing of the border and the deportations bring great hardship to thousands of people, people I've spoken to face to face and care about. I'm not comfortable about this contradiction. I feel like creating a giant funnel or pipeline across the border to bring food to these people.

But I also had tears spring to my eyes when I read about Presi-   5
dent Bush's proposed "Z-card" or "Z-visa." This would be a temporary ID given to working immigrants who've passed through a probationary period, and would be the first step in a path to citizenship. It would be such a relief to so many people.

Bush has always talked about the need both for tightening the   6
border and also for creating a path to legalization for undocumented immigrants. Though I vote Democrat, I've agreed with Bush when he talks about his plans for the border. The problem lies in the fact that the border-tightening is being done and the legalization of workers isn't.

A process of legalization is so important for those crossing the   7
border to work in the fields or wherever, so they won't have to pass through the extraordinarily difficult obstacle course (through hell and high water, literally) to get to the jobs that Americans pay them to do.

But the way public opinion is running these days, I have doubts   8
that a legalization process will happen soon. The *Arizona Daily Star* in Tucson ran a story about an illegal border crosser on Thanksgiving who came across a nine-year-old boy who'd been in a car accident with his mother. The mother eventually died. The man gave the boy his jacket and built a fire as night fell, and in the morning he went and found help, probably saving the boy's life. The border crosser allowed the *migra* to send him home to Sonora, Mexico.

---

[1]*migra*: A Spanish word that refers to the immigration and border patrol officers.

The ghastly thing about this story is that the overwhelming ma-   9
jority of letters to the editor about it were negative, claiming that liberals were trying to make this man into a hero and referring to the
paper as the *Red Star*. There are lots of these letter writers, and they
appear to be well-organized.

There have been demonstrations in Phoenix recently by Latinos   10
protesting US immigration policy. They've been harassed by Minutemen[2] chanting things like "Born in the USA! KKK!" When a trio of
Mexican singers strolled through the crowd, a Minuteman with a
bullhorn shouted, "Make way for monkeys!"

I've worked with Mexicans, both legal and illegal, in the chile   11
processors in Deming and a bit in the fields, and it strikes me that
there's a lot less hatred by Mexicans toward Americans than vice
versa. They aren't spending time either en-
vying or hating Americans. They live in
their own world and have little contact with
Anglos. They just have fun and work hard.

> *It strikes me that there's a lot less hatred by Mexicans toward Americans than vice versa.*

A path toward citizenship for illegal   12
workers is not just a matter of "rewarding
illegality," as understandable as that attitude may be coming from anybody who re-
spects the concept of law. Something like the proposed Z-card is
needed to correct a serious maladjustment in the labor situation,
partly caused by the inability of the US to fulfill its own quotas for
the acceptance of foreign workers. It's estimated that only a third of
the yearly quotas are filled because of the very long process one has
to go through to apply. I've talked to a farmworker in Hatch who
said it took him five years to bring his wife here.

A legalization process is also a necessity for logistical reasons. All   13
you have to do is stop and think for one minute what it would take
to get rid of the 10 million or so illegal immigrants working in the
US. How many trains and buses and army trucks and airplanes and
ships would it take to transport them? For this reason alone—the
fact that it would be impossible—there has to be an amnesty program. It's the only way to bring a state of law.

And you have to think of all the rights violations that would   14
come in the wake of such a witch hunt. There are already Latinos

[2]*Minutemen:* The Minutemen are a group of private citizens who monitor U.S. borders, primarily the border with Mexico. Their goal is to keep out illegal crossers and
draw media attention to immigration.

being taken away at night by policemen. In Long Island on September 27, in a raid on supposed drug dealers in several houses, only one of the 11 Central Americans arrested and put in jail was involved in the drug trade. In Chaparral, New Mexico, and a few nearby towns in early September policemen entered Mexican immigrants' homes on false premises, such as saying they were responding to a 911 call, and then had the people deported.

Think also of the effect that a mass deportation would have on   15
the US economy, which depends to such a large extent on the cheap labor of immigrants, mostly Mexican.

And besides all these reasons, there is the fact that these immi-   16
grants are working hard for low wages in conditions that are often sub-standard. There ought to be more respect for them, and concern for the way their labor rights are neglected.

There needs to be a legalization process for illegal immigrants.   17
Amnesty is not a dirty word. It's a *de facto* necessity.

Vocabulary / Using a Dictionary

1. What does the prefix *mal-* mean? Why does Lilly think there is "maladjustment" in the labor system (para. 12)?

2. What is the root of the word *deportation* (para. 15)?

3. Look up the word *vigil*. How is it related to the noun *vigilance* (para. 3)?

Responding to Words in Context

1. What is a *thicket* (para. 1)? How is Lilly using the word metaphorically?

2. When she imagines a mass deportation, Lilly refers to it as a "witch hunt" (para. 14). Why does she use this term? What does it generally mean?

3. Although Lilly uses the controversial word *amnesty*, she prefers to refer to Bush's specific recommendation of the Z-card. Why do some people consider *amnesty* "a dirty word" (para. 17)?

Discussing Main Point and Meaning

1. How does the Border Agricultural Workers' Union policy complicate the issue of immigrant rights? Why does Lilly refer to that organization?

2. What does Lilly think is wrong with U.S. efforts to address immigration? Why have those efforts failed?

3. What reasons does Lilly give for why we need the Z-card program, or "amnesty" as some are calling it?

Examining Sentences, Paragraphs, and Organization

1. How does the first sentence of paragraph 4 attempt to resolve the complications Lilly has been describing? What is the structure of the sentence?

2. Why does Lilly include the story about the border crosser who saves a young boy's life? What point does it prove?

3. Look at paragraph 13 and determine which is the topic sentence. How do the rest of the sentences in that paragraph support it?

Thinking Critically

1. Why does Lilly compare the border to a wound?

2. Lilly discusses the job market only indirectly in this essay, but her argument is based on some assumptions about the state of employment in the United States. What are these assumptions?

3. After describing readers' responses to the newspaper story, Lilly notes that the letter writers "appear to be well-organized" (para. 9). What does this statement imply?

In-Class Writing Activities

1. Lilly believes that the Z-card would be "a relief to so many people" (para. 5). Write a paragraph or two in which you discuss different groups who would benefit from the program. Would anyone be hurt by it?

2. Why do you think the newspaper printed the controversial article about the illegal border crosser? Write a response to the protest letters in which you offer some reasons for publishing the story.

BRYAN WELCH

Putting a Stop to Slave Labor

[THE UTNE READER / March–April 2007]

Before You Read

What kinds of jobs do undocumented workers usually hold? What are the conditions of these jobs?

Words to Learn

apparent (para. 3): visible or prominent (adj.)
placate (para. 11): to calm (v.)
incarcerate (para. 12): to put in jail (v.)

I remember my feelings of disbelief when, in the fourth grade, we 1
read about the lives of George Washington and Thomas Jefferson.
Until then, I'd been taught to revere Washington's honesty and Jefferson's brilliance. To me, their powdered wigs and knee breeches symbolized a golden era when America's moral mandate and ethical superiority seemed unassailable.

Yet those colonial heroes who wrote that "all men are created 2
equal" and legendarily declared "I cannot tell a lie" owned slaves.
Even at the age of 9, it made no sense to me that we who worshiped
freedom not only tolerated but endorsed human bondage.

---

*Bryan Welch is the publisher and editorial director for The Utne Reader
and runs Ogden Publications, which publishes a collection of magazines "in
the sustainable-lifestyle, rural-lifestyle and collectible categories," including
Mother Earth News, Natural Home, and The Utne Reader. He graduated
with a BA from the University of Denver and received a master's degree from
Harvard University's Kennedy School of Government, where he studied
media policy and media management. In addition to writing and managing
magazines, Welch "raises organic, grass-fed cattle, sheep and goats on his 50-
acre farm" near Lawrence, Kansas.*

I was in high school when the deeper horrors of slavery became   3
apparent: dislocated families, deplorable living conditions, sexual
servitude, torture.

I was just out of college and working for a bilingual newspaper   4
in northern New Mexico by the time I recognized the irony: My
fourth-grade classmates' parents were keeping local farms and businesses afloat by doing work no "legal" laborer would do. Living in
cinderblock hovels hidden away behind the sand hills of southern
New Mexio, they made less than minimum wage, suffered inhumane
working conditions, and could not protest for fear of deportation.

Economically speaking, they served the same purpose as the   5
Africans who slaved for American masters through the first half of
our nation's history. They provided the cheap labor that allowed us
to establish dominance in the international marketplace. And they
were invisible.

Chances are that the roof on your home or the food on your   6
table or the tiles on your floor were put there by undocumented
workers. In the United States, farmers, food processors, roofers,
ranchers, country clubs, contractors, hotels, and mechanics depend
on low-wage "illegal aliens." The United Farm Workers told the *New
York Times* in September that an estimated 90 percent of California's
farmworkers were undocumented. On some construction sites in
Seattle, 90 percent of the workers are native Spanish speakers, according to inspectors, construction foremen, and union organizers interviewed by the *Seattle Times* in 2006. The U.S. Department of
Labor figures that some 85 percent of recent immigrants from Mexico are undocumented.

A U.S. Immigration and Naturalization Service report estimated   7
that there were 7 million undocumented immigrants in the country in
2000. A more recent estimate of 11 million has been discussed in
news accounts. Robert Justich, managing director of Bear Stearns
Asset Management, says that 20 million could be a more accurate
number. In his 2005 paper "The Underground Labor Force Is Rising
to the Surface," Justich estimates that as many as 3 million people
enter the country illegally each year (triple the authorized figure) and
hold somewhere between 12 million and 15 million jobs, which constitute 8 percent of the labor market.

For obvious reasons, the statistics are somewhat unreliable. The   8
reality of the situation, however, is not lost on Wall Street or anyone
else who cares to take a good, hard look. Our nation is full of undocumented workers. We see them every day. We know why they're

here, and most of us are smart enough to figure out why we won't do anything meaningful to change the situation. We don't want to lose the cheap, efficient labor.

"Four to six million jobs have shifted to the underground market, as small businesses take advantage of the vulnerability of illegal residents," Justich concludes in his report. "In addition to circumventing the Immigration Reform and Control Act of 1986, many employers of illegal workers have taken to using unrecorded revenue receipts. Employer enforcement has succumbed to political pressure."

Hiring undocumented workers is illegal. Yet we don't require that employers verify an applicant's documents, and there is no simple system for doing so. How hard would it be to give employers access to a database that would, without violating any privacy rights, check a couple of basic facts related to a Social Security number, such as zip code, name, and work history? In this era of instant online credit, when a teenager working at your local car dealer's parts counter can check a credit score in 15 seconds, it would be neither difficult nor prohibitively expensive. As it is, we don't even check to see that the Social Security number matches a name.

We are systematically tolerating, even encouraging, undocumented workers to come to the United States. Then, in order to placate a vocal and ill-informed minority, enforcement agencies stage various law enforcement dramas at locations across the country. We erect costly and ineffectual fences on the Mexican border.

Some write off undocumented workers as criminals. Factions within the law enforcement establishment stage sporadic raids with little strategic value on high-profile employers like Wal-Mart and Swift & Company. The raids placate the neoconservatives demanding an emphasis on law enforcement, but that's all the raids accomplish. Given that there are somewhere between 10 million and 20 million undocumented workers, if just 10 percent of them were arrested there would be no place to incarcerate them—and the sheer numbers would make deportation logistically impossible. How would we transport a million people to the border? Two million? And how do we fill their jobs when they're gone?

What's most appalling is that we have the audacity to label entrepreneurial immigrants "criminals" when the vast majority of undocumented workers are sincere, skilled, industrious men and women doing what they must to support their families. Just ask the people who hire them. A Texas rancher recently told me he gets 50 percent more work from an "illegal" Mexican day worker than from his legal U.S.

counterpart. The Mexican "is generally a family guy, working for his wife and kids," he said. "The American is some kid who doesn't really care, or he's got other problems—alcohol or whatever—keeping him out of the permanent workforce." (Most honest farmers I've talked to over the years, in fact, will tell you that their Mexican laborers have better skills and work harder than the rest of their documented employees.)

Somehow many of these laborers manage to save a share of their pitiful wages to send home. Justich reports that in 2003, Mexican workers in the United States sent home $13 billion in remittances. That's to Mexico alone, and that's triple the amount recorded in 1995. Talk about family values. 14

The nation's farm shacks, decrepit trailer parks, and urban tenements are packed with people who work long hours every day in illegal working conditions. In agriculture they toil in extreme weather handling toxic chemicals and dangerous heavy equipment. 15

In *Fast Food Nation* (Houghton Mifflin, 2001), author Eric Schlosser calls meatpacking "the most dangerous job in the United States" with an injury rate three times higher than average factory jobs. No one officially complains because the workers desperately want to steer clear of the authorities. As a result, we have no trustworthy information about the undocumented labor force's health, living conditions, education, or beliefs. Even if someone managed to come up with a reliable way of collecting such data, the study's subjects would still be afraid of participating. 16

> *Yesterday, Native Americans and African slaves fell outside our narrow definition of humanity. Today, the undocumented worker does.*

This sort of moral myopia is not a new phenomenon in U.S. culture. Yesterday, Native Americans and African slaves fell outside our narrow definition of humanity. Today, the undocumented worker does. 17

Politicians talk about building fences and sending soldiers to the border, yet they refuse to take the simplest steps to prevent the workers from being hired illegally. They also willfully disregard why immigrants are attracted to the United States in the first place (for the jobs) and why Americans don't want to admit it. 18

If we required good documents starting tomorrow, the nation would plunge into an instantaneous economic crisis. Millions of workers would suddenly be missing. The only practical and ethical solution is to provide legal status to honest, hardworking immigrants. 19

Then we would have to acknowledge how we treat them. We would have to admit that jobs that offer a fair wage and humane working conditions cost money—and that cost would be passed on to consumers, who, for starters, might see an additional 10 percent added to their rent or mortgage payment and pay 15 percent more for groceries.

That's not a change the average consumer would welcome, of course. And it's not going to happen until American citizens are forced to confront the human cost of the system we have built. Then maybe we'll have the guts to change it. 20

I met Max Gonzales in the mountains of northern New Mexico more than 20 years ago. He lived up there in the Cruces Basin Wilderness seven months a year in a canvas tent. Most of the time, he had only his two horses, a border collie, and 1,500 sheep for company. Every two weeks or so, his supplies were carried in on horseback. When there were fresh batteries, he could listen to a Juarez radio station. 21

Sometimes backpackers like me showed up for a few days to hike the trails and fish in the streams, but Max didn't speak English and the campers generally didn't speak Spanish. It was a life of isolation that only a hermit (or a delusional college boy with literary aspirations and a backpack) would choose, and Max was a gregarious 30-year-old without any romantic notions of the sheepherder's lonely vocation. He didn't enjoy the life much. He had a wife and three daughters back in Guanajuato. He was doing it for the money. 22

Max said he was making about $4,500 a year. Even if you adjust for inflation, that's not much of a job, but it was the best a farm kid from Mexico could find without a green card. And without someone like Max, the rancher who owned those sheep might have been out of business. A legal worker would have cost the rancher at least twice what he was paying Max, assuming he could find a competent person willing to move into the mountains alone for six months. That sort of increased overhead would have rendered him vulnerable to competitors at home—unwilling and unmotivated to pay a fair wage—or to wool and meat exporters in Australia and Chile. 23

If we shut down illegal immigration, a program to legalize our "guest workers" would be a matter of necessity to save American agriculture. At that point, the citizenry would have had to acknowledge how we were treating people like Max. But because nothing was done then—and because it doesn't look like anything meaningful is 24 going to happen in the foreseeable future—illegal immigration endures as a testament to our hypocrisy.

We, the citizens of the United States, are lying to ourselves about   25
our labor force. We are lying persistently, and it's hurting everyone involved. The lies rob legitimate workers of needed jobs, they rob industrious immigrants of fair opportunities, and they rob America of its essential morality.

Vocabulary / Using a Dictionary

1. Look up the meaning of *assail*. What does it mean to be *unassailable* (para. 1)?

2. What is the meaning of the prefix *circum-* in *circumventing* (para. 9)? How does that word describe the actions of employers?

3. What is the stem of the word *succumbed* (para. 9)? What is its definition?

Responding to Words in Context

1. Why does Welch put the word *legal* in quotation marks in paragraph 4?

2. What are "undocumented workers" (para. 6)? What documents do they lack?

3. Why does Welch challenge the label "criminal" for undocumented workers (para. 13)?

Discussing Main Point and Meaning

1. In paragraph 5 and again in paragraph 17, Welch compares the jobs of undocumented workers with the labor performed by black slaves in America prior to the Civil War. Why does he make this comparison?

2. What does Welch think is wrong with the government's enforcement tactics?

3. In paragraph 19, Welch offers his solution to the immigration problem. What is this solution, and what does he see as its potential consequences?

Examining Sentences, Paragraphs, and Organization

1. Where does Welch get the quotations in paragraph 2? Why does he cite these lines?

2. Note how Welch begins paragraphs 3 and 4. Why does he use this repetition?

3. Why does Welch turn to the story of Max Gonzalez toward the end of his essay?

Thinking Critically

1. In paragraph 8, Welch claims that most people who pay attention to immigration have a better understanding of the issues than the government would expect. Do you think this is true?

2. In paragraph 10, Welch exposes an inconsistency in immigration policy. What is this inconsistency, and where does he think it comes from?

3. To whom is Welch appealing in this essay? Whom does he hope to convince about his position?

In-Class Writing Activities

1. How do the statistics Welch cites in paragraph 7 present different pictures of immigration? Write an analysis of the different sources he uses and why their numbers differ.

2. In his last paragraph, Welch uses allusion and repetition to reinforce his point about the contradictions of U.S. immigration policy. Write a response in which you discuss how this last paragraph refers back to ideas he brought up earlier in the essay and how the repeated words affect you as a reader.

CHARLES BOWDEN

Our Wall

[NATIONAL GEOGRAPHIC / May 2007]

Before You Read

What is the purpose of building a wall along the border? What are the arguments for and against a more extensive wall between the United States and Mexico?

Words to Learn

zealously (para. 8): devotedly; with intense enthusiasm (adv.)
quinceañera (para. 30): among Latinos, the celebration of a girl's fifteenth birthday (n.)

In the spring of 1929, a man named Patrick Murphy left a bar in Bisbee, Arizona, to bomb the Mexican border town of Naco, a bunny hop of about ten miles. He stuffed dynamite, scrap iron, nails, and bolts into suitcases and dropped the weapons off the side of his crop duster as part of a deal with Mexican rebels battling for control of Naco, Sonora. When his flight ended, it turned out he'd hit the wrong Naco, managing to destroy property mainly on the U.S. side, including a garage and a local mining company. Some say he was drunk, some say he was sober, but everyone agrees he was one of the first people to bomb the United States from the air.

1

Charles Bowden is a contributing editor for GQ *and* Mother Jones *magazines, and his writing has appeared in such publications as* Harper's, New York Times Book Review, Esquire, *and* Aperture. *He is the author of eleven books, including* A Shadow in the City: Confessions of an Undercover Dog *(2006),* Down by the River: Drugs, Money, Murder, and Family *(2004), and* Juárez: The Laboratory of Our Future *(1998). In 1996, Bowden received the Lannan Literary Award for Nonfiction. He was a Lannan Writing Residency Fellow in Marfa, Texas, in 2001.*

Borders everywhere attract violence, violence prompts fences,   2
and eventually fences can mutate into walls. Then everyone pays attention because a wall turns a legal distinction into a visual slap in
the face. We seem to love walls, but are embarrassed by them because
they say something unpleasant about the neighbors—and us. They
flow from two sources: fear and the desire for control. Just as our
houses have doors and locks, so do borders call forth garrisons, customs officials, and, now and then, big walls. They give us divided
feelings because we do not like to admit we need them.

Now as the United States debates fortifying its border with   3
Mexico, walls have a new vogue. At various spots along the dusty,
1,952-mile boundary, fences, walls, and vehicle barriers have been
constructed since the 1990s to slow the surge in illegal immigration.
In San Diego, nine miles of a double-layered fence have been erected.
In Arizona, the state most overrun with illegal crossings, 65 miles of
barriers have been constructed already. Depending on the direction of
the ongoing immigration debate, there may soon be hundreds more
miles of walls.

The 800 or so residents of Naco, Arizona, where Patrick Murphy   4
is part of the local lore, have been living in the shadow of a 14-foot-
high steel wall for the past decade. National Guard units are helping
to extend the 4.6-mile barrier 25 miles deeper into the desert. The
Border Patrol station is the biggest building in the tiny town; the copper roof glistens under the blistering sun. In 2005, a pioneering bit of
guerrilla theater took place here when the Minutemen, a citizen
group devoted to securing the border, staked out 20 miles of the line
and patrolled it. Today about 8,000 people live in Naco, Sonora, on
the Mexican side of the metal wall that slashes the two communities.

Only a dirt parking lot separates the Gay 90s bar from the Naco   5
wall. Inside, the patrons are largely bilingual and have family ties on
both sides of the line. Janet Warner, one of the bartenders, has lived
here for years and is one of those fortunate souls who has found her
place in the sun. But thanks to the racks of stadium lights along the
wall, she has lost her nights, and laments the erasure of the brilliant
stars that once hung over her life. She notes that sometimes Mexicans
jump the new steel wall, come in for a beer, then jump back into
Mexico. The bar began in the late 1920s as a casino and with the end
of Prohibition added alcohol. The gambling continued until 1961,
when a new county sheriff decided to clean up things. On the back
wall are photographs of Ronald and Nancy Reagan when they'd stop
by on their way to a nearby Mexican ranch.

The bar is one of only a handful of businesses left. The commer-   6
cial street leading to the border is lined with defunct establishments,
all dead because the U.S. government sealed the entry to Mexico after
9/11 and rerouted it to the east. Leonel Urcadez, 54, a handsome man
who has owned the bar for decades, has mixed feelings about the
wall. "You get used to it," he says. "When they first built it, it was
not a bad idea—cars were crossing illegally from Mexico and the
Border Patrol would chase them. But it's so ugly."

The two Nacos came into being in 1897 around a border cross-   7
ing that connected copper mines in both nations. By 1901 a railroad
linked the mines. A big miners' strike in 1906, one cherished by Mexicans as foreshadowing the revolution in 1910, saw troops from both
nations facing each other down at the line. The town of Naco on the
Mexican side changed hands many times during the actual revolution—at first the prize was revenue from the customs house. Later,
when Arizona voted itself dry in 1915, the income came from the sa-
loons. Almost every old house in Naco, Arizona, has holes from the
gun battles. The Naco Hotel, with its three-foot mud walls, advertised its bulletproof rooms.

The boundary between Mexico and the United States has always   8
been zealously insisted upon by both countries. But initially Mexicans
moved north at will. The U.S. patrols of the border that began in
1904 were mainly to keep out illegal Asian immigrants. Almost
900,000 Mexicans legally entered the United States to flee the violence of the revolution. Low population in both nations and the need
for labor in the American Southwest made this migration a non-event
for decades. The flow of illegal immigrants exploded after the passage of the North American Free Trade Agreement in the early 1990s,
a pact that was supposed to end illegal immigration but wound up
dislocating millions of Mexican peasant farmers and many small industrial workers.

The result: Naco was overrun by immigrants on their way north.   9
At night, dozens, sometimes hundreds, of immigrants would crowd
into motel rooms and storage rental sheds along the highway. The
local desert was stomped into a powder of dust. Naco residents
found their homes broken into by desperate migrants. Then came the
wall in 1996, and the flow of people spread into the high desert outside the town.

The Border Patrol credits the wall, along with better surveillance   10
technology, with cutting the number of illegal immigrants captured
near Naco's 33-mile border by half in the past year. Before this new

© Diane Cook and Len Jenshel.
Memorial at a border wall in Tijuana, Mexico.

heightening of enforcement, the number caught each week, hiding in arroyos thick with mesquite and yucca, often exceeded the town's population. At the moment, the area is relatively quiet as "coyotes," or people smugglers, pause to feel out the new reality, and the National Guard has been sent in to assist the Border Patrol. At the nearby abandoned U.S. Army camp, the roofs are collapsing and the adobe bricks dribble mud onto the floor. Scattered about are Mexican water bottles—illegals still hole up here after climbing the wall.

Residents register a hodgepodge of feelings about the wall. Even   11
those who have let passing illegal immigrants use their phones or given them a ride say the exodus has to stop. And even those sick of finding trash in their yards understand why the immigrants keep coming.

"Sometimes I feel sorry for the Mexicans," says Bryan Tomlinson, 45, a custodial engineer for the Bisbee school district. His brother Don chimes in, "But the wall's a good thing."   12

A border wall seems to violate a deep sense of identity most Americans cherish. We see ourselves as a nation of immigrants with our own goddess, the Statue of Liberty, a symbol so potent that dissident Chinese students fabricated a version of it in 1989 in Tiananmen Square as the visual representation of their yearning for freedom.   13

> We see ourselves as a nation of immigrants with our own goddess, the Statue of Liberty, a symbol so potent that dissident Chinese students fabricated a version of it in 1989 in Tiananmen Square as the visual representation of their yearning for freedom.

Walls are curious statements of human needs. Sometimes they are built to keep restive populations from fleeing. The Berlin Wall was designed to keep citizens from escaping from communist East Germany. But most walls are for keeping people out. They all work for a while, until human appetites or sheer numbers overwhelm them. The Great Wall of China, built mostly after the mid-14th century, kept northern tribes at bay until the Manchu conquered China in the 17th century. Hadrian's Wall, standing about 15 feet high, 9 feet wide, and 73 miles long, kept the crazed tribes of what is now Scotland from running amok in Roman Britain—from A.D. 122 until it was overrun in 367. Then you have the Maginot Line, a series of connected forts built by France after World War I to keep the German army from invading. It was a success, except for one flaw: The troops of the Third Reich simply went around its northwestern end and invaded France through the Netherlands and Belgium. Now tourists visit its labyrinth of tunnels and underground barracks.   14

In 1859 a rancher named Thomas Austin released 24 rabbits in Australia because, he noted, "the introduction of a few rabbits could do little harm and might provide a touch of home, in addition to a spot of hunting." By that simple act, he launched one of the most extensive barriers ever erected by human beings: the rabbit fences of Australia, which eventually reached 2,023 miles. Within 35 years, the rabbits had overrun the continent, a place lacking sufficient and dedicated rabbit predators. For a century and a half, the Australian government has tried various solutions: imported fleas, poisons, trappers.   15

Nothing has dented the new immigrants. The fences themselves failed almost instantly—rabbits expanded faster than the barriers could be built, careless people left gates open, holes appeared, and, of course, the rabbits simply dug under them.

In Naco all the walls of the world are present in one compact 16 bundle. You have Hadrian's Wall or the Great Wall of China because the barrier is intended to keep people out. You have the Maginot Line because a 15-minute walk takes you to the end of the existing steel wall. You have the rabbit fences of Australia because people still come north illegally, as do the drugs.

Perhaps the closest thing to the wall going up on the U.S.-Mexico 17 border is the separation wall being built by Israel in the West Bank. Like the new American wall, it is designed to control the movement of people, but it faces the problem of all walls—rockets can go over it, tunnels can go under it. It offends people, it comforts people, it fails to deliver security. And it keeps expanding.

Rodolfo Santos Esquer puts out *El Mirador*, a weekly newspaper 18 in Naco, Sonora, and he finds the wall hateful. He stands in his cramped office—a space he shares with a small shop peddling underwear—and says, "It looks like the Berlin Wall. It is horrible. It is ugly. You feel more racism now. It is a racist wall. If people get close to the wall, the Border Patrol calls the Mexican police, and they go and question people."

And then he lightens up because he is a sunny man, and he says it 19 actually hasn't changed his life or the lives of most people in town. Except that the coyotes[1] now drive to the end of the wall before crossing. And as the wall grows in length, the coyotes raise their rates. Santos figures half the town is living off migrants going north—either feeding them and housing them or guiding them into the U.S. Passage to Phoenix, about 200 miles away, is now $1,500 and rising. He notes that after the wall went up in 1996, the migration mushroomed. He wonders if there is a connection, if the wall magically beckons migrants. Besides, he says, people just climb over it with ropes.

Santos fires up his computer and shows an image he snapped in 20 the cemetery of a nearby town. There, there, he points as he enlarges a section of the photo. Slowly a skull-shaped blur floats into view against the black of the night—a ghost, he believes. The border is haunted by ghosts—the hundreds who die each year from heat and

---

[1]*coyotes*: Smugglers paid to take people illegally across the U.S.-Mexico border.

cold, the ones killed in car wrecks as the packed vans of migrants flee the Border Patrol, and the increasing violence erupting between smugglers and the agents of Homeland Security. Whenever heat is applied to one part of the border, the migration simply moves to another part. The walls in southern California drove immigrants into the Arizona desert and, in some cases, to their deaths. We think of walls as statements of foreign policy, and we forget the intricate lives of the people we wall in and out.

We think of walls as statements of foreign policy, and we forget the intricate lives of the people we wall in and out.

Emanuel Castillo Erúnez, 23, takes crime and car wreck photos for *El Mirador*. He went north illegally when he was 17, walked a few days, then was picked up and returned to Mexico. He sits on a bench in the plaza, shielded by a New York Yankees cap, and sums up the local feeling about the wall simply: "Some are fine with it, some are not." He thinks of going north again, but then he thinks of getting caught again. And so he waits. 21

There is a small-town languor about Naco, Sonora, and the wall becomes unnoticeable in this calm. The Minutemen and National Guard terrify people. At the Hospedaje Santa Maria, four people wait for a chance to go over the wall and illegally enter the wealth of the United States. It is a run-down, two-story building, one of many boarding houses for migrants in Naco. Salvador Rivera, a solid man in his early 30s, has been here about a year. He worked in Washington State, but, when his mother fell ill, he returned home to Nayarit, Mexico, and is now having trouble getting past the increased security. He left behind an American girlfriend he can no longer reach. 22

"For so many years, we Mexicans have gone to the U.S. to work. I don't understand why they put up a wall to turn us away. It's not like we're robbing anybody over there, and they don't pay us very much." 23

But talk of the wall almost has to be prompted. Except for those engaged in smuggling drugs or people, border crossers in Naco, Sonora, continue to enter through the main gate, as they always have. They visit relatives on the other side, as they always have. What has changed is this physical statement, a big wall lined with bright lights, that says, yes, we are two nations. 24

Jesús Gastelum Ramírez lives next door to the wall, makes neon signs, and looks like Willie Nelson. He watches people climb the wall and he understands a reality forgotten by most U.S. lawmakers— 25 that simply to go through the wire instantly raises a person's income tenfold. Gastelum knows many of his neighbors smuggle people, and he understands.

Until recently, a volleyball team from the Mexican Naco and a   26
team from the U.S. Naco used to meet once a year at the point where the wall ends on the west side of town, put up a net on the line, bring kegs of beer, and play a volleyball game. People from both Nacos would stream out to the site and watch. And then the wall would no longer exist for a spell. But it always confronts the eye.

Dan Duley, 50, operates heavy equipment and is a native of the   27
Naco area. He was living in Germany after serving in the Air Force when the Berlin Wall came down, and he thought that was a fine thing. But here he figures something has to be done. "We need help," he says. "We're being invaded. They've taken away our jobs, our security. I'm just a blue-collar man living in a small town. And I just wish the government cared about a man who was blue."

But then, as in many conversations on the border, the rhetoric   28
calms down. Duley, along with many other Naco residents, believes the real solution has to be economic, that jobs must be created in Mexico. There is an iron law on this border: The closer one gets to the line, the more rational the talk becomes because everyone has personal ties to people on the other side. Everyone realizes the wall is a police solution to an economic problem. The Mexicans will go over it, under it, or try to tear holes in it. Or, as is often the case, enter legally with temporary visiting papers and then melt into American communities. Of the millions of illegal immigrants living in the United States, few would have come if there wasn't a job waiting for them.

Over in Naco, Sonora, the final night of a fiesta is in full roar.   29
Men drinking beer move by on horseback, groups of girls in high heels prance past. Nearby, folks play bingo, and in the band shell a group does a sound check for the big dance. Looming over the whole party is a giant statue of Father Hidalgo with his bald head and wild eyes. He launched the Mexican Wars of Independence in 1810. Two blocks away, the steel wall glows under a battery of lights.

In the Gay 90s bar in Naco, Arizona, a *quinceañera*, the 15th-   30
birthday celebration that introduces a young girl to the world, is firing up. There are 200 people in the saloon's back room, half from Mexico and half from the U.S. The boys wear rented tuxedo vests, the girls are dressed like goddesses. One man walks in with a baby in a black polka-dot dress with pink trim.

The birthday girl, Alyssa, stands with her family for an official portrait. 31

Walls come and go, but quinceañeras are forever, I say to the man with the baby. He nods his head and smiles. 32

The steel barrier is maybe a hundred feet away. Outside in the darkness, Mexicans are moving north, and Border Patrol agents are hunting them down. Tomorrow, work will continue on the construction of the wall as it slowly creeps east and west from the town. Tourists already come to look at it. 33

I have no doubt someday archaeologists will do excavations here and write learned treatises about the Great Wall of the United States. Perhaps one of them will be the descendant of a Mexican stealing north at this moment in the midnight hour. 34

Vocabulary / Using a Dictionary

1. How does the prefix *fore-* change the meaning of a word? What does it mean in *foreshadowing* (para. 7)?

2. What does *-fold* mean in *tenfold* (para. 25). How does this word describe an immigrant's income?

3. What is the stem of the word *excavations* (para. 34)?

Responding to Words in Context

1. Why does Bowden call recent advocacy for more walls along the border with Mexico a "vogue" (para. 3)? What does he imply?

2. What does the word *battery* mean in "a battery of lights" (para. 29)?

Discussing Main Point and Meaning

1. In paragraph 9, Bowden identifies a turning point in border relations. What is this turning point, and why did it change relations between the two countries?

2. How do the border walls challenge American identity? What ideas do they seem to conflict with?

3. What does Bowden think are the consequences of building a wall? How does it change the surrounding area?

Examining Sentences, Paragraphs, and Organization

1. Why does Bowden begin his essay with the story about the bombing of Naco? What does it suggest about the borderlands?

2. What is the purpose of paragraph 2? What information does Bowden include in it?

3. At the beginning of paragraph 14, Bowden states, "Walls are curious statements of human needs." How do the other sentences in this paragraph support his assertion?

Thinking Critically

1. What does the photograph that accompanies Bowden's essay suggest about walls along the border?

2. Bowden suggests that "the closest thing to the wall going up on the U.S.-Mexico border is the separation wall being built by Israel in the West Bank" (para. 17). Why does he think this is the most accurate comparison? Do you agree?

In-Class Writing Activities

1. How does Bowden describe the wall? What language does he use in characterizing it? Write an essay in which you analyze his choice of words when discussing the border wall.

2. Toward the end of his essay, Bowden claims, "The closer one gets to the line, the more rational the talk becomes" (para. 28). Using this statement as your starting point, write an analysis of the piece, citing examples that illustrate it.

JESSICA CHOU (STUDENT ESSAY)

Undocumented: One Student's Story

[THE DAILY BRUIN, University of California, Los Angeles/February 21, 2008]

Before You Read

What rights do undocumented students have to education in the United States? What is denied to them?

Words to Learn

rosaries (para. 1): series of prayers, often prayed while counting off a string of beads (n.)
mimic (para. 4): to imitate (v).

His mother, holding on to his trembling hand, prayed two rounds of rosaries for luck before the coyotes came. Ernesto Rocha — now a third-year Chicana and Chicano studies and political science student — remembers waiting behind a large rock for hours until the men came to lead the family on a dangerous two-day march away from Mexico. That was just a little over 12 years ago, when Rocha's mother made the decision to move the family to the United States. He remembers being on his aunt's balcony in Tijuana as his mother said

1

Jessica Chou recently graduated from the University of California, Los Angeles, where she majored in history. As a staff photographer for the Daily Bruin, *Chou began working on this essay from a visual standpoint, capturing images of the students she was following. However, what began as a photo essay later evolved into a more comprehensive project that involved writing. Chou says, "I thought it was going to be important to have a writing portion to the series and thought about having another writer work on that — but my editor decided that since I had been working on this for so long, that I would be in the position to write the stories." Topics such as immigration, globalization, and industrial and labor relations interest Chou as a writer and photojournalist, and she hopes to pursue writing in her future, possibly in graduate school.*

"Look, mijo, that's what we have to do. We're going to have to cross that." She was pointing at the border, but Rocha remembers feeling like he was peering down on a battlefield.

"And that's when I started getting really, really scared," Rocha said. "It took us two days and two nights, and the nights were horrible ... It was this constant 'let's go, let's go, we can't stop.' I was just so confused: What are we doing? Jesus."

But Rocha knew that things were supposed to be better in the United States. His single mother, who raised six kids after her husband died of leukemia, hoped there would be more opportunities for the family here. "My mom is the most powerful, strong woman I know," he says. "Six kids ... and she did it with her head up high. She never moped around, she just got up and did things," Rocha said.

Rocha would try to mimic his mother's strength as he grew older and struggled to get a college education in the US, where undocumented immigrants are unable to receive financial aid to help pay their college fees. According to a recent University of California report, there were about 90 undocumented students in the system as of 2006. "I don't have enough money to pay for it," he said. "But you know, you just try to make it work." Rocha knew there would be compromises, but he wouldn't know to what extent until he made the decision to attend his dream school, UCLA, instead of California State University, Long Beach, which was "right in (his) backyard."

"Just because of the fact that I didn't have money," Rocha said. "I felt that that was unfair for me not to give it a chance." But this winter, Rocha, who works at a law office, ran out of funds to pay his student fees. He knew he wanted to stay in school, but the economic burden made it seem almost impossible, until he thought of an unconventional idea. "I have all the resources that I could possibly want—Internet, Facebook, cell phones—and you have everything you could use, and you're not utilizing it?" he said. "My mom raised six kids by herself, and I can't possibly raise $2,000 to stay in school?"

For the next two weeks, Rocha sent out text messages and e-mails and he walked around campus soliciting help. "Look, I'm broke, but I have a desire to stay in school. Please help me. I will be walking around school with a bucket," Rocha told his friends and contacts. He managed to raise enough money to pay his fees before the deadline, "not asking for charity but asking for support ... I think people understood that."

Being undocumented touched almost every aspect of Rocha's college career. "I made it my point that if this was going to affect me, then I would need to know everything about it in order for me to help others and myself." Rocha has now joined Ideas UCLA, a student group for undocumented students at UCLA, where he has worked to bring attention to the challenges facing undocumented students, in part by building support for the California Dream Act, a measure that would allow undocumented students to receive financial aid.

"Our reality is that we are undocumented until something happens," Rocha told me. "Our reality is that everyday, this will affect us until something is changed. So until that happens, there is no reason for me to stop."   8

Vocabulary/Using a Dictionary

1. What are the possible meanings of the verb *peering* (para. 1)? In which sense is Chou using it here?

2. What does the word *compromises* have to do with *promise* (para. 4)?

Responding to Words in Context

1. What does *mijo* mean (para. 1)? If you know, try to define the word. If not, what meaning would you guess from its context in the sentence?

2. What is "unconventional" about Ernesto Rocha's plan for raising money for college (para. 5)?

3. In paragraph 6, Rocha distinguishes support from charity. What does he think the difference is?

Discussing Main Point and Meaning

1. Why does the border look like a battlefield to Rocha (para. 1)?

2. What does Rocha think of the example set by his mother?

3. What is the California Dream Act, and how would it help students like Rocha?

Examining Sentences, Paragraphs, and Organization

1. Chou begins her essay abruptly. What is the effect of this beginning on the reader? Why did she make this choice?

2. Reread the quote from Rocha in paragraph 2. What factual information does it convey? How does it convey emotion?

Thinking Critically

1. Chou uses Rocha's experiences to illustrate facts about undocumented students in general. Does his experience seem representative?

2. How would students like Rocha be affected by legislation that would provide undocumented immigrants with a path to legal status?

In-Class Writing Activities

1. Rocha tells Chou that he used technology such as Facebook and cell phones to raise money for his fees. How do people use such resources to gain support for a cause or spread information? Write a paragraph about their use in general and why you think it worked for Rocha.

2. In paragraph 7, Rocha explains why he decided to join Ideas UCLA. Using this statement as your starting point, write an essay about Rocha's involvement with the program and why you think it is important to him.

ANNOTATION Using Concrete Language

A sure way to make your writing vivid and memorable is to select words that convey specific and concrete meanings. Very often in the process of writing we are confronted with the choice of using either a general noun, such as *tree* or *bird* or *fence*, or a more exact noun, such as *spruce* or *cardinal* or *picket fence*. So it's always a good idea, especially in revising, to look closely at your word choice to avoid language that is so generalized that readers cannot visualize your images or get an exact sense of what you are attempting to convey. The terms *spruce* and *cardinal* can be distinctly pictured, unlike *tree* or *bird*, and *picket fence* conveys a specific type of fence, not just the abstract idea of one.

Observe how Jessica Chou, a student at UCLA, makes a deliberate decision to use concrete words in her essay. Her opening paragraph establishes a specific moment and location that she presents so vividly we can picture it: a frightened Mexican boy clutching his mother's hand as his family prepares to cross the border. We see the mother's concern not because the writer tells us she's worried about the dangers, but because she has "prayed two rounds of rosaries." That specificity *shows* us her fear instead of just telling us about it.

Note how Chou's choice of concrete words helps her create a vivid sense of danger.

His mother, holding on to his trembling hand, prayed two rounds of rosaries for luck before the coyotes came. Ernesto Rocha — now a third-year Chicana and Chicano studies and political science student — remembers waiting behind a large rock for hours until the men came to lead the family on a dangerous two-day march away from Mexico. That was just a little over 12 years ago, when Rocha's mother made the decision to move the family to the United States. He remembers being on his aunt's balcony in Tijuana as his mother said "Look, mijo, that's what we have to do. We're going to have to cross that." She was pointing at the border, but Rocha remembers feeling like he was peering down on a battlefield.

— From "Undocumented: One Student's Story"
by Jessica Chou, page 373

Student Writer at Work: Jessica Chou
On Writing "Undocumented: One Student's Story"

Q: What inspired you to write "Undocumented: One Student's Story"?

A: I think what inspired me in the beginning was just the initial shock of realizing how close to home the immigration debate is. I've always had an interest in the topic, but I don't think I really knew how to interpret what was going on. When I realized how silly it was of me not to have realized there are undocumented students, I decided that this was something that I should be paying attention to. How often do you get bombarded with the importance of policy and politics in the media, but actually understand the reality of what they mean? Since I'm a photographer and not a writer, I thought it was going to be just a photo essay of one person that I would work on for a week. I had all my preconceived—and admittedly superficial—images in my head. Luckily, I began to attend a lot of hearings and rallies around campus, and I started meeting some of the students who were speaking out. It was those first few things that knocked me over my head and told me, "You don't have the slightest idea of what is going on!" and I knew I needed to take my time and fully understand where these stories were coming from. I didn't want to miss the point, and I think for people who are going to be open and vulnerable about their situations, it's only fair to be thorough. It took me a year to finally sit down and say that I was ready to put something together and present it to the *Daily Bruin* for publishing. I thought it was going to be important to have a writing portion to the series and thought about having another writer work on that, but my editor decided that since I had been working on this for so long, I would be in the position to write the stories. The articles, which highlighted four students, accompanied a multimedia package of an audio slideshow where I allowed the students to tell their own stories as the photo essay ran.

Q: Once you sat down to write, what was your main purpose?

A: I think the main purpose of writing this piece was to present a new light on the immigration debate, and to come at it from the perspective of people who are actually affected. It's easy to have an opinion when we lump all of them into one category and explain away all of the legal or economic terms, but it's precisely the human aspect that makes it that much more complex and that much harder to really come together in some sort of "one-size-fits-all" agreement. It's an incredibly multidimensional issue, and I really wanted to address that aspect of it—and if that is already understood, then I want to make sure that it's not forgotten within any discussion of the issue, or at the very least among students.

Q: What response have you received?

A: The responses have been relatively mixed, both good and not so great. It hasn't changed many of my opinions. I think that, given the limited time and space that are usually given to a letter to the editor, there's hardly a chance for a long, drawn-out argument. But that doesn't mean I take readers' opinions lightly; it definitely means something, and I keep their reservations in mind as I continue my research.

Q: Do you generally show your writing to friends before submitting it? Do you collaborate or bounce your ideas off others? To what extent did discussion with others help you develop your point of view on the topic you wrote about?

A: I'm pretty private when it comes to showing my work to friends and family. I just need to not be afraid of criticism for work I know is not fully polished. But I do find that talking about my ideas helps me better articulate my thoughts, tenfold. For this topic, discussing it with my editor really helped me sit down and think about the structure and grab hold of the significance of what I believed each student's story had to offer—and ultimately what their stories were addressing. It was great when my editor would sit down and take the time to ask why I had decided to interview certain people and why I thought certain anecdotes were powerful. As obvious as these questions may seem, they were quite hard for me to answer at first. I think the question "Why?" is a very tough question. It can often make you rethink what you thought you knew as well as find out about things you didn't know you thought, which can be either a "Eureka!" moment or just discomforting. I think all of this really helped me figure out how much of my point of view is just my point of view, and that as confident as I may be about it, I still need to recognize where situations may not fit in with my views and learn to come to terms with that. It's only of service to me to do so.

Q: What advice do you have for other student writers?

A: I don't really have any "words of wisdom" for them, but this is what I have been doing myself: diving in with my eyes shut and taking the chance that I will come out of the other side okay.

Discussing the Unit

Suggested Topic for Discussion

How do the selections in this unit deal with the border as a physical object and as a psychological construct?

Preparing for Class Discussion

1. Each of the essays in this unit suggests some solution to immigration problems. Which authors think those solutions are most imminent or easy to accomplish? Which see the solution as a longer process?

2. Two of the essayists in this unit (Lilly and Bowden) mention the Minutemen, and two (Bowden and Chou) refer to coyotes. How do these selections portray conflict along the border? What parties are involved?

From Discussion to Writing

1. Choose which of the essays from the unit best complements the photo that accompanies "Our Wall." Write a paragraph explaining your choice and how your author portrays the border.

2. Write a message to the new president about what solutions you think would be most effective in solving the problems posed by immigration. Feel free to cite one or more of the essays from this unit as you outline your solution.

Topics for Cross-Cultural Discussion

1. The selections in this unit focus on immigration from Mexico to the United States, but since 2001, the government has been much more restrictive of immigration across the board, especially from predominantly Muslim countries. What different problems do these different kinds of immigration pose? Why has attention to immigration from Islamic countries faded somewhat in comparison to the heated discussions about Mexico?

2. In the history of the United States, the government has placed continually greater restrictions on immigrants. Do some Internet research about these new restrictions. When did they take place? What groups were most affected?

12

The Climate Crisis: Is It Real?

Al Gore won both a Nobel Peace Prize and an Academy Award in 2007 for his work promoting the dangers of global warming, an indication of the primacy of the issue not only in geopolitical circles but also in our popular culture. For three decades now, scientific orthodoxy has held that the earth is getting hotter and that human activity, mostly in the form of carbon emissions, is to blame. But a chorus of skeptics has recently challenged the mainstream view, arguing either that the science behind global warming is faulty or that the threat is overblown. This chapter asks: Is the earth getting warmer at a dangerous rate? Or is the climate crisis just a lot of hot air?

The chapter opens with Bill McKibben's "Let's Act Together on Global Warming," which takes for granted the severity of the problem that many climate scientists say, with varying degrees of certainty and graveness, is at hand. McKibben's essay lays out a few statistics but is foremost a call to arms for activists to do what they can to stem the crisis. McKibben urges the United States to take the lead in reducing carbon emissions but admits to being skeptical that it will happen—our collective inertia is just too strong. "That's why," McKibben concludes, "our only hope is a movement, first in this country and then around the world. This movement must possess at least as much moral urgency and willingness to sacrifice as the Civil Rights movement a generation ago."

Thomas Sowell titles his essay "Cold Water on 'Global Warming,'" and the quotes around the phrase "global warming" intimate

Sowell's stance immediately: He is skeptical of the existence of a crisis. Sowell attributes the public consciousness of climate-change danger to media hype generated by "people who get grants, government agencies who get appropriations, politicians who get publicity and the perpetually indignant who get something new to be indignant about." Sowell gives his blessing to a conference in New York (see the advertisement on page 391) dedicated to alternative theories about planetary climate change, including the possibility of immutable cycles in weather patterns over centuries. There isn't, Sowell admits, "a lot of controversy over temperature readings. What is fundamentally at issue are the explanations, implications and extrapolations of these temperature readings."

Mike Tidwell is one of the people Sowell would label as a global-warming "alarmist." Tidwell writes, in "Snap into Action for the Climate," that even those committed to greening industry and curbing global warming have a false sense of complacency—the earth isn't merely warming, he writes, but "*snapping*, violently, into a whole new regime right before our eyes." Aligning a devastating array of statistics, Tidwell argues that the moment may be forced to its crisis far sooner than any of us imagine, and possibly in the next five years. Tidwell echoes McKibben's call to action, asserting that "the American people need a grassroots political movement that goes from zero to sixty in a matter of months" in order to keep the polar ice caps from melting and inundating Los Angeles by 2013.

Dustin Lushing, a student at Johns Hopkins University, takes a unique position. Lushing concedes that global warming is "most likely caused by humans." What he's incredulous about, however, is the urgency of the problem. "There is consensus that the avian flu exists," Lushing writes, arguing by analogy to a famously overblown menace from the summer of 2007. "But how imminent is the threat? Similarly, how imminent is the nebulous doom that is climate change?" Lushing enjoins us against trusting politicians like Al Gore with our science—an "alarmist politico" like Gore is bound to hype what may be a more modest, solvable problem into a looming catastrophe in order to generate a more compelling sound bite.

Jennifer Oladipo adds a perspective on global warming and race. Environmentalism in general, she says, has been largely understood as a white issue, and minorities are rarely held up as representatives of the movement. Oladipo wants to correct the perception that people of color are apathetic about greening the planet. "Some people think this country is on the precipice of a societal shift that will make environmental stewardship an integral part of our collective moral code," Oladipo writes. "But that is not going to happen as long as we as a nation continue to think and act as if 'green' automatically means 'white.'"

A pair of essays, both by students from the University of Alabama, continues the debate by examining the ways both sides of the issue hold up and scrutinize statistics. Josh Burleson, in "When Politics Meets Science," argues that there is "as much proof" against the virulence of global warming as there is for it. Exposing what he considers gaps in the science surrounding climate change, Burleson asks us to "slow down" and "work on changing the 'proof' of global warming from a widely supported hunch into proven fact." Burleson hints, as many climate-change skeptics do, that the global-warming crowd has a secret political agenda: They want to shut down industry and slow economic growth in the name of rampant environmentalism.

Brett Schoel responds to Burleson by questioning the questioners—in "The Denial of Global Warming Is Just Politics," Schoel suggests the opposite. Considering the power of industry and the position of the Bush administration, Schoel writes, "It seems more likely that any political pressure is coming from an anti-warming position." Schoel also draws a rigid distinction between evidence for a conjecture and absolute proof, an important footnote to a debate in which, when tempers warm, facts tend to melt away.

The chapter concludes with a prophetic 1985 warning about climate change from the late Carl Sagan, one of America's most popular scientists. At that time, Sagan felt the situation, though real, was not urgent: "Fortunately," he said then, "we have a little time. A great deal can be done in decades." Sagan, it should be noted, believed in the potential of "commercial nuclear fusion power."

BILL McKIBBEN

Let's Act Together on Global Warming

[TIKKUN / November–December 2007]

Before You Read

What can you do about global warming? Does this issue feel urgent to you? Do you ever feel helpless, wondering what can be done when faced with such an overwhelming problem?

Words to Learn

hypothesis (para. 1): an assumption or guess (n.)

drought (para. 2): a long period of dry weather that damages crops and plants (n.)

stability (para. 4): firmness in position; permanence (n.)

primates (para. 4): an order of mammals characterized by their large brains and specialized appendages (thumbs), which includes humans, apes, and monkeys (n.)

comprehensive (para. 8): covering completely or broadly (adj.)

subsidize (para. 9): to aid or promote with money (v.)

durable (para. 9): lasting; enduring (adj.)

hybrid (para. 11): something — in this case, a car — that has two different elements performing the same function — in this case, providing fuel (n.)

Bill McKibben is a writer and environmentalist who focuses on issues including "global warming, alternative energy, and the risks associated with human genetic engineering." He graduated in 1982 from Harvard University, where he was president of the Harvard Crimson newspaper, and went on to work as a staff writer for the New Yorker until 1987, contributing to its "Talk of the Town" column. McKibben has authored twelve books, and his writing regularly appears in a variety of publications, including the New York Times, the Atlantic Monthly, Harper's, Orion Magazine, Mother Jones, the New York Review of Books, Granta, Rolling Stone, and Outside.

For years too many people ignored global warming—it wasn't "proven," it was a "hypothesis," it was "doom-saying." It was too small, too distant, to worry about.

But that's not the problem anymore, not since Katrina. Now it's just the opposite—the problem's too big. We all read headlines every few days about the inexorable melt of Arctic ice, about record drought, about big new storms. I'm writing these words the day after the second Category 5 hurricane of the season has made an Atlantic landfall—the first time that's ever happened. And you're going to fix it by *changing your lightbulb?*

Despair is better than disinterest, but it's paralyzing. Let's say we actually wanted to do something meaningful about global warming—about the biggest single threat that the entire earth has ever faced. We'd need, first, to understand a few things:

1) It's coming at us fast. Our foremost climatologist, NASA's James Hansen, said in the autumn of 2005 that his computer model, so far the world's most reliable, indicated that we had ten years to reverse the flow of carbon dioxide into the atmosphere or else we'd guarantee "a totally different planet," one where the stability of the Greenland and West Antarctic ice sheets could no longer be guaranteed. We're already facing, without immediate and dramatic change, huge temperature increases—the consensus estimate is about five degrees Fahrenheit this century, which would make the planet far warmer than any time during the age of primates, and do more harm to poor people, other species, and the fabric of life than anything short of an all-out nuclear exchange.

2) That means we need to transform our energy systems—renewable power, not coal, gas, and oil. That's a tall order (fossil fuels were a kind of magic—cheap, easy to find, easy to transport, loaded with BTUs) but it's only the beginning. The math makes clear that we also need to change the ways we live: stop sprawling, start taking trains; stop shipping our food 1,500 miles, start eating close to home.

3) We need to do this at the toughest possible moment—when the rest of the world, particularly the Chinese and the Indians, are finally starting to use fossil fuel in appreciable quantities. Not American quantities—we'll be the per capita champs for all time. But the rate of their growth, which is pulling people out of poverty, makes the math hard.

It's not *impossible* to square this circle. The biggest international panel of economists and engineers to look at the data concluded last spring that we had just enough time and just enough technology, and that the cost wouldn't break us: they suggested that the window was still open wide enough for us to squeeze through. But we've waited until the last possible second. Here's the consensus among those of us who have been working on this problem for two decades about what needs to happen, a consensus developed over the last year through a coalition called One Sky:

We're the biggest source of the problem — it will be forty years before China's contribution to global warming matches what we've done in the course of our development.

First, the U.S. has to take the lead. We're the biggest source of the problem — it will be forty years before China's contribution to global warming matches what we've done in the course of our development. And for the last two decades we've blocked progress, even as the Europeans and the Japanese have tried to get the world mobilized. In the first few months of the next presidency, we need a piece of comprehensive legislation that commits us to cutting carbon emissions 80 percent by 2050, that guarantees we'll stop building new coal-fired power plants, and that sets up a Green Jobs Corps to start actually making these changes. Tough, mandatory targets drive change.

Second, *once we do that*, we've got to get back in the international game. For many years now the U.S. and China (and now India) have used each other as convenient excuses for not taking action. If there's any hope at all, it will come from those three nations leading the negotiations for a grand global bargain — one that takes some of the wealth the West has built up in two oil-fueled centuries and uses it to subsidize the technologies the poor world needs to develop in a more durable fashion. It's actually fairly simple — everyone holds a knife to everyone else's throat right now, and we need to figure out how to drop them. And then we have to pick up wrenches, and get to work.

If you were placing bets, you'd be ill-advised to wager a whole lot that we'll get these two tasks accomplished. The vested interests are enormously strong (Exxon made more profit last year than any company in the history of profits). The inertia is even stronger (we like to fly in jets). That's why our only hope is a movement, first in this country and then around the world. This movement must possess at least as much moral urgency and willingness to sacrifice as the Civil Rights movement a generation ago. It's a movement that's unimaginable without leadership from people of faith.

It's starting. Last spring we organized 1,400 demonstrations in 11
all fifty states on a single April day. We have the tools—the internet
above all—that might let it spread virally. But it's going to take a
kind of commitment we haven't yet approached. So screw in a new
light bulb. And then screw in a new Congressperson. Drive a hybrid,
sure, but drive change. Do it hard enough and you've earned the right
to hope.

Vocabulary/Using a Dictionary

1. What is the definition of *inexorable* (para. 2)?

2. A recent award-winning documentary about global warming featuring former vice president Al Gore is titled *An Inconvenient
   Truth*. McKibben speaks of the "convenient excuses" (para. 9)
   that different countries have used for not taking action to stop
   global warming. What do *inconvenient* and *convenient* mean?

3. What does *BTU* (para. 5) stand for?

Responding to Words in Context

1. In paragraph 4, McKibben gives us "the consensus estimate" for
   the temperature increase this century. In paragraph 7, he speaks
   about "the consensus" from experts in the field on what needs to
   happen to combat global warming and then about "a consensus
   developed over the last year." How is *consensus* being used in
   each sentence? Does it mean the same thing each time?

2. What does McKibben mean when he says, "We'll be the *per
   capita* champs [in using fossil fuel] for all time" (para. 6)?

3. When "inertia" is discussed in paragraph 10, McKibben adds in
   parentheses "we like to fly in jets." Directly after that, he says,
   "Our only hope is a movement." How do *inertia* and *movement*
   relate to each other? How do you understand McKibben's definition of *movement* here?

Discussing Main Point and Meaning

1. Why does McKibben say that Hurricane Katrina changed our
   view of global warming as an insignificant or distant problem
   (para. 2)?

2. If, as McKibben states, "despair is better than disinterest, but it's paralyzing" (para. 3), which emotion is preferable or will allow us to act?

3. McKibben indicates that the United States won't take the lead on global warming or participate within a global community to end the problem. Why not?

Examining Sentences, Paragraphs, and Organization

1. When experts on global warming are quoted as having recently agreed that "the window [is] still open wide enough for us to squeeze through" (para. 7), what are they saying about our ability to fix the problem of global warming?

2. In paragraph 8, McKibben states that the United States has to lead the rest of the world in solving the problem of global warming. In paragraph 9, he says, "We've got to get back in the international game." Do these two points contradict each other?

3. How does McKibben's use of numbered points early in the essay add to the argument being made?

Thinking Critically

1. It is widely accepted that one of the ways to enact change in our environment is to stop relying on coal, gas, and oil for our energy needs. What are some of the ways in which we have already begun to "transform our energy systems" (para. 5)?

2. According to McKibben, what is the only way to get real action started to end global warming? Do you think he's right?

3. McKibben ends his essay with two statements encouraging big changes to stop global warming: "So screw in a new light bulb. And then screw in a new Congressperson. Drive a hybrid, sure, but drive change" (para. 11). Is there any value to the small changes people make to deal with climate change?

In-Class Writing Activities

1. Hurricane Katrina was a deadly hurricane that hit the southern United States in 2005. Because of the failure of the levees in New Orleans when the storm hit, that city is still recovering from the

massive loss of life, the displacement of approximately a million people, and the overwhelming property damage that occurred. McKibben alludes to the hurricane in paragraph 2 of this essay. Research the causes (particularly the role of global warming) and effects of Hurricane Katrina and write a personal response to what you learn about why the hurricane was so destructive, how government officials and others responded to it, and what has happened to the victims and the city of New Orleans.

2.   McKibben also references the civil rights movement that began in the 1950s (para. 10). Write a brief essay that examines something specific that the civil rights movement affected, whether it is the desegregation of buses, schools, or public facilities; the passage of the Civil Rights Act of 1964, the Voting Rights Act of 1965, or the Civil Rights Act of 1968; or some other event or action.

3.   What have you learned about global warming in your lifetime? Write a list of things you have heard about climate change — what causes it; what it will cause to happen; how you can have an effect on global warming; and what your elected officials, experts in the field, environmental groups, and ordinary people are doing about it. Then do some research on what you've written and verify the items on the list. Write down any facts you find and cite the source that proves or disproves what's on your list.

The Heartland Institute, International Conference on Climate Change

[NEW YORK TIMES/February 27, 2008]

Before You Read

What do you think is the general consensus among scientists about climate change?

The International Conference on Climate Change was held on March 2–4, 2008, in New York City. Sponsored by the Heartland Institute, a Chicago-based think tank, the conference was designed to challenge claims of a global-warming crisis and to prove that "there is no scientific consensus on the causes or likely consequences of global warming." More than 400 scientists, experts, and economists gathered to hear 98 speakers address important issues and to shed light on "another side" to the debate on global warming. Speakers included professors from universities around the world as well as John Stossel, an ABC News correspondent, and the Honorable Václav Klaus, president of the Czech Republic.

Vocabulary / Using a Dictionary

1. What is the root of the word *petition*? What is the aim of the petition this ad refers to?

2. Look up the word *climate* to find its earlier meanings. How has the meaning changed in current usage?

Responding to Words in Context

1. Why does the ad place the word *skeptics* in quotation marks?

2. Why does the ad refer to warming as *natural*? What are the connotations of that word?

Discussing Main Point and Meaning

1. A large part of the ad space is taken up by a long list of names. Why do you think the graphic designers gave so much space to the list?

2. At the end of the ad, there is a recommendation for the book *Unstoppable Global Warming—Every 1,500 Years*. What is the meaning of this title?

Examining Sentences, Paragraphs, and Organization

1. How do you understand the headline of the ad? What is its purpose?

2. Why is the Heartland Institute's logo relatively small and toward the bottom of the ad? How do most ads use logos?

Thinking Critically

1. What is the Heartland Institute? What can you find out about it in an Internet search? What do they have to gain in sponsoring this conference?

2. What is the purpose of the International Conference on Climate Change? What do you think are its goals?

In-Class Writing Activity

1. Look up the full petition at the Web site given in the ad. What exactly have these scientists signed their names to? Write an analysis of the wording of the petition and how it represents the issue of climate change.

THOMAS SOWELL

Cold Water on "Global Warming"

[TOWNHALL.COM / February 28, 2008]

Before You Read

Do you think global warming is an important topic that affects your life? Have you encountered people who don't believe it is a real issue? What facts do you know about climate change, and what do you accept as true and untrue about global warming?

Words to Learn

stampedes (para. 2): rushes of people or animals, usually caused by fear (n.)

mobilize (para. 3): to organize (v.)

appropriations (para. 5): money set aside for a specific use (n.)

indignant (para. 5): characterized by anger over something perceived as unjust or unfair (adj.)

swindle (para. 8): deceit (n.)

dignitaries (para. 9): people who hold honorable positions or offices, usually in government (n.)

consensus (para. 11): agreement (n.)

dire (para. 12): desperate (adj.)

agenda (para. 14): specific plan of things to be done (n.)

fundamentally (para. 17): essentially (adv.)

extrapolations (para. 17): inferences or estimates (n.)

crusade (para. 21): a project or an action aggressively or passionately undertaken (n.)

stake (para. 22): interest in the outcome (n.)

Thomas Sowell is the Rose and Milton Friedman Senior Fellow on Public Policy at the Hoover Institution of Stanford University. He graduated magna cum laude from Harvard University in 1958 with an AB in economics, earned an AM in economics from Columbia University in 1959, and ultimately received his PhD in economics in 1968 from the University of Chicago. Having written more than ten books on economics, Sowell has taught the subject at numerous colleges throughout the years, including Cornell, Amherst, and the University of California at Los Angeles, and was awarded the National Humanities Medal in 2002. When asked about becoming a writer, he replied, "The only way I know to become a good writer is to be a bad writer and keep on improving."

It has almost become something of a joke when some "global warming" conference has to be cancelled because of a snowstorm or bitterly cold weather.

But stampedes and hysteria are no joke—and creating stampedes and hysteria has become a major activity of those hyping a global warming "crisis."

> *Creating stampedes and hysteria has become a major activity of those hyping a global warming "crisis."*

They mobilize like-minded people from a variety of occupations, call them all "scientists" and then claim that "all" the experts agree on a global warming crisis.

Their biggest argument is that there is no argument.

A whole cottage industry has sprung up among people who get grants, government agencies who get appropriations, politicians who get publicity and the perpetually indignant who get something new to be indignant about. It gives teachers something to talk about in school instead of teaching.

Those who bother to check the facts often find that not all those who are called scientists are really scientists and not all of those who are scientists are specialists in climate. But who bothers to check facts these days?

A new and very different conference on global warming will be held in New York City, under the sponsorship of the Heartland Institute, on March 2nd to March 4th—weather permitting.

It is called an "International Conference on Climate Change." Its subtitle is "Global Warming: Truth or Swindle?" Among those present will be professors of climatology, along with scientists in other fields and people from other professions.

They come from universities in England, Hungary, and Australia, as well as from the United States and Canada, and include among other dignitaries the president of the Czech Republic.

There will be 98 speakers and 400 participants.

The theme of the conference is that "there is no scientific consensus on the causes or likely consequences of global warming."

Many of the participants in this conference are people who have already expressed skepticism about either the prevailing explanations of current climate change or the dire predictions about future climate change.

These include authors of such books as *Unstoppable Global Warming: Every 1500 Years* by Fred Singer and Dennis Avery, and *Shattered Consensus*, edited by Patrick J. Michaels.

This will be one of the rare opportunities for the media to hear   14
the other side of the story—for those old-fashioned journalists who
still believe that their job is to inform the public, rather than promote
an agenda.

The subtitle of the upcoming conference—"Global Warming: 15
Truth or Swindle?"—is also the title of a British television program
that is now available on DVD in the United States. It is a devastating
debunking of the current "global warming" hysteria.

Nobody denies that there is such a thing as a greenhouse effect. If   16
there were not, the side of the planet facing away from the sun would
be freezing every night.

There is not even a lot of controversy over temperature readings.   17
What is fundamentally at issue are the explanations, implications and
extrapolations of these temperature readings.

The party line of those who say that we are heading for a global   18
warming crisis of epic proportions is that human activities generating
carbon dioxide are key factors responsible for the warming that has
taken place in recent times.

The problem with this reasoning is that the temperatures rose   19
first and then the carbon dioxide levels rose. Some scientists say that
the warming created the increased carbon dioxide, rather than vice
versa.

Many natural factors, including variations in the amount of heat   20
put out by the sun, can cause the earth to heat or cool.

The bigger problem is that this has long since become a crusade   21
rather than an exercise in evidence or logic. Too many people are too
committed to risk it all on a roll of the dice, which is what turning to
empirical evidence is.

Those who have a big stake in global warming hysteria are un-   22
likely to show up at the conference in New York, and unfortunately
that includes much of the media.

Vocabulary/Using a Dictionary

1. Sowell refers to a television program that is "a devastating de-
    bunking of the current 'global warming' hysteria" (para. 15).
    What does it mean to *debunk* something?
2. What are the origins of the word *hysteria* (para. 2)?
3. How do you define the word *media* (para. 14)? From what lan-
    guage does *media* come?

Responding to Words in Context

1. What does Sowell mean when he says "a whole *cottage industry* has sprung up" (para. 5) around the global-warming crisis?

2. What do professors of *climatology* (para. 8) teach?

3. What is *empirical evidence* (para. 21)?

Discussing Main Point and Meaning

1. Many people accept current data that shows the acceleration of global warming since the beginning of the industrial age. Do you think Sowell believes that people are responsible for climate change? Why or why not?

2. Based on the conference's subtitle, "Global Warming: Truth or Swindle?" how do you think those attending the International Conference on Climate Change view global warming? How do their views differ from those Sowell accuses of creating "hysteria"?

3. Sowell mentions the role of carbon dioxide levels in climate change in paragraphs 18–19. How is carbon dioxide created?

Examining Sentences, Paragraphs, and Organization

1. Why does Sowell add the tag "weather permitting" (para. 7) to his sentence about the upcoming global-warming conference?

2. Sowell spends a great deal of time arguing that those who claim we are in the midst of a global-warming crisis do not "check facts" (para. 6). Based on the construction of the essay, do you feel certain that Sowell has checked his facts? Which paragraphs show evidence that he has? Where might you want more reassurance?

3. Find where Sowell uses the word *hysteria* in this essay. How many times does he repeat it? Why do you think he repeats it, and what is the effect of this repetition on the reader?

Thinking Critically

1. Do you think Sowell believes that the earth is warming? Does his belief have any connection to his feelings about how global warming is being presented by the media?

2. The International Conference on Climate Change was sponsored by the Heartland Institute. Do some research on the Heartland Institute. Do you think this sponsor is a good match for the subject? Explain why or why not.

3. Why do you think Sowell claims that global warming is an issue being used by people for gain? What does he think people get out of the creation of a crisis such as this one? Do you believe him, based on what he says in the essay?

In-Class Writing Activities

1. Do you think, as Sowell does, that "creating stampedes and hysteria has become a major activity of those hyping a global warming 'crisis'" (para. 2)? In writing, discuss why you think this is or is not so (taking both sides is acceptable). If you can find headlines or other information to back up your position, include them in your writing as evidence. Be sure to cite your sources.

2. The greenhouse effect is often mentioned in connection with global warming, but it is more than a by-product of the current global-warming crisis. Write an essay explaining what the greenhouse effect is.

3. Write an essay that outlines what you think will be discussed at a conference called the International Conference on Climate Change: Global Warming: Truth or Swindle? Base some of your conclusions on the participants and other details Sowell mentions.

MIKE TIDWELL

Snap into Action for the Climate

[ORION / May–June 2008]

Before You Read
How pressing is climate change? How many years will it take for there to be a noticeable difference in weather patterns?

Words to Learn
amplifying (para. 9): increasing or making louder (v.)
staunch (para. 14): firm (adj.)
ameliorating (para. 26): making better (v.)
extrapolate (para. 30): to come to a conclusion based on known facts or theories (v.)

Record heat and wind and fire displace nearly one million Southern Californians. Record drought in Atlanta leaves the city with just a few more months of drinking water. Arctic ice shrinks by an area twice the size of Texas in *one* summer. And all over the world—including where you live—the local weather borders on unrecognizable. It's way too hot, too dry, too wet, too weird wherever you go.

All of which means it's time to face a fundamental truth: the majority of the world's climate scientists have been totally wrong.

Mike Tidwell is the director and founder of the Chesapeake Climate Action Network, "a grassroots nonprofit dedicated to raising awareness about the impacts and solutions associated with global warming in Maryland, Virginia, and DC." Tidwell is the author of several books on environmental issues, including Bayou Farewell: The Rich Life and Tragic Death of Louisiana's Cajun Coast *(2003), which began as an assignment for the Sunday travel editor of the* Washington Post. *In addition to writing, he also works as a filmmaker. His latest film is a documentary titled* We Are All Smith Islanders, *and in 2003 he received the Audubon Naturalist Society's Conservation Award.*

They've failed us completely. Not concerning the basics of global warming. Of course the climate is changing. Of course humans are driving the process through fossil fuel combustion and deforestation. No, what the scientists have been wrong about—and I mean really, *really* wrong—is the speed at which it's all occurring. Our climate system isn't just "changing." It's not just "warming." It's *snapping*, violently, into a whole new regime right before our eyes. A fantastic spasm of altered weather patterns is crashing down upon our heads right now.

The only question left for America is this: can *we* snap along with the climate? Can we, as the world's biggest polluter, create a grassroots political uprising that emerges as abruptly as a snap of the fingers? A movement that demands the clean-energy revolution in the time we have left to save ourselves? I think we can do it. I hope we can do it. Indeed, the recent political "snap" in Australia, where a devastating and unprecedented drought made climate change a central voting issue and so helped topple a Bush-like government of deniers, should give us encouragement.

But time is running out fast for a similar transformation here.

A climate snap? Really? It sounds so much like standard fear-mongering and ecohyperbole. But here's proof: One of the most prestigious scientific bodies in the world, the group that just shared the Nobel Peace Prize with Al Gore for its climate work, predicted fourteen months ago that unchecked global warming could erase *all* of the Arctic Ocean's summertime ice as early as 2070. Then, just two months later, in April 2007, a separate scientific panel released data indicating that the 2070 mark was way off, suggesting that ice-free conditions could come to the Arctic as early as the summer of 2030. And as if this acceleration weren't enough, yet another prediction emerged in December 2007. Following the year's appalling melt season, in which vast stretches of Arctic ice the size of Florida vanished almost weekly at times, a credible new estimate from the U.S. Naval Postgraduate School in Monterey, California, indicated there could be zero—*zero*—summer ice in the Arctic as early as 2013.

Five precious years. An eye-blink away.

So the Arctic doomsday prediction has gone from 2070 to 2013 in just eleven months of scientific reporting. This means far more than the likely extinction of polar bears from drowning and starvation. A world where the North Pole is just a watery dot in an unbroken expanse of dark ocean implies a planet that, well, is no longer

3

4

5

6

7

planet Earth. It's a world that is destined to be governed by radically different weather patterns. And it's a world that's arriving, basically, tomorrow, if the U.S. Naval Postgraduate School has it right.

How could this be happening to us? Why is this not dominating every minute of every presidential debate?   8

Actually it's the so-called feedback loops[1] that have tripped up scientists so badly, causing the experts to wildly misjudge the speed of the climate crash. Having never witnessed a planet overheat before, no one quite anticipated the geometric rate of change. To cite one example, when that brilliantly white Arctic ice melts to blue ocean, it takes with it a huge measure of solar reflectivity, which increases sunlight absorption and feeds more warmth back into the system, amplifying everything dramatically. And as northern forests across Canada continue to die en masse due to warming, they switch from being net absorbers of CO_2 to net emitters when forest decomposition sets in. And as tundra melts all across Siberia, it releases long-buried methane, a greenhouse gas twenty times more powerful than even CO_2. And so on and so on and so on. Like the ear-splitting shriek when a microphone gets too close to its amplifier, literally dozens of major feedback loops are screeching into place worldwide, all at the same time, ushering in the era of runaway climate change.   9

"Only in the past five years, as researchers have learned more about the way our planet works, have some come to the conclusion that changes probably won't be as smooth or as gradual as [previously] imagined," writes Fred Pearce in his new book *With Speed and Violence: Why Scientists Fear Tipping Points in Climate Change.* "We are in all probability already embarked on a roller coaster ride of lurching and sometimes brutal change."   10

> Global warming is no longer a hundred-year problem requiring a hundred-year solution.

Global warming is no longer a hundred-year problem requiring a hundred-year solution. It's not even a fifty-year problem. New data and recent events clearly reveal it's a right-here, right-now, white-hot crisis requiring dramatic and comprehensive resolution in the next twenty to thirty years, with drastic but achievable changes in energy consumption required *immediately*. But even a near-total abandonment of fossil fuels might not be enough to save us, given how fast the planet is now warming.   11

[1] *feedback loops*: A system in which the output is fed back in as input.

So the rising whisper even among many environmentalists is this: 12
we might also have to develop some sort of life-saving atmospheric
shield. In a controversial but decidedly plausible approach called geo-
engineering, we could do everything from placing giant orbiting mirrors in outer space to seeding the atmosphere with lots of sulfur dioxide, basically becoming a "permanent human volcano." More on this
in a moment.

But first, if there's any good news surrounding the sudden and un-   13
expected speed of global warming it is this: it's nobody's fault. New
evidence shows that we were almost certainly locked into a course of
violent climate snap well before we first fully understood the seriousness of global warming back in the 1980s. Even had we completely
unplugged everything twenty years ago, the momentum of carbon
dioxide buildup already occurring in the atmosphere clearly would
have steered us toward the same disastrous results we're seeing now.

So we can stop blaming ExxonMobil and Peabody Coal and the   14
father-son Bush administrations. Their frequently deceitful lobbying
and political stalling over the past twenty years didn't wreck the climate. The atmosphere was already wrecked well before the first Bush
took office. These staunch conservatives simply created a "solution
delay" that we can—and must—overcome in a very short time.

The tendency toward denial is still very much with us, of course.   15
From this point forward, however, there can be no hesitation and no
absolution. In a world of obvious climate snap, any obstruction, any
delay, from any quarter, is hands down a crime against humanity.

Amid the sudden need to rethink everything a.s.a.p. comes an-   16
other piece of good news: the clean-energy solutions to global warming grow more economically feasible and closer at hand with each
passing year. Europeans, with a standard of living equal to ours, already use *half* the energy per capita as Americans. If we just adopted
Europe's efficiency standards we'd be halfway to fixing our share of
the problem in America.

We can't do this? We can pilot wheeled vehicles on Mars and   17
cross medical frontiers weekly and invent the iPhone, but we can't
use energy as efficiently as Belgium does today? Or Japan, for that
matter? We can, of course. Wind power is the fastest growing energy
resource in the world, and a car that runs on nothing but prairie grass
could soon be coming to a driveway near you.

But to achieve these changes fast enough, the American people   18
need a grassroots political movement that goes from zero to sixty in a

matter of months, a movement that demands the sort of clean-energy policies and government mandates needed to transform our economy and our lives. We need a mass movement of concerned voters that "snaps" into place overnight—as rapidly as the climate itself is changing. Skeptics need only remember that we've experienced explosive, purposeful change before—quickly mobilizing to defeat Nazism in the '40s, casting off statutory Jim Crowism in a mere decade.

What just took place in Australia could be seen as a dress rehearsal for what might soon happen here in America. The underlying factors couldn't be more similar. A historic drought (similar to current conditions in the U.S. Southwest and Southeast) with an established scientific link to global warming had become so bad by 2007 that 25 percent of Australia's food production had been destroyed and every major city was under emergency water restrictions. The conservative incumbent government, meanwhile, had denied the basic reality of global warming for a decade, refusing to sign the Kyoto Protocol. But voters were increasingly traumatized by the drought and increasingly educated. (Proportionally, twice as many Aussies watched Al Gore's *An Inconvenient Truth* as Americans.) Against this backdrop, Labor Party candidate Kevin Rudd made climate change one of his topmost issues, talking about it constantly as he campaigned toward a landslide victory. It was good politics. The electorate had snapped into place and so had Rudd. His first official act in November was to sign Kyoto and commit his nation to a major clean-energy overhaul.

That time must come soon to America. November 4, 2008, would be a nice start date. And when we go, we must go explosively. Voters, appalled by the increasingly weird weather all across America—weather soon to be made worse by the bare Arctic Ocean and other feedback loops—must finally demand the right thing, laughing all the way to the polls over the recent congressional bill requiring 35 mpg cars by 2020. By 2015, we need to have cut electricity use by at least one third and be building nothing less than *50 mpg* cars. *And* constructing massive and graceful wind farms off most of our windy seacoasts.

That's *our* snap. That's our glorious feedback loop, with political will and technological advances and market transformations all feeding off each other for breathtaking, runaway change.

But will it be enough? As inspiring and unifying and liberating as this World War II–like mobilization will be for our nation, it sadly will not. Getting off carbon fuels—though vital and mandatory—

won't steer us clear of climate chaos. We've delayed action far too long for that tidy resolution. Carbon dioxide lingers in the atmosphere for up to a hundred years, and there's already more than enough up there to erase all the "permanent" ice in the Arctic.

This leaves us with a huge decision to make. Either we fatalistically accept the inability of clean energy alone to save us, resigning ourselves to the appalling climate pain and chaos scientists say are coming, or we take one additional awesome step: we engineer the climate. Specifically, human beings must quickly figure out some sort of mechanical or chemical means of reflecting a portion of the sun's light away from our planet, at least for a while. Whether you're comfortable with this idea or not, trust me, the debate is coming, and we'll almost certainly engage in some version of this risky but necessary tinkering.   23

First of all, forget the giant mirrors in space. Too difficult and expensive. And all those lofty notions of machines that suck CO_2 out of the atmosphere? At best, they are many years away, with significant cost hurdles and engineering challenges still to be resolved. More likely, we'll engage in some combination of cruder efforts, including painting every rooftop and roadway and parking lot in the world white to replace some of the Arctic ice's lost capacity for solar reflectivity.   24

After that, all roads pretty much lead to Mount Pinatubo in the Philippines. In 1991 that volcano erupted, spewing enough light-reflecting sulfur dioxide and dust into the atmosphere to cool the entire planet by one degree Fahrenheit for two full years. Could humans replicate this effect long enough to give our clean-energy transformation a chance to work? Can we artificially cool the Earth, using sulfur dioxide, even while the atmosphere remains full of greenhouse gases? Several very smart climate scientists, including Ralph Cicerone, current president of the U.S. National Academy of Sciences, think the idea is plausible enough to investigate thoroughly right now as a possible "emergency option" for future policymakers.   25

Ironically, we could "harvest" ample supplies of sulfur from modern coal-burning power plants, where it is a byproduct. In liquid form, sulfur could then be added—ironically, again—to jet fuel, allowing passenger aircraft worldwide to seed the atmosphere per scientific calibrations. In theory, we could even use powerful army artillery to shoot sulfur canisters into the atmosphere. But supply and delivery would likely be less of a challenge than the inevitable side effects, including an uptick in acid rain. And then there are the unknown and unintended consequences of subjecting the atmosphere to a multidecade or perhaps multicentury Mount Pinatubo effect. We   26 would need an urgent research effort to assess the possible negative impacts of this process so we can devote resources to ameliorating at least the anticipated outcomes.

But the answer to the question *Can human beings artificially cool the planet?* is almost certainly yes. That answer, I realize, poses a terrible conundrum for conservationists like me who understand it's precisely this sort of anthropocentrism and technological arrogance that got us into the mess we're in. But like it or not, we are where we are. And I, for one, can't look my ten-year-old son in the eye and, using a different sort of ideological arrogance, say, *No, don't even try atmospheric engineering. We've learned our lesson. Just let catastrophic global warming run its course.*   27

What kind of lesson is that? I'd rather take my chances with global engineering and its possible risks than accept the *guarantee* of chaotic warming. As respected climate scientist Michael MacCracken has said, "Human beings have been inadvertently engineering the climate for 250 years. Why not carefully *ad*vertently engineer the climate for a while?"   28

So here we are, stripped of exaggeration and rhetoric, and hard pressed by the evidence right before our eyes. Our destiny will be decided, one way or another, in the next handful of years, either by careful decision-making or paralyzing indecision. We stand at a crossroads in human and planetary history. Or as my southern grandfather used to say, "The fork has finally hit the grits."   29

Try as I might, I truly can't imagine the Arctic Ocean completely free of ice by 2013, nor can I extrapolate all the appalling implications, from the end of wheat farming in Kansas to more record-breaking heat waves in Chicago. It truly is a terrifying time to be alive. But also exhilarating. As the Reverend Martin Luther King Jr. once said, "I know, somehow, that only when it is dark enough, can you see the stars."   30

The part of the picture that I can see is our own snap. I can see potent political change coming to America with our nation passionately joining the Kyoto process. I can see layers and layers of *solution* feedback loops that follow. I can see national policies that freeze and then quickly scale back the use of oil, coal, and natural gas. I see multitudes of Americans finally inspired to conserve at home, their money-saving actions feeding and amplifying the whole process. I then see consumer and governmental demand unleashing the genius of market systems and technological creativity, accelerating everything   31 until we as a society are moving at geometric speed too, just like the climate, and suddenly our use of dirty fuels simply disappears.

Snap!   32

I can see my son coming of age in a world where the multiplier   33
benefits of clean energy go far beyond preserving a stable climate. No more wars for oil. No more mountaintops removed for coal. A plummet in childhood asthma. A more secure, sustainable, and prosperous economy. Although there are surely dark times ahead, I can see him living through them, living deep into the twenty-first century, when most of the lingering greenhouse gases will have finally dissipated from our atmosphere, allowing an orderly end to the geo-engineering process.

Best of all, I see spiritual transformation ahead. We simply can-   34
not make the necessary changes without being changed ourselves. Of this I am sure. With every wind farm we build, with every zero-emission car we engineer, we will remember our motivation as surely as every Rosie the Riveter knew in the 1940s that each rivet was defeating fascism. A deep and explicit understanding of sustainability will dawn for the first time in modern human history, moving from energy to diet to land use to globalization.

We will know, finally, that to live in permanent peace and prosper-   35
ity we must live in a particular way, adhering to a particular set of truths about ourselves and our planet. To borrow from the great architect William McDonough, we will finally become native to this world. We will have lived through the climate threat, *evolved* through it, and our new behavior will emanate from the very core of our humanity.

Vocabulary / Using a Dictionary

1. What is the meaning of the prefix *trans-*? How does it change the meaning of *form* in the word *transformation* (para. 4)?

2. What is the verb form of the noun *absolution* (para. 15)? What does it mean?

3. What is the stem of the word *exhilarating* (para. 30)? How does Tidwell use it?

Responding to Words in Context

1. How does Tidwell revise the idea of the "feedback loop" in paragraph 21?

2. In paragraph 28, Tidwell quotes Michael MacCracken on the idea of global engineering. How does MacCracken use the antonyms *inadvertently* and *advertently* to describe the climate situation?

3. Why does Tidwell use the word *evolved* (para. 35) to describe the way humans will adapt to global warming?

Discussing Main Point and Meaning

1. How does Tidwell want to change the general conception of global warming? How does he hope readers will respond to his essay?

2. How does Tidwell represent the old thinking about how to combat climate change? What does he think we now need to do to address the problem?

3. In paragraph 20, Tidwell gives some specific recommendations for changes we should make. How would you summarize these recommendations?

4. Why does the idea of engineering the environment cause a problem for Tidwell? Why does it seem to contradict his beliefs?

Examining Sentences, Paragraphs, and Organization

1. What is the purpose of Tidwell's list of weather conditions in paragraph 1? Why does he begin his essay with these reports?

2. Tidwell begins paragraph 5 with the two questions: "A climate snap? Really?" What is the purpose of these questions?

3. How does Tidwell use the example of Australia in his essay? What does he think the United States and Australia have in common?

Thinking Critically

1. Why does Tidwell say that a world with no Arctic ice "is no longer planet Earth" (para. 7)?

2. Why is the idea that "it's nobody's fault" crucial to Tidwell's argument (para. 13)? What is the purpose of this assertion?

3. Why does Tidwell mention technologies like the iPhone and the Mars rover? What do these inventions have to do with his overall argument?

In-Class Writing Activities

1. How does Tidwell portray the engineering of the environment? Which methods does he think are plausible, and which does he think are impractical? Write a summary of his recommendations for how to artificially cool the earth, and then explain which methods you think sound most likely.

2. In the course of his essay, Tidwell compares the movement to combat global warming with several other social or political movements. Choose one of these and write an essay in which you discuss how the movement was formed, how it works, and what it might have in common with current activism for the climate.

DUSTIN LUSHING (STUDENT ESSAY)

Global Warming: Is It All Hot Air?

[THE JOHNS HOPKINS NEWS-LETTER, Johns Hopkins University/March 29, 2007]

Before You Read

How have politicians altered the conversation on global warming? Which politicians have been most influential?

Dustin Lushing is a junior at Johns Hopkins University, where he majors in Writing Seminars and occasionally contributes to the Johns Hopkins News-Letter. *"Johns Hopkins is passionately divided between liberals and conservatives, as well as science majors and non-science majors," and so Lushing was drawn to the issue of global warming for his essay because the topic "stirs up ferocious debate among these groups, and I jumped at the opportunity to present an unconventional opinion." To that end, he advises other writers to simply "be yourself."*

Words to Learn

duped (para. 1): fooled (v.)
recounts (para. 2): tells about or narrates (v.)
erroneous (para. 5): wrong; mistaken (adj.)

The gibberish-spewing, liquor-smelling doomsayer on the street   1
corner has a new name: Al Gore. Attention left-leaning students:
You've been duped. At some point during their recent years of impotence, a crack team of Democratic strategists retreated to a backroom
to kick around possible issues. They pondered. What's as scary as
9/11 but scarier? What's just inaccessible enough to average Americans that they won't question it? What will cause people to say "the
scientific community" a lot? Let me throw in one fact before you
crumple this paper up and place it in the nearest recycling bin: Global
warming exists. But it's not that big of a deal.

Benjamin Ginsberg, Professor of Politics at Johns Hopkins Uni-   2
versity, recounts a scene of similar Washington opportunism. The notorious demagogue Joe McCarthy and some of his consultants are sitting in a diner, brainstorming campaign issues. One staffer pitches
anticommunism. McCarthy smiles. The rest is history, spawned from
a simple and recurring formula: take a potentially explosive issue and
exaggerate the hell out of it.

Enter Al Gore. It's easy to fall under Al's charm. Most of us view   3
him through rose-colored glasses. He is the sane, intelligent foil to
Bush's buffoonery. Gore is like that fun uncle who owns a motorcycle
and plays in a rock band on the weekend. In one scene in his film *An
Inconvenient Truth*, Gore is typing away on a fifteen-inch Macbook.
Just like us! It still hurts to think that five hundred Floridians could
have saved us from W.'s disastrous tenure. (Ironically, Florida is one
of the states that Gore predicts will soon be underwater.)

But let us not forget that Gore is a dyed-in-the-wool politician.   4
He may genuinely care about the environment and the fate of our
planet, but we cannot trust him when it comes to urgency. Politics
and science do not mix. A sensitive scientific issue will be exploited,
corrupted and stripped of many layers of truth in the hands of a
politician. Bush once comically stated that the "jury is still out" on
evolution. Former Senate Majority Leader Bill Frist diagnosed Terri
Schiavo—a woman in a vegetative state whose husband wanted to
remove her feeding tube—from what looked like a TiVo. And now
Al Gore cries Armageddon.

A recent *New York Times* article explains that many reputable scientists are calling "Mr. Gore's central point exaggerated and erroneous." Gore rebuts by saying he covered "the most important and salient points" and that "the degree of scientific consensus on global warming has never been stronger." Yes, the consensus is overwhelming that global warming exists, and is most likely caused by humans. But that misses the key question: Should we care? There is consensus that the avian flu exists. But how imminent is the threat? Similarly, how imminent is the nebulous doom that is climate change? The scientific community is not so united on that question. A truly terrifying revelation in the article is that many scientists "commend [Gore's] popularizations and call his science basically sound." *Basically sound?* Science, the last bastion of truth, is compromising itself to be popular.

> *Yes, the consensus is overwhelming that global warming exists, and is most likely caused by humans. But that misses the key question: Should we care?*

So what are college undergrads left to think? A once mildly compelling issue of green earth and clean air has been coopted by an alarmist politico. Those of us who don't buy into it but wish to help the planet are wary of joining a ridiculous doomsday crusade. And what's the point if New York will be under a glacier in six months? There are more important things to focus one's energy and resources on: the war in Iraq, terrorism, stem cell research, poverty, racial equality, unemployment and education among other unexaggerated, authentic causes.

Student organizations at just about every university are handing out fliers and petitioning their administrations to make their campuses more eco-friendly. At my school, crusaders have adopted a logo with a nearly exact reproduction of the iconic image of six Marines raising the American Flag at Iwo Jima, the setting of some of World War II's most hellish combats. Except it's not a flag, it's a giant windmill, and another prime example of the cringe-inducing self-importance of the global warming movement.

Vocabulary/Using a Dictionary

1. Where does the word *gibberish* (para. 1) come from? What does it mean?

2. What is the root of *impotence* (para. 1)? Why does Lushing use this word to describe the Democratic Party?

3. What language does the word *demagogue* (para. 2) come from? What does it mean?

Responding to Words in Context

1. What does it mean to be *dyed-in-the-wool* (para. 4)? What does this phrase suggest about Al Gore?

2. What does it mean that scientists have reached a *consensus* (para. 5) about global warming? Why is Lushing not concerned about the consensus?

3. Why does Lushing criticize the *self-importance* of the global warming movement (para. 7)? How does this term characterize his opinion about it?

Discussing Main Point and Meaning

1. Why does Lushing think politicians have latched onto the idea of global warming? How does it serve their purposes?

2. Why does Lushing turn our attention to other causes in paragraph 6?

Examining Sentences, Paragraphs, and Organization

1. How does the first sentence of Lushing's essay portray Al Gore? How does he use this sentence to challenge our perceptions?

2. How does the last sentence of paragraph 1 summarize Lushing's argument in this essay?

3. In paragraph 4, Lushing mentions actions by several politicians. What are these examples of? What is the point of the paragraph?

Thinking Critically

1. Why does Lushing compare climate-change activism to McCarthyism? Is this a fair comparison?

2. In paragraph 5, Lushing claims that science "is compromising itself to be popular." Do you think Lushing is correct in his assumptions about scientists?

In-Class Writing Activities

1. Do you agree with Lushing's conclusion that students should pay more attention to other issues, such as the ones he lists in paragraph 6, than to global warming? Write a response to his essay in which you either defend the cause of global warming as a primary concern or argue why another issue should take precedence.

2. Write an analysis of the final image Lushing presents in his essay — the student organization logo that plays on a famous World War II photograph. What is the meaning of the picture of Marines raising the flag on Iwo Jima? Why has it become such an icon? And why do the students choose it for the basis of their image?

ANNOTATION Supporting Your Point with Examples

In any discussion or debate, nothing is more persuasive than well-chosen examples. We often use examples to back up a generalization with concrete instances. The examples show what we mean, or they show our readers that we can offer more than a single instance to establish our point. Thus, if we claimed that in the spring of 2008 the costs of numerous consumer goods rose dramatically and all we mentioned was the price of gasoline, our claim would fall short of sufficient evidence; we would need to mention other rising costs, such as for food, heating oil, electricity, tuition, and transportation.

We can see the effectiveness of appropriate examples in Dustin Lushing's "Global Warming: Is It All Hot Air?" Lushing argues in his essay that Al Gore is politicizing the climate-change issue. To back up his generalization that "a sensitive scientific issue will be exploited, corrupted and stripped of many layers of truth in the hands of a politician," Lushing realizes that he requires more than the single example of Al Gore. He then supports his point by introducing two additional examples of politicians who made statements about scientific matters that revealed political biases: George W. Bush's skeptical comment on evolution and Bill Frist's medical diagnosis of a woman in a comatose state.

Lushing helps prove his point about Al Gore's political use of science by introducing two additional examples of politicians who also tried to mix science and politics.

But let us not forget that Gore is a dyed-in-the-wool politician. He may genuinely care about the environment and the fate of our planet, but we cannot trust him when it comes to urgency. Politics and science do not mix. A sensitive scientific issue will be exploited, corrupted and stripped of many layers of truth in the hands of a politician. Bush once comically stated that the "jury is still out" on evolution. Former Senate Majority Leader Bill Frist diagnosed Terri Schiavo — a woman in a vegetative state whose husband wanted to remove her feeding tube — from what looked like a TiVo. And now Al Gore cries Armageddon.

— From "Global Warming: Is It All Hot Air?"
by Dustin Lushing, page 407

JENNIFER OLADIPO

Global Warming Is Colorblind: Can We Say as Much for Environmentalism?

[ORION / November–December 2007]

Before You Read

Do you believe that whites are more involved than minorities in environmental issues? What would happen if minorities became more involved? How would it make a difference to the environmental movement?

Words to Learn

chaperones (para. 2): adults who supervise young people at a gathering in order to assist them and ensure good behavior (n.)

disembark (para. 2): to get out of a vehicle (v.)

predominantly (para. 3): for the most part (adv.)

conjure (para. 4): to produce or bring (v.)

precipice (para. 4): a cliff's edge or brink (n.)

collective (para. 4): characteristic of a number of persons considered as a group (adj.)

assumption (para. 5): a taking for granted that something is true (n.)

amenable (para. 5): open; agreeable (adj.)

solicitations (para. 5): requests or entreaties (n.)

peter out (para. 6): to diminish and then give out (v.)

Jennifer Oladipo, a member of the Society of Professional Journalists, is an independent journalist whose work has appeared in publications including the Utne Reader, Orion, Grist, LEO Weekly, *and* Get Out! *Many of her essays focus on the environment, culture, travel, business, and social justice. No matter what the topic or intended audience, Oladipo writes that she is "driven by the desire to learn, and tell, other people's stories. . . . All writing, in some regard, is a way of embracing that story that has been waiting for its teller."*

organic (para. 7): involving fertiliz-
ers and pesticides of animal or
vegetable origin rather than
manufactured chemicals (adj.)

nuances (para. 7): subtle differences
or distinctions (n.)

In nearly two years of volunteering and working at an urban na-   1
ture preserve, I have never seen another face like mine come through
our doors.

At least, I've not seen another black woman come for a morning   2
hike or native-wildlife program. The few I do encounter are teachers
and chaperones with school groups, or aides assisting people with
disabilities. When I commute by bus to the preserve, located in the
middle of Louisville, Kentucky, I disembark with blacks and other
minorities. Yet none of them ever seems to make it to the trails.

I might have assumed they simply weren't interested, but then I   3
saw that none of the center's newsletters were mailed to predominantly minority areas of town, nor did any press releases go to popular minority radio stations or newspapers. Not ever, as far as I could
tell. Although the nature center seeks a stronger community presence
and feels the same budget pinch as other small nonprofits, it has
missed large swaths of the community with its message.

The terms *environmentalist* and *minority* conjure two distinct   4
images in most people's minds—a false dichotomy that seriously
threatens any chance of pulling the planet out of its current ecological
tailspin. Some people think this country is on the precipice of a societal shift that will make environmental stewardship an integral part of
our collective moral code. But that is not going to happen as long as
we as a nation continue to think and act as if "green" automatically
means "white."

Assumptions about who is amenable to conservation values cost   5
the environmental movement numbers and dollars. Religion, capitalism, and even militarism learned ages ago to reach actively across the
racial spectrum. In terms of winning over minorities, they have left
environmentalism in the dust. Not until I joined an environmental-
journalism organization was my mailbox flooded with information
about serious environmental issues—even though I have been volunteering in organic gardens, hiking, and camping for years. I had received solicitations for credit cards and political parties, fast food
coupons, and a few Books of Mormon—but I had to seek out environmental groups.

Minorities make up one-third of the population, and we are   6
growing as an economic and financial force as our numbers increase.
We are a key to maintaining the energy that environmentalism has
gained as a result of intense mainstream attention. That momentum
will peter out without more people to act on the present sense of urgency. Imagine the power of 100 million Asians, African Americans,
Latinos, and Native Americans invested in sustainable living, joining
green organizations, voting for politicians and laws that protect the
environment.

Nobody benefits from the perception that enjoying and caring   7
for the environment is an exclusively white lifestyle. The truth is that
brown, yellow, red, and black people like to go backpacking, too.
Those of us with the means are buying or-
ganic, local, and hybrid. If environmentalism
continues to appear mostly white and well-
off, it will continue to be mostly white and
well-off, even as racial and economic demographics change. The environmental movement will continue to overlook the nuances,
found in diversity of experience, that reveal
multiple facets of environmental problems —
and their solutions.

> *Nobody benefits from the perception that enjoying and caring for the environment is an exclusively white lifestyle.*

Sooner or later, even global warming will be pushed off magazine   8
covers, television screens, and the Congressional floor. Before that
time, we need to have in place something even more impressive: a
racially diverse, numerically astounding mass of environmentalists
ready to pick up the ball and run with it.

Vocabulary / Using a Dictionary

1. Define the word *minority* (para. 3).

2. What is a *dichotomy* (para. 4)?

3. What does it mean to be a *steward*? What is *environmental stewardship*? (para. 4)?

Responding to Words in Context

1. What is Oladipo referring to when she uses the phrase "current
   ecological tailspin" (para. 4) in regard to our planet?

2. In paragraph 5, Oladipo says that "religion, capitalism, and even militarism learned ages ago to reach actively across the racial spectrum." What is a *spectrum*, and how do you think she's using the word in the context of race?

3. What are the "*conservation* values" Oladipo speaks of in paragraph 5? How does the word *conservation* relate to the political term *conservative*?

Discussing Main Point and Meaning

1. Why does Oladipo feel it's important to mention that many minorities exit the bus with her as she heads to work at the nature preserve, but "none of them ever seems to make it to the trails" (para. 2)?

2. Why might the words *environmentalist* and *minority* bring two very different images into people's minds (para. 4)?

3. Oladipo warns, "If environmentalism continues to appear mostly white and well-off, it will continue to be mostly white and well-off, even as racial and economic demographics change" (para. 7). What are some of the potential drawbacks to an environmental movement that is only "white and well-off"?

Examining Sentences, Paragraphs, and Organization

1. Why does Oladipo begin her essay by saying "I have never seen another face like mine come through our doors" (para. 1) instead of saying "I have never seen another black woman's face come through our doors"?

2. In paragraph 3, Oladipo offers an explanation for why there is so little minority interest in things environmental based on what she notices at the nature preserve where she works. How does this paragraph speak to the question of minorities and environmentalism in the wider sphere?

3. When you read the sentence "The truth is that brown, yellow, red, and black people like to go backpacking, too" (para. 7), who do you think is the intended audience for this essay? What other clues about audience are given in the essay?

Thinking Critically

1. Why might whites be courted by the environmental movement and minorities left out? Does Oladipo, in her essay, suggest any reasons for this difference?

2. Oladipo disputes that environmental work is exclusively of interest to whites, saying, "The truth is that brown, yellow, red, and black people like to go backpacking, too" (para. 7). What clues are you given to what has drawn Oladipo to environmental work?

3. What sort of "environmental problems" (para. 7) are minorities likely to experience? Are they the same problems that whites experience? If not, how are they different?

In-Class Writing Activities

1. Speaking on behalf of minorities, Oladipo states, "Those of us with the means are buying organic, local, and hybrid" (para. 7). Choose one of those options and, in writing, explain what she means. Discuss how the decision of any race to shop in that particular way benefits the environment.

2. Global warming has indeed taken center stage in our national mind as a topic of great importance, although Oladipo warns, "Sooner or later, even global warming will be pushed off magazine covers, television screens, and the Congressional floor" (para. 8). What do you know about global warming, and where is your information coming from? Write an informal essay in which you explain what you know about global warming. Include any concerns you have and consider how input from other sources affects your perceptions and adds to your knowledge about the issue.

3. Oladipo never mentions her urban nature preserve by name, and although she says she is a member of an "environmental-journalism organization," she offers no specifics. What sort of environmental work is out there for someone who is interested? Research jobs, paid and volunteer, high profile or local, with which one might be involved in order to help the environment. Choose one job and write a brief essay that outlines the history of the organization or company, the sort of work offered, and its benefit, as you see it, to the environment.

STUDENT DEBATE

Is Global Warming Scientific?

JOSH BURLESON

When Politics Meets Science

[CRIMSON WHITE, University of Alabama / February 9, 2007]

Before You Read

Where did the first reports about global warming come from? Who has been responsible for publicizing the issue?

Words to Learn

persisted (para. 1): lasted; survived (v.)
obsolete (para. 1): out of date (adj.)
algorithms (para. 2): mathematical processes (n.)

Is global warming real? One of the first scientists to question global warming was Michael Mann, and he was immediately faced with opposition. Questions persisted, and a group of scientists released a review of his work, saying it was "riddled with errors, unjustifiable truncations of extrapolation of source data, obsolete data, geographical location errors, incorrect calculations of principal components and other quality control defects."   1

It took years to force the disclosure of the algorithms used to arrive at Mann's original conclusions. In the meantime, the idea was   2

Josh Burleson graduated from the University of Alabama in 2007 with a degree in computer engineering. Although the writing involved in his job as an engineer is more technical in nature, during his time at UA Burleson frequently wrote on the opinion's Web site of the Crimson White as well as sending in letters to the editor. He first began his essay, "When Politics Meets Science," as a response "to challenge the mainstream beliefs that were constantly being pushed in the student paper." Burleson encourages other student writers, "If you are going to take the time to write, take pride in your work and do your research. Provide facts and evidence to back up your claims if you are writing on a controversial topic."

used to further the political agendas of environmentalists seeking to put restrictions on the "corporate America" they had long despised. Mann was eventually forced to retract some of his data, and it became evident that his methods produced "desired" results when there was no such evidence—but not before the idea of global warming became mainstream.

Opponents of global warming are treated as heretics in the scientific community. One self-proclaimed expert thinks scientists who disagree should be decertified. This politicization of science (on either side of the debate) will only result in bad science. Anybody who has a desired result in mind before they begin a study will inevitably get that result.

Take, for instance, a report released by the United Nations' Intergovernmental Panel for Climate Change, which actually linked a higher suicide rate to global warming. Anybody using deductive logic can quickly see the problem. The cost of televisions has risen over the last ten years, so the same logic would suggest that global warming caused the cost of televisions to rise. When politics fuses with science, this is the result.

Recently, majority opinion has been substituted for real proof of global warming. If the majority of scientists think it is true, then it must be. Unfortunately, a consensus isn't science. If it were, the world would still be considered flat. Consensus is simply a room full of people thinking—or possibly wanting to believe—something is true. Sorry, but I require proof, and currently there is as much proof against global warming as there is for it, and even more questions arise when asking whether or not global warming is caused by man.

> *The problem is that politics has corrupted the science so much that one side refuses to acknowledge the results of the other, and accusations of bias fly.*

In fact, it has been proposed that there was a "global warming period" during the middle ages. If this is true, then it would seem our big SUVs might not be the cause after all. How devastating that must be for the greenies. The problem is that politics has corrupted the science so much that one side refuses to acknowledge the results of the other, and accusations of bias fly. The studies are inconsistent: One says the Antarctic is shrinking. Another says the Antarctic is growing. Yet another says the interior of the Antarctic is growing but the exterior is shrinking. Is it just me, or is this beginning to sound like the debate over whether eggs are healthy?

If we have an unseasonably warm day, then it must be global   7
warming, but when we have record snow, then we should just be
looking at the "trends" over time and not worrying about short-term
changes. Some even argue that global warming caused Katrina.
Katrina has been called a "super-hurricane" and a sign of things to
come. In truth, Katrina wasn't any more powerful than many other
hurricanes. It just happened to hit a city that is shaped like a bowl,
and the levees broke.

And what about the Kyoto Protocol? The United States gets a lot   8
of flack for not signing on. Even if all signatory nations met their
commitments, which is highly unlikely, computer models suggest that
a further human-caused increase in temperature of perhaps two-
tenths of a degree might be averted by 2100. Is 0.2 degree worth the
billions of dollars spent already and the billions more planned?

Do you feel the urge to challenge the results of this study? Will   9
you present alternative results? Doing so only highlights the inconsistency of the science and your own inflexibility when presented with
opposing science.

So here's the deal. I'm not saying global warming isn't real. I'm   10
not even saying that it is impossible for humans to be causing it. All
I'm saying is that the original idea was based on flawed science, has
yet to be proven and has as many scientific studies arguing against it
than for it. So before we burden the economies of the world and put
restrictions on growth and development, let's slow down and work
on changing the "proof" of global warming from a widely supported
hunch into proven fact.

Vocabulary/Using a Dictionary

1. Look up the meaning of the verb *truncate*. What does it mean
   when Burleson claims that the data on global warming has been
   subjected to *truncations* (para. 1).

2. What is the meaning of the prefix *de-* in *decertified* (para. 3)?
   What would that mean for the scientists Burleson is discussing?

3. Look up the meaning of *heretic*. Why does Burleson refer to opponents of the global-warming theory as *heretics* (para. 3)?

Responding to Words in Context

1. What are the *desired* results Burleson mentions in paragraph 3?
   Who desired them?

2. What is *deductive logic* (para. 4)? What does Burleson think it would tell readers about the report put out by the Intergovernmental Panel for Climate Change?

3. In paragraph 6, Burleson refers to global-warming activists as *greenies*. What are the connotations of this term?

Discussing Main Point and Meaning

1. What does Burleson criticize about Michael Mann's research? What does he find problematic?

2. How does Burleson think science and politics interact? How should they?

3. Are there any points to the argument for global warming that Burleson concedes? Where is his main disagreement?

Examining Sentences, Paragraphs, and Organization

1. Burleson begins his essay with a question: "Is global warming real?" (para. 1). How does this question affect readers? Why does Burleson begin with it?

2. Paragraph 6 contains several contradictions. What is the point of these contradictions? What do they mean?

Thinking Critically

1. How does Burleson describe the scientific process in paragraph 4? Does he represent it accurately?

2. In paragraph 5, Burleson asks for proof that global warming exists. What could provide such proof?

3. What is Burleson's understanding of how climate change will work? Looking particularly at paragraph 7, describe his understanding of the forecasted changes.

In-Class Writing Activities

1. How would you answer the question Burleson poses at the end of paragraph 8? Do you think it is worth billions of dollars to make minor changes in the climate?

2. In paragraph 4 of his essay, Burleson discusses a report by the United Nations' Intergovernmental Panel for Climate Change.

Does he give readers enough information to judge the panel's conclusions? Write a paragraph about how Burleson judges the report and what you think of it. Is there anything more you would want to know before you make a decision?

BRETT SCHOEL

The Denial of Global Warming Is Just Politics

[CRIMSON WHITE, University of Alabama/February 16, 2007]

Before You Read
Which parties in the climate-change debate have the most invested? Which have the most power to change public perceptions?

Words to Learn
megalomaniacal (para. 1): related to an inflated belief in one's own importance (adj.)
invariably (para. 1): always; without exception (adv.)
nefarious (para. 5): ill-intentioned or villainous (adj.)

America's confusion about global warming is partly attributable   1
to the near-megalomaniacal self-confidence of our country's pundits,
who think they can sweep aside the issue's complexity and resolve
everything in a few inches of column space. I won't debate the facts
of global warming. However, I would like to offer rebuttal to a few
of the non-factual arguments in Josh Burleson's recent column.
Right-wing politicians and the business magnates who so generously
provide them with the "incentive" to make their case, not scientists,

---

*Brett Schoel is a senior at the University of Alabama, where he is pursu-
ing a degree in civil engineering. After reading another student editorial in the*
Crimson White, *he felt "compelled to write something" in response. Rather
than focus on "specific topical interests" in his work, Schoel is drawn to
writing about a variety of subjects for the opportunity "to communicate
ideas and emotions at the same time."*

have achieved the politicization of global warming. And invariably it is the theory's opponents whose arguments have a political angle.

Many pundits seem particularly engrossed by the idea of collu- 2 sion between scientists and environmentalists. Although I can appreciate the irony of conspiracy theories coming from politicians, it's a little sickening to know that these very "truth warriors" are deep in the pockets of ExxonMobil and friends. Burleson—whether intentionally or not—echoes these conspiracy claims when he writes that "anybody who has a desired result in mind before they begin a study will inevitably get that result." Aside from being incorrect (no, that is not inevitable), this statement assumes that climatologists want global warming to be shown true.

Why? What do they personally have to gain from the existence of 3 global warming? Are we supposed to believe that almost every single one of the world's climatologists chose their career as a means of proactive environmentalism? Or are we to suspect financial conspiracy? If so, consider that the bankroll of the energy industry far exceeds that of the environmentalist movement, which is mostly non-profit. Indeed, the oil industry's attempts to influence popular opinion on global warming are well documented. Moreover, knowing that scientific research is funded primarily by public grant money, and considering that the U.S. government, which has the world's largest funding capacity, has always been environmentally lax, it seems more likely that any political pressure is coming from an anti-warming position.

Burleson writes, "Currently there is as much proof against global 4 warming as there is for it." He means to say evidence, not proof. Proof refers to the validation of a statement by reducing it to, or constructing it from, certain elemental truths or axioms. Proof is only possible within a purely abstract logical framework, like mathematics. All science can provide is evidence. Anthropogenic global warming will never be a "proven fact," because climatology is statistical, not mathematical. Any discussion of "global climate" must involve averages, because climate varies geographically, and because the term itself is defined as the average weather conditions of a place over time. Making precise statements about the climate of even a small area is difficult.

The amount of global climatic data, and the number of factors 5 affecting it, precludes any definitive, irrefutable synopsis. Consequently, conclusions must follow "overwhelming consensus," which is the case with global warming (as well as evolution and quantum mechanics). Towards the end of his article, Burleson speaks of putting "restrictions on growth and development" as if it were one of the most foolish and nefarious things we could do. Restricting growth is necessary when you are living on a planet with a finite surface area and a finite amount of resources.

> *Restricting growth is necessary when you are living on a planet with a finite surface area and a finite amount of resources.*

The single-mindedness with which corporate America (which does form a recognizable power bloc with very real influence on our government, despite Burleson's attempt to de-legitimize the term with quotation marks) pursues profit, and ever-escalating "growth," would be clearly identified as obsession if seen in an individual. Word of advice: When your country holds five percent of the world's population and consumes 25 percent of its resources, expect other countries to ridicule you when you complain about "restricted growth." 6

Restriction on development follows naturally from the realization that every action has a consequence, which is probably the most fundamental scientific truth. And when that development is at the expense of the environment that supports the existence of the civilization supposedly benefiting from it, restriction is the only sane thing to do. 7

Vocabulary / Using a Dictionary

1. Look up the meaning of the verb *attribute*. What does it mean for Americans' confusion about global warming to be *attributable* to commentators (para. 1)?

2. What is the origin of the word *pundit* (para. 1)? What does it connote now?

3. What is the root of *magnate* (para. 1)? What kind of person does the word describe?

Responding to Words in Context

1. Why does School write that commentators are *engrossed* by the idea of scientists who are in league with environmentalists (para. 2)? What is the meaning of that word?

2. Why does Schoel think it is misguided to look for *irrefutable* evidence (para. 5)? What would it mean to *refute* evidence of warming?

3. In paragraph 6, Schoel uses the phrase *restricted growth*. Does he think a restriction on growth is necessary? How might the rest of the world react to those who complain about restricted growth?

Discussing Main Point and Meaning

1. How do Schoel's first and second paragraphs counter Burleson's argument?

2. How does Schoel use economic arguments to respond to Burleson's points? What financial reasons does he give?

3. Why does Schoel say that climate change can't be "proven" (para. 4)?

Examining Sentences, Paragraphs, and Organization

1. What is the purpose of the questions in paragraph 3? Whom are they aimed at?

2. In the first sentence in paragraph 6, Schoel includes a parenthetical comment about corporate America. Why does he include this, and why does he set it off in parentheses?

3. In what order does Schoel respond to Burleson's claims? Where does he place his most important points?

Thinking Critically

1. Why does Schoel challenge Burleson on his understanding of proof and evidence? Is this an effective argument?

2. Do you agree with Schoel's logic when he says that restrictions on growth follow "naturally" from an understanding of causation (para. 7)?

In-Class Writing Activities

1. Write an essay in which you enter into the debate between Burleson and Schoel. Like Schoel, you will probably want to quote from the pieces to which you are responding. Rather than

agreeing with one and disagreeing with the other, try to stake out your own position by finding points you would support and ideas you would challenge in each.

2. Schoel's essay begins with an apology for trying to tackle large issues in the format of a short newspaper column. Write a paragraph explaining why he sees this as a problem. Do you agree? If this isn't the proper forum for discussing global warming, then what is?

Discussing the Unit

Suggested Topic for Discussion

How does each of the authors in this unit portray public opinion? How is it formed, and how does it change? Is public opinion likely to be correct or incorrect? In the specific case of global warming, what ideas do these authors think are most widely held?

Preparing for Class Discussion

1. How do the authors in this unit use scientific language? When do they question it? Choose examples from several different essays to discuss.

2. The advertisement for the International Conference on Climate Change is the one paid message included in this unit. Discuss the difference between the ad and the editorials and feature stories that make up the rest of the unit. How does the medium change the way you read the text or evaluate the author?

From Discussion to Writing

1. Choose two essays from this unit that seem roughly similar in their overall opinions about global warming. Then write an essay in which you discuss their differences. You may find points on which they overtly disagree, but think also about how their focus is different and how the style and the medium of each piece distinguishes it from the other.

2. Although most of the essays in this unit give a central place to discussion of scientific findings, not one of them was written by

an actual scientist or someone with a background in climatology. Can you think of any reasons for this? Write a call for scientists to enter the debate. What would you like to hear from them? What could they clarify about the issue?

Topics for Cross-Cultural Discussion

1. If global warming occurs, which countries or regions will be hardest hit? Which will have the hardest time adapting to the changes?

2. In "Global Warming Is Colorblind," Jennifer Oladipo notes how the movement to combat climate change has largely ignored African Americans. Are there other groups generally excluded from the movement? What is the profile of a stereotypical environmental activist?

AMERICA THEN . . . 1985

The Warming of the World

In a famous short poem in 1920, Robert Frost wondered whether the earth would end in fire or ice—melted by overheating or turned completely into a frozen wasteland. At the time, it appeared that the future climate of the earth could go in either direction. Many dooms-day scenarios, in fact, pictured another ice age, with the earth becoming uninhabitable as glaciers expanded and rivers and seas froze over. In the mid-1970s, such predictions grew popular, and they found scientific support in 1981 when a prominent British astronomer, Sir Frederick Hoyle, published his forecast of a new ice age, Ice: The Ultimate Human Catastrophe.

But by this time, many scientists were also gathering evidence for an opposing worst-case scenario: The earth was seriously overheating

Astronomer Carl Sagan, 1981. Carl Sagan (1934–1996) was for years one of America's best-known scientists, largely because of such popular books as *The Dragons of Eden: Speculations on the Evolution of Human Intelligence* (1977), *Broca's Brain: Reflections on the Romance of Science* (1979), and the enormously successful TV series he hosted, *Cosmos.* Part of his popularity can be attributed to his respect for the general public he was writing for and speaking to. He once said, "The public is a lot brighter and more interested in science than they're given credit for. . . . They're not numbskulls. Thinking scientifically is as natural as breathing."   © Tony Korody/Sygma/Corbis.

as a result of what was called a "greenhouse effect." The crisis was man-made and attributable to the ever-increasing use of fossil fuels (coal, gas, and oil). In 1985, one of America's leading scientists and a prolific scientific writer, Carl Sagan, published a warning in the popular Sunday magazine Parade. *In "The Warming of the World," Sagan—like Hoyle, an astronomer—explained to his readers how fossil fuels produced dangerous levels of carbon dioxide (CO₂) that were "irreversible." "Once the CO₂ is in the atmosphere," Sagan wrote, "human technology is helpless to remove it. So the overall amount of CO₂ in the air has been growing—at least since the industrial revolution. If no other factors operate, and if enough CO₂ is put into the atmosphere, eventually the average surface temperature will increase perceptibly."*

One of the earliest proponents of global warming (a term that was first used in 1969), Sagan asks in his Parade *essay the key questions: "How long, at the present rates of burning wood and fossil fuels, before the global climate becomes significantly warmer? And what would the consequences be?" His answers to those questions— taken from the original 1985 essay—follow. Note that Sagan never sounds panic-stricken and appears generally optimistic that solutions will be found: "Fortunately, we have a little time," he writes.*

It is relatively simple to calculate the immediate warming from a given increase in the CO₂ abundance, and all competent calculations seem to be in good agreement. More difficult to estimate are (1) the rate at which carbon dioxide will continue to be put into the atmosphere (it depends on population growth rates, economic styles, alternative energy sources and the like) and (2) feedbacks—ways in which a slight warming might produce other, more drastic, effects.   1

The recent increase in atmospheric CO₂ is well documented. Over the last century, this CO₂ buildup should have resulted in a few tenths of a degree of global warming, and there is some evidence that such a warming has occurred.   2

The National Academy of Sciences estimates that the present atmospheric abundance of CO₂ is likely to double by the year 2065, although experts at the academy predict a 1-in-20 chance that it will double before 2035—when an infant born today becomes 50 years old. Such a doubling would warm the air near the surface of the Earth by 2°C or 3°C—maybe by as much as 4°C. These are average temperature values; there would naturally be considerable local variation.   3

High latitudes would be warmed much more, although a baked Alaska will be some time coming.

There would be precipitation changes. The annual discharge of rivers would be altered. Some scientists believe that central North America—including much of the area that is now the breadbasket of the world—would be parched in summer if the global temperature increases by a few degrees. There would be some mitigating effects; for example, where plant growth is not otherwise limited, more CO_2 should aid photosynthesis and make more luxuriant growth (of weeds as well as crops). If the present CO_2 injection into the atmosphere continued over a few centuries, the warming would be greater than from all other causes over the last 100,000 years.

As the climate warms, glacial ice melts. Over the last 100 years, the level of the world's oceans has risen by 15 centimeters (6 inches). A global warming of 3°C or 4°C over the next century is likely to bring a further rise in the average sea level of about 70 centimeters (28 inches). An increase of this magnitude could produce major damage to ports all over the world and induce fundamental changes in the patterns of land development. A serious speculation is that greenhouse temperature increases of 3°C or 4°C could, in addition, trigger the disintegration of the West Antarctic Ice Sheet, with huge quantities of polar ice falling into the ocean. This would raise sea level by some 6 meters (20 feet) over a period of centuries, with the eventual inundation of all coastal cities on the planet.

There are many other possibilities that are poorly understood, including the release of other greenhouse gases (for example, methane from peat bogs) accelerated by the warming climate. The circulation of the oceans might be an important aspect of the problem. The scientific community is attempting to make an environmental-impact statement for the entire planet on the consequences of continued burning of fossil fuels. Despite the uncertainties, a kind of consensus is in: Over the next century or more, with projected rates of burning of coal, oil and gas, there is trouble ahead.

The problem is difficult for at least three different reasons:

(1) We do not yet fully understand how severe the greenhouse consequences will be.

(2) Although the effects are not yet strikingly noticeable in everyday life, to deal with the problem, the present generation might have to make sacrifices for the next.

(3) The problem cannot be solved except on an international scale: The atmosphere is ignorant of national boundaries. South African carbon dioxide warms Taiwan, and Soviet coal-burning practices affect productivity in America. The largest coal resources in the world are found in the Soviet Union, the United States and China, in that order. What incentives are there for a nation such as China, with vast coal reserves and a commitment to rapid economic development, to hold back on the burning of fossil fuels because the result might, decades later, be a parched American sunbelt or still more ghastly starvation in sub-Saharan Africa? Would countries that might benefit from a warmer climate be as vigorous in restraining the burning of fossil fuels as nations likely to suffer greatly?

Fortunately, we have a little time. A great deal can be done in decades. Some argue that government subsidies lower the price of fossil fuels, inviting waste; more efficient usage, besides its economic advantage, could greatly ameliorate the CO_2 greenhouse problem. Parts of the solution might involve alternative energy sources, where appropriate: solar power, for example, or safer nuclear fission reactors, which, whatever their other dangers, produce no greenhouse gases of importance. Conceivably, the long-awaited advent of commercial nuclear fusion power might happen before the middle of the next century.   8

However, any technological solution to the looming greenhouse problem must be worldwide. It would not be sufficient for the United States or the Soviet Union, say, to develop safe and commercially feasible fusion power plants: That technology would have to be diffused worldwide, on terms of cost and reliability that would be more attractive to developing nations than a reliance on fossil fuel reserves or imports. A serious, very high-level look at patterns of U.S. and world energy development in light of the greenhouse problem seems overdue.   9

During the last few million years, human technology, spurred in part by climatic change, has made our species a force to be reckoned with on a planetary scale. We now find, to our astonishment, that we pose a danger to ourselves. The present world order is, unfortunately, not designed to deal with global-scale dangers. Nations tend to be concerned about themselves, not about the planet; they tend to have short-term rather than long-term objectives. In problems such as the   10 increasing greenhouse effect, one nation or region might benefit while another suffers. In other global environmental issues, such as nuclear war, all nations lose. The problems are connected: Constructive international efforts to understand and resolve one will benefit the others.

Further study and better public understanding are needed, of course. But what is essential is a global consciousness—a view that transcends our exclusive identification with the generational and political groupings into which, by accident, we have been born. The solution to these problems requires a perspective that embraces the planet and the future. We are all in this greenhouse together.

11

Information for Subscription

Periodicals and Other Media

American Prospect (prospect.org): biweekly. A liberal magazine on politics, culture, and policy. Subscription address: The American Prospect, P.O. Box 601, Mt. Morris, IL 61054-7531; or call (888) 687-8732.

Bitch (bitchmagazine.org): quarterly. A nonprofit, independent, feminist magazine on media culture and analysis. Subscription address: Bitch, P.O. Box 397, Oregon, IL 61061-9917; or call (877) 21-BITCH.

The Boston Globe (boston.com/bostonglobe): daily. General newspaper covering local, national, and international news, business, sports, and arts for Boston, Massachusetts. Subscription address: Boston Globe, P.O. Box 55819, Boston, MA 02205-5819; call (888) MY-GLOBE or (617) 929-2226 if calling from out-of-state.

The Chronicle of Higher Education (chronicle.com): weekly. A news and career-information source for college and university faculty, administrators, and students. Subscription address: Circulation Department, The Chronicle of Higher Education, 1255 23rd Street, NW, Washington, DC 20037; e-mail circulation@chronicle.com; or call (800) 728-2803.

Desert Exposure (desertexposure.com): monthly. Southwest New Mexico local magazine. Subscription address: Desert Exposure, P.O. Box 191, Silver City, NM 88062; or call (505) 538-4374.

Harper's Bazaar (harpersbazaar.com): monthly. Fashion and beauty articles. Subscription address: Harper's Bazaar, P.O. Box 7178, Red Oak, IA 51591-0162; or call (800) 888-3045.

n+1 (nplusonemag.com): biyearly. Print journal featuring politics, literature, and culture. Subscription address: The Editors, 68 Jay Street, #405, Brooklyn, NY 11201; or e-mail subs@nplusonemag.com.

The Nation (thenation.com): weekly. Critical opinions about politics and culture. Subscription address: The Nation, 33 Irving Place, New York, NY 10003; or call (800) 333-8536.

National Geographic (nationalgeographic.com): monthly. Photo features on history, geography, and current events. Subscription address: National Geographic Society, P.O. Box 98199, Washington, DC 20090-8199; or call (800) 647-5463.

National Public Radio (npr.org): daily. Noncommercial radio news, talk, and entertainment. Mailing address: NPR, 635 Massachusetts Avenue, NW, Washington, DC 20001; or call (202) 513-3232.

The New York Times (nytimes.com): daily. Definitive source for national and international news, business, and arts reporting; includes the weekly *New York Times Magazine* on Sunday. Subscription address: The New York Times, 229 West 43rd Street, New York, NY 10036; e-mail circulation@nytimes.com; or call (800) NYTIMES.

Open City (opencity.org): three issues yearly. Journal of poetry and prose. Subscription address: Open City, Inc., 270 Lafayette Street, Suite 1412, New York, NY 10012; or e-mail orders@ opencity.org.

Orion (orionmagazine.org): bimonthly. Features and commentary with an awareness of ecological and social issues. Subscription address: The Orion Society, 187 Mail Street, Great Barrington, MA 01230; or call (800) 254-3713.

The Progressive (progressive.org): monthly. Politics and culture with a pronounced progressive perspective. Subscription address: The Progressive, 409 East Main Street, Madison, WI 53703; e-mail infoprgs@progressive.org; or call (800) 827-0555.

Science (sciencemag.org): weekly. Scientific research, analysis, news, and commentary. Subscription address: AAAS, P.O. Box 96178, Washington, DC 20090-6178; e-mail scienceonline@aaas.org; or call (866) 434-2227.

Tikkun (tikkun.org/magazine): bimonthly. A Jewish magazine on politics, culture, and society. Subscription address: Tikkun Magazine, 2342 Shattuck Avenue, #1200, Berkeley, CA 94704; e-mail magazine@tikkun.org; or call (510) 644-1200.

Townhall.com: online source. Conservative political commentary, analysis, and activism from 120 contributing sources. Subscription address: Townhall.com, 1901 North Moore Street, Suite 205, Arlington, VA 22209; e-mail info@townhall.com; or call (703) 294-6046.

The Utne Reader (utne.com): bimonthly. Independent and alternative writing on politics, art, media, and culture. Subscription address:

Utne Reader, Editorial and Management Offices, 12 North 12th Street, Suite 400, Minneapolis, MN 55403; or call (612) 338-5040.

Vogue (vogue.com): monthly. Fashion and lifestyle magazine. Subscription address: Vogue, P.O. Box 37686, Boone, IA 50037-0686; e-mail VOGcustserv@cdsfulfillment.com; or call (800) 234-2347.

The Washington Post (washingtonpost.com): daily. National newspaper featuring national and international news, politics, business, sports, and arts. Subscription address: The Washington Post, P.O. Box 17370, Arlington, VA 22216; or call (800) 627-1150.

The Week (theweekdaily.com): weekly. International news, media, and arts. Subscription address: The Week, P.O. Box 420235, Palm Coast, FL 32142; or call (386) 447-6312.

Wilson Quarterly (wilsoncenter.org): quarterly. Independent, scholarly features about politics, religion, science, and culture. Subscription address: Subscriber Service, Wilson Quarterly, P.O. Box 4204406, Palm Coast, FL 32142; or call (800) 829-5108.

Wired (wired.com): monthly. Technology news, culture, and politics. Subscription address: Wired, P.O. Box 37705, Boone, IA 50037-0705; e-mail wircustserv@cdsfulfillment.com; or call (800) 769-4733.

Student Sources

The Alligator, University of Florida (alligator.org): daily. Independent student newspaper featuring extensive sports and entertainment sections.

The Bridge, Bridgewater State College (bridgenewspaper.net): monthly. Student publication emphasizing news and cultural pieces of interest to Bridgewater State students and Bridgewater, Massachusetts residents.

Crimson White, University of Alabama (cw.ua.edu): weekly. News, sports, and entertainment serving the University of Alabama and the Tuscaloosa city area.

The Daily Bruin, University of California, Los Angeles (dailybruin.ucla.edu): daily. Covers daily events, sports, and the arts, both on campus and for the surrounding Los Angeles area.

Daily Mississippian, University of Mississippi (thedmonline.com): daily. One of the larger college newspapers in the country, covering university news, sports, and entertainment.

The Daily of the University of Washington, University of Washington (thedaily.washington.edu): daily. International, national, local, and collegiate news, sports, and entertainment in the Seattle area.

Daily Texan, University of Texas at Austin (dailytexanonline.com): daily. One of the oldest and largest independent student newspapers in the country, featuring expansive coverage of international, domestic, and local news.

The Diamondback, University of Maryland (diamondbackonline.com): daily. Independent, student-run publication with an emphasis on campus issues and local news in College Park and Annapolis, Maryland.

The Echo, University of Central Arkansas (ucaecho.net): weekly. University and domestic news and sports.

The Johns Hopkins News-Letter, Johns Hopkins University (jhunewsletter.com): weekly. Campus news and events for Johns Hopkins University and Baltimore, Maryland.

The Lantern, Ohio State University (thelantern.com): daily. Third-largest student-run newspaper in the country, highlighting on-campus news, sports, and entertainment, as well as local events in Columbus, Ohio.

Oregon Daily Emerald, University of Oregon (dailyemerald.com): daily. Independent student newspaper reporting on campus activity and sports, as well as news and entertainment from Eugene, Oregon.

The State Press, Arizona State University (asuwebdevil.com): daily. University, world, and domestic news.

The University Daily Kansan, University of Kansas (kansan.com): daily. Student newspaper addressing on-campus news and sports, as well as issues facing local areas in Lawrence, Kansas.

Vanguard, University of South Alabama (usavanguard.com): weekly. Student-run publication highlighting on-campus issues; events in Mobile, Alabama, and human-interest pieces affecting the collegiate population.

Acknowledgments

Ad Council (advertisement). "Lose Your Love Handles." Courtesy of the Ad Council. Reprinted by permission.

American Civil Liberties Union (advertisement). "The Man on the Left Is 75 Times More Likely to Be Stopped by the Police While Driving Than the Man on the Right." Reprinted by permission of the ACLU and DeVito/Verdi.

Greg Atwan and Evan Lushing (chart). "When You Can Break up with Your Girlfriend via Facebook Message." Copyright © 2008 by Greg Atwan and Evan Lushing. Published by Harry N. Abrams, Inc., New York. All Rights Reserved.

Peter Bagge (comic). "Bums." Copyright © 2007 Peter Bagge. Reprinted by permission of Reason Foundation.

Diane Cook and Len Jenshel (photo). "Tijuana, Mexico." Copyright © Diane Cook and Len Jenshel.

Bettman/Corbis (photographs). "Black Students Integrate Little Rock's Central High School" and "Women Suffrage Parade Supporting Wilson." Copyright © Bettmann/CORBIS. Reprinted with permission.

Charles Bowden. "Our Wall." *The National Geographic Magazine*, May 2007. Copyright © 2007. Reprinted by permission of The National Geographic Society.

Josh Burleson. "When Politics Meets Science." *The Crimson White*, University of Alabama, February 9, 2007. Copyright © 2007 The Crimson White. Reprinted by permission of the author.

Lauren Carter. "Isn't Watermelon Delicious?" *The Bridge*, Bridgewater State College, Volume 2, Spring 2005. Copyright © 2005 Lauren Carter. Reprinted by permission of the author.

Jessica Chou. "Undocumented: One Student's Story." *The Daily Bruin*, UCLA, February 21, 2008. Copyright © 2008. Reprinted by permission of the ASUCLA Student Media and the author.

Kenneth Cole (advertisement). "We All Walk in Different Shoes." Courtesy of Kenneth Cole Productions and Aimee Mullins. Reprinted by permission.

Alan Diaz (photograph). "Armed Federal Agents Seize Elian Gonzalez" by Alan Diaz appears by permission of Alan Diaz/AP/Wide World Photos.

Jeff Dickson. "United We Strive, Divided We Falter." *The Daily of the University of Washington*, April 2, 2008. Copyright © 2008. Reprinted by permission of the author.

Sandy Dover. "How Do You Define You?" *The Lantern*, Ohio State University, January 10, 2007. Copyright © 2007 The Lantern at Ohio State University. Reprinted by permission of the author.

Chelsea Durbin. "Fast Food Is Fat Food." *The University Daily Kansan*, The University of Kansas. November 12, 2007. Copyright © 2007. Reprinted by permission of the author.

Barbara Ehrenreich. "Slaves for Fashion." *The Progressive*. January 1, 2008. Copyright © 2008 by Barbara Ehrenreich. Reprinted by permission from *The Progressive*, 409 E. Main St., Madison, WI 53703. www.progressive.org.

Thomas E. Franklin (photograph.) "Three Firefighters Raising the Flag." Copyright © 2004 Getty Images. Photo by Thomas E. Franklin/The Bergen Record/Getty Images.

Melissa Mapes. "Is Big Brother Watching Your Every Move?" *Arizona State University Web Devil*, February 28, 2008. Copyright © 2008. Reprinted by permission of the Arizona State University Web Devil and the author.

Doug Marlette (cartoon). "That Does It—Tell Iran This Will Be Their Last Warning!" Published September 25, 2006. Copyright 2006. Reprinted by permission of Doug Marlette. www.dougmarlette.com

Bill McKibben. "Let's Act Together on Global Warming." *Tikkun*, November/December 2007. Copyright © 2007 by Bill McKibben. Reprinted by permission of Bill McKibben and the Watkins/Loomis Agency.

Matthais R. Mehl, Simine Vazire, Nairan Ramirez-Esparza, Richard Slatcher, James Pennebaker. "Are Women Really More Talkative Than Men?" *Science, 317:82,* July 6, 2007. Copyright © 2007. Reprinted by permission of the American Association of the Advancement of Science.

Ari Melber. "About Facebook." Reprinted with permission from the January 7, 2008 issue of *The Nation*. For subscription information, call 1-800-333-8536. Portions of each week's *Nation* magazine can be accessed at http://www.thenation.com.

Dinaw Mengestu. "Home at Last." Originally published in *Brooklyn Was Mine*, edited by Chris Knutsen and Valerie Steiker, Riverhead Books, 2008. Copyright © 2008 Dinaw Mengestu. Reprinted by permission of McCormick & Williams Literary, as agents for the author.

Manuel Muñoz. "Leave Your Name at the Border." Copyright © 2007 by Manuel Muñoz. First published in *The New York Times*, August 1, 2007. Reprinted by permission of Stuart Bernstein Representation for Artists, New York, on behalf of the author. All rights reserved.

Robert Nathan and Jo-Ann Mort. "Remembering Norma Rae." Reprinted with permission from the March 12, 2007 issue of *The Nation*. For subscription information, call 1-800-333-8536. Portions of each week's Nation magazine can be accessed at http://www.thenation.com.

Jennifer Oladipo. "Global Warming Is Colorblind: Can We Say as Much for Environmentalism?" Originally published in *Orion* magazine, November/December 2007. Copyright © 2007 Jennifer Oladipo. Reprinted by permission of the author.

Courtney Pomeroy. "The Ethics of What We Wear: Can We Dress Fashionably and Responsibly?" *The Diamondback*, University of Maryland, December 5, 2007. Copyright © 2007 The Diamondback. Reprinted by permission of the author.

Medicine and Madison Avenue On-Line Project (advertisement). "Reduce Easy as ABC! The Same Simple Way the Stars Use to Reduce!" Reprinted courtesy of Medicine and Madison Avenue On-Line Project – Ad #MM0764, John W. Hartman Center for Sales, Advertising & Marketing History, Rare Book, Manuscript, and Special Collections Library, Duke University, Durham, North Carolina. http://library.duke.edu/digitalcollections/mma/ (6/2/2008).

Robert Reece. "Class Struggle Is Race Struggle." *The Daily Mississippian*, University of Mississippi, February 28, 2008. Copyright © 2008 Robert Reece. Reprinted by permission of the author.

Jacob Riis (photograph). "Homeless Boys," (titled "Street Arabs in Their Sleeping Quarters, circa 1890"). Copyright © Museum of the City of New York/Jacob A. Riis Collection (image 121).

Joe Rosenthal (photograph). "Flag Raising at Iwo Jima, February 23, 1945" by Joe Rosenthal appears by permission of Joe Rosenthal/AP/Wide World Photos.

Bryan Welch. "Putting a Stop to Slave Labor." Reprinted with permission from *Utne Reader*, March/April 2007. www.utne.com. Copyright © 2007 Ogden Publications, Inc.

Amy Widner. "The Pursuit of Just Getting By." *The Echo*, University of Central Arkansas, March 12, 2008. Copyright © 2008 The Echo. Reprinted by permission of the author.

Andrew Yates/AFPO/Getty Images (photograph). "Oscar Pistorius Competing at the Paralympic World Cup." By permission of Andrew Yates/AFPO/Getty Images.

Jack Ziegler (cartoon). "Crude Oil from Stem Cells." Copyright © The New Yorker Collection 2006, Jack Ziegler from cartoonbank.com. All Rights Reserved.

Index of Authors and Titles

From Discussion to Writing
Instructional Resources for Teaching

EIGHTH EDITION

America Now

Short Readings

from Recent Periodicals

Robert Atwan

Prepared by
Valerie Duff-Strautmann
Jeffrey Ousborne
Stefanie Wortman

4 3 2 1 0 9
f e d c b a

For information, write: Bedford/St. Martin's, 75 Arlington Street, Boston, MA 02116 (617-399-4000)

ISBN-10: 0–312–48696–0
ISBN-13: 978–0–312–48696–9

Contents

Preface

Using America Now *in Developmental and Composition Classes*

With its strong focus on current issues and its thought-provoking assignments, *America Now* is ideal for both developmental and composition classes. Many of the questions and writing assignments in the book will give students the practice they need to pass basic skills examinations. At the same time, these questions allow students to work within a real context, and all levels of writing classes might use them to practice writing skills, promote discussion, and prepare for take-home essay assignments. Though some questions and writing assignments in the book ask students to focus on just one selection, others require them to synthesize varying opinions and to come to their own conclusions about an issue, drawing on readings and their own observations for support. These more complex assignments might be more appropriate for composition classes or the latter part of developmental classes.

Because *America Now* presents readings on some of today's most important issues and provides all the help students need to understand, discuss, and write on the topics presented, it actively engages the interest of students from a range of courses and skill levels. This book is an excellent choice for developmental students, who need to know more than just where to put a comma or how to handle verb tenses. They need to read critically, to make connections among an author's various points, and to juxtapose these points with those of other authors. They also need to be able to engage in thoughtful classroom discussion and to express and support their own opinions in their writing. Most students can meet these challenges, and instructors report that developmental students effectively analyze texts far more complex than those found in many readers. Their students often say that they can think, but they need advice on how to write in a way that is accepted in academia. Often such students write best when they are asked to discuss topics meaningful to them, and *America Now* and this manual provide contexts for such meaningful expression.

Using This Instructor's Manual

The comments and suggestions that follow invite you to use the eighth edition of *America Now* to expand your students' reading and writing abilities. Each writing class is unique, and labels often do not adequately characterize the abilities, interests, and perspectives of a particular group of students. Therefore, the questions and activities in *America Now* and the suggestions provided here include a variety of options that may be adapted for students with a wide range of reading and writing experiences. We invite you to choose those that best suit your classes, those that best fit your particular teaching style, and those that work best within the curriculum for the specific course you are teaching. We hope that these materials will encourage students to read and write more thoughtfully and critically, challenge them to think about reading and writing in increasingly sophisticated ways, and make planning and organizing classroom activities more manageable for instructors.

This manual is organized to parallel the structure of the student edition of *America Now*. Each chapter begins with a brief introduction to the themes and selections offered in that chapter. Following the introductory material are suggested answers to questions in the text. These suggested answers correspond to the question sets that follow each selection in the student edition — Vocabulary/Using a Dictionary; Responding to Words in Context; Discussing Main Point and Meaning; Examining Sentences, Paragraphs, and Organization; Thinking Critically; In-Class Writing Activities — and those that follow each chapter: Preparing for Class Discussion; From Discussion to Writing; and Topics for Cross-Cultural Discussion. These suggested answers are meant to anticipate possible student responses, to raise further questions for discussion and writing, and to help you better use *America Now* as a tool for classroom discussion and more effective student writing.

Obviously, few classes will be able to read and work with all of the selections in the text in one semester. You may want to focus on thematic groupings of units, or you may prefer to select units that are of particular interest to your students. Some instructors may allow students to choose selections; others will be more comfortable making these selections or taking turns with the class. As an alternative approach, you might ask a group of students to select a unit for the class to read; then the group of students in charge would be responsible for the discussion and the activities in which the class participates.

However you use this manual, we hope that it will help you and your students use the text fully and thoughtfully, think critically about the issues and readings, and consider how these readings fit within the larger context that is America now.

Introduction:
Writing and the Art of Discussion
by Robert Atwan

I enter into discussion and argument with great freedom and ease, inasmuch as opinion finds in me a bad soil to penetrate and take deep roots in. No propositions astonish me, no belief offends me, whatever contrast it offers with my own. There is no fancy so frivolous and so extravagant that it does not seem to me quite suitable to the production of the human mind.

—Michel de Montaigne,
Of the Art of Discussion (1588)

However unwillingly a person who has a strong opinion may admit the possibility that his opinion may be false, he ought to be moved by the consideration that, however true it may be, if it is not fully, frequently, and fearlessly discussed, it will be held as a dead dogma, not a living truth.

—John Stuart Mill,
Of the Liberty of Thought and Discussion (1869)

Students often begin their college writing courses with a popular misconception. They think that writing is an isolating activity demanding extraordinary inner resources. They picture writers as sitting alone at their desks or computers anxiously staring at a blank page or screen until inspiration strikes. Indeed, this romanticized image of anxious solitude followed by a burst of creativity has for centuries served as a powerful model of how literature is produced. But for the average student, who has little understanding of how real writers work and has perhaps never observed people writing professionally, this popular image can lead to a distorted view of writing and the role writing plays in a person's intellectual development.

Most writers work within a lively social context, one in which issues and ideas are routinely discussed and debated. They often begin writing on topics that derive directly from specific professional situations: a journalist covers a murder trial; a professor prepares a paper for a conference; a social worker writes up a case study; an executive reports on a business meeting. Usually, the writer consults with friends and coworkers about the task and solicits their opinions and support, sometimes even asking them to comment on a draft of the work. If the work is to be published, the writer almost always receives additional advice and criticism in the form of editorial comment, copyediting, proofreading, and independent reviews. By the time the work appears, it has probably gone through numerous drafts (for some writers as many as ten or twelve) and has been subjected to a rigorous sequence of editorial support, from fact checking to stylistic fine tuning.

Nearly all the published work a student reads, with the possible exception of work published on the Internet, has gone through this process. Even the most ephemeral article in a magazine has probably been revised several times by several people before publication. But, of course, none of this is visible in the final product. Students have little knowledge of all the various levels of work and collaboration that have gone into a piece of writing—the author's often extensive reading and research; the time spent traveling, interviewing, and discussing; the organization of the information; the composing of several drafts; and the concerted effort of editors and publishers. Unlike a film, a piece of writing shows only the author's name and seldom everyone else who helped make the published work possible (though some books include an acknowledgments page).

The point about student writing should be clear: Students write in a much narrower professional environment than do experienced people whose writing is a significant part of their work. Too often, the student writes in an intellectual vacuum. He or she may feel only minimally engaged by an assigned topic—which may seem to have come out of nowhere—and may not know anyone with whom the topic may be seriously and intelligently discussed. Unlike the professional writer, the student usually sits down alone and tries to write with little intellectual provocation or encouragement. No wonder students find it so hard to begin a paper. Instead of knowing they are writing for a group of interested people, they often feel that their writing will be read by only one other person—the instructor, who will read it not for further discussion but for immediate evaluation.

America Now is designed to help writing students avoid the intellectual and emotional vacuum that confronts them when they begin to write. Two of the biggest problems in composition, finding something to say and getting started, are in large part due to the student's lack of a vital connection with what other people have to say about an issue or idea. The basis of many student writing problems, I believe, is not so much grammatical or rhetorical as social. At their worst, these problems are clearly reflected in the writing, in a disjunctive prose that sounds oddly cut off from most public discourse.

The art of writing and the art of discussion are closely linked. Experienced writers invariably write in a climate of discussion. Their writing is usually embedded in a context of others' ideas and opinions. Many writers, especially in the academic community, are directly responding to other writers—a scientist reexamining the experimental procedures of other scientists; a literary critic taking exception to a prevailing method of interpretation; a sociologist offering an alternative explanation of a colleague's data; a historian participating as a respondent at a conference. Such people are not writing in a vacuum. Their ideas often originate in discussion, their writing is a response to discussion, and their papers are designed to stimulate further discussion.

The Art of Discussion

Discussion is one of those commonly used words from speech and rhetoric — like *essay* and *style* — that remains difficult to define precisely. The word has a long and complex history. It derives from a Latin verb (*discutere*) meaning "to dash, scatter, or shake out," and it gradually came to take on the legal and, later, the rhetorical sense of "breaking" a case or a topic down into its various parts for investigation. Though the word is ordinarily used today to mean "to talk over" or "to consider carefully," it still retains a rhetorical sense of sifting a topic into separate parts for close examination.

It is easier to say what discussion is not: It is neither conversation nor debate. Unlike conversation, discussion is purposefully conducted around a given topic. Unlike debate, it is not formally organized into two competing points of view. Think of discussion as a speech activity that falls between the informalities of conversation and the formalities of debate. For the purpose of this book, discussion is defined as the free and open exploration of a specified topic by a small group of prepared people. The goal of such discussion is not to arrive at a group decision or a consensus, but to investigate as many sides of a topic as possible.

To keep discussion from rigidifying into a debate between two competing sides or from drifting into aimless conversation, a discussion leader or moderator is usually required. The discussion leader may adopt an active role in the discussion or may choose to remain neutral. But regardless of the extent of the leader's role, he or she will ordinarily introduce the topic, encourage participation, maintain an orderly sequence of responses, and ensure that the group sticks to the topic. With its regularly scheduled sessions, its diversified members, and its academic purpose, the typical college composition class of fifteen to twenty-five students makes an ideal discussion group.

It should be noted that there are many different kinds of discussion groups and techniques. Instructors who would like to read more about various discussion groups and methods may want to consult such standard texts as Ernest G. Bormann's *Discussion and Group Methods* or Mary A. Bany and Lois V. Johnson's *Classroom Group Behavior: Group Dynamics in Education*. These and similar texts on discussion can usually be found in the education and psychology sections of most college libraries.

Like writing, discussion is a learned activity. To be adept at group discussion requires the development of a variety of skills — in speaking, listening, thinking, and reading. By encouraging students to participate in group discussion, you can help them become more intellectually mature and better prepared for professional careers. Since participation in group discussion is almost always voluntary, your students can improve their discussion abilities by observing a few ground rules. They should (1) be willing to speak in public, (2) be willing to listen, (3) be willing to examine all sides of a topic, (4) be willing to suspend judgment, and (5) be willing to prepare. These rules are explained further in the introduction for students, "The Persuasive Writer," on page 1 of *America Now*.

Generating Classroom Discussion

Many college teachers in the liberal arts feel that a particular class has gone well when they've been able to generate discussion. This is not surprising. Lively class discussion surely indicates a healthy level of student interest in the course; it also minimizes the burden and monotony of classroom lecturing. I find that even teachers who conduct large lecture courses are pleased when students ask questions and raise relevant points. Anyone who has ever given a public lecture knows how awkward it can be when the moderator invites questions and no hands are raised. Many people instinctively measure the success of a lecture or talk by the number of questions from the audience.

Yet my talks with college instructors in many disciplines indicate that, though they invite class discussion, they don't expect to generate much. "These kids have nothing to say. They just sit there," a professor complained of his introductory European history course. "I do get some students to discuss the reading," a literature teacher told me, "but it's always the same two or three talking every class. The rest are silent." "At the end of class," a writing teacher remarked, "I'll ask, 'Does anyone have any questions about the assignment?' No hands. As I dismiss class and prepare to leave, I notice five or six students gathered around my desk. Each one has a question about the assignment." These experiences, it appears, are quite typical.

Every year hundreds of thousands of college students walk into classrooms throughout America with little knowledge of how to participate in intelligent, informed discussion. One can only speculate about why this is so, but there are clearly several contributing factors: the average student's native shyness and lack of training in extemporaneous speech; an overreliance on lecturing in classrooms; the dismal models of discussion found in the media, especially on radio and television talk shows; and the decline of family conversation as people have less leisure time and as family life grows more fragmented.

One important obstacle to discussion has grown directly out of a seriously misguided educational trend. As schools concentrate more and more on the mastery of isolated and "testable" skills, they leave less and less room in the curriculum for the tentative and exploratory discussion of complex topics. This trend can easily be seen in the growing importance of college and graduate school entrance examinations, which reduce all educational achievement to the "question-answer" level. Such educational instruments not only eliminate discussion and exploration entirely; they foster a mental attitude that is directly opposed to the free and open discussion of ideas: Their rigid format implies that for every question there is always one and only one correct answer.

All of these factors add up to silent college classrooms. In composition courses, lack of discussion can be especially counterproductive to education, since most writing instructors expect their classes to respond to reading assignments and participate in workshop sessions. Few college courses, in fact, are more dependent on class discussion than first-year composition. This often puts a special strain on the instructor, who, in addition to handling a semester's worth of writing assignments, must normally engineer ways to stimulate the discussion of each class's reading material. In more than twenty years of speaking with writing teachers about their teaching, I've noticed how frequently they define a "good class" as one in which the students talk.

The eighth edition of *America Now*, like its predecessors, is specifically designed to get students talking in class. The apparatus following each unit makes it clear to students that the readings are *meant* to be discussed. More important, it gives them questions to consider and small preparatory writing tasks that will help you get class discussion started. The material in this manual is directly linked to the student exercises in the book. The possible "answers" provided here are intended to anticipate student responses to the questions following the selections, and to provide some suggestions for using *America Now* in your course. We hope they will also offer you several ideas for building on what students have prepared and for moving the class discussion of the topic toward the writing assignment.

The book and manual are so directed toward improving class discussion that I'd like to offer a few practical suggestions for generating discussion and using it as a basis for writing. These suggestions are based on the trial and error of my own experience, and on the observations of other instructors and their reports. But because class discussion is so often spontaneous and unpredictable — and is rarely the subject of systematic educational inquiry — I'd like to remind instructors that these suggestions are largely the result of impressions (mine and others') of what works and what doesn't in a classroom. I hope that this book and manual will stimulate the further study of discussion techniques in the field of composition.

Here are a few suggestions designed to generate class discussion and direct it toward the primary goal of the course — student writing:

1. *Emphasize the Importance of Discussion.* Inform students from the start of the course that class discussion is an essential ingredient of the program and that you will be counting on full participation. Remind students that both speaking well and writing well are important factors in anyone's career (it is difficult to think of any profession in which participating in discussion meetings is not essential). Remind students, too, that discussion is neither systematic debate nor aimless conversation but is the free and open exploration of an agreed-upon topic. Since most students are naturally shy, the exploratory nature of class discussion should be emphasized: Questions should be freely asked and points raised without anyone being made to feel stupid.

2. *Create a Climate of Discussion.* Free and open discussion cannot exist in a tense or anxious atmosphere. From the start, therefore, try to know who your students are (learn their names as quickly as possible) and help them become familiar with each other. You might ask your students to stand up and introduce themselves one by one to the entire class and to say something about themselves (where they're from; their major; what they want to be, and so on). This procedure helps break the ice and gets students talking in class. Remember: Productive classroom discussion is not a matter of students talking only to their instructor; they must also talk to each other.

You may have students suggest questions that they believe would make an interesting interview—what they would like to know about a person. Then divide the class into pairs and have students use those questions as a framework for interviews with each other. The students should write down each other's responses (if a class doesn't pair off evenly, a student can do two interviews or two students can handle one). This interview is then read by the interviewer as a way to introduce the other student. Clearly, this method takes the burden off individuals who would feel shy about introducing themselves in front of the class; it also gets the students writing as they learn about each other.

To create a relaxed atmosphere for discussion, it is important to avoid an overbearing manner or a sarcastic tone. Many students are dreadfully afraid of appearing stupid in front of their peers, and an adversarial or sarcastic style of teaching—though it may appeal to a few "knowing" students—may easily lead diffident students to retreat into the safety of silence. A teacher who wants to maintain a lively atmosphere of discussion will also need at times to restrain the sarcasm of the other students toward irrelevant or "stupid" comments. This is easily done by reminding everyone of the exploratory nature of this discussion and the ground rule that no one need be afraid to say anything. I've found that many disarmingly blunt comments or "off-the-wall" questions that I tended to dismiss proved later to be quite good. Questions that sounded ill-informed were merely ill-formed. Many students have not yet learned the art of posing questions, and everything possible should be done to encourage them to do so.

3. *Beware of the Socratic Method.* So many instructors were themselves taught by this method that they often resort to it instinctively in their classrooms. If conducted in the proper dialogic spirit, the method is, of course, a superb tool for both instilling knowledge and creating intellectual drama. But too often it becomes a question-and-answer game in which instructors ask a series of questions for which they possess definite answers. Often, these questions are posed as though the instructor didn't know the answer, but it becomes evident as answer after answer is rejected that this is a pretense of inquiry, that the process is simply leading to the answer the instructor wants. The apparent inquiry is merely a disguised lecture. Students see through this game quickly. Many are put off by it and refuse to play; a few others, adept at reading the instructor's mind, soon become the class's dominant participants. One of the dangers of this type of Socratic method is that it leads to classes in which discussion is limited to the instructor and several "star" pupils.

Quite clearly, some question-and-answer procedures are necessary to generate and direct discussion. But instructors are encouraged to expand class participation by asking more open-ended questions that invite a variety of "right" answers. The topics and instructional apparatus of *America Now* contain many questions designed to elicit more than one answer.

4. *Set Up Collaborative Tasks and Small-Group Activities.* People like to work together—consider how many composition texts are coauthored and coedited. A good way to broaden class participation is to get students working together in small groups. Most composition classes have from fifteen to

twenty-five students. Though groups of this size can accommodate lively general discussion, it is sometimes useful to divide the class into several subgroups (preferably four to five per group) to work on specific tasks. These smaller groups can work together to brainstorm ideas, to consider subdivisions of a topic, or to prepare in-class reports.

Another way to expand participation and to organize discussion is the use of panel sessions or forums. These can take a variety of forms, ranging from the delivery of finished papers to brief statements of positions. One of the most practical ways to conduct panel sessions in the classroom is to divide the class into several groups of four to five students to discuss the various subdivisions of a topic. Either in or outside class, each group collaborates on a written response to the topic or takes a position on it. Each group then selects one of its members to participate on a panel in which papers from all the groups are read for open discussion. Panels introduce students to more organized methods of discussion and expose the class to a wider range of viewpoints. Panel sessions —even very informal ones—take time, however. Instructors who use them should be sure to schedule assignments carefully; a well-constructed panel could take up as many as three class periods.

Though setting up formal debates involves procedures that are outside the scope of this book (and of most composition courses), class discussion can also be enlivened by informal debates. Many topics in *America Now* suggest provocative issues for opposing points of view. If a class is not too large (fifteen students or fewer), it can be divided into two groups for debating purposes; larger classes may need to form smaller groups that come together as teams. As in the panel sessions, each group should select a member to represent its position. If the topic is one students are quite conversant with, impromptu informal debate can be arranged in class. With less familiar topics, outside preparation should be scheduled.

Panels and debates often involve the practical problem of seating arrangements. The most efficient way to set up small groups is to have students cluster their desks together in tight circles. For panel formation and informal debates, several students can bring their desks to the front of the classroom. The average composition classroom, with its instructor's desk set imposingly in front, is perhaps better designed for lecturing than for open discussion. Instructors who want to broaden student participation and interaction may want to experiment with different seating styles. Some instructors, for example, feel that sitting with students at one of their desks facilitates discussion. Others may ask the students to form a large circle of seats and then sit among them. If a class is relatively small and a seminar table is available, its use will generally enhance discussion.

5. *Keep Discussion Linked to Writing.* Though lively group discussion can be an end in itself, the agenda of *America Now* is to use class discussion as a basis for writing. This agenda works two ways: (1) it encourages students to get the composition started in the classroom, and (2) it encourages students to use class discussion as a stimulus and a context for writing.

As you direct class discussion, keep in mind how the discussion can bear directly on the writing assignment. You might want to point out ideas that contain the germ of interesting papers, a tactic that also helps student writers learn how to see ideas emerge. Another way is to periodically focus attention on specific writing strategies as the reading material is discussed. Students almost always want to discuss topics and subjects, rarely techniques and strategies. It is therefore a good idea to initiate discussion by focusing on topics and gradually turn to a consideration of how the writers handled these topics.

From Discussion to Writing

As they prepare to write for college courses, students often confront difficulties that have less to do with the routine tasks of composition—spelling, punctuation, correct grammar—than with the deeper problems of finding something to say and establishing a context in which to say it. It is not uncommon for beginning students to turn in papers that contain few serious errors yet lack intellectual substance and a clear orientation. Using group discussion as a basis for composition can help remedy these problems. Group discussion can serve as a stimulus for an individual's ideas and provide a meaningful context in which to express them. Furthermore, as we will see, the art of discussion can function in many ways as an important model for the art of writing.

Finding something to say about a topic always ranks high on lists of student writing problems. It is the main reason that the blank sheet of paper or computer screen so often triggers a set of anxious questions: "What can I say?" "Where do I begin?" For many, intellectual panic sets in as the page or screen remains blank, the mind remains blank, and the entire writing process suddenly seems to exist in a total vacuum.

Exploratory discussion offers a solution to this dilemma. Years ago, an advertising executive, Alexander F. Osborn, developed a group method of generating ideas that became enormously popular in many fields. With typical advertising savvy, Osborn gave his technique a memorable name—*brainstorming*. Osborn's goal was to stimulate creativity by presenting a small group of people with a problem topic and then encouraging them to toss off as many ideas about it in as short a time as possible. Speed, spontaneity, and free association were essential to his method. But the most important part of his brainstorming procedure was a complete absence of criticism. No one in the group was allowed to criticize or disagree with any idea, no matter how silly or farfetched it seemed. This absence of criticism, Osborn found, kept ideas flowing since people were not afraid to sound ill-informed or just plain stupid.

This brainstorming technique can clearly help students come up with ideas to write about. It could be done in the composition classroom for a brief period, or small groups of students could profitably conduct brainstorming sessions on their own. Moreover, most exploratory discussion—if it is free, open, and relaxed—will contain some degree of spontaneous brainstorming in which ideas can sprout and grow. Students who take note of these ideas will find that when they sit down to write, they will not be starting out in a vacuum but will have a context of discussion out of which their composition can take shape.

An alternative type of brainstorming can also help students move from class discussion to writing. In this type of brainstorming (sometimes referred to by communication researchers as *nominal* brainstorming), each person, instead of vocalizing ideas in a group, works alone, silently jotting down a brief list of ideas. Afterward, all the lists are compared, and after some culling and combining, individual ideas are listed on a blackboard. This brainstorming method is very useful at the start of a class session in opening up various avenues of discussion. The written list also serves as a tangible source of ideas for individuals to pursue later in their papers.

If exploratory discussion can help reduce the anxiety students face in trying to develop ideas for papers, it can also alleviate another major writing problem—the student's alienation. Thinking and writing alone, with little awareness of an actual audience or of a practical situation, the beginning student often composes papers that sound hollow, disembodied, and disengaged. Ideas seem to come out of nowhere; transitions and connections are missing; conclusions that should grow out of the development of an idea are instead little more than blunt, unearned assertions. Though such papers are common, instructors find it difficult to pinpoint precisely what is wrong with them, since the problems are vague, not easily isolated, and therefore hard to identify by the usual marking symbols. The real problem with such papers is not in the writing but in the orientation of the writer. It is not one of style, structure, or content, but of overall *context*.

Experienced writers, as mentioned earlier, invariably work with a clear sense of audience and occasion. For example, a literature or composition teacher working on a critical article is writing within a clearly definable context: He or she has a sense of who the audience will be, where the article could be published, and—most important—why it is being written. No matter what its subject or point of view, the article will be intellectually oriented to a community of readers presumed to be aware of the topic and attuned to the various points of view involved in its discussion. That so many academic papers are first prepared for delivery at professional conferences underscores the vital importance of a concrete audience and situation.

As students discover the connections between discussion and composition, they will also find their bearings as writers. Their writing—no matter what the topic—will be oriented toward response. Their writing will be not only a response to an assigned topic but, more important, a response made in the context of a continuing discussion of that topic. The student, in other words, writes as an active participant, responding, as she or he would in group discussion, to the actual or anticipated responses of others. This texture of mutual response is what so often gives professionally written essays and articles their mature tone and clear orientation. Instructors might further encourage this climate of response by inviting students to cite comments by other class members in their papers.

Once your students see writing as a form of response, they will become more conscious of their social and intellectual attitudes as writers. Are they closed off to other opinions? Are they overbearing in their attitudes? Do they try to see all sides of an issue? Are they patient with complexity? Do they oversimplify difficult problems? Do they skirt issues? Do they base too much on personal experience? These are all considerations learned in group discussion that directly carry over into composition.

As your students work through *America Now*, they will observe how participation in group discussion is relevant to all kinds of writing tasks. It is perhaps easy to see how an awareness of conflicting opinions can play an important part in critical, analytical, and argumentative writing. But personal essays can also profit from exploratory group discussion. By discussing their personal experiences, your students can begin to view them from a broader social perspective and to understand them within a context of divergent human experiences.

Composition that is closely linked to lively group discussion reminds students that they are writing not in a vacuum but as part of a group, part of a community. In a written work, as in discussion, someone is always speaking and someone (or some group) is always being addressed. *America Now* encourages your students to view their writing as an extension of group discussion, to see writing as public, not private, behavior, as a social act rather than a solitary one. To think of writing as an extension of discussion, however, students need to reimagine themselves as writers. When they sit down to write, they should do so not as isolated individuals anxiously awaiting inspiration but as active participants in a process of communication with others. Students then will not expect ideas for writing to "come out of the blue." Rather, they will expect to find their ideas where they are most likely to originate—out of their considered responses to the ideas of others.

Forming Forums:
Student Presentations to Encourage Research, Discussion, and Better Writing
by Liz deBeer

"The forums give a chance for students to participate verbally and not just listen to the teacher."

"Forums enabled students to get to know each other as they worked in groups."

"Forums made people get up in front of class and talk who otherwise didn't talk during class discussion."

"The forums presented lots of good information that I think I would not have learned anywhere else. They provided lots of discussion, and I think that was the best part. The class got a chance to communicate about their cultures and share their experiences or anecdotes, which made the class a much better place to be at 8:30 in the morning."

"Forums: Keep doing this!"

As the student evaluations above reveal, many students seem to enjoy my classes and learn the most when they are asked to work in groups and share their ideas with their peers. Panel presentations or forums help give students authority in the classroom and motivation to write in steps. Perhaps just as important, forums motivate teachers like me to listen more to their students. Even students who feared forums because they didn't like the idea of talking in front of the class acknowledged that they benefited from them, as one student wrote: "I found the forums to be very informative and interesting even though I hated speaking in front of the class."

Forums require students, working in small groups, to research a topic, make presentations, and lead classroom discussion. Forums motivate students to explore topics by interviewing experts, preparing surveys, and analyzing trends, just as many of the writers whose essays appear in *America Now* did. This type of research allows students to observe the controversy implicit in most of the topics in the text and prepares them for writing papers that go beyond clichés. On the first day of class, I tell students that forums allow them to teach part of the class; this comment always gets their interest.

Why Bother? The Value of Forums

After my first few years of teaching composition, I realized that I was doing more research than my students to prepare for my classes. Exhausted and overwhelmed, I decided to create a course where the students were responsible for much of the research and, later, the presentation of it. Although several students balked at the idea of speaking in front of their peers, all followed through, which created the most successful composition classes I had ever taught. In fact, previous students accosted me in the hall demanding to know why we hadn't done forums when they took the course.

There is much research to support the use of collaborative work like forums. Lev Vygotsky's emphasis on collaboration has been well documented; he asserts that students learn from working with others: "With assistance, every child can do more than he can by himself. . . . What a child can do in cooperation today he can do alone tomorrow" (187–88). Douglas Barnes and Frankie Todd reflect on a thirteen-year-old who wonders why the teacher can't just write all the questions and answers on the board so that the students can memorize them. The authors comment that "such students need opportunities and challenges that will enable them to see learning as constructing an understanding, not as reflecting and repeating ready-made formulae whose implications they have not grasped" (14). Talk is the antidote, according to Barnes and Todd, particularly talk that is student-centered, where students can "try out new ways of thinking and reshape an idea midsentence, respond immediately to the hints and doubts of others, and collaborate in shaping meanings they could not hope to reach alone" (15). Forums provide students with time to talk about their projects, reconsider their ideas, and listen to new ideas; forums also hold students accountable for their talk, because the forums eventually involve presentations and term papers, both of which are graded.

Additionally, talk in forums is genuine, unlike much classroom "discussion" where the teacher is searching for someone who can "reproduce what the teacher has presented to them" (Barnes and Todd 15). Jeffrey Wilhelm, reflecting on his own practice and why so many students dislike reading, notes, "If we take the theoretical stance that reading is, in fact, producing meaning, then the way reading education is traditionally practiced in schools must be rethought. . . . [Teachers] must take responses beyond boilerplate questions and 'correct' answers" (10). Wilhelm uses drama and art to teach literature as an active enterprise between students and text; I suggest using forums as an active enterprise between students and *America Now*. Forums rarely disappoint me in my main goal, which is to learn something new—related to the curriculum—from each student, for forums often involve students researching areas beyond the teacher's own knowledge. For example, in past years, students have done forums on immigration and have interviewed people whom I had never met, presenting information that opened my eyes. Other students shared their own stories, such as one student who included an anecdote about how she traveled to the United States from Vietnam on a tiny fishing boat.

Forums also challenge teachers to look differently at the common complaint about lack of resources (Moll). Forums motivated me to embrace the community as a resource, a means to reach out of the classroom door and windows—which are usually shut in college classrooms—and connect student worlds to the texts. Luis Moll calls this "mobilizing funds of knowledge" (231). Although he is referring to a program where community members physically enter the classroom to teach their special skills, forums use students as facilitators of these "funds of knowledge" through their research, which often involves surveys and interviews. For example, in past years, forums on parenting resulted in students presenting research on parenting in other cultures, much of which was unfamiliar to me.

Research strongly suggests that group work can increase tolerance among groups of diverse students, assuming the group work has "highly valued goals that could not be obtained without cooperation" (Schofield 13). However, research also suggests that if group work is not well planned and valued by the teacher, students may not take the tasks seriously (Weinstein). In fact, many teachers suggest that they do not use group work for fear of losing order (Weinstein). I have never experienced difficulty with classroom management when using forums, mainly, I believe, because so many students preferred them to lectures. Moreover, since the group work led to graded work, students knew that if they were unproductive during group work, they might not have a successful forum or a strong paper.

Steps: Preparing Students

Because forums follow the philosophy behind process writing, there are several steps involved. Four major writing activities are involved throughout the semester. First, students brainstorm in small groups for ideas and strategies for researching and presenting information effectively, writing ideas on the sign-up sheet and in their notebooks. Then, they write a two-page paper that summarizes and analyzes the student's individual topic, which is handed in the day of the presentation and is summarized for the student's forum presentation. (Time limits may be necessary.) Each presenter should also prepare a discussion question on the subtopic being presented.

Students who are not presenting must hand in a one-page critical response to each forum other than their own, due the class following each forum. This should evaluate the effectiveness of each presentation — not summarize it. This is excellent practice for students to hone their listening skills and discern the most important aspects of a talk. Recently, I have also asked students to write a one-sentence positive response, telling the presenter what they liked best about the presentation. I do this to help the class feel more like a community; I have found students with eyes brimming upon hearing positive comments from their peers, some telling me that this is the first time they realized anyone was actually paying attention to what they had said in class.

Finally, students in composition classes must write a research paper based on the data gathered for their forum presentation. (Basic skills instructors may choose to eliminate this step.) This paper should involve more sources, more analysis, more detail, and better editing than the two-page paper. After the presentations are all completed, instructors can explain the traditional research paper and how the students' presentations can be revised into longer, more scholarly works.

A typical syllabus for my Composition 101 class, which meets for one semester, includes four or five forum topics, so that about five or six students are members of each group. I organize my syllabus by beginning with a few lectures in which I describe my goals and allow students time to research and prepare their projects. I spend several class periods preparing students for these forums at least two weeks before the first group's topic is due. We spend one class period working on interviewing skills, usually based on a topic from *America Now*. For example, using past editions of the text, I might begin the semester with "Are our news media reliable? Why or why not?" and ask students to conduct an interview of another person about his or her opinions on the objectivity and quality of journalism and television news. Then, I would have students write an essay using a few quotes from the subject of the interview, perhaps also using one essay from *America Now* as a supplement to the paper. Because many of the students interview an expert for their forum presentation, I like to assign one interviewing project well before the forum projects are due.

I schedule one week (or two class periods of eighty minutes each) for each forum topic. For the first class, students are asked to read the unit in *America Now* that covers the assigned topic, and we then analyze the articles and write on each topic in our notebooks. The second class is a student forum based on the same topic. The entire class period is devoted to presentations and discussion led by about five students who are in charge of that topic. I organize my syllabus so that students are working on their projects at the same time. I usually reserve a class period in the middle of the projects for an in-class exam. We spend the rest of the semester concentrating on peer reviews, punctuation, writing, reading and test-taking skills, and work on other small projects like the ones described in units of *America Now*. Usually, I reorganize the order of the table of contents to meet the needs of my syllabus.

I choose forum topics based on which issues I believe will most interest students and create the most compelling forum presentations. Since the material in *America Now* addresses current events, many students are already thinking about the issues they are being asked to write about. Instructors should capitalize on students' interests and concerns when choosing the broad topics for the forums. If students are concerned about obesity or consumerism, then these are good topics for forums. If the issues of social networking, the environment, immigration, or racial conflict have been debated regularly on the news or in the campus paper, then these topics will have special appeal. Much of this evaluation of topics depends on a school's geography and demographics. I rely on past students' essays and discussion to gauge popular topics. Although all topics in *America Now* will interest most students, the ideal forum topic is one that students will be compelled to spend more than one class period discussing. I also avoid topics that are too polarized, such as abortion, which people tend to view as either inherently wrong or right. The topic should be broad enough that several students can explore different angles and should be covered by accessible research sources.

At the beginning of the semester, I write on the board four or five forum topics chosen from issues addressed in *America Now* and ask that each student pick one. Through this process, the small groups are formed. For example, the students who pick the topic obesity will work together on a forum for that topic. Because groups should be approximately the same size to allow for different angles to be addressed on each issue, instructors should limit the number of students allowed to pick each topic.

When groups have been formed, I hand each one a sign-up sheet with the chosen topic written on top. Then, each group member picks a subtopic or angle that relates to the general topic and lists some possible sources that will be used to research it. Students should be reminded that their research may require them to alter the proposed topic or sources.

Although I encourage students to create their own ideas for topics and sources, I provide each small group with some ideas to model how to create a specific topic from a broad one as well as some sources that might be applicable to the general topic. I usually give each group a separate handout along with the sign-up sheet. Examples of my ideas for approaching topics appear at the end of this essay.

At this point, I dedicate a whole class period to reviewing forums so that students know what I expect. Although I have already defined forums briefly before they picked their topics and subtopics, I define them in more detail once students know what area they will be researching. I also make a model presentation to show students the kind of work I expect. I include a visual aid and speak, without reading in a monotone, from my notecards. I pick a topic that is relevant to *America Now*. For example, I once made a presentation on patriotism, for which I interviewed instructors from the political science and journalism departments about their views regarding the role of patriotism in relation to the government, the media, and the public in America today. Students then evaluated my presentation orally as I wrote my expectations on the board; the students themselves provided excellent tips for each other. My use of model presentations has helped my classes improve their presentations over years past. It also reminds me of all the steps students need to take to be prepared for their presentations.

Next, I review how students should prepare their research, presentations, and class discussion. I discuss the importance of asking questions that elicit thoughtful responses and of asking follow-up questions, both during their research and during presentations. I explain how I evaluate forums based on whether presentations — and written reports — are focused and informative, and I discuss the value of current sources. Since students have usually begun to work on their projects, they are encouraged to ask specific questions.

At the next class period, groups meet for the second time so that students can discuss their plans for research and their overall strategy. Instructors should visit each group to learn of individual concerns and should discuss wider concerns with the whole class. Often, group members discuss their fears of talking in front of others. I try to point out the value of speaking skills and sometimes encourage students to participate in later forums so that they can see other students do presentations before they take a turn. Given that many high schools require oral presentations as part of their graduation requirements, many students are already knowledgeable about the basics of preparing forums.

After their second group meeting, students must conduct their research and prepare their presentations. I ask that they write a two-page (typed, double-spaced) report on their forum topic that includes at least one source other than *America Now.* Those sources may include books, magazines, interviews, or even personal experience. If students use personal experience as a source, they must also use one other source. To document their sources, I require a typed "works cited" page. Students may read from their papers, but they may not read the whole paper or they will go over their allotted time. It is imperative to save time for class discussion. Remind students not to use names of people interviewed if the topic involves personal material, as might be the case in a presentation on stereotypes, for instance.

Letting Go: Letting Students Learn

Perhaps instructors' greatest challenge in working with forums is allowing students to research and explore topics on their own and to work in groups during class time. This doesn't *feel* like teaching, but it is. If we want students to actually say something meaningful, as Berthoff suggests in *The Making of Meaning,* we must leave them alone to make their own discoveries. As Bartholomae and Petrosky write in *Facts, Artifacts, and Counterfacts,* "A course in reading and writing whose goal is to empower students must begin with a silence, a silence the student must fill" (7). When students conduct interviews, research their forum topics, or lead class discussion, they are literally filling the silence. Forum projects allow students to think for themselves, to take risks. All this, of course, leads to better writing.

Usually, students ask for little help. Most of them are eager to interview people they know or to find their own sources. Occasionally, students panic and ask me to help with library research, particularly those with limited library experience. (I usually arrange an on-campus library tour before the forums begin.) However, once I have given them enough pointers to get started, I try to leave them alone. Often, during such periods of silence, I observe students working together. Such collaboration confirms my belief that students learn not only from me and from sources but also from each other.

Other experiences have reinforced my belief in the value of forums and have helped me get through the waiting and worrying period. One student, who appeared to be half asleep during much of the class time preceding the forums, became so involved and excited by interviewing his Vietnam-veteran uncle for a forum on the gun-control debate that he suddenly sparkled, waking up enough to complete and pass the course. Similarly, a student from a local subsidized housing development admitted to me later that he planned on dropping my class because of an overloaded schedule. Instead, he stuck it out, comparing and contrasting attitudes about guns from ten men from "the projects" who did not attend college and ten men who did attend college, drawing conclusions about guns and lack of hope. He admitted that the reason he stayed in the course was because he felt impelled to work on his forum project and felt his background and insights were valued in the class.

Teacher as Listener

I like to start with a forum on an accessible topic such as body image because it makes students think critically about something with which they are already familiar. Although (or because) students' experiences vary, these topics should prompt a lot of class discussion. Students who are in these forum groups may interview campus counselors or social workers. One student might survey two generations' attitudes about body image and compare results or split the survey into two social or cultural groups.

Some students may resent it if their group has to present first, but others actually like to "get it out of the way." Once, when a student in the first forum group was unable to finish his research, I moved him to a different topic that was due toward the end of the semester. However, I discourage such behavior by telling the class that I will give an F to students who do not perform on the due date, unless they can be excused because of an extreme circumstance. Only once did a student miss the deadline without an excuse; I allowed her to hand in her written paper, and I averaged the F for the presentation with the written project.

On the day of the presentation, I take attendance and sit in the back of the class. Then, the group presenting moves to the front of the room and presents its reports. At this point, the class asks questions only for clarification so that there is time for everyone to present. Students who are not presenting should be taking notes for their one-page written response to the forum. Instead of a simple summary, I ask students to follow a formula that includes what the main idea was, what they liked best about the presentation, and what they learned. (Students don't have to write such a paper on their own forum topic or on anyone else's in their group. When all the students have presented, I average all of the critical responses of each student to equal one paper grade. Usually everyone who hands in the written response gets a high grade; the only way to fail is to cut class and not hand in any paper.)

After all the students in the group have finished their presentations, the rest of the class may ask questions. Sometimes, presenters need to ask the class a question to prompt discussion. I prefer to keep quiet and let the presenters lead the discussion, but sometimes I'll intervene when I feel it's necessary. Often, I have to remind myself to let the students talk, to let them fill the silence. I usually learn from these discussions. In one class, a student from Nigeria responded to a parenting forum presentation about how divorced American men are fighting to get custody of their children. The Nigerian student commented that in his country it is the norm for divorced men to have custody of the children. This led to a discussion of cultural issues concerning gender roles.

Occasionally, students make poor presentations. In the weakest one I have seen, a bright woman simply chatted for a few minutes without presenting material from any source. Another student twisted data about rape so that it sounded like the violence was justified by the victim's flirtatious behavior. In both instances, the students learned from their peers' responses and my commentary on their short papers, and their final research papers reflected their understanding. Much of this learning process occurs during the discussion following the presentations. Even a blunt comment like "Why do you always call the rape victim 'she'?" can lead to discussion about improving writing.

It is common for students to present too much general information without specific examples, to make rough transitions, or to analyze data inadequately. These problems can also be remedied with helpful commentary from fellow students and the instructor. Because the forum project involves writing in steps, I rarely receive plagiarized or sloppy papers. Before I used the forums, students often had only one chance to write their final research papers and no time to learn from their mistakes. By presenting their ideas and research orally before writing a final research paper, students have time to think and rethink. They learn to value their audience by striving to be clear, concise, and original. Since the projects are staggered, I can spend more time on the two-page papers, offering advice about revising for the final research paper.

When students write critical responses to their peers' presentations, they learn to analyze. One student commented that "I tended to . . . learn more from the people who analyzed their information rather than the ones who dictated the information to the class." Another wrote that "when [presenters] read off a sheet of paper, they were boring. . . . I feel you must get the audience involved." These comments reveal that students were able to learn important writing lessons from the oral presentations.

Other students' comments revealed that they enjoyed the forums. One wrote: "Forums are an excellent learning device. . . . Students taught students about what they had researched." Another reported that "the forums . . . forced the speakers to really know their topics. . . . I feel that a majority of the people got really involved in their subjects, enabling them to learn more about it than if they just read it out of a book. Also, the forums showed that how you say your information is important. You must try to catch the interest of your audience."

These remarks show how eager students are to fill the silence of the classroom, as long as we instructors are willing to give up some of our control. If we empower our students, they can provide the classroom with much more knowledge than any one person alone can.

Works Cited

Barnes, Douglas, and Frankie Todd. *Communication and Learning Revisited: Making Meaning through Talk*. Portsmouth, NH: Boynton/Cook, 1995. Print.

Bartholomae, David, and Anthony Petrosky. *Facts, Artifacts, and Counterfacts: Theory and Method for a Reading and Writing Course*. Portsmouth, NH: Boynton/Cook, 1986. Print.

Berthoff, Ann E. *The Making of Meaning.* Upper Montclair, NJ: Boynton/Cook, 1981. Print.

Moll, Luis. "Literacy Research in Community and Classrooms: A Sociological Approach." *Theoretical Models and the Process of Reading.* 4th ed. Ed. R. B. Ruddell, M. R. Ruddell, and H. Singer. Newark, DE: IRA, 1994. 211–44. Print.

Schofield, Janet W. *Black & White in School: Trust, Tension or Tolerance?* New York: Teachers College Press, 1989. Print.

Vygotsky, Lev. *Thought and Language.* Cambridge, MA: MIT Press, 1987. Print.

Weinstein, Carol S. *Secondary Classroom Management: Lessons from Research and Practice.* New York: McGraw-Hill, 1996. Print.

Wilhelm, Jeffrey D. *"You Gotta Be the Book": Teaching Engaged and Reflective Reading with Adolescents.* Urbana, IL: NCTE, 1995. Print.

1

Is There an Obesity Epidemic?

Are Americans becoming "supersized"? Is there a national weight problem? Recent headlines in *USA Today*, the *Washington Post*, and countless other media outlets seem to shout, "Yes." In her essay "Shame on US," journalist Hannah Lobel captures the fevered rhetoric from national "waistline watchers" when she writes, "Demand for supersized coffins is on the rise! Tubby tykes are clogging schoolyard slides! A costly healthcare crisis looms." But what is the nature of this presumed "epidemic" — in scientific, cultural, and even moral terms?

For Lobel, the problem is overstated: The media reaction seems hysterical, and our tendency to make moral judgments about obesity sends "people into prisons of self-loathing that have them seeking refuge in yo-yo diets that feed a multibillion-dollar weight-loss industry but do nothing to keep the pounds off and, in fact, often contribute to health problems later." She acknowledges that "people have gotten a bit heavier." But Lobel sees a "righteous myopia" in the national preoccupation with fat, a shortsightedness that "stems from our unyielding faith in self-determination." Accordingly, she shifts the focus — and the culpability for our national weight increase — from the presumed gluttony of individuals to a wider context: genetics and ever-present marketing, as well as the surge in prescription drug use and other cultural factors.

Chelsea Durbin, a student columnist for the University of Kansas's *University Daily Kansan* also sees American society as partly culpable in the presumed "obesity epidemic." She writes, "The nation has become a culture of fast food eating and on-the-go living, ultimately creating a "fat" America." But Durbin emphasizes self-awareness and individual choice, arguing that people must learn to forgo the short-term convenience of fast food in view of the long-term liabilities. "Your body will thank you in the future," she writes.

Still, how much control do we actually have over our weight? "The amazing thing is that the general public, of which I used to be a member, does not understand that obesity — even just being overweight — is without question, without need for further debate, a genetic matter," argues lawyer and food writer Jeffrey Steingarten. This knowledge doesn't remove our responsibility for our health, he adds. But given the "infinite combination of genes," he casts doubt on the kind of one-size-fits-all, mass interventions — public education, school exercise programs, shuttering fast food restaurants — that governments and societies want to impose.

HANNAH LOBEL   Shame on US
[*The Utne Reader*/January–February 2008]

Vocabulary/Using a Dictionary

1. The word comes from the Latin *hystericus*, derived from the Greek *hysterikos*, meaning "of the womb" or "suffering in the womb." Hysteria was originally believed to be a neurotic condition peculiar to women.

2. *Fervid* means "impassioned, spirited, or ardent"; it derives from the Latin *fervidus* (glowing or burning) and connotes an emotional state of mind.

3. *Stigma* is from Greek and Latin and means "to puncture, mark, or tattoo." Traditionally, it has meant a mark of disgrace, a visible symptom of disease, or even an identifying mark of slave status. The word is associated with moral or personal failure, so the presumption that heavy people need to be stigmatized or shamed aligns with the perception of them as morally flawed.

4. *Myopia* is a term from ophthalmology (the medical study of the eye) that means "shortsightedness." Metaphorically, it suggests a lack of judgment or long-term perspective in perception, thinking, or planning.

Responding to Words in Context

1. The word *supersized* comes from the language of extra-large fast food portions; as a description of coffins, it connects the prevalence of unhealthy fast food and the health risks of obesity in a darkly comic way. But it also parodies the hysteria and overstatement that Lobel believes are part of our national discussion of weight.

2. *Herculean* means "having the overwhelming strength of the Greek mythological hero Hercules." The word connotes the superhuman, as Hercules was the son of Zeus (the leader of the Greek gods) and a mortal woman. Lobel is implying that for a certain segment of the population, overcoming the biological and cultural inducements to obesity would require supernatural power.

3. In using the term *fatties*, Lobel is trying to make clear—and mock—the unnecessarily judgmental and mean-spirited ways in which some in our culture view obese people. Clearly, she does not agree with this attitude, as one of the main points of her essay is to dispute the shaming and stigmatization of the overweight.

4. Lobel is using this religious language to highlight the moral judgments implicit in the work of writers like William Saletan and others. Here, "original sin" corresponds to the idea that some overweight people are born with a genetic predisposition to obesity and therefore cannot be held completely accountable. "Cardinal sin," on the other hand, refers to the actions (and moral state) of those who become obese through peer pressure, lack of willpower, or other personal failings.

Discussing Main Point and Meaning

1. Lobel begins her essay, in part, by exaggerating and parodying the familiar rhetoric of "waistline watchers in the media, government, and health industry" with alliteration ("tubby tykes") and exclamation points. She points out that according to the *Journal of the American Medical Association*, overweight people do not have higher mortality rates than "normals" (contrary to the image of Americans "committing mass suicide by doughnuts"). She also notes that the growing ranks of the overweight may have less to do with eating habits and more to do with the shifting official standards used to categorize people by weight.

2. For Lobel, the view of obesity as a personal moral failure leads to the practice of shaming people into losing weight. We also obsess over fat. But such attitudes ignore factors that may be beyond the power of individual self-determination and willpower. Such shortsightedness—and narrow-mindedness—about the problem only "send[s] people into prisons of self-loathing" and ineffective yo-yo diets that enrich a large and flourishing "weight-loss industry." This point is reinforced by the backlash against the humorous "Small Steps" advertising campaign, which some among the "health police" did not find sufficiently shaming or frightening (according to Lobel).

3. Lobel has a sophisticated and partially skeptical attitude about science and the way it's reported—for example, the "arbitrary" nature of healthy weight guidelines, or a study in the *New England Journal of Medicine* that set off a "media panic." She also argues that our focus on fat and the morality of obesity leads us to ignore "other culprits." Citing the *Ecologist*, she points to overlooked factors such as environmental pollution, sleep deprivation, and the prevalence of prescription drugs (para. 11). Even as Lobel claims that these areas "desperately need" scientific research, her larger point is that there will be no scientific solution until we change our larger, cultural attitudes about our weight and our bodies.

Examining Sentences, Paragraphs, and Organization

1. Traditionally, many writing instructors have discouraged the use of conjunctions at the beginning of sentences. However, the practice is common in journalism and can be effective, if done with care. In Lobel's essay, this use of *and* reinforces a sense of logical connection and reasoning—both within individual paragraphs and within the essay as a whole (see para. 11). This stylistic device also makes her tone more like that of a spoken argument than like a piece of academic prose. For student writing, the use of conjunctions at the beginning of sentences may or may not be appropriate, depending on the formality of the assignment and the intended audience. Moreover, when overused, it can become a mannerism as well as an attempt to conceal faulty logic or argumentation.

2. Lobel sets up her premises (that we overstate our national weight problem and that the United States is "obsessed" and "hysterical" concerning obesity) in the first two paragraphs. The third paragraph redirects the reader's attention from misunderstandings about the "problem" of obesity to the misunderstandings about "solutions." In terms of Lobel's overall argument and theme, this paragraph also first introduces the idea that factors outside of willpower and "self-determination"—marketing, genetics, class, among others—play a large role in obesity. This is a major aim of Lobel's essay: to look at obesity in a larger, more sophisticated context, rather than seeing it merely as a simple issue of personal morality ("cardinal sin") or genetic programming ("original sin").

3. The essay reflects on the "unyielding faith in self-determination" held by many Americans. Lobel links the obsession with dieting and bodily "renovation" with a certain spiritual (perhaps Puritanical) view of human beings as being in need of perpetual personal improvement (morally and physically)—through constant public judgment and shaming, if necessary. Implicitly, if obesity is stigmatized, then thinness might even be seen as a sign of blessing. Lobel sees these prevailing attitudes as a counterproductive overreaction to the "plain truth": that "people have gotten a bit heavier" and that "fat people make easy targets in public policy and debate, just as they do on the playground."

Thinking Critically

1. Americans have a long tradition of public shaming and social stigmatization, such as the practice of placing people in public stocks or showing people convicted of soliciting prostitutes on television. Students may think about the more subtle ways in which such disciplinary measures work—for example, the push, over the last several years, to reduce smoking generally. This antismoking campaign has included public service announcements, as well as a societal trend toward eliminating places and opportunities for people to smoke, even though it's a legal behavior. Students might want to consider whether there are parallels between obesity and smoking or other issues.

2. Certainly, there is a large, complex, and highly lucrative "industry" around dieting, including glossy magazines offering easy weight-loss tips, diet books, food products, and weight-loss programs. More indirectly, gyms and health clubs benefit from this obsession, which also manifests itself in television shows like *The Biggest Loser*. But students might also distinguish the effectiveness of various weight-loss programs and an "obsession with fat" from a reasonable desire to be relatively fit and healthy.

3. This concluding analogy extends Lobel's claims and implications throughout the article that obese people are subjected to shaming and stigmatization—and even offers a variation on an image in her opening paragraph, "Tubby tykes are clogging schoolyard slides!" It also suggests

the mean-spiritedness present in public discussions and national efforts to curb obesity. At the same time, public health is a legitimate concern, with genuine costs, literally and figuratively; Lobel's analogy here risks labeling any frank discussions of weight or national efforts to curb obesity as mere playground taunting.

In-Class Writing Activities

1. Students may consider the way fat or obesity is represented in advertising, magazines, movies, music, and the media. Inversely, they might look at how thinness is celebrated and transformed into a bodily "renovation project"—whether in specific media representations or in their own lives. What motivates people to go on diets, aside from reasonable considerations of good health? Beyond superficial images, students may also think about how judgments about weight and appearance can also become judgments of morality and character. This might differ across gender lines. In what ways, specifically, are women expected to be less satisfied with their bodies than men are—and how is such an attitude made into a "virtue"?

2. For the assignment, students should examine their own views of "self-determination" in this context and weigh them against external pressures and factors. The principles of individualism and personal responsibility are especially powerful in the perceptions Americans have of themselves. These values have good connotations and associations. But do such "unyielding" convictions have limitations—and can they become counterproductive when dealing with a problem such as obesity? Lobel makes a connection between these ideals and a corresponding tendency to quickly judge the "moral shortcomings" of others, but she does not write at length about the link. Students may want to analyze it in their own writing—whether to push it further, dispute it, or defend it. Additionally, Lobel refers to the "politics of obesity," and students should consider the larger political implications of their views.

3. Lobel provides the example of the study in the *New England Journal of Medicine* about obesity and social networks, which became (according to Lobel) fodder for "Are your friends making you fat?" stories in the commercial media. Students should reflect on how this process works—that is, the way complex issues with multiple aspects, causes, and solutions are reduced, simplified, and made into accessible human-interest stories. Journalists and pundits often bring along the cultural biases that Lobel points out in her essay (for example, the view of obesity as a kind of sin). The Saletan article and the reaction to the humorous public service advertisements from the U.S. Department of Health and Human Services also highlight the media impulse toward conflict and emotionalism. Students can consider how other complex issues might be simplified in the same ways.

CHELSEA DURBIN (STUDENT ESSAY)   Fast Food Is Fat Food
[*The University Daily Kansan*, University of Kansas/November 12, 2007]

Vocabulary/Using a Dictionary

1. Merriam-Webster first included the term *fast food* as an entry in its 1951 dictionary, which suggests that it has been part of American culture for nearly sixty years.

2. A "small calorie" is the amount of heat needed to raise 1 gram of water 1 degree Celsius; a "large calorie," or the "food calorie" commonly used in nutritional measurements, is a unit of 1,000 small calories. The word *calorie* is French, from the Latin *calor* (heat) and *calere* (to be warm).

3. Diabetes is a disease in which the body does not produce or properly use insulin, a hormone necessary to convert sugar, starches, and other food into energy. The term originates in the Greek word for "siphon."

Responding to Words in Context

1. Durbin associates "fast food" and "on-the-go living" with a preoccupation with—and overvaluation of—ease and immediacy. At the same time, such a "culture" would not encourage thought, reflection, or consideration of broader consequences.

2. The quotation marks imply skepticism and irony about these commonly used words—and make us reconsider their meaning in a broader context. For example, the long-term health effects of a diet too reliant on "fast" food may not be "convenient" at all.

3. Although *obese* commonly means "very overweight," the word also has a specific, technical definition developed and used by organizations such as the National Institutes of Health and the World Health Organization. The term is based primarily on a calculation of body mass index (or BMI), but there are other ways of assessing weight that account for variations in age, frame, gender, and other factors. Over the years, the National Institutes of Health has changed the definition of the term *obese*.

Discussing Main Point and Meaning

1. Durbin acknowledges that students are rushed, "because life doesn't always permit enough time to cook a meal" (para. 5). But she also suggests that they are impulsive and not inclined to think about the consequences of their nutritional choices. Consequently, they seem particularly vulnerable to the lure of fast food, whose health "effects are quickly catching up with us" (para. 2).

2. Durbin claims that there is "a direct link in America between obesity and fast food." College students are heedless of the harmful health effects of fast food or simply unaware of them (according to Durbin); they also reach for time- and laborsaving food choices. For Durbin, these two tendencies are contributing to rising obesity levels in the United States. Her

essay claims that the solution — or at least the beginning of a solution — starts with raising awareness of the dangers of fast food and making people more reflective about their eating habits.

3. Durbin views these healthier menu choices in positive terms, as choices that might "encourage healthy eating habits" (para. 6), even if one is tempted to add calories to presumably healthy food. Moreover, she cautions that the availability of healthier menu options in these restaurants will not, in itself, change anyone's eating habits or improve the overall health of Americans. Durbin maintains her emphasis on awareness — that is, "consciously choosing" to eat healthier, which means that a change in attitude must precede a change in specific dietary choices.

Examining Sentences, Paragraphs, and Organization

1. These metaphors make for an effective opening because they ground the essay in a common human experience (the feeling of hunger). The earthquake image is especially startling and visceral. At the same time, the vivid earthquake/rupture analogy may be an overstatement — and it doesn't especially follow from the metaphor in the first sentence. Durbin does not choose to use much, if any, figurative language as the essay develops.

2. The second-person point of view brings immediacy to the opening of the essay; throughout the rest of the article, it suggests that Durbin is perceptive and credible with regard to the eating habits of her fellow college students. By shifting to the first person in paragraph 5, the writer acknowledges that the problem she's discussing applies to herself, as well as others — and thereby avoids the accusatory or preachy tone that can result from the second-person voice. She achieves a similar effect by using first-person plural pronouns when discussing the health problems of "our" nation.

3. The last paragraph focuses the essay on two specific recommendations that follow directly from the points Durbin has made throughout. It also recapitulates her theme that the apparently insignificant choices we make today out of convenience may have long-term consequences, so we need to be more aware in our decision making. That would seem to apply to issues other than food.

Thinking Critically

1. The home-cooked choices Durbin proposes — an image of typical college-student fare — don't appear much healthier or well thought-out than fast food. Durbin thus implies that the dietary considerations or problems of her audience go beyond a tendency to eat at franchises such as McDonald's rather than "eating in." She also implies that a change in attitude about eating healthily would have to go beyond merely avoiding fast food.

2. Durbin cites the ubiquity of fast food, as well as statistics showing that the obesity levels of Americans over the age of twenty rose 25 percent between 2004 and 2006. She also points to health problems such as heart disease,

diabetes, and cancer, which can result from a high-fat, high-calorie diet. More specific, focused data—with regard to the eating habits of college students, the presence of fast food restaurants on (or around) college campuses, and health statistics that apply specifically to a college demographic—would make the link stronger and further Durbin's argument as it directly applies to her readers.

3. Certainly, fast food "is everywhere," as Durbin writes—and that seems true globally, as well. Of course, the practice of eating food quickly (in diners, in Automats, off lunch wagons, and so on) predates the modern chain restaurant. But the standardized, industrialized, modern fast food franchise (as it has evolved over the past half century) seems to represent (and align with) certain common perceptions of Americans and America: a focus on mobility (especially with regard to automobiles), speed, and technological advancement; the centrality of work (rather than time spent eating at leisure); the celebration of mass consumption; and a disregard or indifference to the "food cultures" of older European countries.

In-Class Writing Activities

1. Students may agree with Durbin, or they may challenge her description as a stereotype that doesn't apply to them or to other people they know. Ask them about the factors that determine what they eat, such as time constraints, money, what's available, health considerations, peer pressure, and the desire to lose weight. They might also consider how they "use" food—as a release from stress, for example. The assignment builds on Durbin's assertion that students should become more aware of and reflective about the decisions they make.

2. Students should think about the role of marketing in this context—especially as they constitute a key demographic for fast food restaurants. They might consider how these chains market and advertise directly to students. Businesses exist primarily to sell products and make profits, but do they have any obligations to the public if their products lead to health problems? And should government play a role? The New York City board of health recently banned the use of trans fats from all restaurants, including chains—a controversial move, given that the U.S. Food and Drug Administration has approved trans fats. This trans-fat ban seems to suggest some tension between government regulation, the rights of businesses, and the call for self-awareness and personal responsibility implicit in Durbin's argument.

3. Students might consider sources of inexpensive, fattening, or high-calorie food other than fast food restaurants, especially given the increasing prevalence of high-fructose corn syrup over the past several decades; they could take into account a long-term trend toward bigger portion sizes and a general propensity to consume in America, both literally and figuratively; they might also see the abundance of food as the inevitable by-product of a large, prosperous country. There may be other factors promoting obesity as well—for example, a decline in families eating

together regularly or a trend toward increasingly sedentary lives. You might also leave room for students to disagree with Durbin's premise, as some may argue that America's "weight problem" is overstated.

JEFFREY STEINGARTEN   You Are Not What You Eat
[*Vogue*/April 2008]

Vocabulary/Using a Dictionary

1. *Obesogenic* means "tending to encourage excessive weight gain." Its origins are in the Latin word *obedere* (to eat away) and the Greek *generare* (to create). Other words ending in *-genic* are *carcinogenic, photogenic,* and *mediagenic,* to name a few.

2. A *regimen* is a regulated course of living, including diet and exercise, designed to preserve or restore health. Its roots in the Latin *regere,* "to rule," give associations of government and control, imposed externally or internally, as in self-control.

Responding to Words in Context

1. The word *proprietary* usually means that a proprietor holds private ownership of—or a patent on—processes or products that are sold or operated for profit. Here, however, Steingarten is being ironic: He does not actually have a trademark or ownership rights with regard to this method. The irony is based, in part, on the premise that Americans are unfamiliar with the metric system of measurement, which is used throughout the rest of the world.

2. Barneys is an exclusive, fashionable, and relatively expensive department store identified primarily with New York City. In referring to this specific store (as opposed to simply saying he went shopping for new clothes), Steingarten is signaling his identification with a certain socioeconomic class and culture. He is also presuming that the readers of *Vogue,* a well-known fashion magazine, will understand the reference.

3. Feuerbach lived and wrote during the nineteenth century. In the context of philosophy, materialism is generally the view that matter is the only thing that exists and that all phenomena (such as thoughts) can be reduced to matter. The materialist tradition can be traced back to ancient Greek philosophy. This is a different meaning than the more common definition of *materialist* or *materialism,* which refers to a preoccupation with things and objects in the context of a consumer economy.

4. Steingarten's style is ironic and witty throughout—even on serious subjects like suicide. In this paragraph, he personifies the Food and Drug Administration bureaucracy as a forbidding, scolding figure. He associates the "delectability" of fattening food—eaten without consequences—with an unappetizing-sounding pharmaceutical product. The definition of *suicidality* here does not suggest that his reader needs a dictionary to know the word's meaning; rather, the citation serves as a wry commentary

on the "dreamy" drug's side effects in a culture where thinness and weight loss are so strongly associated with happiness and euphoria. Because students sometimes use dictionary definitions in their college writing, this might be a good opportunity to discuss how to do so effectively.

Discussing Main Point and Meaning

1. By viewing obesity as a medical problem, Steingarten undercuts a prevailing idea (prevalent in the "dieting industry" and the culture at large) that "losing weight is easy and really fun" (para. 10). He asserts that obesity is "without need for further debate, a genetic matter" (para. 25). The disease or disorder model removes some of the stigma associated with excessive weight; although it does not absolve people from personal responsibility for their health, it highlights the degree to which weight is determined by genetics, not individual choice. Additionally, viewing obesity as a medical problem casts the weight-loss industry in a silly light, as no responsible person would advise people with other genetic disorders like diabetes to cure them through fad diets.

2. For Steingarten, the influence of "nurture"—which connotes parenting—is too limited. He points out a societal tendency to "blame the obesity of a child on the family" (para. 8) but asserts that the actual influence of families on the weight of their children is "very small." "Environment," in contrast, encompasses parenting and also a range of other factors.

3. Beginning with its title, Steingarten's essay clearly seeks to upend or debunk the "conventional wisdom" and misinformation prevalent in the discussion of our presumed national "obesity epidemic." The "flood" of magazine articles goes against the "facts": "Diets don't work" (para. 9). Moreover, he sees these things as part of a larger, harmful process in which the dieting industry profits by pandering to the "unrealistic hopes" of people, while "making weight loss into one of the central goals of life" (para. 10).

4. In tracing the misunderstood roots of the aphorism, Steingarten shows how platitudes and clichés become second nature: we no longer think about them or their validity but merely accept them as "true." By putting the words of Jean Anthelme Brillat-Savarin and Ludwig Andreas Feuerbach in context, Steingarten makes us see that this saying originates in discussions of class or philosophical materialism, not dieting advice.

Examining Sentences, Paragraphs, and Organization

1. The list, which includes such topics as "weight change among Chinese schizophrenics," supports his implication that the volume and variety of research done on obesity and genetics is "flabbergasting." It also backs his assertion that "obesity—even just being overweight—is without question, without need for further debate, a genetic matter" (para. 25). This presumption is at the base of all of this esoteric research, and therefore, it is settled science.

2. Steingarten uses the stand-alone, one-sentence paragraph effectively. For example, the second paragraph of the essay essentially contains his entire thesis. Similarly, paragraph 22 ("There seem to be so many ways to become fat and very few to get skinny") brings clarity and concision to his line of argument, as it follows his long, "flabbergasting" section on the comically wide range of obesity research. Such paragraphs may or may not be acceptable in academic discourse, depending on the assignment and the audience.

3. Steingarten becomes somewhat more serious and earnest in this concluding section. He refers to his own presentation at the conference, in which he said that "creating false hopes" about weight loss is "immoral" and that spending government money on national weight-loss initiatives that don't work is "morally wrong." He also defers to "actual experts in obesity" and demonstrates that he's capable of changing his mind when presented with good arguments. Structurally, Steingarten's placement of this anecdote near the end of the essay allows us to see and evaluate the "mass intervention"/"one prescription for all" approach to obesity in light of the argument that he has already made regarding obesity's genetic basis and the inefficacy of diets.

Thinking Critically

1. We may infer that Steingarten means the traditional practices of regulating calories and exercising, seen within the bounds of one's genetic disposition and reasonable expectations. He also notes the varied effectiveness of surgery in certain cases. The main point seems to be to avoid the "unrealistic hopes" of fad diets. But students may notice that Steingarten includes a peculiar diet that he used to lose weight in the 1970s (he did not keep the weight off), which consisted primarily of cottage cheese and scotch. This is far from a "usual method," and few if any people would recommend it as a program to lose weight. However, it does support his broader contention that a "one prescription for all" approach to weight loss is unrealistic, given the "infinite combination of genes and the ways they regulate eating, metabolism, and energy expenditure" (para. 28).

2. Steingarten sees Huckabee as a "freak" and "a sport of nature," thus making him a bad role model for an average person trying to lose weight. Such an example creates unrealistic expectations about what's possible— or probable. At the same time, we might acknowledge that we often like to celebrate and value extraordinary achievements—and see them as admirable and worthy of imitation. Some people would argue that Huckabee's story—especially if he followed the "usual methods of losing weight"—can be seen as inspiring and helpful to a typical dieter.

3. Steingarten is a lawyer and a food writer, not an "actual" expert in obesity (as he acknowledges, self-effacingly). But he relies on a range of experts and sources. He provides a lengthy—and witty—list of studies done by institutions such as Yale University and the National Institutes of

Health in paragraph 3, for example; despite his comic tone, he seems genuinely familiar with the research, which clearly supports his thesis. In addition, he has spoken directly to researchers on obesity (para. 23). Bercause he's a magazine writer, he also appears conversant with the media world and dieting industry that he criticizes. But Steingarten's voice is largely one of a layperson with common sense; after all, we've "heard the facts before" (para. 9). Indeed, he deliberately downplays his own authority in paragraph 28, when he describes his "little talk" at an obesity conference and revises his opinions after hearing other authorities on the subject.

In-Class Writing Activities

1. Part of Steingarten's point is that conventional wisdom and clichés can be not only wrong but also harmful. For this exercise, however, students don't necessarily have to prove that a well-known aphorism is "wrong"; rather, the goal is to take piece of language, a cliché, or an opinion that's accepted as true or valid without much skepticism and to reveal its roots or evaluate its merits. The range of possibilities is broad, from "No pain, no gain" and "The customer is always right" to clichés and aphorisms from politics, family life, and education.

2. Whether or not there is an "obesity epidemic," weight is certainly a national preoccupation. In this assignment, students should consider their personal relationship to this cultural phenomenon. Have they been successful in dieting? Do they struggle to stay thin? Do they view weight management as central to their lives, or to notions of self-improvement, in general? They might also make distinctions between fad diets and programs that are more successful and lasting.

3. Students may think of this in historical terms—for example, the way fat or heaviness has been viewed differently at different times. In the context of morality, the sin of gluttony is associated with being heavy, but perhaps the two qualities can be separated; that is, a person might be obese without being gluttonous, and vice versa. Students might also consider what fat is in material, chemical terms, even as we ascribe various meanings to it. Again, according to the researcher cited, individuals have as much control over their weight as they do over their height, yet we don't tend to ascribe moral, personal, or cultural significance to height—and if we do, it's often positive. Why would that be?

Discussing the Unit

Suggested Topic for Discussion

These fundamental questions underpin each of the three essays. Lobel and Steingarten, in particular, seem to diminish the role of personal choice and autonomy in order to emphasize genetic and cultural factors. Durbin, on the other hand, places primary responsibility on the individual. Students should consider their own assumptions about this tension: Those premises will probably determine how they view the problem of—and possible solutions to—a national "obesity epidemic." Is it a matter of lax self-discipline? Or is our "obesogenic" culture more of a determining factor? This opposition may well inform the way they view other issues—including class, race, and consumerism.

Preparing for Class Discussion

1. Writing in the (generally) politically progressive *Utne Reader*, Lobel's essay seems to have an implicit political subtext for a politically astute audience, who will place her essay in the context of a larger view of American culture, society, and politics. Students should try to be aware of this: How do they read, for example, Lobel's remarks about the need for research on environmental pollution and its effect on people's weight? Steingarten is writing for a sophisticated, fashionable, presumably affluent *Vogue* magazine audience; his droll tone and range of references might be forbidding to some readers. Durbin is clearly writing for a college audience, and her essay may be the most accessible; it also relies less on references to other texts and general knowledge. This provides an opportunity to examine the nature of "sophisticated"—knowing, self-conscious, witty, complex, allusive—writing, and its trade-offs.

2. Generally, the media may simplify, sensationalize, or moralize on the subject of obesity and fitness. Students should think about how and why this occurs. They may also distinguish between different media forms and the demands of each. For example, a story about dieting and weight on the front page of the *New York Times* might suggest a different standard of accuracy and journalistic accountability than a list of diet tips advertised on the cover of a fashion magazine, or a segment on a local news broadcast. Why would that be the case? Furthermore, as both Steingarten and Lobel imply, substantive scientific research, no matter how accurate, does not always have qualities that make it "newsworthy" or easily translatable into the demands of conventional news forms.

3. In some ways, it would appear obvious that a national weight problem would correlate with national prosperity and abundance—especially in a society that's focused on consumption. But fast food has been around for a long time: Does it occupy a different place in American life than it did, say, forty years ago? Why would that be the case? Students might also research other examples of national "worrying" over health problems, throughout history. And how are such preoccupations tied to other cultural trends? For example, food writer Michael Pollan has written about obesity in the context of declining family "food cultures." Is our "obesity epidemic" a root problem, or is it a symptom of something else?

From Discussion to Writing

1. All three essays show that the "obesity epidemic" is not one issue or problem, but a network of interconnected scientific and cultural issues. Each of these writers views it through a different lens—and their works

reflect this. After reading the essays, students should consider what stands out to them: assumptions, patterns, arguments. They may also see what has been overlooked or underdeveloped in these three texts. Students could structure their essay as a response to one or more of the readings, or they can use one (or all) as a starting point for further exploration.

2. The purpose of this assignment is, in part, to analyze and test the generalizations in the readings. For example, what does "pandering" look and sound like, specifically? What does it rely on? What strategies—marketing, branding, journalistic—are at play in dieting trends and products? At the same time, students may use the exercise to find counterexamples, or products and articles that seem to rely less on pandering.

3. To the degree that bodies are always changing and that general health necessarily requires ongoing maintenance and care, we must think of ourselves as "renovation projects." So students may take a closer look at Lobel's metaphor. Beyond reasonable health concerns, is there something inherently wrong with focusing on weight loss or fitness—and making it (in Steingarten's words) "one of the central goals of life"? Are there assumptions at play here about where personal worth and meaning are located (for example, somewhere other than the body and its appearance or fitness)?

Topics for Cross-Cultural Discussion

1. This topic might require some research. It may touch on how notions of heaviness and beauty—as well as attitudes toward food and eating—vary in different cultures. As Steingarten's essay suggests, class differences might also play a role: Who can afford or have access to a Park Avenue therapist? Are disorders such as anorexia and bulimia equally prevalent among all classes, genders, and ethnicities? Why or why not?

2. In some ways, fast food has become a cultural symbol for America itself—as Durbin's essay implies, and as the global presence of American fast food chains demonstrates. Students should think about this in the context of global health, as more countries have adopted certain aspects of the Western diet. But if Steingarten's argument about genetic predispositions is correct, then the scapegoating of brands like McDonald's is overstated (even if such restaurants make the world more "obesogenic"). How are other countries coming to share, if not our health problems, then our preoccupation with fat? Steingarten talks about attending an international conference on obesity, where the success of "public anti-obesity programs" was discussed. Do you think other countries might be more amenable to—and more open to the possible positive effects of—such programs than is the United States? Why or why not?

2
Social Networking:
What are the Risks?

The increasing popularity of social-networking Web sites raises a number of questions both practical (What are the applications of this technology?) and ethical (How will the technology affect the way we interact with one another?). According to the Internet research firm Alexa, in the year from September 2006 to September 2007, Facebook rose from the sixtieth to the seventh most frequently visited Web site. The site was created by a student exclusively for his classmates at Harvard, but it quickly expanded to include all Ivy League schools, all colleges, high schools, and now any users over the age of thirteen. As the site has expanded into other demographics, the ratio of college students to other users has changed. Nonetheless, college students still make up a large part of Facebook users, and a high percentage of students enrolled in college have Facebook pages.

Since students are likely to have experience with Facebook or other social-networking sites, the arguments in this chapter should have some personal resonance. You might begin the unit discussion by asking students how concerned they are about the information they make public over the Internet. The three essays in this section offer very different analyses of the benefits and dangers of electronic communication. The student essay by Melissa Mapes may feel most familiar to students dealing with everyday concerns about how their profiles will affect the way their immediate circles of friends and schoolmates see them. The questions about ethical behavior that underlie some of Mapes's observations are at the center of Regina Lynn's "The New Communication Technology." She offers a challenge to reactionary ideas about the deteriorative effects of technology.

Finally, as a contrast to these essays' focus on personal relationships, Ari Melber surveys the history of Facebook and its discontents in order to examine changing conceptions of privacy in American culture. Taken together, these essays offer both individual-level and broader social readings of communication technologies as well as criticisms and defenses of their increasing importance in our lives.

REGINA LYNN   The New Communication Technology:
A Challenge to Modern Relationships?
[*Wired*/September 21, 2007]

Vocabulary/Using a Dictionary

1. *Pseudo-* means "false" or "in appearance only." Lynn's phrase "pseudo-social networking" summarizes arguments against sites like Facebook that claim they only create the appearance of social interaction but actually isolate individuals from one another.

2. In general, when people say that something "boggles the mind," they mean it is incomprehensible or hard to understand. The word *boggle* originally comes from *bogle*, which means "ghost."

3. *Churl* originally meant "man." The meaning then narrowed to "a man of low status or breeding." To be churlish is to be coarse or vulgar.

Responding to Words in Context

1. People who argue against new media would focus their definition of relationships on how they are conducted—preferably face-to-face. In paragraph 4, Lynn places "for real" in quotes because she finds this to be a shallow definition of what makes a relationship. For her, the connection between two people, not the medium through which they connect, is most important.

2. Lynn sees cell phones as extensions of ourselves. They allow us to connect directly with people we care about and to maintain one-on-one relationships. By contrast, more public and therefore less personal technologies like blogs are suitable for open discourse but do little to cement close relationships.

3. Being "dazzled" is to be almost blinded by something bright, so in her phrasing Lynn suggests that technologies like text-messaging were so exciting and new that we couldn't really see their merits and their problems clearly. Now that we have had time to adjust, she argues for a clearer evaluation of both their positive uses and the etiquette we should employ.

Discussing Main Point and Meaning

1. The primary goal of Lynn's essay is to defend the choice to connect with people she really cares about and not with casual acquaintances. However, she wants to make a distinction between choosing not to pursue relationships with the people she runs into in everyday life and treating them poorly, which she argues is inexcusable. For example, she cannot ignore the hotel employee just because she is engaged in text-messaging. In the end, she hopes that we can keep up our close connections while making "even the most casual of encounters . . . pleasant or at least neutral" (para. 26).

2. Lynn's first counterargument is that, rather than discouraging people from forming new intimate relationships, text-messaging and other technologies allow them to maintain close relationships they have already formed. Her second point is that cell phones and other devices aren't all-encompassing. While technophobes seem to assume that people will be overwhelmed by connectivity, Lynn points out that we can put the phones away when we wish. Both of these points help support her argument that technology facilitates more choice about with whom we have relationships and how we conduct them.

3. In the original context of Daniel Goleman's *Social Intelligence*, the idea of contagious mood explains the harm that rudeness produces as its negativity travels from one person to the next in a "ripple effect" (para. 10). However, Lynn argues that loving interactions can also be contagious and that technology makes spreading caring messages more efficient than ever.

Examining Sentences, Paragraphs, and Organization

1. In Lynn's first paragraph, the idea of universities offering a class about making friends comes off as ridiculous. Students learn such social skills through their interaction with family and friends, not through coursework. However, she points out that friendship has become the subject of university classes, suggesting that the concept of friendship has become more complicated, and more worthy of study, with the advent of social networking.

2. Lynn presents these challenges to critics of electronic communication in order to point out the consequences of an extreme position. Even though greater face-to-face interaction sounds like an unambiguous benefit, Lynn questions whether we should value the quality of relationships over the way in which they are conducted. The imperatives are not meant to expose problems with the critique she is discussing.

3. While the commands starting in paragraph 6 are directed specifically at technology's critics, the ones in paragraphs 26 and 27 are broader. Lynn believes that both she and her readers should exploit the cell phone's ability to connect people. The thesis of her argument is that technology enables rather than prevents intimacy, so the imperative at the end works as a rallying cry to prove just how it can work to spread good feelings.

Thinking Critically

1. In paragraph 24, Lynn claims that the slow process of spelling out text messages has made her a better listener, that the ambiguity of such messages has made her more likely to ask for clarification, and that technology in general has made her more patient. The last of these assertions seems counterintuitive, given that technology has considerably sped up the rate of communication. Also, even though text messages may take some time to compose, they put limits on the complexity of communication, thus calling into question Lynn's idea that they make her a better listener.

2. The acquaintances that Lynn names — "bank tellers, dog walkers, gro-
    cers" (para. 5) — are all in service jobs, and those relationships may be
    unlikely to deepen into greater significance. Constant text-messaging can
    hinder other relationships, too. As a way to get discussion going, you
    might ask students how many of them have ever spent the minutes
    between arriving at a classroom and the start of the period by texting
    friends rather than talking with their classmates. Does this change the
    rapport of the class? Does it make them less likely to form study groups
    or ask someone for notes from a missed class? Is this a problem that Lynn
    fails to take into account?

In-Class Writing Activities

1. Much of the activity on social-networking sites is devoted to finding peo-
    ple with similar interests, so students might think of creative ways that
    workshop participants could find out one another's likes and dislikes and
    create discussion. You might also have them think about the difference
    between being linked through friends online and actually being socially
    introduced to someone new.

2. Rules for mannerly behavior are designed primarily to make social inter-
    actions smoother and avoid any offense or hurt feelings. Any generation
    gap comes not from a change in this basic goal but from different ideas
    about how to reach it. While some parents might think it rude to answer
    a cell phone in a social setting, students may be more likely to accept it as
    long as the person receiving the call is discreet and ends the conversation
    quickly. Lynn draws the line at ignoring the hotel employee helping her in
    order to send a text message, but she doesn't see anything wrong with
    texting while sitting at a coffee shop.

ARI MELBER   About Facebook
[*The Nation*/January 7–14, 2008]

Vocabulary/Using a Dictionary

1. *Quad-* means "four," so to quadruple is to make four times as great.

2. Facebook not only owns the pictures its users post but also has the right
    to sell or transfer them to other entities. This would be a case of sub-
    licensing because the rights would pass from one company, Facebook,
    down to another company it allowed to control them. Therefore, the pre-
    fix *sub-* here means "below" or "secondry."

3. The word *private* comes from the Latin *privatus*, which means "restricted
    for the use of a certain person or certain people."

Responding to Words in Context

1. Our wired culture depends heavily not only on electronic devices like lap-
    top computers and cell phones but also on electronic means of social con-
    nection, such as text-messaging and social-networking sites. Melber also

uses the word *wired* to indicate a society in which both public and private citizens are always being watched and in which notability depends on getting more people to watch you.

2. Melber points out that people are under constant surveillance by video cameras, whether they are owned by the government or by private companies. The long reach of surveillance, he suggests, has made people more likely to allow their information to be collected. Internet users are so used to being watched already that providing their information online doesn't seem like anything new.

3. Facebook's Beacon created a spin on advertising by using content that had been provided by the site's members and broadcasting it to networks they had already formed with friends and acquaintances. To some degree, "social advertising" is euphemistic in that it tries to put a new and positive spin on companies' age-old attempt to sell their products, but Beacon's targeting of customers through personal relationships is something quite different from traditional advertising.

Discussing Main Point and Meaning

1. Though many Facebook users would not think of their profile as offering opportunities for others to spy on them, privacy activists worry that the information people provide on the Internet will reach unintended parties and may even be used against people. Melber describes how this debate came into the public eye in 2007 when Facebook took information posted by its members and broadcast it widely over the internet.

2. Current advertising practices depend heavily on gathering as much information as possible about consumer practices. Some collect information about user purchases without their knowledge, and Facebook even turned user photos into advertisements for products that users had bought.

3. Melber points out that on the Internet, the default is generally to share information rather than to protect it. Users have to actively keep track of their own online profiles and request privacy. He observes that whereas privacy was once automatically granted to individuals, now each person controls the extent to which his or her life is known to others.

Examining Sentences, Paragraphs, and Organization

1. Melber points to the public outcry against Facebook's broadcasting of information as a moment of resistance that has mostly faded away. Throughout the essay, he suggests that people are becoming so acclimated to surveillance that protesting no longer seems reasonable. He mentions the initial controversy again when he discusses Beacon, Facebook's advertising program, but notes that user response to this privacy violation, though negative, was not as strong as the original protests. By citing these two setbacks for the site, Melber writes a narrative of decreasing public resistance to having information gathered and then broadcast.

2. The younger generation's assumption that some information is always public is at the heart of what Melber calls the "new privacy." He cites two sources, one from inside Facebook and another who studies it from an academic perspective. Both of these sources confirm that Internet users have shifted the emphasis from absolute privacy to privacy that is managed and controlled.

3. The sentence begins with an "if" proposition that calls into question whether the "new privacy" is a real phenomenon. The sentence structure allows Melber to maintain his reservations about the "new privacy" while still exploring the consequences. He concludes that such a shift in the concept of privacy would still not explain the way people use Facebook, often counter to their own interests.

Thinking Critically

1. As Melber points out, Facebook makes its explanation of Beacon in "the language of the new privacy," framing the division in terms of shared content and social interaction. Although Zuckerberg casts Beacon as a service to users, it is clear that the real benefit accrues to Facebook in the form of ad revenue.

2. Melber believes that just as Facebook members should take responsibility for what they post, employers and advertisers should be up-front about how they use the information. Thus, he suggests that companies announce their intentions of examining the Web profiles of people they interview. He also believes that Facebook should be more transparent about how widely user information will be available and to what uses it might be put.

In-Class Writing Activities

1. Students will have different responses to these questions, but one line of reasoning that is likely to come up is the widespread popularity of the sites. Students may have a sense of safety in numbers, even if they do retain concerns about their personal information. In fact, some people watching the trend have speculated that in the next decade or so employers and admissions officers will have to be much less picky about what information they find online because public disclosure is so widespread.

2. This question asks students to think about broad policy decisions, but in the process they may wish to refer to personal experience. Have they ever been surprised by how their information was made available or used on social-networking sites? Do they agree that many users are naïve about how the sites work? Naming some specific problems can help them determine who should take action. Would more public awareness of Facebook's privacy settings solve the problem? Or do students believe, like Melber, that the government has some role to play in regulation?

MELISSA MAPES (STUDENT ESSAY)   Is Big Brother Watching Your Every Move?
[*The State Press*, Arizona State University/February 28, 2008]

Vocabulary/Using a Dictionary

1. *Dys-* comes from Greek and generally negates the positive connotations of a word. In this case, the prefix takes the generally positive or at least neutral connotation of the word *function* and suggests a destructive or impaired kind of functioning.

2. The Latin word *fascinare* means "to enchant or put a spell on." Although the word has lost the connotation of magic or witchcraft, it still suggests being transfixed by something.

3. *Rebuttal* comes from the French word *bouter*, "to strike or thrust." With the prefix *re-* added, it suggests a response to an initial strike by one's opponent. More generally, a rebuttal provides countervailing proof or an answer to an argument.

Responding to Words in Context

1. Mapes points out the proliferation on Facebook of relationships that are not necessarily warm or caring but involve surprisingly intimate mutual knowledge. Though the phenomenon of having mixed opinions about acquaintances is certainly not new, Facebook seems particularly apt at creating these ambivalent relationships as people gather Internet "friends" that they wouldn't necessarily spend time with in the real world.

2. A stilted conversation is one that is stiff or awkward. Stilted was originally a metaphorical adjective that suggested something that moved with difficulty, as would someone on stilts.

3. In Internet parlance, *feed* has come to mean a stream of information posted to a site to be e-mailed to selected users. Mapes connects this metaphorical sense of *feed* to the idea of getting nourishment, suggesting that today's college students survive on the information constantly provided to them by Facebook.

Discussing Main Point and Meaning

1. Although Mapes doesn't criticize Facebook directly, the examples from her friends' lives suggest that she thinks that people use Facebook more for demoralizing and mean-spirited purposes than otherwise. She sees that it facilitates harsh judgments, ugly public spats, and unnecessary gossip. She doesn't counsel leaving the site altogether, but she does suggest that students be careful about how their own public personae appear to others.

2. Mapes views Facebook messages positively compared to phone calls, which she argues can take discussion out of the context provided by facial expressions and body language. Even though Facebook messaging

is further removed from the body, it has the benefit of allowing more time for reflection. Mapes also compares Facebook messaging to letter writing because both let the writer take time to craft a message. However, whereas letters are private, messages on the Facebook wall are visible to all users, encouraging not authentic communication but witticisms that will impress everyone in the network.

Examining Sentences, Paragraphs, and Organization

1. The quotations allow Mapes to convey not just what Ashley says about what she reads on Facebook but also a little of her personality and way of speaking. She captures Ashley in a candid moment, using language that she might not use in a public forum. The need to guard such reactions is one of the arguments of Mapes's essay. Mapes also points out that whereas speech can convey emotion and intent, written communications, especially brief ones such as e-mail and Facebook messages, are easy to misconstrue.

2. Mapes's comment about the icons is sarcastic and calls into question the users' role in encouraging "gossip and drama" on the site (para. 4). Mapes's purpose is to criticize the petty behavior she observes among her peers, but this paragraph suggests that to some extent such behavior is inherent in the site's functions.

Thinking Critically

1. On the positive side, Mapes suggests that Facebook messages can be carefully thought out and crafted, as letters were in the past. They might allow for a more measured communication than, for example, a phone call. On the other hand, she suggests that the Facebook message can be a refuge for "cowards" who lack the courage to discuss matters face-to-face (para. 5).

2. The kind of information gathering Mapes describes occurs on an individual level and is motivated by daily dramas or petty vendettas. On the other hand, 1984 describes a government that systematically monitors its citizens for the purpose of solidifying ideology and suppressing dissent. Although the stakes of these two situations are very different, the distance between them is precisely what concerns writers like Ari Melber. Facebook's surveillance might seem benign, but the cleverness of companies in appropriating the site's information suggests that it could easily be put to more worrisome purposes.

In-Class Writing Activities

1. In the event that any students aren't on Facebook, this exercise may work best in groups, but they can choose from many features of the site: the ability to tag other people in photos you post, the games you can challenge other users to play, or applications that allow people to rate your desirability as a friend or date. Each of these functions creates different social interactions within the site.

2. The fact that Facebook gets its name from a physical artifact that colleges used to pass out to students suggests that it does have non-Internet origins. Leaving notes on someone's Facebook wall is similar to writing messages in a yearbook. The games people play on the site have a direct relation to games both electronic and traditional (such as Scrabble). The labeled pictures are a digital form of scrapbooks. Students can likely come up with many ways in which Facebook uses technology to facilitate activities that have been around for a long time.

Discussing the Unit

Suggested Topic for Discussion

Each of the authors in this unit is weary of potential threats caused by the progression of technology. While Melber believes that the threat is within technologies such as Facebook, Lynn and Mapes agree that it is how people use technology that needs to be controlled. You can start class discussion by asking students what they think about new communication technologies such as Facebook. Do they agree with Melber that these social networking sites obstruct our right to privacy? Or do they think, like Lynn, that they have made it easier to stay in touch with friends and loved ones? The question of privacy is an interesting one and may start off a debate. Remind your students to use evidence to back up their arguments, perhaps even using citations from the articles in this unit. What do they think about employers and faculty having access to their profiles? Would this make them think twice about what they put online? How does it make them feel to know that posted content could prevent them from getting a job?

Preparing for Class Discussion

1. The essays that are more focused on personal relations draw more on personal anecdotal experience for their evidence. Mapes uses primarily observations of her friends, and Lynn cites her own practices, although she also refers to academic writers to lend theoretical value to her defense. Melber's essay uses the most empirical data, such as news items and statistics, but he also relies on analysis of statements from Facebook executives to reveal their intentions.

2. Lynn's essay counters the second argument, and she dispatches the concern fairly quickly, arguing that the change in communication only appears to have lessened personal connection. Mapes deals with both questions, considering the way students use Facebook to manipulate one another as well as the need to exercise caution in creating an online persona. Melber focuses on the issue of surveillance rather than connection, and of the three authors, he makes the gloomiest predictions about the future of technology.

From Discussion to Writing

1. In response to this question, students may choose either to praise the merits of the technology they choose or to express concerns about the changes it will bring to communication. Either way, their arguments should be based on a precise description of how the technology works and a comparison of its features to previous innovations.

2. As of this writing, recent stories about Facebook have considered the complications that arise when coworkers or even bosses and their employees are connected on Facebook, the possibility of using the site for notification in emergency situations, and the addition of chat to its features. These stories suggest that both creative new uses and potential new problems are constantly evolving on the site.

Topics for Cross-Cultural Discussion

1. Just as Facebook quickly spread from Ivy League schools to other colleges, it also spread from its country of origin because of demand elsewhere. Outside the United States, the site is most popular in the English-speaking countries Canada and the United Kingdom, but Turkey, Colombia, and South Africa are all in the top ten for number of users.

2. Governments that have banned Facebook have cited several different reasons. Both Syria and Iran believed that people were using the Web site for subversive purposes, promoting attacks on the government. Some of the site's pages were being used to criticize state authorities. The United Arab Emirates claimed that the site was being used for online dating, which the country has banned.

3

How Important Is Ethic Identity?

The essays in this chapter take varied approaches to the question of how immigrants adapt to American life. Dinaw Mengestu's essay considers how people who come to the country find a home for themselves, making from scratch the connections that others might take for granted. He is rooted in his Brooklyn neighborhood not by the past or by ethnic identification but by his own choice of the place and his love for it. Manuel Muñoz uses given names as a lens through which he can examine the process of assimilation, which proves to be both a goal for immigrant families and a burden to them. He offers a nuanced reading of the changes he has seen in the names Mexican American parents pick for their children. Nathan Huang explains the customs that surround an important holiday in his native Taiwan and relates how his family's traditions had to adapt to their new lives in America. Finally, Sandy Dover examines both his largely homogeneous campus population and images from the media to see the complex ways in which people identify themselves.

Though the four authors in this chapter take different perspectives, three of them are at least partially concerned with children and how they experience immigration. Huang has the child version of himself relate the story of the red envelopes and their loss, and both Mengestu and Muñoz take time to narrate childhood experiences. The former recalls walks with his father that pointed out the deep differences in how the two of them relate to Ethiopia. Muñoz remembers a high school graduation that illustrated just how much was at stake in the pronunciation of Spanish names. You might wish to have students discuss why the child's perspective is central to each of these works. What does it provide that gets left out of the parents' views about cultural identity?

The essays in this chapter could be paired usefully with more argumentative pieces from Chapter 11. Even though none of the writers in this chapter offer overt analysis of immigration issues, each of their works is informed by the ongoing national debate. As your students read the essays in this chapter, have them keep this political context in mind. How might the appearance of immigration on the front pages of the newspaper have prompted or inspired these essays? How do the writer's personal experiences deepen a discussion of immigration issues?

DINAW MENGESTU Home at Last
[*Open City*/Winter 2008]

Vocabulary/Using a Dictionary

1. *De facto*, meaning "in fact," is opposed in legal usage to *de jure*, meaning "by law." The term signifies something that is acknowledged as true even if it is not officially established.

2. The stem *simil-* means "like." To assimilate is to become like something else—in this context, to become like the culture into which you migrate.

3. Mengestu's Brooklyn neighborhood is named after a borough of London. The label attests to the fact that the area's original inhabitants were British, adding another layer to the history of migrations that the author tracks through the kinds of shops and restaurants he finds in Kensington.

Responding to Words in Context

1. Mengestu experiences racial prejudice in high school, even to the point of physical violence. The fights he describes are based solely on his appearance. However, when he goes to college, he finds different expectations placed on him, based not on looks but on identity. He places the word *black* in quotation marks to signal a set of assumptions about what blackness means. Because this definition is based on African American attitudes and practices, his peers consider the African-born Mengestu an outsider.

2. A close-knit fabric is one in which the yarns are interlocked tightly, without a lot of open space. A community is close-knit if its individual members are not just related as parts of a whole but are in close contact and form a relatively cohesive unit.

3. A reenactment involves acting out a prior event for the purpose of remembering it. Mengestu's use of the word *reenactment* suggests that the life these men lead in Kensington is not an original act but a performance of a more authentic life that they previously knew. However, his sense of what the gathering means to them is not really that cynical. In the last paragraph, he admires people's ability to "rebuild and remake" communities in whatever way suits them.

Discussing Main Point and Meaning

1. One quality of the neighborhood Mengestu values is its diversity. He notes that on his way to the train station, he passes Latin American, Chinese, and halal markets as well as Pakistani and Bangladeshi restaurants. The fact that successive waves of immigrants have made Kensington their home gives Mengestu hope that he will be able to do the same. It is not a beautiful neighborhood, but he has a feeling of community with the men who gather on the sidewalk to drink tea and talk.

2. Although he is ethnically Ethiopian, Mengestu left his parents' country early enough in his life that he doesn't have any memories of it. The memories of their friends and family tie his parents to their country of origin,

but without anything to "remember," the author feels disconnected from Ethiopia.

3. For Mengestu's father, the evening walks are contemplative. During this time, he considers what he has lost, especially the brother whose name he whispers. His son wants to accompany him on these walks, but he has not experienced the same kind of loss, and so the father remains "alone" (para. 3) in his grief while his son remains apart from his parents' culture. Although the walks are an attempt to share experiences, they actually underline the gap between the parents' lives and those of their children.

Examining Sentences, Paragraphs, and Organization

1. Mengestu opens the essay by stating that he is twenty-one because it points out the fact that he has arrived at adulthood without a clear sense of home. While most people identify with the places where they were born or grew up, Mengestu has to take a more active role in finding a place to call home.

2. In the beginning of "Home at Last," Mengestu provides the necessary background so that he can later explain his attachment to his Brooklyn neighborhood. By discussing his parents' sense of both belonging and loss, he highlights the fact that he lacks a clear sense of where he comes from. Starting with paragraph 4, Mengestu analyzes his expectations for Kensington and the relationship he has established with it.

3. As Mengestu observes the crowd of South Asian men who commune in a language he can't understand, it reminds him of the Ethiopian community in Washington, D.C. Although he shared an ethnic background with the Ethiopian men who gathered outside coffee shops, he could not speak Amharic. In both cases, Mengestu watches from the outskirts, hoping that "the simple act of association and observation was enough to draw [him] into the fold" (para. 9).

Thinking Critically

1. Before he starts to form relationships with people in his neighborhood, Mengestu first tries to master the geography of the place. He walks all the streets and memorizes all the place names, convinced that his knowledge of the place will prevent anyone from claiming that he "didn't belong" (para. 5).

2. Mengestu entertains the idea of having friends out to Kensington for cheap biryani and beers, but he decides that his connection to the neighborhood is too personal. Even though the components of this "Kensington night" might be representative of its offerings, the neighborhood's appeal does not lie in charms that would be apparent to a visitor. Mengestu admits that it's not the most attractive area of the city. However, he loves it for the relationships he has formed with the people and places it contains, and those relationships are precisely what a visitor would not be able to experience.

3. Mengestu sees the "remnants" of the Jewish community as evidence that the successive waves of immigrants eventually become more seamlessly incorporated into the larger society. When they first arrive, the immigrants are relatively isolated, but as their children grow up, they move out of the insular community because they feel more comfortable than their parents did in American culture. By Mengestu's logic, the Pakistani and Bangladeshi communities that have developed in Brooklyn will eventually dissipate because their members will be assimilated. Finally, he takes this pattern as assurance that he will one day feel at home in America.

In-Class Writing Activities

1. Since campus life might challenge the notion of a neighborhood, students could choose to write about their family homes. Alternatively, this assignment may give them a chance to consider how communities are formed at college. If they live on campus, would they consider their dorm a kind of "neighborhood"? Does off-campus living create unusually homogeneous neighborhoods, made up entirely of twenty-year-olds? How does the kind of neighborhood they live in affect the way they act toward their neighbors?

2. This assignment might work well as a group activity. Have students brainstorm by thinking of local places that stand out in some way—by architecture, by name, or by function. Then have them choose one to write about. What was the place's original purpose? Has it changed? Or have things changed around it?

MANUEL MUÑOZ   Leave Your Name at the Border
[*New York Times*/August 1, 2007]

Vocabulary/Using a Dictionary

1. The root *Angl-* means "English," so a name that is Anglicized is made to sound more like an English-language name.

2. The Latin stem *lingua-* means "tongue" or, figuratively, "language."

3. "Nombres del rancho" literally translates as "names of the ranch." This phrase establishes a connection between the traditional names Muñoz's stepfather misses and an agrarian lifestyle, which has been largely replaced by industrialization in both Mexico and the United States.

Responding to Words in Context

1. Muñoz notes that in other places, people might carefully differentiate among people of Mexican descent, those who were born in Mexico, people from other Latin American countries, and so on. In Fresno, however, the distinctions are less precise—people are considered either white or Mexican.

2. In this paragraph, Muñoz imagines that he and other children of immigrants play into the desire of American culture to erase their ethnicity.

However, he claims that he was "unwittingly complicit," suggesting that although he may have gone along with assimilation, he did not really know what was at stake in small choices such as the way to pronounce a name.

3. *Corrosive* refers to the process of wearing something down, as rust eats away at metal. By using this word, Muñoz describes a situation in which one culture gradually destroys the integrity of another by displacing its customs, products, and other cultural artifacts.

Discussing Main Point and Meaning

1. Though Muñoz has political reasons for objecting to the change in pronunciation, he also has clear aesthetic objections to what he describes as the butchering of Spanish names. When mispronounced or replaced by English equivalents, the names lose the beauty of the Spanish language and become "clunky" and "ugly" (para. 12).

2. For Muñoz and his peers, the question of names comes down primarily to a desire to fit in, but for the generation of their parents, a name could mean the difference between finding work and staying unemployed. For his stepfather, going by the name "Tony" was a signal that he was competent in English and could communicate well with his employer.

3. Muñoz claims that rather than embracing both languages, he and others in Dinuba segregated their lives into English- and Spanish-speaking situations. English was for school and public discourse while Spanish was for the privacy of home, and as he recounts, Spanish was devalued as "privacy quickly turned to shame" (para. 16).

Examining Sentences, Paragraphs, and Organization

1. Muñoz uses the gate agent as an illustration of how Mexican names change when their bearers immigrate to the United States. She is a concrete example of how the pronunciation becomes more "American," and it is important to his discussion that her job puts her in the position of having her voice amplified and heard by a large group of travelers.

2. Muñoz lists his cousins' names assuming that the reader can easily separate them into traditional Spanish names (Estella, Dubina) that likely indicate a familiarity with the language and Anglo-American names (Eric, Melanie) that probably belong to children who grew up speaking only English.

3. The lists of names in "Leave Your Name at the Border" serve as evidence, but they also give texture to the writing. Muñoz clearly delights in the sounds of names like Luis (para. 11). He also wants to give a place to the old "nombres del rancho" that may be disappearing (para. 13).

Thinking Critically

1. As an adult, Muñoz assumes that the teacher was well-meaning and that his pronunciation was a sign of respect for the children's parents. He implies

that, at the time, hearing their names pronounced with a Spanish accent was embarrassing to his classmates because it ran counter to their attempts to appear "American."

2. The students of color Muñoz encounters in college find it easier to express ownership over and pride in their ethnicity. He feels embarrassed about his small-town upbringing, presumably because it forced him to make concessions to mainstream culture that he would not have had to make if he had lived in a city big enough to have cohesive ethnic communities within the larger population.

3. Muñoz imagines Eugenio Reyes as an older man with a cowboy hat because he thinks the name is traditional and belongs to a more rural past. However, after he makes this assessment, Muñoz realizes that his characterization of Eugenio Reyes is largely unfounded and that he is making the mistake of assuming too much based on a name.

In-Class Writing Activities

1. The desire to take a different name often comes from the feeling that the name you were given does not match the person you are. It often appears at times of transition, such as when students leave home to go to college. However, the motivation for these thoughts of change is mainly internal. The pronunciation changes and substitutions made by Muñoz's friends and family members have both internal causes (the desire to fit in) and external ones (the pressure to assimilate).

2. Language use is governed by rules, but, paradoxically, to express something elusive speakers or writers sometimes have to push the boundaries set by language. Muñoz's statement is informed by his sense that both Spanish and English have limitations, and his ability to use both in a single conversation, which he calls "code-switching" (para. 19), makes it possible for him to work against those limitations.

NATHAN HUANG   A Red Envelope Day
[*New York Times*/February 18, 2007]

Vocabulary/Using a Dictionary

1. The root -*gram* comes from the Greek word *gramma*, which means "to write" or, by extension, "to draw." A hologram uses light to produce the illusion of a "whole" or three-dimensional image.

2. A custom is any habitual act, but today people use the word primarily to indicate cultural practices rather than simple habits. *Custom* shares its origin with the word *costume*, and this connection underlines the relation between custom and a fashion or manner of doing something.

Responding to Words in Context

1. Huang explains in panel 2 that his family is large, and in the first panel many adults and children are visible. He imagines that the sheer number of his relatives has the potential to be intimidating.

2. Huang's use of the word *particularly* indicates that even though there were other annoying boys in school, this one is especially irksome to him. This word choice shows why Huang singles him out in the comic and why the boy plays an important role in what the main character learns in this story.

Discussing Main Point and Meaning

1. Huang appreciates the fact that his big family helps him remember and observe Taiwanese customs. He also realizes that having a big family means that he should reap more red envelope money during the holiday. However, the size of the family makes that custom prohibitively expensive, a limitation that proves to be a disappointment to the narrator.

2. While the narrator is plotting how he will spend the greater quantities of money he will get from his large family, his parents and the other adults are making decisions about their financial position in their new country. Seeing his Chinese classmate show off his possessions after the New Year is even more onerous to Huang because he imagined he would have an opportunity to get back at the boy.

Examining Sentences, Paragraphs, and Organization

1. Because the comic is focused on the child's experiences, the drawings of the adults emphasize their distance from him. In panel 7, their backs are turned to him because they have their own concerns to think about while he plots his revenge on a classmate. In panel 9, adults are pictured from a child's perspective, with their heads cut off and only the lower parts of their bodies visible. This child's-eye view also emphasizes their gesture of agreement, the handshake.

2. Huang uses a busy composition to convey the bustle of family life and of the preparations for the holiday, particularly in panels 1 and 3. He uses more open space in the panels that contain only a single figure — either the main character or his nemesis. In the last two panels of the comic, the negative space emphasizes the speaker's isolation.

Thinking Critically

1. The "particularly annoying Chinese boy" (panel 4), in addition to giving Huang a more pressing reason for wanting the red envelope money, also serves as a foil to the main character. Even though this boy is the villain of the story, his greed reflects back on Huang himself as he gets caught up in the need to show off.

2. Huang tells his story from his own point of view as a child, but there are moments when an adult, or at least a more mature, consciousness intrudes. His discussion of the adults' decision not to keep up the custom of giving red envelopes is one instance. He can now clearly explain this decision as a matter of "financial survival" (panel 9), a form of reasoning that he probably would not have fully understood as a child.

3. Although the narrator might experience some childish resentment at not getting any red envelope money, the tone of his last statement seems to be resigned to the family's difficult decision. He is sad not to participate in the custom, but he at least partially knows that the adults have larger problems to consider.

In-Class Writing Activities

1. The traditions that Huang describes have two primary purposes: banishing bad luck or bad feelings and welcoming good things for the coming year. Students might wish to compare the symbolism of the Chinese traditions with their own New Year's observations.

2. Huang resists giving his story an easy ending that affirms the value of familial love over material goods. Making such a statement would undermine the real disappointment of the young protagonist. The comic's message seems to be less about the comforts of family than about the corrupting influence of jealousy.

SANDY DOVER (STUDENT ESSAY)   How Do You Define You?
[*The Lantern*, Ohio State University/January 10, 2007]

Vocabulary/Using a Dictionary

1. *Con-* is a variant of *co-*, which means "together." Dover uses the word concurrent to indicate that Stein can have different identities that are present at the same time.

2. *Distinguish* come from the Latin verb *distinguere*, which means "to separate." In current use, to distinguish is to recognize something as different, or to single one thing out from others.

Responding to Words in Context

1. Many colleges hope to have a mix of students from different socioeconomic backgrounds and cultural experiences as well as different racial and ethnic groups. Achieving this balance gives opportunities to groups historically underrepresented in college, and it also provides a more varied student body for all collegians.

2. The idea that black and white are physical designations whereas identities such as Jewish are more cultural categories shows the logic on which Stein bases her varied identifications. It seems to justify her possibly contradictory claims.

Discussing Main Point and Meaning

1. The multiplicity of identities with which some of the students associate themselves suggests that identity is more malleable than people might think. It also indicates that there is a complex taxonomy of categories: for example, white is a broader designation that is not mutually exclusive of "Jewish" and "Israeli" (para. 2).

2. Dover's claims and the examples he chooses are meant to challenge simplistic notions about race and ethnicity. He introduces complicating factors not to discredit the way his peers identify themselves but to show that such identifications are often quite individual and personal.

Examining Sentences, Paragraphs, and Organization

1. The third paragraph of Dover's essay begins by showing why Stein's belief that she is both Israeli and white could be considered self-contradictory. In the rest of the paragraph, he reveals some other ways in which ethnicity can be complicated, including references to both of the comedians he mentioned in the introduction.

2. The first sentence of paragraph 5 states outright Dover's main point: that the ways people associate themselves with ethnicities and cultures are many and varied. In his final paragraph, he arrives at a conclusion for his peers: They should be more aware of how identities are formed.

Thinking Critically

1. Dover includes these two examples in order to show how much the media influence our understanding of ethnic difference and identity. This is particularly true for people who live in largely homogeneous communities, like Dover's university. However, by putting the two together he obscures the point that the anti-Semitism in *Borat* is a deliberate part of the satire, while Richards's comments were unscripted and spontaneous.

2. Dover seems to suggest in paragraph 3 that everyone has a complex identity, even those who deal in stereotypes. However, these two comedians' individual ethnicities seem to have relatively little to do with either their elaborate and layered parody of how people signify identity (in Cohen's case) or the specific prejudices their comments might reveal (in Richards's case).

In-Class Writing Activities

1. Whereas Jodi Stein's self-determined identity is additive, the identity that is placed on Dan Wandrey by others is based on subtracting — on figuring out what he is not. You might ask students to consider in their writing whether this external identification reveals something about human nature. Does it generally seek to exclude rather than to include?

2. Students will no doubt come up with their own examples, but one relatively recent film that comments extensively on stereotypes is Spike Lee's

Bamboozled (2000), in which a disgruntled black actor puts on a minstrel show in protest but is surprised to find that it become a huge hit.

Discussing the Unit

Suggested Topic for Discussion

The United States is often referred to as a "melting pot"—defined as people of different ehnicities, races, and religions merging into a single, united society. The articles in this unit show that Americans come from all over the world, such as Ethiopia, Mexico, and Taiwan to name a few. Ask your students to look around them, not only in the classroom but also on the streets, in the grocery store. Is there a certain prevalent ethnicity? Depending on your college and/or state locations, this might give your students insight on the migration patterns of the area. Is your city or state diverse?

The "promise of diversity" is a debatable issue. Talk to your students about the assimilation that Muñoz describes in his article. Does assimilation enable or hinder diversity? What about ghettos like Chinatown? Can isolation of cultural equals be defined as diversity or as segregation?

Preparing for Class Discussion

1. Of the essays in this unit, Mengestu's is the most overtly concerned with what it means to feel at home somewhere, and his definition is based less on origins than on ideals. He feels at home in Kensington because he approves of its unpretentious mix of cultures and customs. Muñoz examines a border culture in which residents negotiate between two homes, the dominant English-speaking culture and the influence of Spanish-speaking Mexico. Huang closely associates tradition with home, but his narrator comes to realize that traditions have to adapt to new surroundings. Finally, even though Dover does not discuss home in a literal sense, his essay is concerned with how young people come to feel comfortable in their multiple identities.

2. Muñoz focuses on how the dominant language, English, can distort other languages and in the process change the pronunciation of Spanish names. He also discusses how bilingual speakers may divide their lives between the languages, resulting in a conflicted relationship with both. Mengestu, on the other hand, feels more comfortable with English than any other language. The languages spoken by older Ethiopians and by his South Asian neighbors are equally foreign to him.

From Discussion to Writing

1. The introduction suggests the ways in which each of these authors uses childhood in his work. For all of them, the child's perspective offers a naïveté that reveals common assumptions about immigration. The young Mengestu's observations of his father's behavior remind readers of its emotional impact. The shame Muñoz and his classmates feel is testimony

to the intense pressure to assimilate. Finally, Huang's child narrator points out some of the smaller sacrifices that immigrant families make, which, although they might be overlooked, are sometimes just as heartbreaking.

2. Of the four writers, Muñoz seems most concerned about what may be lost in the process of assimilation. He shows how the need to exist in two cultures can produce the feeling of being a divided self. Mengestu seems to see assimilation as a more natural process, one that occurs gradually when immigrants become accustomed to America and move out of their concentrated neighborhoods. Although Huang's perspective is more focused in his shorter piece, he sees assimilation as a process of loss. Dover traces American identities to their historical roots and suggests that cultural blending, which has been going on for thousands of years, may be inevitable.

Topic for Cross-Cultural Discussion

Because people from Mexico and other Latin American countries make up the bulk of immigrants to the United States, the problems that Muñoz considers have much to do with public perception. He notes that in his part of California, all distinctions among Latinos are reduced to the designation "Mexican." By contrast, Mengestu sometimes finds himself being deliberately alienated from African Americans, who don't see him fitting into their culture. Of the three, Huang's piece seems most universal in the problems it addresses: financial hardship and the struggle to hold onto traditions.

4

Gender Differences:
Can You Trust the Scientific Reports?

As Beth Skwarecki writes in "Mad Science: Deconstructing Bunk Reporting in 5 Easy Steps," "traditional gender roles are an evergreen subject in the science pages." The presumed differences between men and women—in ways of thinking, feeling, and behaving—are a source of enduring fascination. They also have practical consequences when they are used to justify stereotypical behavior as "male" or "female," explain why more men than women pursue mathematics as a profession, or determine whether women talk more than men do.

No doubt, most of our perceptions about gender roles come from customs, personal experience, and our everyday interactions with people and are therefore subjective and unsystematic. What happens, however, when researchers bring the tools of the scientific method to bear on gender differences? Indeed, science can apply its strategies to the subject and offer fresh insights. But despite its connotations of empiricism and objectivity, science sometimes brings along cultural biases and limitations. It can also simply be wrong or incomplete, as legitimate scientists will openly acknowledge. Furthermore, nonexperts generally encounter this research not in scientific journals but filtered through the popular, mainstream media, which may distort claims and findings in pursuit of sensational stories. As the essays in this chapter demonstrate, students should not simply accept the lofty endorsement of "science" without reading—and thinking—critically about the authority, validity, and context of scientific claims.

That is especially true with regard to gender and gender roles. The first three selections in this chapter look closely at the case of neurobiologist Louann Brizendine's book *The Female Brain* (2006). In it, she claims that "a woman uses about 20,000 words per day while a man uses about 7,000." As Matthias R. Mehl and his colleagues point out in "Are Women Really More Talkative Than Men?" those numbers were widely "circulated throughout television, radio, and print media" and took on "the status of a cultural myth." But Mehl's study of male and female conversations—the first that has ever systematically recorded the "total daily output" of men and women—shows that Brizendine's assertions were unfounded. Indeed, this experiment not only debunked "bad" science and science reporting but also concluded, "on the basis of available empirical evidence, that the widespread and highly publicized stereotype about female talkativeness is unfounded." Two stories from National Public Radio and the *Wilson Quarterly* discuss Brizendine's claim, scientific responses to it, and the effects of such stereotypes as they filter into popular culture after being given the stamp of scientific credibility. These essays also touch on the real possibilities for insight that science can bring to the study of gender difference. As a whole, these three articles suggest a provocative discussion about the complex relationship among science, the media, and cultural beliefs.

But how do we distinguish "good" science from "bad," credible research from sensational popular journalism? Skwarecki's essay provides a checklist of questions to help readers spot "mangled" scientific findings, suspicious sources, and blatant misrepresentation in such reporting. For example, she urges us to beware of stories that use scientific research to confirm cultural stereotypes. Such reports may offer readers the satisfaction of claiming, "Yes! I knew it all along!" But these accounts can be misleading. Skwarecki claims that we should make sure that the study being covered actually supports a story's attention-grabbing headline; she also shows how double standards about men and women creep into accounts in the popular media. Although her focus is on gender differences, students might consider how other complex and controversial scientific issues, from genetic engineering to global warming, are reported in the mainstream press.

In "Where Are All the Women Mathematicians?" Joseph Vandehey looks at gender assumptions as they're shaped by the belief that difference implies hierarchical, "better"/"worse" value judgments. He also argues that our need to see social distinctions between men and women as either a function of biology or the result of sexism lead to unsatisfactory answers to questions like the one in his essay's title. Beginning with the premise that there are more male mathematicians than female ones, Vandehey shows how most current accounts of this phenomenon are incomplete or, in the case of presumably "objective" scientific explanations, merely reinforce the "'differences are hierarchies' mindset" in scientific terms. He claims that society's generally negative attitude toward the math profession may discourage *anyone* from choosing it as a field of study, but that negativity might affect women even more than men. Students may use Vandehey's essay as a starting point to examine how gender assumptions—their own and society's—have shaped their academic interests and career pursuits.

MATTHIAS R. MEHL ET AL.   **Are Women Really**
More Talkative Than Men?
[*Science*/July 6, 2007]

RICHARD KNOX   **Study: Men Talk Just as Much as Women**
[National Public Radio, *All Things Considered*/July 5, 2007]

EDITORS, WILSON QUARTERLY   **He Said, She Said**
[*Wilson Quarterly*/Autumn 2007]

Vocabulary/Using a Dictionary

1. *Ambient* means "of the surrounding area or environment," and ambient sound is often considered background noise. For example, conversation is the ambient sound the EAR picks up in this study, but many things can be considered ambient sound, such as the sound of the wind blowing, the hum of a refrigerator, or the sound of cars in the street.

2. *Homogeneity* means "the state of being the same or similar in nature." Other words that use the prefix *homo-* include *homologous, homographic, homosexual,* and *homogeneous.*

3. When someone is disadvantaged, he or she lacks the comforts or opportunities afforded to others. Synonyms of *disadvantaged* include *deprived, impaired, disabled,* and *impoverished."*

Responding to Words in Context

1. The adjective *lexical* is derived from the word *lexicon,* which refers to a dictionary or vocabulary. Budgets most often have to do with sums of money that are set aside or needed. A lexical budget is the number of words allotted to a person.

2. *Everyday* is an adjective that means "ordinary." It is often confused with the two words *every day,* meaning "each day." Everyday, or ordinary, conversation is not the same as "daily utterances," which take place daily, or each day.

3. Someone who is taciturn is disinclined to talk. Someone who is reticent is inclined to be silent. The words refer to the same kind of person.

Discussing Main Point and Meaning

1. One message of Knox's article is that men and women are inclined to believe in stereotypes. Mehl's study and Knox's article "prove" that men and women hold deeply ingrained assumptions about gender-specific behavior and that these are hard to dispel even with scientific evidence. Mehl's study mentions that the idea that women are more talkative than men has "achieved the status of a cultural myth." As Knox says in his essay, "Mehl acknowledges that many will have trouble believing the results, since it contradicts their own perceptions."

2. If women were significantly more verbal than men, then at some point women would no longer be able to converse because men would run out of words, in a sense. Because women are assumed to talk more, psychologists have produced books on the subject, positing that this discrepancy cound lead to conflict between the sexes. The discrepancy in talkativeness would affect men and women in their personal lives and probably in their professional lives as well. Stereotypes abound about the talkative female and silent male, but it is impossible to imagine a situation in which every woman talks significantly more than every man, and every man is significantly more silent than every woman.

3. The study acknowledges that the similarity of all subjects (they are all college students) is a possible limitation. It is also important to note that the number of words spoken per day is an estimated average and that the students studied are a small sample of the population. The study of a higher percentage of total daily conversation or a wider, more diverse population would make the results of the study even more comprehensive.

Examining Sentences, Paragraphs, and Organization

1. That sentence offers important information to those who don't have the study in front of them (and National Public Radio listeners wouldn't have it in front of them). It shows how thorough the research is, and it gives people a chance to make up their minds about the validity of the study.

2. The word *study* suggests a level of examination and analysis; the word *claim* does not. A claim need not have facts behind it. Knox may have included the periodical name to add scholarly weight to the Mehl study — *Science* magazine is published by the American Association for the Advancement of Science. He may have omitted relevant publication information about the book in an attempt to make it appear less rigorous or academic (he also neglects to give the author's distinguished credentials as a neuropsychiatrist). These particular word choices and the inclusion and omission of certain information influence the reader's perception of the Mehl study and the book by Louann Brizendine.

3. The Knox article and the *Wilson Quarterly* summary review the findings of the Mehl study. They give the same background information and repeat the basic findings of the study. However, the Knox article also includes feedback from one of the study's main researchers, quoting him extensively. In this way, Knox gives the researcher the chance to evaluate his data conversationally and offer more insight on the subject being studied.

Thinking Critically

1. A stereotype is a generalization, fair or unfair, about a group of people. Stereotypes help us evaluate, because they can characterize a group in a way that makes it easier to understand that group — whether it be a stereotype of gender, race, ethnic background, or chosen profession; however, we should be aware that groups are made up of individuals and that stereotypes can often reflect our prejudices toward another group.

2. A man can talk as much or more than a woman and still not want to talk about emotional issues or relationship problems with a woman. According to Knox, research shows that men and women talk about different things, although it doesn't show that one gender talks more or less than the other. In the "demand/withdrawal pattern," the woman wants to talk about a particular topic, but the man withdraws from the topic.

3. The Mehl study provides useful information because it gives a scientific view on a subject about which many people hold unscientific assumptions. It contains data that holds up under scrutiny, as opposed to putting forth untested claims. Studies often present conflicting results depending on research conditions and the goals of the researchers, so it is helpful to consider many studies when coming to a scientific conclusion about something. Systematic study can give us answers that we can believe, but it is important not to be blind to other answers and possibilities.

In-Class Writing Activities

1. Students may choose from negative or positive stereotypes that distinguish men from women. They may choose complex and psychological differences: men's and women's expression of aggression, their academic strengths, or their relationships with their parents. Students might focus on a stereotype of what men and women choose to spend their money on or how they nurture their children differently. Some students may believe there are no intrinsic differences in the behaviors of men and women, despite the perceived stereotypes. Any thesis should be backed up with relevant examples.

2. The summary should simplify the information in Knox's article and present its main points. The opening paragraph should introduce Knox and his article in the same way that Knox introduces the Mehl study. The summary should not be a simple paraphrase of the article.

3. The electronically activated recorder has become a versatile, easy-to-use machine as technology has advanced. Students should be able to find information on the device and its usefulness on the Web and elsewhere. Based on their research, students will decide for themselves how effective the machine is for such a study and what improvements, if any, would give future studies more validity. They can decide if the other variables in the study make the research seem stronger or weaker. Mehl's study also gives a brief history of the methods of past studies, which students can also take into consideration.

BETH SKWARECKI   Mad Science: Deconstructing Bunk
Reporting in 5 Easy Steps
[*Bitch*/Spring 2008]

Vocabulary/Using a Dictionary

1. A bias is a person's judgment about something and frequently reveals a personal preference or prejudice.

2. *Curative* can be either a noun or an adjective. In this context, it is used as an adjective and means "used to heal, cure, or treat." It can also be a noun and means "a remedy or a cure." If a dictionary wasn't handy, you might look at the root of the word and assume it has to do with curing or caring for something. Curative properties are qualities that promote healing.

3. *Calibrate* is a scientific term that means "to measure something precisely or to measure against a standard." The word *miscalibrate* is formed by joining *calibrate* and the prefix *mis-*, which means "wrongly" or simply negates the word it precedes. *Miscalibrate* means "to make an incorrect calibration."

Responding to Words in Context

1. The word *mainstream* (a compound of *main* and *stream*) means "a prevailing current or direction of activity or influence." Mainstream media are news sources that reach the largest audiences. They are the television, radio, and print sources that most people know. Anything mainstream is considered more vulnerable to the reactions of its mainstream audience and to the influence of government and advertising sources. Students may be able to offer examples of mainstream media: CNN, NBC, the *Los Angeles Times*, the *New York Times*, and others. Skwarecki also names several mainstream journals and radio broadcasts in her article.

2. *Hardwired* usually refers to permanent electronic circuitry, such as that in a computer or a phone. In this case, though, it has to do with human behavior patterns and inborn responses. In the essay, Skwarecki questions a study that suggests women are hardwired to like pink because of how our earliest female ancestors lived.

3. Ogle means "to stare." Most often, oglers are assumed to be men who lustfully or rudely look at women.

Discussing Main Point and Meaning

1. Evergreens are trees that stay green year-round, and Skwarecki is saying that there is an endless supply of questions to be answered about traditional gender roles. Gender roles fascinate because men want to understand or explain unfamiliar female behavior and vice versa. Now that traditional roles are being examined and questioned, people want to know when they originated and what is behind them. Because science supposedly provides facts and hard evidence, we look to science to clarify gender related issues for us.

2. We are all affected by stereotypes, although one hopes scientists will work hard to overcome these prejudices in their pursuit of a truthful answer. Skwarecki notes double standards that many of us are oblivious to when thinking about men and women — for example, double standards involving sexual promiscuity that skew one's perception of such topics. As Skwarecki points out, even scientists can lose sight of other

possible answers and meanings as they follow a particular theory, and so can lay people, who are more likely to stand by what they've heard about men and women, with or without proof.

3. The citation of sources is one way to decide whether a study is using good science. Good science requires proof to back up its claims, whereas bad science does not. In addition, bad science often contains logic errors, such as sweeping generalizations and *post hoc, ergo propter hoc* fallacies. Good science is more careful in drawing conclusion.

Examining Sentences, Paragraphs, and Organization

1. By including the interjection "duh," Skwarecki shows that she is firmly behind the idea that housework is hard—and she suggests the ridiculousness of not including it with traditionally "male" examples of strenuous work. If the sentence simply read "it turns out that domestic tasks are hard work" or "this proves that domestic tasks are hard work," the sentence would feel more neutral: however, with the inclusion of a simple interjection, Skwarecki establishes herself as someone clearly angered by cultural stereotyping. She pushes her own feminist stance into her writing here and elsewhere in the essay.

2. The sentence relates to the one preceding it, but it is set apart for emphasis. In paragraphs 39 and 40, Skwarecki describes a study that involved a phony formula that was then published with no accompanying information about the study's source. By following the story with a moral, she adds further stress to the point she hoped would be revealed through the anecdote.

3. By numbering the points, Skwarecki highlights them and draws her readers' attention to them in much the same way that the headlines of mainstream articles draw in their readers. More important, the numbered points organize the information just as an outline does. They become a checklist that readers can apply to their reading in the same way that a good researcher would apply them to his or her scientific data.

Thinking Critically

1. Students may approach this question with great faith in cultural stereotypes. It is important to challenge these assumptions and examine such beliefs from a variety of angles. Students can question assumptions about men and women based on basic physical differences and then look to studies of the measurable effects of estrogen and testosterone—and then consider whether these physical differences can be said to have an effect on all men and all women in terms of how they see the world and act in it.

2. A hook is like a sound bite in the news. It grabs the attention of the anticipated audience. Mainstream media are more interested in generating attention for their stories than they are in reporting the dry facts of science. The media also cultivate an audience and generate revenue based on

the size of their audience, and so they have a monetary stake in the most interesting hook. The hook is not necessarily about good or truthful reporting.

3. Some students will think that gender differences should be studied, and some will argue they should be left as topics of interest that hold no scientific weight. After reading this essay, many students might believe that questions (and assumptions) about men's and women's color preferences are best left to puff and opinion pieces; however, students may believe that questions about reducing breast cancer risk (or prostate cancer risk) are worthy of a scientist's time and that the differences between men and women should be studied to shed light on these issues. After reading Skwarecki's essay, students may feel that commonly held views and claims about men and women must be tested first before gender differences can be studied effectively.

In-Class Writing Activities

1. Students can choose from a wealth of stereotypical male and female behavior for this essay. They can discuss physical or psychological stereotypes or stereotypes about intelligence or social behavior. Skwarecki offers a variety of examples in the essay itself, but students should be encouraged to find something they have wondered about or held to be true. When they explore the possible "scientific validity" of the stereotype they have chosen, they should do research and cite sources. Students should apply Skwarecki's questions to their opinions and to the studies they have chosen when they decide whether their evidence is based on sound science.

2. Skwarecki briefly mentions other studies performed by biased researchers—one, in particular, that "claims that African-Americans have higher IQs than Africans because they have Caucasian genes that make them smarter." Race and ethnicity are other areas that are prone to stereotyping. Students could come up with any number of studies that would benefit from Skwarecki's questions, because anything that involves a comparison and generalizes about an entire group should be suspect—comparing children and adults, comparing people who live in warm climates and those who live in a cold climates, comparing premature infants and full-term babies, to name a few.

3. Students may note that she is writing about gender issues, and this makes the article a good fit for such a magazine. They may also note her feminist slant, revealed in her examples and her tone. She takes on the sort of stereotypes that are of greatest concern to feminists—assumptions about femininity and sexuality and "women's work" (namely, housework). Students may suggest other kinds of articles one would find in a magazine like *Bitch* and compare them to Skwarecki's piece. Her ending, too, may deserve mention, because she points out a recent scientific study entitled "Men and women found more similar than portrayed in popular media."

JOSEPH VANDEHEY (STUDENT ESSAY)   Where Are All the Women Mathematicians?

[*Oregon Daily Emerald*, University of Oregon/November 8, 2007]

Vocabulary/Using a Dictionary

1. *Hierarchy* comes from the Greek *hierarch*, meaning "a steward, priest, or high religious authority in charge of sacred rites."

2. *Gender* originates in the Latin *gener*, which means "kind" or "sort." Words such as *generic* and *homogeneous* share the same origin.

3. The term *cognitive* comes from the Latin *cognoscere*, (to know, to learn). Related words include *recognize* and *cognizant*.

4. The term *chauvinism* comes from Nicolas Chauvin, a French soldier in Napoleon's army, who was notorious for his brash, outspoken patriotism and devotion to Napoleon. With the word *male* as a modifier, it now most commonly refers to the presumption of male superiority over women.

Responding to Words in Context

1. By using the qualification "automatically," Vandehey allows for the possibility that sometimes differences do imply hierarchies. The use of the word *instinct* suggests that people apply this hierarchical view of oppositions without thought or consideration.

2. The term *connotation* refers to a word's meanings and associations beyond its explicit or primary definition. By using the phrase *negative connotations*, Vandehey is referring to the negative images, meanings, or associations evoked by the idea of a mathematician in our culture.

3. Vandehey means that we view mathematicians as impractical and unnecessary, although they're allowed to practice their profession.

Discussing Main Point and Meaning

1. Vandehey argues that we see the contrasting mathematical inclinations of men and women in the context of a "'differences are hierarchies' mindset" (para. 4). Moreover, observers either tend to explain this difference in terms of sexism—which doesn't account for successful female mathematicians and requires "the vast majority of males to be bigots" (para. 3)—or ignore sexism entirely, focusing instead on reductive biological explanations.

2. In relying on presumed "cognitive differences between men and women" (para. 4), these explanations suggest that the superior (and therefore hierarchical) spatial and quantitative abilities of men explain the larger number of male mathematicians. Vandehey also points out that math requires abilities other than spatial and quantitative skills, so this "cognitive" account not only is biologically reductive and hierarchical but also misrepresents the nature and profession of mathematics.

3. According to Vandehey, "Society as well as biology must be taken into account, and society has attached many negative connotations to mathematicians" (para. 6). He describes the negative image ascribed to mathematicians as well as his own struggles to pursue the profession against the wishes of his parents. He concludes that, given how hard it is for anyone to choose this career (let alone get encouragement to do so), women may have been prevented from joining the field "not because of a lack of ability, but because of a lack of support" (para. 6). That's especially true if historically (or even now), people haven't viewed jobs in mathematics as "womanly" (para. 6).

Examining Sentences, Paragraphs, and Organization

1. Vandehey believes our "difference as hierarchy" thinking is reflexive and ingrained. Even though he has already said that two things can be different without one being "better" or "worse" than the other, the repetition reinforces his idea that we will react instinctively to his next statement and impose a hierarchical framework on the assertion that, "men and women are different" (para. 1).

2. Vandehey mostly uses anecdotal evidence and personal observation to make generalizations, whether describing the "skewed" male-to-female ratio in his own classes (para. 2) or articulating an argument about math and gender that he has learned from his own female colleagues (para. 5). He does refer to research done by the Educational Testing Service in his final paragraph, but this evidence is not essential to his position. Vandehey presumes that his audience is familiar with this discussion and its premises; he doesn't need to "prove" that some people think this gender disparity is the result of sexism and that others think it's caused by innate cognitive differences between men and women. Similarly, when he writes that, "this subject is too politicized" (para. 3), he takes it for granted that the claim will be accepted without the support of specific examples. His sense of his readers suggests that they will see his essay as part of an ongoing — and long-standing — conversation.

3. After establishing the general premise that difference does not automatically imply hierarchy, he ends his introductory paragraph with a generalization: "Men and women are different." He then sharpens his focus to an apparently indisputable fact: "The numbers of men and women who like numbers are different" (para. 2). His observational evidence backs this statement — as does the very existence of a controversy over the lack of women mathematicians. Vandehey then demonstrates how the two main, current accounts of this discrepancy (biological determinism versus sexism) are unsatisfactory if taken by themselves. Ultimately, he concludes that the real reasons lie "somewhere between the extremes of non-hierarchical differences and societal expectations" (para. 7).

Thinking Critically

1. Certainly, as Vandehey makes clear, this kind of binary thinking is preva-
    lent with regard to differences between men and women—for example,
    the distinction between "reason" and "emotion," which has often been
    put in gender terms (usually with "reason" in the superior, "male" posi-
    tion), or the difference between the "domestic sphere" (associated with
    women) and the "public sphere" (usually male). The history of race rela-
    tions is also bound up in this issue, from the basic privileging of "white"
    over "black" to the legal and social concept of "separate but equal." But
    Vandehey's essay provides another good example. In his discussion of the
    math profession, he says that society treats mathematicians as an "indul-
    gence," as they "provide nothing and make nothing of use" (para. 6).
    Implicit here is a binary, hierarchical—and likely false—opposition
    between ideas and action, between thinking and doing, between the mathe-
    matician and the "engineer," in which the latter categories are seen as
    superior to the former.

2. When a subject is politicized, it means that some larger political or social
    interest or agenda is at stake in the debate. As such, participants may have
    more of an investment in supporting their agendas (consciously or uncon-
    sciously) than in finding more disinterested accounts or explanations of an
    issue—especially if that evidence goes against their interests. As Vandehey
    points out, even presumably "objective" scientific approaches to gender
    difference can reiterate cultural and social biases. He highlights how diffi-
    cult it is to remove such debates from society and culture.

3. Vandehey's assertions could be broadened to include any profession that
    is perceived to produce "nothing of use" (para. 6). That would encompass
    those (in academia, for example) who supposedly pursue ideas for their
    own sake and anyone else who engages in an activity without obvious,
    practical applications. As he seems to suggest that a stereotype exists, he
    might make that point clearer with examples from popular culture—for
    example, films such as *A Beautiful Mind* or *Good Will Hunting*, which
    use stereotypical images of mathematicians. He might also refer to the rela-
    tive wages of those in the math profession, as evidence of their perceived
    value.

In-Class Writing Activities

1. The explanation provided by Vandehey's female colleagues is appealing,
    yet it would require further testing to make it more valid. It also partakes
    of stereotyping, whereby men are active and women are more passive.
    Moreover, it leaves unresolved the fundamental question of whether such
    differences are ultimately the product of socialization (for example, men
    are "rewarded" for their aggressiveness), or whether there are also essen-
    tial biological qualities in men and women that determine this difference
    in behavior. Students should consider whether they tend to view gender
    differences more through a biological framework or more as the result of
    culture and society.

2. As Vandehey implies and the Summers example demonstrates, the inter-section of science and society is frequently controversial. Students should think about the consequences of scientific inquiry: What happens when research leads to theories or conclusions that are not compatible with conventional social arrangements or the way we're accustomed to viewing people? Students might also review Summers's specific remarks in context in order to see if the controversy was justified. Vandehey writes about how reflexive the "'differences are hierarchy' mindset" is: Was Summers a purveyor of this "mindset," or was he the victim of it, as people mis-understood or misapplied his comments?

3. Students should explain how they have reconciled personal desires (to do what they enjoy or what interests them) with other considerations — financial, social, parental. They should try to become fully conscious of how and why they're making the educational and professional choices that they do. They may see how gender has have shaped these decisions and also how certain jobs — nurse, preschool teacher, airline pilot, and so on — seem "gendered."

Discussing the Unit

Suggested Topic for Discussion

Students should consider how the science courses they have taken have prepared them to distinguish "good" science from "bad" science. They might also think about how science has been presented to them — what values it stresses, what limitations it acknowledges, and so on. Given that general cul-tural concern about science education in the Uinted States dates back at least to the cold war, students might also evaluate the accuracy and validity of this concern: What evidence do journalists, politicians, scientists, and educators cite to back their claims about the state of the scientific training of students? Do journalists, in particular, bring some of the same biases (for example, the need for a hook) to this reporting that they do to their science coverage, more generally? In a sense, these worried accounts — whether they're accurate or not — share some of the characteristics of the "scare story" genre that Skwa-recki refers to in her article.

Preparing for Class Discussion

1. The Mehl study is largely shaped and restrained by the limits of the sci-entific method, rather than by the imperatives of attracting readers with sensationalism or a provocative human-interest angle. The authors of this study are careful to acknowledge the limitations of their research (for example, "all participants were university students"). They conclude, ultimately, that differences between the talkativeness of men and women are not "statistically significant." Although the study concludes that a popular stereotype is "unfounded," it lacks the characteristics that make for a popular science story: It doesn't scare, it's not "wacky," and it doesn't reaffirm some cultural preconception.

2. Mehl's study shows how an unfounded empirical claim can be tested through the scientific method, thus providing a more accurate, objective assessment of a cultural stereotype. National Public Radio was one of the media sources that initially reported Brizendine's unfounded figures; here, however, we see the same outlet revising its coverage to include new and presumably more accurate and valid information. Skwarecki provides a checklist and a series of critical questions to help her readers sort through scientific claims. Vandehey tests prevailing cultural and biological explanations of gender differences in the math profession against his own experience as a mathematician. In every case, these claims are subject to revision in light of new information and are part of an ongoing process—imperfect, messy, and provisional, but open to self-correction.

From Discussion to Writing

1. In this sentence, the word *perceptions* would seem to include thoughts, feelings, and preconceptions about a subject, which override empirical or "objective" considerations. As a whole, the statement suggests that the notion of human beings as largely rational actors, sorting disinterestedly through empirical data using their reason and their senses, is, at best, incomplete, and, at worst, fundamentally wrong. Students might consider the various sources of knowledge they rely on in their day-to-day lives, ranging from tradition and emotional intuition, to more "empirical" forms. This aspect of human behavior has larger implications beyond science—for example, it can help explain how we make political and consumer decisions.

2. Science reporting abounds in places like the Yahoo news site, which aggregates stories from Reuters and the Associated Press. Similarly, television coverage would also be a fertile place to look, as the demands of a visual medium might influence such reports. Students should consider the ways in which research may be sensationalized or "spun," or whether different formats (news briefs, for example) limit how accurately or thoroughly a study can be reported and explained. They might also determine which news sources (or media forms) do a better or worse job of such coverage.

Topics for Cross-Cultural Discussion

1. As the Knox article points out, researching whether various cultural stereotypes exist can have a useful purpose if, say, gender research lends insight into the "demand/withdrawal pattern" among men and women. In contrast, such analysis can be crudely reductive, as in Skwarecki's example of the researcher "who claims that African-Americans have higher IQs than Africans because they have Caucasian genes that make them smarter" (para. 35). Students might make connections with the unit on redesigning humanity—especially concerning the subject of eugenics.

2. America would seem to be divided on the subject of scientism. On the one hand, our culture tends to value and embrace innovation, technology, and

progress—implicitly, the fruits of science. The sciences, arguably, also hold the most prestigious place in our educational system—especially in higher education. On the other hand, there's a deeply religious strain in American life, which is evident in the large number of Americans who believe the biblical account of creation rather than evolutionary theory. Students should consider how they evaluate these competing ways of knowing and explaining the world—and the conflicts and opportunities for reconciliation between them.

5

Do We Need an Ethics of Consumption?

Consumerism and consumer culture are central to American life. Indeed, it often seems as though our roles as consumers take precedence over our roles as citizens, and our political—and perhaps even ethical—identities are subsumed by our freedom of choice as buyers. Moreover, the pleasures of consumption are often antithetical to conscientious thinking: We want what we want. But what are the moral implications of those consumer choices? Does the apparently harmless purchase of a shirt at Gap or a knock-off Louis Vuitton handbag from a street vendor implicate buyers in child labor practices in Asia or even organized crime? How accountable are corporations to those who buy—and to those who make—their products? What role should government regulatory agencies play in protecting consumers? How do we sort out these questions in the context of a complex, global, consumer market? All of the writers in this unit address these difficult issues.

Dana Thomas takes an in-depth look at the $600 billion trade in counterfeit and pirated goods, from fake Ferraris to copies of Rolex watches and Polo shirts. That illicit trade also includes counterfeit medications, which, according to the Food and Drug Administration, could account for up to 10 percent of all drugs worldwide. But beyond highlighting the obvious dangers of unregulated pharmaceutical knock-offs, Thomas shows how the act of buying an innocuous fashion accessory may bring a consumer into a morally dubious, "dark and dangerous world" of international crime syndicates that "deal in money laundering, human trafficking, and child labor." And participating in this underground economy, whether we do it knowingly or not, costs us all in the form of lost jobs and tax revenue. Thomas also demonstrates that shopping at well-known chain stores doesn't guarantee brand authenticity: Even Wal-Mart has faced legal action because it was selling fake products. For students (and all consumers), Thomas's essay provides not only insight into this illicit trade and the ways that law enforcement officials are countering it but also a provocative view of the very notion of a "victimless crime."

In "Slaves for Fashion," Barbara Ehrenreich views reports about Gap's use of child slave labor with indignation and irony: "But let's try to look at this dispassionately—not as a human rights issue, but as a PR disaster." Her target is not just the indifference or malfeasance of corporations but also the rhetorical, logical, and ethical justifications used to explain away or minimize such practices. Using an ironic—and darkly comic—technique akin to Jonathan Swift's "A Modest Proposal," Ehrenreich's essay challenges readers to infer the profound seriousness of her argument. She also sees this issue in a broad social and political context: an interconnected world where child slavery in India is

50

linked, through the writer's elliptical ironies, to children lacking health insurance in the United States.

Jim Hightower also considers child labor and corporate doublespeak in "The Price of Cheap Goods," but he focuses more on the role of federal regulatory agencies in charge of protecting consumers. Beginning with a recent case in which toxic Chinese products entered the U.S. market, Hightower suggests that our indignation about the incident would be better directed at our own "toothless" watchdogs, such as the Consumer Product Safety Commission, than at manufacturers in China. He points out how corporate giants like Wal-Mart benefit from the cheap production costs in countries with low (or non-existent) labor standards, lobby for looser regulation on consumer protections, and then wish to be seen as "moral exemplars" for bringing inexpensive products to families in the United States. But he also provokes American consumers to evaluate their own choices—and measure the real, ethical costs of "cheap goods."

According to Courtney Pomeroy's "The Ethics of What We Wear: Can We Dress Fashionably and Responsibly?" at least some college students are willing to accept such considerations and buy more ethically. Part of the problem, of course, is apathy, the power of consumer desire, and our general love of shopping convenience. But even if we're socially conscious, how do we know when our consumer choices are responsible? As one undergraduate interviewed claims, "I would imagine it would be pretty difficult to find clothes that don't violate somebody's rights." But Pomeroy suggests that while some clothing companies have built ethics into their brand image, others would prefer to keep any questions about child labor—and the value of human life—on the "down-low." Because she's writing about, and for, a college audience, her essay provides students an opportunity to see other undergraduates wrestling with these difficult issues.

DANA THOMAS   The Fake Trade
[*Harper's Bazaar*/January 2008]

Vocabulary/Using a Dictionary

1. *Pirated* here is used as an adjective, meaning "used without authorization." To *pirate* something means to take or copy it illegally. Most students will be very familiar with the noun *pirates* (lawless men who steal from ships).

2. A supply chain is a network of people and organizations linked together to provide materials to consumers. A transporter carries or transports goods (students will recognize the root in words such as *transportation*), and a wholesaler is someone who sells goods wholesale or in quantity to a retailer (who then sells them to the public in small quantities).

3. Something legitimate is in conformance with the law. Something fraudulent is characterized by deceit or dishonesty. Here, the trademark application is legitimate, so it is legal; however, it has been fraudulently secured,

so its attainment violated a law. Anyone, including a counterfeiter whose intention is to commit fraud, can apply through proper channels for a trademark.

Responding to Words in Context

1. Thomas explains that if there is no demand for these counterfeit goods, there will be no supply. She means that if people stop buying them, the sellers will stop selling. The term *supply and demand* refers to an economic model of a competitive market. If a buyer wants something, or demands it, a seller will supply it.

2. In a victimless crime, there is no one particular victim, so no one gets hurt. Thomas argues that counterfeiting is not, in fact, a victimless crime, although this is our perception of it. She goes on to say that "we're all victims of counterfeiting," citing the loss of jobs and revenue and the support of international crime organizations.

3. *Deluxe* refers to the height of luxury, and *luxury* has to do with elegance and comfort. Both contain the same French root: *lux*. *Luster*, although it sounds like the other words, does not share their root. *Luster* derives from the situation Latin *lustrare* (to purify ceremonially) and has to do with something's shine. The title could be translated to "The Height of Luxury: How Luxury Lost Its Brilliance." Thomas is concerned with exposing the dark side of counterfeiting, which has been encouraged by the public's interest in appearing wealthy without having to pay for it.

Discussing Main Point and Meaning

1. Thomas creates an atmosphere of American prosperity in the first paragraph. A wealthy child living in a rich suburb of northern California is quite at home carrying a "designer" bag. Her "blonde blunt" haircut suggests that she is Caucasian and well groomed. Thomas also includes adjectives such as "preppy" and "all-American" to give a sense of where and by whom these counterfeit materials are enjoyed. She also might be trying to create a connection with the readers of the essay, which originally appeared in an upscale fashion magazine.

2. Thomas is making the point that it's not just handbags and apparel that are counterfeited. The stakes of counterfeiting are much higher and perhaps feel more important when one realizes that medications and car brakes are also counterfeited with disastrous consequences. Most people don't realize just how many fake products they might possibly come in contact with.

3. The surging business for counterfeiters means that more workers, including children, will be exploited. Trade and U.S. jobs are at stake if cheaper counterfeit products are being produced and sold overseas. Businesses lose revenue when consumers actively seek out knock-offs. And as Thomas points out, public health and safety are at risk in the case of certain counterfeit products.

Examining Sentences, Paragraphs, and Organization

1. *Law & Order* is a popular television show that attempts to model itself on real issues involving police and the legal system. The inclusion of the show as "evidence" of the problem of counterfeiting shows how relevant the topic must be if the show's producers thought it would appeal to a television audience. It is also a show most *Harper's* readers would be familiar with, at least by hearsay.

2. Thomas quotes a security expert who is skeptical that women from the suburbs don't know what they're dealing with when they shop at these wholesale markets. The quotation adds yet another perspective that backs up Thomas's point — use your common sense and don't go out of your way to support potential counterfeiters. The women in the anecdote have ample clues that they are not buying "the real thing" at these markets.

3. By returning to the little girl of the opening paragraph, Thomas brings the essay full circle and solidifies the girl's place as a "consumer" of counterfeit goods, albeit through her parents. She is seemingly innocent in the beginning of the essay, but by the end it is clear how purchases of knockoff bags are part of the greater cycle of counterfeiting. Thomas starts with a personal story; widens her scope to include all the evils of counterfeiting, including commentary from officials who fight those evils daily; and then returns to the little girl after outlining what we can do to break the counterfeiter's grip on the market.

Thinking Critically

1. The Internet is itself a wide market, and it is not located down a hidden alley. There is nothing unusual about using the Internet as a tool to find a low price, and people often turn to it as the best and fastest way to find a price that is "too good to be true." Ease is a big factor: People can shop from their bedrooms for almost any goods they want, and they don't feel there's anything necessarily seedy about the transactions taking place. All of these aspects mean that the Internet provides a comfortable venue for counterfeiters.

2. People are not generally inclined to think that the products they use are counterfeit; in fact, many people don't give any thought to how their products came to them. Thomas's statement forces readers to consider what items are potential counterfeits because she isn't talking just about handbags and clothing. Readers are more likely to speculate about the history of counterfeiting, and they are more likely to wonder how the counterfeiters' hold has become so deep and tenacious as to possibly affect them.

3. Answers may vary. Some students may feel that the human rights issues involved are the most terrible; others may worry about their own safety. Some students may think the most devastating effect is our blindness to the problem or the American public's need to cultivate the appearance of

wealth at such a cost. Thomas offers insight into several pieces of the problem created by counterfeiting, including monetary and social ramifications.

In-Class Writing Activities

1. Students can research one of Thomas's examples or one they find on their own. Students will also find a good deal of information on other specific manufactured goods that have been counterfeited, and these stories may appeal if the student is familiar with a particular brand name. Counterfeiting money is not highlighted in this essay, but there are many examples of counterfeiting operations throughout history (in the United States and elsewhere). Students may find this a particularly interesting type of operation to research.

2. Students may disagree with Thomas's outcry against counterfeiting, but they must be prepared to back up their points with the same strong and wide-ranging evidence that she provides. It will be helpful if students are able to rebut some of the arguments she uses in the essay. Students who agree with Thomas can stick with one of her arguments and deepen it instead of trying to incorporate as many reasons to fight counterfeiting as Thomas does.

3. Brands provide status. Because of our consumer culture, we often think of the world and ourselves in terms of brands — our lives are filled with them. Imagine going into a store with no brand-name merchandise on sale. What would that look like? Students should be encouraged to examine what brands fill their lives (from food to clothing to medicine to cars) and why. They should also consider the reasons for seeking out counterfeit versions of those brands.

BARBARA EHRENREICH   Slaves for Fashion
[*The Progressive*/January 2008]

Vocabulary/Using a Dictionary

1. If you look at something dispassionately, you are looking at it with little feeling. The root of the word is *passion*, which means "intense emotion," and the prefix *dis-*, which means "not."

2. *Demented* means "insane." The word is often used to describe the behavior of people in insane asylums or those who commit atrocious acts. Ehrenreich uses the example of a child piling up blocks just to knock them down. In children, this sort of behavior is normal and is in fact a form of learning; however, because she is speaking of child labor, she is making the point that such activities are unproductive. If an adult behaved like that all day, his or her behavior would be called into question.

3. *Impregnated* is related to the word *pregnant*, which means "rich or full," but it most commonly refers to making a woman pregnant.

Responding to Words in Context

1. Ehrenreich describes children rubbing "Krazy Glue into their siblings' hair" and spilling "apple juice onto your keyboard" as acts of children's vandalism. A vandal is someone who destroys another person's property, and vandalism is the destruction or defacement of property. Usually vandals and vandalism are associated with malicious intent, and vandalism is often considered something that a person with no occupation or sense of values would do.

2. Children depend on their parents for food, clothing, and their general well-being and are not expected to take care of themselves in the world as adults do. In infancy, children are dependent on their parents for everything. They become more independent the more they can care for their basic needs (mobility, eating, and drinking for starters) on their own. The child laborers in this essay are dependent on their work supervisors for food and shelter, although the circumstances around their dependency on a corporation instead of a parent have not been fully explained. They are dependent both because they are children and because they have been enslaved. Ehrenreich ironically insists that the child laborers are independent (whereas American children are not), because they are working for a living and not enjoying the idle dependency of childhood.

3. A *dhoti* is a loincloth worn by men in some parts of India. The reader might guess that it's an article of clothing because earlier in the sentence Ehrenreich discusses shopping for clothing at American Apparel. *Dhoti* is a foreign word, and since the essay refers to a sweatshop in India, the reader might assume the clothing is Indian.

Discussing Main Point and Meaning

1. Ehrenreich uses strong adjectives and verbs in the opening paragraph of her essay. Images such as "mosquito-covered rice" and "oily cloths" give the offensive picture of life in the sweatshops its full impact. Her opening sentence uses the descriptive and unpleasant verb *vomit*, referring to how the reader will react, and the verbs *forced*, *beaten*, and *cried* add violence to the story being told. These glimpses into the reality of child labor give the reader a better understanding of the sarcastic tone of the rest of the essay.

2. The 1982 discovery of cyanide in Tylenol capsules was a tragedy in which several people died. The national news story caused widespread fear, and the product was removed from store shelves. The makers of Tylenol suffered greatly as a result of the product's implication in these deaths (Tylenol had been tampered with), but the real tragedy was that several people lost their lives. Ehrenreich is equating the child labor situation with the cyanide story because both are terrible tragedies. She calls them PR disasters, suggesting that the real victims are Tylenol and Gap, rather than the innocent people involved in the stories. By noticing that Ehrenreich has placed such a heinous crime back-to-back with Gap's child labor scandal, the reader understands that calling them PR disasters is tongue-in-cheek.

3. When some people say "I'm a slave for fashion," they mean that they
    need to keep up with the latest fashion trends. Other people mean that
    they have to own the most fashionable, and often the priciest, clothing
    styles. In either case, the phrase is a figure of speech, not literal.

Examining Sentences, Paragraphs, and Organization

1. Another version of that sentence might read: "If they pile up blocks and
    knock them down all day, then they might as well sew on buttons and
    bring home a little cash." Ehrenreich might have made it even simpler
    and less detailed by saying, "They're doing things already, so they might
    as well sew on buttons and bring home a little cash." Students may grav-
    itate more toward the "if . . . then" construction, either as a rhetorical
    question or as a statement. They might notice that the rhetorical question
    adds to the sarcasm of Ehrenreich's tone, particularly as it has more
    emphasis at the end of a paragraph. Ehrenreich does a great deal of sug-
    gesting in this essay, rather than stating, so a student might feel that the
    simple statement is too pushy or hard-hearted—more along the lines of
    the statement she quotes in paragraph 9.

2. Because Hansen includes the qualification of "our garments," Ehrenreich
    feels that Hansen did not completely condemn the use of child labor by
    manufacturers. She twists Hansen's use of the word *condone* in her state-
    ment by saying it is clear that Gap does not pardon or forgive much from
    its child laborers, given their recorded treatment.

3. On several occasions, Ehrenreich offers a clear statement on the great
    wrong being done in child labor sweatshops. First, she begins the essay
    with a gruesome picture of conditions experienced by the children work-
    ing for Gap. She returns to the plight of those children in paragraph 15,
    indicating that first "cookies and milk" will be refused to American chil-
    dren sent to work, and then, "as in India, the toilets and beds," alluding
    to the extent of abuse child laborers suffer. In paragraph 16, she com-
    ments that the opposition to such labor will always include those "who
    would rather wear skirts than blue jeans impregnated with the excrement
    and tears of ten-year-olds."

Thinking Critically

1. Just as Jonathan Swift, in his "Modest Proposal," never meant for anyone
    to eat a child, Ehrenreich does not intend for people to start a welfare-to-
    work program for children. Her essay is, in fact, an attempt to show the
    absurdity of enforced child labor. No American wants his or her child to
    end up experiencing conditions like those in Gap's sweatshop, and by
    imagining a situation reversal, Ehrenreich drives home the point that
    nobody's children should be forced to work.

2. When thinking about the current day, students might say that situations
    of extreme poverty can lead to untenable living or working conditions
    here, and it is possible to talk about the abuse of children, but it is impor-

tant to recognize that laws been put in place to protect children from the sorts of abuses suffered overseas. At one time, the United States had no child labor laws, and children often worked in terrible situations in American factories. Children were regularly employed before the twentieth century, and many deplorable sweatshop conditions were documented during the Industrial Revolution. Rural children frequently experienced long hours and poverty while working on farms. The treatment of black slaves in this country can be compared to the treatment of the sweatshop children in India today.

3. Ehrenreich looks at the worst facet of American business — the desire to cut corners and turn a profit no matter what the cost to others. Gap no doubt set up sweatshops using child laborers in India because it was cheap for the company and because executives thought they could get away with it. Although there are, no doubt, some ethical people in charge of manufacturing companies, many of the best-known brands have shipped their work overseas in search of the cheapest labor, and several have been found guilty of human rights abuses. Because no American children work in these sweatshops, it may be much easier to look the other way — because such working conditions are allowed in other countries.

In-Class Writing Activities

1. Students may address Ehrenreich's criticism of the fashion giants responsible for child labor situations, or they may speak to her criticism of those of us who support child labor situations by buying clothes from manufacturers who do not go far enough in their condemnation of such labor. Students might argue that the essay is a criticism of the United State's approach to children in general by noting the specific hypocrisy mentioned in her final paragraph: "In a nation that cannot bring itself to extend child health insurance to all children in need, child-made clothes make a fine fashion statement."

2. Students may mention basic rights involving sanitary conditions, unquestioned use of the bathroom, and mandatory breaks for food. They may include a right to sick days or situations that call for leave with pay. They may even go so far as to invoke the Bill of Rights, minimum-wage laws, or other legislation that has been passed to help the citizens of this country. It's important to note what a basic right is, and which requests go beyond basic rights. If student's feel they should be granted something beyond a basic right, they should argue why such a right is inalienable or why it is in the employer's best interest to grant it.

3. There is a wealth of information on sweatshops, some of it dating back to the Industrial Revolution. Sweatshops were staffed by the poorer classes in growing urban areas in this country and others. Students may find the literal derivation of the word *sweatshop* or choose to examine the connotations of the word. When discussing what present-day sweatshops are, students should consider the issue of globalization and the arguments for and against their use today.

JIM HIGHTOWER   The Price of Cheap Goods
[*The Progressive*/March 2008]

Vocabulary/Using a Dictionary

1. The word *toxic*, which means "poisonous," originates with the Greek term *toxikon*, which refers to the poison used on arrows. Other words with the same root include *intoxicated*, *toxicology*, and *toxin*.

2. *Procuring* means "obtaining with great care." It derives from the Latin *procurare*, "to take care of." It also has a secondary meaning that refers to obtaining prostitutes.

3. Antibiotics, such as penicillin, are substances that destroy or inhibit the growth of microorganisms; they are produced by fungi, bacteria, or other organisms. They are frequently used to treat infectious diseases. The word *antibiotic* derives from the Greek *anti-* (against) and *biotikos* (fit for life).

Words in Context

1. The metaphor suggests that, left to their own devices or the determinations of the market, businesses and corporations will act in ways that may be harmful to consumers—and citizens. Here, government regulation is seen as a necessary restraint that, according to Hightower, needs to be even stronger. A person with a more explicitly pro-business point of view might not use this metaphor.

2. Both *profit* and *profiteer* mean "to make financial gains," but *profiteer* means "to make exorbitant or unreasonable profits through the sale of scarce or rationed goods." The word allows Hightower to suggest that immoderate corporate avarice—as distinguished from the practice of making a reasonable amount of money—is a problem.

3. Hightower is being ironic. A moral exemplar would set a high moral standard to be copied. Given the essay as a whole, in which Hightower targets corporations and their "chieftains" for criticism, we can determine that his words actually mean the opposite of what they appear to say.

4. *Bean counter* is a disparaging term used for accountants and financial officers—that is, the people who keep track of dollars, cents, and profits. The term implies that such people focus entirely on financial quantification to the exclusion of every other concern.

Discussing Main Point and Meaning

1. Hightower argues that much of the blame should be placed on our own government's "regulatory watchdogs" (para. 1), which should be more stringent, effective, and thorough in determining what products can (and cannot) enter the country. For Hightower, these agencies are "toothless," and our current consumer protection laws are "riddled with loopholes" that allow unsafe products into the country—products that pose a threat to the welfare of Americans.

2. According to Hightower, large corporations lobby the government in Washington to make consumer protections more lax and to ease corporate regulation, generally; implicitly, these corporations do not show due regard for the necessity of such laws, which are intended to keep buyers safe. At the same time, companies move their production facilities to places like China (where wages are low and working conditions are poor) so that they can take advantage of cheap manufacturing. Then, as Hightower views it, "the top executives insist that they should get credit for serving the moral good" by bringing cheap products to American families (para. 6).

3. By using manufacturers in countries with looser laws, American corporations take profitable advantage of lax regulations around practices such as child labor, even as their executives wish (according to Hightower) to get credit for "serving the moral good." If U.S. companies contract with — or own — foreign plants that operate outside the bounds of American labor laws, one can argue that they are complicit in exploitation. Furthermore, Hightower asks: "You want cheap? What's a finger worth?" (para. 8). His point is that the American consumer, who expects inexpensive products without considering the human costs, may also be part of this ethically dubious process.

Examining Sentences, Paragraphs, and Organization

1. The last sentence in paragraph 5 encapsulates Hightower's point about lax regulations and corporate influence over consumer protection laws in the United States. It summarizes the argument of the first half of the essay and creates the transition to the second half, where he focuses on corporations, more generally, and the ethics of their practices in the context of globalism. The last sentence sums up his second point. In a way, both of these sentences can be seen as thesis statements, even though neither one is in the first paragraph of the essay.

2. The tone of this paragraph is dry, not emotional, even as Hightower is clearly appealing (in part) to our emotional responses. He begins the paragraph with the conjunction *or*, which suggests that the section could be an afterthought (even though it is not). The use of the word *stuff* diminishes the significance and meaning of the cheap products the boy helps produce, thus contributing to the writer's point that we may value "stuff" more than human lives. The injured boy's quotation, taken from the *New York Times*, is also bland: The machines he uses are "quite hot." The overall effect of the paragraph is provocative, yet Hightower uses no explicitly emotionally charged or angry rhetoric to accomplish this. Consider how the paragraph could have been rewritten with a more overtly emotionalized or indignant tone.

3. Clearly, Hightower is not writing academic discourse for an academic audience, even though his essay uses some of the techniques (such as citing sources and studies) that we associate with academic writing. Nor is writing neutral, "objective" journalism. Perhaps the most notable aspect

of his style is its conversational or spoken quality. It creates the sense of a person talking—even in its rhythms. For example, consider the last sentence of the first paragraph: "But wait a minute—where, oh where, are our own country's regulatory watchdogs?" The second "oh where" is obviously unnecessary for his argument, but it's a stylistic choice that sounds as though Hightower is speaking. It's also a rhetorical question that reads like a conversational question, as does his provocative "You want cheap? What's a finger worth" (para. 8), which he uses to set up his reference to a study of factory injuries. Additionally, Hightower keeps his sentences relatively short, a technique that also contributes to this conversational style—especially the two-letter sentence "BS!" in paragraph 10.

Thinking Critically

1. Hightower refers primarily to a book on the dangers of everyday products, a study of factory accidents in Hong Kong, and a story from the *New York Times*. He integrates them deftly, as when he describes the boy at the beginning of paragraph 9 (after citing the study of factory injuries) and then moves to direct quotation. For a short, polemical opinion column in a magazine, the sourcing seems adequate; different writing forms have different requirements. Hightower does use the rhetorical strategy of speaking for the corporate interests he's criticizing—for example, "Look, they say, we are helping American families by bringing cheap products to them" (para. 6) and "Corporate officials here claim they're appalled by these conditions" (para. 10). The article might have benefited from direct quotations from these sources.

2. Hightower makes effective use of this example from Mark Schapiro's *Exposed: The Toxic Chemistry of Everyday Products and What's at Stake for American Power*. First, phthalate is a slightly sinister-sounding chemical additive that's potentially dangerous to children, who are generally perceived as being most in need of protection. Second, Schapiro compares the effectiveness of U.S. regulation and consumer protection laws unfavorably with those in Europe, suggesting that our system leaves us vulnerable in ways that citizens in other countries are not.

3. This language contributes to the column's conversational quality: "BS!" is the kind of exclamation usually spoken, not written. Hightower's use of this expression also indicates the degree of comfort that he has with his audience. The exclamation is effective in this context because the writer backs it up by highlighting a major—and serious— contradiction. On the one hand, corporate officials (according to Hightower) say they're appalled by the working conditions in foreign factories but claim that they "simply can't keep track of what goes on" in all of them (para. 10). On the other hand, "Wal-Mart boasts that it's able to track every penny of cost in its sprawling system of procuring and marketing products" (para. 11). This disconnect is an ideal example (at least, rhetorically) to show the relative value of people and profits in the business practices of a company like Wal-Mart.

In-Class Writing Activities

1. People regularly use the word *corporate* with a negative connotation associated with blandness, avarice, and conformity. But students should consider what a corporation is and does, specifically. For example, they may discover that a corporation has the legal status of a person and that publicly traded companies are ultimately beholden to shareholders, not their customers, their employees, or their executives. Students can consider the power and influence of corporations, both good and bad: How did they become such a dominant institution? Additionally, increased globalization complicates the relationship between corporation and nation, as when an "American company" outsources work overseas or is operated as a multinational entity. This raises the question not only of whether such institutions have social obligations (to be environmentally safe, to treat their workers well) but also of whether the goals or practices of corporations may run counter to national interests.

2. Students may have different reactions to this exercise, especially because so many products are now made overseas (this fact, in itself, might be a revelation). But the assignment should get them thinking about buying in a broader context, even if the ethical dimensions are complex or even frustrating. They might also consider how companies have reacted to controversies over issues such as sweatshops or child labor in other countries (for example, Nike) or have even built ethical considerations into their brand identities. For instance, American Apparel clothing is created and marketed as a "sweatshop-free" American-made product; this has both marketing and ethical dimensions.

3. Although we may react viscerally to child labor and other such practices, we must consider them in social, regional, and economic contexts. For example, in the early 1990s, Senator Tom Harkin (D-Iowa) proposed legislation banning imports from countries employing underage workers. As a result, textile factories in Bangladesh fired their child employees, leaving an enormous number of them out of work, in worse jobs, or (infamously) driven to prostitution. How do we weigh such considerations in a complex global economy? Can students research and formulate useful ways of dealing with these complicated issues?

COURTNEY POMEROY (STUDENT ESSAY)   The Ethics of What We Wear: Can We Dress Fashionably and Responsibly?
[*The Diamondback*, University of Maryland/December 5, 2007]

Vocabulary/Using a Dictionary

1. *Corporation* comes from the Latin word *corporare*, which means "to form into a body." In basic terms, a corporation is a group of individuals who form a "body," either by law or under legal authority, that has a continuous existence independent of the individual existence of its members and has powers and liabilities distinct from those of its members.

The root of the word is *corpus*, Latin for "body." Related words include *corpse*, *corpulence*, and *corporeal*.

2. *Inhumane* means "lacking in humanity, kindness, or compassion" (presuming those are innate human qualities). The word derives from the Latin *in-*, which means "not," and *humanus*, meaning "human." Other words that use the prefix *in-* are *inconsiderate* and *inconsequential*.

3. *Apathy* comes from the Greek *a-* (without) and *pathos* (emotion, feeling). *Apathy* originally had a positive meaning of "freedom from suffering," but now it has a negative meaning of "indifference or lack of concern." Words such as *sympathy* and *empathy* share the same root.

Responding to Words in Context

1. "Cheap labor" refers to people who work for little money and under bad conditions, often in a factory. The term has taken on new connotations in the context of globalization. Many companies outsource manufacturing to "cheap labor countries" that have different workplace standards than the United States has, thereby cutting production costs.

2. Although *laborer* is a synonym for *worker*, the word *laborer* suggests a person who has an unskilled, low-paying, manual, menial job.

3. Pomeroy uses the word *trendy* to describe chain stores and brand names preferred by college consumers. The word evokes a sense of shallowness, impermanence, and perhaps triviality; this contrasts with the seriousness of the "abuse of workers" and "inhumane factory conditions" that make such trendy goods possible.

Discussing Main Point and Meaning

1. Pomeroy's opening paragraph contrasts the glamorous, welcoming interior of the store and its abundant, colorful products with the "dirty secret" of overseas factory laborers who manufacture these clothes. The disparity between a brand's public image and the hidden realities of working conditions in cheap-labor countries makes it difficult to recognize which companies use ethical business practices. This is one of the main points of the essay, and Pomeroy returns to her introductory contradiction in her final sentence.

2. Pomeroy highlights companies like Gap, Urban Outfitters, and American Apparel in part because they reflect the consumer habits of her college reading audience (in addition to the fact that they're ethically questionable, according to the writer). What emerges in this essay is an image of companies that value profits over people. Students should consider their own relationship to—and views of—companies in this context.

3. The essay suggests that trying to be an ethical consumer can be problematic and frustrating. As one of Pomeroy's sources claims, "I would imagine it would be pretty difficult to find clothes that don't violate somebody's

rights" (para. 5). Beyond the difficulty of locating and vetting ethically produced clothing, other problems include consumer apathy, corporate misinformation, and the sense that even supposedly ethical companies (such as American Apparel) may not live up to their professed ideals.

Examining Sentences, Paragraphs, and Organization

1. Pomeroy's essay is journalistic: It raises an issue and examines student attitudes toward it through interviews. It also reports indirectly on the business practices of companies such as Gap. Yet the essay also has a definite point of view and an agenda that emerges clearly: Corporations engage in questionable ethics, students should become more aware in their buying habits, and options for ethical buying are limited at the moment. Note that she doesn't use the first-person singular in her writing, nor does she offer any personal experience. But her phrasing and language reveal a position, as when she writes about "the vicious cycle that takes place amongst consumers" and the companies that offer "stylish threads while keeping [their] abuse of workers on the down-low" (para. 6).

2. The essay is as much about the attitudes and habits of undergraduate consumers as it is about the ethics of corporations such as Gap. First, Pomeroy quotes two student activists to establish the political and social terms of the issue. Then she cites two undergraduates who are concerned about the problem, and another who describes the difficulty of being an ethical consumer. The overall effect is to portray students who are socially aware and well-meaning, but unsure how to act on those impulses other than to "try [their] best" to shop in places that claim not to use sweatshop labor.

3. Pomeroy raises the major theme of her essay in the first paragraph: the relationship among the public image of stores like Gap, the sweatshop labor that produces their clothing, and the obliviousness of shoppers who may be complicit in the companies' unethical practices. Paragraphs 3, 4, and 5 provide various opinions on the subject from interviews, which expand on her general theme and show specific individuals trying to make ethical choices. The last paragraph offers limited and (as Pomeroy acknowledges) unsatisfactory solutions to the problem—as well as hope that "sometime in the near future students will be able to get their trendy, brand-name gear from companies that value humanity more than cheaply made goods" (para. 6).

Thinking Critically

1. Generally, few consumers or corporate officials are going to claim explicitly, "Profits are more important than people's lives." But there's often a gap between rhetoric and ideals (on the one hand) and actual buying and business practices (on the other), especially given the institutional impersonality of big corporations and economic markets. However, there may be examples that reconcile these two principles in practice.

2. The woman interviewed is describing the rationalization process, whereby people have convictions or principles but then act against them (in this case) through apathy or the desire for convenience.

3. A union is an organization of workers who join together to achieve common goals such as better wages and working conditions; it represents a counterweight to the interests of the owners and operators of businesses. Historically, unions have been important for establishing standards and rights for workers. Arguably, their power and prestige have diminished in the United States over the last several decades. They have also been subject to criticism.

In-Class Writing Activities

1. The word *ethics* in this context suggests that our choices in buying clothing partake of fundamental moral issues of right and wrong. For this assignment, students could choose a common activity or issue — the ethics of education, dating, eating, or voting, for example. The goal is to get them to consider the wider, ethical implications of a particular practice — considerations that are usually hidden or ignored.

2. Pomeroy touches on several large subjects here in a very short essay — the general ethics of consumption, "cheap labor," the attitudes of college students, labor laws, the moral obligations of corporations, the implications of globalization and economic markets, and the ways in which certain corporations are incorporating an ethical image into their brands. For this assignment, students can investigate any one of these issues and tease out complexities or counterarguments that Pomeroy overlooks.

3. For this assignment, students should consider their own behavior and attitudes, as well as those of their peers. Do they view consumer ethics as a problem of innate or intractable apathy, or do they believe that students will behave ethically if given the opportunity? Information plays a key role: Pomeroy includes an account of a British newspaper that alleged Gap was using child labor in one of its factories in India, and the company was forced to respond and take action. Do articles such as Pomeroy's have any effect on the behavior of readers?

Discussing the Unit

Suggested Topic for Discussion

Both of these essays acknowledge, overtly and subtly, that this is not an entirely safe presumption. Thomas's account of suburban women buying counterfeit goods after being led down "dark corridors, through locked doors" is a good example — obviously, these women were aware, on some level, that something was amiss, even if they were unaware of the working conditions of the laborers who made the products they were buying. Student responses to this might reveal their fundamental views about people or themselves: that is, whether we're essentially good and responsible, if given the right information, or whether we tend to be selfish and ready to rationalize our decisions. Students might also discuss how to make consumption more ethical—even if that means bringing ethical choices more in line with our perceived self-interest.

Preparing for Class Discussion

1. Ehrenreich's acerbic, Swiftian essay frames the behavior of companies such as Gap in part as a symptom of broader societal and economic tendencies, from the focus on public relations and celebrities, to "welfare-to-work" programs and children without health insurance. Compare this with Pomeroy's essay, which covers similar material but doesn't try to be as broadly suggestive as "Slaves for Fashion." Is it possible to agree with Ehrenreich's argument about child labor without completely accepting the larger implications of her politics? She's writing in the *Progressive*, so her original audience was probably sympathetic to most, if not all, of her premises. Is that a problem for her essay as it applies to a wider readership?

2. Describing certain behaviors as "victimless crimes" is commonly done to justify those behaviors. But several of these essays reveal the hidden or ignored ethical consequences of actions that appear harmless on their surface. Students can look for such issues or practices that may become more morally problematic when viewed closely and in a wider context (personal drug use, for example).

From Discussion to Writing

1. The use of irony allows William Kristol to make a darkly comic point about emotional political rhetoric, but as Ehrenreich suggests, such comments can seem glib and genuinely mean-spirited when looked at in a different context (in this case, child labor). Irony can be obvious, as when Hightower refers to corporate executives as "moral exemplars." But Ehrenreich's sustained use of irony is more demanding. It forces readers to slow down, examine the writing, and question their own responses, as when she writes of a Gap executive, "The other, more serious problem, is that Hansen got defensive about child labor." On what level is Ehrenreich being serious, and on what level is she being ironic? The trade-off is that ironic writers risk being misunderstood, or even subverting the premises or seriousness of their own arguments if they're not careful. Irony can also become tedious and predictable if it's too obvious. Students should consider their own writing styles and preferences as readers. They may also explain their attitude toward irony in an essay that uses irony.

2. Several essays in this unit refer to the need to raise awareness in consumers. Students may want to think about how public relations fits into this scheme, as one of the main goals of PR is to raise public "awareness." In one sense, public relations suggests spin, rationalizations, propaganda, and disingenuous denials (as implied in Ehrenreich's article). In another sense, PR represents another voice disseminating information, a

particular point of view, and — in the case of a corporate spokesperson — an image of accountability. Students may also want to argue that the practice is essentially neutral in its implications and consequences.

Topics for Cross-Cultural Discussion

1. Students should think about the meaning and significance of brands and branding in our consumer culture. For example, does a brand's meaning come from those who choose to buy it, therefore reflecting the community and presumed values of its consumers? Or is a brand's identity determined by the company that designs and sells the product? Do students use certain brands to establish aspects of their own identity? This issue becomes more complex when we consider how certain brands can be marketed to specific racial or ethnic cultures — FUBU, for example, is a clothing line originally aimed at African Americans. More recently, Nike unveiled a line of shoes marketed to Native Americans, but brand identity and cultural identity may overlap or interconnect in more subtle ways as well.

2. This assignment asks students to reflect broadly on ethics and responsibilities, as well as how they view and apply their ethical responsibilities. Ehrenreich, for example, implicitly upholds one ethical standard when she addresses the question of unemployed children in other countries, however ironic her approach may be: She applies the logic and ethics of those who justify child labor in other countries to "idle" children in the United States, thereby highlighting the ridiculousness of such arguments. But in criticizing these practices on a systematic and economic level, does she overlook the practical implications of eliminating such jobs as they apply to specific people? Do certain ethical and moral standards need to be recalibrated depending on specific circumstances and locations?

6
Redesigning Humanity — What Are the Limits?

Scientific, technological, and medical advances provide innumerable — and obvious — opportunities and benefits for humanity. But our embrace of these achievements may overlook the ways in which progress creates new problems and raises difficult cultural, social, ethical, and legal questions. Indeed, such "improvements" frequently lead us to face the "big questions about human nature," as Michael Sandel writes in his essay included in this chapter. The pursuit of perfection — athletic, physical, cosmetic, genetic — has an almost irresistible fascination; in some ways, the quest to gain mastery over nature has frequently represented what is most creative or courageous about humanity. Yet we might also agree that we must place limits on that pursuit, especially with regard to technologies like eugenics and bioengineering — practices that have had hazardous consequences in the past. The essays and advertisement in this unit explore the possibilities and limitations of redesigning human beings, from the risks of getting cosmetic surgery to questions about how "enhanced" athletes change the meaning of athletic competition and human achievement. Sandel writes about the "Promethean" qualities of some of these advancements, and students may want to think about the dual nature of the Prometheus myth as it applies currently: On the one hand, the story suggests boldness, ambition, and originality; on the other hand, it connotes hubris, presumption, and transgression.

Ellen Goodman's "Remanufacturing Athletes" focuses on redesigning humanity in the context of amateur and professional sports, but her essay suggests wider implications for the pursuit of perfection. Athletes have an increasing number of ways to gain a competitive edge or challenge our conventional notions of human capability — and these go well beyond the realm of the steroid controversy. For example, should disabled athletes with high-tech prosthetics be allowed to compete in the Olympics against the nondisabled? We may admire the determination and skill of such competitors, but do such devices represent a human and technological triumph over adversity, or an unfair performance enhancement that we should reject? These questions become more complex if we grant that people have been using "enhancements" ever since (in Goodman's words) "the first runner put on a shoe." If we find beauty and meaning in the essentially human achievements of sports, what are the consequences of tampering with our notions of what is "human" and what is not? Students should be encouraged to test their own sense of these limitations. They should consider not only where they draw the line between what seems acceptable and what seems like cheating but also how their views of these issues reflect their larger assumptions about human beings.

Kenneth Cole features Aimee Mullins, athlete, actress, model, and president of the Women's Sports Foundation, as part of its "25 years of non-uniform thinking" advertising campaign. Mullins is a double amputee with prosthetic legs, and her provocative image challenges us to think about identity, difference, individuality, and our attitudes toward the disabled in the context of athletics, fashion, and feminine beauty itself. The ad seems less like a campaign to sell a particular product and more like an attempt to evoke a complex set of associations and responses; the model's image is one in which it's hard to tell where her "humanity" ends and her "artificial" limbs begin. Indeed, the advertisement might imply that Mullins's prosthetics are as much an expression of her human individuality as the shoes that she's promoting. The ad is also a good opportunity to look critically at the sophisticated techniques and strategies of advertising and branding. How do ads borrow from arts such as rhetoric, poetry, photography, and painting? What role do such brand messages and identifications play in the way students think about their own identities and lives?

For Rebecca Ganzak in "Is Cosmetic Surgery Worth the Risk?" the problems with redesigning humanity bring practical hazards along with moral ones. Writing about teenagers who undergo elective cosmetic surgery, she argues that young people are taking unnecessary risks—and spending enormous amounts of money—in a vain attempt to fit into a celebrity-fixated popular culture that places too much emphasis on personal appearance. Indeed, her essay provides an occasion to discuss the nature of physical beauty itself as well as its place in our society, which values it highly. Ganzak writes as an undergraduate who considered plastic surgery for herself, weighed the risks, and decided not to undergo the procedure. Her argument demonstrates the ways in which young writers can turn their reactions to personal experiences into arguments with wider and more general applications.

Ganzak argues that parents who approve of or fund cosmetic surgery for the children are avoiding the responsibilities of parenting. Michael Sandel, in "Designer Babies: The Problem with Genetic Engineering," is also concerned with the ethics of parenting, particularly the ways in which genetic engineering could drastically alter the relationship between parents and children. Rather than viewing these new technologies in terms of human progress and mastery, Sandel asserts that such tampering—whether chosen by individual parents or mandated by society as a means for social uplift—falls in the dangerous tradition of the eugenics movement of the first half of the twentieth century. He argues that the desire to "exercise dominion over the genetic traits of the next generation" poses large and "morally troubling" questions for parents and for our society as a whole. But just as Goodman wrestles to define what constitutes an unfair athletic "enhancement," Sandel acknowledges that there are not always clear lines between engaging in a hubristic "Promethean assault" and merely bestowing the advantages that parents have traditionally wanted to give their children. He explicitly brings a "religious sensibility" to the issue, although his argument is meant to appeal to secular readers, and this tension is worthy of discussion. His essay is allusive, nuanced, historically minded, and deeply serious, yet it's also lucid and accessible. Students should consider how the writer achieves that balance.

ELLEN GOODMAN   Remanufacturing Athletes
[*Boston Globe*/May 25, 2007]

Vocabulary/Using a Dictionary

1. *Manufacture* means "to make or produce something." *Remanufacture* means "to manufacture or make into a new product" (the prefix *re-* means "again").

2. *Phenom* is a shortening of the word *phenomenon*. In this context, a phenomenon is a person with unusual or exceptional talents. *Phenom* is a slang form of the word and implies that the person involved is an extraordinary athlete.

3. *Cyborg* (short for "cybernetic organism") means a "bionic human." The noun *transhuman* refers to someone who is superhuman in some way (the prefix *trans* means "across" or "beyond"). Both terms suggest images of science fiction or futuristic technology.

Responding to Words in Context

1. Marathon is a place in Greece. According to ancient Greek legend, a runner ran from Marathon to Athens to inform the Greeks of their victory over the Persians. He died from exhaustion shortly after delivering his message. With the beginning of the modern Olympics, the name *marathon* was given to the long-distance footrace. Currently, the length of a marathon is 26 miles 385 yards.

2. *Enhancement* means "an improvement in quality or value." Athletes can enhance their performance in sports through practice, by using trainers and better equipment, or through chemical or physical enhancers. Surgical and physical enhancements are the main concern of Goodman's essay because they raise ethical questions and potentially devalue the principles of athletic activities.

3. *Cheetah* is a suggestive word. It brings to mind the animal, a swift-moving cat, and is indicative of the speed and "superhuman" quality that these prosthetic legs give to Pistorius. Goodman also plays with the phonetics of *Cheetah* when she writes, "I don't think that Cheetahs are cheating." She is very concerned with the issue of fairness surrounding the use of such enhancements.

Discussing Main Point and Meaning

1. Those who agree that Woods's Lasik surgery gives him an unfair advantage will call his victories into question. Woods was extremely nearsighted before his surgery, and his eyesight may well have been a disadvantage for many years. No one would argue with him for using glasses or contacts to restore his vision to 20/20. But because the Lasik surgery granted him

better than average eyesight, one might wonder if creating such good vision is similar to the use of steroids or other drugs to create great muscles or added stamina. Surgical enhancements are less common than drug enhancements in the sports world, so the question of whether they constitute cheating is clouded.

2. Bonds and Pistorius both use "enhancements" because they want to excel in their sport. Pistorius, however, could not even compete without his Cheetahs because of the amputation of his legs. Bonds knew full well that the use of steroids was illegal and would give him an added advantage over his competitors. Still, if the Cheetahs give Pistorius an advantage over his competitors (that has nothing to do with other, more natural factors), then he is not "playing by the rules" or winning because he is the better athlete.

3. Some athletes, in the name of fairness, may wish to compete separately in an arena with others who have similar disabilities, although some athletes who have worked hard in a variety of ways to overcome a particular disability may take offense at being asked to compete separately. Students should consider what constitutes an unfair "enhancement," and what goal the athlete is trying to achieve.

Examining Sentences, Paragraphs, and Organization

1. Goodman wants to make the distinction that Pistorius will be using something other than "his own two feet," as the saying goes, if he competes in the Olympics. Goodman's choice of words is also important because it normalizes what Pistorius wants to do — his Cheetahs are his feet.

2. It is sometimes difficult to prove that an athlete has purposely cheated at a sport. Landis's case is complicated because he is accused of having extraordinarily high levels of testosterone in his body that helped him win the Tour de France. Testosterone is a naturally occurring hormone in the body, and so it is hard to prove that his testosterone levels were intentionally and unnaturally elevated. Athletes have also been known to question the reliability of the drug tests themselves.

3. There are many areas in which humans compete, with sports being just one such area. A woman competing in a beauty pageant who claims that she underwent plastic surgery was used to treat a medical condition or disfigurement is using much the same argument as Pistorius, who wants to run on his Cheetahs in the Olympics. Soejima's wheelchair gives him added speed on the Boston Marathon track, and a nose job or lip enhancement gives a beauty contestant added attractiveness in a beauty pageant. Both achieve, by means of the wheelchair and the surgical alteration, a certain perfection otherwise lacking.

Thinking Critically

1. Answers will vary depending on how students perceive the ethics behind such enhancements and technology. Many may be persuaded by Good-

man's argument; others may feel that disabled athletes deserve special consideration or that all athletes work to enhance themselves through natural or artificial means.

2. Again, one might argue that Pistorius's advantage would be fair because he has simply compensated for the loss of his legs. It is important for the students to note when the enhancement gives a clear advantage to the athlete and when the enhancement is being used specifically to cheat at an event. Students should examine the rules governing particular sports, as well as rules dealing with the use of performance enhancements.

3. Participants in dance, music, and drama competitions might be inclined to use the same performance enhancements as athletes use. Goodman notes plastic surgery as another type of enhancement in the world of beauty pageants. Students should consider competitions that involve intelligence: Are there enhancements for those who need to study more, remember more, and think more clearly during such competitions? Competitors in all areas who suffer from a "disability" such as anxiety or from chronic disabling conditions such as arthritis might use medications as an "enhancement" during competition.

In-Class Writing Activities

1. Goodman offers a range of athletes whose use of enhancements might be considered admirable or worthy of censure. She mentions Masazumi Soejima, Oscar Pistorius, Barry Bonds, Hank Aaron, Floyd Landis, Tiger Woods, and others as potential subjects for further scrutiny. Goodman spends a good deal of time on Pistorius, so if students choose him as a subject, their essays should go well beyond Goodman's argument.

2. A disabled athlete might choose to compete with abled athletes as a way to show triumph over a particular disability. Soejima races on the same track as Cheruiyot because the Boston Marathon route is challenging to both the man in the wheelchair and the man on foot. However, Soejima is not actually racing against Cheruiyot, because the wheelchair provides a much faster speed than what can be achieved naturally by a runner. If an abled athlete's equipment or venue is impossible for a disabled athlete to use or compete in, then it makes sense for the equipment or venue to be altered to accommodate the disability.

3. Students should investigate who was allowed to compete in the Olympic Games of ancient Greece, what sports took place, what awards were offered, and what penalties were in place for any cheating that occurred. They can then compare their findings with those same aspects of the modern games. Students should also consider location since today's games rotate from country to country. The inclusion of anecdotes about particular competitors would also be interesting points of comparison.

KENNETH COLE   **We All Walk in Different Shoes**
[*Vogue*/March 2008]

Discussing Main Point and Meaning

1. Kenneth Cole is advertising shoes—and also a brand message of non-conformity. The slogan links one's choice in footwear to the essence of individual identity and personal distinction. It also calls to mind the saying "Walk a mile in another person's shoes," which is usually meant as an appeal to empathy: Shoes become analogous to the misfortunes or disadvantages of others, who deserve our compassion or understanding. But in the ad, Aimee Mullins is presented not as unfortunate or disadvantaged but as empowered, admirable, and even defiant: different, perhaps, but certainly not worse off. There also might be other, more indirect associations of walking and individuality, such as Robert Frost's "The Road Not Taken."

2. Doubtless, many students see their clothing choices as reflections of personal style. Others, however, may feel that the link between clothing and identity is superficial, or artificial. This question takes a more complex aspect in the context of the ad, as Mullins wears Kenneth Cole high-heel shoes on prosthetic limbs, thus complicating the issue of defining what is "really" her. Students may also consider the way their choice of brands—and the various associations that those brands aspire to—reflects their sense of who they are.

3. On one level, the advertisement relies on our perception of—and response to—the fact that Mullins has artificial limbs. On another level, the ad obscures this by alluding to it only subtly and indirectly. There are many perceptions of people with disabilities, but this ad seems to play off the viewer's sense that succeeding despite physical handicaps is admirable. The ad suggests that one must be a strong, distinctive individual to triumph over adversity, even as it simultaneously diminishes the importance of her prosthetic limbs and turns them into something that makes Mullins different, not disabled.

Examining Details, Imagery, and Design

1. Unsmiling, with her hands on her hips, her hair pulled back, and her chin raised as she looks directly at the camera, Mullins's pose is defiant and assertive. This is a contrast to clothing ads in which women may appear flirtatious or mysterious. Female legs are frequently eroticized in this context; Mullins's prosthetics play off this expectation in a way that appears daring. Her pose (and her clothing) seems to suggest both defiance and female seductiveness, undiminished—or even heightened—by her attitude toward her disability. This reinforces the message of difference and individuality.

2. The typeface makes the text appear as though it was handwritten quickly with a felt-tipped pen. In contrast to the standardized lettering of many ads, the font seems nonuniform and spontaneous; there are even individual

differences between the same letters, which is not the case with most standard fonts. This nonuniform writing suggests part of the brand's message: "25 years of non-uniform thinking."

3. The order of the descriptors is significant. Implicitly, it addresses the relationship between Mullins's identity in her disability and her other identities. The ad lists first her role as a paralympic athlete and then her other professional roles. But rather than marking her as "disabled" or "handicapped," the term *Paralympic athlete* reframes her disability in the positive terms of an accomplishment.

Thinking Critically

1. The ad does seem to encourage and celebrate difference and "nonuniform" thinking, but its ultimate purpose is to get the viewers both to accept the brand image and to buy the product. So in a sense, its goal is to make viewers more uniform as consumers. Students could even argue that Kenneth Cole clothing is itself a "uniform," which the advertisement ultimately wants the viewer to wear. Students might also question more closely the connection between buying clothing and "thinking," as the ad suggests this link but does not really demonstrate it.

2. The text makes no explicit reference to her prosthetic legs, other than to say that Mullins is a Paralympic athlete. The picture itself is also relatively subtle, as the joints of her prosthetics are partially hidden by her dress. Thus, the ad requires the viewer to look closely to determine the meaning. The shoes themselves are not prominently displayed, suggesting that the ad is selling an attitude and a message as much as a specific product.

3. Students should consider what demographics or types of people this ad is supposed to appeal to. For example, the image of a defiant, assertive, successful woman might resonate with women as an admirable role model. At the same time, Mullins is also presented in a way that is stylized and feminine—which might appeal to men. Models and actresses frequently use their innate (or enhanced) attractiveness, as well as the beauty of their specific body parts (legs, eyes, physique, and so on). Is Mullins simply doing the same thing? It might be pointed out that she is a professional fashion model, although that is not listed as one of her occupations.

In-Class Writing Activities

1. Students should incorporate visuals, effective language, quotations, cultural references, and evocative images—all the usual strategies of advertising. They should have a clear sense of how their choices are related to their audience. They should be able to see that advertisements use many of the same techniques that writing and visual art do, but with a difference. For example, both an ad and an argumentative essay are meant to persuade, but the former may rely less on clear logic than on associations or emotional appeals. Like poetry, ad copy may reflect careful attention to sound, rhythm, allusion, and connotation. But how does

the ultimate aim of such writing—to sell products—change its nature or limit it?

2. Students should consider this language in a historical context. For example, words such as *lame* and *crippled* are not generally acceptable or in use anymore. Why is that the case? Have we become more culturally sensitive? Does this different language reflect a different view of the people and disabilities themselves? Such words may also have different purposes—to describe, diagnose, or even celebrate. In a way, people with mental, physical, sensory, or other disabilities may constitute various cultures of their own. As such, should they decide, as a group or individually, what terms are appropriate? Students might also think about the function of euphemisms in this context.

3. The widespread cultural and academic practice of studying and analyzing advertisements using strategies from literary and art criticism, psychology, contemporary philosophy, and history is a relatively recent development. Advertising has usually been seen as part of mass culture or popular culture and therefore less worthy of study than "high" culture or art. Students should consider that advertising is not only ubiquitous and enormously influential but also carefully crafted to achieve certain goals and have certain effects on consumers. With that in mind, students should see the importance of looking critically at advertisements and understanding advertisement techniques and strategies.

REBECCA GANZAK (STUDENT ESSAY)   Is Cosmetic Surgery Worth the Risk?
[*The Alligator*, University of Florida/March 27, 2008]

Vocabulary/Using a Dictionary

1. The term *celebrity* derives from the Latin *celebritas* (fame, multitude) and *celeber* (populous, frequented). According to the *Oxford English Dictionary*, the first usage of *celebrity* defined as "a famous person" was in 1849—relatively recently.

2. *Malignant* comes from the Latin *malignus* (wicked or bad natured). Other words with the root *mal* (from *male*, meaning "badly" in Latin) include *malign*, *malice*, and *malefactor*.

3. Hyperthermia is an increase in body temperature that can stop metabolic functioning and cause death. Hypothermia is a decrease in body temperature. *Hypo-*, meaning "under," and *hyper-*, meaning "over," are from Greek.

Responding to Words in Context

1. The word *cosmetic* implies something decorative, beautifying, or superficially adorning. In contrast, *corrective* suggests that a flaw is being fixed.

2. In this context, *graphic* means "depicted vividly and realistically."

3. Plastic comes from the Greek *plastikos* (that which can be molded). It can refer to a synthetic, artificial material, but in the context of plastic surgery it means "capable of being molded or receiving form." In a discussion of cosmetic surgery, though, the word also connotes a sense of artificiality.

Discussing Main Point and Meaning

1. Ganzak argues that the main reason more teens are going "under the knife" is the influence of Hollywood celebrities. She acknowledges that teenage issues such as self-consciousness and self-esteem are common reasons but implies that they did not commonly lead to drastic surgery in the past. Now, the standards of beauty are determined by movie stars, and if "no one in Hollywood has a hooked nose, then why should a young girl find hers attractive?" (para. 2).

2. Ganzak believes that parents who approve of or fund such procedures are shirking their responsibilities. Rather than providing the kind of guidance that she imagines she will give her own daughter, parents (according to Ganzak) are using surgery "as a way to avoid actually being a parent," which might require setting limitations and helping children use good judgment.

3. Although Ganzak touches on the negative influence of celebrities and enabling parents, her primary argument against these procedures is that they entail health risks—a fact that teenagers don't seem to take into account. She makes this clear when she refers to the death of Stephanie Kuleba at the beginning of the essay. In her account of her own decision not to get corrective surgery, she claims that she changed her mind after she "researched the pain and cost involved" (para. 5). But later, she realized she hadn't taken into account the more alarming fact that "the chance of death due to anesthesia is pretty common" (para. 6).

Examining Sentences, Paragraphs, and Organization

1. Ganzak uses rhetorical questions in her introductory and concluding paragraphs, and in the body of her essay. They work to raise issues of concern or curiosity for Ganzak, for example: "So why would parents willingly put their children through such a risk?" (para. 5). The questions also seem to function more like transitional sentences than topic sentences for paragraphs: They lead from thought to thought, or to counter-arguments, rather than setting up a specific question to be answered.

2. Ganzak waits until paragraph 5 to bring up her own experience, after she has established her premises and her point of view using statistics and other examples. Her account of being self-conscious about her nose as a teen, weighing the possibility of a corrective procedure, and then deciding against it makes her credible on the subject—and also sets an example.

3. In paragraph 2, Ganzak uses statistics to establish a major premise of her essay—that plastic surgery is a growing trend among girls and boys under the age of eighteen. Including data from earlier years and showing an

obvious increase would make this point stronger, but the numbers Ganzak provides are already striking. She also relies effectively on statistics in paragraph 6 to emphasize the risks of general anesthesia; this follows from her statement that "you probably won't catch anyone admitting they would risk their life" for such procedures (para. 1). The numbers demonstrate that people do in fact take this risk.

Thinking Critically

1. Celebrities and pop culture certainly do exert influence over what's acceptable, especially with regard to appearance and notions of beauty. The direct link between that fact and the rise in plastic surgery is less clear. Students should consider how such images and standards affect them, either directly or more subtly. There may be other contributing factors as well: a culture more invested in appearances, generally; higher expectations of what is possible by way of medical procedures and even pharmaceuticals; a widespread increase in (and availability of) such surgeries for all demographics, not just younger people.

2. Ganzak seems to view the current teen culture as shallow and easily swayed by pop culture trends, and she characterizes an increasing number of teens as being either ignorant or heedless of the risks of their choices. She also says that many parents are not imposing proper limits on their children and are avoiding their parental responsibilities. Perhaps these are perennial concerns, but in the context of risky surgical procedures, the consequences are now greater. Additionally, Ganzak's reference to the "swipe of a credit card" (para. 4) implies that surgery is now just another consumer product.

3. Ganzak is pointing out the heightened, persistent, stereotypical self-consciousness of teenagers with regard to their bodies. As such, focusing on the surgical correction of one perceived flaw will not change teens temperamentally. This observation is important for her argument because it highlights problems with the adolescent perception of "issues like body image and self-esteem" (para. 3).

In-Class Writing Activities

1. Students should consider their perceptions of their own appearances and try to understand the rationale of those who choose surgery. They should also think about the standards they're applying to their appearance — what they are, where they come from. Why do certain body parts take on more significance in this context than others? For students who would not undergo such procedures, what would hold them back? Health risks? Costs? Parental disapproval? For students who would consider plastic surgery, what do they hope to achieve with such surgery? Self-acceptance? Acceptance by others?

2. Students should think about what constitutes a "reasonable" emphasis on physical appearance, especially given the ways in which society often

claims to value "substance" over "style" while at the same time celebrating and rewarding physical attractiveness. This tendency transcends celebrity culture and its influence. Ganzak is writing about teenagers here. But does our relationship with outward appearances or physical beauty vary according to our age?

3. This assignment might require some research to determine the relative numbers of men and women who get cosmetic surgery and the different kinds of procedures that men and women choose. But students should consider how men and women differ in their relationship with their bodies and emphasis on appearance. For example, women might need to rely (or think they need to rely) on certain physical attributes (such as ample breasts) in ways that men do not.

MICHAEL SANDEL   Designer Babies: The Problem with Genetic Engineering
[*Tikkun*/September–October 2007]

Vocabulary/Using a Dictionary

1. *Aptitude* means "skill or ability, either innate or acquired." Its roots are in the Latin *aptus*, meaning "jointed" or "fitted."

2. Eugenics is the science of hereditary improvement by controlled, selective breeding. The word *eugenics* derives from the Greek *eu* (good) and *genos* (birth). Genocide is the deliberate extermination of a national, political, racial, or cultural group. The word *genocide* comes from the Greek *genos* (which also means "type" or "kind") and the Latin *cidere* (to kill).

3. Prometheus was a titan in Greek mythology. He stole fire from the gods, and in defiance of Zeus, the king of the gods, he gave it to human beings. He was punished for his actions. The adjective *Promethean* means "boldly creative" or "original," but it can also carry a connotation of "overreaching," especially in the sense of humans striving to have god-like power.

4. *Humility* comes from the Latin *humilitas*, which means "lowness" or even "insignificance." Sandel is arguing for a concept of human beings as finite, limited, and ungodlike, and against human arrogance and self-importance.

Responding to Words in Context

1. Sandel includes the word *feeble-minded* because it was a standard part of the language of supposedly well-meaning eugenicists who wished to reduce the number of less intelligent or disabled people ("imbeciles," in Supreme Court Justice Oliver Wendell Holmes's words) through selective breeding. The quotation marks around the word signal Sandel's non-endorsement of the term, as does the modifier *so-called* that precedes it.

2. Sandel's essay is, ultimately, about the morality of eugenics and genetic engineering, so he persistently turns the reader's attention to fundamental

matters of right and wrong. He insists that our attitude toward—and our culture's response to—his subject necessarily has a moral component.

3. *Secular* means "pertaining to worldly things" or "not religious." Although Sandel refers to God and religion, he also makes sure that his argument is not reliant on religion, revealed truth, or the supernatural. Thus, he frames the "moral stakes" of the debate in a way that will appeal to nonbelievers.

Discussing Main Point and Meaning

1. Sandel's objections to genetic engineering are not based primarily on fears that a state would require it or even that it's a danger to health and safety. Instead, he sees the issues in terms of "a set of moral considerations that go beyond safety and fairness" (para. 7). According to Sandel, the methods and even the goals of eugenics are secondary to his fundamental moral objection to genetic engineering as "a Promethean assault" (para. 12) that might fundamentally alter—for the worse—our conception of society and what it means to be human.

2. Sandel sees "individualistic eugenics" and "free market eugenics" as a "deflation" of the public ideal of the practice, as flawed as that original ideal was. Formerly an "uplift" for humanity, it is now a way for parents to give their kids a competitive edge. But in both its public and private forms, genetic engineering is wrong for the same reasons: It tries to "control or exercise dominion over the genetic traits of the next generation" (para. 4). Sandel is aware that contemporary proponents of eugenics think in terms of "free markets" and "individualism," as if it's entirely a matter of personal choice and therefore beyond broad judgments like the ones in this essay. But his point, in part, is that these "privatized" choices could have enormous and complex public consequences.

3. Sandel is not referring to the special talents or abilities of gifted children but rather to the idea that children are, in and of themselves, "gifts" to parents. For the writer, it follows that the fundamental aspect of this relationship is that parents accept and appreciate their children "not as products of [the parents'] design or instruments of [their] ambition" (para. 10). Parental love—unlike, perhaps, the love for those we may love because of their qualities—is not "contingent" on any attributes a child happens to have. As Sandel sees it, genetic engineering tampers with this elemental ethical aspect of family relationships.

4. Sandel does not view eugenics as increasing freedom but instead sees it as creating an "explosion of responsibility" (para. 21). If we see ourselves as created by God or by nature, it follows that we are not always responsible for the way we are. But "the more we become masters of our genetics the greater burden we bear for the talents we have and the way we perform" (para. 19). Similarly, parents of children with Down syndrome are now judged because of the "burden of choice" created by new genetic technologies, as they could have chosen not to bring a disabled child into the world.

Examining Sentences, Paragraphs, and Organization

1. Sandel presents a supple and sophisticated argument. Part of its effectiveness is in the way he anticipates objections and positions other than his own. Here, he openly acknowledges that eugenics appeals to aspects of human nature that we often value highly: ambition, the belief in "progress" through knowledge, and human aspiration itself. But even granting this appeal, the fundamental moral problems inherent in genetic engineering outweigh its attractiveness.

2. This historical account of eugenics fits in with Sandel's overall approach to the subject. He notes that eugenics was discredited by horrific practitioners such as the Nazis, whose intentions and methods we obviously reject. But his larger theme is that genetic engineering is wrong regardless of intentions or methods. To that end, he highlights its appeal to "respectable" people who have embraced eugenics "in the name of those who have been burdened or disadvantaged" (para. 2). Both well-meaning and genocidal eugenicists are ultimately part of the same "dark history," as both the quotation from Oliver Wendell Holmes and the forced sterilization laws that once existed in America suggest.

3. According to Sandel, if genetic engineering allowed us to "override the results of the genetic lottery," we might lose "our capacity to see ourselves as sharing a common fate" (para. 22). In a meritocracy, the successful would be more likely to see themselves as entirely self-made (as opposed to being fortunate) and would view those with lesser gifts or status "simply as unfit"—and unworthy of solidarity, forgiveness, or compassion. In a sense then, the notion of "privatized" genetic engineering is false: Such practices, whether private or public, would have social consequences for everyone in society. This connects to his concluding assertion that eugenics ultimately "deadens the impulse for social and political improvement" (para. 26).

Thinking Critically

1. By focusing on humility, the dangers of "Promethean" ambition, and the need to understand humans as being "creatures of nature or God," Sandel wants to remind his reader that human beings are finite and bound by natural (or supernatural) contingencies beyond their power. Moreover, the latter limitation—and our awareness of it—is one of the foundations of compassion, forgiveness, acceptance, and solidarity with other people. This is what he means by a "religious sensibility," and it does not require belief in God or a particular religion. It stands in opposition to the desire for unlimited "mastery and control" (para. 26). Throughout the essay, from his use of the word *dominion* (which has connotations from the book of Genesis) to his allusion to Prometheus, Sandel projects this sensibility.

2. Sandel acknowledges that there is no "bright line" between genetic enhancement and "the kind of heavily managed, high pressure child rearing

practices that are common these days" (para. 15). But he turns this ambiguity to his rhetorical advantage. The "frenzy" he sees in contemporary parenting—the desire for control and mastery—suggests the same kind of "overreaching" that bioengineering does. Therefore, the similarity between these two forms of parental control does not vindicate eugenics. Rather, it casts a negative light on both.

3. It's difficult to exactly formulate a "substantive, normative conception of what human flourishing consists of." It's a question that could touch on philosophy, psychology, religion, politics, culture, biology, and innumerable other disciplines, approaches, and points of view. From the context of the essay as a whole, we might assume it would look like the "political and social realms that are more hospitable to the gifts and also to the limitations of imperfect human beings" (para. 26). But these are still generalities—as Sandel implicitly acknowledges near the end of his article, when he says that his subject "has something to do with our big questions about human nature" (para. 26). As it connects to his argument about eugenics, parents who live according to—and with acceptance of—the "ethic of giftedness" might provide an example of this standard of "human flourishing."

In-Class Writing Activities

1. Variations of the narrative of Prometheus have been told for thousands of years, from the biblical story of the Fall and other Greek myths (the story of Icarus and Daedalus), to Mary Shelley's *Frankenstein* and the 1997 science fiction film *Gattaca* (Sandel has referred to this film in his other writing on the subject of eugenics). Students should consider why this story is so persistent—and what it seems to say about human nature. They may also contrast it with a counter strain in history and culture that celebrates extraordinary ambition or achievement.

2. The purpose of this assignment is to get students to examine their own assumptions and views on this issue. For example, they might consider whether they approach genetic engineering from a religious or a secular perspective, and how that difference affects their position, if at all. At several points in Sandel's essay, he acknowledges that certain distinctions are difficult to determine—for example, between active parents who provide various advantages to their children, and those who would genetically enhance their offspring. How do students resolve or wrestle with these ambiguities? Moreover, if "designer babies" became a standard practice, then depriving one's own children of genetic advantages or a competitive edge might bring another set of moral problems and dilemmas into play.

3. Students who disagree with Sandel might say that laws regulating genetic engineering are unnecessary. Those who agree that genetic engineering is potentially harmful and in need of regulation would have to consider how such laws would be enacted and enforced. Would the American public be in favor of such regulation? Would such limits—ones that Sandel presumably would support—infringe on any individual rights, reproductive

and otherwise? Given the "free market eugenics" that Sandel identifies, certain business interests also might lobby against such restrictions. In part, the purpose of this exercise is to see how an informed, passionate public debate about a complex, difficult issue might lead to a specific political action.

Discussing the Unit

Suggested Topic for Discussion

In part, the gap seems to be between what we can do and what we ought to do (or not do). Students should think about newer scientific developments on the horizon (human cloning, for example). Or they may want to consider other, historical cases of scientific or technical advancements that brought new ethical dilemmas and debates—as well as new opportunities for humanity and society. As a recent example, our current ethics and laws regarding the uses and abuses of the Internet (such as music file sharing) are still evolving and incomplete.

Preparing for Class Discussion

1. Fundamentally, Sandel is making an argument about the morality—and the moral hazards—of bioengineering and genetics. In contrast, Ganzak is making a case against cosmetic surgery based primarily on the practical risks of such procedures, although she does make judgments about parents—and a popular culture—that encourage people to undergo them. For Sandel, the problem lies in tampering with the genetics of future generations, which entails a massive public risk. Although cosmetic surgery can be dangerous and its prevalence may have a negative influence, Ganzak is mostly concerned with how this personal choice affects individuals, not the general public, the culture as a whole, or future generations. Still, are there moral considerations about cosmetic surgery that she overlooks?

2. Students should think about where they draw their own lines on these issues. Setting aside legal and safety considerations, how are illegal steroids different from nutritional supplements or other "enhancements?" How are hair-dyeing or other alterations different from plastic surgery? The question of genetic engineering seems to bring with it a different order of moral problems than Goodman or Ganzak raise: Why is that the case?

From Discussion to Writing

1. Sandel writes with an overt religious sensibility that privileges modesty and resignation in the face of the limitations in the persuit of human perfection. Even though there are certain and obvious limits on humans, students might consider—and draw upon—the long history of human achievement and how scientific progress has overcome perceived limitations in ways that have benefited people or provided new and powerful knowledge. Sandel characterizes bioengineering as "a Promethean assault," but if the

story of Prometheus is about the dangerous desire for godlike powers, it's also a story about boldness, originality, and creativity.

2. Students — even those who are not sports fans — should be able to articulate the reasons that people have found athletics so compelling for so long. They should consider what qualities sports are supposed to represent or embody, or at least what they claim to represent (as in the Kenneth Cole ad, in which Aimee Mullins's athletic achievement suggests part of her "difference"). Do students agree with Sandel that "part of what we admire about great athletes is that we are able to see ourselves in their human achievements"? Do drugs like steroids and prosthetics such as those worn by Oscar Pistorius (from Goodman's article) or Aimee Mullins (from the Kenneth Cole ad) make it harder for us to "see ourselves" in those athletes?

Topics for Cross-Cultural Discussion

1. This question has grown in significance in recent years, especially as disabled groups have become more politically and socially aware and active. Students might consider the example of "Deaf [with a capital *D*] culture," whose members view their deafness not as a disability but merely as a different kind of human experience. This notion of shared community has significant implications for the practice of redesigning human beings. As cochlear hearing implants — devices implanted in infancy or childhood that can essentially remedy deafness for many people — become more widely used, some members of Deaf culture have referred to their use as "cultural genocide"; that is, by eliminating or reducing the prevalence of deafness, the implants pose a threat to sign language, deaf schools, and other aspects of the deaf community. In a sense, then, Deaf culture understands deafness less as an objective flaw or handicap to be "fixed" and more as a cultural construct — and a difference to be appreciated and preserved. Can this be seen as akin to, say, an ethnic culture?

2. Sandel's example of the Nazis highlights a historical tendency — obvious in the Holocaust — of viewing racial, ethnic, or other differences between groups in terms of "inferior" or "superior" genetics. This standpoint turns what may be a cultural difference into a biological difference — even to the point of labeling some groups as less fully "human" than others. Clearly, this kind of biological determinism can be dangerous when used to justify eugenics.

7

Will We Ever Transcend Race?

Alhough it might be tempting to believe that we live in a post-racist society, the problems of race are clearly still with us. During the 2008 presidential campaign, the possibility of an African American being elected president for the first time brought to the surface racial issues that never entirely disappear from American life. This chapter examines the extent to which race still influences how we view one another and communicate with one another. As a way of starting discussion, you might have your students talk about how important race is to our national conversation. How much does our society talk about it, and how much should we? Will there ever be a day when race is no longer an issue? What might cause that change?

The America Then feature for this chapter reminds students about past struggles for equality by recalling the push for desegregation that followed the Supreme Court decision in *Brown v. Board of Education*. In 1954, the federal government took a stand against states' illegal segregation practice. Today, some of the measures taken to provide more opportunities to students of color are under fire from groups that find them unnecessary or even unfair. Affirmative action has been challenged in a number of states, and several court cases have focused on university admissions policies. The fact that colleges have been a prime battleground for fights over affirmative action may underline for students the relevance of this issue to their lives.

The selections in this chapter engage both the political and the personal implications of racial identity. In the excerpt from Barack Obama's speech, the 44th American President talks honestly about the racial bitterness of both blacks and whites and acknowledges how difficult racial discourse can be. Jerald Walker uses anecdotes from his experience at a largely white university to argue for a more open conversation about race. Lauren Carter opens her essay with an anecdote showing how her identity is mirrored back to her, and then moves to a larger discussion of how race is assigned or read by society. All three of these writers suggest both the ways in which our understanding of race has progressed and what we still need to do to improve our policies, our mindsets, and our relationships.

JERALD WALKER   Teaching, and Learning, Racial Sensitivity
[*Chronicle of Higher Education*/March 20, 2008]

Vocabulary/Using a Dictionary

1. *Bene-* comes from the Latin word meaning "well" and *-volent* means "wishing." Walker suggests that the only reason the church basketball league allowed him to play was that they had good wishes for him, not because he had any skill.

2. *Predominant* describes a subset or a trait that dominates a group. It refers primarily to numerical abundance, but it can also suggest an ideological majority. It means "prevailing" or "being most frequent or common."

3. The word *fabric* originally referred not only to cloth but also to any material made by workmanship. With the addition of the suffix *-ate*, it became a verb meaning "to create something using skill." Gradually, the word took on a negative connotation, and now *fabricating* can mean "making something up for the purpose of deception."

Responding to Words in Context

1. The word *gaffe* is heard primarily in the realm of politics, in which a relatively minor instance of mis-speaking can result in scandal. In general, a gaffe is a mistake that arises out of ignorance or stupidity rather than ill-will.

2. *Trounced* means not only "beaten" but also "defeated decisively." Walker chooses this word to show just how fully he departs from the stereotype of the "black male from Chicago's inner city" with impressive basketball skills (para. 17). He notes that the other players look at him suspiciously because they expected him to fulfill that stereotype.

3. For Walker, encouraging sensitivity involves debunking stereotypes, such as his college roommate's idea that African Americans have small tails. He also wants people to become more empathetic and better listeners. For example, he wants his roommate to understand that he likes to be referred to as "black" but that there are many opinions on the subject, which people can learn only through individual contact.

Discussing Main Point and Meaning

1. Although Walker argues to his administrator that posting the picture was necessary, by the end of the essay he believes that he could have made a better choice. Rather than reacting out of frustration, he thinks he should have been more conscientious about helping his colleague or his roommate achieve a better racial understanding. Perhaps he should have modeled his behavior on that of his fellow basketball player, whose willingness to talk about race resulted in a productive conversation.

2. Walker's claims that he has "game" are a form of posturing that, he eventually argues, get in the way of honest discussions about race. Not only do they feed into stereotypes, but also they block deeper conversation.

3. Although the story outrages other minority professors, some of whom even imagine ways of retaliating, the white professors refuse to believe the story. Given the number of similar incidents Walker is able to cite, his minority colleagues likely have encountered similar frustrations and can, as he says, put themselves in his shoes (para. 3). The white faculty members, on the other hand, are predisposed to believe the white professor's denial of the incident. Some even believe that Walker lied about the conversation.

Examining Sentences, Paragraphs, and Organization

1. Walker uses understatement or euphemism at several points in his essay. For example, rather than saying his children are black or African American, he describes them as being "of the Negro persuasion" (para. 1), a phrase that pokes fun at misguided political correctness. He also points to the ridiculousness of the white professor's request by mentioning that he might be able to help with "any racially deprived felines" (para. 2). Walker turns the humor on himself when he contrasts his own self-image as someone who has "game" (para. 25) with the fact of being "trounced" at basketball (para. 26).

2. All three of the incidents reveal a moment of potentially tense discussion about race with a white acquaintance. Walker begins with the conversation about the dogs to illustrate how such discussions can go wrong when people aren't honest about their ideas and reactions. The second incident with a colleague offers a more positive example of how both parties can benefit from open communication. Finally, Walker's conversation with his roommate leads the way to his self-critique. Although his roommate's ideas about African Americans were outrageous, Walker recognizes that Lenny was trying to find a better racial understanding and that his own over-the-top reaction didn't help Lenny along the way.

Thinking Critically

1. Walker's argument in this essay is based on the virtue of open communication, so it follows that he would identify the problem not in ignorant speech but in dishonesty. In their discussion, students may wish to speculate about why the professor would lie. What pressures would cause him to do so?

2. Walker seems to believe that both minorities and whites are equally responsible for engaging in an open dialogue about race. Minorities need to inform people and counteract stereotypes, and whites need to examine their prejudices and to actively seek better understanding.

In-Class Writing Activities

1. Although some white students may not have had much exposure to minorities, each student should have some experience in which he or she had to address potentially uncomfortable racial subjects. Have them think about whether that discomfort prevents people from opening up or whether there are other reasons for that reticence.

2. This writing assignment should get students thinking about how individual voices add to the discourse. By narrowing their focus to the campus, students can concentrate on how their particular experiences—not just as whites or blacks but also as small-town/big-city dwellers, commuters/dorm residents, first-generation collegians/legacy students—alter their perspective.

LAUREN CARTER (STUDENT ESSAY)   Isn't Watermelon Delicious?
[*The Bridge*, Bridgewater State College/Spring 2005; revised with bibliography 2008]

Vocabulary/Using a Dictionary

1. *Ingenious* (meaning "clever or talented") comes to English through French from the Latin root *ingenium* (natural capacity).

2. *Dis-* has the sense of removing or reversing action, so to discover something is to remove what is hiding it or to undo the act of covering it up.

3. *Ordinare* means "to put in order," so *subordinate* means "to treat someone or something as lower in rank or importance."

Responding to Words in Context

1. In Reagan's eyes, and for many people, cultural choices or affinities are racially marked, and conversely, a person signifies race by his or her choices. Carter points out that if blackness is tied to these markers, then she is "behind in the race for true blackness" (para. 9); however, it is clear that she actually believes that the notion of a single "true" blackness is both erroneous and destructive.

2. Weldon's narrator passes for white by conducting himself as a white man and having others respond to him as such. In the novel, the decision about whether to identify as an African American or to lead an easier life as a white man is deeply complex for the narrator. Carter introduces this example as an illustration of someone who switches back and forth between cultural codes.

3. *Arbitrary* means "based only on opinion or preference and not on fact." Carter's point in this paragraph is that race, as a way of dividing people into categories, has no more validity than characteristics like eye color or other physical attributes.

Discussing Main Point and Meaning

1. As Carter puts it, Stacey's remark suggests that "a behavior related to a skin tone" and, moreover, that her own behavior is "related to two different ones" (para. 7). What she finds strange about this idea is that it seems to mean that she is not one person, but two halves, each of which asserts itself at different times.

2. Like Carter herself, the narrator of Weldon's *Autobiography* identifies with multiple races. She is interested in the narrative because the character is able to switch back and forth between appearing white and living as an African American. The question this raises for her is whether racial categories matter much at all, given the ease with which some people cross them.

3. When she talks about her sister, Carter questions whether her racial identity is determined by ancestry or by the way others perceive her. Both the story of Johnson's Ex-Colored Man and her sister's experience suggest that the latter definition can be malleable and quite inaccurate. On the other hand, the former definition refers solely to genetics and not to social interaction. Nonetheless, neither of these ways of reading race can account for an individual's complex identity.

Examining Sentences, Paragraphs, and Organization

1. Carter uses parallel structure in these sentences to replace one inadequate idea about racial identity ("The size of my nose is not my inheritance") with a more internal and complex one ("The will to survive is").

2. Carter's opening paragraph presents a very common scenario to show that questions and misconceptions about race don't always show up in a public forum or in a highly dramatic manner. For her, the questions came up during a typical evening with a friend she trusted. At other points in the essay, Carter is reminded of these questions by her reading and by the personal experiences of her family members.

3. In paragraph 8, Carter takes the idea that appearance defines identity to an extreme. She suggests that if that were true, African Americans could just move en masse back to Africa to be among people with similar appearances. However, this imagined scenario supports her claim that racial identity is internal as well as external because, as she points out, Africans in countries like Uganda would easily recognize the differences in experience and values between themselves and African Americans.

Thinking Critically

1. The idea that Carter is black, regardless of how she behaves, makes her internal sense of identification the defining characteristic of racial identity. However, it also seems to throw her back on genetics as a determiner of race, a way of defining people that she suggests earlier in the essay is somewhat limiting.

2. Carter's essay is idealistic, and at times the argument she is making reflects the way the world should be rather than the way it is. Although students will probably agree with her that identity is much more complicated than appearance, some might also argue that the way people treat you based on your physical traits deeply affects the way you relate to the world.

3. Although the essay re-creates Carter's thought processes as she tries to figure out how a person can be divided between white and black aspects, by the end she claims that this question no longer bothers her. What she implies is that she has matured into a sense of her own racial identity and doesn't have to worry so much about how other people perceive her.

In-Class Writing Activities

1. Even though Carter is curious about Stacey's comment, she quickly decides that a loud club is not the place for a thoughtful and possibly difficult discussion of race. She imagines asking Stacey about it later in a coffee shop, a place culturally coded as more contemplative and conducive to communication than a club. However, no conversation happens there either. Eventually Carter finds that a personal essay is the right place to explore her questions. Perhaps the medium of writing, with its more deliberate composition process and sense of permanence, is a better way to work out her ideas than is the medium of conversation.

2. Thes first chapter ("Of Our Spiritual Strivings") of DuBois's book is widely available online (including at www.bartleby.com/114/1.html). Not only is this a foundational text for African American letters, but it also provides a theoretical basis for some of the questions that Carter raises. You might point out to students that *The Souls of Black Folk* was published in 1903, more than one hundred years before Carter wrote her essay.

Discussing the Unit

Suggested Topic for Discussion

The articles in this unit are all written in the first-person. Ask your students if these would have the same impact or convey the same message were they written in third-person narrative. As the narrators tell us their stories, we put ourselves in their shoes and react the way they do. Recounting personal experiences makes the narrators more personable and their experiences more relatable. Ask your students to recall an experience when their racial identity or someone else's was the center of discussion. Do they see race as an issue today? In what situations or locations does race present more of an issue?

Preparing for Class Discussion

1. In one respect, the 2008 Democratic primary race between Barack Obama and Hillary Clinton brought a resurgence in identity politics, raising questions about whether African Americans support Obama just because of his race and whether women support Clinton just because of her gender. However, Obama's success also increased discussion about the continued need to right whenever possible the deep injury done by slavery and racism. In his speech, Obama shows that he understands both the frustration of the black community and the resentment of whites.

2. Of the three authors, Walker is clearest in presenting his solution, which is to have open discussions even when they may feel uncomfortable. His approach to the problem is interpersonal, although it has larger implications for public discourse. Obama, speaking more at the public level than the private, certainly doesn't argue against open communication, but he seems more concerned with taking legislative steps to narrow the gap between white and black Americans. Specifically, he thinks that effective solutions to problems that stress both groups, including unemployment and failing schools, will help reduce tensions. Finally, Carter's essay addresses racial division on a theoretical level. She engages with both anecdotal evidence and literary works in order to challenge essentialist notions about race.

From Discussion to Writing

1. A large part of Walker's essay revolves around the idea that black men, particularly black men from the inner city, know how to play basketball. Of course, Walker reveals that in his case this is far from the truth. However, the media-driven stereotype (which is reiterated in numerous movies and songs) about the urban black male is so strong that Walker even thinks his colleagues get suspicious when he doesn't fit it. In "Isn't Watermelon Delicious?" Carter also looks to images of blackness in the media, but she adds the idea that blackness is something marketable, a quality that gets attached to clothing and shoes in order to sell them.

2. Students might be quick to notice that the speech has a more elevated tone than either of the essays, which, perhaps paradoxically, are more "talky." Both Obama and Walker repeat an idea to tie their works together, but for Obama the repeated references to historical grievances in this excerpt become especially important for helping his listeners follow his argument. He also avoids many references, like the ones that Carter makes to James Weldon Johnson, Richard Wright, and others. While she is writing to an academic audience that might know these authors, Obama is appealing to the more general audience of voters.

Topics for Cross-Cultural Discussion

1. Because the United States used slave labor on a massive scale, its problems with race have seemed more overt than, for example, those in European countries. However, France, Britain, and other European countries have had a resurgence of tension surrounding racial issues, often refigured as problems with immigration. The genocide in Sudan has been driven largely by conflict between Arab and African ethnic groups. Ethnic violence has also plagued a number of Asian countries, including Sri Lanka, with its ongoing civil war between Tamil separatists and the Sinhalese majority.

2. The growing Latino population is changing the face of American politics and will continue to do so in the coming decades. Latinos are now as

important a segment of the electorate as African Americans; however, some commentators suggest that Latinos are a less cohesive voting bloc than are African Americans. Although Latino voters and middle- and working-class African Americans and whites share many of the economic concerns, some Latinos also adhere to traditional and historically conservative values.

8

Education Today:
Is Underachieving the Norm?

Legislators and political commentators seem to agree that the United States needs to make improvements in the education system; debates about the issue now revolve around how to encourage and track those improvements. The No Child Left Behind Act, passed in 2001, created a battery of tests to assess students' progress, but the tests have proved to be controversial. Many state governments are now concerned about whether their schools can meet the benchmarks set for the 2013–2014 school year. In addition to these changes in goals and assessments, the twenty-first century has brought changes in the atmosphere of schools.

The two student essays in this chapter discuss how the problem with low achievement can extend to higher education. Amy Widner uses anecdotal evidence from her peers to create a larger argument about the reasons for attending college. She looks at the anti-intellectualism of underachieving college students as a problem of personal ambition and motivation. Jason Shepherd, on the other hand, discusses a technology that he thinks could distance college students even further from their professors. He worries that technological developments could take away the class interaction necessary for learning.

Allen Kanner's essay points out what he believes is a problematic trend — the increasing influence of corporations on school resources and even instructional materials. This blending of commercial with educational aims turns classrooms into captive audiences for cleverly disguised advertising.

While these three essays look at the way contemporary schools work, Susan Jacoby addresses an even broader problem with education in America. She uses the occasion of an election year to plead for a more engaged and informed public. Like Widner, she traces the education crisis to a problem of values, arguing that our country has a history of anti-intellectual feeling. This range of essays should help your students engage questions about the problems plaguing American education. Where should we start if we want to fix them? How much can public policy change the system, and how much of that change will rely on individual students or families?

SUSAN JACOBY   How Dumb Can We Get?
[*The Week*/February 29, 2008]

Vocabulary/Using a Dictionary

1. The suffix *-phile* is from the Greek word *philia* (meaning "friendship" or "love"). A technophile is someone who loves technology.

2. *Cumber* has several obsolete meanings, including "to overwhelm or overthrow," but in current use the verb means "to weigh down" or "to clutter up." The textual comparison of political messages is cumbersome because it involves more work and more detailed thinking. It is the difficulty (or weightiness) of this work, according to Crain, that makes negative political ads more effective because they don't require careful analysis.

3. *Rational* means "endowed with reason" or "able to make judgments based on reason." Jacoby criticizes Americans not only for being ignorant but also for devaluing the use of thought to make decisions and relying only on emotion.

Responding to Words in Context

1. By altering the words of Lincoln's famous speech, she calls attention to the word *folks* as undignified and improper for public discourse. If the word *folks* sounds so out of place in a political speech, then by extension, are self-conceived "just folks" really an important part of the body politic? Jacoby objects to the word because it suggests a simplicity that works counter to a nuanced understanding of political affairs.

2. *Infotainment* is a portmanteau word combining *information* and *entertainment*. In Jacoby's view, Americans have become so neglectful of intellectual life that basic news has to be couched in the form of entertainment in order to appeal to audiences.

3. Jacoby suggests that anti-intellectualism is spreading in America and doing so in a way that could be hard to control. She uses the word *epidemic* to introduce the idea that we need more radical ways to combat these tendencies, beyond the inadequate measure of standardized testing.

Discussing Main Point and Meaning

1. Jacoby argues that what constitutes "dumb" in American culture has hit ever-lower levels in recent years. She attributes the lowering of standards to a switch from print to video culture, which decreases literacy.

2. She suggests that as news stories about the Iraq War decreased, the war faded out of people's minds, a phenomenon directly related to Americans' shortening attention spans. She attributes our lack of concentration to the kind of reading we do—short summaries of information found on the Internet rather than complex narratives or arguments, which require long stretches of absorption.

3. Jacoby finds the extremely brief sound bites and pat explanations of recent presidents to be inferior to the more detailed discussions that Franklin Roosevelt and other twentieth-century presidents had with their citizens. For a point of comparison, she mentions Roosevelt's fireside chats, which gave Americans detailed and complex information about the country's involvement in World War II.

Examining Sentences, Paragraphs, and Organization

1. The statistic on how many Americans read for pleasure shows a steady decline over the years of the study, a fact that Jacoby ties to the increasing suspicion of intellectualism. It is also significant, she points out, that the study covered the years of significant growth for video games and the Internet.

2. Jacoby suggests that even though Americans today have greater access to technologies such as "satellite-enhanced Google maps" that would help them learn, they are less likely to use them to understand politics and the news than their grandparents would have been.

3. At the end of her argument, Jacoby suggests that in order to change the climate of anti-intellectualism, we need to ask ourselves whether "we truly value intellect and rationality." She also indicates that the 2008 election year is an especially important time to have this discussion. The candidates are promising change, and she believes that the issue of anti-intellectualism is one of the most pressing in American life.

Thinking Critically

1. America was founded on the rhetoric of representative democracy, in which all voters have a voice in government. However, the writers of the Constitution insisted that voters' views be filtered through the body of Congress, a system that refines the common opinion. A literal reading of representative democracy, added to a spirit of exceptionalism, might suggest that all voices are equally valuable, no matter how thoughtful or informed.

2. Caleb Crain suggests that because it is harder to keep track of context in video reports as opposed to written ones, viewers are left to judge not with reason but with emotion. Jacoby links this way of assessing information with the negative political ads that contain little argument but a lot of emotional force.

3. Students may be more likely than Jacoby to see merit in Steven Johnson's argument (cited in para. 7) that video games and other technology actually pose cognitive challenges. In discussing this issue, you might also have them focus on some of Jacoby's statistics. For example, does the percentage of people who read books for pleasure reflect what students see among their own friends and family? Are these measures the best ones for gauging Americans' intellectual involvement?

In-Class Writing Activities

1. Almost all colleges have forums such as student newspapers and government in which students can voice ideas about college events and policies. However, the extent to which these spaces are used for public comment and how much effect they have vary widely. In writing their essays, students should think about how informed the student body is about school issues and whether any public matters require more discussion.

2. Especially for young college students, recently out of high school, standardized tests are likely a subject on which they have an opinion, either pro or con. For this assignment, remind them that their argument about the tests may be based on personal experience but should engage Jacoby's larger questions about Americans' lack of education and how that shortfall can be remedied.

AMY WIDNER (STUDENT ESSAY)   The Pursuit of Just Getting By
[*The Echo*, University of Central Arkansas/March 12, 2008]

Vocabulary/Using a Dictionary

1. *Procrastination* is based on the Latin word *crastinus*, which means "belonging to tomorrow." *Procrastination* means "putting off doing something that should be done."

2. *Cognize*, a term used primarily in law or philosophy, means "to notice or become conscious of." *Recognize* means "to become aware of something previously known," although the sense of "again" added by the prefix *re-* in this word is weaker than in other words containing the prefix.

3. In Greek, *diploma* originally meant "a piece of paper folded double." In Latin, it came to mean "an official state document or letter of recommendation." Today, the word also refers to a document recording graduation from an educational institution.

Responding to Words in Context

1. In calling for "professionalism," Widner is referring primarily to relationships among students and between students and their professors. Even though attending college is not a profession, she thinks that students should approach their education with a level of seriousness and effort that they would give to a job.

2. For Widner, the "normal" way to approach the college experience is for students to get the most they can out of it by performing to the best of their abilities. What is "abnormal" about these students' attitudes is that they call into question the purpose of going to college — to become an educated person.

3. Because so many employers now expect a college education, many students are under pressure from their parents, high schools, and society as a whole to attend college, whether they are invested in the education or

not. Students don't make an active choice, and so going to college becomes a kind of automatic response.

Discussing Main Point and Meaning

1. Widner accepts that the conversation between the students might serve the purpose of "stress relief, nervous small talk, academic confessionals" (para. 5), all of which are ways to make light of underachievement. However, the deeper problem is a lack of concern for or even a devaluation of achievement.

2. In past generations, attending college was not as common as it is today and was held in great esteem. Now, so many jobs require a bachelor's degree that college, though not mandatory, seems necessary for success. Widner believes that because such a large number of students end up attending college, many have lost sight of the real goals of higher education and devalue the learning experience.

3. Widner argues that students who act proud of underachieving learn bad habits, such as procrastination and a poor work ethic. Although she personally finds these traits distasteful in college, they will present an even greater problem in the real world when students look for jobs and find employers who expect much more out of them than they may be used to giving.

Examining Sentences, Paragraphs, and Organization

1. Widner's sarcastic quotation points out the problems with students' underachievement. People who believe that "D is for diploma" (para. 4) assume that the degree is all that matters. Widner, however, ridicules the assumption that employers care only about the diploma and not the skills students are supposed to have learned while getting it.

2. Widner begins with a question she imagines readers might ask her and then gives a list of five answers to that question. She uses parallel structure, beginning each sentence with "it" and then a different verb, to emphasize the five reasons that she finds underachievement so upsetting.

3. Through much of the essay, Widner is chastising other students for behavior that she would never engage in. At the end, however, she makes a rhetorical turn to group herself with all college students. Although her tone is still warning, the switch to the pronoun *we* moves toward solidarity and indicates the universality of the consequenes of underachievement.

Thinking Critically

1. Because high school attendance is state-mandated, some students may be there against their will. College attendance, however, is voluntary, so it is reasonable to expect that college students would be highly motivated to benefit from their education. Moreover, the cost of college to either students or their parents increases all the time. Given the big investment of

both time and money that students put into college, Widner thinks it is foolish to applaud underachieving.

2. The obstacle course analogy helps Widner explain the attitude that some students have about their professors' intentions. It suggests that college is just a series of hoops to jump through and also that the goals of the process are hidden or ambiguous. She sees this as a faulty comparison because she believes that college actually teaches relevant skills and has clear applicability for later occupations.

In-Class Writing Activities

1. For this assignment, you might encourage students to actually re-create a conversation of their own—either one that shows a similar attitude or one that challenges Widner's argument about current trends among college students. This conversation should provide a basis from which to respond to "The Pursuit of Just Getting By."

2. Students might want to make this list specific to their particular coursework or major and to think about what skills they will likely need for a future career. Or they might approach the assignment more generally, considering how the whole college experience helps prepare students for their working lives.

JASON SHEPHERD (STUDENT ESSAY)   Should Professors Podcast Their Lectures?
[*Vanguard*, University of South Alabama/February 19, 2007]

Vocabulary/Using a Dictionary

1. *Pathos* is an emotion of sympathetic pity, and the prefix *a-* means "without." To be apathetic is to be without strong feelings.

2. In this instance, *pro-* means "in support of." Proponents are supporters of a person or idea.

Responding to Words in Context

1. *Podcast* is a play on the word *broadcast*. Podcasts are audio or video recordings distributed to listeners' iPods or computers, often through subscription.

2. By saying that his fellow students "admitted" their likelihood of skipping classes, Shepherd suggests that such a response is slightly embarrassing or shameful.

3. Shepherd believes that the best learning happens in the classroom when professors and their students can interact with one another face-to-face. In this case, both parties are actively trying to come to an understanding. He argues that coursecasts are passive by nature, allowing students to just sit back and watch a lecture that the professor had already created, without actively engaging the professor.

Discussing Main Point and Meaning

1. One of the reasons for introducing coursecasting is to provide a more flexible form of instruction. It can provide background information for students who need it, but those who don't need it could skip that part of a lecture. Students who need time to absorb concepts could watch parts of the lecture as many times as they liked. Some proponents of course-casting also suggest that it will help professors connect to student culture and bridge the student-teacher gap.

2. First of all, Shepherd argues that coursecasting will cause a drop in atten-dance because it will make it easier for students to skip class. Second, not only will it make students lazier, but it might also lead professors to slacken in their teaching because they don't have to explain themselves as fully to students who might want to ask questions. And finally, he argues that podcasts would not be the most efficient way to provide background information to students who need to catch up in a course.

3. Given his reservations about the technology and its effects, Shepherd hopes that professors strictly limit the use of coursecasts. Coursecasts may work as supplements to traditional courses but should in no way replace them.

Examining Sentences, Paragraphs, and Organization

1. The first paragraph of this essay establishes reasons that coursecasting might benefit both students and teachers. Shepherd lays out these reasons first so that in the rest of his essay he can systematically counter them with his own predictions about how the technology would work.

2. Shepherd marks the beginning of his arguments against coursecasting with "first" (para. 2). The transitions "besides" and "better yet" help him point to the real question at hand and to suggest a solution (para. 5). He includes "of course" (para. 6) to show that he makes some concessions to the arguments for coursecasting but maintains his basic position that they should not replace traditional instruction.

Thinking Critically

1. Shepherd likely asked his friends or classmates how they would respond if professors moved from lectures to coursecasts. Although he did learn something from their answers, a more rigorous survey would require interviewing a random sample of students to get a true cross section of opinions.

2. Even though he doesn't say specifically what uses for coursecasts he would find acceptable, clearly Shepherd does not want them to carry the burden of conveying important course information to the students. Therefore, coursecasts might complement classroom work by supplying additional nonessential information or by furthering discussion of how the ideas could be applied.

In-Class Writing Activities

1. Some universities have pushed to get iPods into the hands of their students for educational use, but students might be unfamiliar with this particular application of podcasting. Have them think about what kind of information could be usefully conveyed in this medium. What type of teaching would be better handled in class?

2. In thinking about this question, students might compare their experience in college with that of older siblings or friends. Even a few years' difference can encompass major changes. For example, the use of course management programs like Blackboard was relatively rare until recent years. Many colleges have created "smart" rooms with technology such as projectors and DVD players. Have students think about how much these changes have altered the way classes are run and the kind of material that courses now include.

ALLEN D. KANNER   Today's Class Brought to You By . . .
[*Tikkun*/January–February 2008]

Vocabulary/Using a Dictionary

1. Here the word *pervert* is used as a verb and in this context means to "corrupt or misdirect." The word is also a noun, meaning "a deviant" (usually someone with a sexual preversion). The adjective *perverted* means "corrupt" or "marked by perversion."

2. The root of *discretionary* is the noun *discretion*, which is related to the adjective *discreet*. Discretion is an individual choice or judgment, having the quality of being discreet. If one is discreet, one shows good judgment, and often means one is capable of wisely keeping silent on an issue.

3. The word *ban* means "to prohibit" or "to exclude." If advertising is banned from schools, it would be completely removed from any such setting.

Responding to Words in Context

1. Students may be most familiar with television commercials, or paid advertising. Students with business backgrounds might be more aware of the word *commercial*'s relation to all things having to do with commerce, or the buying and selling of commodities. These definitions of the word will probably suggest that the "commercialization of childhood" means that childhood has been mixed with the business world and material gain in some way.

2. *Implicit* and *explicit* have opposite meanings. An implicit endorsement is an implied endorsement—one not expressly stated. An explicit endorsement is one that is fully and clearly expressed.

3. *Inadequate* means "insufficient." Adequately trained teachers probably have access to the resources needed to do their job satisfactorily, whether those resources are money, personal support, materials, or education. They

would not need to rely as heavily on prepackaged materials from corporations, whereas inadequately trained teachers might feel that they have no other choice but to lean on SEMs as a resource.

Discussing Main Point and Meaning

1. The bottom line for corporations is to get consumers to buy their products. There may be educational value to a particular corporation's sponsorship of SEMs, but it is important to realize that SEMs are a vehicle for advertising and that advertisers are investing huge sums of money to win over the consumer. Are students aware of vending machines in their halls or corporate logos in their learning materials? Ask them to imagine a school without any corporate fingerprints. If your school has been untouched by corporate sponsorship, ask students to consider the difference between watching shows on public broadcasting stations (which now accept some limited corporate sponsorship, but less than other stations) and watching shows on commercial television or to imagine the disappearance of billboards they know well. Once they appreciate the impact of corporate marketing, ask them to apply that to the learning environment they experience in school.

2. Students will probably mention entertainment media such as television, the Internet, movies, radio, and magazines as areas of commercialization. Ask them to consider more "learned" media such as newspapers and scholarly journals. Is there a corporate presence even in these media? Advertisers fund sports events and other social happenings. Commercialization in modern life may be so pervasive that students are not aware of the advertising they take in as they ride a bus, stroll in a shopping mall, or walk down the street. Ask whether they have taken part in any events or visited any public places that have been free from commercialization, and test those assumptions.

3. Having the input of many individuals in the educational system provides certain benefits because it invites a diversity of information and approaches to learning and also sets up a system of checks and balances similar to what we have in our government to avoid absolute power and corruption. If education is privatized, profit might be valued above the education and welfare of the children, and those running a particular school might be more likely to be swayed, or "bought," by a corporation trying to gain a foothold. In privatized education, there would be no checks and balances and no need for consensus from a board or other body representing parents.

Examining Sentences, Paragraphs, and Organization

1. The words *exclusive* and *exclude* share the same root, and the repetition within this sentence emphasizes the idea that some sort of restriction is taking place. If only a restricted number of companies are allowed to sell their products on campus (in this case, soft-drink giants Pepsi or Coke), student choices are very limited.

2. The Revlon curriculum is a clear-cut example of how companies sell to students through SEMs. If Revlon puts its name on a curriculem that asks students to name which hair products are essential to them, the curriculum is implicitly or explicitly pushing the company's products. Even if students want to take other products to a desert island, they will now at least think about choosing a Revlon product, just from name recognition alone. Because of the prevalence of commercialization, people are constantly exposed to brand names, whether they appear in ads or in learning materials. By using this example so early in the essay, Kanner lets the reader know that SEMs contain a certain level of marketing, even if only the company name or logo appears in the materials.

3. Kanner's essay provides a wealth of examples and creates a persuasive picture of what can happen in the schools thanks to the proliferation of SEMs. The essay shifts in paragraphs 8 and 9 as Kanner turns his attention from what SEMs are and how they affect education to what his readers can do to stop them. Ultimately, he is against advertising in the schools, and in paragraph 8 he calls on readers to act and outlines the steps they can take to eliminate the problem.

Thinking Critically

1. By being aware of what children watch on television or whom they interact with, parents help shape their children's world. Although parents cannot shield children from all things, involved parents can be effective censors of what their very young children encounter. Once children start attending school, parents in part turn over their role as censors to their children's teachers. If the school uses an SEM from a corporate sponsor, parents might not be aware of this commercialization of education or be able to stop their children from learning from those materials. Often school is the last place parents expect their children to encounter marketers. Marketing is, by its nature, biased, and teachers are supposed to provide students with an unbiased atmosphere in which to learn.

2. Student answers will vary. Some students will sense the presence of marketing more strongly, in vending machines or other physical manifestations of products. Other students will point to prizes offered by corporations for contests. Still others will be aware of the mention of products in texts and other lesson plans. Students should consider whether they took anything of value from the experience and how their perception of the product changed as a result of its presence in the school.

3. Kanner suggests three ways to combat SEMs: outright banning of advertising, screening SEMs for accuracy and relevance, and providing schools with more money so that they will not need to rely on SEMs. Some students may think that the problem is all about money and that without enough money, schools will always be susceptible to the outside influence of corporations. They should examine what areas in particular need funding, where this funding might come from, and how this money will shut out SEMs. Other students may believe that the problem lies not with money, but with the

SEMs presentation of material and their distortion of the "truth." These students should construct definitions of "truth" in learning materials and explore how those truths are agreed upon. Still other students may think that advertising simply has no place in the schools. They should consider whether advertising can be totally banned in schools. Such a ban may present drawbacks that students need to consider.

In-Class Writing Activities

1. Student answers will vary. The description should be as detailed as possible, and students should consider the benefits to both the advertiser and the learner that the SEM provides.

2. There are many reasons why young people might be more vulnerable to marketers than are older age groups. Very young children are often not able to discriminate between "truth" and "advertising." They may be drawn to packaging (the use of familiar cartoon characters, for example) or some other reward being offered with the product (such as toys in a cereal box). Older children may be more influenced by peers and peer pressure. Teenagers may be more influenced by advertising that uses sex or connections to the adult world (ads for cars, for example) or that promises to alleviate the concerns and distresses of adolescents (such as ads for acne cream). Some students might argue that other populations are equally vulnerable to marketing: the elderly (advertising for medications and pain relief, for example) or professional adults (advertising for products that promote status or the image of wealth). Make sure students provide some clear ideas of the interests of various age groups and how marketers appeal to those interests.

3. Students will have to examine what they think they are getting out of their education in order to define *knowledge* and *values*. You might consider asking them to formulate the definitions of these words before they address the issue of SEMs. This assignment also asks them to judge the effect of commercialization on their lives, in school and elsewhere. Students may choose a particular SEM example because of their familiarity with the company's product, regardless of whether their contact with it has been positive, negative, or neutral.

Discussing the Unit

Suggested Topic for Discussion

Before forecasting how education will change, ask your students how education has changed thus far. What was school like back when their parents were students? One example of a big change in education is the development and popularity of online courses. Now, students can get their degrees from the comfort of their own homes. Do your students think that such a development is an improvement or a sign of America's laziness and "dumbing down"?

When thinking about education and technology, it is important to consider America as a whole. Not all Americans have access to computers and the Internet. Knowledge is still a luxury and something that takes work and effort. What does that say about the future of education? Ask your students if they believe that, as Widner states, "college is starting to feel more like extended high school" (para. 6)? Or do they see the rise of college tuition as a sign of the decreased popularity of college education?

Preparing for Class Discussion

1. Kanner's piece discusses the youngest students, so he is most concerned about the commercial messages they absorb without even knowing it. Shepherd's argument about coursecasting reveals the greater independence of college students — he is not worried that they will be manipulated, but he is concerned that coursecasting will deprive them of contact with their instructors. Both Jacoby and Widner discuss the public perception of education and are concerned by the tone that adults, both the young adults in college and the general voting population, set for the country.

2. Jacoby's essay draws on a wide range of sources, from recent opinion surveys to analyses of presidential speeches. Kanner surveys the corporate programs that exist in schools to back up his assertion that educational materials are sometimes supplied for marketing purposes. The shorter student essays draw mostly on campus discourse, both casual exchanges between students and more official discussion about curriculum.

From Discussion to Writing

1. This assignment asks students to put two essays in conversation with each other and therefore will require them to extend the positions the authors put forward. For example, they might think about how Widner or Jacoby would respond to Shepherd's assertion that face-to-face interaction is necessary to education, or how Shepherd's concerns about coursecasting would apply to the kinds of materials Kanner discusses in his essay.

2. In their writing, students sometimes rush to offer opinions, so this assignment asks them to dwell on the first task of identifying a problem. The problem they discuss need not be huge or overarching — it could be something as specific as the way requirements are structured for a major or the placement of breaks in the school calendar. In any event, they should try to look at the problem from as many angles as possible. What is its source? How long has it existed?

Topics for Cross-Cultural Discussion

1. Discussion of these questions will be largely anecdotal, but if students have traveled to other countries, they might have insights into other educational systems and how rigorous they are compared to America's educational system. Alternatively, you might discuss how "universal" American education really is. How does it compare to countries in which education is reserved for only part of the population, as determined by gender or by class?

2. A 1982 Supreme Court decision requires states to provide primary and secondary education to the children of immigrants without legal status. However, when these students reach college age, many of them hit a barrier. Although some states have passed laws offering in-state tuition to students without legal status, the students might not be eligible for financial aid.

9

Signs of Change:
What Can We Expect America to Be?

From John Winthrop's 1630 sermon about the "city upon a hill" and Thomas Jefferson's arguments with James Madison, right up to many current public and political debates, people in America have always had strong convictions—and expectations—about what this country is supposed to be. Indeed, at times it seems as if the United States exists as a set of ideas and ideals as much as it does as a country. Because those ideals are bound up with concepts of individual freedom, self-determination, and the democratic process, the real work of putting them into practice is supposed to fall on us, as citizens. But how civically and politically engaged are we, really? And what is the quality of that engagement? What obligations do we have to one another as Americans? What kind of country do we want to live in? All the essays in this unit focus on these questions, in one way or another.

In "Lower the Voting Age!" Marco Roth argues that the franchise should be expanded to include sixteen-year-olds—and perhaps citizens even younger than that. He recalls the sentiments of the campaign that lowered the voting age in 1971, during the Vietnam War: "Old enough to fight, old enough to vote!" For Roth, though, the current voting age is still too high: "at 18, you could still suddenly be drafted, fight, and die in a war started by a government you had never previously voted for." His argument goes beyond these military considerations, however. For Roth, expanding the electorate might cure our nation's current political apathy as well as release America's "stalled" democratic and revolutionary impulses; such expansions have often led to social change in the past. But where other people have tied voting age to qualifications like property ownership, assumptions about the nature of "reason," or the prerogatives of military service, Roth makes a more contemporary—and more provocative—claim: If teens can participate in consumer society, then they can vote, as the two activities have become so similar in character. Moreover, after looking back at the last few election cycles, he asks, "Could a bunch of 16-year-olds choose any worse?" Students can consider whether they would support such a measure; at the same time, they should think about whether teens have untapped democratic energies that could be directed toward politics.

Young people might also wonder who votes with their particular interests in mind, if they cannot. That lack of representation may have significant consequences. According to Paul Starr's essay, "A New Deal of Their Own," the great federal programs and government reforms of the twentieth century "failed to establish durable policies in support of the young." As a result, the

United States has relatively high levels of poverty and other problems affecting children and adolescents, when compared with other prosperous and developed countries. For Starr, the solution to this lies in social investment along the lines of the GI Bill, possibly linked to voluntary national service.

Both Roth and Starr offer proposals that work through existing government institutions. In "Protest Is Dead. Long Live Protest," Joseph Hart looks at the recent state of political dissent and civil disobedience and finds it lacking in power and originality. Whether considering the "impotent" antiwar movement or the "unimaginative" protests that surrounded the 1999 World Trade Organization conference in Seattle, the essay suggests that such actions have become ritualized and largely irrelevant to real political change. But Hart finds inspiration and imagination in groups like the Critical Art Ensemble, which stages provocative public protests, and people such as Ji Lee, who left his job in advertising to initiate the anticorporate Bubble Project. The essay challenges students to evaluate the merits of such methods, even as it approves of them; it also raises questions about the nature of civil disobedience, and forces readers to consider the differences between activities such as culture jamming and just plain vandalism. Ultimately, Hart is calling for creativity and originality, as much as he is urging political commitments to specific issues.

Jeff Dickson sees the main problem with the United States not as a lack of political engagement but as a lack of unity. According to Dickson, too often we see ourselves as hyphenated Americans, separated by race, faith, political affiliation, or other demographic differences rather than as one people united by shared values and a common purpose. He looks back at the solidarity of the World War II generation and its accomplishments and then argues that similar unity now could help our country deal with challenges such as foreign oil dependence, global warming, and health care. As with the other writers in this chapter, Dickson sees great potential in the young for a powerful, civic revival.

MARCO ROTH   Lower the Voting Age!
[N+1/Winter 2008]

Vocabulary/Using a Dictionary

1. The adjective *civic* refers to citizens. *Engagement* means "the act of being involved." "Civic engagement" refers to a person's participation in public activities.

2. A bagatelle is an insignificant thing. It comes from the French word *bagatelle* (trinket), which is derived from the Italian word *bagatella*.

3. *Discern* means "to recognize as separate or distinct" or "to detect with the senses."

Responding to Words in Context

1. *Franchise* in this context means "a privilege given to an individual or a group," in this instance the right to vote. *Enfranchising* means "endowing

with the privileges of a citizen," especially the right to vote. *Disenfranchise* means "to deprive of a privilege," in this case the right to vote. Each word shares the same root. The prefixes in the latter two words shape and change their meanings, although all have to do with suffrage.

2. The prefix *an-* means "not" or "without," and the Greek word *archos* means "ruler." Literally translated, anarchy means "the state of being without a ruler." Anarchists advocate against any authority or established order. Globalists want to recognize a single, global authority, placing the interests of the world over individual nations. (Students may be familiar with the term *globalization*, which has to do with free trade and the creation of a global economy.) Environmentalists are concerned with the well-being of the earth's environment. Libertarians are concerned with individual liberties, or freedoms, and are particularly interested in safeguarding private property.

3. *Defraud* means "to deprive someone of money or property by dishonest means (fraud)." *Defund* means "to withdraw funding from something."

Discussing Main Point and Meaning

1. Roth believes that younger voters would revitalize elections and be more interested in the process than are some apathetic older adults. He states that we are afraid that younger voters would be more radical or less reasonable in their choice of officials and policies, but he believes that their enthusiasm and diversity would help neutralize that problem. Scientific evidence now shows that the teenage brain isn't fully developed, adding some credence to the theory that young people lack the maturity to make wise decisions in elections; however, teenagers do participate in society in other valuable ways and are expected to behave more like adults by age eighteen. Roth adds that teenagers are usually learning about the democratic process and the history of their nation, and with that knowledge fresh in their minds, they are better equipped than adults to participate in the election process.

2. Roth's description of teenage voters helps destroy stereotypes and misconceptions that we might hold. Because teenagers "are harder to predict, harder to homogenize" (para. 3), it's impossible to make the generalization that their votes would be more radical, according to Roth. Not all teenagers would make snap decisions. Some would be facing the prospect of fighting in an imminent or ongoing war, and some would be serious students who would carefully weigh the pros and cons of all the candidates—just as older voters do. Roth also cites cynicism and apathy as two of the greatest problems afflicting older voters; lowering the voting age would allow younger, more impassioned voters to counteract that cynicism and apathy.

3. "Political inheritance" refers to our nation's long democratic tradition, particularly the texts we learn in school that have shaped the voting process. Roth cites the Constitution, the Voting Rights Act, and the con-

cept of separation of powers as part of that "inheritance." Students in high school regularly take history, civics, and political science classes and learn a great deal about the voting and governing processes they have yet to participate in. Their recent contact with such information might make them better voters than adults, who are less likely to have such concepts fresh in their minds.

Examining Sentences, Paragraphs, and Organization

1. Trench warfare, a form of fighting that was common in the Civil War and in World War I, was used as a defensive strategy. Trenches were dug for troops to slow the advance of an attacking force while the troops tried to find a way to break through the opposing force's line. Because of advances in the technology of war, soldiers no longer had to face each other on a battlefield and shoot at specific individuals in order to inflict damage. Life and war in the trenches could be protracted and static, with neither side making much progress. By using the metaphor of "trench warfare," Roth implies that the struggle to win over swing voters has persisted over a long period of time and has been brutal but futile.

2. In his last paragraph, Roth includes a series of declarative sentences, notable for their use of anaphora: "We've licensed a growing national debt . . . ," "We've participated in . . . ," "We've guaranteed . . . ," "We've tolerated . . . ," "We've allowed . . ." Both the use of anaphora and the sentence construction change the overall style of the essay, which has been varied, and give the writing in that paragraph a particular force. Anaphora is used often for effect in speeches (one of the most popular examples is Martin Luther King Jr.'s "I Have a Dream" speech). Roth wants his argument to carry the most weight at the very end of the essay, as he comes to a close and has his last chance to persuade his readers. His use of the third-person plural includes his readers in each statement but also lets them know that he too holds himself accountable (he makes the argument personal, avoiding a divisive "I/you" or "they" construction). He ends the paragraph with a rhetorical question (a device used elsewhere in the essay), inviting readers to consider the argument for themselves.

3. Because voting requirements have been changed in the past, Roth knows that his request to lower the voting age is not an impossible one. Setting up his essay with the example of the change in voting age in 1971, he also firms up his argument with clear evidence as to why such changes are important and warranted. He then goes on to show how younger voters would strengthen the election process and also why they are due the right to vote. If he had omitted the information about the first change in the voting age, readers might feel that his suggestion is too radical (even given his description in para. 5 of the exclusionary voting practices in "pre-Jacksonian democracy"). The example of the constitutional amendment lowering the voting age gives readers a sense of history and their place in it and lets them imagine why, in the current climate, another change in voting age might be equally warranted.

Thinking Critically

1. Students are already part of the consumer culture, Roth notes, and in some ways, voters are simply consumers. Candidates reach voters through the same media (television, magazines, the Internet) that companies use to push their products, and often politicians' "messages" are reduced to sound bites—and impress themselves on voters the same way commercials do. Teenagers might not have their own bank accounts or hold property, but they can be fairly independent, hold a job, and have discretionary income.

2. Roth distinguishes between an intellectual definition of the "age of reason (being able to think for oneself) and an American definition of the "age of reason" (reasoning out what serves one's best interest). He points out that Americans are often swayed by "special interests." In the past, certain groups (women and blacks) were thought to always fail the intellectual definition because they were subject to others and therefore would never reach the intellectual "age of reason." In contemporary America, the voter "age of reason" could have to do with making decisions for oneself or knowing what serves one's best interests. It could also be linked to other factors, such as having attained a level of learning in school or being able to participate intelligently in debates on a candidate's position.

3. Students may think that Roth's argument about the draft, or at least enlistment age, is an important factor in deciding the voting age. Some students might argue that with sexual activity occurring earlier, childbearing age should be a factor because reproduction rights are an important issue. Climate change and education are pressing issues today, and some students may feel that adolescents should have a say in which officials will represent them on such topics. However, students can also make the case that the voting age should be raised if they disagree with the points Roth makes in his essay. Some will make a convincing case that eighteen is the right voting age.

In-Class Writing Activities

1. Answers will vary depending on which issues students think are the most pressing. Students should research the issue and include specific examples to strengthen their argument. Encourage students to narrow the argument to include only one or two issues (rather than simply glossing several "hot topics") so that they can focus on how each one affects a range of voters.

2. Students may or may not be familiar with the role of the electoral college in U.S. presidential elections. Researching the 2000 presidential election and its aftermath may help students get a better understanding of how the president and vice president come to office. Because the dynamics are complicated, essays can include information on how the current electoral system works and then argue which vote should decide an election. Students can make acceptable arguments on both sides of this issue.

3. Students may feel heartened or disheartened by various aspects of elections, from candidate positions to candidate funding and advertising. During the course of an election, they may change their party allegiances or be confused about whom to believe and what each party represents. They may object to the media's or another group's role in swaying voters before an election. Students should focus on the 2008 campaign and election which will be freshest in their minds.

PAUL STARR   A New Deal of Their Own
[*American Prospect*/March 2008]

Vocabulary/Using a Dictionary

1. *Median*, which means "in the middle" or "pertaining to the middle," comes from the Latin *medianus* (in the middle). It is related to words such as *mediocre* and *medium*.

2. *Universality*, meaning "the state of existing everywhere, or being applicable to everyone," derives from the Latin *universalis* (of or belonging to all) and *universes* (all together). It is related to words such as *university* and *universe*.

3. *Reciprocity* means "the state or act of mutual exchange." Its origins are in the Latin word *reciprocus* (alternating), which joins the Latin *re* (back) and *pro* (forward).

Responding to Words in Context

1. The New Deal was a series of social programs for financial reform, economic recovery, and public assistance in response to the Great Depression. It was enacted in the 1930s by President Franklin Roosevelt. By using this phrase, Starr is evoking one of the "great waves of social reform" and placing it in a contemporary context.

2. Capital is the wealth, whether in money or property, that a business or person owns or employs and which can be used to generate more wealth. Human capital refers to the people who are capable of contributing to a society's prosperity. Starr views his public investment proposals not only as a means of economic assistance but also as a way of creating more wealth in the United States generally.

3. Starr wants to revive a sense of public spiritedness that he associates with the energetic, reform-minded politics of American figures such as Franklin Roosevelt and John Kennedy. This quote from Kennedy's inaugural address also reflects on the notion that economic assistance might be tied to various forms of public service.

Discussing Main Point and Meaning

1. Starr writes about the New Deal, the GI Bill, and the Great Society social programs of the 1930s, 1940s, and 1960s. He approves of all these pro-

grams but notes that, whatever their successes, they mostly left out universal support and aid for young people in America. As he is writing about the current need for such programs targeted at the young, he is seeking a viable model from the past and believes that the GI Bill might serve that purpose.

2. Starr cites studies showing that even though young workers shared the economic prosperity and growth in the three decades after World War II, this demographic has lost ground since the 1970s. Young people are less likely than their 1960s counterparts to find stable, long-term jobs with benefits; if they do find work, they will also earn less money (compared to older workers in the same jobs) than did previous generations. Weekly earnings for these people have dropped since the 1970s. One consequence is that younger workers are waiting longer to start families.

3. According to Starr, the major reform programs have mostly left out younger workers, even as they have benefited the poor and especially the elderly, as "social spending has shifted increasingly toward seniors" (para. 8). The young have also been affected by the decline (in real value) of unemployment benefits and the minimum wage. Tuitions at public universities and other education expenses have risen, but "a failure to bring public policy into line has left young adults to bear the burden" (para. 13). The big challenge in reversing this trend in "social investment" is to find ways of supporting the young that reconcile the "two ideals" of "reciprocity" and "universality" (para. 17). That is, we must create programs that unite benefits in exchange for service (like the GI Bill) with a more comprehensive approach that will cover more young adults than just those who serve in the military.

Examining Sentences, Paragraphs, and Organization

1. Starr's first sentence is a keynote for his essay, setting up his main premise and theme. At the same time, it's also a topic sentence: He makes one general assertion and then backs it up with the rest of the paragraph. He frequently deploys this strategy throughout the article. For example, paragraph 16 begins with a generalization about the relevance of the GI Bill; Starr then supports this claim with a more concrete examination of the government program.

2. Starr uses paragraph 4 both to bring up the "three great waves of social reform since the 1930s" and to assert generally that they have "failed to establish durable policies in support of the young." In the next three paragraphs, he looks closely at each program (in chronological order) and demonstrates the limitations of each as far as benefits for young adults. This highly structured approach has the benefit of being methodical, linear, and easy to follow.

3. Starr's prose seems to strive for clarity, linearity, and transparency, as opposed to wittiness or the crafting of memorable or original phrases. He chooses to use little or no figurative language in the essay and largely

avoids rhetorical flourishes and allusion. Instead, the style calls the reader's attention almost entirely to the substance of his argument—particularly in his extensive reliance on statistics and economic data, as well as his description of historical trends. Starr takes the subject matter seriously—in terms of both real problems and possible solutions—and his writing voice reflects that quality of mind.

Thinking Critically

1. Starr's use of data to support his argument requires us to slow down and think through the numbers, as when he explains how the income of young people has declined over the past four decades. We must consider the meaning of phrases such as "median real weekly earnings" (para. 2) as well as the statistics that Starr provides. He uses precise data to back up his positions, a technique that makes his argument persuasive, even as it may contribute to the density and complexity of the article. His clear, linear prose style—in which he makes an assertion, supports it with relevant statistics, and then moves on to another assertion—is an asset in this context. Starr is writing in the *American Prospect*, a publication largely concerned with economic issues in the United States, so his audience is economically and historically sophisticated and more likely to be familiar with concepts such as discretionary spending programs (para. 8) than readers of a general-interest magazine would be.

2. Students might consider the difference between the word *welfare*, which has a range of connotations, some of them negative, and specific welfare programs such as TAANF. What images does the word *welfare* evoke? How accurate are those images as applied to the reality of the people who rely on such programs and how these programs are used? As Starr's essay implies, with its references to programs such as the New Deal and the Great Society, over the last several decades there has been a fundamental shift in the way Americans view government assistance. See, for example, the Welfare Reform Act of the 1990s. Students should also think about the degree to which they believe government should intervene to help citizens economically.

3. Starr suggests that, with some exceptions, the social programs of the twentieth century largely left young adults behind. He also shows how this demographic has lost ground economically over the past four decades. At the same time, he remains hopeful that they will become politically and socially aware enough to change these trends, possibly through a renewed emphasis on national public service. Not only does Starr want the economic prospects of young adults to improve, but he also sees their renewed prosperity in terms of public spiritedness—the notion of an "American revival" (para. 18) that resonates with John F. Kennedy's call to think about what we can do for our country. Students might especially consider how they might "use their energies and talents for the public good," as well as the meaning of the term "public good" in itself (para. 18).

In-Class Writing Activities

1. Discussions of government spending and the value of social programs are central to many of our contemporary political debates, as well as to the formation of our political identities. Students should consider their own views about these issues and the proper role of government, as well as how those views are shaped—by class, race, education, the media, and so on. Students may discover they have misperceptions about programs of public assistance; they may also make connections between their attitude toward these programs and their broader notion of the "public good."

2. Starr sees the prospect of harnessing the "energies and talents" of young people for the "public good" in ways that would be reciprocally beneficial for the teenagers and young adults involved. What would be the best way to do that? The goal of the exercise is not merely to focus on how more people can acquire more financial benefits from the government but also to consider the relationship between citizenship and public service. Students may research programs already in existence, such as AmeriCorps, to get ideas, or they may even propose mandatory military service. They should think about whether such programs should operate at the local, state, or national level.

3. Students should consider not only what level of wealth they consider qualifies as middle class but also the values and associations of the social category—such as hard work, thrift, aspiration, education, security, and property. Politicians frequently make appeals to these ideas. Why? Students may already consider themselves members of the middle class, or they may see education as a means of entering the middle class. They may also aspire to moving beyond the middle class and see social mobility as an essential aspect of being American. Students might also think about why the country benefits from having a large middle class that allows entry and upward mobility. Do they believe public policy should be brought in line with this goal?

JOSEPH HART   Protest Is Dead. Long Live Protest.
[*The Utne Reader*/May–June 2007]

Vocabulary/Using a Dictionary

1. *Cul-de-sac* comes from French and literally translates as "bottom of the bag." A cul-de-sac is a type of street—in particular, a blind alley or a dead-end street.

2. In its literal sense, the adjective *visceral* means "pertaining to the viscera" (viscera are internal organs of the body). Figuratively, *visceral* means "dealing with coarse or base emotions."

3. A progressive is someone who favors change or reform in political matters (unlike a conservative, who favors tradition and maintaining the status quo). A progressive favors progress, which forms the base of the word *progressive*.

Responding to Words in Context

1. Someone who is prone to exhibitionism behaves in a way that attracts attention. Those with the psychiatric disorder called exhibitionism gain sexual gratification by exposing their genitals in public. Calling protest "political exhibitionism," then, implies that protest is a disorder that brings self-gratification simply through displays of one's political feeling.

2. A vacuum is a void, or a space that contains nothing. It is, in fact, impossible to operate in a vacuum. The expression is most often phrased in the negative — "such-and-such cannot operate in a vacuum." By using this phrase, Hart shows the futility of the activities of today's protesters.

3. A monologue is a lengthy talk by a single speaker; a dialogue is a conversation between two or more people. The Bubble Project offers a way to shut down advertisers' monologues, and to open up a dialogue with the public.

Discussing Main Point and Meaning

1. The civil rights movement the Vietnam antiwar movement gained a great deal of attention in a time of social and political upheaval in this country. Hart points out that demonstrations were only one way these groups gained attention. More important, these two movements viewed the rallies as just one way to work toward change. Hart suggests that today's war protesters see rallies and demonstrations as ends in themselves, even as a "lifestyle."

2. For the antiwar movement to become forceful, a certain unity is needed. Current demonstrations in this country seem scattered and fragmented. Protest is also taking place in Iraq, but it is violent resistance — the ongoing war — that is in the forefront. "Middle-aged war opponents" and "aging hippies" in this country appear to be a throwback to a different time, as if they are just continuing a now-stale protest. However, they are not the only representatives of current antiwar sentiment, given that 67 percent of Americans disapprove of the handling of the war. But for younger, more mainstream people to speak out, new forms of protest must enter the nation's consciousness.

3. Hart's essay deals with various forms of nonviolent protest. Although he says that the nonviolent protest perfected in the 1960s is becoming obsolete, he is interested in finding new approaches to add to that type of protest. He firmly believes in civil disobedience as a way to enact change. Violent protest is mentioned only once in the essay, in the paragraph about the World Trade Organization protests in 1999, which he condemns because they were "unimaginative and overshadowed the cause" (para. 11).

Examining Sentences, Paragraphs, and Organization

1. Because the Bubble Project involves highly visual protest, the inclusion of the Web site address is helpful for students who are unfamiliar with it and also adds a certain relevance — students can realize that protest is in fact

happening around them, and they can connect with the Bubble Project's protest by visiting the site.

2. Hart gives some background on historic civil rights and antiwar protests and other methods of resistance that students may not be aware of. The inclusion of that information shows how newer groups such as the Yes Men and Forest Ethics are creatively following in their predecessors' footsteps. It is also interesting to note the gravitas of those earlier protests — a group of black protesters whose well-being is jeopardized by authority figures while protesting for their civil rights carries a certain moral weight, whereas a protest in which older, well-off Americans gather in a field while police officers look on has little meaning or effect.

3. Hart offers many examples of creative protest in this essay. Even though he does not offer a particular instance of creative protest related to stopping the Iraq War, he does show how new forms of protest can be more effective than the antiwar movement's current strategy. Hart wants the antiwar movement to find a way to "take back" the power it had in the 1960s, and so he shows where the movement has stalled out in its own desire to repeat history, or at least how it is failing to accumulate the massive support and vibrant leaders generated by the 1960s protests.

Thinking Critically

1. If enough people share antiwar sentiment in this country and decide to act, the antiwar movement could gain momentum through creative acts of disobedience. The Bubble Project could work against the war if those participating focus solely on that issue. The tactics of the Yes Men could be used to show the absurdity of arguments in favor of continuing the war. The Forest Ethics model would help people become more aware of the war's effects and how the country's money is being spent. Hart hopes that these examples will be used as a springboard to other creative endeavors that would help end the war.

2. In a country with representational government, people can make their wishes known through protest (many Europeans expressed their feelings about their country's participation in the Iraq war by engaging in nonviolent demonstrations, although in Great Britain this tactic had little immediate effect). However, Hart makes a good case for combining protest with actions that facilitate solutions in order to avoid the current "antiwar movement's impotence." Although activists taking a stand and voicing a position hold a certain power, the point of protest is to create change. If they protest and at the same time lead the opposition to the desired outcome, the protesters gain in strength and authority.

3. Some students may view the Bubble Project as an act of vandalism bcause it destroys advertisers' property. Other students may argue that advertisers are invading public space and manipulating our thoughts and desires; therefore, these students might see the Bubble Project as subversive but within Ji Lee's and the public's rights as a form of protest.

In-Class Writing Activities

1. Answers will vary based on students' interests. Students should not use examples given on the Bubble Project Web site. This activity will give students a chance to experience firsthand the level of creativity that Hart calls for from protesters.

2. United for Peace and Justice sponsors events across the country, and its work is not limited to ending the war in Iraq. The group calls for involvement in its causes and suggests three primary ways to voice protest: through direct connection with public officials; through donations; and through events of nonviolent protest, largely of the kind that took place in the 1960s through public demonstration. Students can explore the Web site, especially the "grassroots action" link, to get a sense of how United for Peace and Justice operates and whether it is trying to find new ways to lodge protest.

3. Any number of rallies and protests from the 1960s might form the subject of students' essays. They can focus on a variety of people who participated in these events, including civil rights leaders, musicians, clergy, and student activists. It might be helpful to consider how the media have changed since the 1960s, what other activities were connected with these events, and how the events were publicized and funded. Students should also examine the protesters commitment to their cause—many people went to jail or took great risks by standing up for what the they believed in.

JEFF DICKSON (STUDENT ESSAY)   United We Strive, Divided We Falter
[*The Daily*, University of Washington/April 2, 2008]

Vocabulary/Using a Dictionary

1. *Affiliation* means "association" or "connection." The word derives from the Latin *affiliare* (to adopt); *filius* means "son."

2. The word *demographic*, which refers to a portion of a population, originates in the Greek *demo* (people) and *graphos* (something drawn or written). Words such as *democracy* and *biography* share these roots.

3. *Petty* comes from the French *petit* meaning "small." In this context, it means "having little or no significance."

Responding to Words in Context

1. In saying that Americans now "segregate" themselves, Dickson means that they tend to separate, restrict, or define themselves in terms of specific groups. He evokes the term *segregation* as it has applied historically in the United States. In the past, racial segregation was enforced by law and custom; now, as Dickson sees it, our current trend toward division is voluntary.

2. Dickson here is emphasizing the differences in the American population that result from immigration. By using the term *hodgepodge* (rather than *tapestry* or *mosaic*), he is suggesting that America's immigrant composition is a muddle or even a mess of dissimilar ingredients.

3. *Harmonious* means "marked by agreement in feeling, attitude, or action." It comes from musical terminology: harmonious music is melodious and forms a pleasant, consistent whole. Dickson believes that "harmonious effort" on the part of Americans would create more cohesion and unity of national purpose.

Discussing Main Point and Meaning

1. Dickson's main thesis is located in the final sentence of paragraph 1: "But there is one issue plaguing our country that receives little or no press coverage, an issue that negatively distinguishes us from the golden years: There is a lack of unity between Americans." All the paragraphs that follow serve to support this primary assertion and to show its implications.

2. According to Dickson, America's diversity as an immigrant nation makes it fundamentally heterogeneous, but he offers several reasons to explain why Americans seem especially divided now. He cites a tendency for people to define themselves according to categories such as race, religion, ethnicity, or political affiliation; to Dickson, many of these differences are "petty" (para. 6). He places some of the responsibility on controversial media figures who thrive on and exacerbate division, such as Rush Limbaugh and Al Sharpton. More generally, he blames the media for focusing so much on divisive stories. Moreover, the partisan polarization of the government "has trickled down and permeated even the smallest of communities" (para. 5).

3. Dickson argues that a large-scale sense of civic solidarity would increase our recycling efforts; would help us deal with climate change, healthcare issues, and social security; would lead us to develop alternative fuels (and end our dependence on foreign oil); and would lower the crime rate. Dickson acknowledges that we need division and competition to drive a "capitalistic economy," but he believes that "some tasks . . . are simply too large and too important and require a cooperative effort" (para. 4).

Examining Sentences, Paragraphs, and Organization

1. As a figure of speech, the famous "melting pot" metaphor traditionally evokes an ideal whereby immigrants from different countries lose their distinctive cultures and ethnic traditions and assimilate into a more homogeneous society to become "Americans." The metaphor is still commonly used, but there are alternative, competing analogies as well, such as the "salad" and the "mosaic" anologies, which imply that various cultures and ethnicities maintain significant parts of their various heritages. However, even though other countries might have more homogeneous populations, their citizens may view various regional, historical, and cul-

tural distinctions within their country as significant differences—ones that we as outsiders cannot perceive.

2. Dickson's essay has elements of a compare-and-contrast essay. He is comparing and contrasting the unity of the past with the disunity of the present. Paragraph 3—the last half, in particular—serves as a specific example of past national solidarity and achievement. It supports his point that some challenges require cooperative effort and that Americans are capable of coming together for a united purpose when necessary.

3. Students should think about the way "generations" are characterized and the connotations of generational labels: the Greatest Generation, the Silent Generation, the Baby Boom Generation, Generation X, the Millennial Generation. These labels may be useful, whether as a means to organize historical or social analysis (or arguments like Dickson's) or even as a means to target marketing efforts. Generational designations also suggest how historical events can shape—or at least appear to shape—large groups of people in certain age ranges.

Thinking Critically

1. Issues such as the cost of the Iraq War and economic problems in the United States are, unquestionably, newsworthy, whether the resulting stories are positive or negative. Some students might argue that the news media focus more on the negative aspects of American life because such stories (especially if they are sensational or frightening) tend to draw more readers, viewers, and listeners. Moreover, conflict is generally more mediagenic than are harmony and contentment—whether on a reality TV show or a cable news program. Students should especially consider who benefits from our political discourse being so polarized by media and political figures, even if such divisions don't accurately represent the views of most Americans. Students might also present counterexamples to Dickson's assertion that the media do not report on such divisions. For example, the media have carried many stories about the bitterness of political partisanship over the last several years.

2. Dickson says that our tendency to "overly define ourselves" by race, religion, and political affiliation contributes to divisiveness. Similarly, we "categorize ourselves as fill-in-the-blank–Americans" rather than "simply as 'Americans'" (para. 2). From a historical perspective, the comparison between "then" and "now" is problematic, especially with regard to race. By law and custom, blacks were second-class citizens in the 1940s, so would race have been a "petty" difference at the time? Is it now? Similarly, it can be difficult to distinguish between a subtle political difference and an irreconcilable one, as they apply to the large tasks and "obvious challenges" that Dickson wants our country to address. If some citizens don't believe in global warming or think there is a problem with health care in this country, do they need to put aside those convictions? Students may want to think about how we achieve consensus on these issues—and also to consider that division and conflict can be a source of progress.

3. As evidence of the country's deterioriation, we can measure certain cul-
    tural or social trends (for example, we can compare crime statistics from
    different eras), however, the tendency to idealize or romanticize the past
    can make the past seem better than it actually was. This impulse has pro-
    found implications: If we view society as being in a continual state of
    degeneration from some lost golden era, our social, political, and cultural
    convictions may differ greatly from those of people who see our country
    in terms of "progress." In any case, it can be difficult to generalize about
    this historical process, as most people will probably acknowledge both
    the "good" and the "bad" inherent in different time periods.

In-Class Writing Activities

1. As Dickson notes, America has traditionally defined itself as a country of
    immigrants, so—at least theoretically—it doesn't have the strong (or
    even ancient) binding notions of blood, race, ethnicity, and historical
    nationalism that some other, more "homogeneous" nations can draw
    upon for unity. Although discussions of "what it means to be an Ameri-
    can" can lend themselves to cliché, students should think about how
    "American-ness" is, in many ways, bound up with ideas and abstract
    principles—which may not be the case in many other countries. And
    fierce debates about immigration and the "making of Americans" are
    perennial, from the founding of the United States to the waves of immi-
    grants in the nineteenth and early twentieth centuries, to current political
    controversies on the subject.

2. Some students may have strong ties to the ethnic, racial, or national
    aspects of their backgrounds; this might be affected by whether they
    (or their parents) are recent immigrants. Similarly, religious faith can be a
    strong part of identity in this context, as some people might consider
    themselves Christians or Muslims before they consider themselves Amer-
    icans.

3. For this assignment, students should take a close and critical look at the
    media's role in the divisions that Dickson describes. They should also
    consider the implicit distinction that he makes between "unwanted" or
    "unnecessary" controversies and those that are legitimate or newsworthy.

Discussing the Unit

Suggested Topic for Discussion

Roth argues that young people are often "flush" with knowledge of their
"political inheritance." Therefore, at least some would probably be interested
in political and social issues, as well as the political process. Ask students how
they view their own political efficacy and whether they trust the government or
the public at large to address broad problems or create genuine reform. If
they're unsatisfied with, or cynical about politics, does that dissatisfaction gen-

erally make them radical, or merely indifferent? If they are apathetic, they should be able to articulate the specific causes of their apathy and passivity and propose possible solutions.

Preparing for Class Discussion

1. Fundamentally, these questions ask how much faith students place in the nation's political institutions and the democratic and legal process. Even if much contemporary protesting has become (as Hart says) "ritualized" and ineffectual, protests still occur regularly on issues ranging from abortion to the war in Iraq. Students should consider their reactions to — and judgments of — the disruptive campaigns of people such as Ji Lee: Is this legitimate dissent or mere vandalism? Moreover, such activities seem more like cultural protest than political protest. The United States certainly has a long tradition of civil disobedience, from abolitionism through the civil rights movement. How do we decide when laws are unjust, civil institutions are moving too slowly, and therefore conscience or conviction requires breaking the law?

2. Dickson refers to soldiers fighting in World War II as representing part of the "glory days" of America. Is the military viewed differently now than it was then? Activists who wanted to lower the voting age in the 1960s and 1970s recognized the obvious link between national service and citizenship: "Old enough to fight, old enough to vote!" Ask students to consider how the political awareness, commitment, and activity of teens and young adults would be different today if there was a military draft. They should also consider the possibility and value of nonmilitary and voluntary service.

From Discussion to Writing

1. Students should consider the implications of this analogy between consumers and voters. Are there really no differences? For example, consumption is frequently based on the desire for immediate gratification, even if the pleasures of shopping and spending are ephemeral; this doesn't seem compatible with Roth's notion that young people could turn out to be a group of voters with no discernible interests except the general welfare. Similarly, we rarely think of consumerism in terms of wider obligations and sacrifices — other than the need to make enough money to spend on products. Students should also compare and contrast liberty in the marketplace (the freedom to make purchasing choices) and liberty as a political idea and practice.

2. Obviously, the proposed campaigns should be legal, but students should be free to determine the goal of their campaigns. The point of the assignment is to get students engaged in an issue that matters to them and that is also socially, politically, or culturally relevant; then, they can think about the campaign's strategy, their audience, the medium for their message, and the ways that their campaign could effect real action and change.

Topics for Cross-Cultural Discussion

1. This assignment should get students to think beyond their own personal politics, to that of their peers more generally. The Vietnam War defined "boomer politics"; but what issues, events, or ideas are shaping the current generation of young people? Dickson discusses climate change, energy dependence, the wars in Iraq and Afghanistan, economic recessions, and social and political polarization—do these issues resonate? Or are cultural trends more influential and definitive (for example, how the Internet has changed the nature of politics and political engagement)? Students may also question the premise that generations can be defined or labeled in this way.

2. These questions might be usefully linked to Roth's speculation about what kinds of new voters might emerge if the voting age were lowered. In any case, students should consider that our political identities aren't formed in a cultural vacuum—and they usually don't follow from Dickson's neutral notion of our simply being "Americans." Instead, our political identities are influenced by our family and peers as well as innumerable other factors, including religion, gender, ethnicity, race, and class.

10

What Does the New
Class Struggle Look Like?

The notion of a class system seems, on the surface, antithetical to the idea of America. Indeed, the United States is supposed to represent egalitarianism, democracy, lack of hereditary privilege, individual achievement, and social mobility. But even though the United States has never had the traditional social hierarchies or feudal arrangements of older countries, class *does* matter here—and always has. Commenting in the nineteenth century, the British writer Frances Trollope wryly and evocatively referred to the "fable of equality" that exists in the United States; similarly, observers from Alexis de Tocqueville to innumerable contemporary intellectuals, political officials, journalists, and social scientists have struggled to elucidate how class operates in America.

All the pieces in this unit address class issues from different perspectives —and even define class in different ways. Peter Bagge's comic strip "Bums" takes an unflinching look at the chronically homeless as a distinct social class. He begins with his own responses to homeless people in San Francisco— reactions that include fear, incomprehension, and even indignation when he sees "bums" in a park receiving free gourmet food from volunteers. Bagge's focus is not on the vast majority of homeless people, whom he views as "there-but-for-the-grace-of-God" figures, temporarily impoverished and displaced by domestic abuse, medical expenses, or other personal catastrophe. Instead, he is concerned with examining—and representing—the permanent, chronic 10 percent of the homeless population, who often struggle with mental illness and addiction. He also sheds light on a controversial but apparently effective policy called "Housing First," which gives these terminally homeless people free housing with no requirements for their sobriety. In the process, he portrays their subculture, debunks stereotypes of the "carefree hobo," and grants homeless people common human dignity, without sentimentalizing them or denying his own honest responses. Students may consider how the comic strip form allows Bagge to accomplish these things in ways that an essay perhaps could not.

Bagge's comic turns a personal response to a specific experience into a discussion that touches on wider public issues and problems, and Robert Reece's column "Class Struggle Is Race Struggle in U.S." has similar origins: He begins the essay with an anecdote about race from his childhood. He examines this puzzling experience by thinking, reading, and writing about it; in doing so, he provides an excellent example of how to connect the personal and the political.

In looking at the persistence of "white privilege" in the United States, he also suggests links between class and race. The lingering effects of racism, according to Reece, are not so much at the level of individual attitudes and behavior, but rather are more systematic in American life. He sees a need for Americans to acknowledge that this privilege still exists in our major institutions; only then can we eliminate it and become the true meritocracy we claim to be.

In "Hollywood Flicks Stiff the Working Class," Robert Nathan and Jo-Ann Mort discuss how Hollywood and the entertainment industry view working-class people and class struggles. The writers begin with an examination of the 1979 film *Norma Rae,* which stars Sally Field as a union activist in a textile mill. Nathan and Mort show that the film—with its subversive message and platonic romance between a factory worker and a Jewish intellectual—was difficult to make at the time, and largely forgotten since. More important, they argue that it would be nearly impossible to make such a movie now, as images of struggling workers don't fit Hollywood formulas or entertainment marketing demographics. Similarly, the mainstream film industry, which prefers "conventional wisdom" and inoffensive, can't-we-all-just-get-along social statements, would never make a film with such a daring, subversive political message today. Nathan and Mort suggest that Hollywood's political timidity and unwillingness to represent real working-class people mean that the subject of class is missing not just from our entertainment, but also from our shared cultural and political consciousness.

As Nathan and Mort do now, the photographer and reformer Jacob Riis understood the links between class and cultural visibility—only his subjects were the slums, the poor, and the homeless in late nineteenth century New York City. Riis saw that one of the most significant characteristics of these places and this class of people was their relative invisibility to the more affluent residents of the city. In his book *How the Other Half Lives,* he portrayed these subjects with shocking realism; the result disturbed readers, helped encourage reform movements, and led to a legacy of muckraking journalism.

PETER BAGGE   Bums
[*Reason*/April 2007]

Vocabulary/Using a Dictionary

1. The word *noxious,* which means "harmful," is the root of the word *obnoxious.*

2. Here the word *hammered* means "drunk." The adjective hammered also can mean "having been shaped with a hammer." When used as a verb, it can mean "pounded" ("She hammered on the door until someone heard her").

3. An abyss is a bottomless chasm or void. *Abysmal* means "immeasurably wretched" and also "limitless"; both definitions stem from the root word *abyss.*

Responding to Words in Context

1. The word *Messiah* refers to Jesus Christ, so this man is making the grandiose claim that he is an incarnation of Christ. Bagge has created an apparently delusional character, evident from the look on the man's face and his body language a well as what he says.

2. A chronic condition (such as homelessness or an illness) is one that recurs constantly (and is never expected to disappear entirely). Bagge is making the case that some people will never escape the situation of homelessness.

3. Life expectancy is the average number of years a person is expected to live. Life expectancies can vary widely among different groups of people.

Discussing Main Point and Meaning

1. Bagge first tries to distinguish between chronically homeless people and those who will eventually go back to more normal lives. He also makes a distinction between homeless people and those who pretend to be homeless (but are actually con artists). For Bagge, the true homeless are those on the street who have no family support and suffer from some form of mental illness. He also makes a case that homeless people cost taxpayers quite a bit of money, and he mentions the ways some have tried to alleviate this cost ("bunks for drunks," for example). The problem, according to Bagge, is that most people don't understand the situation of chronically homeless people who will never entirely escape their homelessness because of personal and mental problems.

2. Bagge's drawings do not seem to convey great sympathy (he usually appears frightened or repelled in the drawings of himself, and his hobos are not particularly appealing in their physique or expression). However, as he gets to know some homeless people, they start to speak with him (and not just at him), and he humanizes them by creating characters. By the fourth page, they are much easier to fathom than the "crazed street people" who are shouting in panel 1.

3. Bagge paints a dark picture of the lives of homeless people. He mentions their short life expectancy and presents statistics about the violent and disordered lives such people usually live. Bagge emphasizes the undesirability of such a life, in both words and pictures, by showing his own terror of becoming a homeless person in the last cartoon panel.

Examining Sentences, Paragraphs, and Organization

1. Because this is a cartoon and not an essay, Bagge wants his thoughts to appear to flow from panel to panel. The normal convention of the paragraph is not really effective in a graphic art form. Ellipses usually indicate a pause in thought or a trailing off of thought. This form of punctuation allows Bagge the freedom to "float" from panel to panel above his pictures. If he used periods rather than ellipses, his commentary might be crisper, but it would lack the free-flowing quality that ellipses create.

2. Because he is working within a cartoon, Bagge can provide points of view other than his own. One can hear the thoughts of other characters through their speech bubbles. In a way, using speech bubbles is like introducing quoted material or dialogue into an essay. The incorporation of other characters is much more fluid here because Bagge's commentary rides above and plays off his cartoon or pictorial commentary. He can present his, the hobo's, or the mainstream public's viewpoint (or any viewpoint he chooses) simply by drawing the character along with a speech bubble.

3. If we lift Bagge's commentary from his cartoon, we find rather dark and straightforward information about who the homeless are and what issues they face. The caricatures make us laugh, but the facts presented are bleak. Bagge does not shy away from images that are distressing to viewers, such as the homeless man being killed with a bullet or the man in the trash can who says, "I wish I was dead."

Thinking Critically

1. Students may not accept Bagge's claim that some apparently homeless people are not actually homeless or that such people are "well-fed." Students may wish he had provided more supporting evidence in either words or pictures for his claim. Bagge is trying to clarify who the homeless are, and he does not have the time or space to go into differences between the homeless and the very poor, or the very poor and the working poor. Still, some students might wonder if his generalizations about "all those people" being "well-fed" and "lazy jerks" are accurate; more factual, distanced research (like the research he presents elsewhere) would strengthen this section of the cartoon. Bagge plants himself and his opinion squarely in the argument, and it's easier to do this in a medium that is also meant to entertain. An essay would require that such assertions be supported.

2. In his cartoon, Bagge represents himself as a man who is frightened and repulsed by the bums he comes in contact with, and does not try to make himself a particularly likable character in his cartoon. However, no really likeable characters appear in "Bums." The people he works with in San Francisco are angry and bitter; the others who respond (or don't respond) to the homeless are also self-absorbed and unempathetic. The bums themselves are pathetic and unpleasant. The elements of cruelty and despair in the cartoon keep anyone from being particularly likable. Perhaps it is this very lack of sentimentality and attractiveness that makes Bagge's portrait of homelessness so effective. Calling the piece "Bums" instead of "The Homeless" strikes a certain tone that carries through the cartoon.

3. Unlike an essay, a cartoon doesn't necessarily have a concluding paragraph, although Bagge could have ended his cartoon with a summarizing statement. Students should be encouraged to think about why Bagge ended as he did. Perhaps he wanted to leave readers with the disturbing possibility of becoming homeless and how that might feel. If he had

ended with a simple fact about homelessness, his ending would have been more intellectual and less emotional. It is important to note that he both begins and ends his cartoon from a personal standpoint, thus giving the piece some closure.

In-Class Writing Activities

1. *Reason* publishes articles that deal with politics and social issues, and it probably appeals to a younger, more open-minded, politically active audience. The cover is glossy and usually features a provocative image, either a photograph or graphic art. A recent issue covered a variety of topics, including workplace drug testing, nanotechnology, Mitt Romney, and Dana Thomas's book *How Luxury Lost Its Luster*. Students will find *Reason*'s mission statement, its history, and information on its audience on the magazine's Web site (www.reason.com).

2. Associations relating to the word *hobo* will probably come from sources such as folktales, music, pictures, cartoons, and Halloween costumes. The hobo is classically pictured as a worn-down man with patches on his clothes and carrying his belongings in a bag on a stick. Images of out-of-work men during the Great Depression may come to mind; the person eating beans beneath a bridge or hopping rides on freight trains might be the typical impression of a hobo. Students should consider whether such images are mild or menacing and whether the impression of a hobo gets conflated with what Bagge calls "crooks and con artists." Students should gather impressions of the present-day homeless person and compare them with the image of the hobo. In some ways, the images may match; for the most part, however, the "hobo" is a person of the past or of myth, whereas the "homeless person" is a stark reality of the modern world.

3. Letters will vary. Some students may prefer to learn this sort of information from a cartoon, whereas others will prefer the essay format. Some may find Bagge's caricatures appealing because they add a certain life to the subject; other students may find the harsh caricatures off-putting. In considering what other subjects they would like Bagge to tackle in the future, students should decide whether they view him as an authority on this kind of subject. Some students may want to see him deal satirically with topics that are not as grave as the subject matter of "Bums."

ROBERT NATHAN AND JO-ANN MORT Hollywood Flicks
Stiff the Working Class
[*The Nation*/March 12, 2007]

Vocabulary/Using a Dictionary

1. Advocacy is the act of pleading, supporting, or recommending. It comes from the Latin *advocare*, which means "to call (to one's aid)." The Latin root *-voc* (a form of *vox*) is also shared words such as *voice*, *vocal*, and *vocation*.

2. To call something iconic means that it is an enduring and important image, picture, or other representation. *Iconic* derives from the Greek word *eikon*, meaning "image" or "portrait."

3. A renaissance is a renewal or revival of life, vigor, or interest. The word *renaissance* derives from the Latin *nasci* (to be born) and *re* (again). Words such as *nascent*, *natal*, and *nature* share *nasci* as a root.

Responding to Words in Context

1. The adjective *poetic* suggests that the line from the movie partakes of certain striking qualities associated with poetry: compression and originality of language, sonorousness, and metaphor. The effect of this line of dialogue is evocative and memorable.

2. "Economic justice" refers to fairness and equity in economic matters and transactions, generally, or in the workplace, as in the specific case in *Norma Rae*.

3. Platonic love is an intimate relationship characterized by an absence of sexual involvement. The term originally comes from the philosopher Plato, who believed that spiritual and ideal beauty are superior to physical, material beauty. It is significant that the film portrays this type of love because (according to Nathan and Mort) successful Hollywood films (and audiences) usually require their heroes to "end up in bed" (para. 8). By not conforming to Hollywood's formulaic plot lines, *Norma Rae* is an "aberration."

Discussing Main Point and Meaning

1. There were many difficulties surrounding the production of *Norma Rae*. Several leading actresses who could have given star power to the film turned it down before Sally Field accepted the lead role. The movie included an unconventional platonic love story between a Jewish intellectual and a factory worker—which worked against the expectation that the "audience wants the heroes to end up in bed" (para. 8). The real-life company that served as the basis for the story's fictional, anti-union textile mill made it difficult to find shooting locations. Perhaps most important, the film contained "a profound and, for its time, disturbing political message" (para. 6). Nathan and Mort recount these challenges and point out that such a movie would be even more difficult to make today.

2. Nathan and Mort highlight "the invisibility of working people fighting to better their lives" (para. 13) in the products of the entertainment industry. Films may try to provide socially or politically substantive content, but their messages cannot be blunt. Instead, presumably political films such as *Babel* can only bring themselves to pose a "rather mild question" (para. 6). With a few exceptions, these productions are rarely "politically daring," they "don't fundamentally threaten the established order," and they merely deliver relatively safe, comforting "conventional wisdom"

(para. 7). Nathan and Mort single out the film *Blood Diamond* for praise, but they acknowledge that it was a disappointment at the box office. They also note that some contemporary TV shows have focused on workers and workers' issues.

3. According to Nathan and Mort, Hollywood studios "have a mega-hit mentality" (para. 13) and don't want to make smaller pictures that deal with the plight of working-class people. But perhaps more important, the United States has a problem with social apathy and fragmentation. That makes it harder to "build a mass movement for social and economic change" now, and also more difficult to "find large numbers of Americans who care about social solidarity" (para. 13). Therefore, there doesn't seem to be a broad, politically engaged audience for movies like *Norma Rae*. The implicit paradox here, as the authors see it, is that there are large numbers of struggling working-class people who would be represented and brought into the public consciousness by such films.

Examining Sentences, Paragraphs, and Organization

1. Nathan and Mort are discussing images of a certain kind of working-class struggle — representations that are conspicuously rare on television. From their point of view, the images and connotations surrounding firefighters are no longer simply "working class"; instead, such rescue workers are already perceived (culturally and symbolically) as heroic, admirable, exceptional, and therefore worthy of media portrayal and public visibility. Therefore, in a sense, they don't actually represent the day-to-day lives of average, struggling, working-class people.

2. Although their immediate, motivating subject is a film from 1979, along with media images of workers and the state of the entertainment business, Nathan and Mort have a much broader agenda. Their concluding paragraph connects their specific analysis of *Norma Rae* and their brief survey of popular culture to fundamental social and political issues. Their point that workers have disappeared from television shows and movies leads to a larger conclusion, namely, that such figures are disappearing from our popular consciousness altogether, even as they exist in great numbers in our country. In passively allowing this loss, we jeopardize not so much the quality or significance of our movies, but "the future of our society itself" (para. 15). This move outward to broader issues, along with other arguments in the essay, makes their reading of *Norma Rae* and its history not only clever and perceptive but also socially significant.

3. Several sections of the essay reveal a compare-and-contrast structure. For example, the introduction implicitly contrasts an excerpt from the script of *Norma Rae* with what we would normally expect from film clips shown at the Academy Award ceremonies; the next paragraph contains a close analysis of the dialogue's specific language, which supports the authors' point effectively. This sets up the theme of "then versus now" which shows up throughout the article. Paragraph 7 compares and contrasts American filmmakers and European filmmakers such as Ken Loach

and Mike Leigh. Paragraph 8 introduces the disparity between *Norma Rae* and contemporary "message" films with a deceptively simple but effective four-word topic sentence: "*Norma Rae* was different."

Thinking Critically

1. For Nathan and Mort, class issues—disparities in wealth, the disadvantages of the poor, the daily struggles of typical workers, the notion that working-class people have political and economic interests that are different and from possibly antagonistic to those in more affluent classes—matter profoundly, but the writers feel that these subjects are not given a proper place in our popular entertainment. Arguably, America has had a different relationship to class than European countries have had. At least theoretically and ideologically, if not always in practice, Americans have mythologized social mobility, individual autonomy, self-making, and the notion that there is no "natural" aristocracy or class system in this country. By way of contrast, England has always had a more traditional—and openly acknowledged—class system. This fact may help explain why it's easier to make class the subject of films there.

2. "Conventional wisdom" refers to some commonly accepted truth or point of view. But the phrase carries with it the negative connotation of something safe, secondhand, obvious, unoriginal, and unquestioned. When a film aspires to challenge viewers or even change society but then merely dispenses a conventional, comfortable, widely accepted point or message, it undercuts its own power to provoke the audience. In contrast, Nathan and Mort want movies to make genuine demands on viewers—and perhaps even make them uncomfortable.

3. Implicit in paragraph 13 is a provocative argument. On the one hand, this "Hollywood" view of filmmaking (and of culture, in general) is essentially an appeal to democracy and the free market. It also fits with a consumer model in which the customer is always right—or at least is made to feel that that is the case. Such a position claims that public demand determines what kind of art is produced and that the movie industry is just giving the people what they want. This consumer model gets more complicated when we consider that the profit-driven film industry not only reflects public desires but also shapes them through marketing, advertising, and many other channels. On the other hand, making movies in this way caters to the blandest common denominator and undercuts the filmmaker's role of expressing an unusual vision in a film. The consumer model also implies that the viewer should never be challenged too much or made to feel uncomfortable.

In-Class Writing Activities

1. Students should reflect on and clarify their own views of the nature and purposes of movies (or television programs). They should use specific examples to support their argument. The idea of a "message" film might connote preachiness, clumsiness, or humorlessness; at the same time, stu-

dents may acknowledge that movies can be more than mere escapism or entertainment. Of course, students' arguments could connect to larger, long-standing debates about what art should be or should accomplish. For example, students could consider this discussion in light of Oscar Wilde's famous dictum that all good art should be perfectly useless.

2. The purpose of this assignment is, in part, to show (as Nathan and Mort do) that popular culture products are open to close reading and interpretation in the same way that poetry and novels are. Students will get a more thorough awareness of class and images of class and will be able to test their responses against those of Nathan and Mort. The exercise will also get them engaged as active watchers who approach films and television shows critically, with a substantive, genuine point of view.

3. Ask students to think beyond the simple categories of lower, middle, and upper class. Class background—their own or their parents'—may have influenced the schools they have attended, the jobs they have held, the careers they desire, and other aspects of their lives. It may also affect how they view money, education, culture, and other people. If they have had experience, directly or indirectly, with the kinds of struggles that preoccupy Nathan and Mort, they should consider that experience. At the same time, if students have been relatively affluent and comfortable, how has that shaped their lives and expectations?

ROBERT REECE (STUDENT ESSAY)   Class Struggle Is Race Struggle in U.S.

[*Daily Mississippian*, University of Mississippi/February 28, 2008]

Vocabulary/Using a Dictionary

1. The word *prejudiced* derives from the Latin *prae-* or *pre-* (before) and *iudicium* (judge).

2. *Meritocratic*, which means "based on ability or talent (rather than class privilege or wealth)," comes from the Latin *meritum* (worthy of praise or blame) and the Greek *kratia* or *kratos* (rule or strength). The suffix *-cratic* is used similarly in words such as *democratic* and *autocratic*.

3. The word *stereotype* comes from the printing profession and refers to a plate with a raised surface for lettering or other imprinting. Its origins are in the Greek *stereo* (solid) and the Latin *typus* (image) or Greek *tupos* (impression).

Responding to Words in Context

1. McIntosh is using the word *white* less as a literal description of skin color and more as a marker of a certain kind of dominant standard in the United States, both historically and currently.

2. For Reece, all these terms are indicative and reflective of the dominant powers in American society; these prerogatives are also exclusive or even

repressive to others outside their norms, even when such "privileges" are practiced unconsciously.

3. Racial profiling usually refers to an alleged practice of some police officers and other law enforcement officials who stop and search people belonging to particular racial groups. It can also be used to single out presumably identifiable members of certain religious or ethnic groups.

Discussing Main Point and Idea

1. Reece cites the writer and scholar Peggy McIntosh, who suggests that whites are "taught to think that racism could end if white individuals changed their attitude" (para. 2). But the nature of racism and its effects are not determined solely by the attitudes, intentions, or behavior of specific individuals: Whiteness grants privileges and opens doors "whether or not we approve of the way dominance has been conferred upon us" (para. 2). This is significant because Reece is arguing that racism can still exist and have widespread consequences, even if most white people are not "consciously racist" (para. 3).

2. Reece sees a direct link between race and class, as minorities have higher rates of poverty and incarceration than whites do. But he suggests that "poor whites" who are socially mobile and acquire wealth and social status will also benefit from "white privilege" in ways that African Americans cannot, regardless of their class.

3. Because Reece sees racism as deeply entrenched, he wants Americans to acknowledge and disavow the systematic benefits of being white; that means not so much changing individual behavior as it does reconsidering the more subtle and prevalent racism inherent in "nearly every institution in our country" (para. 7).

Examining Sentences, Paragraphs, and Organization

1. Reece's opening story shows how whites benefit from institutional racism, a theme that is the foundation of his essay. His initial difficulty in making sense of the incident also reflects the more general difficulty of defining this kind of racist practice. By beginning his essay this way, Reece illustrates his theme and draws the reader into his personal story and his emotional response. At the same time, such anecdotes must be credible, and a persuasive writer trying to make a larger point must be able to generalize convincingly from a particular experience and also support those generalizations with more objective evidence.

2. Reece expects some of his readers to be skeptical, resistant, or even hostile to his argument. He even acknowledges that he identifies with that skepticism when he says "I completely understand"(para. 4). He anticipates objections and counterarguments, and this tendency shapes his writing throughout—from his qualification about whites not being "consciously racist," to his care not to "diminish the accomplishments of white people" (para. 5).

3. In paragraph 5, Reece makes connections between poverty rates and race, as well as incarceration rates and race. Both of these statistics show a correlation that supports his larger argument about race and class. Because he begins with personal, anecdotal evidence and relies on generalizations at various points ("We all make those little prejudiced remarks and stuff people into stereotypes" [para. 3]), hard, objective data is essential to his case.

Thinking Critically

1. Reece is writing about institutional racism: It is systematic, historical, and largely unrelated to overtly racist acts by individuals or overtly racist laws, which existed in the United States into the 1960s. In some ways, the very nature of institutional racism makes it more difficult to isolate, identify, and discuss. It also makes assigning moral responsibility and finding a remedy more complex because, according to Reece and McIntosh, whites still benefit from racial privilege, whether or not they approve of it. That is why, at the end of his essay, Reece asserts the need for systematic change: Inequalities spring less from individuals and more from the prevalence of racism "in nearly every institution in our country" (para. 7).

2. To look at the issue of race objectively, whites would have to view it from a completely disinterested, detached, and impersonal point of view. For Reece, that would require them to face unpleasant facts and possibly lose the privileges of racial, social, and economic dominance. At the same time, his own essay is deeply personal and rooted in his own subjective experience. He counters this bias mainly by claiming that he too has only recently begun to acknowledge—more "objectively," perhaps—the advantages he has been given in life (para. 4), and also by citing statistical evidence that supports his point of view.

3. Reece sees the relationship between the classes in a capitalist economy as inherently antagonistic. Implicitly, the dominant socioeconomic classes seek to maintain their privilege and defend the system that secures their dominance, regardless of the inequalities that result. Reece sees a parallel—and overlap—between this economic power and the benefits of being white. Ultimately, he indicts the whole notion that the United States is a "meritocratic society," in which only individual talent, initiative, and achievement assures success, independent of race or class.

In-Class Writing Activities

1. The moments that Reece describes in the first two paragraphs are among the most significant a person can have when developing as a reader: learning to make sense of one's subjective and personal experience by abstracting from it and making connections to a wider world of books, ideas, and culture. Students should think about memorable, formative, or even haunting occasions in their lives that seemed important, even if they did not have the language or ideas to describe these events as they were happening. They should also give examples of how reading (broadly understood)

has informed their lives and identities and enabled them—like Reece—to make sense of their place in the world.

2. Although Reece is writing in the context of race and class, the practice of stereotyping transcends those categories. Students should think about how often they rely on generalizations and superficial judgments to categorize people. Stereotypes can serve as a kind of shorthand and a way of making sense of our social lives and other people. Students might consider a case in which they presumed that a certain person fit a stereotype, but then developed a more nuanced appraisal as they became familiar with that person as an individual and not a "type." What was revealed in this process? Conversely, they may also include occasions in their lives when stereotypes turned out to be accurate. Does the existence of such examples vindicate the practice of stereotyping?

3. For decades, sociologists, historians, political scientists, journalists, and others have analyzed the connections between race and poverty, as well as other topics related to that link. Students should get a sense of the wider, ongoing discussion of this complex, enormous, and often controversial subject. Reece frames his argument so that either his suggestions about racism and poverty are correct or the correlation is merely a coincidence. However, there may be other, more precise explanations or perspectives.

Discussing the Unit

Suggested Topic for Discussion

Students should consider the well-worn metaphor of the "level playing field" and determine how well it applies to socioeconomic status in the United States. They might also think about where the United States, compared with other Western countries, ranks in terms of the social mobility of its citizens. The ideal of the "rugged individual" and the notion that "anyone can become president" remain incredibly powerful tropes in America's image of itself. Students can test these concepts against their own perceptions of class in America.

Preparing for Class Discussion

1. Many historical reasons—most obviously, the legacy of slavery and race relations in the United States—account for this focus on race. Because of this legacy, American filmmakers over the years have produced countless films—*Birth of a Nation*, *To Kill a Mockingbird*, *Boyz n the Hood*, and *Crash*, to name just a few—that have addressed racial issues, no matter how mild or daring their messages were. However, Hollywood has made far fewer films that directly confront class issues. But this tendency goes beyond flimmaking to larger questions about the content of our social and public discourse. For example, why is it so difficult for politicians to discuss disparities in wealth or class without being accused of engaging in "class warfare"?

2. In a way, both Riis and Bagge address the same question. Riis writes, "Whence this army of homeless boys? is a question often asked." Bagge asks, "Who are these people? Where did they all come from?" In its portrayal of homeless children, the extract from *How the Other Half Lives* unavoidably has a sentimental aspect; the boys seem innocent, harmless, and beyond reproach for their condition. Although Bagge is sympathetic, his portrayals are often grotesque and elicit judgmental responses, even if he notes that chronically homeless people struggle with mental illness and use toughness as a pose. "Bums" also has a level of irony (evident in the last panel, for example) that is clearly absent from Riis's work; this irony might allow for a more complex and sophisticated response from readers, yet it also might make them less inclined to respond emotionally in an unqualified way.

From Discussion to Writing

1. The "Housing First" policy provokes a complex response. On the one hand, people might oppose it from a moral position: On some level, it just seems "wrong" to "reward" what appears to be bad behavior. On the other hand, from a purely economic or pragmatic point of view, such an approach to a chronic problem might make a lot of sense.

2. This assignment should help students move from the process of recounting or simply narrating "what happened" in their lives, to the more complex process of interpreting and drawing conclusions from events or experiences. Once they have done this, they can connect meaningful events in their own lives to broader issues. Encourage students to choose smaller or less obvious experiences, as they often tend to gravitate to major events (such as graduation day).

Questions for Cross-Cultural Discussion

1. These issues suggest that television shows and movies not only hold a mirror up to society but also shape views of our own culture, as well as other cultures. For example, studies done over the last several years have investigated the low visibility of Latino characters on prime-time television. What is at stake in such limited representation? Is it significant? What are the risks of stereotyping? And how have media stereotypes of different cultures changed over the years? Applying Nathan and Mort's principles to these questions, we can see that media visibility may be connected to real social, political, and cultural consequences.

2. The word *culture* generally has positive connotations, yet we may not wish to celebrate or embrace the "culture" of chronic homelessness, even if we recognize both its existence and the humanity of homeless people. In a sense, by observing the behavior of a distinctive group and then articulating its particular customs, values, and behaviors (however seriously), Bagge is informally engaging in sociocultural anthropology. Students should consider whether they accept his generalizations and whether "Bums" has changed their views of homeless people.

11

The Border: Can We Solve the Illegal Immmigration Problem?

Immigration has been a contentious issue in recent years because of attempts by Congress to reform immigration legislation. Comprehensive immigration reform acts were introduced in both 2006 and 2007 but failed to pass both times. Debate in the Senate and House of Representatives about immigration mirrored concerns in the population at large. Tightened restrictions, including the requirement that U.S. citizens on the border have passports, have placed great strain on administrative departments. In fact, in 2007 the government had to temporarily suspend the new rule because the wait for passports got so long. While some groups used news about the immigration issue to call for greater security measures on the U.S. border, others argued that the conversation about this topic often became discriminatory and even racist. Immigration remains a central issue in the campaigns leading up to the 2008 presidential election.

Americans and Mexicans who live along the border have a special understanding of immigration issues. They are the ones most directly affected by changes in law or policy, and most likely to have connections on both sides of the line. The essays in this chapter are rooted in communities close to the border, and they offer nuanced analyses of how immigration is regulated and policies are enforced. Marjorie Lilly begins in the chile fields of Texas, Bryan Welch refers to his childhood experience in New Mexico, Charles Bowden looks at two towns on either side of the Arizona-Sonora border, and Jessica Chou observes a crossing from Tijuana into California. As your students read the selections, remind them to think about why the locations each author refers to are important. How would people from states that don't border Mexico have a different understanding of immigration?

MARJORIE LILLY   The A-Word
[*Desert Exposure*/January 2008]

Vocabulary/Using a Dictionary

1. The prefix *mal-* means "bad." Lilly is suggesting that the current labor situation is badly adjusted to the needs of the country. Without immigrant workers, U.S. companies would face a severe labor shortage.

2. The root of *deportation* is the Latin verb *portare*, which means "to carry."

3. A vigil is a period of staying awake, usually at night to keep watch. *Vigilance,* meaning "alert watchfulness," shares the same root as *vigil.* When Lilly writes about the vigilance of the border patrol officers, she suggests that they are constantly watching for illegal crossings.

Responding to Words in Context

1. A thicket is an area of dense vegetation. Lilly refers to the immigration issue as a thicket because its complications make it confusing and difficult to navigate.

2. The term *witch hunt* refers to the trials and executions of women and men accused of witchcraft in Europe and Puritan New England. More generally, a witch hunt is a fear-based campaign of persecution based on scant evidence. Lilly points out that Latinos have already been subject to unfounded police scrutiny, and to criminalize immigrants without legal status would certainly worsen the problem.

3. The word *amnesty* emphasizes the illegal nature of border crossing and suggests that allowing migrant workers to stay would be giving them pardon for a crime. Even though Lilly recognizes the need to enforce our laws, she thinks that dealing with workers is a more practical matter and should be resolved by changing policy, not by blindly enforcing it.

Discussing Main Point and Meaning

1. By mentioning the UTAF's stand on immigration, Lilly illustrates how difficult it can be to claim one coherent position on border policy. As she points out in paragraph 2, people who sympathize with underpaid farmworkers are also likely to feel sympathy for those who cross the border illegally looking for better opportunities. However, the UTAF's stand on border policy shows why the question is not so simple — as more illegal workers enter the country, their wages are pushed lower.

2. Lilly agrees with President Bush's two-part plan for improving the immigration situation, but she argues that the government is working on only half of the equation. While law enforcement attempts to tighten control of the border, Congress has failed to pass any measures to allow illegal workers to gain legal status.

3. First, the Z-card program would keep workers that the U.S. economy cannot afford to lose. Second, it would solve logistical problems about how to get those workers into the country effectively, and it would eliminate the disaster that would follow from a mass deportation. Finally, it would afford more respect to people who work extremely hard at thankless, low-paying jobs.

Examining Sentences, Paragraphs, and Organization

1. Although Lilly admits that immigration policy is confusing and often contradictory, at this point in the essay she tries to set forth a black-and-white statement. Using parallel structure, she argues that obeying the law has one consequence (stability), whereas disobeying it has the opposite effect (chaos).

2. Lilly recounts this story not to illustrate the dangers and cruelties of border crossing (which are apparent) but to describe the public's reaction to

it. The heated responses the newspaper received after printing the story reveal the fraught political climate surrounding immigration.

3. In paragraph 13, the first sentence is the topic sentence, which argues that we need a legalization process for logistical reasons. The rest of the paragraph is devoted to playing out the scenario of a mass deportation effort in order to show how impossible it would be.

Thinking Critically

1. Lilly compares the border to a wound in order to liken the flow of immigrants into the United States to the flow of blood. However, on a more fundamental level, she uses this metaphor because the border is a site of pain, primarily for the Mexicans who try to cross but to a lesser extent for the Americans who can't find an entirely acceptable solution to border problems.

2. Lilly believes, as do many commentators, that Mexican laborers fill jobs that Americans are reluctant to take. Therefore, she believes that they play a crucial role in our economy, one that would have devastating consequences if it were suddenly reduced.

3. Lilly sees the responses to the story not as individual reactions but as part of a racist campaign against immigrants. In paragraph 10, she mentions the Minutemen, and apparently she assumes that they, or a similar group, organized the letter-writing campaign that accused the paper of being communist.

In-Class Writing Activities

1. The temporary worker program would certainly benefit those who want to immigrate to the United States for work or who are already here without legal status. It would also help employers who rely on immigrant labor to keep their businesses running. Some might argue that those employers would eventually see a problematic increase in wages and that Mexican workers would take jobs away from Americans. However, Lilly says that the program would also be a relief to most American citizens, especially those in border areas who are torn between sympathy and the need to enforce the law.

2. The fact that the article was published on Thanksgiving suggests that the newspaper intended it to serve as an example of selfless giving to a stranger. This would indicate that the paper was motivated not by the politics of the story but by its human interest. The writers of the protest letters, however, assumed that the newspaper printed the story in an attempt to foist a partisan agenda on readers.

BRYAN WELCH   Putting a Stop to Slave Labor
[*The Utne Reader*/ March–April 2007]

Vocabulary/Using a Dictionary

1. *Assail* comes from a Latin verb meaning "to leap or spring," but now it means "to attack." If something is unassailable, it is impervious to attack, either physical or verbal.

2. The prefix *circum-* means "around." When employers circumvent the law, they do not directly confront it but find ways to get around it.

3. The stem of *succumbed* is the Latin verb *cumbere* (to lie). In this context, *succumbed* means "gave in" or "failed to resist."

Responding to Words in Context

1. Although the workers Welch refers to do not have official legal status, he finds it ironic that the incredibly hard and low-paying jobs they do—jobs that other workers shun—somehow don't count.

2. The primary problem for undocumented workers is that they lack a visa, which is the document that permits people from other countries to live and work in the United States temporarily, or a green card, which the government requires for permanent residents.

3. Even though crossing the border to work without a visa is illegal, the people who do so often do not fit our conception of what a criminal is. As Welch points out, undocumented workers tend to be hardworking people supporting their family. In fact, according to the employers he talks to, the Americans who would take similar jobs more closely conform to what we usually think of as criminals.

Discussing Main Point and Meaning

1. By comparing the jobs of undocumented workers to slave labor, Welch not only underscores the harshness of both but also suggests that the country is suffering from a moral blindness when it comes to dealing with immigrants, much the same way it was blind to the immorality of slavery for many years.

2. Welch believes that the raids on big companies are staged primarily for show. Although they garner a lot of media attention, they cannot put a dent in the high numbers of workers who enter the country illegally and whose labor is crucial to the economy.

3. Welch believes that the only real solution to the immigration problem is to provide some way for immigrants to gain legal status. This would require employers to treat them fairly under the law, giving them the same wages and benefits required for U.S. citizens. Even though Welch admits that such a move could eventually raise prices, he thinks that paying this cost is necessary if Americans want a fair and ethical system.

Examining Sentences, Paragraphs, and Organization

1. Welch uses these quotations from American history and folklore in order to invoke the country's ideals. Thomas Jefferson wrote the first quote into the Declaration of Independence, and George Washington reportedly said the second. Welch brings in these figures to point out the discrepancy between our ideas about them and the facts of their lives.

2. Welch's use of anaphora — "I was in high school," "I was just out of college" — draws attention to the development that he is outlining in these paragraphs. He shows the reader how his consciousness of racial and ethnic inequality deepened as he matured.

3. Gonzalez's story serves several purposes. It personalizes the more abstract questions Welch has been considering in his essay; it illustrates the undesirability of many of the jobs filled by undocumented workers; and it helps support his conclusion that reform of the immigration system would provide fairer compensation for workers like Gonzalez.

Thinking Critically

1. This is a good question for discussion because students may have broadly different answers. People who are invested in the immigration issue or who spend a lot of time thinking about it may agree with Welch's assessment, but students may be quick to point out that the issue is so complicated that even relatively well-informed citizens might feel confused about the consequences of proposed policies.

2. The government requires businesses to comply with immigration laws, but it does not provide an easy way for them to check social security numbers, even though the technology is available and in use elsewhere. According to Welch, this shows that the government knows that our economy relies on undocumented labor. His essay suggests that the government pretends to enforce laws while actually making it possible for employers to hire the workers they need.

3. Welch is certainly speaking to readers who share his ideas about immigration, but he also seems to have a conservative audience in mind. He refers to "family values," which are dear to many conservatives, but he does so to point out the ironic fact that some of the immigrants conservative groups are so eager to deport display strong traditional family values.

In-Class Writing Activities

1. Welch's figures suggest that the government downplays the number of workers who have entered the United States illegally and that private-sector organizations have higher, and more accurate, numbers. This disparity reveals both the difficulty of counting undocumented workers and the fact that the government prefers low estimates.

2. At the end of his essay, Welch recalls where he began, with the founding fathers and their vision for the country. He repeats the words *lying* and

rob as a counterpoint to his discussion of Jefferson and Washington, who are revered for their fairness and honesty. Once again, he draws our attention to the tension between America's self-image and its current policies.

CHARLES BOWDEN   Border Wall
[*National Geographic*/May 2007]

Vocabulary/Using a Dictionary

1. *Fore-* means "before" or "prior to," so *foreshadowing* means "representing or typifying something beforehand." Usually writers use the word to indicate a premonition of some negative turn of events.

2. The suffix *-fold* added to a number indicates multiplication. Bowden uses the word *tenfold* to indicate that a Mexican worker who enters the United States makes ten times as much money as he did in Mexico.

3. The stem of *excavations* is the Latin verb *excavare*, meaning "to hollow out."

Responding to Words in Context

1. A vogue is something trendy or fashionable, so using the word *vogue* in the context of recent demands to extend the border walls suggests that this is a temporary concern and also perhaps that it is somewhat frivolous.

2. In this context, a battery is a grouping of similar objects. Here Bowden is referring to a large number of lights all pointed at the border.

Discussing Main Point and Meaning

1. The picture Bowden paints of the borderlands in the early twentieth century is of a sparsely populated place where no one paid much attention to the dividing line. He notes that the passage of NAFTA in the early 1990s changed the situation drastically, putting many Mexican laborers out of work and pushing them toward the United States.

2. Bowden points out the Statue of Liberty as an icon that represents America not only to its citizens but also to people around the world. The statue symbolizes open doors and free opportunity, which are crucial to the ideology of the nation. The inscription on the Statue of Liberty welcomes immigrants, whereas the walls are a visual signal that they are unwelcome.

3. Building a border wall has some immediate economic consequences. It doesn't necessarily stop illegal crossers, but it makes them rely more on coyotes, who raise their rates for their services. A border wall also forces crossers to go deeper into the desert, making the trip more dangerous, and increasing the number of deaths that occur.

Examining Sentences, Paragraphs, and Organization

1. The story about Patrick Murphy mistakenly bombing the wrong Naco leads into the assertion that begins Bowden's second paragraph: "Borders

everywhere attract violence." It also establishes an identity between the two towns: Although they are on opposite sides of the line, they mirror each other. They share a name, and from the air Murphy couldn't tell them apart.

2. In paragraph 2, Bowden analyzes the border not as a geographic division but as a concept or even a psychological construct. Most of the information he includes in this paragraph has negative connotations.

3. Paragraph 14 includes a list of famous historical walls, through which Bowden hopes to reveal their deeper function. His examples show both how walls work to separate people, and how frequently they fail.

Thinking Critically

1. The wall pictured in this photo essay looks old and rusted out. It appears to have been designed to prevent crossers on foot, and a cross marks an unknown person who died in the crossing. The image suggests that the border is intensely dangerous, bleak, and unfeeling toward those who seek prosperity in the United States. At a time when some are calling for massive reform, it serves as a reminder that the current method of prevention is not consistently humane.

2. Bowden notes that both of the walls he compares in paragraph 17 were built to keep people out, but as he states earlier in the essay, that is true of most walls. Perhaps he makes this comparison because both are very controversial—many Americans and Israelis have qualms about their construction. Also, both are a locus for ethnically charged violence.

In-Class Writing Activities

1. In the beginning of his essay, Bowden describes the wall in Naco as cold, forbidding, and monolithic. The bright lights to which one resident "has lost her nights" (para. 5) seem blinding, and another resident points out that the wall is "so ugly" (para. 6). Even though some on the Arizona side of the wall think it is a necessity, no one seems to like having it there, and Bowden's language reflects their feeling.

2. Throughout "Our Wall," Bowden talks with local people who have to balance their political views about immigration with their personal sympathy for people on the other side of the border. The fact that they attribute the problem to economics speaks to their understanding of the factors that motivate illegal crossers, and the solution suggested by one Naco resident, job creation in Mexico, imagines a positive response rather than the negative methods of the "police solution" (para. 28).

JESSICA CHOU (STUDENT ESSAY)   Undocumented: One Student's Story

[*The Daily Bruin*, University of California, Los Angeles/February 21, 2008]

Vocabulary/Using a Dictionary

1. *Peering* can mean "coming slightly into view" or "emerging partly." However, here Chou uses the word *peering* to describe Rocha looking closely or with concentration.

2. A compromise is literally a co-promise, or a mutual promise made by two people. This origin explains how *compromise* came to mean "an agreement reached by making mutual concessions."

Responding to Words in Context

1. *Mijo* is a contraction of *mi hijo* (my son). It can also be a more general form of address, expressing affection for a male. (The feminine form is *mija*.) Even if students don't speak Spanish, they will probably be able to guess from the context that Rocha's mother is using the word as a term of endearment.

2. Rocha's plan for raising money for college is unconventional in that it doesn't follow any of the usual, established paths. In addition, he uses new media such as Facebook, making his fund-raising even less conventional.

3. Although Rocha does not define the two words outright, he seems to believe that asking for charity is asking someone to take care of you. His fund-raising did not have that goal, but he did ask people to give him the assistance he needed in order to keep pursuing his college education.

Discussing Main Point and Meaning

1. The barricades along the border resemble the fortifications used in war, so there is a visual similarity between the border and a battlefield. The border is also the site of much conflict and suffering; thus, even though this might not be immediately apparent, knowledge of violence also informs Rocha's vision of the border.

2. Rocha has profound admiration for his mother's hard work to support the family on her own. Inspired by her determination, he believes that raising the money for his school fees will be not only possible but also relatively easy compared to the hardships she faced.

3. Currently, undocumented students in California are ineligible for financial aid. Even if they are accepted to college, they may not be able to finance it. If the California Dream Act passes, it will allow students like Rocha to apply for aid.

Examining Sentences, Paragraphs, and Organization

1. The beginning of Chou's essay throws the reader directly into the most dramatic part of Rocha's story. Although it may be slightly disorienting because we don't yet know who "he" is, this technique has the benefit of quickly getting the reader emotionally involved.

2. This particular quote from Rocha, with its repetitions and fragments, functions not so much to provide information but rather to show the impact the crossing had on him. The elliptical nature of his speech suggests that, even in recollection, the crossing is emotionally charged for him.

Thinking Critically

1. Rocha's attendance at UCLA separates his experience from that of many undocumented immigrants, but among those who attend college the challenges he has had to face are quite common. Rocha's involvement with Ideas UCLA showed him just how many other undocumented students there were at his university.

2. Proposals for legalization are aimed largely at adult workers in low-wage jobs, but they would also benefit young people whose parents immigrated illegally and whose futures are made uncertain by their immigration status. Such a program would likely make them eligible for financial aid.

In-Class Writing Activities

1. Although they might seem impersonal at first, social-networking sites such as Facebook and devices like cell phones actually allow people to make one-on-one connections quickly and easily. Rather than being confronted with an abstract cause, people who supported Rocha probably saw him as a bright and ambitious individual.

2. Rocha sounds like a highly motivated student whose aspirations extend beyond just getting by in college; he also wants to do well, learn about his situation, and help others with similar problems. He believes that by educating himself about the laws and policies that pertain to undocumented students, he not only will help himself but also can inform other students.

Discussing the Unit

Suggested Topic for Discussion

The border in Bowden's article is the most obviously physical — it is marked by a metal wall that separates Mexico and the United States. Although no specific demarcations are referenced in the other articles (except for a brief mention in Welch's piece), the border is still visible. All of the articles in the chapter mention the border as a line to cross in hopes of better paying jobs to help support Mexican families. Although border crossers may not see the line with their eyes, they know of the dangers they risk of getting caught and deported.

Psychologically, the Mexican-American border represents many things for people on both sides. For hopeful Mexicans, the border symbolizes a chance for better wages and bigger opportunities, such as a college education in Rocha's case. He describes it as a "battlefield" (Chou, para. 6), and interviewees from Bowden's article call it "ugly" and "racist" (para. 6 and18). The border represents the difference between an illegal immigrant and a U.S. citizen; for American employers, it represents the difference between low-wage workers and expensive, legal labor. Ask your students if they can think of any other kind of border in their surroundings—either psychological, physical, or both. What purpose does it have? Is it keeping someone inside or outside? Why?

Preparing for Class Discussion

1. Lilly believes that President Bush's proposed Z-visa represents positive change, and she hopes it is enacted into law. Welch agrees that a legalization process is necessary, but he pays more attention to the outcomes of a policy change and how citizens will have to adjust. Bowden turns his eye not to what the United States can do but to what changes in Mexico would encourage more workers to stay.

2. These essays describe a stratified border society. On one level are the citizens on either side who, for the most part, go about their lives, largely ignoring the border or crossing back and forth casually. Then there are law enforcement officials of both countries who are responsible for upholding border laws. Finally, private groups and individuals, such as the Minutemen and coyotes, become involved, in legal and illegal ways, in the system of exchange and conflict on the border.

From Discussion to Writing

1. The essays in this unit give students a range to choose from. Their choices may be literal, finding arguments that most closely describe the danger of the border as portrayed in the photograph, or they could be more impressionistic, representing the authors' feelings about the dividing line.

2. As students work on this assignment, you might remind them that first they will need to identify the most pressing or widespread problems posed by immigration. Once they have determined what problems most need to be addressed, they will have a better basis from which to argue for their solutions. Students should also consider the long-range consequences of their recommendations.

Topics for Cross-Cultural Discussion

1. Immediately after September 11, any debates surrounding immigration revolved around security and the need to close the borders to anyone with intentions of carrying out violent attacks. The arguments against immigration from Mexico are much more closely tied to economics. Although there are some security issues, what agitates most people when discussing Mexican immigrants is the possibility that they will take too many jobs from Americans.

2. Starting in the late nineteenth century, Congress passed a number of acts that increasingly restricted how many immigrants could enter the country. Aside from Latinos, those facing the harshest restrictions were immigrants from Asian countries (with the exception of the Philippines). In 1917, Asian immigrants were prohibited entirely from entering the country.

12

The Climate Crisis: Is It Real?

As news stories about unusual weather phenomena increase, climate change is rapidly becoming one of the most widely discussed issues in world politics. A search of recent news on the topic is likely to turn up stories in countries from Canada to Pakistan. As concern about the issue spreads around the world, it has also hit home for more and more Americans. Al Gore's documentary *An Inconvenient Truth*, which Dustin Lushing discusses at length, is just one public statement that has helped turn the issue of climate change from a concern limited to environmental activists into a mainstream political issue. Several of the essayists in this chapter see global warming as a real and pressing problem, whereas others, such as Thomas Sowell, believe its dangers are being blown out of proportion.

As is the case with other hot-button issues, such as evolution and genetic engineering, global warming is intricately connected to science. The arguments both for and against more active measures to combat global warming are based on scientific data and conclusions that are often obscure or hard for laypeople to understand. One point you might bring up in discussion of these works is how each of the writers deals with observations of climate change and how they are interpreted by scientists. The essay by Josh Burleson and the response by Brett Schoel revolve around questions about how science works, and the advertisement for the International Conference on Climate Change depends on scientific testimonials. What types of scientific evidence convince the authors in this chapter, and when do they believe it falls short? How much does the science of global warming complicate our discussion of possible solutions?

The climate-change debate inspires emotionally charged exchanges, and the essays in this chapter are no exception. The selections here, perhaps even more than in the other chapters, provide a good opportunity to talk about how writers use emotional appeals in addition to logical argument. As students read, have them highlight words or sentences that play on readers' emotions rather than their reasoning. When you discuss these points, ask students why this issue might be a particularly emotional one. Both Bill McKibben and Mike Tidwell find moral and even spiritual purpose in the movement against global warming. What is it about the possibility of climate change that inspires such passions?

BILL MCKIBBEN   Let's Act Together on Global Warming
[*Tikkun*/November–December 2007]

Vocabulary/Using a Dictionary

1. *Inexorable* means "not to be moved or stopped" or "relentless."

2. *Convenient* means "comfortable" or "easy." *Inconvenient* means "not convenient, even to the extent of being troubling or annoying."

3. BTU stands for British thermal unit. It represents the amount of heat required to raise one pound of water by one degree Fahrenheit.

Responding to Words in Context

1. *Consensus* means "general agreement." *Consensus* has basically the same definition in all three instances. In the first example, McKibben uses *consensus* as an adjective meaning "generally agreed upon." In the second example, he uses *consensus* to mean "general agreement." In the same paragraph, the second use of *consensus* could be refined to mean "unanimity," because the closeness of the repetition of the word could be seen to strengthen the implied meaning.

2. *Per capita* is a Latin phrase that means "by or for each person." McKibben means that the United States still outstrips other countries in its consumption of fossil fuels, despite other countries' increasing use of these fuels.

3. Inertia is inactivity or a resistance to movement. Movement is inertia's opposite: When one moves, one changes place or position. McKibben is playing with the meaning of the word *movement* here: He is referring to an organized group of people working toward a common goal (he mentions that such a movement must be as strong as the civil rights movement of the 1950s and 1960s).

Discussing Main Point and Meaning

1. Before Hurricane Katrina, Americans could shrug off reports of global warming coming from distant, isolated places like Antarctica. They might have noticed changes in weather patterns or reports of devastating storms in other parts of the world without realizing their significance. But Katrina was an unusually strong hurricane that hit the coast of the United States, wreaking great havoc and attracting national notice. Whether or not one believes that global warming spawned Katrina, it is hard to overlook more frequent and intense changes in the weather when they happen in our own country and when they cause as much pain and suffering as did that particular hurricane.

2. The flip side of despair is hope, and McKibben wants us to feel hopeful about the sort of change we can make regarding climate change, if only we will hold on to that emotion and act. He is not interested in sorrow or regret or anger. Because ending climate change requires the efforts of many

people, he hopes that we will begin to organize for real change: "Do it hard enough and you've earned the right to hope" (para. 11).

3. McKibben understands that large corporations have huge investments in the use of fossil fuels in this country. He mentions that "Exxon made more profit last year than any company in the history of profits" (para. 10). He also mentions that we as a people will be very reluctant to give up the lifestyle we lead, which depends largely on fossil fuels. These two reasons will prevent the U.S. government (backed by the companies and empowered by the people) from taking the lead or acting with other governments to stop global warming.

Examining Sentences, Paragraphs, and Organization

1. The experts are playing with the phrase "window of opportunity" and using a metaphor of an open window that we can just barely squeeze through (if we can do it, we have just enough time, money, and resources to fix the problem of global warming). The experts are saying that getting through the rapidly closing window will be a huge challenge but that it is still possible to do so—for now.

2. McKibben is suggesting that to work on global warming, the United States has to be both a leader and a follower. It has to lead because it is the biggest contributor to global warming. The United States also has to follow in the sense that it has to cooperate with other nations and work toward a global solution; not doing so will keep all nations at odds with one another.

3. Using numbered points to outline what we need to understand about global warming is an effective way to set up the essay's argument. It allows McKibben to provide the darker details of how global warming is happening, what needs to happen to fix the problem, and why it is still so difficult for us to act together as a global community. By setting these points aside as he does, instead of making them the focus of his essay, he has given the reader crucial information, and he can then go on to explain how the United States should act in the global community and how change will begin. He then moves to his main point in the final paragraph when he exhorts the reader to act and to hope, providing a real sense of the action that will effect change.

Thinking Critically

1. Change has begun in the auto industry with the development and mass marketing of hybrid cars. Researchers are investigating renewable energy sources as a way to replace our reliance on fossil fuels. Nuclear power, which has its own drawbacks, and hydrogen power are being considered as better sources of energy. Wind and waterpower are already being used to provide energy, though not yet in a significant way,.

2. McKibben believes that organized groups of people are key to fighting and reversing global warming. He does not believe that governments will

suddenly stand up and do what's right. He is a proponent of movements—both in this country and around the world—which have a tradition of creating wider change (he uses the civil rights movement as an example). It may be helpful to examine a variety of social movements with the class in order to show the effectiveness of groups that have made significant change for various causes, from labor to the environment to human rights and justice.

3. Small change is valuable, but the breadth of the problem of climate change requires action on a macro, not a micro, scale. The value to small change is that it begins to affect the inertia McKibben refers to in paragraph 10. If we change our lifestyle through recycling, conservation efforts (such as more fuel-efficient cars and fluorescent lightbulbs), and other small acts, we become more aware of our effect on the earth, and our mind-set will start to change. This may lead to bigger action—to living simply and reducing our "carbon footprint" in other ways, while encouraging others to do so as well. Eventually, McKibben hopes, a change in mind-set will lead to the development of a movement that may force governments throughout the world to take charge of the problem before it is too late.

In-Class Writing Activities

1. Much information about Katrina is available on the Web and elsewhere, and students may have personal recollections of the event itself. The debate about how much global warming can be blamed for Katrina is ongoing; the focus has been largely on the government's poor response to the catastrophe. Post-Katrina New Orleans continues to rebuild, but the victims who lost family and property have all but faded from the media's view.

2. Students can write about the growth of the civil rights movement and how it created change in a specific way. Essays can focus on particular leaders or on the ordinariness of the movement's rank-and-file participants. Students should examine the circumstances and impediments surrounding a particular victory of the civil rights movement.

3. During the past several years, students may have heard a variety of myths and truths about global warming. It will be interesting to note where a presumed fact has been turned on its head or where a truth students hoped was false is supported. Discuss any revelations students had during this activity, and find out if they came to this activity with similar or dissimilar ideas about global warming.

ad: Heartland Institute, International Conference on Climate Change
[*New York Times*/February 27, 2008]

Vocabulary/Using a Dictionary

1. *Petition* comes from the Latin verb *petere*, which means "to seek or ask for." Most petitions that people sign usually involve some kind of

request, such as a request for a candidate to be put on the ballot. This petition does not seem to have an immediate request attached to it but simply demonstrates the scientists' opinion on climate change.

2. *Climate* once meant "a region of the earth between two lines of latitude." With better scientific knowledge of weather patterns and ecosystems, the word *climate* became more closely associated with the prevailing atmospheric conditions in a region.

Responding to Words in Context

1. In this sentence, the ad writers are using the language of scientists who do believe in human-created global warming and who believe that their colleagues who reject the theory are stubbornly ignoring the facts. The point the ad wants to make is that some scientists doubt the conclusions about climate change not just for the sake of doubting but through a process of reasoning.

2. *Natural* has positive connotations that imply that global warming is a normal and unavoidable process. By suggesting that climate change is natural, the ad makes it seem not only less urgent but also less threatening.

Discussing Main Point and Meaning

1. Part of the point of the ad is that large numbers of scientists disagree with the idea that climate change has been caused by human factors. By listing some of the names rather than just giving the number of scientists, the ad's creators both reinforce that these are individual opinions and emphasize that there are many like-minded people.

2. The title of this book, which the Heartland Institute endorses, suggests that climate change does occur but that it is a natural phenomenon. By connecting current climate trends to past cycles, the book's title suggests that the changes are natural and must be allowed to take their course.

Examining Sentences, Paragraphs, and Organization

1. The headline ("Can 19,000 scientists be wrong about global warming?") is purposefully ambiguous. It leads us to expect that the ad is for a conference in support of the idea that humans are causing climate change, so we are surprised to learn that the conference actually has the opposite objective.

2. In most ads created by for-profit companies, the logo would be much more prominent. However, the Heartland Institute's goal is not to make money or even to draw attention to itself but to provide information. By using a small logo, the ad's creators put more emphasis on the headline and the list of names.

Thinking Critically

1. The Heartland Institute, based in Chicago, is a nonprofit think tank. Although it is not affiliated with a political party, it promotes free markets,

individualism, and limited government involvement. Because the institute holds conservative views, it tends to argue against any government intervention that might be advocated by those who believe that humans are causing climate change.

2. Since the Heartland Institute's petition has already established that these scientists are generally like-minded on the issue of climate change, the function of the conference seems not so much to exchange and discuss ideas but rather to gain publicity and public support for the scientists' particular take on global warming.

In-Class Writing Activity

1. The petition's primary aim is to consolidate opposition to the Kyoto protocols, which would require governments to restrict the use of fossil fuels and to find alternative energy solutions. In addition, the petition suggests not only that climate change is not a crisis but also that it may in fact be beneficial to plant life.

THOMAS SOWELL   Cold Water on "Global Warming"
[*townhall.com*/February 28, 2008]

Vocabulary/Using a Dictionary

1. When something is debunked, it is exposed as a lie.

2. *Hysteria* derives from the Greek word *hysterikos*, which means "suffering in the womb." The Greeks thought that women displayed hysteria because of uterine problems.

3. The word *media* refers to communication sources, including newspapers, radio, television, and now the Internet. It comes from Latin and is plural — the singular form is *medium*.

Responding to Words in Context

1. In this context, Sowell means that people have created a small industry out of the climate-change crisis and that they engage in it fervently. He implies that those involved receive some kind of gain, monetary or otherwise, from this activity.

2. Professors of climatology teach about weather conditions, weather patterns, and the history of climate changes.

3. *Empirical* means "based on, or verifiable by, observation." Empirical evidence comes from scientific research and is revealed through experience or as the result of an experiment.

Discussing Main Point and Meaning

1. Sowell never states outright that people are not responsible for climate change, but he firmly believes we should not accept as fact that they are.

He focuses on a conference that hosts people "who have already expressed skepticism" (para. 12) about the prevailing theories on climate change, and he alludes to ideas about climate change as a natural phenomenon. Sowell takes issue with the current "explanations, implications and extrapolations" (para. 17) that the media transmit about global warming, and he suggests that no one is looking at prior instances and natural causes of such warming.

2. Many of the conference's attendees are probably more skeptical of the reality of global warming than are the environmentalists and scientists who are creating "the current 'global warming' hysteria" (para. 15). Sowell notes that many of the participants have doubts about "either the prevailing explanations of current climate change or the dire predictions about future climate change" (para. 12). He also mentions the participation of the authors of two books whose titles register their doubt about prevailing beliefs on global warming. Sowell does not explicitly state who is creating "hysteria," but he presents them as people who are convinced in their viewpoints and want to create a sense of panic about climate change.

3. Carbon dioxide, a greenhouse gas, is created in a variety of ways. Living things produce it by breathing. It is also a by-product of burning fossil fuels and of some natural geothermal processes. The output of carbon dioxide can be affected by deforestation (because plants use carbon dioxide during photosynthesis).

Examining Sentences, Paragraphs, and Organization

1. Sowell is adding a bit of ironic humor to his essay by including the tag "weather permitting" in paragraph 7. Global warming is, ultimately, about the weather, and according to Sowell, our current views on global warming lead us to believe that any bad weather is significant. The tag echos his opening paragraph, which reads, "It has almost become something of a joke when some 'global warming' conference has to be cancelled because of a snowstorm or bitterly cold weather."

2. A number of "facts" are offered in this essay, but Sowell does not provide many citations. The vagueness of many statements leaves readers wondering whether he is presenting a fact or a claim. Paragraph 6 mentions that "not all those who are called scientists are called scientists are really scientists and not all of those who are scientists are specialists in climate." The statement is fine on the surface, but it would hold more weight if Sowell gave specific examples to support his claims. His information about the upcoming global-warming conference is most compelling because he includes names and numbers. In the last few paragraphs, he discusses some natural causes of climate change, but phrases such as "some scientists say" (para. 19) don't create a solid, factual argument. Providing more citations or supporting evidence for such facts would strengthen his position.

3. Sowell uses the word *hysteria* four times when referring to the treatment of global warming by the media and by those who believe it is a human-made crisis. By using the word *hysteria* when referring to "those hyping a global warming 'crisis,'" Sowell implies that they are experiencing such overwhelming emotion that they are out of control and beyond reason. Through repetition of the word, he underscores how irrational and over-heated the global-warming debate has become.

Thinking Critically

1. Sowell does not deny that the earth is warming. In his final paragraphs, he mentions the possible natural causes for such warming. He believes that the media are exaggerating the effects of global warming and are claiming that we have caused it and that we can do something about it because there is some sort of gain to be had from doing so: "A whole cottage industry has sprung up among people who get grants, government agencies who get appropriations, politicians who get publicity and the perpetually indignant who get something new to be indignant about" (para. 5).

2. The Heartland Institute, a Chicago-based think tank, is a nonprofit organization. Using the Heartland Institute's Web site and other information available on the Web, students should make some educated guesses about how the institute aligns itself politically and socially. Some students may be skeptical of a global-warming conference sponsored by the Heartland Institute because of the organization's conservative bent. Based on their positions on climate change and other issues, other students may believe that the institute is a good choice. Students should also consider who sponsors (funds) the institute. Does that information affect their opinion?

3. Sowell believes that the media profit from the global-warming crisis because it generates fear and interest, sells more papers, and draws a bigger audience. According to Sowell, individuals and organizations receive funding and politicians get publicity for such "crises"; this is a problem if the crises lack validity. Moreover, some self-proclaimed global-warming experts use the issue to gain recognition, even though they lack any credentials. The statement "It gives teachers something to talk about in school instead of teaching" (para. 5) smacks of opinion, and Sowell doesn't back it up with evidence.

In-Class Writing Activities

1. Students' opinions on global warming will vary, as will their reactions to what they hear from the media. Students may think that a more moderate approach should be taken by those who are skeptical of the crisis as well as by those who believe that ignoring or disbelieving the crisis is unacceptable. No matter what position they take, students will find a wealth of material in the news and on the Web to back up their arguments.

2. The greenhouse effect is the trapping of the sun's warmth in the earth's lower atmosphere. Students should outline how energy gets absorbed by the atmosphere and is then released again. They may want to discuss greenhouse gases or what might happen if the greenhouse effect goes beyond our control.

3. Sowell names two book titles and their authors and provides some information on the conference's attendees. Students' outlines should show that this conference will debate not only what to do about climate change but also the accuracy and legitimacy of claims currently being made about global warming. Students should feel free to be creative with their outline, suggesting panel titles and participants based on Sowell's claims in his essay.

MIKE TIDWELL   Snap into Action for the Climate
[*Orion*/May–June 2008]

Vocabulary/Using a Dictionary

1. *Trans-* means "across" or "over." This prefix in *transformation* gives the word its meaning of "the act or process of moving from one form or shape to another."

2. The verb form of *absolution* is *absolve*. Absolution is the act of clearing someone of guilt, blame, or sin.

3. *Exhilarating* is based on the stem *hilar-*, which means "cheerful." Tidwell suggests that this is an exhilarating time to be alive because he is excited and glad about the opportunity for human invention, despite his fears about climate change.

Responding to Words in Context

1. Up to this point, Tidwell has been using the term *feedback loop* to describe the exponential increases in carbon dioxide. Here he imagines positive loops, in which small acts of conservation will lead to ever bigger results.

2. In this quote, MacCracken defends the idea of deliberately ("advertently") engineering the climate by pointing out that humans have accidentally ("inadvertently") been changing it for years. Although there are concerns about intervening, he believes that for once we should make our changes to the climate purposeful.

3. Tidwell's use of the word *evolved* suggests that the change will not be superficial. Rather, he expects a deep and lasting change in the way humans relate to their environment.

Discussing Main Point and Meaning

1. In this essay, Tidwell argues that scientists have drastically underestimated how much time broad climate changes will take. He believes that

the only solution to this rapidly evolving problem is an equally rapid mobilization of activists who will push for government support of the Kyoto protocol and other carbon-reducing measures.

2. At the end of paragraph 11, Tidwell notes that finding alternatives to fossil fuels, which has been the focus of efforts to combat global warming, may not be enough to solve the problem. He believes that we are at a point where it will become necessary to use "geo-engineering" to deliberately cool the planet (para. 12).

3. Tidwell thinks that voters have to demand much greater change from politicians. For example, Congress should require the auto industry to make cars that get 50 miles to the gallon instead of 35. He also suggests that we construct wind farms in all feasible positions along the coasts and reduce electricity use by one-third by 2015.

4. As a conservationist, Tidwell generally seeks to minimize the impacts humans have on the natural world, so it seems ironic that in this essay he advocates for human intervention in climate conditions. However, he argues that such drastic measures are necessary because humans have already had a profound impact on the climate.

Examining Sentences, Paragraphs, and Organization

1. In the beginning of his essay, Tidwell anticipates the possible criticism that isolated weather events do not necessarily point to climate change. He includes several of these individual incidents of extreme weather in order to suggest a pattern: Even though none of them alone can serve as evidence of global warming, together they seem to indicate that some change is under way.

2. At this point in his essay, Tidwell imagines readers' responses to the points he has made so far. Because he challenges the usual timeline of how climate change is expected to happen, he feels that his ideas may meet with some resistance and disbelief. By including these questions, he gives himself an opportunity to provide more evidence for why he thinks climate change is happening so quickly.

3. Tidwell points to Australia as a country that has experienced a "snap" in public opinion about climate change. Although Australia, like the United States, has recently been controlled by conservatives, a more liberal candidate who made global warming his central issue gained massive support. Also, recent droughts in the United States have mirrored the droughts in Australia that brought climate change to the forefront of public affairs.

Thinking Critically

1. Tidwell's statement reveals his belief that our definition of "planet Earth" is based on a set of conditions specific to the planet. If global warming changes these conditions significantly, that definition will no longer apply, and we will be living on a planet we don't recognize.

2. For those who believe that global warming is real, threatening, and urgent, it often seems important to place blame for resistance to change. Tidwell's claim that global warming was well on its way by the time we recognized it allows him to avoid the task of assigning responsibility and instead to focus on the more pressing need to mobilize solutions.

3. Tidwell believes that we have reached the point at which engineering has to step in and help solve the global-warming problem. He points out that humans have enough ingenuity to create these technologies as a way of convincing readers that "geo-engineering" could be within our reach.

In-Class Writing Activities

1. Tidwell dismisses one of the most talked-about solutions, machines that draw carbon dioxide out of the air, as too far in the future to matter. He also thinks that the idea of using giant orbiting mirrors is far-fetched and prohibitively expensive. However, he does believe that painting rooftops and roadways a reflective white might be one relatively easy, if crude, solution. He also believes that some chemical means of cooling, such as introducing more sulfur dioxide into the atmosphere, will become both possible and necessary.

2. One of the comparisons Tidwell cites is the civil rights movement in America. It is an example of a movement that was opposed by a large part of the population (especially in the southern states) but that made gains based on its deep moral authority. Another comparison he mentions is support for World War II, which required individual citizens to make sacrifices in order to attain a greater good.

DUSTIN LUSHING (STUDENT ESSAY)   Global Warming: Is It All Hot Air?

[*The Johns Hopkins News-Letter*, Johns Hopkins University/March 29, 2007]

Vocabulary/Using a Dictionary

1. Gibberish is unintelligible speech, not belonging to any language. It is formed from the verb *gibber*, which means "to chatter or talk nonsense," and the suffix *-ish* (meaning "relating to"), which is often used to denote a language.

2. The root of *impotence* is the Latin *potent* or *posse*, "to be powerful or able." Lushing argues that the Democrats, after being out of the political majority for several years, plotted to regain power by exploiting the issue of climate change.

3. *Demagogue* derives from the Greek *demagogos*, which means "leader of the people." In current use, a demagogue is someone who arouses the passions of the populace or a mob, perhaps to ignoble ends.

Responding to Words in Context

1. The phrase *dyed-in-the-wool* comes from the textile industry. A fabric that is made from dyed wool, rather than being dyed after it has already been woven together, holds its color better. It is used metaphorically to suggest a deep and permanent association. In other words, Lushing suggests that Al Gore is a politician through and through.

2. A consensus is a general agreement, or an opinion reached by a group as a whole. Although Lushing concedes that most scientists believe both that the climate is changing and that humans have caused it to change, he doesn't believe that global warming will be as disastrous as some predict.

3. Lushing believes that those hyping the global-warming issue are self-important in that they have turned a legitimate topic of discussion into a shrill and exaggerated complaint at the center of American politics. Throughout the essay, he is concerned that the motives of the global-warming movement are political and self-serving.

Discussing Main Point and Meaning

1. Lushing argues that Democrats in particular have used global warming to mobilize their supporters. What makes this particular issue effective for politicians is that it is frightening and yet difficult for laypeople to understand.

2. Part of the point of Lushing's essay is to refocus attention on issues that he thinks are more pressing and can be confronted in a more immediate fashion. By listing these issues, he points out topics worthy of political activism, other than advocating for legislation about climate change.

Examining Sentences, Paragraphs, and Organization

1. Al Gore is generally perceived to be very intelligent, if slightly wooden as a politician. Here Lushing associates him with the stereotype of a crazed and drunken person who rails about the end of the world. He suggests that Gore's beliefs about global warming are based on fanaticism instead of reason.

2. By saying that global warming exists but that "it's not that big of a deal" (para. 1), Lushing establishes the grounds for his argument. He doesn't want to debate whether there is evidence of warming. Instead, he wants to consider why it has inspired such a vocal group of politicians and voters.

3. Lushing includes Bush's comical quote about evolution, Frist's hasty diagnosis, and Gore's fears about the climate as a way of showing that politicians have a shallow understanding of, or don't care about, science. His point is that scientific problems like climate change should not be entrusted to politicians, who have their own motives.

Thinking Critically

1. Lushing believes that the current debates about global warming, as in the communist scares of the 1950s, are playing up fears in order to make political gains. In their effects, however, McCarthyism and global-warming activism are quite different. McCarthy's hearings singled out individuals that he associated with communism, often leaving them unemployed or worse. The debate about climate change is aimed at much broader regulation, which would place responsibility for change on governments and corporations.

2. Lushing takes the quotation about Al Gore's science of global warming being "basically sound" (para. 5) as evidence that scientists are going along with an idea that has gained currency, even though they have reservations about it. However, there are other ways to read this phrase. For instance, scientists might be hesitant to challenge highly technical points of an argument presented in a form that is friendly to laypeople.

In-Class Writing Activities

1. For this assignment, students who feel that global warming could prove to be disastrous will likely focus on the fact that a radical change in living conditions would only exacerbate or make moot the other political issues Lushing lists in paragraph 6. However, students who question the speed or the scope of climate change might feel that other issues, ones that affect citizens in an immediate way, are more deserving of attention.

2. The famous photo from Iwo Jima represents patriotism, combined effort, and victory. One of the reasons the student group chose it might have been to offer an image of a number of people working together to accomplish a task. More deeply embedded in the image is the moral justification for World War II. Environmentalists argue that global warming is a similar moral battle.

JENNIFER OLADIPO   Global Warming Is Colorblind: Can We Say as Much for Environmentalism?
[*Orion*/November–December 2007]

Vocabulary/Using a Dictionary

1. Strictly speaking, a minority is a number that forms less than half of the whole. The word has come to mean a group that differs somehow, in race, religion, or ethnic background, from the majority of the population. In this essay in particular, it refers to the nonwhite part of the population.

2. A dichotomy is a division into two parts, especially two opposed or contradictory groups.

3. A steward is someone who manages or directs. On ships, buses, and trains, stewards are those who attend to and supervise passengers. Stewardship

refers to the obligations and responsibilities of the steward; therefore, *environmental stewardship* means "the careful management of the environment."

Responding to Words in Context

1. A tailspin is a decline or downturn (the word literally refers to the fast descent of an aircraft in a steep spiral spin). Ecology is the study of the relations and interactions between organisms and their environment—Oladipo's essay deals with the environmental movement. The phrase "current ecological tailspin" refers to global warming, a difficult human-made problem that has the potential to leave our planet increasingly inhospitable and uninhabitable.

2. A spectrum is a range that forms a continuous sequence or series (the word *spectrum* often refers to the continuum of color when light is dispersed through a prism). When Oladipo refers to a "racial spectrum," she is speaking of the various racial and ethnic communities found throughout this country. Instead of just lumping people into the category "white" or "black," she includes people of fall colors and racial backgrounds.

3. Conservation values are those espoused by environmental activists. In the context of this essay *conservation* refers to the careful preservation and protection of our environment. The term *conservative* is used in political spheres to mean someone who favors perserving existing or traditional conditions (as opposed to a liberal, who favors progress or reform). A political conservative does not necessarily share Oladipo's conservation values.

Discussing Main Point and Meaning

1. By making these statements, Oladipo confirms that she works in an area where minorities live and could have access to the nature preserve and that their absence confuses her. This specific observation leads to the broader theme of her essay—the question of why minorities do not participate in greater numbers in the environmental movement.

2. An environmentalist is someone interested in the protection of air, water, animals, plants, and other natural resources. A minority is a racial group different from the majority of the population (usually white). There is no fundamental reason for these two words to be in opposition to each other in people's minds, but Oladipo says that they are. Minorities are often thought to be less affluent than whites, and environmentalists are often thought to have greater financial means with which to support their cause. Both of these stereotypes are often untrue. It would be false to assume that minorities have any less at stake in the preservation of the environment than do whites. Oladipo's essay deals with the fact that environmental groups provide little, if any, information to minorities and rarely solicit their participation.

3. Because minority populations are growing, an environmental movement that is only "white and well-off" ignores the concerns and ideas of a large segment of the population and loses the backing of potential financial contributors (Oladipo mentions that "minorities make up one-third of the population, and we are growing as an economic and financial force as our numbers increase" [para. 6]). If a "white and well-off" environmental movement alienates one-third of the population, it disables itself by not addressing the concerns of a large group of people.

Examining Sentences, Paragraphs, and Organization

1. By beginning with this sentence, Oladipo makes it clear that she is both an environmentalist and a member of a minority. She speaks for a group that is not represented in this movement. The phrase "another face like mine" is inclusive. However, if she had said "I have never seen another black woman's face come through our doors," she would have created an "us versus them" or "I versus other" tone.

2. Oladipo speaks from personal experience in this paragraph, noting that mailings from her organization do not go to areas where minorities live and that press releases do not go to the radio stations or newspapers minorities are most likely to listen to or read. Because minorities do not get information about her organization, they are highly unlikely to notice or express an interest in it. Oladipo is concerned that minorities are not involved in her environmental organization, but she's more concerned with the fact that they seem much less involved than whites in any environmental organizations. By noticing what happens in her own workplace, she is able to generalize: It is likely that most environmental organizations do not provide adequate outreach to minorities.

3. Oladipo wants to disabuse whites of the notion that minorities do not share their interests. Members of minority groups are much more likely to be aware, from personal experience, that they enjoy (or have the potential to enjoy) activities like backpacking than are members of the majority, who perhaps assume that only whites enjoy these activities. Minorities are not excluded as an audience for this essay, but Oladipo is speaking primarily to whites: She wants to encourage them to be more inclusive regarding environmental concerns. She provides information about herself and her interests ("I have been volunteering in organic gardens, hiking, and camping for years" [para. 5]) to show that a member of the minority can be just as passionate about environmental issues and activities as whites are. She also includes some information about minorities' growing power as "an economic and financial force" (para. 6), not to be overlooked by a white audience still holding on to outdated assumptions.

Thinking Critically

1. The prevailing assumption is that whites have the money and power and can effect change as members of the environmental movement, whereas minorities are considered less valuable or less interested constituents.

Challenging such assumptions, Oladipo makes a few statements to clarify the currently voiceless minorities' interests in the environment ("Brown, yellow, red, and black people like to go backpacking, too" and "Those of us with the means are buying organic, local, and hybrid" [para. 7]). She does not go into greater detail about the history of minorities and the majorities' perception of them in this country, or about the history of the environmental movement, which might shed more light on why "green" equals "white" for most people.

2. Oladipo does not give a great deal of information about her interest in environmental work, except to say that she has been an outdoors type of person for a long time: "I have been volunteering in organic gardens, hiking, and camping for years" (para. 5). Her experience suggests that she is well versed in environmental issues and fairly active in the movement as well: She "joined an environmental-journalism organization," leading environmental groups to take her more seriously. Her essay itself is a call to action—to whites to change how they view minorities' relationship to the environment, and to minorities to take pride in what they have to offer the movement.

3. Minorities breathe the same air, drink the same water, and experience the same changes in climate as whites, but because minorities have traditionally lived in inner cities (as opposed to the more affluent suburbs), they may experience environmental problems more intensely—poorer air and water quality, for example. Minorities and whites who live below the poverty line are less likely to be able to afford the organic or local foods that Oladipo buys, and therefore they are more likely to be exposed to pesticides or to harm the environment by buying foods that use more natural resources to produce and ship. And as Oladipo points out, if minorities are not provided with information on environmental issues, they are much less likely to try to preserve the environment or fight global warming, simply out of ignorance of the problems they face.

In-Class Writing Activities

1. Students' answers will vary. Those who choose the "organic" option will focus on the use of pesticides on most fruits and vegetables, the introduction of antibiotics and other materials in livestock feed, and the movement to find healthier ways to produce food. They may write about how the consumption of nonorganic food affects all races of people, particularly children, and how the organic food industry has grown in this country. Buying "local" restricts food choices, but it uses far fewer natural resources for growing and shipping—thus having an effect on global warming—and benefits small local farmers. Students who choose the "hybrid" option should research the work being done to produce energy-efficient cars. They can study the market for these cars and explore how they reduce emissions.

2. Students may get their information from news sources, politicians, or environmental groups. They may have seen a movie about global warming or experienced a change in weather (severe or gradual) that led them to look

up information on the topic. Because this is an informal essay, students may include myths or misinformation about global warming—if this happens, be sure to suggest that students do further research to challenge their assumptions. They may feel that outside sources help enlighten them about the issue and what they can do, or those sources may cause them to be fearful or to doubt the information they have received about this issue.

3. Encourage students to write about an organization they know by name, either locally or nationally (it can be anything from a local recycling plant to an international environmental group such as Greenpeace). They may be able to find information about the organization on the Web; many groups post their job listings and volunteer opportunities on their Web sites. Ask students to imagine that they are working in the job they have selected. What are their duties? How are they having an effect on the environment? Then they can do further detailed research into how this job will protect and preserve the environment.

JOSH BURLESON (STUDENT DEBATE)   When Politics Meets Science
[*Crimson White*, University of Alabama/February 9, 2007]

Vocabulary/Using a Dictionary

1. *Truncate* means "to shorten or cut off." Burleson is claiming that scientific studies were shortened, or that elements of them were taken out of context, when they were used in the case for global warming.

2. The prefix *de-* signifies undoing or taking something away. Burleson notes that "one self-proclaimed expert" has argued that scientists who disagree with the consensus on global warming should have their credentials as scientists taken away from them.

3. A heretic is someone who dissents from commonly held ideas, particularly on religion. Because so many scientists believe that global warming is occurring, those who speak out against it stand out as dissenters. However, Burleson's comment also carries the sense of unjust persecution, to which he believes dissenting scientists have been subjected.

Responding to Words in Context

1. Burleson argues that the case for global warming was made in order to call attention to environmental issues. He thinks that this effort was the work of scientists and politicians with a particular environmentalist agenda.

2. Deductive logic is the process of deriving a conclusion based on facts or principles already known. Burleson thinks that by using logic, readers can see the fallacy in the report's link between climate change and an increased suicide rate.

3. The term *green* has been associated with the environmental movement and is used to describe buildings, products, and programs that are ecologically sound. Here Burleson applies the word *greenies* in a trivializing manner.

Discussing Main Point and Meaning

1. Burleson claims that in a review of Mann's work conducted by other scientists, his data and conclusions appeared to be careless and hasty. He also notes that Mann's methods were not always transparent and that it took much prodding to get him to release them to the public.

2. In this essay, Burleson argues that political goals have motivated the conclusions about global warming and that this "politicization of science" (para. 3) calls into question their scientific validity. He seems to believe that science and politics should be entirely separate or at least that political aims should come into play much later, after scientists have done their work without any bias.

3. Burleson does not want to argue that global warming is not real, nor is he prepared to say that it is definitely not linked to human activity (para. 8). His primary claim is that the science on climate change is incomplete and flawed and that governments should not take drastic action based on it.

Examining Sentences, Paragraphs, and Organization

1. One of the points Burleson argues in his essay is that the general public has been too quick to accept isolated incidents of severe weather as evidence of global warming and to assume that drastic measures should be taken to address it. He begins his essay by going back to the fundamental question of whether the weather patterns we're seeing really do add up to an overall global change.

2. Burleson cites contradictory reports on the conditions in Antarctica in order to suggest that the science on climate change is still in its early stages. By comparing climate change to differing opinions on whether eggs are healthy, he indicates that ideas on the subject of global warming change so often that people just end up ignoring the debate.

Thinking Critically

1. Burleson claims that having a result in mind when you begin a study or experiment will necessarily sway the results. However, most scientists do begin experiments with hypotheses about how they will turn out, and no one would claim that a hypothesis constitutes a bias.

2. Because the scope of climate change is so great and because weather conditions are always subtly changing, it would be exceedingly difficult to provide irrefutable proof that it is directly related to human activity. This is one of the points that Brett Schoel addresses in the next selection.

3. In this paragraph, Burleson claims that people are quick to attribute any warm day to climate change but that they simply ignore unseasonable cold. He points out that global warming is a huge change that can't accurately be tracked in terms of individual highs and lows. However, he associates climate change solely with increasing temperatures, whereas some

scientists argue that it will alter weather patterns in unpredictable ways, causing lower temperatures in some areas.

In-Class Writing Activities

1. For those who believe that climate change poses an immediate problem for human life, the billions of dollars spent in counteracting global warming will probably seem like a fair price to pay. Many commentators note that very small changes in global temperatures can have a huge impact. Also, these monies will go partially toward maintaining or reducing carbon levels, which will prevent further warming rather than achieving dramatic reductions in temperatures. However, some students might believe, as Burleson does, that the tiny impact on actual temperature change is not worth the large amounts of money the Kyoto protocol would pledge to the issue.

2. Burleson believes that the Intergovernmental Panel for Climate Change jumps to a conclusion about the influence of global warming on the suicide rate. However, from his brief mention of the report, it is difficult to judge the reasoning the panel used. Before students write, have them think about what would show a stronger link between the two factors. What evidence would they find convincing?

BRETT SCHOEL (STUDENT DEBATE)   The Denial of Global Warming Is Just Politics
[*Crimson White*, University of Alabama/February 16, 2007]

Vocabulary/Using a Dictionary

1. *Attribute* means "to ascribe" or "to explain something by indicating a cause. Schoel essentially says that Americans are confused about the complex issue of global warming because commentators are too self-confident in their ability to explain it in a brief column.

2. The word *pundit* derives from the Hindi word *pandit* (a learned person, particularly in the law or religion). It has come to refer to an expert in a particular field who gives his or her opinion to the public.

3. *Magnate* comes from the Latin word *magnus*, which means "great." The word refers to someone wealthy and influential. It was once applied primarily to the nobility but now refers generally to someone very successful in business.

Responding to Words in Context

1. To be engrossed in something is to be totally consumed by it or to give it all of one's attention. Schoel suggests that the pundits are so obsessed by the idea of politicized science that they ignore other aspects of the global-warming issue.

2. To refute evidence is to show it to be false or erroneous. Because of the nature of climate science, not only would it be impossible to prove the

global-warming theory in a way that could not be challenged, but it would also be difficult to unambiguously refute conclusions.

3. School believes that "restricted growth" is necessary, as the United States consumes one-quarter of the world's resources. And, according to School, because "every action has a consequence," the United States is expected by the international community to take responsibility by placing restrictions. Complaining about the practice is an invitation for ridicule by other countries.

Discussing Main Point and Meaning

1. Whereas Burleson believes that scientists with a particular agenda have turned global warming into a political rather than an ecological issue, School argues that it is conservative politicians and business leaders who have politicized the science.

2. School points out that much scientific research is sponsored by government grants, which are unlikely to put pressure on researchers to exaggerate their claims about climate change. That pressure, he argues, would be more likely to come from the business interests that would be hurt by restrictions on growth and emissions.

3. Because weather is always changing, statements about climate have to be based on averages and trends. Thus, it doesn't make sense to ask for definite proof that the earth's temperature is rising. A more effective task would be to compare recent rises to previous ones and to try, where possible, to determine causes.

Examining Sentences, Paragraphs, and Organization

1. In this paragraph, School poses rhetorical questions to the reader, but they are also a direct answer to Burleson's argument that the scientists who initiated the global-warming debate had clear political intentions. By asking these questions, School suggests that it is unlikely that so many scientists would be motivated by political aims when they derive no obvious or immediate gains by believing in the existence of global warming.

2. School's comment about corporate America is a direct response to Burleson, who, according to School, tries to "de-legitimize the term" (para. 6). School sets off this part of the sentence in prentheses because he does not want to get away from his main point, but he includes it because he wants to establish that the term *corporate America* logically describes a real factor in American life.

3. School first addresses Burleson's idea that scientists have been politically motivated to theorize global warming. Then he challenges Burleson's understanding of the scientific process and his desire for "proof." Both of these points are important, but School places his fundamental argument—that humans have to restrict growth in order to preserve the resources of the planet—at the end of his essay.

Thinking Critically

1. In his essay, Burleson insists on proof that global warming is happening and that it is being caused by human factors. Schoel suggests that in doing so, Burleson radically misunderstands the nature of scientific inquiry into problems like climate change. By asking for proof, Burleson finds a disingenuous way around the actual evidence that does exist.

2. By using the word *naturally* in this sentence, Schoel suggests that his conclusion—that growth should be restricted—follows from an understanding of consequences almost automatically. He seems to gloss over the process of reasoning that might follow a realization that our planet has limited resources and a decision about the proper course of action for humans to take in response.

In-Class Writing Activities

1. This exercise is good practice for students who are used to thinking in simple pro/con frameworks. When you introduce it, you may wish to point out that they don't necessarily have to find a third position in the middle. They may agree mostly with one of the authors but have a few minor quibbles or some points to add. They may argue for a more extreme position than either essayist. In any case, remind them to make clear when they are quoting or paraphrasing and when they are putting their own ideas forward.

2. Schoel regrets that the complicated issues of global warming are often reduced to short polemics written by professional opinion-givers. He writes his response despite this perception because he wants to rebut Burleson. However, the question stands about where a nuanced discussion of climate change is taking or could take place. One possible forum for discussing global warming is conferences or meetings devoted to the subject, such as the ones at Kyoto and the United Nations. Although Schoel does not go into detail about the ideal forum, readers might infer from his essay that solutions need to come from scientists who understand the scope and nature of the earth's resources and politicians who have the power to regulate and control them.

Discussing the Unit

Suggested Topic for Discussion

Many authors of this chapter present politicians as a main influence on public opinion. When it comes to global warming in particular, politicians, big corporations, and scientists are the most trusted sources; however, some of the articles refer to the dangers of underlying political agendas that could distort the reality and facts about the issue. Both Tidwell and Oladipo make a call out to the media to get involved and inform the public. As a source of information that can reach everyone, the media can change public opinion—where its ethical question and duty lie.

Ask your students what they think about the news media. Do they believe everything that they read or hear? Public opinion can be compared, at a smaller scale, to the spread of gossip in your students' social circles. Is everything they hear true? What makes a piece of gossip true? What makes it interesting?

Preparing for Class Discussion

1. You might direct students to look first at the paired essays by Burleson and Schoel, since they deliberately discuss terms of experimental science such as "evidence" and "proof." Once students have discussed this debate, they may be more likely to pick out the scientific language in other essays.

2. Because it is a paid advertisement, the notice from the Heartland Institute has to be evaluated in terms of what the buyers of the ad space want to achieve. While it is true that readers also have to analyze the purposes and motivations of essayists and columnists, the writers' identities and opinions are more transparent. Because the ad doesn't have a single named author, students should look at it in the context of the Heartland Institute's mission.

From Discussion to Writing

1. Possible pairings for this assignment are the essays by Sowell and Lushing; Sowell and Burleson; McKibben and Tidwell; or McKibben and Schoel. No matter which pair they choose, students should begin their essays with a brief statement about the common ground between the two, which will provide a basis for examining where the essays diverge.

2. Several of the authors in this unit lament that the discussion of climate change, at least the one in the general press, is happening mostly in short, politically charged opinion pieces rather than detailed analyses. This exercise gives students an opportunity to ask for greater depth and to imagine how voices from the scientific community might clarify the issues in the debate.

Topics for Cross-Cultural Discussion

1. Many commentators have pointed out that the areas of the world that could be most hurt by a rapid change in weather patterns are those that are already the poorest and the least prepared—such as sub-Saharan Africa, India, and other parts of South Asia. Additionally, the burden of restrictions on carbon output could fall disproportionately on developing nations like China and India. This is one of the points of contention in the continuing discussion of the Kyoto protocol.

2. The environmental movement has been largely associated with young white liberals. As Oladipo points out, African Americans have rarely been mobilized in support of climate-change issues, and this is likely true for other ethnic minorities. Also, environmentalism has rarely been a cause supported by conservatives, although in recent years some conservative religious groups have made care of the planet and its resources and important part of their mission.

Your students get more online and in print.

Order *Re:Writing Plus* with *America Now* at a significant discount or purchase them separately (package ISBN-10: 0-312-56229-2; ISBN-13: 978-0-312-56229-8). To find out more, visit **bedfordstmartins.com.**

Re:Writing Plus neatly gathers our collections of premium digital content into one online library for composition. Check out *i•cite visualizing sources*, tutorials and hands-on source practice; *ModelDoc Central*, hundreds of model documents; and *Peer Factor*, the first-ever peer review game.

bedfordstmartins.com/rewritingplus

Ready to order? You can package this book with additional resources at a discount. Visit **bedfordstmartins.com** for details.

America Now with *i•cite* (CD-ROM)
ISBN-10: 0-312-48754-1; ISBN-13: 978-0-312-48754-6

America Now with *i•claim visualizing argument* (CD-ROM)
ISBN-10: 0-312-48756-8; ISBN-13: 978-0-312-48756-0

America Now with *ix visual exercises* (CD-ROM)
ISBN-10: 0-312-48757-6; ISBN-13: 978-0-312-48757-7

America Now with *Writing and Revising* by X.J. Kennedy,
Dorothy M. Kennedy, Marcia F. Muth (PRINT)
ISBN-10: 0-312-56228-4; ISBN-13: 978-0-312-56228-1